Survival Communications in Virginia: Cities A – L

John E. Parnell, KK4HWK

ISBN 978-1-62512-090-8

Cover design by:
Lynda Colón
FREELANCE GRAPHIC DESIGN &
MARKETING COMMUNICATIONS
www.hirelynda.webs.com

Titles available in this series:

Survival Communications in Alabama
Survival Communications in Alaska
Survival Communications in Arizona
Survival Communications in Arkansas
Survival Communications in California
Survival Communications in Colorado
Survival Communications in Connecticut
Survival Communications in Delaware
Survival Communications in Florida
Survival Communications in Georgia
Survival Communications in Hawaii
Survival Communications in Idaho
Survival Communications in Illinois
Survival Communications in Indiana
Survival Communications in Iowa
Survival Communications in Kansas
Survival Communications in Kentucky
Survival Communications in Louisiana
Survival Communications in Maine
Survival Communications in Maryland
Survival Communications in Massachusetts
Survival Communications in Michigan
Survival Communications in Minnesota
Survival Communications in Mississippi
Survival Communications in Missouri

Survival Communications in Montana
Survival Communications in Nebraska
Survival Communications in Nevada
Survival Communications in New Hampshire
Survival Communications in New Jersey
Survival Communications in New Mexico
Survival Communications in New York
Survival Communications in North Carolina
Survival Communications in North Dakota
Survival Communications in Ohio
Survival Communications in Oklahoma
Survival Communications in Oregon
Survival Communications in Pennsylvania
Survival Communications in Rhode Island
Survival Communications in South Carolina
Survival Communications in South Dakota
Survival Communications in Tennessee
Survival Communications in Texas
Survival Communications in Utah
Survival Communications in Vermont
Survival Communications in Virginia
Survival Communications in Washington
Survival Communications in West Virginia
Survival Communications in Wisconsin
Survival Communications in Wyoming

The above titles are available from your favorite online or brick-and-mortar bookstore or directly from the publisher at Tutor Turtle Press LLC, 1027 S. Pendleton St. – Suite B-10, Easley, SC 29642.

TABLE OF CONTENTS

Appendix A – Virginia Ham Radio Clubs

ARRL Affiliated Amateur and Ham Radio Clubs – By City

Appendix B – Virginia: Cities A – L Ham Licensees by City

Survival Communications in Virginia

Perhaps you have prepared for WTSHTF or TEOTWAWKI with respect to food, water, self-defense and shelter. But what about communication?

Whenever there is a disaster (hurricane, earthquake, economic collapse, nuclear war, EMF, solar eruption, etc.), the normal means of communication that we're all reliant upon (cell phone, land line phone, the Internet, etc.) will probably be, at best, sporadic and at worst, non-existent.

As this author sees it, short of smoke signals and mirrors, there are three options for communication in "trying times": (1) GMRS or FRS radios; (2) CB radios; and (3) ham or amateur radio. Let's consider each of these options to come up with the most acceptable one.

GMRS (General Mobile Radio Service) / FRS (Family Radio Service)

GMRS (General Mobile Radio Service) / FRS (Family Radio Service) radios work optimally over short distances where there is minimal interference. Originally designed to be used as pagers, particularly inside a building or other such confined area, these radios are low-cost and convenient to carry. Unfortunately their small size and light weight comes with a trade-off – short range and short battery life. These radios are supposed to be able to communicate for up to 25-30 miles. Right. That's on level terrain, without buildings or trees getting in the way. While battery life technology is constantly improving, you will need spare batteries to keep communicating or someway of recharging the ones in the radio. In this author's opinion, GMRS/FRS radios are not first choice when concerned with medium or long range communication.

CB (Citizens Band)

CB (Citizens Band) radios operate in a frequency range originally reserved for ham or amateur radio operation. Because of the overwhelming number of people wishing quick, low-cost, regulation-free communication, the FCC (Federal Communication Commission) split off a portion of the frequency spectrum and allowed anyone to purchase a CB radio and start communicating. No test. No license. Just personal/business communication. Today, CB radios are readily available in such outlets as eBay and Craigslist. This author has seen them at yard/garage/tag sales and at flea markets.

CB radios come in a variety of "flavors." Fixed units, sometimes referred to as base units are intended for home use. For the most part, they derive their power from the utility company. In the event of loss of electricity, most base units can also be connected to a 12-volt battery, like that in your car/truck. If you choose to obtain a fixed unit, make sure you know how to connect the unit to the battery – ahead of time. Trying to figure this out when you're under extra stress is not a good situation.

A second type of CB radio is designed to be mobile, that is, installed in your car/truck. It gets its power from the vehicle's battery. You can either attach an antenna permanently to the vehicle or have a removable, magnetic type antenna.

The third type of CB radio is designed for handheld use. They are small and light. Most weigh less than a pound and operate on batteries. Yes, using batteries in a CB poses the same limitations as those by the GMRS/FRS radios, but have the added advantage that most handheld units come with a cigarette lighter adapter. Comes in handy when you are on the move and wish to be able to communicate both from a vehicle and also when you have to abandon it.

While they have a greater range than GMRS/FRS radios, CB radios are, legally, limited to operate on 40 channels, with a power rating of four (4) watts or less. Yes, it is possible to alter CB radios to get around these limitations, but not legally,

Ham/Amateur Radio

Ham/Amateur radio is very appealing. With a ham radio, you are not limited to less than 50 miles, but can communicate with anyone in the world (who also has access to a ham radio, of course).

Standardized Amateur Radio Prepper Communications Plan

In the event of a nationwide catastrophic disaster, the nationwide network of Amateur Radio licensed preppers will need a set of standardized meeting frequencies to share information and coordinate activities between various prepper groups. This Standardized Amateur Radio Communications Plan establishes a set of frequencies on the 80 meter, 40 meter, 20 meter, and 2 meter Amateur Radio bands for use during these types of catastrophic disasters.

Routine nets will not be held on all of these frequencies, but preppers are encouraged to use them when coordinating with other preppers on a routine basis. Routine nets may be conducted by The American Preparedness Radio Net (TAPRN) on these or other frequencies as they see fit. However, TAPRN will promote the use of these standardized frequencies by all Amateur Radio licensed preppers during times of catastrophic disaster. The promotion of this Standardized Amateur Radio Communications Plan is encouraged by all means within the prepper community, including via Amateur Radio, Twitter, Facebook, and various blogs.

Standardized Frequencies and Modes
80 Meters – 3.818 MHz LSB (TAPRN Net: Sundays at 9 PM ET)   40 Meters – 7.242 MHz LSB   40 Meters Morse Code / Digital – 7.073 MHz USB (TAPRN: Sundays at 7:30 PM ET on CONTESTIA 4/250)   20 Meters – 14.242 MHz USB   2 Meters – 146.420 MHz FM

Nets and Network Etiquette

In times of nationwide catastrophic disaster, the ability of any one prepper to initiate and sustain themselves as a net control may be limited by the availability of power and other resource shortages. However, all licensed preppers are encouraged to maintain a listening watch on these frequencies as often as possible during a catastrophic disaster. Preppers may routinely announce themselves in the following manner:

• This is [Your Callsign Phonetically] in [Your State], maintaining a listening watch on [Standard Frequency] for any preppers on frequency seeking information or looking to provide information. Please call [Your Callsign Phonetically]. Preppers exchanging information that may require follow up should agree upon a designated time to return to the frequency and provide further information. If other stations are utilizing the frequency at the designated time you return, maintain watch and proceed with your communications when those stations are finished. If your communications are urgent and the stations on frequency are not passing information of a critical nature, interrupt with the word "Break" and request use of the frequency.

For More Information

Catastrophe Network: http://www.catastrophenetwork.org or @CatastropheNet on Twitter The American Preparedness Radio Network: http://www.taprn.com or @TAPRN on Twitter

© 2011 Catastrophe Network, Please Distribute Freely

In order to use a ham radio, legally, one must be licensed to do so by the FCC (other countries have analogous governmental bodies to regulate ham radio). To obtain a license is quite easy – take a test and pay your license fee. There are currently three classes of license – Technician, General, and Amateur Extra. With each of these licenses come specific abilities.

Technician class is the beginning level. The exam consists of 35 multiple choice questions randomly drawn from a pool of 395 questions. The question pool is readily available online for free downloading (http://www.ncvec.org/downloads/Revised%20Element%202.Pdf) or in such publications at *Ham Radio License Manual Revised 2nd Edition* (ISBN 978-0-87259-097-7). The current Technician pool of questions is to be used from July 1, 2010 to June 30, 2014. Be sure the question pool you are studying from is current. You will need to score at least 26 correct to pass. (Do not worry, Morse Code is no longer on the test, although many ham operators use it anyway.) You do not need to take a formal class in order to qualify to take the exam. You can learn the material on your own. Most people spend 10-15 hours studying and then successfully take the exam. The cost of taking the exam is under $20. The exam is given in MANY locations throughout the US. Usually the exam is given by area ham clubs. You do not have to belong to the club to take the exam. Check Appendix A for a listing of clubs in Virginia.

Topics for the Technician License in Amateur Radio

The Technician license exam covers such topics as basic regulations, operating practices, and electronic theory, with a focus on VHF and UHF applications. Below is the syllabus for the Technician Class.

Subelement T1 – FCC Rules, descriptions and definitions for the amateur radio service, operator and station license responsibilities

[6 Exam Questions – 6 Groups]

T1A – Amateur Radio services; purpose of the amateur service, amateur-satellite service, operator/primary station license grant, where FCC rules are codified, basis and purpose of FCC rules, meanings of basic terms used in FCC rules

T1B – Authorized frequencies; frequency allocations, ITU regions, emission type, restricted sub-bands, spectrum sharing, transmissions near band edges

T1C – Operator classes and station call signs; operator classes, sequential, special event, and vanity call sign systems, international communications, reciprocal operation, station license licensee, places where the amateur service is regulated by the FCC, name and address on ULS, license term, renewal, grace period

T1D – Authorized and prohibited transmissions

T1E – Control operator and control types; control operator required, eligibility, designation of control operator, privileges and duties, control point, local, automatic and remote control, location of control operator

T1F – Station identification and operation standards; special operations for repeaters and auxiliary stations, third party communications, club stations, station security, FCC inspection

---

Subelement T2 – Operating Procedures

[3 Exam Questions – 3 Groups]

T2A – Station operation; choosing an operating frequency, calling another station, test transmissions, use of minimum power, frequency use, band plans

T2B – VHF/UHF operating practices; SSB phone, FM repeater, simplex, frequency offsets, splits and shifts, CTCSS, DTMF, tone squelch, carrier squelch, phonetics

T2C – Public service; emergency and non-emergency operations, message traffic handling

---

Subelement T3 – Radio wave characteristics, radio and electromagnetic properties, propagation modes

[3 Exam Questions – 3 Groups]

T3A – Radio wave characteristics; how a radio signal travels; distinctions of HF, VHF and UHF; fading, multipath; wavelength vs. penetration; antenna orientation

T3B – Radio and electromagnetic wave properties; the electromagnetic spectrum, wavelength vs. frequency, velocity of electromagnetic waves

T3C – Propagation modes; line of sight, sporadic E, meteor, aurora scatter, tropospheric ducting, F layer skip, radio horizon

Subelement T4 - Amateur radio practices and station setup

[2 Exam Questions – 2 Groups]

T4A – Station setup; microphone, speaker, headphones, filters, power source, connecting a computer, RF grounding

T4B – Operating controls; tuning, use of filters, squelch, AGC, repeater offset, memory channels

Subelement T5 – Electrical principles, math for electronics, electronic principles, Ohm's Law

[4 Exam Questions – 4 Groups]

T5A – Electrical principles; current and voltage, conductors and insulators, alternating and direct current

T5B – Math for electronics; decibels, electronic units and the metric system

T5C – Electronic principles; capacitance, inductance, current flow in circuits, alternating current, definition of RF, power calculations

T5D – Ohm's Law

Subelement T6 – Electrical components, semiconductors, circuit diagrams, component functions

[4 Exam Groups – 4 Questions]

T6A – Electrical components; fixed and variable resistors, capacitors, and inductors; fuses, switches, batteries

T6B – Semiconductors; basic principles of diodes and transistors

T6C – Circuit diagrams; schematic symbols

T6D   Component functions

Subelement T7 – Station equipment, common transmitter and receiver problems, antenna measurements and troubleshooting, basic repair and testing

[4 Exam Questions – 4 Groups]

T7A – Station radios; receivers, transmitters, transceivers

T7B – Common transmitter and receiver problems; symptoms of overload and overdrive, distortion, interference, over and under modulation, RF feedback, off frequency signals; fading and noise; problems with digital communications interfaces

T7C – Antenna measurements and troubleshooting; measuring SWR, dummy loads, feedline failure modes

T7D – Basic repair and testing; soldering, use of a voltmeter, ammeter, and ohmmeter

Subelement T8 – Modulation modes, amateur satellite operation, operating activities, non-voice communications

[4 Exam Questions – 4 Groups]

T8A – Modulation modes; bandwidth of various signals

T8B – Amateur satellite operation; Doppler shift, basic orbits, operating protocols

| T8C – Operating activities; radio direction finding, radio control, contests, special event stations, basic linking over Internet |
| T8D – Non-voice communications; image data, digital modes, CW, packet, PSK31 |

Subelement T9 – Antennas, feedlines

[2 Exam Groups – 2 Questions]

T9A – Antennas; vertical and horizontal, concept of gain, common portable and mobile antennas, relationships between antenna length and frequency

T9B – Feedlines; types, losses vs. frequency, SWR concepts, matching, weather protection, connectors

Subelement T0 – AC power circuits, antenna installation, RF hazards

[3 Exam Questions – 3 Groups]

T0A – AC power circuits; hazardous voltages, fuses and circuit breakers, grounding, lightning protection, battery safety, electrical code compliance

T0B – Antenna installation; tower safety, overhead power lines

T0C – RF hazards; radiation exposure, proximity to antennas, recognized safe power levels, exposure to others

Once your name and call sign are available in the FCC database, you have the privilege of operating on all VHF (2 m) and UHF (70 cm) frequencies above 30 megahertz (MHz) and HF frequencies 80, 40, and 15 meter, and on the 10 meter band using Morse code (CW), voice, and digital mode. For a Technician license in Virginia, your call sign will consist of a two-letter prefix beginning with K or W, the number four (4), and a three-letter suffix. The single digit number in the call sign is determined according to which area of the US you obtain your first license. Even though you may move to another state, you keep this number in your call sign. This is also true should you upgrade to a higher license and get a new call sign. The numeral portion of your call sign stays the same.

Call Sign Numbers

Below is a chart showing the various numbers and the state(s) in which you would obtain the number.

Call Sign Number	State(s)
0	CO, IA, KS, MN, MO, NE, ND, SD
1	CT, ME, MA, NH, RI, VT
2	NJ, NY
3	DE, DC, MD, PA
4	AL, FL, GA, KY, NC, SC, TN, VA
5	AR, LA, MS, NM, OK, TX
6	CA
7	AZ, ID, MT, NV, OR, WA, UT, WY
8	MI, OH, WV
9	IL, IN, WI

Residents of Alaska may have any of the following call sign prefixes assigned to them: AL0-7, KL0-7, NL0-7, or WL0-7. Likewise, residents of Hawaii may have the prefix AH6-7, KH6-7, NH6-7, or WH6-7 assigned.

Once you obtain your Technician license, do not stop there. Go and get your General license.

General is the second of three ham license classes. Like the Technician license, to get a General license, you merely have to take a 35-question multiple choice exam and pay your license fee. Passing is still at least 26 correct answers and the fee is the same (less than $20). Again the question pool is available for free online (http://www.ncvec.org/page.php?id=358). It is also available in such print publications as *The ARRL General Class License Manual 7th Edition* (ISBN 978-0-87259-811-9). The current General pool of questions is to be used from July 1, 2011 to June 30, 2015. Be sure the question pool you are using is current. Being a bit more comprehensive than the Technician license, the General license usually requires 15-20 hours of study to learn the material. Check Appendix A for a listing of clubs in Virginia where you might take your exam. Once your name and NEW call sign is listed in the FCC database, you're good to go. For a General license in Virginia, your call sign will consist of a one-letter prefix beginning with K, N or W, the number four (4), and a three-letter suffix.

Topics for the General License in Amateur Radio

The General license exam covers regulations, operating practices and electronic theory. Below is the syllabus for the General Class.

Subelement G1 – Commission's Rules
(5 Exam Questions – 5 Groups)
G1A – General Class control operator frequency privileges; primary and secondary allocations
G1B – Antenna structure limitations; good engineering and good amateur practice, beacon operation; restricted operation; retransmitting radio signals
G1C – Transmitter power regulations; data emission standards
G1D – Volunteer Examiners and Volunteer Examiner Coordinators; temporary identification
G1E – Control categories; repeater regulations; harmful interference; third party rules; ITU regions

Subelement G2 – Operating procedures
(5 Exam Questions – 5 Groups)
G2A – Phone operating procedures; USB/LSB utilization conventions; procedural signals; breaking into a OSO in progress; VOX operation
G2B – Operating courtesy; band plans, emergencies, including drills and emergency communications
G2C – CW operating procedures and procedural signals; Q signals and common abbreviations; full break in
G2D – Amateur Auxiliary; minimizing interference; HF operations

G2E – Digital operating; procedures, procedural signals and common abbreviations

Subelement G3 – Radio wave propagation

(3 Exam Questions – 3 Groups)

G3A – Sunspots and solar radiation; ionospheric disturbances; propagation forecasting and indices

G3B – Maximum Usable Frequency; Lowest Usable Frequency; propagation

G3C – Ionospheric layers; critical angle and frequency; HF scatter; Near Vertical Incidence Sky waves

Subelement G4 – Amateur radio practices

(5 Exam Questions – 5 Groups)

G4A – Station Operation and setup

G4B – Test and monitoring equipment; two-tone test

G4C – Interference with consumer electronics; grounding; DSP

G4D – Speech processors; S meters; sideband operation near band edges

G4E – HF mobile radio installations; emergency and battery powered operation

Subelement G5 – Electrical principles

(3 Exam Questions – 3 Groups)

G5A – Reactance; inductance; capacitance; impedance; impedance matching

G5B – The Decibel; current and voltage dividers; electrical power calculations; sine wave root-mean-square (RMS) values; PEP calculations

G5C – Resistors; capacitors and inductors in series and parallel; transformers

Subelement G6 – Circuit components

(3 Exam Questions – 3 Groups)

G6A – Resistors; capacitors; inductors

G6B – Rectifiers; solid state diodes and transistors; vacuum tubes; batteries

G6C – Analog and digital integrated circuits (ICs); microprocessors; memory; I/O devices; microwave ICs (MMICs); display devices

Subelement G7 – Practical circuits

(3 Exam Questions – 3 Groups)

G7A – Power supplies; schematic symbols

G7B – Digital circuits; amplifiers and oscillators

G7C – Receivers and transmitters; filters, oscillators

Subelement G8 – Signals and emissions

(2 Exam Questions – 2 Groups)

> G8A – Carriers and modulation; AM; FM; single and double sideband; modulation envelope; overmodulation
>
> G8B – Frequency mixing; multiplication; HF data communications; bandwidths of various modes; deviation

Subelement G9 – Antennas and feed lines

(4 Exam Questions – 4 Groups)

G9A – Antenna feed lines; characteristic impedance and attenuation; SWR calculation, measurement and effects; matching networks

G9B – Basic antennas

G9C – Directional antennas

G9D – Specialized antennas

Subelement G0 – Electrical and RF safety

(2 Exam Questions – 2 Groups)

G0A – RF safety principles, rules and guidelines; routine station elevation

G0B – Safety in the ham shack; electrical shock and treatment, safety grounding, fusing, interlocks, wiring, antenna and tower safety

With a General license, you can use all VHF and UHF frequencies and most of the HF frequencies. You would have access to the 160, 30, 17, 12, and 10 meter bands and access to major parts of the 80, 40, 20, and 15 meter bands. Of course, this is in addition to all bands available to Technician license holders.

Amateur Extra is the third of three ham license classes. Like the Technician and General classes, you merely have to pass a test and pay your fee to get your Amateur Extra license. This class of license is more comprehensive than the lower license classes. The exam is longer – 50 questions – and the minimum passing score is higher – 37. However, once you get your Amateur Extra license, all ham frequencies, VHF, UHF and HF are available for your enjoyment. The Extra exam covers regulations, specialized operating practices, advanced electronics theory, and radio equipment design.

Like for the other license classes, the question pool for the Amateur Extra license is available online for downloading (http://www.ncvec.org/downloads/REVISED%202012-2016%20Extra%20Class%20Pool.doc). It is also available in print form in such publications as *The ARRL Extra Class License Manual Revised 9th Edition* (ISBN 978-0-87259-887-4).

Topics for the Extra License in Amateur Radio

Below is the syllabus for the Amateur Extra Class for July 1, 2012 to June 30, 2016.

Subelement E1 – Commission's Rules

[6 Exam Questions – 6 Groups]

E1A – Operating Standards: frequency privileges; emission standards; automatic message forwarding; frequency sharing; stations aboard ships or aircraft

E1B – Station restrictions and special operations: restrictions on station location; general operating restrictions, spurious emissions, control operator reimbursement; antenna structure restrictions; RACES operations

E1C – Station control: definitions and restrictions pertaining to local, automatic and remote control operation; control operator responsibilities for remote and automatically controlled stations

E1D – Amateur Satellite service: definitions and purpose; license requirements for space stations; available frequencies and bands; telecommand and telemetry operations; restrictions, and special provisions; notification requirements

E1E – Volunteer examiner program: definitions, qualifications, preparation and administration of exams; accreditation; question pools; documentation requirements

E1F – Miscellaneous rules: external RF power amplifiers; national quiet zone; business communications; compensated communications; spread spectrum; auxiliary stations; reciprocal operating privileges; IARP and CEPT licenses; third party communications with foreign countries; special temporary authority

Subelement E2 – Operating procedures

[5 Exam Questions – 5 Groups]

E2A – Amateur radio in space: amateur satellites; orbital mechanics; frequencies and modes; satellite hardware; satellite operations

E2B – Television practices: fast scan television standards and techniques; slow scan television standards and techniques

E2C – Operating methods: contest and DX operating; spread-spectrum transmissions; selecting an operating frequency

E2D – Operating methods: VHF and UHF digital modes; APRS

E2E – Operating methods: operating HF digital modes; error correction

Subelement E3 – Radio wave propagation

[3 Exam Questions – 3 Groups]

E3A – Propagation and technique, Earth-Moon-Earth communications; meteor scatter

E3B – Propagation and technique, trans-equatorial; long path; gray-line; multi-path propagation

E3C – Propagation and technique, Aurora propagation; selective fading; radio-path horizon; take-off angle over flat or sloping terrain; effects of ground on propagation; less common propagation modes

Subelement E4 – Amateur practices

[5 Exam Questions – 5 Groups]

E4A – Test equipment: analog and digital instruments; spectrum and network analyzers, antenna analyzers; oscilloscopes; testing transistors; RF measurements

E4B – Measurement technique and limitations: instrument accuracy and performance limitations; probes; techniques to minimize errors; measurement of "Q"; instrument calibration

E4C – Receiver performance characteristics, phase noise, capture effect, noise floor, image rejection, MDS, signal-to-noise-ratio; selectivity

E4D – Receiver performance characteristics, blocking dynamic range, intermodulation and cross-modulation interference; 3rd order intercept; desensitization; preselection

E4E – Noise suppression: system noise; electrical appliance noise; line noise; locating noise sources; DSP noise reduction; noise blankers

Subelement E5 – Electrical principles

[4 Exam Questions – 4 Groups]

E5A – Resonance and Q: characteristics of resonant circuits: series and parallel resonance; Q; half-power bandwidth; phase relationships in reactive circuits

E5B – Time constants and phase relationships: RLC time constants: definition; time constants in RL and RC circuits; phase angle between voltage and current; phase angles of series and parallel circuits

E5C – Impedance plots and coordinate systems: plotting impedances in polar coordinates; rectangular coordinates

E5D – AC and RF energy in real circuits: skin effect; electrostatic and electromagnetic fields; reactive power; power factor; coordinate systems

Subelement E6 – Circuit components

[6 Exam Questions – 6 Groups]

E6A – Semiconductor materials and devices: semiconductor materials germanium, silicon, P-type, N-type; transistor types: NPN, PNP, junction, field-effect transistors: enhancement mode; depletion mode; MOS; CMOS; N-channel; P-channel

E6B – Semiconductor diodes

E6C – Integrated circuits: TTL digital integrated circuits; CMOS digital integrated circuits; gates

E6D – Optical devices and toroids: cathode-ray tube devices; charge-coupled devices (CCDs); liquid crystal displays (LCDs); toroids: permeability, core material, selecting, winding

E6E – Piezoelectric crystals and MMICs: quartz crystals; crystal oscillators and filters; monolithic amplifiers

E6F – Optical components and power systems: photoconductive principles and effects, photovoltaic systems, optical couplers, optical sensors, and optoisolators

Subelement E7 – Practical circuits

[8 Exam Questions – 8 Groups]

E7A – Digital circuits: digital circuit principles and logic circuits: classes of logic elements; positive and negative logic; frequency dividers; truth tables

E7B – Amplifiers: Class of operation; vacuum tube and solid-state circuits; distortion and intermodulation; spurious and parasitic suppression; microwave amplifiers

E7C – Filters and matching networks: filters and impedance matching networks: types of networks; types of filters; filter applications; filter characteristics; impedance matching; DSP filtering

E7D – Power supplies and voltage regulators

E7E – Modulation and demodulation: reactance, phase and balanced modulators; detectors; mixer stages; DSP modulation and demodulation; software defined radio systems

E7F – Frequency markers and counters: frequency divider circuits; frequency marker generators; frequency counters

E7G – Active filters and op-amps: active audio filters; characteristics; basic circuit design; operational amplifiers

E7H – Oscillators and signal sources: types of oscillators; synthesizers and phase-locked loops; direct digital synthesizers

Subelement E8 – Signals and emissions

[4 Exam Questions – 4 Groups]

E8A – AC waveforms: sine, square, sawtooth and irregular waveforms; AC measurements; average and PEP of RF signals; pulse and digital signal waveforms

E8B – Modulation and demodulation: modulation methods; modulation index and deviation ratio; pulse modulation; frequency and time division multiplexing

E8C – Digital signals: digital communications modes; CW; information rate vs. bandwidth; spread-spectrum communications; modulation methods

E8D – Waves, measurements, and RF grounding: peak-to-peak values, polarization; RF grounding

Subelement E9 – Antennas and transmission lines

[8 Exam Questions – 8 Groups]

E9A – Isotropic and gain antennas: definition; used as a standard for comparison; radiation pattern; basic antenna parameters: radiation resistance and reactance, gain, beamwidth, efficiency

E9B – Antenna patterns: E and H plane patterns; gain as a function of pattern; antenna design; Yagi antennas

E9C – Wire and phased vertical antennas: beverage antennas; terminated and resonant rhombic antennas; elevation above real ground; ground effects as related to polarization; take-off angles

E9D – Directional antennas: gain; satellite antennas; antenna beamwidth; losses; SWR bandwidth; antenna efficiency; shortened and mobile antennas; grounding

E9E – Matching: matching antennas to feed lines; power dividers

E9F – Transmission lines: characteristics of open and shorted feed lines: 1/8 wavelength; 1/4 wavelength; 1/2 wavelength; feed lines: coax versus open-wire; velocity factor; electrical length; transformation characteristics of line terminated in impedance not equal to characteristic impedance

E9G – The Smith chart

E9H – Effective radiated power; system gains and losses; radio direction finding antennas

Once your new call sign is listed in the FCC database, you are good to go. For an Amateur Extra license in Virginia, your call sign will consist of a prefix of K, N or W, the number four (4), and a two-letter suffix, or a two-letter prefix beginning with A, N, K or W, the number four (4), and a one-letter suffix, or a two-letter prefix beginning with A, the number four (4), and a two-letter suffix.

Ham radio equipment can be expensive or you can do it "on the cheap." The cost will run from a couple hundred dollars to well in the thousands, depending on what you have available. eBay, and Craigslist are good places to start looking. Most ham clubs do some sort of hamfest annually wherein club members or others are willing to part with older equipment. See Appendix A for a list of clubs in Virginia.

Another excellent source of equipment, as well as advice on setting the equipment up and how to use it properly, is current ham operators. In Appendix B, the author has listed all the FCC licensed ham operators in Virginia, listed by city, and then sorted by street and house number on the street. Who knows, maybe someone who lives close to you is a ham operator. Be a good neighbor, stop by and have a chat with him/her.

Like CB radios, ham radios come in three formats – base, mobile, and handheld. They can use the electric company for power, or operate off a car battery. In the opinion of this author, in spite of the slightly higher cost of the equipment and having to take a test to legally use the equipment, ham radio is the way to go when concerned about communication during times of crisis.

Canadian Call Sign Prefixes

Because of our proximity to Canada, many times ham contact is made with our northern neighbors. Below is a chart showing the origin of Canadian call sign prefixes.

Call Sign Prefix	Provence or Territory
CY0	Sable Island
CY9	St. Paul Island
VA1, VE1	New Brunswick, Nova Scotia
VA2, VE2	Quebec
VA3, VE3	Ontario
VA4, VE4	Manitoba
VA5, VE5	Saskatchewan
VA6, VE6	Alberta
VA7, VE7	British Columbia
VE8	North West Territories
VE9	New Brunswick
VO1	Newfoundland

VO2	Labrador	
VY0	Nunavut	
VY1	Yukon	
VY2	Prince Edward Island	

Common Radio Bands in the United States

Certain radio bands are more popular with ham radio enthusiasts than others. Below is a chart showing these bands and when they are most popular.

	Band (meter)	Frequency (MHz)	Use
HF	160	1.8 – 2.0	Night
	80	3.5 – 4.0	Night and Local Day
	40	7.0 – 7.3	Night and Local Day
	30	10.1 – 10.15	CW and Digital
	20	14.0 – 14.350	World Wide Day and Night
	17	18.068 – 18.168	World Wide Day and Night
	15	21.0 – 21.450	Primarily Daytime
	12	24.890 – 24.990	Primarily Daytime
	10	28.0 – 29.70	Daytime during Sunspot highs
VHF	6	50 – 54	Local to World Wide
	2	144 – 148	Local to Medium Distance
UHF	70 cm	430 – 440	Local

Common Amateur Radio Bands in Canada

160 Meter Band - Maximum bandwidth 6 kHz
1.800 - 1.820 MHz - CW
1.820 - 1.830 MHz - Digital Modes
1 830 - 1.840 MHz - DX Window
1.840 - 2.000 MHz - SSB and other wide band modes

80 Meter Band - Maximum bandwidth 6 kHz
3.500 - 3.580 MHz - CW
3.580 - 3.620 MHz - Digital Modes
3.620 - 3.635 MHz - Packet/Digital Secondary
3.635 - 3.725 MHz - CW
3.725 - 3.790 MHz - SSB and other side band modes*
3.790 - 3.800 MHz - SSB DX Window
3.800 - 4.000 MHz - SSB and other wide band modes

40 Meter Band - Maximum bandwidth 6 kHz
7.000 - 7.035 MHz - CW
7.035 - 7.050 MHz - Digital Modes
7.040 - 7.050 MHz - International packet

7.050 - 7.100 MHz - SSB
7.100 - 7.120 MHz - Packet within Region 2
7.120 - 7.150 MHz - CW
7.150 - 7.300 MHz - SSB and other wide band modes

30 Meter Band - Maximum bandwidth 1 kHz

10.100 - 10.130 MHz - CW only
10.130 - 10.140 MHz - Digital Modes
10.140 - 10.150 MHz - Packet

20 Meter Band - Maximum bandwidth 6 kHz

14.000 - 14.070 MHz - CW only
14.070 - 14.095 MHz - Digital Mode
14.095 - 14.099 MHz - Packet
14.100 MHz - Beacons
14.101 - 14.112 MHz - CW, SSB, packet shared
14.112 - 14.350 MHz - SSB
14.225 - 14.235 MHz - SSTV

17 Meter Band - Maximum bandwidth 6 kHz

18.068 - 18.100 MHz - CW
18.100 - 18.105 MHz - Digital Modes
18.105 - 18.110 MHz - Packet
18.110 - 18.168 MHz - SSB and other wide band modes

15 Meter Band - maximum bandwidth 6 kHz

21.000 - 21.070 MHz - CW
21.070 - 21.090 MHz - Digital Modes
21.090 - 21.125 MHz - Packet
21.100 - 21.150 MHz - CW and SSB
21.150 - 21.335 MHz - SSB and other wide band modes
21.335 - 21.345 MHz - SSTV
21.345 - 21.450 MHz - SSB and other wide band modes

12 Meter Band - Maximum bandwidth 6 kHz

24.890 - 24.930 MHz - CW
24.920 - 24.925 MHz - Digital Modes
24.925 - 24.930 MHz - Packet
24.930 - 24.990 MHz - SSB and other wide band modes

10 Meter Band - Maximum band width 20 kHz

28.000 - 28.200 MHz - CW
28.070 - 28.120 MHz - Digital Modes
28.120 - 28.190 MHz - Packet

28.190 - 28.200 MHz - Beacons
28.200 - 29.300 MHz - SSB and other wide band modes
29.300 - 29.510 MHz - Satellite
29.510 - 29.700 MHz - SSB, FM and repeaters

160 Meters (1.8-2.0 MHz)

1.800 - 2.000 CW
1.800 - 1.810 Digital Modes
1.810 CW QRP
1.843-2.000 SSB, SSTV and other wideband modes
1.910 SSB QRP
1.995 - 2.000 Experimental
1.999 - 2.000 Beacons

80 Meters (3.5-4.0 MHz)

3.590 RTTY/Data DX
3.570-3.600 RTTY/Data
3.790-3.800 DX window
3.845 SSTV
3.885 AM calling frequency

40 Meters (7.0-7.3 MHz)

7.040 RTTY/Data DX
7.080-7.125 RTTY/Data
7.171 SSTV
7.290 AM calling frequency

30 Meters (10.1-10.15 MHz)

10.130-10.140 RTTY
10.140-10.150 Packet

20 Meters (14.0-14.35 MHz)

14.070-14.095 RTTY
14.095-14.0995 Packet
14.100 NCDXF Beacons
14.1005-14.112 Packet
14.230 SSTV
14.286 AM calling frequency

17 Meters (18.068-18.168 MHz)

18.100-18.105 RTTY
18.105-18.110 Packet

15 Meters (21.0-21.45 MHz)

21.070-21.110 RTTY/Data

21.340 SSTV

12 Meters (24.89-24.99 MHz)

24.920-24.925 RTTY
24.925-24.930 Packet

10 Meters (28-29.7 MHz)

28.000-28.070 CW
28.070-28.150 RTTY
28.150-28.190 CW
28.200-28.300 Beacons
28.300-29.300 Phone
28.680 SSTV
29.000-29.200 AM
29.300-29.510 Satellite Downlinks
29.520-29.590 Repeater Inputs
29.600 FM Simplex
29.610-29.700 Repeater Outputs

6 Meters (50-54 MHz)

50.0-50.1 CW, beacons
50.060-50.080 beacon subband
50.1-50.3 SSB, CW
50.10-50.125 DX window
50.125 SSB calling
50.3-50.6 All modes
50.6-50.8 Nonvoice communications
50.62 Digital (packet) calling
50.8-51.0 Radio remote control (20-kHz channels)
51.0-51.1 Pacific DX window
51.12-51.48 Repeater inputs (19 channels)
51.12-51.18 Digital repeater inputs
51.5-51.6 Simplex (six channels)
51.62-51.98 Repeater outputs (19 channels)
51.62-51.68 Digital repeater outputs
52.0-52.48 Repeater inputs (except as noted; 23 channels)
52.02, 52.04 FM simplex
52.2 TEST PAIR (input)
52.5-52.98 Repeater output (except as noted; 23 channels)
52.525 Primary FM simplex
52.54 Secondary FM simplex
52.7 TEST PAIR (output)
53.0-53.48 Repeater inputs (except as noted; 19 channels)
53.0 Remote base FM simplex
53.02 Simplex
53.1, 53.2, 53.3, 53.4 Radio remote control

53.5-53.98 Repeater outputs (except as noted; 19 channels)
53.5, 53.6, 53.7, 53.8 Radio remote control
53.52, 53.9 Simplex

2 Meters (144-148 MHz)

144.00-144.05 EME (CW)
144.05-144.10 General CW and weak signals
144.10-144.20 EME and weak-signal SSB
144.200 National calling frequency
144.200-144.275 General SSB operation
144.275-144.300 Propagation beacons
144.30-144.50 New OSCAR subband
144.50-144.60 Linear translator inputs
144.60-144.90 FM repeater inputs
144.90-145.10 Weak signal and FM simplex (145.01,03,05,07,09 are widely used for
   packet)
145.10-145.20 Linear translator outputs
145.20-145.50 FM repeater outputs
145.50-145.80 Miscellaneous and experimental modes
145.80-146.00 OSCAR subband
146.01-146.37 Repeater inputs
146.40-146.58 Simplex
146.52 National Simplex Calling Frequency
146.61-146.97 Repeater outputs
147.00-147.39 Repeater outputs
147.42-147.57 Simplex
147.60-147.99 Repeater inputs

1.25 Meters (222-225 MHz)

222.0-222.150 Weak-signal modes
222.0-222.025 EME
222.05-222.06 Propagation beacons
222.1 SSB & CW calling frequency
222.10-222.15 Weak-signal CW & SSB
222.15-222.25 Local coordinator's option; weak signal, ACSB, repeater inputs, control
222.25-223.38 FM repeater inputs only
223.40-223.52 FM simplex
223.52-223.64 Digital, packet
223.64-223.70 Links, control
223.71-223.85 Local coordinator's option; FM simplex, packet, repeater outputs
223.85-224.98 Repeater outputs only

70 Centimeters (420-450 MHz)

420.00-426.00 ATV repeater or simplex with 421.25 MHz video carrier control links and
   experimental
426.00-432.00 ATV simplex with 427.250-MHz video carrier frequency

432.00-432.07 EME (Earth-Moon-Earth)
432.07-432.10 Weak-signal CW
432.10 70-cm calling frequency
432.10-432.30 Mixed-mode and weak-signal work
432.30-432.40 Propagation beacons
432.40-433.00 Mixed-mode and weak-signal work
433.00-435.00 Auxiliary/repeater links
435.00-438.00 Satellite only (internationally)
438.00-444.00 ATV repeater input with 439.250-MHz video carrier frequency and re-
    peater links
442.00-445.00 Repeater inputs and outputs (local option)
445.00-447.00 Shared by auxiliary and control links, repeaters and simplex (local option)
446.00 National simplex frequency
447.00-450.00 Repeater inputs and outputs (local option)

33 Centimeters (902-928 MHz)

902.0-903.0 Narrow-bandwidth, weak-signal communications
902.0-902.8 SSTV, FAX, ACSSB, experimental
902.1 Weak-signal calling frequency
902.8-903.0 Reserved for EME, CW expansion
903.1 Alternate calling frequency
903.0-906.0 Digital communications
906-909 FM repeater inputs
909-915 ATV
915-918 Digital communications
918-921 FM repeater outputs
921-927 ATV
927-928 FM simplex and links

23 Centimeters (1240-1300 MHz)

1240-1246 ATV #1
1246-1248 Narrow-bandwidth FM point-to-point links and digital, duplex with 1258-
    1260.
1248-1258 Digital Communications
1252-1258 ATV #2
1258-1260 Narrow-bandwidth FM point-to-point links digital, duplexed with 1246-1252
1260-1270 Satellite uplinks, reference WARC '79
1260-1270 Wide-bandwidth experimental, simplex ATV
1270-1276 Repeater inputs, FM and linear, paired with 1282-1288, 239 pairs every 25
    kHz, e.g. 1270.025, .050, etc.
1271-1283 Non-coordinated test pair
1276-1282 ATV #3
1282-1288 Repeater outputs, paired with 1270-1276
1288-1294 Wide-bandwidth experimental, simplex ATV
1294-1295 Narrow-bandwidth FM simplex services, 25-kHz channels
1294.5 National FM simplex calling frequency

1295-1297 Narrow bandwidth weak-signal communications (no FM)
1295.0-1295.8 SSTV, FAX, ACSSB, experimental
1295.8-1296.0 Reserved for EME, CW expansion
1296.00-1296.05 EME-exclusive
1296.07-1296.08 CW beacons
1296.1 CW, SSB calling frequency
1296.4-1296.6 Crossband linear translator input
1296.6-1296.8 Crossband linear translator output
1296.8-1297.0 Experimental beacons (exclusive)
1297-1300 Digital Communications

2300-2310 and 2390-2450 MHz

2300.0-2303.0 High-rate data
2303.0-2303.5 Packet
2303.5-2303.8 TTY packet
2303.9-2303.9 Packet, TTY, CW, EME
2303.9-2304.1 CW, EME
2304.1 Calling frequency
2304.1-2304.2 CW, EME, SSB
2304.2-2304.3 SSB, SSTV, FAX, Packet AM, Amtor
2304.30-2304.32 Propagation beacon network
2304.32-2304.40 General propagation beacons
2304.4-2304.5 SSB, SSTV, ACSSB, FAX, Packet AM, Amtor experimental
2304.5-2304.7 Crossband linear translator input
2304.7-2304.9 Crossband linear translator output
2304.9-2305.0 Experimental beacons
2305.0-2305.2 FM simplex (25 kHz spacing)
2305.20 FM simplex calling frequency
2305.2-2306.0 FM simplex (25 kHz spacing)
2306.0-2309.0 FM Repeaters (25 kHz) input
2309.0-2310.0 Control and auxiliary links
2390.0-2396.0 Fast-scan TV
2396.0-2399.0 High-rate data
2399.0-2399.5 Packet
2399.5-2400.0 Control and auxiliary links
2400.0-2403.0 Satellite
2403.0-2408.0 Satellite high-rate data
2408.0-2410.0 Satellite
2410.0-2413.0 FM repeaters (25 kHz) output
2413.0-2418.0 High-rate data
2418.0-2430.0 Fast-scan TV
2430.0-2433.0 Satellite
2433.0-2438.0 Satellite high-rate data
2438.0-2450.0 WB FM, FSTV, FMTV, SS experimental

3300-3500 MHz
3456.3-3456.4 Propagation beacons

5650-5925 MHz
5760.3-5760.4 Propagation beacons

10.00-10.50 GHz
10.368 Narrow band calling frequency 10.3683-10.3684 Propagation beacons 10.3640 Calling frequency

Now that you have your license (you do, don't you?), and your equipment, you are ready to go live. Below is a suggested start.

1) Assuming you have the HT set up to the appropriate frequency, and offset, press the mic button on the HT and say, "KK4HWX listening." Replace the KK4HWX with your own call sign, the one assigned to you by the FCC (it's the law). If no one responds to your call, you may wish to try again. Hopefully someone will respond to your call.

2) Once you get a response, it will be in the form of something like, "KK4HWX this is ??1??? in Eastport returning. My name is Florence. Back to you. ??1???" then a tone. Let us examine the response more closely. She first acknowledged your call sign (KK4HWX), then identified hers (??1???). From the 1 in her call sign, you know that she first got her license in Region 1, meaning she got it while a resident of CT, ME, MA, NH, RI, or VT. She then told you where she's transmitting from (Eastport). The term "returning" means that she is returning your call. Her name is Florence. The phrase, "Back to you" indicates that she is turning over the conversation to you. She then repeats her call sign. The tone indicates to you that it is okay to proceed with your response. BTW if she had used the term "Over" instead of "Back to you," it would mean the same thing, just fewer words.

3) At this point, press the mic button and continue with the conversation. You should restate your call sign often during the conversation (perhaps every 10 minutes or less and whenever you begin transmitting). Don't forget to say, "Over" or "Back to you" whenever you are giving Florence control of the conversation again.

4) When you are ready to stop the conversation, you should say goodbye or use the phrase "73", meaning "best wishes." Your conversation would end something like, "??1??? 73, this is KK4HWX clear and monitoring." The "clear and monitoring" indicates that you are going to continue to monitor the frequency. If you are not going to continue monitoring, you may wish to end the conversation with Florence with, "clear and QRT" instead. The QRT means that you are stopping transmissions.

Call Sign Phonics

Because of different accents of various people, sometimes it is difficult to understand call sign letters when spoken. For this reason, most ham operators verbalize their call sign using phonics. Below is a table listing the accepted phonics for letters and numbers.

A = ALFA

B = BRAVO

C = CHARLIE

D = DELTA

E = ECHO

F = FOXTROT

G = GOLF

H = HOTEL

I = INDIA

J = JULIETT

K = KILO

L = LIMA

M = MIKE

N = NOVEMBER

O = OSCAR

P = PAPA (PA-PA')

Q = QUEBEC (KAY-BEK')

R = ROMEO

S = SIERRA

T = TANGO

U = UNIFORM

V = VICTOR

W = WHISKEY

X = X-RAY

Y = YANKEE

Z = ZULU (ZED)

1 = ONE

2 = TWO

3 = THREE (TREE)

4 = FOUR

5 = FIVE (FIFE)

6 = SIX

7 = SEVEN

8 = EIGHT

9 = NINE (NINER)

0 = ZERO

The words in parentheses are the pronunciation or the alternate pronunciations for the words or numbers, but you will hear both used. With the letter Z, (ZED) is by far the most commonly used. With the number 9, NINER is the most common and easiest to understand ON THE AIR.

If you wish to use Morse code (CW) instead of voice communication, the "conversation" would follow the same steps, with a few modifications. To type out each word would require a lot of typing and translating. If you are like this author, more means more, i.e., more typing means more typos are likely. To help with this situation, CW enthusiasts have developed a language all their own – they use abbreviations for common phrases. Below is a chart showing some of these abbreviations.

Abbreviation	Use
AR	Over
de	From or "this is"
ES	And
GM	Good Morning
K	Go
KN	Go only
NM	Name
QTH	Location
RPT	Report

R	Roger
SK	Clear
tnx	Thanks
UR	Your, you are
73	Best Wishes

Morse Code and Amateur Radio

If you wish to use CW, but are concerned about accuracy, you might consider purchasing a Morse code translator. This is an electronic device that you place in front of your speakers. It takes the CW sounds and translates them into English and displays the transmission on an LCD display. For the reverse, you can pick up a CW keyboard. With the keyboard, you type in your message and it converts the text to Morse code. The translator does not need to be attached to your ham equipment, whereas the keyboard would.

For your convenience, below is a table showing the Morse code signals and their meaning.

Character	Code
A	· —
B	— · · ·
C	— · — ·
D	— · ·
E	·
F	· · — ·
G	— — ·
H	· · · ·
I	· ·
J	· — — —
K	— · —
L	· — · ·
M	— —
N	— ·
O	— — —
P	· — — ·
Q	— — · —
R	· — ·
S	· · ·
T	—
U	· · —
V	· · · —
W	· — —
X	— · · —
Y	— · — —
Z	— — · ·

0	— — — — —
1	• — — — —
2	• • — — —
3	• • • — —
4	• • • • —
5	• • • • •
6	— • • • •
7	— — • • •
8	— — — • •
9	— — — — •
Ampersand [&], Wait	• — • • •
Apostrophe [']	• — — — — •
At sign [@]	• — — • — •
Colon [:]	— — — • • •
Comma [,]	— — • • — —
Dollar sign [$]	• • • — • • —
Double dash [=]	— • • • —
Exclamation mark [!]	— • — • — —
Hyphen, Minus [-]	— • • • • —
Parenthesis closed [)]	— • — — • —
Parenthesis open [(]	— • — — •
Period [.]	• — • — • —
Plus [+]	• — • — •
Question mark [?]	• • — — • •
Quotation mark ["]	• — • • — •
Semicolon [;]	— • — • — •
Slash [/], Fraction bar	— • • — •
Underscore [_]	• • — — • —

An advantage of using Morse Code is that when broadcasting CW, you are using reduced power, thereby saving your battery. Your battery is used only while actually transmitting or receiving.

International Call Sign Prefixes

As was stated earlier, all ham radio call signs begin with letters (or numbers) taken from blocks assigned to each country of the world by the *ITU - International Telecommunications Union,* a body controlled by the United Nations. The following chart indicates which call sign series are allocated to which countries.

Call Sign Series	Allocated to
AAA-ALZ	**United States of America**
AMA-AOZ	Spain
APA-ASZ	Pakistan (Islamic Republic of)
ATA-AWZ	India (Republic of)

AXA-AXZ	Australia
AYA-AZZ	Argentine Republic
A2A-A2Z	Botswana (Republic of)
A3A-A3Z	Tonga (Kingdom of)
A4A-A4Z	Oman (Sultanate of)
A5A-A5Z	Bhutan (Kingdom of)
A6A-A6Z	United Arab Emirates
A7A-A7Z	Qatar (State of)
A8A-A8Z	Liberia (Republic of)
A9A-A9Z	Bahrain (State of)
BAA-BZZ	China (People's Republic of)
CAA-CEZ	Chile
CFA-CKZ	Canada
CLA-CMZ	Cuba
CNA-CNZ	Morocco (Kingdom of)
COA-COZ	Cuba
CPA-CPZ	Bolivia (Republic of)
CQA-CUZ	Portugal
CVA-CXZ	Uruguay (Eastern Republic of)
CYA-CZZ	Canada
C2A-C2Z	Nauru (Republic of)
C3A-C3Z	Andorra (Principality of)
C4A-C4Z	Cyprus (Republic of)
C5A-C5Z	Gambia (Republic of the)
C6A-C6Z	Bahamas (Commonwealth of the)
C7A-C7Z	World Meteorological Organization
C8A-C9Z	Mozambique (Republic of)
DAA-DRZ	Germany (Federal Republic of)
DSA-DTZ	Korea (Republic of)
DUA-DZZ	Philippines (Republic of the)
D2A-D3Z	Angola (Republic of)
D4A-D4Z	Cape Verde (Republic of)
D5A-D5Z	Liberia (Republic of)
D6A-D6Z	Comoros (Islamic Federal Republic of the)
D7A-D9Z	Korea (Republic of)
EAA-EHZ	Spain
EIA-EJZ	Ireland
EKA-EKZ	Armenia (Republic of)
ELA-ELZ	Liberia (Republic of)
EMA-EOZ	Ukraine
EPA-EQZ	Iran (Islamic Republic of)
ERA-ERZ	Moldova (Republic of)
ESA-ESZ	Estonia (Republic of)
ETA-ETZ	Ethiopia (Federal Democratic Republic of)
EUA-EWZ	Belarus (Republic of)

EXA-EXZ	Kyrgyz Republic
EYA-EYZ	Tajikistan (Republic of)
EZA-EZZ	Turkmenistan
E2A-E2Z	Thailand
E3A-E3Z	Eritrea
E4A-E4Z	Palestinian Authority
E5A-E5Z	New Zealand - Cook Islands (WRC-07)
E7A-E7Z	Bosnia and Herzegovina (Republic of) (WRC-07)
FAA-FZZ	France
GAA-GZZ	United Kingdom of Great Britain and Northern Ireland
HAA-HAZ	Hungary (Republic of)
HBA-HBZ	Switzerland (Confederation of)
HCA-HDZ	Ecuador
HEA-HEZ	Switzerland (Confederation of)
HFA-HFZ	Poland (Republic of)
HGA-HGZ	Hungary (Republic of)
HHA-HHZ	Haiti (Republic of)
HIA-HIZ	Dominican Republic
HJA-HKZ	Colombia (Republic of)
HLA-HLZ	Korea (Republic of)
HMA-HMZ	Democratic People's Republic of Korea
HNA-HNZ	Iraq (Republic of)
HOA-HPZ	Panama (Republic of)
HQA-HRZ	Honduras (Republic of)
HSA-HSZ	Thailand
HTA-HTZ	Nicaragua
HUA-HUZ	El Salvador (Republic of)
HVA-HVZ	Vatican City State
HWA-HYZ	France
HZA-HZZ	Saudi Arabia (Kingdom of)
H2A-H2Z	Cyprus (Republic of)
H3A-H3Z	Panama (Republic of)
H4A-H4Z	Solomon Islands
H6A-H7Z	Nicaragua
H8A-H9Z	Panama (Republic of)
IAA-IZZ	Italy
JAA-JSZ	Japan
JTA-JVZ	Mongolia
JWA-JXZ	Norway
JYA-JYZ	Jordan (Hashemite Kingdom of)
JZA-JZZ	Indonesia (Republic of)
J2A-J2Z	Djibouti (Republic of)
J3A-J3Z	Grenada
J4A-J4Z	Greece
J5A-J5Z	Guinea-Bissau (Republic of)

J6A-J6Z	Saint Lucia
J7A-J7Z	Dominica (Commonwealth of)
J8A-J8Z	Saint Vincent and the Grenadines
KAA-KZZ	**United States of America**
LAA-LNZ	Norway
LOA-LWZ	Argentine Republic
LXA-LXZ	Luxembourg
LYA-LYZ	Lithuania (Republic of)
LZA-LZZ	Bulgaria (Republic of)
L2A-L9Z	Argentine Republic
MAA-MZZ	United Kingdom of Great Britain and Northern Ireland
NAA-NZZ	**United States of America**
OAA-OCZ	Peru
ODA-ODZ	Lebanon
OEA-OEZ	Austria
OFA-OJZ	Finland
OKA-OLZ	Czech Republic
OMA-OMZ	Slovak Republic
ONA-OTZ	Belgium
OUA-OZZ	Denmark
PAA-PIZ	Netherlands (Kingdom of the)
PJA-PJZ	Netherlands (Kingdom of the) - Netherlands Antilles
PKA-POZ	Indonesia (Republic of)
PPA-PYZ	Brazil (Federative Republic of)
PZA-PZZ	Suriname (Republic of)
P2A-P2Z	Papua New Guinea
P3A-P3Z	Cyprus (Republic of)
P4A-P4Z	Netherlands (Kingdom of the) - Aruba
P5A-P9Z	Democratic People's Republic of Korea
RAA-RZZ	Russian Federation
SAA-SMZ	Sweden
SNA-SRZ	Poland (Republic of)
SSA-SSM	Egypt (Arab Republic of)
SSN-STZ	Sudan (Republic of the)
SUA-SUZ	Egypt (Arab Republic of)
SVA-SZZ	Greece
S2A-S3Z	Bangladesh (People's Republic of)
S5A-S5Z	Slovenia (Republic of)
S6A-S6Z	Singapore (Republic of)
S7A-S7Z	Seychelles (Republic of)
S8A-S8Z	South Africa (Republic of)
S9A-S9Z	Sao Tome and Principe (Democratic Republic of)
TAA-TCZ	Turkey
TDA-TDZ	Guatemala (Republic of)
TEA-TEZ	Costa Rica

TFA-TFZ	Iceland
TGA-TGZ	Guatemala (Republic of)
THA-THZ	France
TIA-TIZ	Costa Rica
TJA-TJZ	Cameroon (Republic of)
TKA-TKZ	France
TLA-TLZ	Central African Republic
TMA-TMZ	France
TNA-TNZ	Congo (Republic of the)
TOA-TQZ	France
TRA-TRZ	Gabonese Republic
TSA-TSZ	Tunisia
TTA-TTZ	Chad (Republic of)
TUA-TUZ	Côte d'Ivoire (Republic of)
TVA-TXZ	France
TYA-TYZ	Benin (Republic of)
TZA-TZZ	Mali (Republic of)
T2A-T2Z	Tuvalu
T3A-T3Z	Kiribati (Republic of)
T4A-T4Z	Cuba
T5A-T5Z	Somali Democratic Republic
T6A-T6Z	Afghanistan (Islamic State of)
T7A-T7Z	San Marino (Republic of)
T8A-T8Z	Palau (Republic of)
UAA-UIZ	Russian Federation
UJA-UMZ	Uzbekistan (Republic of)
UNA-UQZ	Kazakhstan (Republic of)
URA-UZZ	Ukraine
VAA-VGZ	Canada
VHA-VNZ	Australia
VOA-VOZ	Canada
VPA-VQZ	United Kingdom of Great Britain and Northern Ireland
VRA-VRZ	China (People's Republic of) - Hong Kong
VSA-VSZ	United Kingdom of Great Britain and Northern Ireland
VTA-VWZ	India (Republic of)
VXA-VYZ	Canada
VZA-VZZ	Australia
V2A-V2Z	Antigua and Barbuda
V3A-V3Z	Belize
V4A-V4Z	Saint Kitts and Nevis
V5A-V5Z	Namibia (Republic of)
V6A-V6Z	Micronesia (Federated States of)
V7A-V7Z	Marshall Islands (Republic of the)
V8A-V8Z	Brunei Darussalam
WAA-WZZ	**United States of America**

XAA-XIZ	Mexico
XJA-XOZ	Canada
XPA-XPZ	Denmark
XQA-XRZ	Chile
XSA-XSZ	China (People's Republic of)
XTA-XTZ	Burkina Faso
XUA-XUZ	Cambodia (Kingdom of)
XVA-XVZ	Viet Nam (Socialist Republic of)
XWA-XWZ	Lao People's Democratic Republic
XXA-XXZ	China (People's Republic of) - Macao (WRC-07)
XYA-XZZ	Myanmar (Union of)
YAA-YAZ	Afghanistan (Islamic State of)
YBA-YHZ	Indonesia (Republic of)
YIA-YIZ	Iraq (Republic of)
YJA-YJZ	Vanuatu (Republic of)
YKA-YKZ	Syrian Arab Republic
YLA-YLZ	Latvia (Republic of)
YMA-YMZ	Turkey
YNA-YNZ	Nicaragua
YOA-YRZ	Romania
YSA-YSZ	El Salvador (Republic of)
YTA-YUZ	Serbia (Republic of) (WRC-07)
YVA-YYZ	Venezuela (Republic of)
Y2A-Y9Z	Germany (Federal Republic of)
ZAA-ZAZ	Albania (Republic of)
ZBA-ZJZ	United Kingdom of Great Britain and Northern Ireland
ZKA-ZMZ	New Zealand
ZNA-ZOZ	United Kingdom of Great Britain and Northern Ireland
ZPA-ZPZ	Paraguay (Republic of)
ZQA-ZQZ	United Kingdom of Great Britain and Northern Ireland
ZRA-ZUZ	South Africa (Republic of)
ZVA-ZZZ	Brazil (Federative Republic of)
Z2A-Z2Z	Zimbabwe (Republic of)
Z3A-Z3Z	The Former Yugoslav Republic of Macedonia
2AA-2ZZ	United Kingdom of Great Britain and Northern Ireland
3AA-3AZ	Monaco (Principality of)
3BA-3BZ	Mauritius (Republic of)
3CA-3CZ	Equatorial Guinea (Republic of)
3DA-3DM	Swaziland (Kingdom of)
3DN-3DZ	Fiji (Republic of)
3EA-3FZ	Panama (Republic of)
3GA-3GZ	Chile
3HA-3UZ	China (People's Republic of)
3VA-3VZ	Tunisia
3WA-3WZ	Viet Nam (Socialist Republic of)

3XA-3XZ	Guinea (Republic of)
3YA-3YZ	Norway
3ZA-3ZZ	Poland (Republic of)
4AA-4CZ	Mexico
4DA-4IZ	Philippines (Republic of the)
4JA-4KZ	Azerbaijani Republic
4LA-4LZ	Georgia (Republic of)
4MA-4MZ	Venezuela (Republic of)
4OA-4OZ	Montenegro (Republic of) (WRC-07)
4PA-4SZ	Sri Lanka (Democratic Socialist Republic of)
4TA-4TZ	Peru
4UA-4UZ	United Nations
4VA-4VZ	Haiti (Republic of)
4WA-4WZ	Democratic Republic of Timor-Leste (WRC-03)
4XA-4XZ	Israel (State of)
4YA-4YZ	International Civil Aviation Organization
4ZA-4ZZ	Israel (State of)
5AA-5AZ	Libya (Socialist People's Libyan Arab Jamahiriya)
5BA-5BZ	Cyprus (Republic of)
5CA-5GZ	Morocco (Kingdom of)
5HA-5IZ	Tanzania (United Republic of)
5JA-5KZ	Colombia (Republic of)
5LA-5MZ	Liberia (Republic of)
5NA-5OZ	Nigeria (Federal Republic of)
5PA-5QZ	Denmark
5RA-5SZ	Madagascar (Republic of)
5TA-5TZ	Mauritania (Islamic Republic of)
5UA-5UZ	Niger (Republic of the)
5VA-5VZ	Togolese Republic
5WA-5WZ	Samoa (Independent State of)
5XA-5XZ	Uganda (Republic of)
5YA-5ZZ	Kenya (Republic of)
6AA-6BZ	Egypt (Arab Republic of)
6CA-6CZ	Syrian Arab Republic
6DA-6JZ	Mexico
6KA-6NZ	Korea (Republic of)
6OA-6OZ	Somali Democratic Republic
6PA-6SZ	Pakistan (Islamic Republic of)
6TA-6UZ	Sudan (Republic of the)
6VA-6WZ	Senegal (Republic of)
6XA-6XZ	Madagascar (Republic of)
6YA-6YZ	Jamaica
6ZA-6ZZ	Liberia (Republic of)
7AA-7IZ	Indonesia (Republic of)
7JA-7NZ	Japan

7OA-7OZ	Yemen (Republic of)
7PA-7PZ	Lesotho (Kingdom of)
7QA-7QZ	Malawi
7RA-7RZ	Algeria (People's Democratic Republic of)
7SA-7SZ	Sweden
7TA-7YZ	Algeria (People's Democratic Republic of)
7ZA-7ZZ	Saudi Arabia (Kingdom of)
8AA-8IZ	Indonesia (Republic of)
8JA-8NZ	Japan
8OA-8OZ	Botswana (Republic of)
8PA-8PZ	Barbados
8QA-8QZ	Maldives (Republic of)
8RA-8RZ	Guyana
8SA-8SZ	Sweden
8TA-8YZ	India (Republic of)
8ZA-8ZZ	Saudi Arabia (Kingdom of)
9AA-9AZ	Croatia (Republic of)
9BA-9DZ	Iran (Islamic Republic of)
9EA-9FZ	Ethiopia (Federal Democratic Republic of)
9GA-9GZ	Ghana
9HA-9HZ	Malta
9IA-9JZ	Zambia (Republic of)
9KA-9KZ	Kuwait (State of)
9LA-9LZ	Sierra Leone
9MA-9MZ	Malaysia
9NA-9NZ	Nepal
9OA-9TZ	Democratic Republic of the Congo
9UA-9UZ	Burundi (Republic of)
9VA-9VZ	Singapore (Republic of)
9WA-9WZ	Malaysia
9XA-9XZ	Rwandese Republic
9YA-9ZZ	Trinidad and Tobago

Third-Party Communications and Amateur Radio

If all of this information about ham radios is somewhat intimidating, do not despair. "You" can still use ham radios for communications without being a licensed operator. Yes, you do have to have a ham license in order to legally transmit by ham equipment (or be under the direct supervision of someone else who is licensed), but there is an alternative – third-party communication.

Third-party communications occur when a licensed operator sends either written or verbal messages on behalf of unlicensed persons or organizations. There are two "controls" on third-party communication.

First, the communication must be noncommercial and of a personal nature. Asking a ham operator to contact another ham operator located in an area just hit by tornados and, because of being without power, phones do not work in Grandma Sally's city so you can check up on her, is okay. Asking a ham to send a message out that you have an old Chevy for sale would not be okay.

Second, the message must be going to a permitted area. Transmitting from a US location to another US location is okay, but transmitting from the US to another country may not. Because third-party communications bypass a country's normal telephone and postal systems, many foreign governments forbid such communications. In order to transmit from one country to another, the other country must have signed a third-party agreement with the US. What follows is a list of those countries that do have third-party a communications agreement with the US.

V2	Antigua / Barbuda
LU	Argentina
VK	Australia
V3	Belize
CP	Bolivia
T9	Bosnia-Herzegovina
PY	Brazil
VE	Canada
CE	Chile
HK	Colombia
D6	Comoros (Federal Islamic Republic of)
TI	Costa Rica
CO	Cuba
HI	Dominican Republic
J7	Dominica
HC	Ecuador
YS	El Salvador
C5	Gambia, The
9G	Ghana
J3	Grenada
TG	Guatemala
8R	Guyana
HH	Haiti
HR	Honduras
4X	Israel
6Y	Jamaica
JY	Jordan
EL	Liberia
V7	Marshall Islands
XE	Mexico
V6	Micronesia, Federated States of

YN	Nicaragua
HP	Panama
ZP	Paraguay
OA	Peru
DU	Philippines
VR6	Pitcairn Island
V4	St. Christopher / Nevis
J6	St. Lucia
J8	St. Vincent and the Grenadines
9L	Sierra Leone
ZS	South Africa
3DA	Swaziland
9Y	Trinidad / Tobago
TA	Turkey
GB	United Kingdom
CX	Uruguay
YV	Venezuela
4U1ITUITU	Geneva
4U1VICVIC	Vienna

Remember, before TSHTF, keep your pantry well stocked, your powder dry, and your batteries fully charged. 73

APPENDIX A

American Radio Relay League

Affiliated Amateur Radio Clubs in

Virginia

ARRL Affiliated Club	Mountain Empire Amateur Radio Society
City:	Abingdon, VA
Call Sign:	K4PAY
Section:	VA
Links:	www.home.earthlink.net/~mears_arrl

ARRL Affiliated Club	Arlington Radio Public Service Club
City:	Alexandria, VA
Call Sign:	W4AVA
Section:	VA
Links:	www.w4ava.org

ARRL Affiliated Club	Mt Vernon Amateur Radio Club
City:	Alexandria, VA
Call Sign:	K4US
Section:	VA
Links:	www.mvarc.org

ARRL Affiliated Club	Lynn C Wilson Memorial Amateur Radio Venturing Crew 80
City:	Alexandria, VA
Call Sign:	W3BSA
Section:	VA

ARRL Affiliated Club	Alexandria Radio Club Inc.
City:	Alexandria, VA
Call Sign:	W4HFH
Section:	VA
Links:	www.w4hfh.org

ARRL Affiliated Club	National Capitol DX Association
City:	Annandale, VA
Call Sign:	NC3DX
Section:	VA
Links:	www.ncdxa.org/

ARRL Affiliated Club	Pentagon Amateur Radio Club
City:	Arlington, VA
Call Sign:	K4AF
Section:	VA
Links:	www.k4af.org

ARRL Affiliated Club	Arlington Amateur Radio Club
City:	Arlington, VA
Call Sign:	W4WVP
Section:	VA
Links:	www.w4wvp.org

ARRL Affiliated Club   Network Engineers Repeater Assn.
City: Arlington, VA
Call Sign: WA3KOK
Section: VA
Links: www.neradc.org

ARRL Affiliated Club   Lynchburg Amateur Radio Club
City: Bedford, VA
Call Sign: K4CQ
Section: VA
Links: www.k4cq.org

ARRL Affiliated Club   North Shenandoah DX Assn.
City: Boyce, VA
Call Sign: NS4DX
Section: VA

ARRL Affiliated Club   Lake Country Amateur Radio Service
City: Brodnax, VA
Call Sign: W4LCA
Section: VA
Links: www.lcarsonline.org

ARRL Affiliated Club   Lake Braddock Secondary School Amateur Radio Club
City: Burke, VA
Call Sign: KI4JSV
Section: VA

ARRL Affiliated Club   Virginia Young Radio Amateurs Assoc.
City: Charlottesville, VA
Call Sign: W4YRA
Section: VA

ARRL Special Service Club   Albemarle Amateur Radio Club Inc.
City: Charlottesville, VA
Call Sign: WA4TFZ
Section: VA
Links: www.albemarleradio.org

ARRL Affiliated Club   Floyd Amateur Radio Society
City: Check, VA
Section: VA
Links: www.floydamateurradiosociety.org

ARRL Affiliated Club	K4AMG Memorial Amateur Radio Club
City:	Chesapeake, VA
Call Sign:	K4AMG
Section:	VA

ARRL Affiliated Club	Chesapeake Amateur Radio Service
City:	Chesapeake, VA
Call Sign:	W4CAR
Section:	VA
Links:	www.w4car.org

ARRL Affiliated Club	Virginia Mountain Amateur Radio Club
City:	Covington, VA
Call Sign:	W4COV
Section:	VA

ARRL Affiliated Club	Culpeper ARA
City:	Culpeper, VA
Call Sign:	W4CUL
Section:	VA
Links:	www.w4cul.com groups.yahoo.com/group/W4CUL

ARRL Affiliated Club	New River Valley Amateur Radio Club
City:	Dublin, VA
Call Sign:	N4NRV
Section:	VA
Links:	www.qsl.net/n4nrv

ARRL Affiliated Club	Stafford Area Radio Association, Inc.
City:	Fredericksburg, VA
Call Sign:	WW4VA
Section:	VA
Links:	www.ww4va.org

ARRL Affiliated Club	Rappahannock Valley Amateur Radio Club
City:	Fredericksburg, VA
Call Sign:	K4TS
Section:	VA
Links:	www.qsl.net/rvarc

ARRL Affiliated Club	Middle Peninsula Amateur Radio Club
City:	Gloucester Point, VA
Call Sign:	W4HZL
Section:	VA
Links:	www.mparc.net

ARRL Affiliated Club	Eastern Mennonite College Amateur Radio Club
City:	Harrisonburg, VA
Call Sign:	W4RBC
Section:	VA

ARRL Affiliated Club	MASSANUTTEN Amateur Radio Association, Inc.
City:	Harrisonburg, VA
Call Sign:	K4MRA
Section:	VA

ARRL Affiliated Club	New Kent 4 D Star Amateur Radio
City:	Lanexa, VA
Call Sign:	NK4DS
Section:	VA
Links:	www.nk4ds.net

ARRL Affiliated Club	Russell County Amateur Radio Club, Inc.
City:	Lebanon, VA
Call Sign:	WR4RC
Section:	VA
Links:	www.russellcoarc.org

ARRL Affiliated Club	Rockbridge Amateur Radio Club
City:	Lexington, VA
Section:	VA
Links:	www.rockbridgeamateurradioclub.com

ARRL Affiliated Club	Page Valley Amateur Radio Club
City:	Luray, VA
Call Sign:	K4PMH
Section:	VA
Links:	www.k4pmh.org

ARRL Affiliated Club	Terrain Wireless Society
City:	Luray, VA
Section:	VA

ARRL Affiliated Club	Ole Virginia Hams Amateur Radio Club Inc.
City:	Manassas, VA
Call Sign:	W4OVH
Section:	VA
Links:	www.w4ovh.net

ARRL Affiliated Club	South Piedmont Amateur Radio Klub
City:	Martinsville, VA
Call Sign:	N4FU
Section:	VA
Links:	www.sparkarc.org

ARRL Affiliated Club	Amateur Radio Research & Development Corp.
City:	McLean, VA
Call Sign:	W4CIA
Section:	VA
Links:	www.amrad.org/

ARRL Affiliated Club	Northern Virginia FM Association Inc.
City:	Mclean, VA
Call Sign:	NV4FM
Section:	VA
Links:	www.nvfma.org

ARRL Affiliated Club	Central Virginia Contest Club
City:	Mechanicsville, VA
Call Sign:	W4ML
Section:	VA
Links:	CVCC Web Page

ARRL Affiliated Club	Southern Peninsula Amateur Radio Klub
City:	Newport News, VA
Call Sign:	W4QR
Section:	VA
Links:	qsl.net/w4qr/

ARRL Affiliated Club	Peninsula Amateur Radio Club
City:	Newport News, VA
Call Sign:	W4MT
Section:	VA
Links:	www.qsl.net/w4mt

ARRL Affiliated Club	Radio Amateur Society Of Norfolk, Inc.
City:	Norfolk, VA
Call Sign:	W4NPS
Section:	VA
Links:	rasonva.com/index.html

ARRL Affiliated Club	Portsmouth Amateur Radio Club
City:	Portsmouth, VA
Call Sign:	W4POX
Section:	VA
Links:	www.W4POX.org

ARRL Affiliated Club	Loudoun Amateur Radio Group
City:	Purcellville, VA
Call Sign:	K4LRG
Section:	VA
Links:	www.k4lrg.org
ARRL Affiliated Club	Richmond Amateur Telecommunications Society
City:	Richmond, VA
Call Sign:	W4RAT
Section:	VA
Links:	www.rats.net
ARRL Affiliated Club	Dominion DX Group
City:	Richmond, VA
Call Sign:	K4VAC
Section:	VA
Links:	www.ddxg.net
ARRL Affiliated Club	Richmond Amateur Radio Club
City:	Richmond, VA
Call Sign:	W4ZA
Section:	VA
Links:	www.rarclub.net
ARRL Affiliated Club	Roanoke Valley Amateur Radio Club Inc.
City:	Roanoke, VA
Call Sign:	W4CA
Section:	VA
Links:	www.W4CA.us
ARRL Affiliated Club	Franklin County Amateur Radio Club
City:	Rocky Mount, VA
Call Sign:	W4FCR
Section:	VA
Links:	www.qsl.net/w4fcr
ARRL Affiliated Club	Sterling Park Amateur Radio Club
City:	Sterling, VA
Call Sign:	K4NVA
Section:	VA
Links:	www.qsl.net/sterling
ARRL Affiliated Club	Potomac Valley Radio Club
City:	Vienna, VA
Call Sign:	W3GRF
Section:	VA
Links:	www.pvrc.org

ARRL Affiliated Club	Potomac Valley Radio Club
City:	Vienna, VA
Call Sign:	W3GRF
Section:	VA
Links:	www.pvrc.org

ARRL Affiliated Club	Virginia DX Century Club
City:	Virginia Beach, VA
Call Sign:	K4IX/W4DZ
Section:	VA
Links:	www.vadxcc.com

ARRL Affiliated Club	Virginia Beach Amateur Radio Club
City:	Virginia Beach, VA
Call Sign:	W4UG
Section:	VA

ARRL Affiliated Club	USS Wisconsin Radio Club
City:	Virginia Beach, VA
Call Sign:	N4WIS
Section:	VA
Links:	www.n4wis.org

ARRL Affiliated Club	Fauquier Amateur Radio Association
City:	Warrenton, VA
Call Sign:	W4VA
Section:	VA
Links:	www.w4va.org

ARRL Affiliated Club	Williamsburg Area Amateur Radio Club
City:	Williamsburg, VA
Call Sign:	K4RC
Section:	VA
Links:	www.k4rc.net

ARRL Affiliated Club	Shenandoah Valley Amateur Radio Club
City:	Winchester, VA
Call Sign:	W4RKC
Section:	VA
Links:	www.w4rkc.org

ARRL Affiliated Club	Winchester Amateur Radio Society
City:	Winchester, VA
Call Sign:	WA4RS
Section:	VA
Links:	www.nsdxa.org/

APPENDIX B

Amateur Radio License Holders

in

Virginia: Cities A – L
(by City)

FCC Amateur Radio Licenses in Abingdon

Call Sign: KD4NGL
Ralph A Hughes
426 Arnold St
Abingdon VA 24210

Call Sign: KG4KEN
William P Walker
22220 Azure Ln
Abingdon VA 24211

Call Sign: KC4WRB
Martha A Walker
22220 Azure Ln
Abingdon VA 242115934

Call Sign: KX4DX
Robert W Walker
22220 Azure Ln
Abingdon VA 242115934

Call Sign: KR4NW
Wayne R Lane
368 Beverly Dr
Abingdon VA 24210

Call Sign: KD4VEW
Charlie Casey
Rt 8 Box 1130
Abingdon VA 24210

Call Sign: KE4FCE
Scottie Coleman
Rt 1 Box 1264
Abingdon VA 24210

Call Sign: KD4TME
Joseph R Simmons III
Rt 6 Box 154
Abingdon VA 24210

Call Sign: KD4EEZ
George W Ketron
Rt 7 Box 267
Abingdon VA 24210

Call Sign: KD4EEY

Helen J Ketron
Rt 7 Box 267
Abingdon VA 24210

Call Sign: N4SEW
Raymond J Lutzo
Rt 3 Box 338
Abingdon VA 24210

Call Sign: KD4UZM
Delmar W Parks
Rt 5 Box 677
Abingdon VA 24210

Call Sign: N4OIU
Michael G Barker
Rt 4 Box 782
Abingdon VA 24210

Call Sign: N4VAU
Thomas L Bailey
Rt 4 Box 842
Abingdon VA 24210

Call Sign: AK4MT
Michael L Terry
19058 Celebrity Ln
Abingdon VA 24211

Call Sign: AC4IA
Charles W Edmonds
12311 Chip Ridge Rd
Abingdon VA 24210

Call Sign: W4NTF
Russell L Shearrow
15253 Cliffhanger Rd
Abingdon VA 24210

Call Sign: KB4JUN
William R Mc Cracken
13437 Countiss Rd
Abingdon VA 242108707

Call Sign: K4DPG
John D Bonham
495 Court St
Abingdon VA 24210

Call Sign: KN4DPF
Peggy L Adams
801 Crosscreek Dr
Abingdon VA 24210

Call Sign: K1PEG
Peggy L Adams
801 Crosscreek Dr
Abingdon VA 24210

Call Sign: KF4UEL
Thomas M Hale
849 Crosscreek Dr
Abingdon VA 24210

Call Sign: KF4UJB
Thomas D Hale
849 Crosscreek Dr
Abingdon VA 24210

Call Sign: W4ZYD
Michael A Steele
23808 Denton Valley Rd
Abingdon VA 242114224

Call Sign: KF4FKQ
Eddy D Clevinger
27220 Denton Valley Rd
Abingdon VA 24211

Call Sign: KE4BHQ
Frederick E Conrad
418 E Main St
Abingdon VA 24210

Call Sign: N4FEC
Frederick E Conrad
418 E Main St
Abingdon VA 24210

Call Sign: KJ4QYL
Michael A Boardwine
831 Falcon Dr
Abingdon VA 24210

Call Sign: K4HRO
James M Cole
240 Gillespie Dr
Abingdon VA 24210

Call Sign: WA4WKX
James E Fleenor
241 Gillespie Dr
Abingdon VA 24210

Call Sign: KI4QOP
William W Wasson
23250 Golden View Dr
Abingdon VA 24211

Call Sign: WA2BCZ
William W Wasson
23250 Golden View Dr
Abingdon VA 24211

Call Sign: WD4BYB
Jack D Blackson
1155 Hillview Dr
Abingdon VA 24210

Call Sign: KI4RYK
Dorris B Salyers
19491 Johnson Dr
Abingdon VA 242116901

Call Sign: KF4DWB
Tim G Smith
18007 Kenwarn Ln
Abingdon VA 24210

Call Sign: KB4TNT
Melvin R Adams
18364 Lacy Ln
Abingdon VA 24211

Call Sign: KC4ATS
Avery R Mc Clellan
18501 Landridge Way
Abingdon VA 24211

Call Sign: KD4CZE
Robert L Jones
25350 Lee Hwy
Abingdon VA 24211

Call Sign: W4YRB
Carl H Steele
25510 Lee Hwy

Abingdon VA 24211

Call Sign: KF4VBF
Ronnie L Layne
16482 Lindy Dr
Abingdon VA 24211

Call Sign: KE4VAQ
David M Brillhart
12551 Maiden Creek Rd
Abingdon VA 24210

Call Sign: WA4JRV
David M Brillhart
12551 Maiden Creek Rd
Abingdon VA 24210

Call Sign: N4BDQ
Robert L Pugh
16261 Mary St
Abingdon VA 242108415

Call Sign: KB4NHA
Richard E Mullins
17203 Marylee Dr
Abingdon VA 24210

Call Sign: WB8RXW
Randy E Asbury
17203 Marylee Dr
Abingdon VA 24210

Call Sign: KG4BGB
Mary J O Quinn
11145 Mendota Rd
Abingdon VA 24210

Call Sign: KE4KMY
Jason B Price
24525 Mock Knob Rd
Abingdon VA 24210

Call Sign: KF4FHT
Sheila J Widner
538 Norfolk St
Abingdon VA 24210

Call Sign: KB4WLY
Willis E Blevins

425 Oakland St
Abingdon VA 24210

Call Sign: KF4NFZ
Brenda S Mc Clellan
19358 Oakwood Dr
Abingdon VA 24211

Call Sign: KJ4WAC
Beverly F Wright
19387 Oakwood Dr
Abingdon VA 24211

Call Sign: KD6UOI
Todd M Tholl
17746 Old Jones Boro Rd
Abingdon VA 242116626

Call Sign: N4YHW
Michael J Canter
14394 Peaceful Valley Rd
Abingdon VA 24210

Call Sign: AE4GL
Gilbert Kiser
14176 Poterfield Hwy
Abingdon VA 24210

Call Sign: KJ4WAD
Paula K Wright
15033 Quail Ridge Way
Abingdon VA 24210

Call Sign: KJ4UXX
Don Cipriani
14282 Rattle Creek Rd
Abingdon VA 24210

Call Sign: KJ4UXW
Nina M Cipriani
14282 Rattle Creek Rd
Abingdon VA 24210

Call Sign: N5LWV
Charles P Jones
23244 Richvalley Rd
Abingdon VA 24210

Call Sign: N4SEY

Ernest F Sutherland
Rte 3
Abingdon VA 24210

Call Sign: KF4DRO
Fred M Sutherland Jr
21011 Russell Rd
Abingdon VA 24210

Call Sign: WA4IZC
Lewis A Dye
333 Shady St
Abingdon VA 24210

Call Sign: AD4WM
Carl M Mitchell
467 Shady St
Abingdon VA 24210

Call Sign: KE4QZT
Bridget E Mitchell
467 Shady St
Abingdon VA 24210

Call Sign: KE4QZU
Jeremy B Mitchell
467 Shady St
Abingdon VA 24210

Call Sign: KF4DWC
William I Slagle
16094 Spring Valley Rd
Abingdon VA 242108266

Call Sign: KJ4WAG
Gregory W Osborne Jr
16312 Spring Vlley Rd
Abingdon VA 24210

Call Sign: KD4MBS
Rebecca L Hayter
541 Sutton St
Abingdon VA 24210

Call Sign: N4BTR
Benjamin T Rice
960 Timberland Ct
Abingdon VA 24210

Call Sign: KB8CIY
F David Wilkin
19230 Triple Crown Dr
Abingdon VA 24211

Call Sign: KG4LAM
Brian W Canada
19478 Triple Crown Dr
Abingdon VA 24211

Call Sign: KG4MAZ
Whitney B Canada
19478 Triple Crown Dr
Abingdon VA 24211

Call Sign: KG4SVA
James R Harris
155 Valley St NW
Abingdon VA 242102800

Call Sign: KF4GOJ
Douglas E Debusk
26333 Watauga Rd
Abingdon VA 242117345

Call Sign: KI4BWC
Matthew K Thrift
26469 Watauga Rd
Abingdon VA 24211

Call Sign: KD4SHX
John P Ferratt
254 Whites Mill Rd
Abingdon VA 242102900

Call Sign: N4LZO
Julian R Lowe
371 Winterham Dr
Abingdon VA 24211

Call Sign: KD4TMI
Jack C Phelps Jr
Woodland Hills
Abingdon VA 24210

Call Sign: KD4JUS
Luedell S Bailey
19060 Woodland Hills Rd
Abingdon VA 24210

Call Sign: WB4ENN
William A Bailey
19060 Woodland Hills Rd
Abingdon VA 242109644

Call Sign: WA4JME
Howard Jack M Taylor
979 Woodlawn Ter
Abingdon VA 24210

Call Sign: W4FXT
Clifford M Turner
16294 Worthing Way
Abingdon VA 242101686

Call Sign: KD4JDJ
Robert L Carbary
Abingdon VA 24210

Call Sign: K4HUF
Jimmy L Countiss
Abingdon VA 24212

Call Sign: KF4GCV
Thomas J Crise
Abingdon VA 24212

Call Sign: WD4DCX
Daniel E Nicewander
Abingdon VA 24212

Call Sign: KI4PAY
Inc Mountain Empire ARS
Abingdon VA 242121971

Call Sign: K4PAY
Inc Mountain Empire ARS
Abingdon VA 242121971

FCC Amateur Radio Licenses in Accomac

Call Sign: KF4DHN
Alan B Hooker
23309 Back St
Accomac VA 23301

Call Sign: WD4JBG

J Williamso Brown Jr
Back St Hwy 1503
Accomac VA 23301

Call Sign: N4SNM
Susan M Morgan
26430 Baylys Neck Rd
Accomac VA 23301

Call Sign: WA4AZB
Herbert Morgan
26430 Baylys Neck Rd
Accomac VA 23301

Call Sign: KF4SNC
Michael C Cropper
24114 Charlotte St
Accomac VA 23301

Call Sign: KC4UOH
Henry A Lewis
24385 Dix Farm Dr
Accomac VA 23301

Call Sign: KD4NVQ
Gregory A Lewis
24511 Dix Farm Dr
Accomac VA 23301

Call Sign: KD4NWC
Nathaniel B Williams Sr
24549 M N Smith Rd
Accomac VA 23301

Call Sign: KD4NVJ
Robert M Brownlie Jr
23341 Merry Branch Rd
Accomac VA 23301

Call Sign: KF4KOO
Angelo L Chandler
Accomac VA 23301

Call Sign: K3DM
Robert T Frost
Accomac VA 23301

Call Sign: N4DND
William R Lewis III

Accomac VA 23301

Call Sign: KG4YYJ
Cecil R Marshall III
Accomac VA 23301

Call Sign: AI4VD
Cecil R Marshall III
Accomac VA 23301

Call Sign: W5CRM
Cecil R Marshall III
Accomac VA 23301

FCC Amateur Radio Licenses in Achilles

Call Sign: KU4AU
Philip L Smith
Achilles VA 23001

FCC Amateur Radio Licenses in Afton

Call Sign: KF4ZBK
James D Bowers
Rt 1 Box 481 D
Afton VA 22920

Call Sign: WD4NEB
Larry K Akers
710 Crawfords View Rd
Afton VA 22920

Call Sign: KR4BG
Matthew C Brill
797 Crawfords View Rd
Afton VA 22920

Call Sign: KI4NTN
Nathan E Houser
8230 Dick Woods Rd
Afton VA 22920

Call Sign: KG4FYF
Howard C Gay
9062 Dick Woods Rd
Afton VA 229201543

Call Sign: KA3MWD
M Paul Knear
420 Fox Hollow Rd
Afton VA 22920

Call Sign: KA3MWE
Cathy M Knear
420 Fox Hollow Rd
Afton VA 22920

Call Sign: KG4ZSR
Thomas J Broeski
32 Mt View Dr
Afton VA 22920

Call Sign: NM9S
Mark A Bowers
137 Mt View Dr
Afton VA 22920

Call Sign: KJ4CCX
Hillbilly DxErs
351 Mtn Rd
Afton VA 22920

Call Sign: K4HDX
Hillbilly DxErs
351 Mtn Rd
Afton VA 22920

Call Sign: K4BDR
Kevin K Ward
351 Mtn Rd
Afton VA 22920

Call Sign: KG4OBC
Henry Bisgaier
1128 Ortman Rd
Afton VA 22920

Call Sign: KF4TKJ
Matthew E Bisgaier
1128 Ortman Rd
Afton VA 229201852

Call Sign: N3UV
Matthew E Bisgaier
1128 Ortman Rd
Afton VA 229201852

Call Sign: W8GTA
Robert L Canody
837 Pounding Branch Rd
Afton VA 229203121

Call Sign: KI4VLC
Elbert L Halterman
1290 Pounding Branch Rd
Afton VA 22920

Call Sign: W4VLC
Elbert L Halterman
1290 Pounding Branch Rd
Afton VA 22920

Call Sign: KF4UTC
Jeffrey W Howe
7158 Rockfish Valley Hwy
Afton VA 22920

Call Sign: KJ4RPS
Carol H Hunt
139 Towler Way
Afton VA 22920

Call Sign: KB4WWH
Dee P Almquist
Afton VA 22920

Call Sign: KG4TWQ
Howard C Gay
Afton VA 22920

Call Sign: N4SYH
John C Bottemiller
Afton VA 229200071

FCC Amateur Radio Licenses in Alberta

Call Sign: KE4SPU
Diane F Gott
3764 Old Poole Rd
Alberta VA 23821

Call Sign: AG4GE
Diane F Gott
3764 Old Poole Rd

Alberta VA 23821

Call Sign: AF4AE
Andrew C Gott Jr
3764 Old Poole Rd
Alberta VA 23821

FCC Amateur Radio Licenses in Aldie

Call Sign: KJ4SSW
Sara Robinson
24701 Byrne Meadow Sq 411
Aldie VA 20105

Call Sign: KJ4OIP
Mehrdad Maroofi
24701 Byrne Meadow Sq Apt
411
Aldie VA 20105

Call Sign: KJ4VRY
Nicolas A Cremeans
25205 Destination Sq
Aldie VA 20105

Call Sign: KJ4MTH
Jason A Stripling
25274 Diligence Ct
Aldie VA 20105

Call Sign: KD6ADY
Frank N Lapato
25373 Frosty Meadow Ln
Aldie VA 20105

Call Sign: AJ4IW
Frank N Lapato
25373 Frosty Meadow Ln
Aldie VA 20105

Call Sign: KK4FYU
Andrew Gizinski
41827 Inspiration Ter
Aldie VA 20105

Call Sign: KG4MAU
Dean E Rudge
40881 John Mosby Hwy

Aldie VA 201052823

Call Sign: KD4ZUY
Randall S Benn
40719 Lenah Run Cir
Aldie VA 20105

Call Sign: KG4ZCB
David T Mullins
24075 New Mtn Rd
Aldie VA 20105

Call Sign: KE4WBY
Michael R Lang
21545 Oatlands Rd
Aldie VA 201051703

Call Sign: KG4TIH
Paulson G Mcintyre
21663 Oatlands Rd
Aldie VA 20105

Call Sign: WB2AYE
Howard S Sterling
25480 Tomey Ct
Aldie VA 20105

Call Sign: KA4DCS
Marvin B Cranshaw Jr
Aldie VA 201050295

FCC Amateur Radio Licenses in Alexandria

Call Sign: KF4DMM
Paula J Fetterman
6507 10th St A 2
Alexandria VA 223076505

Call Sign: KI4IFP
Miles H Mcginnis
718 4 Mile Rd
Alexandria VA 22305

Call Sign: KD4VYT
Joseph K Fordham Jr
6325 8th St
Alexandria VA 22312

Call Sign: KF6DCM
Jason T Luttgens
6247 Abbottsbury Row
Alexandria VA 22315

Call Sign: KB6DMP
Erika S Falk
305 Adams Ave
Alexandria VA 22301

Call Sign: W4HEK
Jerry F Murphree
3802 Adrienne Dr
Alexandria VA 22309

Call Sign: KJ4FUW
Michael Murphree
3802 Adrienne Dr
Alexandria VA 22309

Call Sign: N4XJY
Edwin H Copenhaver
3205 Alabama Ave
Alexandria VA 22305

Call Sign: KI4PHH
Samuel H Laane
3314 Alabama Ave
Alexandria VA 22305

Call Sign: N1BV
George K Coyne
1102 Alden Rd
Alexandria VA 22308

Call Sign: KF4NDR
Joseph J Butasek
1120 Alden Rd
Alexandria VA 22308

Call Sign: KI4QNE
William H Hillard Jr
4506 Apple Tree Dr
Alexandria VA 22310

Call Sign: N8IWT
William H Hillard Jr
4506 Apple Tree Dr
Alexandria VA 22310

Call Sign: KA0SEY
John E Queen
6747 Applemint Ln
Alexandria VA 22310

Call Sign: N4QQQ
John E Queen
6747 Applemint Ln
Alexandria VA 22310

Call Sign: KH6JDW
Salustiano Q Devela
6026 Archstone Ct Apt 102
Alexandria VA 22310

Call Sign: KK4FFR
Joseph Cunetta
6005 Archstone Way 104
Alexandria VA 22310

Call Sign: KB3QMU
Soren T Harward
6011 Archstone Way 303
Alexandria VA 22310

Call Sign: N4TKM
Jaroslav Rohleder
824 Arcturus On The Potomac
Alexandria VA 22308

Call Sign: W3WKP
David J Reese II
824 Arcturus On The Potomac
Alexandria VA 22308

Call Sign: KG4YEC
Jason S Grigsby
4521 Arendale Sq
Alexandria VA 22304

Call Sign: KG4YEB
Thomas W Grigsby
4521 Arendale Sq
Alexandria VA 22304

Call Sign: W4IAL
Albert Karasz
456 Argyle Dr

Alexandria VA 22305

Call Sign: KJ4RBE
Edwin B Sare
2260 Arlington Ter
Alexandria VA 22303

Call Sign: KC4ZYP
Hal T Miller
12 Ashby St A
Alexandria VA 223052817

Call Sign: KG4FSQ
March A Beall
7850 Audubon Ave
Alexandria VA 22306

Call Sign: KI4COB
Robert L Wilkinson Jr
3446 Austin Ave
Alexandria VA 22310

Call Sign: KA4GFY
Richard C Adamy
3408 Austin Ct
Alexandria VA 22310

Call Sign: K4GAA
Raymond Cole Jr
3410 Austin Ct
Alexandria VA 22310

Call Sign: KI4KXH
Benjamin E Turk
3408 Austin Ct
Alexandria VA 22310

Call Sign: N1CYA
Eric C Johnson
1861 Ballenger Ave
Alexandria VA 22314

Call Sign: N7XUI
Stanley R Pryga
5223 Ballycastle Cir
Alexandria VA 22315

Call Sign: KG4UNQ
Richard J Hayes II

5269 Ballycastle Cir
Alexandria VA 22153

Call Sign: K1CAR
Collegiate ARA
5900 Barclay Dr
Alexandria VA 22315

Call Sign: W4SSS
Collegiate ARA
5900 Barclay Dr
Alexandria VA 22315

Call Sign: N3BF
Bradley A Farrell
5900 Barclay Dr
Alexandria VA 22315

Call Sign: WB4QPW
Gilbert L Patton III
7132 Barry Rd
Alexandria VA 22315

Call Sign: KG4IEI
Ramsey D Gorchev
529 Bashford Ln Apt 4
Alexandria VA 22314

Call Sign: KA4CRO
James G Manning
3025 Batter Sea Ln
Alexandria VA 223092158

Call Sign: KB4APM
Chester S Clifford
8806 Battery Rd
Alexandria VA 223082801

Call Sign: W4PJA
Bernard A Neuman
8902 Battery Rd
Alexandria VA 22308

Call Sign: KC4HSJ
Edward H Takken
7905 Bayberry Dr
Alexandria VA 22306

Call Sign: KK4CBK

Timothy J Brown
7910 Bayberry Dr
Alexandria VA 22306

Call Sign: WA7HPK
Omar Y Spaulding
6124 Bayliss Pl
Alexandria VA 22310

Call Sign: KW7OS
Omar Y Spaulding
6124 Bayliss Pl
Alexandria VA 22310

Call Sign: KJ4IMX
Eric R White
6912 Baylor Dr
Alexandria VA 22307

Call Sign: KJ4IMS
Jacolyn White
6912 Baylor Dr
Alexandria VA 22307

Call Sign: KA4KPC
Murray E Ward
9004 Beatty Dr
Alexandria VA 22308

Call Sign: KF4KJP
Jean G Delort
5134 Beauregard St
Alexandria VA 223121936

Call Sign: KG4MJT
James P Sauers Jr
6614 Beddo St
Alexandria VA 22306

Call Sign: KJ4PRZ
Brian C Norton
6613 Beddoo St
Alexandria VA 22306

Call Sign: KI4NBS
Christopher M Huffine
6623 Beddoo St
Alexandria VA 22306

Call Sign: KC7ITC
Steven J Nosich
6705 Beddoo St
Alexandria VA 223066607

Call Sign: KG6JLH
Rudy G Murray
5375 Bedford Ter A
Alexandria VA 22309

Call Sign: W4MV
Sidney T Smith
4514 Bee St
Alexandria VA 22310

Call Sign: KG4JHZ
William P Sullivan
1913 Belfield Rd
Alexandria VA 223071109

Call Sign: N2VVG
William D Rogers Jr
1911 Belle Haven Rd
Alexandria VA 22307

Call Sign: N4LYR
Chastain B Stone
2102 Belle View Blvd
Alexandria VA 22307

Call Sign: KE4IUH
James K Batchelor
2112 Belle View Blvd
Alexandria VA 22307

Call Sign: KC4XX
Henry W Petruskewic
1402 Belle View Blvd B1
Alexandria VA 22307

Call Sign: KF4BBT
Kevin T Kellbach
5960 Berkshire Ct
Alexandria VA 22303

Call Sign: KA4UNR
Luis A Lama
6226 Berlee Dr
Alexandria VA 22312

Call Sign: K4BNY
Walter A Cullen
6213 Bernard Ave
Alexandria VA 22310

Call Sign: KJ4BQT
Cecelia Vergaretti
7112 Bertram Ln
Alexandria VA 22306

Call Sign: KC4ZPW
Jack E Jackson
6314 Beryl Rd
Alexandria VA 22312

Call Sign: KN4TY
Wm Michael Dante
6321 Beryl Rd
Alexandria VA 22312

Call Sign: N7SJZ
Kathryn L Knight
5238 Bessley Pl
Alexandria VA 22304

Call Sign: KI4GOL
Arlington VA ARC
5262 Bessley Pl
Alexandria VA 22304

Call Sign: W4AVA
Arlington Radio Public Service
Club
5262 Bessley Pl
Alexandria VA 22304

Call Sign: KF4LMB
Patrick S Pendleton
5262 Bessley Pl
Alexandria VA 22304

Call Sign: KF4QQM
Timothy D Jordan
5262 Bessley Pl
Alexandria VA 22304

Call Sign: KA4BQB
Adrienne S Fox

4927 Birch Ln
Alexandria VA 22312

Call Sign: WA4SVC
Jay A Fox
4927 Birch Ln
Alexandria VA 22312

Call Sign: KG4WET
James H May II
7009 Birkenhead Pl Unit C
Alexandria VA 22315

Call Sign: KA3TIS
John C Place
7013 Birkenhead Pl Unit E
Alexandria VA 22315

Call Sign: KD4JND
Louis J Krause
6023 Bitternut Dr
Alexandria VA 22310

Call Sign: KC4TAU
Mario M Almeida
7554 Blanford Ct
Alexandria VA 22315

Call Sign: K1PHS
James M Riley
4010 Blue Slate Dr
Alexandria VA 22306

Call Sign: W3DM
Frederick M Galloway
6507 Blue Wing Dr
Alexandria VA 22307

Call Sign: KB4WSG
Jonathan C Bierce
7932 Bolling Dr
Alexandria VA 22308

Call Sign: KG4IRI
James W Pravel
7948 Bolling Dr
Alexandria VA 22308

Call Sign: AI4ZD

Frederick B Kuhn Jr
5906 Bond Ct
Alexandria VA 22315

Call Sign: KJ4JMQ
Dvin Adalian
5925 Bond Ct
Alexandria VA 22315

Call Sign: KI4IPK
Douglas J Jemison
2804 Boswell Ave
Alexandria VA 22306

Call Sign: KK4AWI
Philip B Mulford
8504 Bound Brook Ln
Alexandria VA 22309

Call Sign: AK4KM
Philip B Mulford
8504 Bound Brook Ln
Alexandria VA 22309

Call Sign: KD4PES
Richard D Dove
1201 Braddock Pl 612
Alexandria VA 22314

Call Sign: KC9AVX
Adam T Carpenter
1200 Braddock Pl Apt 315
Alexandria VA 223141665

Call Sign: KI4PIW
Thomas Jefferson ARC
6560 Braddock Rd
Alexandria VA 22312

Call Sign: KJ4CJN
John F Francis
8230 Brady St
Alexandria VA 22309

Call Sign: KC4IQZ
Charles H Shaw
9324 Brambly Ln
Alexandria VA 22309

Call Sign: AK4KQ
Andrew H Lavanway
5228 Brawner Pl
Alexandria VA 22304

Call Sign: NW0N
Andrew H Lavanway
5228 Brawner Pl
Alexandria VA 22304

Call Sign: KI4IPQ
Gyrwen Ni
6478 Brick Hearth Ct
Alexandria VA 22306

Call Sign: KI4IPT
Henry L Yung
6478 Brick Hearth Ct
Alexandria VA 22306

Call Sign: KI4MWQ
Randal J Laporte
8908 Bridgehaven Ct
Alexandria VA 22308

Call Sign: KI4QNG
Sandra D Laporte
8908 Bridgehaven Ct
Alexandria VA 22308

Call Sign: KI4ZGW
Albert F Kaminsky
7461 Brighouse Ct
Alexandria VA 22315

Call Sign: KI4WKX
Albert F Kaminsky Jr
7461 Brighouse Ct
Alexandria VA 223153835

Call Sign: KD4LTI
Ren E Nehls
6828 Brindle Heath Way
Alexandria VA 22315

Call Sign: KE4RBQ
Paul L Viani
9400 Brookmay Ct
Alexandria VA 22309

Call Sign: WB4CDX
Raymond C Fisher
4424 Brookside Dr
Alexandria VA 22312

Call Sign: KE4MKB
Evan C Campbell
9033 Buckner Rd
Alexandria VA 22309

Call Sign: KJ4SZM
Kevin B Knapp
6002 Burdon Ct Apt 302
Alexandria VA 22315

Call Sign: KI4MLV
William H Embrey
5602 Burgundy Pl
Alexandria VA 223031157

Call Sign: W4WHE
William H Embrey
5602 Burgundy Pl
Alexandria VA 223031157

Call Sign: N3SAT
Randall L Coleman
2405 Burke Ave
Alexandria VA 22301

Call Sign: N4TCI
Mary J Morris
6111 Burnett St
Alexandria VA 22310

Call Sign: WZ4A
John L Forrest Jr
6111 Burnett St
Alexandria VA 22310

Call Sign: W6IVH
John H Buchbach
7405 Burtonwood Dr
Alexandria VA 22307

Call Sign: KF4OSJ
Dominick S Caridi
8802 Camden St

Alexandria VA 223082367

Call Sign: KD4YRK
Joel S Miayo
5840 Cameron Run Ter
Alexandria VA 22303

Call Sign: KD4OAR
Nenita C Miayo
5840 Cameron Run Ter 208
Alexandria VA 22303

Call Sign: KI4GRX
Corbett B Coburn III
5850 Cameron Run Ter 515
Alexandria VA 22303

Call Sign: N4YKR
Nicole L Adaniya
5850 Cameron Run Ter 912
Alexandria VA 22303

Call Sign: KG4RCM
Barbara A Barry
5850 Cameron Run Ter Apt
1521
Alexandria VA 22303

Call Sign: KE5DBG
Athappan Kannan
5850 Cameron Run Ter Apt
1613
Alexandria VA 22303

Call Sign: KF4AJW
Henry P Coleman
509 Cameron St
Alexandria VA 22314

Call Sign: KB7VYF
David P Fitchitt
185 Cameron Station Blvd
Alexandria VA 223047783

Call Sign: N4HAM
Krieger W Henderson Jr
8837 Camfield Ct
Alexandria VA 22308

Call Sign: KC9I
Allan M Dickson
8813 Camfield Dr
Alexandria VA 22308

Call Sign: KG4RKF
George C Kirby III
8819 Camfield Dr
Alexandria VA 22308

Call Sign: KG4RKG
Benjamin C Kirby
8819 Camfield Dr
Alexandria VA 22308

Call Sign: KF4MNE
Charles F Crizer Jr
3207 Campbell Dr
Alexandria VA 22303

Call Sign: KC4NDJ
Marguerite G Kendall
5208 Cannes Ct
Alexandria VA 22310

Call Sign: W4PB
John A Springer
5731 Cannon Ln
Alexandria VA 22303

Call Sign: W3IGZ
Louis W Heacock
5805 Cannon Ln
Alexandria VA 22303

Call Sign: KC4KSU
Caroline L Quinn
31 Canterbury Sq
Alexandria VA 22304

Call Sign: KA5TUU
John C Von Senden
18 Carriage House Cir
Alexandria VA 223046338

Call Sign: KJ4LBX
Matthew C Johnson
3719 Carriage House Ct
Alexandria VA 22309

Call Sign: N1IIX
Christopher R Watts
5009 Caryn Ct Apt 102
Alexandria VA 22312

Call Sign: KF4FMM
Harvey J Glowaski
6125 Castletown Way
Alexandria VA 22310

Call Sign: KJ4CNM
Sohrab A Rezvan
5923 Cauba Ct
Alexandria VA 22310

Call Sign: KA9WOI
Michael L Fontaine
4332 Cedarlake Ct
Alexandria VA 22309

Call Sign: AK4QY
Douglas M Rose
5100 Celtic Dr 104
Alexandria VA 22310

Call Sign: KD4AOF
Eileen M Boettcher
1602 Chapel Hill Dr
Alexandria VA 22304

Call Sign: W4AF
Gary M Patterson
1602 Chapel Hill Dr
Alexandria VA 22304

Call Sign: W3AUR
Edwin A Speakman
9018 Charles Augustine Dr
Alexandria VA 22308

Call Sign: KB5RNQ
Clyde W Spence Jr
8434 Cherry Valley Ln
Alexandria VA 22309

Call Sign: W4JDC
James D Compton III
6475 Cheyenne Dr Unit 301

Alexandria VA 22312

Call Sign: K4SHD
James T Gobbel Jr
2607 Childs Ln
Alexandria VA 22308

Call Sign: W4LVD
Edward B Crossman
2621 Childs Ln
Alexandria VA 22308

Call Sign: KJ4FDH
Christopher B Chaney
2624 Childs Ln
Alexandria VA 22308

Call Sign: KI4FOL
Laurent F Delfosse
5229 Chippewa Pl
Alexandria VA 22312

Call Sign: KX4W
George D Farmer III
5721 Clermont Dr
Alexandria VA 223101402

Call Sign: KB3QEQ
Nathaniel H Wilson
323 Clifford Ave
Alexandria VA 22305

Call Sign: KI4CQC
Urai C Ackerbauer
7023 Clifton Knoll Ct
Alexandria VA 22315

Call Sign: KC4OMV
Blair Ackerbauer
7023 Clifton Knoll Ct
Alexandria VA 22315

Call Sign: KA4JGP
Michael C Lewis
327 Cloudes Mill Dr
Alexandria VA 223043080

Call Sign: K7BLT
Kurt W Weiler

6232 Cockspur Dr
Alexandria VA 22310

Call Sign: KJ4DGB
Carl D Bird IV
7009 Cold Spring Ln
Alexandria VA 22306

Call Sign: N4NNS
Lillian S Vasilas
1801 Collingwood Rd
Alexandria VA 22308

Call Sign: KF4WLC
Joseph C Smith Jr
3805 A Colonial Ave
Alexandria VA 22309

Call Sign: N4JCS
Joseph C Smith Jr
3805 A Colonial Ave
Alexandria VA 22309

Call Sign: KI4EOF
William A Tarpeh
6932 Columbia Dr
Alexandria VA 22307

Call Sign: KB1EVT
Devin G Fisher
1606 Concord Pl
Alexandria VA 22308

Call Sign: N9ZTM
Colin P Chandler
1506 Cool Spring Dr
Alexandria VA 22308

Call Sign: KA4MFF
John N Street
4210 Corcoran St
Alexandria VA 22309

Call Sign: KG4ROA
Douglas A Mccuistion
4229 Corcoran St
Alexandria VA 22309

Call Sign: KG4SCG

Ian W Mccuistion
4229 Corcoran St
Alexandria VA 22309

Call Sign: KG4URM
Judith M Mccuistion
4229 Corcoran St
Alexandria VA 22309

Call Sign: W4TDT
Luther T Cruse Jr
5607 Cornish Way
Alexandria VA 22310

Call Sign: KS4KW
Laurence C Parfitt Jr
6612 Cottonwood Dr
Alexandria VA 22310

Call Sign: KC4GCQ
Paul Watkins
7012 Coventry Rd
Alexandria VA 22306

Call Sign: KI4MAF
Scott A Horsfield
5905 G Coverdale Way
Alexandria VA 22310

Call Sign: KJ4IKH
Jane E Callahan
7530 Coxton Ct
Alexandria VA 22306

Call Sign: KJ4OXN
Encarnita S Arguelles
7530 Coxton Ct Unit C
Alexandria VA 22306

Call Sign: KJ4HSS
Patrick M Callahan
7530 Coxton Ct Unit C
Alexandria VA 22306

Call Sign: N4RPI
Patrick M Callahan
7530 Coxton Ct Unit C
Alexandria VA 22306

Call Sign: KJ4LBZ
Brian M Patten
5260 Cozy Glen Ln
Alexandria VA 223123900

Call Sign: WV4Q
Brian M Patten
5260 Cozy Glen Ln
Alexandria VA 223123900

Call Sign: W4RUS
Kenton W Van Lue
9304 Craig Ave
Alexandria VA 22309

Call Sign: WB6ABN
Byron L Powers
2314 Creek Dr
Alexandria VA 22308

Call Sign: KI4DXM
James M Buchanan
1720 Crestwood Dr
Alexandria VA 22302

Call Sign: K3BUC
James M Buchanan
1720 Crestwood Dr
Alexandria VA 22302

Call Sign: KJ4OCH
Brad A Johnson
6216 Crestwood Dr
Alexandria VA 22312

Call Sign: KJ4IMV
Robert L Reynolds
6017 Cromwell Pl
Alexandria VA 22315

Call Sign: KG4YJZ
Brian A Ferguson
8223 Crown Ct Rd
Alexandria VA 223081524

Call Sign: WM4S
James H Foresman III
8310 Crown Ct Rd
Alexandria VA 223081526

Call Sign: WA3EJL
Lawrence M Hurzon
6080 Crown Royal Cir
Alexandria VA 223101747

Call Sign: KA8UCX
Alan J Doi
309 Crown View Dr
Alexandria VA 22314

Call Sign: KB4EUY
Robert C Suggs
2507 Culpeper Rd
Alexandria VA 22308

Call Sign: N3GK
George N Kamm
2508 Culpeper Rd
Alexandria VA 22308

Call Sign: W4SWP
Lewis L Bradley
8520 Culver Pl
Alexandria VA 223082012

Call Sign: K3IZ
Stephen M Schneider
8602 Cushman Pl
Alexandria VA 22308

Call Sign: K4US
Mount Vernon ARC
8602 Cushman Pl
Alexandria VA 22308

Call Sign: KJ4IKE
Theodore F Kirby
6511 Cygnet Dr
Alexandria VA 22307

Call Sign: KF4YKD
Ryan B Comes
8507 Cyrus Pl
Alexandria VA 22308

Call Sign: N4GDF
Thomas A Dickson
4005 Dakota Ct

Alexandria VA 22312

Call Sign: W4LOR
Allan B Rochford
1052 Dalebrook Dr
Alexandria VA 22308

Call Sign: AF4W
Richard N Lynn
3624 Dannys Ln
Alexandria VA 22311

Call Sign: W8MSC
Roger G Hunter
7603 Darden Row
Alexandria VA 223153734

Call Sign: W4FAA
Roger G Hunter
7603 Darden Row
Alexandria VA 223153734

Call Sign: W3MQ
Roger G Hunter
7603 Darden Row
Alexandria VA 223153734

Call Sign: W4LU
Roger G Hunter
7603 Darden Row
Alexandria VA 223153734

Call Sign: KO4IO
Keith B Ward
4509 Dartmoor Ln
Alexandria VA 22310

Call Sign: KO4IQ
Lucas D Ward
4509 Dartmoor Ln
Alexandria VA 22310

Call Sign: KF4RUX
C Oscar H Yankey Jr
2800 Dartmouth Rd Apt 5
Alexandria VA 22314

Call Sign: KA6AKH
Donald F Clark

906 Darton Dr
Alexandria VA 22308

Call Sign: KI4FPZ
Veronica F Clark
906 Darton Dr
Alexandria VA 22308

Call Sign: WK4T
Edward S Cribbs
4024 David Ln
Alexandria VA 22311

Call Sign: KF4TJG
J Whipple Dutton
2609 Dawn Dr
Alexandria VA 22306

Call Sign: KJ4BQE
Walter J Munyan Jr
1006 De Wolfe Dr
Alexandria VA 22308

Call Sign: KJ4KAY
Brent M Simpson
4708 Deer Run Ct
Alexandria VA 22306

Call Sign: K2AGR
Brent M Simpson
4708 Deer Run Ct
Alexandria VA 22306

Call Sign: KD4QCL
Alan C Kepple
3800 Densmore Ct
Alexandria VA 22309

Call Sign: KC4YNC
Kevin N Miller
1322 Dewitt Ave
Alexandria VA 22301

Call Sign: KG4YIV
Andrew T Wesley
8461 Diablo Ct
Alexandria VA 22309

Call Sign: KJ4DFU

Jodi Terhorst
1500 Dogwood Dr
Alexandria VA 22302

Call Sign: K4JLT
Jodi L Terhorst
1500 Dogwood Dr
Alexandria VA 22302

Call Sign: KF4YXU
Brian K Mason
6402 Dorset Dr
Alexandria VA 223103016

Call Sign: W4OUZ
Neil R Sheeley Jr
913 Dresden Ct
Alexandria VA 22308

Call Sign: KC4WCV
Ritchie W Miller
1810 Duffield Ln
Alexandria VA 22307

Call Sign: KG4NIE
Patricia A Myers-Hayer
117 Duke St
Alexandria VA 22314

Call Sign: KJ4FDL
Robert K Breece
4004 Duke St
Alexandria VA 223042608

Call Sign: K4RKB
Robert K Breece
4004 Duke St
Alexandria VA 223042608

Call Sign: AB4QJ
Elfriede Urani
Alexandria Rad Clb 401 Duke
St
Alexandria VA 22314

Call Sign: KG4UCR
Zekarias Gebeyehou
4600 Duke St 1330
Alexandria VA 22304

Call Sign: KB0KME
Silas V Darden
5240 Duke St 218
Alexandria VA 22304

Call Sign: KK4FPF
Jose R Beitia
4600 Duke St 706
Alexandria VA 22304

Call Sign: WD4ORI
Charles S Barrett
5203 Duke St Apt 303
Alexandria VA 22304

Call Sign: KA0PRP
Judith A Stockhouse
5375 Duke St Apt 620
Alexandria VA 22304

Call Sign: KI4DXO
Angel L Gonzalez
5375 Duke St Apt 710
Alexandria VA 22304

Call Sign: KI4DXQ
Isabel A Gonzalez
5375 Duke St Apt 710
Alexandria VA 22304

Call Sign: KI4DXP
Olivia A Gonzalez
5375 Duke St Apt 710
Alexandria VA 22304

Call Sign: N8SIJ
Robert A King
4600 Duke St Apt 807
Alexandria VA 22304

Call Sign: KA4YZT
Jack Ben Rubin
4600 Duke St Ste 716
Alexandria VA 22304

Call Sign: KI4JEH
Gary L Peters
5546 Dunsmore Rd

Alexandria VA 22315

Call Sign: KJ4JED
Lauren S Davis
1201 E Abingdon Dr Ste 400
Alexandria VA 22314

Call Sign: KJ4SFC
Kevin F Jura
300 E Bellefonte Ave
Alexandria VA 22301

Call Sign: WA4RBE
Thomas B Lucas
410 E Bellefonte Ave
Alexandria VA 22301

Call Sign: W4TBL
Thomas B Lucas
410 E Bellefonte Ave
Alexandria VA 22301

Call Sign: KE4IUF
Martha M Fruehwald
7009 E Birkenhead Pl
Alexandria VA 22310

Call Sign: KC6RON
Dennis A Coriell
545 E Braddock Rd 406
Alexandria VA 22314

Call Sign: WB4NFO
Pradyumna S Rana
29 E Chapman St
Alexandria VA 223012201

Call Sign: KG4BYL
Robert D Ballenger
15 E Cliff St
Alexandria VA 22301

Call Sign: KU8V
Robert D Ballenger
15 E Cliff St
Alexandria VA 22301

Call Sign: KI4BNQ
David L Stephens

102 E Glendale Ave
Alexandria VA 22301

Call Sign: KK4HMU
Paul G Kudarauskas
116 E Glendale Ave
Alexandria VA 22301

Call Sign: WA4MZB
Herbert H Toney
114 E Linden St
Alexandria VA 223012222

Call Sign: WD4SGC
Dale R Schmidt
3 E Luray Ave
Alexandria VA 22301

Call Sign: KA4COQ
Ronald E Reafs
111 E Luray Ave
Alexandria VA 223012027

Call Sign: WA4CCF
James R Schwitz
519 E Luray Ave
Alexandria VA 22301

Call Sign: WA3YUF
Thomas H Murphy
561 E Nelson Ave
Alexandria VA 22301

Call Sign: K3SL
Steven W Lett
21 E Oak St
Alexandria VA 223012207

Call Sign: KG4WVD
Ronald A Gunn
305 E Oxford Ave
Alexandria VA 22301

Call Sign: KE4MKC
Rafael E Lemaitre
213 E Raymond Ave
Alexandria VA 22301

Call Sign: KF4OSQ

Robin R Bryant
2908 E Side Dr
Alexandria VA 22306

Call Sign: KF4RUR
Jim Bryant
2908 E Side Dr
Alexandria VA 223061713

Call Sign: WA6KYE
Mark D Rotter
715 E Timber Branch Pkwy
Alexandria VA 22302

Call Sign: KE4WLJ
Kathy L Thorpe
211 E Uhler Ave
Alexandria VA 223011319

Call Sign: KE4WLK
Timothy S Thorpe
211 E Uhler Ave
Alexandria VA 223011319

Call Sign: KC4WWK
Jean P Davis
1922 Earldale Ct
Alexandria VA 22306

Call Sign: W4NNG
Robert A Brubaker
1922 Earldale Ct
Alexandria VA 22306

Call Sign: K1JXT
Joseph M Dolan Jr
4388 Eaton Pl
Alexandria VA 22310

Call Sign: KJ4MTE
Joseph M Dolan III
4388 Eaton Pl
Alexandria VA 22310

Call Sign: K5LEX
Lexow Grant
5310 Echols Ave
Alexandria VA 22311

Call Sign: KE4LCQ
Martin S Gunn
5922 Edgehill Ct
Alexandria VA 22303

Call Sign: KB5QGQ
Carson C Evans
6209 Edison Dr
Alexandria VA 22310

Call Sign: KI4IPN
William P Hamlin Jr
6225 Edison Dr
Alexandria VA 22310

Call Sign: KI4KXE
Glenda B Davis
3732 Edison St
Alexandria VA 22305

Call Sign: N3TNU
George T Mc Neill
6260 Edsall Rd 102
Alexandria VA 22312

Call Sign: KC4YMH
Kevin K Dahlke
6168 Edsall Rd 20
Alexandria VA 22304

Call Sign: KG4CKK
Christopher C Dickinson
6439 Edsall Rd Apt 101
Alexandria VA 22312

Call Sign: N4JUD
David C Kelly
6161 Edsall Rd Apt 103
Alexandria VA 223044126

Call Sign: N3UMI
Ronald P Denton Jr
5911 Edsall Rd Apt 913
Alexandria VA 223044119

Call Sign: W3IRD
Ronald P Denton Jr
5911 Edsall Rd Apt 913
Alexandria VA 223044119

Call Sign: KG4NOS
Geoffrey G Hermanstorfer
6100 Edsell Rd
Alexandria VA 22304

Call Sign: KJ4VSC
Ruben A Legaspi
3831 Eisenhower Ave
Alexandria VA 22304

Call Sign: KE4PUI
Alan B Phillips
5400 Eisenhower Ave
Alexandria VA 22304

Call Sign: KB1GDG
Kathleen M Cain
4850 Eisenhower Ave 212
Alexandria VA 22304

Call Sign: KB7TVZ
Diane L Bishop
2251 Eisenhower Ave Apt 1018
Alexandria VA 22314

Call Sign: WA7LB
Larry A Bishop
2251 Eisenhower Ave Apt 1018
Alexandria VA 22314

Call Sign: N5YRE
Kelly Marie H Carter
2251 Eisenhower Ave Apt 1610
Alexandria VA 22314

Call Sign: KG4SGP
James D Carter
2251 Eisenhower Ave Apt 1610
Alexandria VA 22314

Call Sign: KK4EPP
Jeffrey C Scaparra
4854 Eisenhower Ave Unit 444
Alexandria VA 22304

Call Sign: KK4EPN
Wesley Huang
4854 Eisenhower Ave Unit 444

Alexandria VA 22304

Call Sign: WA3YQJ
Lloyd F Rohrbach
3800 El Camino Pl
Alexandria VA 22309

Call Sign: KB4JGE
Mark A Guidi
7718 Elba Rd
Alexandria VA 22306

Call Sign: AK4HX
Jeffery R Wickens
3809 A Elbert Ave
Alexandria VA 22305

Call Sign: KF4GDC
Richard P Taschler
3803 Elbert Ave
Alexandria VA 22305

Call Sign: KD9SP
Luis A Duran
6608 Elk Park Ct
Alexandria VA 22310

Call Sign: KA3ZBM
James T Moore
4015 Ellicott St
Alexandria VA 22304

Call Sign: KB4YHO
Richard S Marks Jr
3409 Elmwood Dr
Alexandria VA 22303

Call Sign: KB4AVN
Dennis C Mc Craney
6513 Enfield Dr
Alexandria VA 22310

Call Sign: K1ULK
Richard A Morgan
5381 Essex Ct 252
Alexandria VA 22311

Call Sign: KE4EPF
Michael R Cooper

6111A Essex House Sq
Alexandria VA 22310

Call Sign: KD4NSD
Judy A Metcalf
5742 Evergreen Knoll Ct
Alexandria VA 22303

Call Sign: KJ4EAD
Geoffrey S San Antonio
5700 Evergreen Knoll Ct
Alexandria VA 22303

Call Sign: KA3GPX
Amy E Baggott
7206 Fairchild Dr 102
Alexandria VA 22306

Call Sign: KI4IFQ
Don C Terrill
3836 Fairfax Pkwy
Alexandria VA 223121145

Call Sign: N4ZTS
James J Nugent
7922 Fairfax Rd
Alexandria VA 223081140

Call Sign: KG4QWF
Daniel B Rosenfeld
2503 Fairview Dr
Alexandria VA 223066404

Call Sign: W4DBR
Daniel B Rosenfeld
2503 Fairview Dr
Alexandria VA 223066404

Call Sign: KJ4JHL
Eric T Kramer
1220 Falster Rd
Alexandria VA 22308

Call Sign: WJ0T
Alan P Oliver
1230 Falster Rd
Alexandria VA 22308

Call Sign: KB2CJI

Christopher M Schimenti
2503 Farm Rd
Alexandria VA 223022820

Call Sign: K4NKN
Edwin G Newberger
2909 Farm Rd
Alexandria VA 22302

Call Sign: KJ4FUU
Thomas F Kirby Jr
2631 Farmington Dr
Alexandria VA 223031352

Call Sign: N5UNW
Harry L Frizzell
2103 Farrington Ave
Alexandria VA 22303

Call Sign: KD4CNZ
Michele T Moorhouse
9406 Ferry Landing Ct
Alexandria VA 22309

Call Sign: KJ4WJC
Edward Jones
4200 Ferry Landing Rd
Alexandria VA 22309

Call Sign: KJ4JHK
Larry E Dawes
4312 Ferry Landing Rd
Alexandria VA 22309

Call Sign: KF4VVV
Susan T Concannon
4701 Ferry Landing Rd
Alexandria VA 223093118

Call Sign: KI4IDW
Thomas P Concannon
4701 Ferry Landing Rd
Alexandria VA 223093118

Call Sign: KJ4JNB
Neil K Dawes
4312 Ferry Landing Rd
Alexandria VA 22309

Call Sign: KE4TDX
Benaiah P Williams
4201 Fielding St
Alexandria VA 22309

Call Sign: KA4KNH
John O Murphy
5320 Fillmore Ave
Alexandria VA 223111338

Call Sign: W4EGU
William B Knight
4800 Fillmore Ave Apt 1354
Alexandria VA 22311

Call Sign: KE4WYG
Ogal P Crews
1621 Fitzgerald Ln
Alexandria VA 22302

Call Sign: KJ4UYA
Alexander L Carr
2705 Fleming St
Alexandria VA 22306

Call Sign: KJ4UXZ
Steven B Carr
2705 Fleming St
Alexandria VA 22306

Call Sign: WA7MLZ
Jeffrey D Greene
6206 Florence Ln
Alexandria VA 223102213

Call Sign: KE4IRV
Thomas E Dengler
5422 Forest Ave
Alexandria VA 22310

Call Sign: KE4BAD
Peter D Reynolds
1605 Fort Hunt Ct
Alexandria VA 22307

Call Sign: WB4CYR
ARChie L Julian
6921 Fort Hunt Rd
Alexandria VA 22307

Call Sign: KC4IBQ
Alfred E Sommers
7401 Fort Hunt Rd
Alexandria VA 22307

Call Sign: KC4IJE
Nina B Sommers
7401 Fort Hunt Rd
Alexandria VA 22307

Call Sign: WH6SU
Stephen D Macleod
8820 Fort Hunt Rd
Alexandria VA 22308

Call Sign: N4BBS
Robert S Schwartz
3828 Fort Worth Ave
Alexandria VA 22304

Call Sign: N4CDG
Chris D Grabiel Sr
5307 Foxboro Ct
Alexandria VA 22315

Call Sign: KG4URQ
Chris D Grabiel Jr
5307 Foxboro Ct
Alexandria VA 22315

Call Sign: N5CDG
Chris D Grabiel Jr
5307 Foxboro Ct
Alexandria VA 22315

Call Sign: WC6P
William J Schworer III
6200 Foxcroft Rd
Alexandria VA 22307

Call Sign: N4WYG
Milton V Richards
6203 Foxcroft Rd
Alexandria VA 22307

Call Sign: KG4QWD
Mike C Crowe
7421 Foxleigh Way

Alexandria VA 22315

Call Sign: KC4LGT
John C Nicholson
6105 Franconia Forest Ln
Alexandria VA 22310

Call Sign: N4XWG
John C Nicholson
6105 Franconia Forest Ln
Alexandria VA 22310

Call Sign: KJ4BQN
Paul J Blemberg
6120 Franconia Station Ln
Alexandria VA 22310

Call Sign: WB7UEV
Lee R Anderson
2634 Ft Farnsworth Dr Apt 2D
Alexandria VA 22303

Call Sign: WB7TZH
David J Mc Cloud
8316 Ft Hunt Rd
Alexandria VA 22308

Call Sign: KK4GLU
Matthew S Miller
5125 Gardner Dr
Alexandria VA 22304

Call Sign: W8ZM
Tyssen W Becker
8647 Gateshead Rd
Alexandria VA 22309

Call Sign: N4GHK
Warren B Johnson
8653 Gateshead Rd
Alexandria VA 22309

Call Sign: KI4YPG
Gerald A Seeley
8655 Gateshead Rd
Alexandria VA 22309

Call Sign: WB4OLN
Joseph D White

8702 Gateshead Rd
Alexandria VA 22309

Call Sign: KI4OBN
Barry J Carlisle
8721 Gateshead Rd
Alexandria VA 22309

Call Sign: KD4IDZ
Stanley L Carts Jr
8812 Gateshead Rd
Alexandria VA 22309

Call Sign: WD4ALP
Sylvia S Carts
8812 Gateshead Rd
Alexandria VA 22309

Call Sign: WD4ARO
Jeffrey T Olson
8822 Gateshead Rd
Alexandria VA 22309

Call Sign: KJ4HDA
Cameron H Piper
1300 Gatewood Dr
Alexandria VA 22307

Call Sign: KI4LOQ
Peter Town
1306 Gatewood Dr
Alexandria VA 22307

Call Sign: KE4POM
James F Deucher
3302 Gentle Ct
Alexandria VA 22310

Call Sign: KC4HED
David M Milligan
6239 Gentle Ln
Alexandria VA 22310

Call Sign: KC4JTS
Patricia M Milligan
6239 Gentle Ln
Alexandria VA 22310

Call Sign: N0OQT

Christopher J Mc Cormack
6251 Gentle Ln
Alexandria VA 22310

Call Sign: KC4UON
Victor Muller
6473 Gildar St
Alexandria VA 22310

Call Sign: AD4B
David J Buress
1115 Gladstone Pl
Alexandria VA 22308

Call Sign: KA4RYK
Patricia M Gold
1201 Gladstone Pl
Alexandria VA 22308

Call Sign: KD4MFE
Taydon C Mandt
5305 Glen Green Ct
Alexandria VA 22310

Call Sign: KD4NSE
Gregory A Mandt
5305 Glen Green Ct
Alexandria VA 22310

Call Sign: W4SHK
Harry B Pettit
5704 Glenwood Ct
Alexandria VA 22310

Call Sign: KJ4DFR
Dennis C Lowe
3399 Governors Crest Ct
Alexandria VA 22310

Call Sign: N5OLL
Richard A Cooper
5591 Governors Pond Cir
Alexandria VA 22310

Call Sign: N4NKO
Dennis E Gersomino
4302 Granada St
Alexandria VA 22309

Call Sign: WD6DPU
Keith E Krombel
4305 Granada St
Alexandria VA 22309

Call Sign: KK4DEE
Robert E Senkel
5988 Grand Pavilion Way
Alexandria VA 22303

Call Sign: KK4DOS
Brenden W Taylor
5950 Grand Pavillion Way Apt
422
Alexandria VA 22303

Call Sign: KE4WYD
Richard O Norris
1104 Greenway Rd
Alexandria VA 22308

Call Sign: KG4NIH
Gaylon L Smith
6006 Grove Dr
Alexandria VA 22307

Call Sign: AA4IC
David S Wollan
6026 Grove Dr
Alexandria VA 22307

Call Sign: K4DBW
Robert T Platt Jr
7704 Grovenor Ct
Alexandria VA 223154005

Call Sign: KG4YDY
Austin T Jones
7711 Grovenor Ct
Alexandria VA 22315

Call Sign: KI4DKV
Karen L Jones
7711 Grovenor Ct
Alexandria VA 22315

Call Sign: KW1LTS
Karen L Jones
7711 Grovenor Ct

Alexandria VA 22315

Call Sign: KG4YDZ
Mark A Jones
7711 Grovenor Ct
Alexandria VA 22315

Call Sign: KI4IPV
Valerie A Jones
7711 Grovenor Ct
Alexandria VA 22315

Call Sign: KE4PON
Jason C Geist
2625 Groveton St
Alexandria VA 22306

Call Sign: K5QMA
Neal B Carter
7433 Grumman Pl
Alexandria VA 22306

Call Sign: KJ4UND
Rachel L Murphy
7833 Gum Springs Village Dr
Alexandria VA 22306

Call Sign: KI4NFC
Eric S Heis
3450 Gunston Rd
Alexandria VA 22302

Call Sign: KE4JPE
Leslie I Rosenbaum
3774 Gunston Rd
Alexandria VA 22302

Call Sign: KD5GQS
William M Hartley
206 Guthrie Ave
Alexandria VA 223051817

Call Sign: KA4UWC
Phillip L Simpson
7949 Hammond St
Alexandria VA 22309

Call Sign: KD4YOB
Samuel P Brutcher Jr

6709 Harrison Ln
Alexandria VA 22306

Call Sign: KI4UGB
Alexander R Higbee
3112 Hatcher St
Alexandria VA 22303

Call Sign: KD4VUM
Hector L Correa
7435 Hatherleigh Ct
Alexandria VA 223153846

Call Sign: AI4TG
Hector L Correa
7435 Hatherleigh Ct
Alexandria VA 223153846

Call Sign: K7VCG
William J Broome
7451 Hatherleigh Ct
Alexandria VA 22315

Call Sign: KJ4GPM
Michael Kato
723 Hawkins Way
Alexandria VA 22314

Call Sign: NP3C
Stephen J Werner
7722 Hayfield Rd
Alexandria VA 223153954

Call Sign: KG4RFN
Christopher W Mckee
7706 Haynes Point Way Unit L
Alexandria VA 22315

Call Sign: K4UHQ
Charles S Wimberly
6506 Haystack Rd
Alexandria VA 22310

Call Sign: WD4PWG
Timothy J Slattery
4503 Hazeltine Ct Apt J
Alexandria VA 22312

Call Sign: WA4KZY

William R Dellinger Sr
9324 Heather Glen Dr
Alexandria VA 22309

Call Sign: KF4PSZ
Rodney D Pendleton
6813 Heatherway Ct
Alexandria VA 22315

Call Sign: K3MCC
Michael C Cumpton
321 Helmuth Ln
Alexandria VA 22304

Call Sign: K1FR
Jesse T Mc Mahan
5149 Heritage Ln
Alexandria VA 22311

Call Sign: KK4FQY
William G Burton Jr
2950 Hickory St
Alexandria VA 223052513

Call Sign: KI4BNK
Blair W Thompson
302 High St
Alexandria VA 22302

Call Sign: K8BVH
Wayne C Johnson Jr
6370 Hillary Ct
Alexandria VA 22310

Call Sign: AA4ZS
Francis W Lempicki
5606 Hilldale Dr
Alexandria VA 22310

Call Sign: WA4DJH
Curtis L Lamb
6202 Hillview Ave
Alexandria VA 22310

Call Sign: KB8PYM
Patrick A Ouellette
6219 Hillview Ave
Alexandria VA 22310

Call Sign: KJ4BQF
Aletha A Ouellette
6219 Hillview Ave
Alexandria VA 22310

Call Sign: KC8WLJ
James E Ouellette
6219 Hillview Ave
Alexandria VA 22310

Call Sign: NE4PO
Patrick A Ouellette
6219 Hillview Ave
Alexandria VA 22310

Call Sign: KD4ZLG
Joel S Armstrong
2803 Holland Ct
Alexandria VA 22306

Call Sign: AG4YB
Joel S Armstrong
2803 Holland Ct
Alexandria VA 22306

Call Sign: KG4ATH
Anna C Tyler
401 Holland Ln Apt 1326
Alexandria VA 22314

Call Sign: KJ4PRY
Sheila A Mcgough
3112 Holly St
Alexandria VA 22305

Call Sign: K4HQK
John W Fuller
3403 Holly St
Alexandria VA 22305

Call Sign: KG4LOM
Christine Couldrey
3702 Holmes Ln
Alexandria VA 22302

Call Sign: N7NGW
Elizabeth T Cady
5300 Holmes Run Pkw 710
Alexandria VA 22304

Call Sign: KJ4MFI
Steven M Goodwin
5500 Holmes Run Pkwy
Alexandria VA 22304

Call Sign: KJ4MFH
Jennifer Goodwin
5500 Holmes Run Pkwy 1508
Alexandria VA 22304

Call Sign: W4PAY
Northern VA RC
5300 Holmes Run Pkwy 606
Alexandria VA 22304

Call Sign: WB4LAC
Howard D Jones Jr
5300 Holmes Run Pkwy 706
Alexandria VA 22304

Call Sign: W3CY
James F Mc Donough
5500 Holmes Run Pkwy Apt
1615
Alexandria VA 22304

Call Sign: N4HRB
Duane M Tollaksen
5300 Holmes Run Pkwy Unit
604
Alexandria VA 22304

Call Sign: W4TKR
James A Murray Jr
6215 Houston Ct
Alexandria VA 22310

Call Sign: KF4DIR
Richard E Jernigan
6172 Howell Rd
Alexandria VA 22310

Call Sign: N3RSP
Harry C Clay
2059 Huntington Ave 1400
Alexandria VA 22303

Call Sign: W5JMC

John M Carpenter
2902 Huntington Grove Sq
Alexandria VA 22306

Call Sign: N0ILN
Robert D Olson
7068 Huntley Run Plave
Alexandria VA 22306

Call Sign: KK4DBC
Joshua N Nunn
2507 Hunton Pl
Alexandria VA 22311

Call Sign: KP4ZX
Luis A Villalobos
5804 Huron Pl
Alexandria VA 22310

Call Sign: KK4GBS
Clayton M Dobbs
8551 Hyman Way Apt 362
Alexandria VA 22309

Call Sign: KB4MEL
Kerri Brady
5729 Independence Cir
Alexandria VA 22312

Call Sign: AB5QR
Anthony J Hickey
2604 Indian Dr Apt 1D
Alexandria VA 22303

Call Sign: N4JKJ
Nancy H Cady
3731 Ingalls Ave
Alexandria VA 22302

Call Sign: KF4QXO
Keith W Akins
3828 Ingalls Ave
Alexandria VA 22302

Call Sign: K8KAQ
Paul J School
1803 Ingemar Ct
Alexandria VA 22308

Call Sign: KI4RZH
Giancarlo M Calderolli
5816 Iron Willow Ct
Alexandria VA 22310

Call Sign: KB9BMQ
Douglas D Kung
2651 Jamestown Ln 303
Alexandria VA 22314

Call Sign: KI4MSF
Florence P Haseltine
2181 Jamieson Ave 1606
Alexandria VA 22314

Call Sign: KI4IFO
Lester Ravitz
2181 Jamieson Ave 909
Alexandria VA 22314

Call Sign: N3LES
Lester Ravitz
2181 Jamieson Ave 909
Alexandria VA 22314

Call Sign: WA0WOZ
Gregory N Larsen
2121 Jamieson Ave Condo 2003
Alexandria VA 22314

Call Sign: N4OUN
Roger C Bucholz
1301 Janneys Ln
Alexandria VA 22302

Call Sign: KD4NZP
James E O Neal
4104 Jarins Dr
Alexandria VA 22310

Call Sign: AG4DH
James E O Neal
4104 Javins Dr
Alexandria VA 22310

Call Sign: KI4TLJ
Andrew J ONeal
4104 Javins Dr
Alexandria VA 22310

Call Sign: K4XAR
James E O Neal
4104 Javins Dr
Alexandria VA 22310

Call Sign: K4TXU
Lee A Delson
5924 Jewell Ct
Alexandria VA 22312

Call Sign: W9TCE
Theodore C Einersen
6409 Joyce Rd
Alexandria VA 223102617

Call Sign: KE4HPF
Kirk E Wilke
6047 Kathmoor Dr
Alexandria VA 22310

Call Sign: KJ4VSW
Michael T Burns
4662 Kell Ln
Alexandria VA 223114917

Call Sign: KI4FOJ
George J Wallace
4637 Kemp Ct
Alexandria VA 22311

Call Sign: KJ4WWP
Lon E Callen
4836 Kenmore Ave 103
Alexandria VA 22304

Call Sign: KC8ERP
Jesse M Barton
4701 Kenmore Ave Apt 1202
Alexandria VA 22304

Call Sign: N3PDK
Thomas M Carter
4801 Kenmore Ave Apt 805
Alexandria VA 22304

Call Sign: KJ4TQS
Hugh M Eaton III
6 Kennedy St

Alexandria VA 22305

Call Sign: AJ4YZ
Hugh M Eaton III
6 Kennedy St
Alexandria VA 22305

Call Sign: KI4SCK
Spencer Williams
1675 Kenwood Ave
Alexandria VA 22302

Call Sign: WB7SFB
Robert E Fulton III
6054 Kestner Cir
Alexandria VA 22310

Call Sign: KB4ADI
Christopher A Kidd
1120 Key Dr
Alexandria VA 22302

Call Sign: KG4NIK
Christopher A Kidd
1120 Key Dr
Alexandria VA 22302

Call Sign: KD4LTD
Gary J Post
1408 Key Dr
Alexandria VA 22302

Call Sign: WB0ORC
Steven J Weigel
7944 Kidd St
Alexandria VA 22309

Call Sign: N3QB
Edward M Cabic
8114 Kidd St
Alexandria VA 22309

Call Sign: KJ4SFA
Jeffrey L Price
2402 King St
Alexandria VA 22301

Call Sign: KB8OAU
Ryan E Mc Coy

3730 King St
Alexandria VA 22302

Call Sign: KE4POP
Barton W Taube
3686 King St 102
Alexandria VA 22302

Call Sign: KC8ASW
Anthony A Barone
4380 King St 1104
Alexandria VA 22302

Call Sign: N4ASX
Richard R Bunn
6402 Kings Landing Rd
Alexandria VA 223103119

Call Sign: KK4BWN
William Chong
7007 Kings Manor Dr
Alexandria VA 22315

Call Sign: WA6AAI
Stanley H Grigsby
7638 Kingsbury Rd
Alexandria VA 22315

Call Sign: WD6EJI
Donna J Grigsby
7638 Kingsbury Rd
Alexandria VA 223154157

Call Sign: KF4GOY
Alden H Ose
4611 Kling Dr
Alexandria VA 22312

Call Sign: KI4YQB
Benjamin J Jones
5350 Knole Ct Apt 240
Alexandria VA 22311

Call Sign: N6MAX
William L Eischens
7143 Lake Cove Dr
Alexandria VA 22315

Call Sign: KJ4ZTM

Richard Speckart
312 Lamond Pl
Alexandria VA 22314

Call Sign: KB4USM
Stephen D Wiles
7010 Lamp Post Ln
Alexandria VA 22306

Call Sign: KG4SCF
Arnom H Harris III
2913 Landover St
Alexandria VA 22305

Call Sign: KK4HMT
Wyatt W Davis
3201 Landover St 1108
Alexandria VA 22305

Call Sign: N3USK
Stephen T Glose
3201 Landover St Apt 1121
Alexandria VA 22305

Call Sign: KJ4IVC
Jared A Watson
6505 Langleigh Way
Alexandria VA 22315

Call Sign: KT4KS
Robert R Raevis
4541 Lantern Pl
Alexandria VA 22306

Call Sign: W4HIT
Brian D Mayberry
4910 Larno Dr
Alexandria VA 22310

Call Sign: N4KRR
Kevin L Mc Elhone
200 Laverne Ave
Alexandria VA 22305

Call Sign: KI4MAG
Donovan J Lewis Sr
3191 Lawsons Hill Pl
Alexandria VA 22310

Call Sign: KI4D
Donovan J Lewis Sr
3191 Lawsons Hill Pl
Alexandria VA 22310

Call Sign: WB4NYZ
Dale F Anderson
8733 Lea Ln
Alexandria VA 223094026

Call Sign: KF4WLF
Charles A Belanger
7900 Lee Ave
Alexandria VA 22308

Call Sign: AE7GW
Robert T Vanhook
4980 Leesburg Pike Apt 620
Alexandria VA 223021109

Call Sign: KJ4BRB
Michael M Fijalka
1920 Leo Ln
Alexandria VA 22308

Call Sign: KJ4BRA
Sharon W Fijalka
1920 Leo Ln
Alexandria VA 22308

Call Sign: KC4SMM
Daniel E Landis
5733 Leverett Ct Apt 372
Alexandria VA 22311

Call Sign: KG4QBK
David W Scheuermann
6905 Lichen Ct
Alexandria VA 22306

Call Sign: WA4VAQ
Robert H Thornton Jr
2217 Lida Ct
Alexandria VA 22306

Call Sign: KI4CYL
Brett T Sigmundsson
6381 Lincolnia Rd
Alexandria VA 22312

Call Sign: KJ4WCT
Jerome O Rosimo
5520 Linnean St
Alexandria VA 22303

Call Sign: KB4EBM
Robert S Sylvest
3107 Little Creek Ln
Alexandria VA 22309

Call Sign: W4HEE
Robert W Carter
3118 Little Creek Ln
Alexandria VA 22309

Call Sign: KD4QWG
Norman S Brown
6574 Lochleigh Ct
Alexandria VA 22310

Call Sign: WD4EKL
Johnnyson P Jones Sr
3300 Lockheed Blvd Apt 102
Alexandria VA 22306

Call Sign: KA4TZL
Fred A Morley
2207 Londonderry Rd
Alexandria VA 22308

Call Sign: W4IOR
Venizelos Mallis
207 Longview Dr
Alexandria VA 22314

Call Sign: KE4POQ
Thomas A Hennig
7714 Lookout Ct
Alexandria VA 223062519

Call Sign: W4YSK
Leonard J Seal
219 Luna
Alexandria VA 22306

Call Sign: KJ4MSW
Eric P Roos
7503 Lund Ct

Alexandria VA 22315

Call Sign: N2UEK
Meir Menes
400 Madison St 204
Alexandria VA 22314

Call Sign: K3LSQ
Henry M Johnson III
400 Madison St 701
Alexandria VA 223141755

Call Sign: WA4WLK
Charles E Fox
5605 Magnolia Ln
Alexandria VA 22311

Call Sign: KB1IM
Vilhelm Gregers Hansen
7709 Maid Marian Ct
Alexandria VA 22306

Call Sign: KK4DPS
Aaron R Newman
6464 Manhasset Ln
Alexandria VA 223122339

Call Sign: N4UUI
Kazi A Hafeez
7532 Manigold Ct
Alexandria VA 22315

Call Sign: WP4DSX
Felix J Diaz
902 Manor Dr 301
Alexandria VA 22305

Call Sign: KJ4BQO
Christopher W Mcbroom
926 Manor Rd 202
Alexandria VA 22305

Call Sign: KG4VMY
Haworth P Bromley
302 Mansion Dr
Alexandria VA 223022903

Call Sign: N4BNQ
Leslie Cohen

8801 Mansion Farm Pl
Alexandria VA 223092216

Call Sign: KE4KGP
Billy D Hamilton
3854 Manzanita Pl
Alexandria VA 22309

Call Sign: KF5PB
Robert W Mc Cord
5617 Marble Arch Way
Alexandria VA 22315

Call Sign: KQ4XS
Lawrence E Wickliffe
5706 Marble Arch Way
Alexandria VA 223154014

Call Sign: W5EUE
Earl J Holliman
4301 Marionet St
Alexandria VA 22312

Call Sign: KC4QXZ
Ning C Sung
3946 Mariposa Pl
Alexandria VA 22309

Call Sign: KB1DSM
Geoffrey J King
3731 Mark Dr
Alexandria VA 223052426

Call Sign: W4CCI
Richard L Cheeseman Sr
7025 Marlan Dr
Alexandria VA 22307

Call Sign: KG4NIG
Heather A Dalby
2256 Mary Baldwin Dr
Alexandria VA 22307

Call Sign: W0QED
Genell K Hausauer
1807 Mason Hill Dr
Alexandria VA 223071934

Call Sign: W0CN

Daniel J Hausauer
1807 Mason Hill Dr
Alexandria VA 22307

Call Sign: KD4BMJ
Frances Y Cowhig
6317 May Blvd
Alexandria VA 22310

Call Sign: NS4G
Monroe E Hill
2900 Mayer Pl
Alexandria VA 22302

Call Sign: KN4TU
Robert D Crea
3105 McGeorge Ter
Alexandria VA 22309

Call Sign: KD4CXB
Jared K Johnson
6160 McLendon Ct
Alexandria VA 22310

Call Sign: KA1BKM
John P Mattia Jr
6504 Medinah Ln
Alexandria VA 22312

Call Sign: KG4CKJ
Howell G Crim III
3321 Memorial St
Alexandria VA 22306

Call Sign: KA3MEE
Carl L Bittenbender
6311 Merle Pl Apt A
Alexandria VA 22312

Call Sign: K4OIJ
Joseph W Eshelman III
7613 Midday Ln
Alexandria VA 22306

Call Sign: KC4JKC
Keith S Crabtree
7802 Midday Ln
Alexandria VA 22306

Call Sign: N4DBE
Robert E Huneycutt Jr
1501 Middlebury Dr
Alexandria VA 22307

Call Sign: KB3TSG
Aaron W Linville
2109 Mill Rd Apt 207
Alexandria VA 223145323

Call Sign: KJ4MSY
Robert L Kopelen
2109 Mill Rd Apt 423
Alexandria VA 22314

Call Sign: N4BV
Robert M Sawyer
4515 Millburn Ct
Alexandria VA 22309

Call Sign: KI4IPJ
Hugo Teufel III
5204 Mitchell St
Alexandria VA 22312

Call Sign: KC8EJA
Jay T Purvis
5244 Mitchell St
Alexandria VA 22312

Call Sign: KF7IJZ
Jeremy R Kolonay
2741 Monacan St Apt 202
Alexandria VA 22314

Call Sign: KG4AYE
John R Carlisle
2730 Monacan St Apt 304
Alexandria VA 22314

Call Sign: K4DHB
Lynn C Wilson
160 Moncure Dr
Alexandria VA 22314

Call Sign: AA4HS
A Maitland Bottoms
216 Moncure Dr
Alexandria VA 22314

Call Sign: KA4ZOI
Paul A Harouff
304 Moncure Dr
Alexandria VA 22314

Call Sign: KJ4OCF
John E Duvall Jr
508 Monticello Blvd
Alexandria VA 22305

Call Sign: KC4VW
James H Barnes
5920 Monticello Rd
Alexandria VA 22303

Call Sign: KJ4OXK
W Tate Heuer Jr
6015 Monticello Rd
Alexandria VA 22303

Call Sign: K4AVF
Kenneth R Duvall
6436 Montrose St
Alexandria VA 22312

Call Sign: WB7ERU
Alexander A Masone
937 Moody Ct
Alexandria VA 22312

Call Sign: KB4EBK
Daryl B Bolstad
8402 Morey Ln
Alexandria VA 22308

Call Sign: KK4EWK
Christopher Howard
6809 Morning Brook Ter
Alexandria VA 22315

Call Sign: N4CTH
Christopher Howard
6809 Morning Brook Ter
Alexandria VA 22315

Call Sign: KI4QIK
Keith A Tyeryar
8074 Morning Meadow Ct

Alexandria VA 22315

Call Sign: KG4TJT
Elwood P Sheetz
5902 416 Mt Eagle Dr
Alexandria VA 22303

Call Sign: KG4WXF
Elwood P Sheetz
5902 416 Mt Eagle Dr
Alexandria VA 22303

Call Sign: KE4FWZ
Frederick B Schwartz
5902 Mt Eagle Dr 1004
Alexandria VA 22303

Call Sign: KD4IEE
John F Larison
5901 Mt Eagle Dr 1209
Alexandria VA 22303

Call Sign: KC4REQ
Alan D Jordan
5902 Mt Eagle Dr 1514
Alexandria VA 22303

Call Sign: KG4AKJ
Miles R Walbrecht
5901 Mt Eagle Dr 308
Alexandria VA 22303

Call Sign: KE4LNF
James W Schofield
5904 Mt Eagle Dr 402
Alexandria VA 22303

Call Sign: KI4IAN
Howard Prescott
5902 Mt Eagle Dr 818
Alexandria VA 22303

Call Sign: AA4QY
Boynton G Hagaman
5904 Mt Eagle Dr Unit 904
Alexandria VA 22303

Call Sign: KA3DMS
Michael J Yokitis

123 Mt Vernon Ave
Alexandria VA 223012322

Call Sign: N4QOS
Daniel P Mc Clafferty
3022 Mt Vernon Ave
Alexandria VA 22305

Call Sign: W4FQ
Timothy S Thorpe
2308 Mt Vernon Ave 120
Alexandria VA 22301

Call Sign: N4KLT
Kathy L Thorpe
2308 Mt Vernon Ave 120
Alexandria VA 22301

Call Sign: KG4GZE
James M Topolski
2415 Mt Vernon Ave 4
Alexandria VA 22301

Call Sign: KC4TPW
Della J Rutledge
3110 Mt Vernon Ave 910
Alexandria VA 22305

Call Sign: WA3NNI
Charles Luddeke Jr
9503 Mt Vernon Landing
Alexandria VA 22309

Call Sign: KK4DBF
Christian B Burnette
6110 Mulberry Ct
Alexandria VA 22310

Call Sign: KE4WLB
Emory L Laskin
401 N Amistead St 511
Alexandria VA 22312

Call Sign: WB4NCH
Amanda E Lee
645 N Armistead St
Alexandria VA 223122942

Call Sign: WB1CWU

Frank S Helmes Sr
481 N Armistead St 103
Alexandria VA 22312

Call Sign: KI4MWT
William J Hranicky
511 N Armistead St T 2
Alexandria VA 22312

Call Sign: K5OTZ
William J Hranicky
511 N Armistead St T 2
Alexandria VA 22312

Call Sign: KE4DBZ
Gilberto Pietri
493 N Armisted St Apt 303
Alexandria VA 22304

Call Sign: W4LKU
Bernard A Terrien
906 N Ashton St
Alexandria VA 22312

Call Sign: KJ4HCY
Leslie J Slaght
2254 N Beauregard St 1
Alexandria VA 22311

Call Sign: KF4BNN
Scott L Snyder
301 N Beauregard St 707
Alexandria VA 22312

Call Sign: N2KFA
Peter M Laager
301 N Beauregard St 714
Alexandria VA 22312

Call Sign: KI4VYI
David S Darland
1517 N Chambliss St
Alexandria VA 22312

Call Sign: N0DSD
David S Darland
1517 N Chambliss St
Alexandria VA 22312

Call Sign: KF4EAN
Jonathan E Lee
32 N Donelson St
Alexandria VA 22304

Call Sign: KT4FX
Stanley E Lee
32 N Donelson St
Alexandria VA 22304

Call Sign: KW1E
Stanley E Lee
32 N Donelson St
Alexandria VA 22304

Call Sign: K4SUM
Joseph J Moraski Sr
2324 N Early St
Alexandria VA 22302

Call Sign: KC6BBQ
James F Trost
1460 N Greenmount Dr 308
Alexandria VA 22311

Call Sign: KB7MGA
Matt N White
3101 N Hampton Dr
Alexandria VA 22302

Call Sign: KC4TJV
William T Cox Jr
3101 N Hampton Dr Apt 701
Alexandria VA 22302

Call Sign: KE4SLN
Heather L Graham
1528 B N Highview Ln
Alexandria VA 22311

Call Sign: KA3TIK
Donald R Torrence Jr
212 N Howard St 104
Alexandria VA 22304

Call Sign: KG4GHO
Susan E Jacobs
211 N Howard St Apt 204
Alexandria VA 22304

Call Sign: WB2STR
Thomas V Mukai
1300 N Ivanhoe St
Alexandria VA 22304

Call Sign: KI4DJQ
Grant K Mukai
1300 N Ivanhoe St
Alexandria VA 22304

Call Sign: KE4TOI
James B Rice
5741 N Kings Hwy
Alexandria VA 223031402

Call Sign: W2ISM
David M Liebergott
6026 N Kings Hwy
Alexandria VA 22303

Call Sign: KI4THJ
William P Eckel
321 N Langley St
Alexandria VA 22304

Call Sign: KJ4BQK
Peter S Eckel
321 N Langley St
Alexandria VA 22304

Call Sign: WA3UMR
Howard Pyle
125 N Lee St
Alexandria VA 223143264

Call Sign: K4TXD
Ralph J Schneider
718 N Overlook Dr
Alexandria VA 22305

Call Sign: WB4KZV
C Leslie Golliday Jr
608 N Owen St
Alexandria VA 22304

Call Sign: N3RL
Robert C Landis
433 N Patrick St

Alexandria VA 22314

Call Sign: KG4TSX
Jason B Jenkins
713 N Paxton St
Alexandria VA 22304

Call Sign: KI4YPI
Robert W Cross
930 N Paxton St
Alexandria VA 22304

Call Sign: KG2BSA
Kristofer M Ostergard
519 N Payne St
Alexandria VA 22314

Call Sign: KI4PRL
Alex M Wheeler
125 N Peyton St
Alexandria VA 22314

Call Sign: K5IRS
Ernest L Sheffield Jr
200 N Pickett St 512
Alexandria VA 22304

Call Sign: KE6TC
Phyllis M Gilmore
200 N Pickett St 811
Alexandria VA 223042115

Call Sign: KB8LUV
Ryan W Noyes
226 N Pitt St
Alexandria VA 22314

Call Sign: KD5BSZ
Walter M Goode
534 N Pitt St
Alexandria VA 22314

Call Sign: KG4NIL
Don C Chapman
801 N Pitt St 1510
Alexandria VA 22314

Call Sign: K4FIF
Charles Laniak

202 N Quaker Ln
Alexandria VA 22304

Call Sign: KB4QGJ
Gerald J Rose
524 N Quaker Ln
Alexandria VA 22304

Call Sign: KC4YMD
Kenneth R Farris
3708 N Rosser St 203
Alexandria VA 22311

Call Sign: N0CCF
Fred Van Remortel
400 N Union St
Alexandria VA 22314

Call Sign: KD6HUT
John A Bly
418 N Union St
Alexandria VA 22314

Call Sign: N4JSL
Marion C Dalby
428 N Union St
Alexandria VA 22314

Call Sign: KC4HSH
Lynn J Jacobson Kriegel
2601 N Van Dorn 103
Alexandria VA 22302

Call Sign: WJ4VA
Jesse M Barton
1449B N Van Dorn St
Alexandria VA 22304

Call Sign: KE4MXV
William A Vaughan Jr
921 N Van Dorn St 100
Alexandria VA 22304

Call Sign: KK4FFK
George T Snyder
2500 N Van Dorn St 1024
Alexandria VA 22302

Call Sign: KC4KIZ

Cameron H Fish
921 N Van Dorn St Apt 100
Alexandria VA 22304

Call Sign: KA1VLZ
Matthew R Scott
2601 N Van Dorn St Apt 203
Alexandria VA 22302

Call Sign: KI4KEC
Matthew R Scott
2601 N Van Dorn St Apt 203
Alexandria VA 22302

Call Sign: KJ4WKE
William L Wiley
210 N View Ter
Alexandria VA 22301

Call Sign: KI4EKI
Richard A Rivenbark
5243 Navaho Dr
Alexandria VA 223122034

Call Sign: N8NFK
Mark W Reilly
828 Neal Dr
Alexandria VA 22308

Call Sign: N4ENP
Robert W White
1011 Neal Dr
Alexandria VA 22308

Call Sign: KC7OVS
David A Miskimens
4417 Neptune Dr
Alexandria VA 22309

Call Sign: WR3Z
Barry J Shapiro
6507 Nevitt Way
Alexandria VA 22315

Call Sign: KE4MFI
Jonahtan A Kidney
2574 Nicky Ln
Alexandria VA 22311

Call Sign: KG4SCD
Cecil E Haithcock
2593 Nicky Ln
Alexandria VA 22311

Call Sign: AJ4ZD
Andrew J Pomerance
2597 Nicky Ln
Alexandria VA 22311

Call Sign: KD4GJZ
Ira G Vail II
9015 Nomini Ln
Alexandria VA 22309

Call Sign: KA0LZD
David A Souza
5816 Norham Dr
Alexandria VA 223154729

Call Sign: KI4THN
Ryan C Glasgow
5726 Norton Rd
Alexandria VA 22303

Call Sign: KB9CU
E Michael Hansen
6624 Oak Dr
Alexandria VA 22306

Call Sign: KJ4EAF
John A Babcock
6701 Oak Dr
Alexandria VA 22306

Call Sign: KI4EOG
Justin Bard
8725 Oak Leaf Dr
Alexandria VA 22309

Call Sign: N4RQL
Murray Scheine
3614 Oakland Dr
Alexandria VA 22310

Call Sign: KG4NMC
Delbert K Matlock
6498 Old Carriage Ln
Alexandria VA 223155029

Call Sign: KI4KXI
Michael C Murphy
6510 Old Coach Ct
Alexandria VA 22315

Call Sign: KI4PCN
John G Witzel
8762 Old Colony Way 3 D
Alexandria VA 22309

Call Sign: KE4ULN
David A Sirignano
7902 Old Marsh Ln
Alexandria VA 22315

Call Sign: KJ4NPM
Emil K Banks
7914 Old Marsh Ln
Alexandria VA 22315

Call Sign: WA4DGB
James L Sohn
5112 Old Mill Rd
Alexandria VA 22309

Call Sign: W5TID
James L Sohn
5112 Old Mill Rd
Alexandria VA 22309

Call Sign: KE4KDZ
Arthur H Collier
8721 Old Mt Vernon Rd
Alexandria VA 22309

Call Sign: N3OHS
James W Freeman
5905 Old Rolling Rd
Alexandria VA 223101828

Call Sign: KR4AT
Glenn W Rickman
6001 Old Rolling Rd
Alexandria VA 22310

Call Sign: KC4ASE
James L Price
7352 Old Telegraph Rd

Alexandria VA 22310

Call Sign: K4AXQ
Roy L Wright
415 Old Town Ct
Alexandria VA 223143543

Call Sign: KD7TWE
Robert W Noonan Jr
5704 Olde Mill Ct 144
Alexandria VA 22309

Call Sign: KJ4JHF
Matthew D Blower
1751 Olde Towne Rd
Alexandria VA 22307

Call Sign: KJ4BQX
Melanie L Blower
1751 Olde Towne Rd
Alexandria VA 22307

Call Sign: KJ4BQU
Susan L Kelly-Mccarthy
1751 Olde Towne Rd
Alexandria VA 22307

Call Sign: K3LEG
Susan L Kelly-Mccarthy
1751 Olde Towne Rd
Alexandria VA 22307

Call Sign: KD7LMF
Christa J Laser
6803 Oregano Ln
Alexandria VA 22310

Call Sign: KG4FIE
Carl E Espeland Jr
8116 Orville St
Alexandria VA 22309

Call Sign: KD4DWQ
Daniel G Lagasse
8304 Orville St
Alexandria VA 22309

Call Sign: N0GLF
Joel J Bertrand

5903 Otley Dr
Alexandria VA 22310

Call Sign: W4BRF
Le Roy Thompson Jr
6450 Overlook Dr Pinecrest
Alexandria VA 22312

Call Sign: W4IKA
Ola D Thompson
6450 Overlook Dr Pinecrest
Alexandria VA 22312

Call Sign: KD4COA
Matt C Wilson
5716 Overly Dr
Alexandria VA 22310

Call Sign: KE4JPA
William D Robey Jr
5723 Overly Dr
Alexandria VA 22310

Call Sign: N4ZGI
Jeanne S Rexroad
5723 Overly Dr
Alexandria VA 22310

Call Sign: KG4UNP
Thomas V Strickland
6082 Palladium Ct P2
Alexandria VA 22315

Call Sign: KG4TKU
Michael C Homsi
2601 Park Center Dr Apt C
1207
Alexandria VA 22302

Call Sign: KC5EOC
Leland E Price
2601 Park Center Dr Apt C1010
Alexandria VA 22302

Call Sign: KI4BNN
Michael C Homsi
2601 Park Center Dr Apt C1207
Alexandria VA 22302

Call Sign: W4YEH
Howard L Clark Jr
7420 Park Terrace Dr
Alexandria VA 223072000

Call Sign: KI4SXZ
Damon T Baldini
6379 Patience Ct
Alexandria VA 22315

Call Sign: KB4ZOD
Arthur S Spencer
9101 Patton Blvd
Alexandria VA 22309

Call Sign: N0NYN
Dave W Fletcher
5450 Patuxent Knoll Pl
Alexandria VA 22312

Call Sign: KG4WNI
Victor B Blanchard
2113 Paul Spring Rd
Alexandria VA 22307

Call Sign: KA4DUU
Robert W Morgan
4512 Peacock Ave
Alexandria VA 22304

Call Sign: N3LHG
William C Pulver III
5859 Pearson Ln
Alexandria VA 22304

Call Sign: KG4VKM
Paul H Kittridge Jr
4394 Pembroke Dr
Alexandria VA 22309

Call Sign: KI4BNP
Gregory S Danes
4424 Pembrooke Village Dr
Alexandria VA 22309

Call Sign: KJ4DGE
Gregory S Danes
4424 Pembrooke Village Dr
Alexandria VA 22309

Call Sign: KF4KHL
Harlan H Vinnedge
399 Pendleton St Apt 612
Alexandria VA 22314

Call Sign: KG4NIJ
Michael W Dewalt
2427 Phillips Dr
Alexandria VA 223066427

Call Sign: KJ4BQJ
Stephan S Rose
10 Phoenix Mill Pl
Alexandria VA 22304

Call Sign: KD4RNG
David W Tucker
4503 Picot Rd
Alexandria VA 223102049

Call Sign: KN4JZ
Thomas R Garlington
6602 Potomac Ave Apt B1
Alexandria VA 22307

Call Sign: K4RQZ
Michael Kato
1843 Potomac Greens Dr
Alexandria VA 22314

Call Sign: KR4CZ
Joseph P Salemi
1217 Powhatan St
Alexandria VA 22314

Call Sign: WA4MHB
Lee R Hawkins
5914 Poyntz Pl
Alexandria VA 22310

Call Sign: KE4POK
Richard G Harman Jr
5810 Pratt Ct
Alexandria VA 22310

Call Sign: KG4RKE
Lisa M Harman
5810 Pratt Ct

Alexandria VA 22310

Call Sign: WE4BSA
Lisa M Harman
5810 Pratt Ct
Alexandria VA 22310

Call Sign: WA4USB
Richard G Harman
5810 Pratt Ct
Alexandria VA 223101842

Call Sign: KE4POO
Michael J Gallagher
2810 Preston Ave
Alexandria VA 22306

Call Sign: KE4SNE
Robert G Walsh
2825 Preston Ave
Alexandria VA 22306

Call Sign: KJ4ZJX
Nova Island Hunters Club
809 Princess St
Alexandria VA 22314

Call Sign: KF4WOA
Sons Of Confederate Veterans
Amat Rad Clb
809 Princess St
Alexandria VA 22314

Call Sign: N2ALQ
L Graham Newton
1009 Priscilla Ln
Alexandria VA 22308

Call Sign: WC4TT
Edwin N Myers
1010 Priscilla Ln
Alexandria VA 22308

Call Sign: KA3ZQY
Alan L Gehl
521 Putnam Pl
Alexandria VA 22302

Call Sign: KC2UQZ

Richard J Munz
7004 Quander Rd
Alexandria VA 22307

Call Sign: N4VJG
Charles H Hendren III
5800 Quantrell Ave Ste 1616
Alexandria VA 22312

Call Sign: KQ4YK
Daniel J Sehnal
124 Quay St
Alexandria VA 22314

Call Sign: KG4SFR
Karen H Sehnal
124 Quay St
Alexandria VA 22314

Call Sign: KE4GKP
Andrew E Vellenga
8527 Radford Ave
Alexandria VA 22309

Call Sign: KF6LYG
John R Peterson
2002 Rampart Dr
Alexandria VA 223081637

Call Sign: KE4ER
Michael E Larkin
2118 Rampart Dr
Alexandria VA 22308

Call Sign: KI4OBS
Andrew W Stebbins
3401 Ramsgate Ter
Alexandria VA 22309

Call Sign: N4BFJ
James L Keena
7501 Range Rd
Alexandria VA 223062423

Call Sign: N4MHK
Douglas L Megenity
7403 Recard Ln
Alexandria VA 22307

Call Sign: WB2EVL
Stephen Weissman
2622 Redcoat Dr Apt 2B
Alexandria VA 223032629

Call Sign: KE4GMW
John W Turner
9307 Reef Ct
Alexandria VA 22309

Call Sign: KJ4SER
James S Commeree
5312 Remington Dr
Alexandria VA 223093344

Call Sign: K1VMC
James S Commeree
5312 Remington Dr
Alexandria VA 223093344

Call Sign: KJ4NP
Ted L Parr
5903 Reservoir Heights Ave
Alexandria VA 22311

Call Sign: KD4IED
Jimmy R Hickey Sr
5408 Richenbacher Ave 101
Alexandria VA 22304

Call Sign: KI4YBO
Daniel A Stuard
5980 Richmond Hwy 1416
Alexandria VA 22303

Call Sign: KJ4GPK
Rachid Maouda
6429 Richmond Hwy 204
Alexandria VA 22306

Call Sign: KC7SGN
Nathan P Richmond
6034 Richmond Hwy 716
Alexandria VA 22303

Call Sign: W3NKB
Nicholas K Boedecker
6034 Richmond Hwy Apt 1005
Alexandria VA 22303

Call Sign: KD4EBM
George R Scott
5980 Richmond Hwy Apt 607
Alexandria VA 22303

Call Sign: KC0EWN
Lori K Mattison
5980 Richmond Hwy Apt 818
Alexandria VA 22303

Call Sign: KF4FOR
Paul A Bernhardt
5704 Ridge View Dr
Alexandria VA 22310

Call Sign: KE4ALX
Dale L Pope
5912 Ridge View Dr
Alexandria VA 22310

Call Sign: WA4NKQ
George A Riscili
7703 Ridgecrest Dr
Alexandria VA 22308

Call Sign: KA4FDH
Helen Abadzi
7822 Ridgecrest Dr
Alexandria VA 22308

Call Sign: WA2BNJ
Alan Mankofsky
6336 River Downs Rd
Alexandria VA 22312

Call Sign: KJ4JHG
Jonathan C Holmes
2403 Riverview Ter
Alexandria VA 22303

Call Sign: KC8KHL
Mark C Haffner
6006 Rock Cliff Ln Apt C
Alexandria VA 22315

Call Sign: KT4DV
Jesse E Bush
7139A Rock Ridge Ln

Alexandria VA 22310

Call Sign: KB6OXJ
Philip J Wilkin
7137 Rock Ridge Ln Apt M
Alexandria VA 22315

Call Sign: KD4CNT
Chartay Marbell
6480 Rockshire St
Alexandria VA 22310

Call Sign: KI4IBV
Brian R Mcdonald Jr
6870 Rolling Creek Way
Alexandria VA 22315

Call Sign: WA4URR
James L Richey
4402 Roundhill Rd
Alexandria VA 22310

Call Sign: AG4MA
James L Richey
4402 Roundhill Rd
Alexandria VA 22310

Call Sign: KF4TIR
Douglas C Shelton Jr
4403 Roundhill Rd
Alexandria VA 22310

Call Sign: KI4PCL
Billy J Shilling
1304 Roundhouse Ln 305
Alexandria VA 22314

Call Sign: KG4WNG
David L Whitney
808 Russell Rd
Alexandria VA 22301

Call Sign: W1AYJ
John W Wulff
3201 Russell Rd
Alexandria VA 223051723

Call Sign: W4KSA
Alan J Coiro

1112 S Alfred St
Alexandria VA 22314

Call Sign: KG4GIX
Thomas B O Reilly
1202 S Alfred St 233A
Alexandria VA 22314

Call Sign: KA1HGC
Jeannine S Swift
655 S Columbus St
Alexandria VA 22314

Call Sign: KJ4FUZ
Terrence E Buxton
234 S Jenkins St
Alexandria VA 22304

Call Sign: KI4KSV
Aloin H Sobel
6712 S Kings Hwy
Alexandria VA 22306

Call Sign: KB4MCC
David B Marcus
406 S Lee St
Alexandria VA 22314

Call Sign: KA1ICP
Charles B Newlin
414 S Lee St
Alexandria VA 22314

Call Sign: KD4GGP
Mark L Filteau
917 S Lee St
Alexandria VA 22314

Call Sign: WB8LCR
James W Metzger
704 S Overlook Dr
Alexandria VA 22305

Call Sign: KD8GEO
James M Fleshman
261 S Pickett St 201
Alexandria VA 22304

Call Sign: KK4AIB

John D Cordone
269 S Pickett St 202
Alexandria VA 22304

Call Sign: KI4CYK
Jamie Ainsleigh
340 S Pickett St Box 22734
Alexandria VA 22304

Call Sign: N6ITG
Jamie Ainsleigh
340 S Pickett St Box 22734
Alexandria VA 22304

Call Sign: KK4EAV
George H Phillips III
5609 S Quaker Ln
Alexandria VA 22303

Call Sign: KB3KH
Charles E Ficklin
125 S Reynolds St
Alexandria VA 22304

Call Sign: KI4FOM
Gregory D Young
260 S Reynolds St 408
Alexandria VA 22304

Call Sign: WD0BLL
James L Passauer
250 S Reynolds St Apt 1505
Alexandria VA 22304

Call Sign: KC6BEG
Susan C Arbogast
175 S Reynolds St K101
Alexandria VA 22304

Call Sign: W4XG
Robert J Macnab
408 S Royal St
Alexandria VA 22314

Call Sign: KG4YIS
Arnold S Miller
517 5 S Royal St
Alexandria VA 22314

Call Sign: N0ASM
Arnold S Miller
517 5 S Royal St
Alexandria VA 22314

Call Sign: WA4IST
Harry L Brock Jr
314 S Saint Asaph St
Alexandria VA 22314

Call Sign: KI4YHB
Anandhi Mani
719 S Saint Asaph St Apt 205
Alexandria VA 22314

Call Sign: KC4RJB
Edward C Mc Connaughey Jr
209A S Union St
Alexandria VA 22314

Call Sign: KJ4DZU
Margaret A Szalajeski
300 S Van Dorn St Apt R102
Alexandria VA 22304

Call Sign: K1VTY
James T Szalajeski
300 S Van Dorn St Apt R102
Alexandria VA 22304

Call Sign: KI4KSS
Connie L Buchanan
100 S Van Dorn St C 418
Alexandria VA 22314

Call Sign: KJ4WCQ
Benedick C Gratil
40 S Van Dorn St D301
Alexandria VA 22304

Call Sign: KI4BXU
Erik Misavage
60 S Van Dorn St F505
Alexandria VA 223044249

Call Sign: KI4FON
Donald E Smith
602 S View Ter
Alexandria VA 22314

Call Sign: W5UCE
James P Mitchell
1250 S Washington St 106
Alexandria VA 22314

Call Sign: KE4LYK
Charles H Schoon
1204 S Washington St 26
Alexandria VA 223144447

Call Sign: W3OHV
Charles F Scheid Jr
1250 S Washington St 716
Alexandria VA 22314

Call Sign: KJ4BQM
Joanne M Mcbride
1202 S Washington St 809
Alexandria VA 22314

Call Sign: KA3IEC
Brett A Crouse
905 S Washington St Apt 117
Alexandria VA 22314

Call Sign: KI4SCI
Melinda L Surratt
1202 S Washington St Apt
425C
Alexandria VA 22314

Call Sign: KI4SCJ
Tim J Meehan
1202 S Washington St Apt
425C
Alexandria VA 22314

Call Sign: KK4FQX
Marland C Thurston
1250 S Washington St Unit 714
Alexandria VA 22314

Call Sign: N4TVX
Joanne M Orsena
342 S West St
Alexandria VA 223145916

Call Sign: KI3O

Robert G Lepelletier Jr
107 S West St 321
Alexandria VA 223142891

Call Sign: AB4YP
James T Hurysz
107 S West St 489
Alexandria VA 22314

Call Sign: KF4NMN
William P Gewiss
5809 Sable Dr
Alexandria VA 22303

Call Sign: KJ4NIB
Kirk A Wimer
5515 Sacramento Mews Pl
Alexandria VA 22309

Call Sign: KJ4CYE
K4 National Wildlife Refuge
ARC
7423 Salford Ct
Alexandria VA 22315

Call Sign: KG4UHE
Collegiate ARA
7423 Salford Ct
Alexandria VA 22315

Call Sign: KG6MSQ
Matthew E Weiss
4541 Sawgrass Ct
Alexandria VA 22312

Call Sign: N4FKH
Richard E Weiss
4541 Sawgrass Ct
Alexandria VA 22312

Call Sign: KB4OKC
Jack H Goodwin
3979 Seminary Rd
Alexandria VA 22304

Call Sign: KI4BTA
Raymond C Stoner
5001 Seminary Rd 1419
Alexandria VA 22311

Call Sign: KB5LMT
Regina K Kennedy
4635 Seminary Rd 203
Alexandria VA 22304

Call Sign: W4ZAW
Kenneth J Graham
5001 Seminary Rd 630
Alexandria VA 22311

Call Sign: AF4YO
John B Nuelsen
5001 Seminary Rd Apt 1524
Alexandria VA 223111922

Call Sign: KJ4LYB
Shawn R Babbitt
4693 Seminary Rd Apt T1
Alexandria VA 22304

Call Sign: KF4NAN
Abdul Hakeem H Muhammad
7950 F Seven Woods Dr
Alexandria VA 223091475

Call Sign: KF4OHJ
Juan M Burwell
3603 Sexton St
Alexandria VA 22309

Call Sign: KD4FBS
Stephen L Buck
3420 Sharon Chapel Rd
Alexandria VA 22310

Call Sign: N4SUP
Jonathan T Cain
1220 Shenandoah Rd
Alexandria VA 22308

Call Sign: WB4IHC
Herman B Schmid
1805 Shenandoah Rd
Alexandria VA 22308

Call Sign: N4RVC
Sue S Baker
2006 Shenandoah Rd

Alexandria VA 22308

Call Sign: KG4YED
Jonathan M Baker
2006 Shenandoah Rd
Alexandria VA 22308

Call Sign: KG4MCN
William P Stillman
4552 Shetland Green Rd
Alexandria VA 22312

Call Sign: KA3V
John S Mason Jr
1931 Shiver Dr
Alexandria VA 223071631

Call Sign: WB4DC
Stephen D Courtney Jr
117 Shooters Ct
Alexandria VA 22314

Call Sign: WC9A
Paul E Jacob
6843 Signature Cir
Alexandria VA 223104373

Call Sign: KI4FYJ
Marnie M Dicristi
6385 Silver Ridge Cir
Alexandria VA 22315

Call Sign: KD4STI
Robert K Coit
6405 Sixteenth St
Alexandria VA 22307

Call Sign: KA6UBS
Pamela J Bertin
307 Skyhill Rd
Alexandria VA 22314

Call Sign: KJ4OCC
Bruce R Mccolley
171 Somervelle St 403
Alexandria VA 22304

Call Sign: KD7CUJ
Agha J Durrani

4250 Sonia Ct
Alexandria VA 22309

Call Sign: KE4JEM
John K Miller
3137 Southgate Dr Apt 203
Alexandria VA 22306

Call Sign: KD4WSZ
Julie S Abrams
8538 Southlawn Ct
Alexandria VA 22309

Call Sign: KD4YMT
Charles A Rexroad
7919 Spotswood Dr
Alexandria VA 22308

Call Sign: KE4WGK
Charlotte H Rexroad
7919 Spotswood Dr
Alexandria VA 22308

Call Sign: W4QXO
George A Paull
6637 Spring Valley Dr
Alexandria VA 223122136

Call Sign: N4AXI
Charlie L Ross
8056 St Annes Ct
Alexandria VA 22309

Call Sign: KE4GCX
Jules C Romalho
2751 St Elliott Ct
Alexandria VA 22306

Call Sign: KD4ILT
Sophia S Pao
5906 St Giles Way
Alexandria VA 22310

Call Sign: KC7USW
Wayne E Leach
8511 Stable Dr
Alexandria VA 22308

Call Sign: W4SBQ

J Carl Seddon
8720 Standish Rd
Alexandria VA 22308

Call Sign: KD4ZLJ
Paul A Miller Jr
8120 Steadman St
Alexandria VA 22309

Call Sign: AA8O
Paul A Miller Jr
8120 Steadman St
Alexandria VA 22309

Call Sign: KA6IOO
G Scott Mc Intyre
6123 Stegen Dr
Alexandria VA 223102277

Call Sign: KI4WKG
Pbs ARC
6455 Stephenson Way
Alexandria VA 22312

Call Sign: WA4PBS
Pbs ARC
6455 Stephenson Way
Alexandria VA 22312

Call Sign: KA4HSL
Allan L Kamerow
3504 Sterling Ave
Alexandria VA 22304

Call Sign: AJ4TP
Russell A Magnuson
3513 Sterling Ave
Alexandria VA 22304

Call Sign: KF1K
Russell A Magnuson
3513 Sterling Ave
Alexandria VA 22304

Call Sign: N3IJW
Sean M Faith
6300 Stevenson Ave 1001
Alexandria VA 22304

Call Sign: KF4OSI
Neil T Boertlein
8815 Stockton Pkwy
Alexandria VA 22308

Call Sign: KC4DH
James R Wiggins
8803 Stockton Pky
Alexandria VA 22308

Call Sign: KG4KWR
Gary F Shortencarrier
6020 Stoddard Ct 303
Alexandria VA 22315

Call Sign: KC4UIZ
Aaron T Claxton
2604 Stone Hedge Dr
Alexandria VA 22306

Call Sign: WD4PDP
James T Claxton
2604 Stone Hedge Dr
Alexandria VA 22306

Call Sign: K4GFM
John F Dellinger
2608 Stone Hedge Dr
Alexandria VA 22306

Call Sign: N1DVZ
Ellen D Briscoe
1709 Stonebridge Rd
Alexandria VA 22304

Call Sign: W1IAY
Melbourne G Briscoe
1709 Stonebridge Rd
Alexandria VA 22304

Call Sign: KF4AGM
Better Amateur Radio
Federation
2608 Stonehedge Dr
Alexandria VA 22306

Call Sign: KI4NVX
Gregory A Mccain
8902 Stratford Ln

Alexandria VA 22308

Call Sign: KT4XY
Leonard P Houser
4337 Stream Bed Way
Alexandria VA 22306

Call Sign: KF4RRK
Robert J Pavilonis
3811 Sulgrave Dr
Alexandria VA 22309

Call Sign: KF4SJQ
Mildred S Pavilonis
3811 Sulgrave Dr
Alexandria VA 22309

Call Sign: WD4MFU
Mildred S Pavilonis
3811 Sulgrave Dr
Alexandria VA 22309

Call Sign: KI4IPX
Adrian S Lehnen
502 Summet Ct
Alexandria VA 22301

Call Sign: KB3CGI
Jaime Velis
6007 Sumner Rd
Alexandria VA 22310

Call Sign: K4PDA
Franklin B Love
3837 Taft Ave
Alexandria VA 22304

Call Sign: KF4GTV
Daniel C Savage
6709 Tahalla Dr
Alexandria VA 22306

Call Sign: KA1IKV
David R Smith
5236 Tancreti Ln
Alexandria VA 22304

Call Sign: K4MBE
Sterrett J Carter

2412 Taylor Ave
Alexandria VA 223023306

Call Sign: K4CG
Uscg Radio Sta
7323 Telegraph Rd
Alexandria VA 223153940

Call Sign: N4USE
Frederic C Leiner
3900 Terry Pl
Alexandria VA 22304

Call Sign: KC4REW
Richard L Stockstill Jr
6201 The Pkwy
Alexandria VA 22310

Call Sign: KA9CMI
William P Blase
6430 The Pkwy
Alexandria VA 22310

Call Sign: K4IAV
William L Womack
6617 The Pkwy
Alexandria VA 223103056

Call Sign: KI4CIZ
Barry E Eastman
8801 Thomas Stockton Pkwy
Alexandria VA 22308

Call Sign: K9EIS
Dennis Dzierzawski
6210 Thornwood Dr
Alexandria VA 223102961

Call Sign: KA1UWE
Douglas K Turecek
5923 Tilbury Rd
Alexandria VA 22310

Call Sign: KD4NEX
Carl J Potter
8073 Topper Ct
Alexandria VA 223155016

Call Sign: KG4RNZ

Eldo Daniel
6705 Tower Dr Apt 104
Alexandria VA 22306

Call Sign: KG4IQY
John W Wulff
6700 Tower Dr Apt 205
Alexandria VA 223066718

Call Sign: NA1JW
John W Wulff
6700 Tower Dr Apt 205
Alexandria VA 223066718

Call Sign: N8OQA
Brian C Hicks
6501 Tower Dr Apt 303
Alexandria VA 22306

Call Sign: N9RRC
Burt A Wagner III
6519 Tower Dr T2
Alexandria VA 22306

Call Sign: KI4BED
Kimberli D Eaton
5511 Trent Ct 211
Alexandria VA 22311

Call Sign: WA7UIE
James R Budge
3706 Trigger Ct
Alexandria VA 22310

Call Sign: KF4FON
Thomas F Thompson
4128 Tulsa Pl
Alexandria VA 223042427

Call Sign: KD4WTQ
Leo A Brooks
4909 Tunlaw St
Alexandria VA 22312

Call Sign: KI4RSE
Robert A Hoey
4934 Tunlaw St
Alexandria VA 223122139

Call Sign: WB4YVX
Scott M Fox
210 Uhler Ter
Alexandria VA 22301

Call Sign: KO4HH
James E Nestell Jr
408 Underhill Pl
Alexandria VA 22305

Call Sign: KE4HPI
David R Fruehwald
7009 Unit E Birkenhead Pl
Alexandria VA 22310

Call Sign: W3HSW
Charles N Haser
6926 University Dr
Alexandria VA 22307

Call Sign: KE4LCP
Charles T Armstrong Jr
220 VA Ave
Alexandria VA 22302

Call Sign: KF4JPC
Arlington Radio Public Service
Club Inc
220 VA Ave
Alexandria VA 22303

Call Sign: K4CRA
Ralph M Hoke
6316 VA Hills Ave
Alexandria VA 22310

Call Sign: KD5CLL
Andrew S Duet Jr
3522 Valley Dr
Alexandria VA 22302

Call Sign: KJ4DLX
Alan Wormser Memorial Code
Warriors
5250 Valley Forge Dr 503
Alexandria VA 22304

Call Sign: KD4UJG
Theodore C Einersen

5250 Valley Forge Dr 503
Alexandria VA 223035611

Call Sign: KG4JLK
Ian H Keith
5250 Valley Forge Dr Apt 503
Alexandria VA 223045611

Call Sign: N8IK
Ian H Keith
5250 Valley Forge Dr Apt 503
Alexandria VA 223045611

Call Sign: KE4CKZ
Joshua S Bowman
5832 Valley View Dr
Alexandria VA 22310

Call Sign: KB6DQH
Robert D Lefever
4015 Van Dorn St Apt 104
Alexandria VA 22304

Call Sign: KG4WNJ
Joseph A Stahl
6816 Vantage Dr
Alexandria VA 22306

Call Sign: KD4CNW
Candadai K Madhavan
7003 Vantage Dr
Alexandria VA 22306

Call Sign: KD4EKD
Vishal C Madhavan
7003 Vantage Dr
Alexandria VA 22306

Call Sign: K2GJT
George J Trimble
7100 Vantage Dr
Alexandria VA 22306

Call Sign: KJ4BQI
George M Crabill
809 Vassar Rd
Alexandria VA 22314

Call Sign: WB4QDQ

George D Farmer Jr
7414 Vernon Sq Dr
Alexandria VA 22306

Call Sign: KO4NX
Richard J Miler II
9005 Vernon View Dr
Alexandria VA 22308

Call Sign: AJ3G
Richard J Miler II
9005 Vernon View Dr
Alexandria VA 22308

Call Sign: WA4YZD
Frank C Mallinson
9100 Vernon View Dr
Alexandria VA 22308

Call Sign: AF4NT
Charles R Keller Jr
403 Victoria Dr
Alexandria VA 223101832

Call Sign: KA4RHA
Joseph Marsten II
8690 Village Sq Dr
Alexandria VA 223094718

Call Sign: AK4QG
Arthur W Meeks Jr
9101 Volunteer Dr
Alexandria VA 223092922

Call Sign: KJ4ZMQ
Jack W Norray
1420 W Abingdon Dr 339
Alexandria VA 22314

Call Sign: KB2ZNG
Gregory A D Alessio
4840 W Braddock Rd
Alexandria VA 223114886

Call Sign: KB4ZNG
Gregory A D Alessio
4840 W Braddock Rd
Alexandria VA 223114886

Call Sign: AG4GV
Jose A Ferrer
4849 W Braddock Rd 204
Alexandria VA 22311

Call Sign: KC2UJY
Alan B Hershkowitz
4835 W Braddock Rd Apt 203
Alexandria VA 22311

Call Sign: KJ4LYG
Arnold G Mooney III
4749 W Braddock Rd Apt 204
Alexandria VA 22311

Call Sign: KI4IPS
Gerald L Patterson
13 W Cedar St
Alexandria VA 22301

Call Sign: N3LK
Ormon E Bassett
22 W Chapman St
Alexandria VA 223012502

Call Sign: N2OAV
Michelle M Koeth
5 W Glebe Rd Apt C6
Alexandria VA 22305

Call Sign: N2LPN
Timothy W Koeth
5 W Glebe Rd Apt C6
Alexandria VA 22305

Call Sign: K0ETH
Timothy W Koeth
5 W Glebe Rd Apt C6
Alexandria VA 22305

Call Sign: KI4MWP
Marshall M Deberry Jr
18 W Masonic View Ave
Alexandria VA 223012413

Call Sign: KE4ULI
Jo Rachel Jordan
306 W Masonic View Ave
Alexandria VA 22301

Call Sign: KG4GBH
Northern Neck ARC
306 W Masonic View Ave
Alexandria VA 223012419

Call Sign: KA4GOI
John F Boyd
407 W Masonic View Ave
Alexandria VA 22301

Call Sign: KE4BUM
Beth E Patridge
9 W Oak St
Alexandria VA 22301

Call Sign: K6PKD
Ernest M Smith
800 W Timber Branch Pky
Alexandria VA 223023627

Call Sign: W6MS
Ernest M Smith
800 W Timber Branch Pky
Alexandria VA 223023627

Call Sign: KI4BYI
Paul Lippner
6723 W Wakefield Dr Apt A2
Alexandria VA 22307

Call Sign: KJ4JGY
Michael P Marsh
8348 Wagon Wheel Rd
Alexandria VA 22309

Call Sign: KJ4JHE
Anne M Marsh
8348 Wagon Wheel Rd
Alexandria VA 223092154

Call Sign: WB4VBJ
Billy W Collins
8418 Wagon Wheel Rd
Alexandria VA 22309

Call Sign: W3ZWY
Kenneth H Rasmussen
8517 Wagon Wheel Rd

Alexandria VA 22309

Call Sign: KI4UFY
Roger W Allers
8527 Wagon Wheel Rd
Alexandria VA 22309

Call Sign: KG4BDS
Carolyn G Aaronson
6621 Wakefield Dr 509
Alexandria VA 22307

Call Sign: KC5REJ
William A Mc Intyre
6621 Wakefield Dr 904
Alexandria VA 22307

Call Sign: N5NCA
Daniel D Burget
6359 Walker Ln Ste 210
Alexandria VA 22310

Call Sign: KJ4UZX
Hans P Blondeel Timmerman
6507 Walter Dr
Alexandria VA 22315

Call Sign: NB2T
Hans P Blondeel Timmerman
6507 Walter Dr
Alexandria VA 22315

Call Sign: KJ4SSY
Margreet M Blondeel
Timmerman
6507 Walter Dr
Alexandria VA 22315

Call Sign: K2XYL
Margreet M Blondeel
Timmerman
6507 Walter Dr
Alexandria VA 22315

Call Sign: W8QPN
Richard E Spielmaker
8611 Waterford Rd
Alexandria VA 22308

Call Sign: KB4DPV
Kenneth R Pomeroy Sr
8612 Waterford Rd
Alexandria VA 223082350

Call Sign: KJ4HDB
Forrest E Waller Jr
913 Waynewood Blvd
Alexandria VA 223082609

Call Sign: KG4NMB
Patricia S Collins
1305 Waynewood Blvd
Alexandria VA 22308

Call Sign: KM4NM
Thomas L Peterson
4808 Welford St
Alexandria VA 22309

Call Sign: KG4QWC
James A Deyoung
3218 Wellington Rd
Alexandria VA 223022229

Call Sign: WA4AEI
George E Mather Sr
7907 Wellington Rd
Alexandria VA 22308

Call Sign: N2GAQ
John A Gerig
7909 Wellington Rd
Alexandria VA 22308

Call Sign: KE4BUN
Laurel L Singletary
6013 Wescott Hills Way
Alexandria VA 22315

Call Sign: KJ4JHH
Nathan W Liebman
5783 Westchester St
Alexandria VA 22310

Call Sign: KJ4JHI
Daniel A Liebman
5783 Westchester St
Alexandria VA 223101147

Call Sign: KB4VRG
Oi T Sciuto
5910 Westchester St
Alexandria VA 22310

Call Sign: N4MQX
Joseph F Sciuto
5910 Westchester St
Alexandria VA 22310

Call Sign: KD4NSF
Matthew L Keegan
7335 Wichford Dr
Alexandria VA 22310

Call Sign: KJ4TAU
Thomas M Griffiths
7219 Wickford Dr
Alexandria VA 22315

Call Sign: K4NWR
K4 National Wildlife Refuge
ARC
7229 Wickford Dr
Alexandria VA 22315

Call Sign: K4RT
Bradley A Farrell
7229 Wickford Dr
Alexandria VA 22315

Call Sign: KD4CNQ
Sally A Keegan
7335 Wickford Dr
Alexandria VA 22310

Call Sign: KD4CNU
David J Keegan
7335 Wickford Dr
Alexandria VA 22310

Call Sign: KD4CNY
Daniel L Keegan
7335 Wickford Dr
Alexandria VA 22310

Call Sign: KJ4EYT
Joe G Foreman

4214 Wiljton Woods Ln
Alexandria VA 22310

Call Sign: KF4GQV
Frederick S Benson III
216 Wilkes St
Alexandria VA 22314

Call Sign: KE4FEP
Marshall T Mays Jr
601 Wilkes St 203
Alexandria VA 22314

Call Sign: KJ4WWQ
Amy P Mcfee
2213 William And Mary Dr
Alexandria VA 22308

Call Sign: KI4GRW
Troy E Mcfee
2213 William And Mary Dr
Alexandria VA 22308

Call Sign: AK4AP
Troy E Mcfee
2213 William And Mary Dr
Alexandria VA 22308

Call Sign: KA3FTY
Bruce L Minnick
6450 Windham Ave
Alexandria VA 22315

Call Sign: KC4HMM
William N Mc Crosky
6484 Windham Ave
Alexandria VA 22310

Call Sign: WD4IQE
James P Geib
6229 Windham Hill Run
Alexandria VA 22315

Call Sign: N4GOJ
Karen W Tyson
7402 Windmill Ct
Alexandria VA 22307

Call Sign: NW4D

Herbert L Tyson III
7402 Windmill Ct
Alexandria VA 22307

Call Sign: KK4ADP
John M Eiseman
2001 Windsor Rd
Alexandria VA 22307

Call Sign: AC4WC
John N Geracimos
2104 Windsor Rd
Alexandria VA 223071016

Call Sign: KI4KST
Margaret H French
114 Wolfe St
Alexandria VA 22314

Call Sign: N3FNQ
Alan J Golombek
4605 Wood Dr
Alexandria VA 22309

Call Sign: KG4RKD
Marc T Apter
3506 Wood Pile Ct
Alexandria VA 22310

Call Sign: N4LBN
William B Harris
1219 Woodcliff Ct
Alexandria VA 22308

Call Sign: K4FPE
James R Parker
1101 Woodcliff Dr
Alexandria VA 223081059

Call Sign: KF4HGF
Carlos M Ilarregui
6001 Woodlake Ln
Alexandria VA 22315

Call Sign: KE4HPJ
John P Green
8422 Woodlawn St
Alexandria VA 22309

Call Sign: KD4CBC
Derrill W Ballenger
2804 Woodlawn Trl
Alexandria VA 22306

Call Sign: KA9TRI
James R C Miller
2904 Woodlawn Trl
Alexandria VA 22306

Call Sign: KG4QMR
Charles P Daly
3709 Woodley Dr
Alexandria VA 22309

Call Sign: WZ4C
Robert S Burns
4310 Woodway St
Alexandria VA 22312

Call Sign: KJ4IKI
Paul I Jaffe
5817 Wyomissing Ct
Alexandria VA 223031635

Call Sign: KF4RUV
Michael D Vance
6508 Yadkin Ct
Alexandria VA 22310

Call Sign: KG4RCC
Jon L Cook
203 Yoakum Pkwy 1014
Alexandria VA 22304

Call Sign: KE6RPT
Fred S Feer
203 Yoakum Pkwy 1611
Alexandria VA 22304

Call Sign: W4NTA
Leona C Hudgins
203 Yoakum Pkwy Apt 1810
Alexandria VA 22304

Call Sign: KA9FFI
Robert N Tucker Jr
309 Yoakum Pkwy Apt 510
Alexandria VA 22304

Call Sign: KA9QEI
Don S Bowers Jr
309 Yoakum Pky 1603
Alexandria VA 22304

Call Sign: K7RUW
Dean D Baird
309 Yoakum Pky 901
Alexandria VA 22304

Call Sign: WB5LSZ
Bruce E Dunn
309 Yoakum Pky Apt 909
Alexandria VA 22304

Call Sign: WB0TOB
Gary D Strohm
Alexandria VA 22304

Call Sign: KE4HPL
Kenneth C Garvey
Alexandria VA 22309

Call Sign: KG4BYV
Matthew C Mead
Alexandria VA 22301

Call Sign: KI4FBG
Jeffrey S Behrbaum
Alexandria VA 22302

Call Sign: K4GFO
Jeffrey S Behrbaum
Alexandria VA 22302

Call Sign: KF4OSN
Philip Sternberg
Alexandria VA 22303

Call Sign: KI4FOK
Gerald W Young Sr
Alexandria VA 22304

Call Sign: KJ4HSP
Thomas E Jennings
Alexandria VA 22304

Call Sign: KK4GEI

Alexandria RC
Alexandria VA 22310

Call Sign: W4HFH
Alexandria RC
Alexandria VA 22310

Call Sign: KG4KWU
Lee A Falcon
Alexandria VA 22310

Call Sign: KI4GHN
Lee A Hekking
Alexandria VA 22313

Call Sign: KI4GHM
Matthew A Tanner
Alexandria VA 22313

Call Sign: KI4BYX
Alexandria Seaport Foundation
RC
Alexandria VA 22313

Call Sign: K3GMS
Gregory M Stone
Alexandria VA 22313

Call Sign: WB9PHA
Gregory M Stone
Alexandria VA 22313

Call Sign: KI6DZF
Robert Traylor
Alexandria VA 22315

Call Sign: KE4HAA
Michael J Newman
Alexandria VA 22315

Call Sign: WA4ZJR
Robert T S Colby
Alexandria VA 22320

Call Sign: KG4PJC
Donna L Reese
Alexandria VA 223020001

Call Sign: K7LU

Scott E Parker
Alexandria VA 223028380

Call Sign: KD7END
Gabriela C Parker
Alexandria VA 223028380

Call Sign: N2PSN
Donnie Lewis
Alexandria VA 223049218

Call Sign: KL0KC
William J Broome
Alexandria VA 223150156

FCC Amateur Radio Licenses in Altavista

Call Sign: KG4DDN
Arthur Ray Caldwell Jr
1007 7th St
Altavista VA 24517

Call Sign: WA4ISI
Edward D Dudley
905 9th
Altavista VA 24517

Call Sign: KF4FCU
Lee M Shirlen
1605 Avondale Dr
Altavista VA 24517

Call Sign: K4VXY
John C Eubank
1411 Bedford Ave
Altavista VA 24517

Call Sign: KF4EGP
Chad A Shelton
1800 Bedford Ave
Altavista VA 24517

Call Sign: N4RTJ
Fletcher P Witt
Rt 2 Box 146
Altavista VA 24517

Call Sign: KF4MNL

Wayne A Childress
Rt 1 Box 200A
Altavista VA 24517

Call Sign: KF4UKL
June C Carpenter
1415 Broad St
Altavista VA 24517

Call Sign: N3LV
Robert P Hasson
1703 Dale Ave
Altavista VA 24517

Call Sign: KF4FYJ
Joshua D Roach
1202 Lola Ave
Altavista VA 24517

Call Sign: N4RTI
Elizabeth A Witt
118 Lynch Ln
Altavista VA 24517

Call Sign: KF4CQY
Marion E Williamson
307 Ogden Rd
Altavista VA 24517

Call Sign: N4YPW
Daniel P Mc Laughlin
1929 Tabby Ln
Altavista VA 24517

Call Sign: KB4OYC
Bunny F Woodson
1795 Wards Rd
Altavista VA 245174017

Call Sign: KE4ISF
Keith A Aguila
3738 Wards Rd
Altavista VA 24517

Call Sign: KB4BNW
John P Barnard
3738 Wards Rd
Altavista VA 245174051

Call Sign: KF4EGO
Lori D Barnard
3738 Wards Rd
Altavista VA 245174051

Call Sign: N4NB
John P Barnard
3738 Wards Rd
Altavista VA 245174051

Call Sign: KD4WHG
Gary K Bolling
92 Woodrow Ln
Altavista VA 24517

Call Sign: N6HIK
Carl T Williams
Altavista VA 24517

Call Sign: WA4OGZ
Herbert M Reedy
Altavista VA 24517

FCC Amateur Radio Licenses in Alton

Call Sign: KF4UIO
James E Long
1170 Alton Post Office Rd
Alton VA 24520

Call Sign: KD4IPF
Christopher N Wilmouth
Rt 1 Box 161 E
Alton VA 24520

Call Sign: KD4ISL
John R Brandon Jr
Rt 1 Box 203
Alton VA 24520

Call Sign: KD4GXL
David W Gillespie Jr
Rt 2 Box 215
Alton VA 24520

Call Sign: KD4HFB
Paul A Walker
Rt 1 Box 27

Alton VA 24520

Call Sign: KE4EDJ
Jason S Talbott
Rt 1 Box 512A
Alton VA 24520

Call Sign: N4ZIZ
Christopher O Talley
Rt 1 Box 63A
Alton VA 24520

Call Sign: KE4EDM
Michael K White
Rt 1 Box 68G
Alton VA 24520

Call Sign: KF4TGB
Henry B Daniel III
1202 Calvary Rd
Alton VA 24520

Call Sign: K2PSK
David M Yates
3155 Mt Carmel Rd
Alton VA 24520

Call Sign: KE4WVY
Christopher Robinson
17054 Philpott Rd
Alton VA 24520

Call Sign: KF4HUB
Michelle M Robinson
17054 Philpott Rd
Alton VA 24520

Call Sign: KE4WVZ
Seth Robinson
17181 Pilpott Rd
Alton VA 24520

Call Sign: KF4FTK
Timothy S Westbrooks
Alton VA 24520

FCC Amateur Radio Licenses in Amelia

Call Sign: KD4GKU
Ruth F Cowherd
Rt 4 Box 129B
Amelia VA 23002

Call Sign: N4VRU
George A Barnett
Rt 3 Box 149C
Amelia VA 23002

Call Sign: KC4TYA
Rebecca B Giella
Rt 5 Box 3060
Amelia VA 23002

Call Sign: KD4DSC
Tara L Giella
Rt 5 Box 3060
Amelia VA 23002

Call Sign: KD4DSD
Brian M Giella
Rt 5 Box 3060
Amelia VA 23002

Call Sign: KD4YVG
Kenneth W Hodges
Rt 5 Box 920
Amelia VA 23002

Call Sign: KG4BGS
Cathy B Redman
12777 Butlers Rd
Amelia VA 23002

Call Sign: KG4JMY
Stanley R Sitnik II
10750 Christopher Ln
Amelia VA 23002

Call Sign: KK4HTY
Jeffrey E Showalter
4520 Cralles Rd
Amelia VA 23002

Call Sign: K4KIT
Malcolm E Kitchen
10581 Dutchess Ln
Amelia VA 23002

Call Sign: KB4JXS
Robert E Anderson
11231 Genito Rd
Amelia VA 23002

Call Sign: KD4YOK
James E Anderson
11231 Genito Rd
Amelia VA 23002

Call Sign: KF4EFZ
Shirley C Anderson
11231 Genito Rd
Amelia VA 23002

Call Sign: N4REA
Robert E Anderson
11231 Genito Rd
Amelia VA 23002

Call Sign: KG4FFZ
Richard L Blankenship
13401 Horseshoe Loop
Amelia VA 23002

Call Sign: K4LMY
Henry N Hassell
17251 Ingram Ln
Amelia VA 23002

Call Sign: KJ4IDM
Diane V Hassell
17251 Ingram Ln
Amelia VA 23002

Call Sign: KB4YKV
William R Cowherd Sr
15531 Kennons Ln
Amelia VA 23002

Call Sign: KF4DHT
Elisabeth G Cowherd
15531 Kennons Rd
Amelia VA 23002

Call Sign: KI4KDJ
Michelle D Holder
14501 Little Patrick Rd

Amelia VA 23002

Call Sign: KF4YZS
Albert V ARCher
12720 Lodore Rd
Amelia VA 23002

Call Sign: KI4UFS
Greg R Miller
13105 Lodore Rd
Amelia VA 23002

Call Sign: WB3R
Philip J Giella
9607 Military Rd
Amelia VA 23002

Call Sign: KD4YOL
Robert J Anderson
4706 Mills Ln
Amelia VA 23002

Call Sign: KF4TCI
George L Vaughan Jr
13620 Namozine Rd
Amelia VA 23002

Call Sign: KD4ADV
David S Ingram
10910 Pridesville Rd
Amelia VA 23002

Call Sign: KJ4VSG
Donald F Brown
10601 Redfield Dr
Amelia VA 23002

Call Sign: KF4WSO
Nancy F Baumgardner
12200 Rodophil Rd
Amelia VA 23002

Call Sign: KC4VMX
Timothy W Bentz Sr
16831 Royalton Rd
Amelia VA 23002

Call Sign: KG4KHB
Roy D Gunter

8020 S Amelia Ave
Amelia VA 23002

Call Sign: KF4WLZ
Curtis D Woodard
Amelia VA 23002

Call Sign: KI4TSY
Marcus L Ovando
Amelia VA 23002

Call Sign: W8MLO
Marcus L Ovando
Amelia VA 23002

Call Sign: WV4Y
Marcus L Ovando
Amelia VA 23002

FCC Amateur Radio Licenses in Amelia Court House

Call Sign: N2IAI
Walter W Patrick
14701 Clemontown Rd
Amelia Court House VA 23002

Call Sign: K4ULV
William E Jones Jr
13400 Dykeland Ter
Amelia Court House VA 23002

Call Sign: KF4ZOM
Aaron J Irons
17860 Eggelstetton Rd
Amelia Court House VA
230024921

Call Sign: KK4HBT
Troy J Poore Sr
17740 Genito Rd
Amelia Court House VA 23002

Call Sign: WN4IXR
Don M Baumgardner
11200 Howard Rd
Amelia Court House VA 23002

Call Sign: KE4UMV

Harold L Walsh Sr
6739 Military Rd
Amelia Court House VA 23002

Call Sign: KF4ZOO
Leonard L Wiggins Jr
15710 Pope Ln
Amelia Court House VA 23002

Call Sign: KQ4FC
Blaine L De Haven
14121 Whispering Oaks Ln
Amelia Court House VA 23002

FCC Amateur Radio Licenses in Amherst

Call Sign: KI4AXY
Laura K Floss
193 Angus Dr
Amherst VA 24521

Call Sign: KI4CMX
Thomas A Floss
193 Angus Dr
Amherst VA 24521

Call Sign: WD4IDW
David B Woodson Jr
228 Bellevue Ln
Amherst VA 24521

Call Sign: KA1GU
Jefferson L Purcell
279 Blue Ridge Ln
Amherst VA 24521

Call Sign: K2REI
Jefferson L Purcell
279 Blue Ridge Ln
Amherst VA 24521

Call Sign: KF4EGN
Jeremy S Staton
Rt 5 Box 193A
Amherst VA 24521

Call Sign: KE4TJF
James L Thompson Jr

Rt 2 Box 338D
Amherst VA 24521

Call Sign: K2RKJ
Robert P Tomko
147 Briarwood Dr
Amherst VA 24521

Call Sign: KF4YGE
Kean T Myron
314 Covey Rd
Amherst VA 24521

Call Sign: KU4HS
Edwin P Christensen
155 Dairy Rd
Amherst VA 24521

Call Sign: KG4FGS
John E Connolly
281 Dyestone Ridge Ln
Amherst VA 24553

Call Sign: KG4FLO
Patricia A Connolly
281 Dyestone Ridge Ln
Amherst VA 24553

Call Sign: KJ4RTM
Ronald R Crosby Sr
1904 Early Farm Rd
Amherst VA 24521

Call Sign: KD4EMU
David F Mears
305 Father Judge Rd
Amherst VA 245213324

Call Sign: K4CNO
Galen A Wright
151 Glenway Dr
Amherst VA 24521

Call Sign: KG4R
William Vanderlaan
1235 Grandmas Hill Rd
Amherst VA 245214497

Call Sign: W4AEX

Arthur L Richards Jr
216 Huff Creek Trl
Amherst VA 245219603

Call Sign: KD4SSD
David W Cash
189 Little Hawk Ln
Amherst VA 24521

Call Sign: KI4PVD
Ben J Trefsgar
683 Maple Run Rd
Amherst VA 24521

Call Sign: KG4FSY
David S Riley
182 Misty Hollow Rd
Amherst VA 24521

Call Sign: KJ4RIV
Charles A Greve
235 N 5 Forks Rd
Amherst VA 24521

Call Sign: K4IXL
Douglas C Atchison
382 N Main St
Amherst VA 24521

Call Sign: K4IXL
Randall D Atchison
382 N Main St
Amherst VA 24521

Call Sign: N7LYO
Randy Davis
514 Pendleton Dr
Amherst VA 24521

Call Sign: KD6AAV
Dennis G Iverson
840 Richmond Hwy
Amherst VA 24521

Call Sign: K4VE
James D Cameron
Box 207 Rt 2
Amherst VA 24521

Call Sign: KI4FGS
Julius A Jennings
345 Sprouse Dr
Amherst VA 245213356

Call Sign: KD4CQW
Linzy O Evans Jr
186 Summerhill Rd
Amherst VA 24521

Call Sign: KC4TQE
Michael T Brown
266 Sunset Dr
Amherst VA 24521

Call Sign: K4XL
Kenneth D Grimm
686 Sunset Dr
Amherst VA 245212547

Call Sign: KB4AZX
Phillip E Steege
179 Walnut Hill Rd
Amherst VA 24521

Call Sign: K4SKA
Phillip E Steege
179 Walnut Hill Rd
Amherst VA 24521

Call Sign: KD4ARV
Troy R Nipper
Amherst VA 24521

Call Sign: W4MXH
Maurice T Jordan
Amherst VA 24521

Call Sign: KF4GHW
Samuel T Morcom Jr
Amherst VA 24521

**FCC Amateur Radio Licenses
in Amissville**

Call Sign: N8EPO
Thomas H Worswick
1466 Ashley Ct
Amissville VA 20106

Call Sign: KJ4DXS
John H Kim
5194 Beach Ridge Ln
Amissville VA 20106

Call Sign: KB4PRF
Daniel L Barbeau
R Rt 1 Box 235
Amissville VA 22002

Call Sign: W4KFS
Charles H Davis
Rfd 1 Box 425
Amissville VA 22002

Call Sign: K4SO
Mark C Killmon
14087 Carsons Way
Amissville VA 20106

Call Sign: WB3KAV
Merle L Rough
2324 Colvin Rd
Amissville VA 20106

Call Sign: KA3RAC
Jann M Rough
2324 Colvin Rd
Amissville VA 20106

Call Sign: K3PSO
Scott D Smith
15644 Covey Cir
Amissville VA 20106

Call Sign: K1HTV
Richard V Zwirko
16143 English Setter Ct
Amissville VA 20106

Call Sign: K1WSN
Phyllis G Zwirko
16143 English Setter Ct
Amissville VA 20106

Call Sign: N7OFP
Bonnie S Almond
16143 English Setter Ct

Amissville VA 22002

Call Sign: W4VOO
Alvin R Almond
16143 English Setter Ct
Amissville VA 22002

Call Sign: KE4TMA
William F Tapp
15 Hinsons Ford Rd
Amissville VA 20106

Call Sign: NA4N
Gregory H Drzyzga
1190 Kristin Ln
Amissville VA 20106

Call Sign: KI4MNJ
Everett D Nesselrodt
14802 Lee Hwy
Amissville VA 20106

Call Sign: KI4QKU
Thomas A Walther
1155 Old Bridge Rd
Amissville VA 20106

Call Sign: AA4ZM
Arthur Ziehm Jr
15025 Priest Ln
Amissville VA 20106

Call Sign: KK4ARI
Christopher M Cuyler
16264 Quail Ridge Dr
Amissville VA 20106

Call Sign: KI4EKJ
Tim W Macquarrie
3296 Running Quail Tr
Amissville VA 20106

Call Sign: WB4RSW
Roy R Ludvigsen Jr
117 Shurgen Ln
Amissville VA 20106

Call Sign: WD4GOW
Bonnie J Murphy

7116 Tapps Ford Rd
Amissville VA 201063414

Call Sign: WD4KOJ
George T Murphy
7116 Tapps Ford Rd
Amissville VA 201063414

Call Sign: AD4SA
Thomas J Dennis
4071 Waterford Rd
Amissville VA 201061703

Call Sign: KE4YXQ
Eleanor M Dennis
4071 Waterford Rd
Amissville VA 201061703

Call Sign: K3FR
Ronald C Todd
17190 Waterloo Rd
Amissville VA 201062067

Call Sign: KG4TOC
Richmond B Henriques
2730 Wildwood Cir
Amissville VA 20106

Call Sign: K7CAV
Richmond B Henriques
2730 Wildwood Cir
Amissville VA 20106

Call Sign: KG4DGM
John W Guyant
30 Woods Edge Ln
Amissville VA 20106

Call Sign: KG4FLE
Charlotte C Guyant
30 Woods Edge Ln
Amissville VA 20106

Call Sign: WB4UZM
Kenneth D Ring
Amissville VA 22002

Call Sign: WB4D
Lewis E Wharton

Amissville VA 20106

Call Sign: KJ4UYE
Kenneth D Ring
Amissville VA 20106

FCC Amateur Radio Licenses in Annandale

Call Sign: AB4CG
Arthur J Walsh
7472 Adams Park Ct
Annandale VA 22003

Call Sign: WB4ZIG
Worth V Anderson
4936 Andrea Ave
Annandale VA 22003

Call Sign: W4ACN
Harry Z Kaklikian
4941 Andrea Ave
Annandale VA 22003

Call Sign: KG4KXQ
Craig A Mccubbin
4202 Ann Fitz Hugh Dr
Annandale VA 22003

Call Sign: N4FLN
Charles R Scott
3626 Annandale
Annandale VA 22003

Call Sign: KH6JJD
Theodore F Rogers Jr
8533 Ardfour Ln
Annandale VA 220034507

Call Sign: N4BNF
Warren D Deem
7707 Arlen St
Annandale VA 22003

Call Sign: KD4PYL
Emmanuel Dimitriadis
7719 Arlen St
Annandale VA 22003

Call Sign: N2TBX
Lawrence W Katz
7301 Auburn St
Annandale VA 22003

Call Sign: KE4TXQ
Mark E Nichols
4741 Backlick Rd
Annandale VA 22003

Call Sign: KB4ZSS
Robert D Shuck
3603 Balin Ct
Annandale VA 22003

Call Sign: KO4SE
Ernest B Vanarsdall Jr
7220 Beverly St
Annandale VA 22003

Call Sign: KK4HD
Paul J C Van Der Eijk
4900 Bradford Dr
Annandale VA 22003

Call Sign: WB4HTL
Martha L Andrews
5105 Bradford Dr
Annandale VA 22003

Call Sign: WB4VMB
Leonard S Andrews
5105 Bradford Dr
Annandale VA 22033

Call Sign: KE3BK
William C Wuttke Jr
8907 Braeburn Dr
Annandale VA 22003

Call Sign: KI4TZB
Robert E Kovacs
3909 Brenda Ln
Annandale VA 22003

Call Sign: KD4GSD
Lloyd F Glenn III
8459 Broken Arrow Ct
Annandale VA 22003

Call Sign: N4GNQ
Richard D Law
8508 Bromley Ct
Annandale VA 22003

Call Sign: KJ4RBD
Robert E Anderson
7914 Brunswick Forest Pass
Annandale VA 22003

Call Sign: NY4W
Robert C Watson
3623 Buckwood Ct
Annandale VA 22003

Call Sign: N4DO
Walter C Pumo
9205 Burnetta Dr
Annandale VA 22003

Call Sign: KJ4VSZ
Douglas K Reece
3630 Camelot Dr
Annandale VA 22003

Call Sign: AK4AO
Douglas K Reece
3630 Camelot Dr
Annandale VA 22003

Call Sign: KJ4BWP
Alfred H O Brien
8532 Canterbury Dr
Annandale VA 22003

Call Sign: K7HAP
Alfred H Obrien
8532 Canterbury Dr
Annandale VA 22003

Call Sign: K5VRX
Roger L Stephens
6717 Capstan Dr
Annandale VA 22003

Call Sign: KE4TKR
David M Burk
8220 Capt Hawkins Ct

Annandale VA 220034602

Call Sign: KC4GLQ
Charles W Murray Jr
8521 Chapel Dr
Annandale VA 22003

Call Sign: K4KRE
Paul J Mooney
8449 Chapelwood Ct
Annandale VA 22003

Call Sign: KE5UX
Kenneth E Yucka
7915 Charles Thomson Ln 203
Annandale VA 22003

Call Sign: KE4YTV
Khang A Nguyen
7903 Charles Thomson Ln 4
Annandale VA 22003

Call Sign: KD4IWE
Robert C Arman
3412 Charleson St
Annandale VA 22003

Call Sign: N4DEB
Michael J Kirchner
4439 Chase Park Ct
Annandale VA 22003

Call Sign: N4GHC
Paul O Henry
4118 Chatelain Rd
Annandale VA 22003

Call Sign: W4UIL
William D Erickson Sr
3905 Cherrywood Ln
Annandale VA 220031901

Call Sign: KD4RED
Lawrence F May
7406 Chester Dr
Annandale VA 22003

Call Sign: K5AGI
John R Rivoire

8104 Chivalry Rd
Annandale VA 22003

Call Sign: KE4TXO
Jeffrey D Wright
8205 Chivalry Rd
Annandale VA 22003

Call Sign: WA4SEH
Allen C Johnson III
6925 Columbia Pike 630
Annandale VA 22003

Call Sign: KK4GOQ
Brian A Woodward
6811 Crossman St
Annandale VA 22003

Call Sign: K4BAW
Brian A Woodward
6811 Crossman St
Annandale VA 22003

Call Sign: KK4GOP
Zachary R Woodward
6811 Crossman St
Annandale VA 22003

Call Sign: KD4RGZ
Clark D Newell Jr
8421 Damian Ct
Annandale VA 22003

Call Sign: KJ4YHB
Clark D Newell Jr
8421 Damian Ct
Annandale VA 22003

Call Sign: KU4XA
Walter J Molony Jr
7558 Davian Dr
Annandale VA 22003

Call Sign: KI4EBC
Jeffrey R West
7116 Dejohn Ct Dr
Annandale VA 22315

Call Sign: N4YFA

Michael E Card
5004 Dodson Dr
Annandale VA 22003

Call Sign: KG4ONR
Rolland A Felton
7023 Donna Cir
Annandale VA 22003

Call Sign: WA3ORG
Mark S Irwin
7704 Donnybrook Ct 201
Annandale VA 22003

Call Sign: KA3WFW
Ardin H Marschel
4473 Edan Mae Ct
Annandale VA 220035704

Call Sign: W4BU
Roger E Baldwin
4912 English Dr
Annandale VA 22003

Call Sign: KI4NFB
Richard G Hall
4208 Evergreen La 234
Annandale VA 22003

Call Sign: K4YHQ
Richard G Hall
4208 Evergreen La 234
Annandale VA 22003

Call Sign: WA4ZAX
Richard A Clark
8953 Falling Creek Ct
Annandale VA 22003

Call Sign: N4YE
Christopher B Ramsay
4465 Forest Glen Ct
Annandale VA 22003

Call Sign: KF4AJZ
Philip V Schroeder
5124 Fortune Ct
Annandale VA 220034333

Call Sign: KB4KTF
Ingobert S Brauning
7417 Fountain Head Dr
Annandale VA 22003

Call Sign: KI4DHD
Heather M Tinsman
7482 Fountain Head Dr
Annandale VA 22003

Call Sign: K7CMZ
Melvin I Woods
4509 Guinea Rd
Annandale VA 22003

Call Sign: K4BIX
Norman L Carroll
8314 Highcliffe Ct
Annandale VA 22003

Call Sign: N0DM
Dennis E Mc Laughlin
8216 Hillcrest Rd
Annandale VA 22003

Call Sign: NO4F
Richard J Miner
4707 Holborn Ave
Annandale VA 22003

Call Sign: KK4HKB
Gavin R Lambert
4305 Holly Ln
Annandale VA 22003

Call Sign: WD4IAD
Ronald L Herold
3612 Hummer Rd
Annandale VA 22003

Call Sign: KB4MRY
Linda L Lay
7904 Inverton Rd 302
Annandale VA 22003

Call Sign: KB4MUI
Wolcott E Lay III
7904 Inverton Rd Unit 302
Annandale VA 22003

Call Sign: KE4GNA
Gina Rivas
4408 Island Pl 103
Annandale VA 22003

Call Sign: N4WN
Wilbur C Nyberg
3713 Ivydale Dr
Annandale VA 22003

Call Sign: AA4BE
Warren J Danzenbaker
7104 Jayhawk St
Annandale VA 22003

Call Sign: W5SMT
John W Gallagher
8300 Kay Ct
Annandale VA 22003

Call Sign: KB4LTG
Robert L Tyler
4911 Killebrew Dr
Annandale VA 22003

Call Sign: KG4LTC
Thomas C Martindale
5012 Killebrew Dr
Annandale VA 22003

Call Sign: K4TCM
Thomas C Martindale
5012 Killebrew Dr
Annandale VA 22003

Call Sign: KC4RVK
Harry F Sieber III
5162 Kimscott Ct
Annandale VA 22003

Call Sign: KB4WID
William C Steketee
3518 King Arthur Rd
Annandale VA 22003

Call Sign: KA5KMN
Gerald C Kelleher
3717 King Arthur Rd

Annandale VA 22003

Call Sign: W4ZC
Gerald C Kelleher
3717 King Arthur Rd
Annandale VA 22003

Call Sign: K4JBB
Floyd D Hedrick
3824 King Arthur Rd
Annandale VA 22003

Call Sign: KC2DA
William P Suffa
3904 King Arthur Rd
Annandale VA 22003

Call Sign: N4DED
Tommy K Meeker
5004 King David Blvd
Annandale VA 22003

Call Sign: AG4FJ
Ronald P Sherwin
5022 King David Blvd
Annandale VA 22003

Call Sign: KK4ARA
Peter L Merkel
5001 King Richard Dr
Annandale VA 22003

Call Sign: WB5CYM
Kent P Avery
7560 Kingman Dr
Annandale VA 22003

Call Sign: W4MAC
Merle J Beachy
4205 Kings Mill Ln
Annandale VA 22003

Call Sign: KI4ZYM
Gerald R Garren
3706 Krysia Ct
Annandale VA 22003

Call Sign: N9ABG
Gerald R Garren

3706 Krysia Ct
Annandale VA 22003

Call Sign: KX4D
Gerald R Garren
3706 Krysia Ct
Annandale VA 22003

Call Sign: WB4CVY
Stephen G Creeden
7138 Lanier St
Annandale VA 22003

Call Sign: KK4GB
Robert J Dooley
3602 Larchmont Dr
Annandale VA 22003

Call Sign: N4EGJ
John C Lozinyak
7812 Libeau Ln
Annandale VA 22003

Call Sign: KJ4WTZ
Elon N Smith
8213 Light Horse Ct
Annandale VA 22003

Call Sign: KI4TLK
Erik Von Baumgarten
3816 Linda La
Annandale VA 22003

Call Sign: WA4UFO
Erik Von Baumgarten
3816 Linda La
Annandale VA 22003

Call Sign: N4WMV
Kenneth P Mittelholtz
3804 Linda Ln
Annandale VA 220031512

Call Sign: KI4THO
Barbara J Von Baumgarten
3816 Linda Ln
Annandale VA 22003

Call Sign: W4BIO

Barbara J Von Baumgarten
3816 Linda Ln
Annandale VA 22003

Call Sign: KI4THK
Julia E Von Baumgarten
3816 Linda Ln
Annandale VA 22003

Call Sign: KD4SEA
Julia E Von Baumgarten
3816 Linda Ln
Annandale VA 22003

Call Sign: KC4SVF
George S Von Baumgarten
3816 Linda Ln
Annandale VA 22003

Call Sign: K4BIO
George S Von Baumgarten
3816 Linda Ln
Annandale VA 22003

Call Sign: WA4SKC
James D Coffman
3823 Linda Ln
Annandale VA 22003

Call Sign: KB3CUM
Timothy H Butler
5045 Linette Ln
Annandale VA 22003

Call Sign: KI4FQD
Steve J Hailey
7138 Little River Tnpk 1410
Annandale VA 22003

Call Sign: WB4MQZ
Jack S Blevins
8705 Little River Tpke
Annandale VA 22003

Call Sign: WA4QNX
Raymund V Nolan
6615 Locust Way
Annandale VA 22003

Call Sign: KD4ZLK
Edward C Mahen Jr
3908 Longstreet Ct
Annandale VA 22003

Call Sign: KG4URR
Edward P Davitt Jr
3442 Luttrell Rd
Annandale VA 22003

Call Sign: W4PDW
Thomas A Graves
7456 Madeira Pl
Annandale VA 22003

Call Sign: KJ4BMZ
Jean Dumay
4548 Maxfield Dr
Annandale VA 22003

Call Sign: KB4RTY
Jason A Copson
4606 Medford Dr
Annandale VA 22003

Call Sign: WB4FOJ
Ernest R Mc Daniel
4021 Medford Dr 201
Annandale VA 22003

Call Sign: KB6UPR
Lois M Rogers
3709 Merlin Way
Annandale VA 220031326

Call Sign: N4UUA
Thomas M Louden
3714 Merrimac Trl
Annandale VA 22003

Call Sign: WB4WLW
Jeffrey D Brennan
3718 Merrimac Trl
Annandale VA 22003

Call Sign: KB4SI
Francis J Burke Jr
8208 Mockingbird Dr
Annandale VA 22003

Call Sign: W8MOX
Robert C Dodt Jr
8902 Moreland Ln
Annandale VA 22003

Call Sign: KI4WFW
Benjamin L Rollins
3903 Moss Dr
Annandale VA 22003

Call Sign: KD4ILI
Richard C Ehlke
4216 N Valiant Ct
Annandale VA 22003

Call Sign: KD4ILJ
Nancy K Ehlke
4216 N Valiant Ct
Annandale VA 22003

Call Sign: KD4ILK
Daniel C Ehlke
4216 N Valiant Ct
Annandale VA 22003

Call Sign: KI4IFT
Evan R Kwerel
4105 Necostin Way
Annandale VA 22003

Call Sign: K2CPF
Thomas J O Brien
7553 New Castle Dr
Annandale VA 22003

Call Sign: KB9MCP
Dmitri V Baraban
4302 Oak Hill Dr
Annandale VA 22003

Call Sign: K4DUL
William O Hershberger
4212 Old Columbia Pike
Annandale VA 220032111

Call Sign: N4ISR
Harold G Blodgett
3813 Oliver Ave

Annandale VA 22003

Call Sign: N5LF
Alan J Wormser
3826 Oliver Ave
Annandale VA 22003

Call Sign: K4UBZ
Norman L Black
4011 Oxford St
Annandale VA 22003

Call Sign: N0IIU
Daniel C May
7544 Park Ln
Annandale VA 22003

Call Sign: N4SEQ
George S Magenta Jr
4731 Parkman Ct
Annandale VA 22003

Call Sign: KG4GYX
Lawrence P May
7544 Parks Ln
Annandale VA 22003

Call Sign: W2BSA
William W Stewart Sr
7825 Patriot Dr
Annandale VA 22003

Call Sign: KG4RKK
Erin M Stewart
7825 Patriot Dr
Annandale VA 22003

Call Sign: KI4DXS
Kelsey L Stewart
7825 Patriot Dr
Annandale VA 22003

Call Sign: KI4IPR
Deborah D Stewart
7825 Patriot Dr
Annandale VA 220034852

Call Sign: N2RMX
Brooks L Moatz

7877 Patriot Dr
Annandale VA 22003

Call Sign: KB4ZWL
Thomas D Sine
9025 Phoebe Ct
Annandale VA 22003

Call Sign: WA4CGU
George W Garand
7201 Pine Dr
Annandale VA 220035846

Call Sign: K3VD
Robert M Lundien Jr
4113 Pineridge Dr
Annandale VA 220032337

Call Sign: KB4OTN
Suzanne A Pastura
3705 Pleasant Ridge Rd
Annandale VA 22003

Call Sign: WB8WFV
Francis J Pastura
3705 Pleasant Ridge Rd
Annandale VA 22003

Call Sign: KA4IGP
Craig B Mccurdy
3808 Pleasant Ridge Rd
Annandale VA 22003

Call Sign: W4WNB
Warren C Sharp
7509 Pleasant Way
Annandale VA 22003

Call Sign: KJ4JPQ
Samuel A Yarashus
4825 Ponderosa Dr
Annandale VA 22003

Call Sign: KJ4BXT
Zachary A Yarashus
4825 Ponderosa Dr
Annandale VA 22003

Call Sign: KG4YQL

David R Yarashus
4825 Ponderosa Dr
Annandale VA 220034225

Call Sign: KF4JQE
James H Hartselle
8516 Raleigh Ave
Annandale VA 22003

Call Sign: KV4CJ
James H Hartselle
8516 Raleigh Ave
Annandale VA 220033631

Call Sign: KD4AQQ
Kikook Han
4327 Ravensworth Rd 601
Annandale VA 22003

Call Sign: KB4BJV
Mildred M Pace
4327 Ravensworth Rd Apt 611
Annandale VA 22003

Call Sign: KA4DZN
John H Hagstrom
4952 Regina Dr
Annandale VA 22003

Call Sign: KA4JZB
Alice J Hagstrom
4952 Regina Dr
Annandale VA 22003

Call Sign: KD4EPA
Richard Schiller
6920 Richard Pl
Annandale VA 22003

Call Sign: K6ETM
George M Sinclair
3901 Ridge Rd
Annandale VA 220031834

Call Sign: KD4LTB
Todd D Mitchell
3911 Ridge Rd
Annandale VA 22003

Call Sign: WX4VA
Todd D Mitchell
3911 Ridge Rd
Annandale VA 22003

Call Sign: KI4MWR
John B Mitchell
3911 Ridge Rd
Annandale VA 220031834

Call Sign: K4FKM
Jerry Coretti
3604 Rose Ln
Annandale VA 22003

Call Sign: N4JSM
John E Dodge
3915 Rose Ln
Annandale VA 22003

Call Sign: KE4CSF
Peter J Park
7705 Royston St
Annandale VA 22003

Call Sign: KC4YMS
Altaf Ahmad
7803 Royston St
Annandale VA 22003

Call Sign: K4IPV
Joseph J Carr
7804 Royston St
Annandale VA 22003

Call Sign: KI4EAU
Ferdinand J Heider
7120 Sanford Ct
Annandale VA 22003

Call Sign: W1FQH
Ferdinand J Heider
7120 Sanford Ct
Annandale VA 22003

Call Sign: KF4MBB
Lisa N Varga
4923 Sauquoit Ln
Annandale VA 22003

Call Sign: WA6CKB
Arthur J Brantz
8735 Shadow Lawn Ct
Annandale VA 22003

Call Sign: K4HKW
William D Sheehan
3904 Shelley Ln
Annandale VA 22003

Call Sign: KD6LAA
Paul D Blumstein
6820 Shrine Ct
Annandale VA 220036155

Call Sign: KD6NDA
Joan S Blumstein
6820 Shrine Ct
Annandale VA 220036155

Call Sign: KD4FBT
Arthur A Pond III
6821 Silver Ln
Annandale VA 22003

Call Sign: KB4UYY
Barry G Vecchioni
4504 Sleaford Rd
Annandale VA 22003

Call Sign: W4SNL
Charles S Mc Keon
4913 Springbrook Dr
Annandale VA 22003

Call Sign: N4FG
Fred M Griffee
8809 Stark Rd
Annandale VA 22003

Call Sign: KJ4LWL
Alexander F Karman
8845 Stark Rd
Annandale VA 22003

Call Sign: WB4WAJ
Robert B Clark IV
4927A Sunset Ln

Annandale VA 22003

Call Sign: KE4ULR
William F Hendricks
4807 Tabard Pl
Annandale VA 220034054

Call Sign: KD4TBS
Joanne M Keys
4012 Terrace Dr
Annandale VA 22003

Call Sign: WA4QVT
Harold Tunick
6921 Terrace Pl
Annandale VA 22003

Call Sign: WB2BFI
Michael J Sobel
8328 The Midway
Annandale VA 22003

Call Sign: NA4HI
Michael J Sobel
8328 The Midway
Annandale VA 22003

Call Sign: KB4VLC
Mark A Zettler
8316 Tobin Rd 12
Annandale VA 220036835

Call Sign: W4VHG
Roy G Siske
8208 Toll House Rd
Annandale VA 22003

Call Sign: N4BZQ
Luther F Hux Jr
7620 Trammell Rd
Annandale VA 22003

Call Sign: W4SCS
David P Floyd
4717 Trotting Ln
Annandale VA 22003

Call Sign: KF4SNX
Scott E Hiland

7217 Valleycrest Blvd
Annandale VA 22003

Call Sign: KA4GSG
James P Mornone
7315 Valleycrest Blvd
Annandale VA 22003

Call Sign: KA4RFZ
Augustus J Mornone
7315 Valleycrest Blvd
Annandale VA 22003

Call Sign: KF4IRS
Arthur L House
3441 Valor Ct
Annandale VA 22003

Call Sign: KG4MCK
Navdeep Singh
3900 Victoria Oaks Trl
Annandale VA 22003

Call Sign: N4ECI
Sherwood C Randall II
4208 Wadsworth Ct 104
Annandale VA 22003

Call Sign: K4GCM
Wilfred J Gregson II
4104 Wadsworth Ct Apt 202
Annandale VA 220037005

Call Sign: WB4JJE
Kathleen J Gregson
4104 Wadsworth Ct Apt 202
Annandale VA 220037005

Call Sign: KF4BAM
Trang Diem Nguyen
4810 Wakefield Chapel Rd
Annandale VA 22003

Call Sign: K4NWE
James R Simpson
7721 Weber Ct
Annandale VA 220035133

Call Sign: KB4LPJ

Russell H Slater
3381 Whipple Ct
Annandale VA 22003

Call Sign: KD4UCO
Eric W Witzig
4106 Whispering Ln
Annandale VA 22003

Call Sign: K1MU
Richard H Murphy
3842 Whitman Rd
Annandale VA 22003

Call Sign: NC3DX
National Capitol Dx Assn
3842 Whitman Rd
Annandale VA 22003

Call Sign: WD4NKX
Harrison P Butturff
7225 Wilburdale Dr
Annandale VA 22003

Call Sign: AA4I
Walter J Stewart
6831 Winter Ln
Annandale VA 22003

Call Sign: N4ZH
Terrance R Hines
3505 Woodburn Rd
Annandale VA 22003

Call Sign: N3NTU
Elisabeth V Byrne
3358 Woodburn Rd Apt 21
Annandale VA 22003

Call Sign: KI4ISS
Arthur J Leeper
8206 Woodland Ave
Annandale VA 22003

Call Sign: K4JN
Robert Arrowsmith
Annandale VA 22003

Call Sign: N4XNA

Robert E Millard
Annandale VA 22003

Call Sign: W9ABS
Camelot Wireless Club
Annandale VA 22003

Call Sign: W9XC
Woodburn Wireless Group
Annandale VA 220030166

FCC Amateur Radio Licenses in Appalachia

Call Sign: KG4UEJ
Eric B Fisher
1817 Derby Rd
Appalachia VA 24216

Call Sign: KG4RXH
Thomas E Mellon
367 Henry St
Appalachia VA 24216

Call Sign: KI4USA
Thomas E Mellon
367 Henry St
Appalachia VA 24216

Call Sign: KE4DQR
Mark S Hollyfield
304 Spruce St
Appalachia VA 24216

Call Sign: KG4HUP
Thomas E Fisher
5015 Stonega Rd
Appalachia VA 24216

Call Sign: KG4SGM
Charles S Fisher Jr
5023 Stonega Rd
Appalachia VA 24216

Call Sign: W4PGS
Wilson D Cornett Jr
225 Wise St
Appalachia VA 24216

Call Sign: KE4UUS
Joe D Brown
Appalachia VA 24216

Call Sign: KI4FGE
Ansel L Payne
Appalachia VA 242160027

FCC Amateur Radio Licenses in Appomattox

Call Sign: KE4SWS
Wesley B Baldwin
Rt 5 Box 12
Appomattox VA 24522

Call Sign: KC4HEE
Arnold B Ewers
Rt 5 Box 124 Charles Dr
Appomattox VA 245229313

Call Sign: KC4HJL
Patsy R Thompson
Rt 3 Box 168
Appomattox VA 24522

Call Sign: KD4JFF
Michael A Smith
Rt 5 Box 184
Appomattox VA 24522

Call Sign: KD4JXS
William D Cook
Rt 1 Box 228
Appomattox VA 24522

Call Sign: KE4VCW
Robert H Lucado
Rt 3 Box 349
Appomattox VA 24522

Call Sign: KF4RJR
Michael D Workman
Rt 3 Box 388
Appomattox VA 24522

Call Sign: W2ICU
Harold Abatte
Rr 1 Box 481

Appomattox VA 24522

Call Sign: WD4CXJ
Clarence N Tolley
Rt 2 Box 486
Appomattox VA 24522

Call Sign: KG4VLK
Justin N Harvey
Rt 1 Box 564A
Appomattox VA 24522

Call Sign: KG4POY
Amy K Bates
Rt 6 Box 588
Appomattox VA 24522

Call Sign: KG4RZF
Donald W Dery
Rte 3 Box 592Aa
Appomattox VA 24522

Call Sign: KF4LHK
Clayton T Powers
Rt 1 Box 601 A
Appomattox VA 24522

Call Sign: W3MPG
Michael F Gillam
Rr 3 Box 607
Appomattox VA 24522

Call Sign: K4TD
Francis C Gillam
Rt 3 Box 607
Appomattox VA 24522

Call Sign: WA4HBO
Michael F Gillam
Rt 3 Box 607 Gladwood Dr
Appomattox VA 24522

Call Sign: KF4GMQ
Ximene O Fortin
Rt 3 Box 619
Appomattox VA 24522

Call Sign: KD4JFG
Tyree B Lee

Rt 3 Box 646
Appomattox VA 24522

Call Sign: N4CIE
Morris T Wagner
Rrt 2 Box 727
Appomattox VA 245229238

Call Sign: KC4HYZ
John D Canada
Rt 1 Box 778
Appomattox VA 24522

Call Sign: KF4SKN
Lisa A Franklin
2018 Central Church Rd
Appomattox VA 24522

Call Sign: KF4TCD
Kenneth L Franklin
2018 Central Church Rd
Appomattox VA 24522

Call Sign: KE4TR
John W Ewers Jr
254 Chestnut Grove Rd
Appomattox VA 245225401

Call Sign: KF4WXI
James T Jones
530 Church St
Appomattox VA 24522

Call Sign: N4JTJ
James T Jones
530 Church St
Appomattox VA 24522

Call Sign: N4KDF
Brian J Gillam
183 Gladwood Dr
Appomattox VA 24522

Call Sign: KC4SF
James E Mcclary Jr
291 Matthews Rd
Appomattox VA 24522

Call Sign: KF4RJN

Richard C Adams
706 Morning Star Rd
Appomattox VA 24522

Call Sign: K4JGR
Billy B Mc Coy
373 Oakleigh Ave
Appomattox VA 24522

Call Sign: AB1EE
James Cadorette
4748 Old Courthouse Rd
Appomattox VA 24522

Call Sign: WA3RSL
Frank A Perdew
8367 Old Courthouse Rd
Appomattox VA 24522

Call Sign: K4ZN
Rodney H Longmire Jr
186 Patricia Anne Ln
Appomattox VA 24522

Call Sign: KG4VLH
Benjamin K Martin
4425 Pumping Station Rd
Appomattox VA 24522

Call Sign: WD4BPW
John A Mathews
Rt 24
Appomattox VA 24522

Call Sign: KI4LIW
Shannon L Whiteley
311 Soybean Dr
Appomattox VA 24522

Call Sign: N4DB
David H Blake
342 Soybean Dr
Appomattox VA 24522

Call Sign: KJ4IGD
John F Davids Sr
174 Twin Tunnel Ln
Appomattox VA 24522

Call Sign: KB4RXI
Catherine L Elder
518 Walton Dr
Appomattox VA 24522

Call Sign: KF4YI
Breck W Elder
518 Walton Dr
Appomattox VA 24522

Call Sign: KJ4EEH
Clark R Brown
1036 Whippoorwill Rd
Appomattox VA 24522

Call Sign: KG4VTB
Nicholas L Waddell
130 Woodland Rd
Appomattox VA 24522

Call Sign: KJ4EJR
Lorenzo R Saenz
720 Woodlawn Trl
Appomattox VA 24522

Call Sign: KD4BVM
Joseph R Mottley Jr
Appomattox VA 24522

Call Sign: KE4SVT
Alfonse V Cestaro Jr
Appomattox VA 24522

Call Sign: KJ4QCA
Brent E Peterson
Appomattox VA 24522

Call Sign: N4DKM
Joseph R Mottley Jr
Appomattox VA 24522

Call Sign: KI4CMT
Ollie T Harris Jr
Appomattox VA 24522

FCC Amateur Radio Licenses in Ararat

Call Sign: K4JIM

James B Padden
668 Green Spring Rd
Ararat VA 24053

Call Sign: KI4RVJ
James B Padden
66B Green Spring Rd
Ararat VA 24053

Call Sign: KG4HEP
Travis J Scales
1463 Rabbit Ridge Rd
Ararat VA 24053

Call Sign: N4BTE
Lloyd J Scales
1463 Rabbit Ridge Rd
Ararat VA 24053

Call Sign: WB4TSK
Joseph G Sloop
4180 Willis Gap Rd
Ararat VA 24053

Call Sign: AE4NE
Jerry W Whitaker Sr
4368 Willis Gap Rd
Ararat VA 27030

Call Sign: N4VYG
Judith E Whitaker
4368 Willis Gap Rd
Ararat VA 240533460

Call Sign: KD4WHY
Jimmy E Thompson
Ararat VA 24053

Call Sign: KG4PVL
Nathan T Gentry
Ararat VA 24053

FCC Amateur Radio Licenses in Ark

Call Sign: AC4HB
Donald R Hensley
Ark VA 23003

Call Sign: KF6RCZ
Richard T Loda
Ark VA 230030230

Call Sign: AJ4FU
Richard T Loda
Ark VA 230030230

FCC Amateur Radio Licenses in Arlington

Call Sign: KI4UFZ
Ben L Harwood
1603 11th St S
Arlington VA 22204

Call Sign: AD5PC
Scott M Litvinoff
2200 12th Ct N Apt 507
Arlington VA 222016512

Call Sign: KI4VYJ
David J Nelson
1633 12th St S
Arlington VA 22204

Call Sign: KI4VYK
Donna M Difelice
1633 12th St S
Arlington VA 222044708

Call Sign: N8HYO
Edward N Schneider Jr
2700 12th St S
Arlington VA 222044889

Call Sign: KK4EPO
Gregory J Redmann
550 14th Rd S Apt 537
Arlington VA 22202

Call Sign: WB6YGX
Lewis W Doss
3716 14th St S
Arlington VA 22204

Call Sign: KD7ZMS
Marc L Buursink
5863 15th Rd N

Arlington VA 22205

Call Sign: K1PW
Robert W Faris
5915 15th St N
Arlington VA 22205

Call Sign: KB2ERV
Peter S Eitingon
901 15th St S 615
Arlington VA 22202

Call Sign: KJ4ETK
Paul Saunders
936 16th St S
Arlington VA 22202

Call Sign: KD7RBQ
Eric L Smith
614 18th St S 1
Arlington VA 22202

Call Sign: KG4LOO
William H Somerville
3207 19th St N
Arlington VA 22201

Call Sign: KJ4BQQ
Judie A Armington
1119 19th St S
Arlington VA 222021613

Call Sign: KJ4OCA
Patricia S Lengle
3126 1st St N
Arlington VA 22201

Call Sign: N4CNR
Curtiss D Werner
4409 1st St S
Arlington VA 22204

Call Sign: N4COP
Richard B Engelman
5614 1st St S
Arlington VA 22204

Call Sign: W4LAV
Ernest S Teutschbein

4452 20th Rd N
Arlington VA 22207

Call Sign: WA3WXW
Stephen J Francis
3504 21st Ave N
Arlington VA 22207

Call Sign: KG4NZG
Gary S Russo
5418 21st St N
Arlington VA 22205

Call Sign: K4IJD
Fred N Wimberly
617 21st St S
Arlington VA 22202

Call Sign: KJ4WCL
Donald A Whiteside
1035 21st St S
Arlington VA 22202

Call Sign: KE4CYY
Davidson C Miller
2538 23rd Rd N
Arlington VA 22207

Call Sign: KB3HIU
David A Staples
320 23rd St S Apt 1527
Arlington VA 22202

Call Sign: KC4UHO
John H Mc Glosson
320 23rd St S Apt 801
Arlington VA 22202

Call Sign: KJ4QEG
Chris Sullivan
2300 24th Rd S 223
Arlington VA 22206

Call Sign: NW3V
Michael B Callaham
5900 25th Rd N
Arlington VA 222071207

Call Sign: K4GR

Robert J Slagle
3515 25th St N
Arlington VA 22207

Call Sign: KJ4UYH
Joseph L Dupesko Jr
2311 25th St S 302
Arlington VA 22206

Call Sign: KJ4UYC
Cristina A Dupesko
2311 25th St S Apt 302
Arlington VA 22206

Call Sign: KJ4ZMS
Timothy J Tomlinson
521 26th Rd S
Arlington VA 22202

Call Sign: KG4PXF
Paul R Gibson
4901 26th St N
Arlington VA 22207

Call Sign: WG4M
Paul R Gibson
4901 26th St N
Arlington VA 22207

Call Sign: KJ4ZER
Albert A Robbert III
913 26th St S
Arlington VA 22202

Call Sign: K3AAR
Albert A Robbert III
913 26th St S
Arlington VA 22202

Call Sign: KJ4BQV
Cynthia L Kellams
1207 26th St S
Arlington VA 222022202

Call Sign: KJ4CLK
Cynthia L Kellams
1207 26th St S
Arlington VA 222022202

Call Sign: KC4RKW
Peter D Blair
3946 27th Rd N
Arlington VA 22207

Call Sign: KB3EVA
Frank M Palumbo
3811 27th St N
Arlington VA 22207

Call Sign: KK4DPX
Lester R Gerber
1408 28th St S Apt 5
Arlington VA 22206

Call Sign: KA4KEL
Ray H Darling Jr
4925 29th St N
Arlington VA 22207

Call Sign: N4AJN
Claudine S Banton
5301 2nd St N
Arlington VA 22203

Call Sign: KI4DHW
Charles E Norton
5944 2nd St N
Arlington VA 22203

Call Sign: KK4GBR
Billy B Brown Jr
4652 2nd St S
Arlington VA 22204

Call Sign: N4OQX
Zen J Stevens
6801 30th Rd N
Arlington VA 22213

Call Sign: KK4GOL
Judah L Rosner
3855 30th St N
Arlington VA 222075303

Call Sign: KA2UVH
Donald H Stewart Jr
4411 33rd St N
Arlington VA 22207

Call Sign: KD4KMR
Richard J Fleeson
4108 34th St N
Arlington VA 222074425

Call Sign: W4RAU
Larry S Nixon
4651 35th St N
Arlington VA 22207

Call Sign: KK4FLE
Steven S Strasburg
5500 36th St N
Arlington VA 22207

Call Sign: W5DRP
James A Brown Jr
6317 36th St N
Arlington VA 222131409

Call Sign: W0FHS
David F Morehouse
4522 36th St S
Arlington VA 22206

Call Sign: W6APM
Noah C New
4032 41st St
Arlington VA 222074647

Call Sign: KA3NDW
Herman R Jensen
5908 4th Rd N
Arlington VA 22203

Call Sign: KJ4YHF
John G Brannon
4119 4th St N Apt 2
Arlington VA 22203

Call Sign: KB4WKH
Robert H Crist
6016 5th Pl N
Arlington VA 22203

Call Sign: AJ4EJ
Dale J Robertson
5609 5th Rd S

Arlington VA 222041212

Call Sign: KI4KFA
Christopher F Donahue
3202 5th St N
Arlington VA 22201

Call Sign: KE4FXZ
Carl H Layno
5613 5th St S
Arlington VA 22204

Call Sign: N4BIP
Gary R Thayer
6034 6th St N
Arlington VA 222031017

Call Sign: KD4JTZ
Nancy K Voigtsberger Ms
3908 6th St S
Arlington VA 22204

Call Sign: KI4UGG
Roland K Springer
5732 7th St N
Arlington VA 22205

Call Sign: N4BVF
Leo B Hurst
5316 8th Rd S Apt 9
Arlington VA 22204

Call Sign: KJ4AZR
Charles E Williams
2803 8th St S 351 A
Arlington VA 22204

Call Sign: KJ4PSB
Philip A DAmbrosio
3835 9th St N 303W
Arlington VA 22203

Call Sign: KB9SCM
Pamela L Toman
4001 9th St N Apt 1025
Arlington VA 22203

Call Sign: W4ZIF
George D Stanton

4508 9th St S
Arlington VA 22204

Call Sign: N8YSZ
Daniel H Brown
31 Aberdeen St S
Arlington VA 22204

Call Sign: W4GKI
Michael L Reese
1021 Arlington Blvd 1116
Arlington VA 22209

Call Sign: N4NTC
Robert S North
4501 Arlington Blvd 124
Arlington VA 22203

Call Sign: KB4LXG
Maxwell B Hirshorn
4501 Arlington Blvd 125
Arlington VA 22203

Call Sign: KA6RZW
Mary A Wright
1021 Arlington Blvd Apt 1020
Arlington VA 22209

Call Sign: KK4CYW
Dana E Leavitt
4501 Arlington Blvd Apt 310
Arlington VA 22203

Call Sign: WA6EKM
Eric Hagerstrom
1111 Arlington Blvd Apt 637
Arlington VA 22209

Call Sign: W0OTL
James P Horgen
2810 Arlington Ridge Rd
Arlington VA 22202

Call Sign: KJ4BQL
Elizabeth Y Scott
1111 Army Navy Dr 106
Arlington VA 22202

Call Sign: AD4Y

Si Hong Lin
1111 Army Navy Dr 714
Arlington VA 22202

Call Sign: KD4ODT
Ghada F Abu Rahmeh
1300 Army Navy Dr 815
Arlington VA 22202

Call Sign: KJ4IDY
Robert T Leith Jr
1111 Army Navy Dr Apt 424
Arlington VA 22202

Call Sign: KJ4ZTN
Eric D Green
1300 Army Navy Dr Apt 710
Arlington VA 22202

Call Sign: KI4YBI
Charles P Conn
2250 Clarendon Blvd 2012
Arlington VA 22201

Call Sign: W3XU
William M Remington
2400 Clarendon Blvd 604
Arlington VA 22201

Call Sign: N1ODW
Carolyn F Hunt
2400 Clarendon Blvd 713
Arlington VA 22201

Call Sign: KD4FRI
Jimmy N Clarke
2400 Clarendon Blvd 811
Arlington VA 22201

Call Sign: N4JEW
Jason E Wilhelm
2500 Clarendon Blvd Apt 221
Arlington VA 22201

Call Sign: KI4KXK
Daniel D Goodson
2800 Clarendon Blvd W 303
Arlington VA 22201

Call Sign: K4KMX
Daniel D Goodson
2800 Clarendon Blvd W 303
Arlington VA 22201

Call Sign: KI4YBN
Christopher K Mitarai
1603 Colonial Ter
Arlington VA 22209

Call Sign: N3FSH
Joel W Rochow
1527 B Colonial Ter
Arlington VA 22209

Call Sign: KJ4GPJ
Joel W Rochow
1527 B Colonial Ter
Arlington VA 222091400

Call Sign: N3FSH
Joel W Rochow
1527B Colonial Ter
Arlington VA 22209

Call Sign: N3ZVJ
Harvey E Walters
1555 Colonial Ter 400
Arlington VA 22209

Call Sign: KI4UGF
Michael A Peers
5547 Columbia Pike 218
Arlington VA 22204

Call Sign: KI4DOD
Michael E Gouge
3850 Columbia Pike 304
Arlington VA 22204

Call Sign: KJ4WWO
Rebecca D Blasdell
2301 Columbia Pike 319
Arlington VA 22204

Call Sign: KD4FC
John S Tyler
2121 Columbia Pike 408
Arlington VA 22204

Call Sign: KE4PKM
Michael L Reese
5010 Columbia Pike 5
Arlington VA 22204

Call Sign: KI4IFR
Kenneth R Carter
2005 Columbia Pike 733
Arlington VA 22204

Call Sign: KC6ZNH
Kim A Thomas
2005 Columbia Pike 830
Arlington VA 22204

Call Sign: W4NHB
Matthew Pierzchala
4420 Columbia Pike Apt 1006
Arlington VA 222044420

Call Sign: KD4RNE
Robert C Markham
2200 Columbia Pike Apt 1218
Arlington VA 22204

Call Sign: AI4Z
Edward T Konechny Jr
5100 Columbia Pike Apt 3
Arlington VA 222043262

Call Sign: KB1DJK
Steven G Carlson
1939 Columbia Pike Apt 41
Arlington VA 22204

Call Sign: W4PDQ
Alex Y Lee Jr
5550 Columbia Pike Apt 462
Arlington VA 222043155

Call Sign: KB1IEQ
Patrick T Dolan
5535 Columbia Pike Apt 504
Arlington VA 22204

Call Sign: K4ATZ
William N Anton
4301 Columbia Pike Apt 627

Arlington VA 22204

Call Sign: KB3DQI
Michael F Tyner
4301 Columbia Pike Apt 721
Arlington VA 22204

Call Sign: KF4LLX
Norma R Dunn
1505 Crystal Dr 410
Arlington VA 22202

Call Sign: KF4LNL
Bruce A Dunn
1505 Crystal Dr 410
Arlington VA 22202

Call Sign: KE4HYO
J Perry Smith
1801 Crystal Dr 718
Arlington VA 22202

Call Sign: KO5V
Charles P Forrest
1501 Crystal Dr 930
Arlington VA 22202

Call Sign: W5SFF
Charles R King Jr
1505 Crystal Dr Apt 205
Arlington VA 22202

Call Sign: KI4BNJ
Gary W Taylor
1805 Crystal Dr Apt 914
Arlington VA 22202

Call Sign: KB9GJV
Corey Adam Baye
2101 Crystal Plz Arcade Ste 202
Arlington VA 222024616

Call Sign: KI4BDZ
Rohit R Modi
1600 Eads St Apt 635N
Arlington VA 22202

Call Sign: KK4GOM
Donald J Guffey

2841 Fort Scott Dr
Arlington VA 22202

Call Sign: N3DCT
Craig S Peterson
4141 Henderson Rd N 1102
Arlington VA 22203

Call Sign: W4CTR
Craig S Peterson
4141 Henderson Rd N 1102
Arlington VA 22203

Call Sign: N3DCT
Craig S Peterson
4141 Henderson Rd N 1102
Arlington VA 22203

Call Sign: KG4GQP
Lucas Guchu
1986 Horse Shoe Rd
Arlington VA 22922

Call Sign: WH6AZA
James S Carr
Hqbn Home Hh Mmea Box 8
Arlington VA 22214

Call Sign: KF7LHE
Sean V Docken
2111 Jefferson Davis Hwy
1010N
Arlington VA 22202

Call Sign: K4NGB
Timothy L Russer
2111 Jefferson Davis Hwy
1111s
Arlington VA 22202

Call Sign: KJ4PSD
Joanna M Pineda
2711 Jefferson Davis Hwy 1200
Arlington VA 22202

Call Sign: KA4JMP
Joanna M Pineda
2711 Jefferson Davis Hwy 1200
Arlington VA 22202

Call Sign: KF4ZGV
Steven E Rusak
1515 Jefferson Davis Hwy Apt
1021
Arlington VA 22202

Call Sign: WA2HLO
Jon S Marshall
1515 Jefferson Davis Hwy Apt
405
Arlington VA 22202

Call Sign: W4ZSU
James G Black
2111 Jefferson Davis Hwy Apt
717S
Arlington VA 22202

Call Sign: N0UGB
Mark D Griffith
1515 Jefferson Davis Hwy Apt
719
Arlington VA 22202

Call Sign: KK4DPZ
David M Sims
2111 Jefferson Davis Hwy Apt
81514
Arlington VA 22202

Call Sign: KD4HBP
Edward D Powers Jr
3201 John Marshall Dr
Arlington VA 22207

Call Sign: K9JKN
David L West
1530 Key Blvd St 1216
Arlington VA 22209

Call Sign: N4VBA
Timothy B Wolgast
5590 Lee Hwy
Arlington VA 22207

Call Sign: KF6GNZ
Zaziouxe D Zadora
4400 Lee Hwy Apt 202

Arlington VA 22207

Call Sign: N7BEJ
Peter S Wood
6548 Little Falls Rd
Arlington VA 22213

Call Sign: KJ4GOH
John Rohland
6758 Little Falls Rd
Arlington VA 22213

Call Sign: WA6LTP
Michael G Kozak
5501 Little Falls Rd
Arlington VA 22207

Call Sign: N4GA
Gerald D Adkins
1206 Livingston St
Arlington VA 22205

Call Sign: KF6HMQ
Leslie G Bond
3904 Military Rd
Arlington VA 22207

Call Sign: KJ4HXQ
Christopher J Bannon
5718 N 10th Rd 10
Arlington VA 22205

Call Sign: KK4CJB
Christopher J Bannon
5718 N 10th Rd 10
Arlington VA 22205

Call Sign: N2JXJ
Jeffrey M Klaiman
2525 N 10th St Apt 504
Arlington VA 22201

Call Sign: WB0TEG
Ann Bennett
3812 N 14th St
Arlington VA 22201

Call Sign: KB1DKV
Joseph E Dennis

5006 N 14th St
Arlington VA 22205

Call Sign: AE4AO
Nikolai S Shirko
5916 N 15th St
Arlington VA 22205

Call Sign: KE4UNQ
Peter Lemken
5916 N 15th St
Arlington VA 22205

Call Sign: KC9BCJ
David M Thomas
1523 N 16th Rd Apt 3
Arlington VA 22209

Call Sign: N1DMT
David M Thomas
1523 N 16th Rd Apt 3
Arlington VA 22209

Call Sign: N4FSI
David J Collins Jr
4729 N 16th St
Arlington VA 22205

Call Sign: KG4PTC
Richard L Biby
4900 N 16th St
Arlington VA 222052627

Call Sign: KF4HGD
Ronnie L Costello
6006 N 16th St
Arlington VA 22205

Call Sign: KI4CJO
William R Albertolli
6411 N 16th St
Arlington VA 22205

Call Sign: KJ4L
Frank C Emerson
4707 N 17th St
Arlington VA 22207

Call Sign: KE4AJM

James C Perry
5629 N 18th Rd
Arlington VA 22205

Call Sign: KE4GJW
Harry R Blacksten
4413 N 18th St
Arlington VA 22207

Call Sign: KD3WW
Ray C Stringfellow
4427 N 18th St
Arlington VA 22207

Call Sign: KD4AXW
Frances T Milligan
6608 N 18th St
Arlington VA 22205

Call Sign: KI4MB
Robert D Milligan
6608 N 18th St
Arlington VA 22205

Call Sign: KA1KWP
Mary A Milligan
6608 N 18th St
Arlington VA 222051802

Call Sign: KA4WPS
Robert N Milligan
6608 N 18th St
Arlington VA 222051802

Call Sign: KA9QMV
Leonard H Milligan
6608 N 18th St
Arlington VA 222051802

Call Sign: KG4EIJ
Michael A Milligan
6608 N 18th St
Arlington VA 222051802

Call Sign: KF4RUW
William L Taylor
3214 N 1st St
Arlington VA 22201

Call Sign: KD4WTA
Michael E Shoupe
4635 N 20th Rd 10
Arlington VA 22207

Call Sign: KA3JCD
Whayne H Haffler
4014 N 20th St
Arlington VA 222073010

Call Sign: KA3JCE
Sandra H Haffler
4014 N 20th St
Arlington VA 222073010

Call Sign: WB4AYT
Robert W Biddle
4678 N 20th St
Arlington VA 22207

Call Sign: K4ARC
National Capital Ares Council
5832 N 20th St
Arlington VA 22205

Call Sign: KO4ALA
L Alan Bosch
5832 N 20th St
Arlington VA 22205

Call Sign: KC4LHC
John M Middleton
6032 N 20th St
Arlington VA 22205

Call Sign: KC4MON
Brian W Bardsley
5608 N 22nd St
Arlington VA 22205

Call Sign: W4MVW
Robert R Ebbs
6227 N 22nd St
Arlington VA 22205

Call Sign: KI4PCP
Desiree G Fey
4623 N 23rd St
Arlington VA 22207

Call Sign: KC4ISD
Richard A Hoska
5025 N 25th Pl
Arlington VA 22207

Call Sign: KC4KSJ
Christine M Hoska
5025 N 25th Pl
Arlington VA 22207

Call Sign: WA3UEA
Lukas E Hoska III
5025 N 25th Pl
Arlington VA 22207

Call Sign: KE4HPM
Catherine L Hoska
5025 N 25th Pl
Arlington VA 22305

Call Sign: KF4HGE
John F Ghizzoni
4551 N 25th Rd
Arlington VA 22207

Call Sign: KJ4IKJ
Thom W Vincent
5821 N 25th Rd
Arlington VA 22207

Call Sign: KJ4UNW
Carole G Newman
3607 N 25th St
Arlington VA 22207

Call Sign: KJ4TMZ
Crit J Cook
3607 N 25th St
Arlington VA 22207

Call Sign: KD9XB
Kim A Elliott
5001 N 25th St
Arlington VA 22207

Call Sign: KJ4HXV
Ian Elliott
5001 N 25th St

Arlington VA 22207

Call Sign: KC4YMK
Michael W Pinkerton
6012 N 25th St
Arlington VA 22207

Call Sign: K3SFP
Peter B Broida
3610 N 26th St
Arlington VA 22207

Call Sign: KJ4UBX
Mitchell B Mellen
4522 N 26th St
Arlington VA 22207

Call Sign: KF4EWG
Oliver P Coudert
6432 N 26th St
Arlington VA 222071045

Call Sign: KB4VCO
Dennis L Scholl
6927 N 26th St
Arlington VA 22213

Call Sign: KC4RKU
Stephen F Wurfel
2914 N 27 St
Arlington VA 22207

Call Sign: KC4PLV
Kenneth A Swain
4827 N 27th Pl
Arlington VA 22207

Call Sign: W4KAS
Kenneth A Swain
4827 N 27th Pl
Arlington VA 22207

Call Sign: KG4WMT
Stephen J Duall
6731 N 27th St
Arlington VA 22213

Call Sign: N4DRA
Rodney L Swearingen

6821 N 27th St
Arlington VA 22213

Call Sign: W4YDA
James S Mc Corkle
6821 N 28 St
Arlington VA 22213

Call Sign: WD4MIS
John Maher
6032 N 28th St
Arlington VA 222071237

Call Sign: KB4PVJ
Damon E Nesselrodt
6577 N 29th St
Arlington VA 22213

Call Sign: KB4VHM
Tamara L Wexler
5314 N 2nd St
Arlington VA 22203

Call Sign: KJ4OXL
Judith E Norton
5944 N 2nd St
Arlington VA 22203

Call Sign: KE4FND
Bradford M Smith
3808 N 30th St
Arlington VA 22207

Call Sign: KJ4PUR
Matthew V Skowronski
6331 N 30th St
Arlington VA 22207

Call Sign: KG4PLP
Ellis Kim
6319 N 31st St
Arlington VA 22207

Call Sign: KD4UJV
Patricia A Rourke
4609 N 32nd St
Arlington VA 22207

Call Sign: W4BMW

Robert J Rourke
4609 N 32nd St
Arlington VA 22207

Call Sign: KC4RKV
Edward S Buckler III
4913 N 33rd Rd
Arlington VA 22207

Call Sign: WA4QMS
Dennis B Voegler
4500 N 33rd St
Arlington VA 22207

Call Sign: K4DSD
Thomas N Pyke Jr
4887 N 35th Rd
Arlington VA 22207

Call Sign: N4MEW
Donnan E Basler
5046 N 35th Rd
Arlington VA 22207

Call Sign: KI4RTE
Daniel F Caughran
4400 N 36 St
Arlington VA 22207

Call Sign: W3DZK
Dennis A Bodson
5600 N 36th St
Arlington VA 22207

Call Sign: WB4AKK
Kenneth L Heitner
6116 N 36th St
Arlington VA 22213

Call Sign: K4HDL
Oscar M Garcia
5808 N 37th St
Arlington VA 22207

Call Sign: WB4RFA
Ernestine E Garcia
5808 N 37th St
Arlington VA 22207

Call Sign: WB4MCJ
Carl A Rochelle
4618 N 41st St
Arlington VA 222072964

Call Sign: KI4AFI
David Bodner
3208 N 5th St
Arlington VA 22201

Call Sign: N4KWI
Roland A Mattmueller
5015 N 6th St
Arlington VA 22203

Call Sign: KE4JEP
Douglas O Svendsen
5717 N 6th St
Arlington VA 22207

Call Sign: N4ZVZ
Constance W Cox
4001 N 9th St Apt 1023
Arlington VA 222021973

Call Sign: KG4GTX
Ronald S Senykoff
4001 N 9th St Apt 1910
Arlington VA 22203

Call Sign: ND4O
Ronald S Senykoff
4001 N 9th St Apt 1910
Arlington VA 22203

Call Sign: KC4REM
Matthew P Carter
4001 N 9th St Apt 521
Arlington VA 222031959

Call Sign: N4ENM
James D Cross Cole
208 N Abingdon St
Arlington VA 22203

Call Sign: N3FDP
Christian V Moreau
620 N Abingdon St
Arlington VA 22203

Call Sign: WB4BAW
Gail W Boseley
725 N Abingdon St
Arlington VA 22203

Call Sign: KF4VCA
David E Henderson
2042 N Abingdon St
Arlington VA 222072255

Call Sign: KE4IUI
Joseph J Novak
2001 N Adams St 205
Arlington VA 22201

Call Sign: N6IHC
David G Mandelkern
2000 N Adams St 605
Arlington VA 22201

Call Sign: KK4COQ
Albert H Behnke
2001 N Adams St 614
Arlington VA 22201

Call Sign: K4AHB
Albert H Behnke
2001 N Adams St 614
Arlington VA 22201

Call Sign: KB0QNS
Hans P Lellelid
2001 N Adams St 803
Arlington VA 22201

Call Sign: KJ4NJD
Michael R Egbert
2001 N Adams St Apt 917
Arlington VA 22201

Call Sign: KD4QQD
Christiana T Brewer
735 N Albemarle St
Arlington VA 222031424

Call Sign: KG4UHN
Paul P Kiendl
752 N Albemarle St

Arlington VA 22203

Call Sign: KB4LIR
Thuy T Brewer
735 N Albemarle St
Arlington VA 222031424

Call Sign: K8DIU
Dennis G Brewer
735 N Albemarle St
Arlington VA 222031424

Call Sign: KJ4EAC
David C Huckabee
3804 N Albemarle St
Arlington VA 22207

Call Sign: N7YMO
Timothy J Evans
1121 N Arlington Blvd Apt 630
Arlington VA 22209

Call Sign: N4FNZ
Barry L Travis
201 N Barton St
Arlington VA 22201

Call Sign: KC4HPO
Lee A Glover
804 N Barton St
Arlington VA 22201

Call Sign: KE4KLA
Robert S G Lennox
1630 N Barton St
Arlington VA 22201

Call Sign: W3JTA
Phil Schneider
263 N Bryan St
Arlington VA 22201

Call Sign: KJ4RNP
Peter F Vanderpoel
1713 N Bryan St
Arlington VA 22201

Call Sign: K1OYG
Jerry Delli Priscoli

1714 N Bryan St
Arlington VA 22201

Call Sign: KO4MI
David H Skolnick
5432 N Carlin Springs Rd
Arlington VA 22203

Call Sign: WB3FNS
David H Hunsberger
3827 N Chesterbrook Rd
Arlington VA 22207

Call Sign: KJ4VZO
Kenneth P Sarzynski
1227 N Cleveland St
Arlington VA 22201

Call Sign: KJ4JHD
Clinton J OHara
1931 N Clevelnd St 500
Arlington VA 22201

Call Sign: KJ4HXU
Bernard Huon-Dumentat
1552 N Colonial Ter
Arlington VA 222091442

Call Sign: K4BHD
Bernard Huon-Dumentat
1552 N Colonial Ter
Arlington VA 222091442

Call Sign: KF4VNS
Michael G Davidson
10 N Columbus St
Arlington VA 222032650

Call Sign: KI4FWE
Richard P Cincotta
230 N Columbus St
Arlington VA 222032619

Call Sign: KI4FW
Richard P Cincotta
230 N Columbus St
Arlington VA 222032619

Call Sign: W4PWF

Charles D Bodson
233 N Columbus St
Arlington VA 22203

Call Sign: W4WVP
Arlington ARC
233 N Columbus St
Arlington VA 22203

Call Sign: KS4CU
Marc Anderson
1233 N Courthouse Rd 102
Arlington VA 22201

Call Sign: KI4THH
Catherine N Dorset
1017 N Daniel St
Arlington VA 22201

Call Sign: KA6TIE
Catherine N Dorset
1017 N Daniel St
Arlington VA 22201

Call Sign: KG3R
Jane B Dorset
1017 N Daniel St
Arlington VA 22201

Call Sign: WB4J
Thomas H Dorset
1017 N Daniel St
Arlington VA 22201

Call Sign: W4THD
Thomas H Dorset
1017 N Daniel St
Arlington VA 22201

Call Sign: N0EZR
David L Lee
4650 N Dittmar Rd
Arlington VA 22207

Call Sign: K4JJP
Dorothy M Easton
367 N Edison St
Arlington VA 22203

Call Sign: KD4QMR
David R Randall
805 N Emerson St
Arlington VA 22205

Call Sign: KI4RI
Alfred N Berry
3459 N Emerson St
Arlington VA 22207

Call Sign: N1BFU
Andrew A King
3488 N Emerson St
Arlington VA 22207

Call Sign: KC3WD
Matthew J Butcher
213 N Evergreen St
Arlington VA 22203

Call Sign: KF4NOL
Elizabeth J Pennisi
213 N Evergreen St
Arlington VA 22203

Call Sign: KJ4UCA
Jesse G Cassibba
4001 N Fairfax Dr
Arlington VA 22203

Call Sign: W4UAI
Michael B Banacki
5715 N Fairfax Dr
Arlington VA 22205

Call Sign: KD4SIC
Jessica R Creech
3800 N Fairfax Dr 909
Arlington VA 22203

Call Sign: KK4ELF
Bryan T Sparkman
2507 N Florida St
Arlington VA 22207

Call Sign: AJ4VO
James R Murphy
2638 N Florida St
Arlington VA 22207

Call Sign: AA0J
James R Murphy
2638 N Florida St
Arlington VA 22207

Call Sign: KJ4SEZ
John Murphy
2638 N Florida St
Arlington VA 22207

Call Sign: KC4UYA
Amable P Ocampo
1028 N Frederick St
Arlington VA 22205

Call Sign: KD7ENK
Birgitta M C Beuthe
1616 N Garfield St
Arlington VA 22201

Call Sign: N4YGN
James K Simmons
1624 N Garfield St
Arlington VA 22201

Call Sign: N4QX
Brennan T Price
1021 N Garfield St Apt 432
Arlington VA 222012565

Call Sign: W8MAU
Robert M Cullen
101 N George Mason Dr 2
Arlington VA 22203

Call Sign: KI4N
Thomas G Mc Williams
2600 N Glebe Rd
Arlington VA 222073549

Call Sign: W4REE
Whit M Bishop
3526 N Glebe Rd
Arlington VA 22207

Call Sign: AI4GO
Roy L Nickelson Jr
851 N Glebe Rd 1512

Arlington VA 22203

Call Sign: W4HU
John H Swafford
2000 N Glebe Rd Apt 210
Arlington VA 22207

Call Sign: WB4KLJ
Robert E Bowis
335 N Granada St
Arlington VA 222031323

Call Sign: WD4PTF
Richard J Cmiel
207 N Greenbrier St
Arlington VA 22203

Call Sign: KD4ET
Orman G Charles
1310 N Greenbrier St
Arlington VA 22205

Call Sign: AA7NE
Jose A Perez
2546 N Greenbrier St
Arlington VA 22207

Call Sign: KG4PSY
Gary K Bogle
700 N Greenfrier St
Arlington VA 22205

Call Sign: KD4KMS
Joanne M Hughes
1325 N Harrison St
Arlington VA 22205

Call Sign: KJ4HXR
Rene Costales
1412 N Harrison St
Arlington VA 222052700

Call Sign: KA4YPK
Stafford W Wilbur
2116 N Harrison St
Arlington VA 22205

Call Sign: K4LRU
Olin R Houston

2614 N Harrison St
Arlington VA 22207

Call Sign: K4IC
Thomas H Miller
3689 N Harrison St
Arlington VA 22207

Call Sign: W1EWF
Richard C Dunham
1819 N Hartford St
Arlington VA 22201

Call Sign: WB3HYZ
Richard G Simpson
4411 N Henderson Rd
Arlington VA 22203

Call Sign: WD4JOL
Malcolm B Sippy
1813 N Herndon St
Arlington VA 22201

Call Sign: KI4IFS
Sarah R Ramsey
1200 N Herndon St 333
Arlington VA 22201

Call Sign: N4YOE
Richard S Muffley
605 N Highland St
Arlington VA 22201

Call Sign: KA4KUU
Paul N Wengert
1511 N Highland St
Arlington VA 22201

Call Sign: KC6KUE
James R Strube
1727 N Huntington St
Arlington VA 22205

Call Sign: KG4KXA
Jay M Peters
805 N Illinois St
Arlington VA 22205

Call Sign: WB4QAX

Howard D Dunlap
1208 N Inglewood St
Arlington VA 22205

Call Sign: KG4HZC
John M Mcnamara
40 N Irving St
Arlington VA 22201

Call Sign: KK4EBG
John W Melvin
620 N Ivy St
Arlington VA 22201

Call Sign: KI4IPM
William J Murray
519 N Jackson St
Arlington VA 22201

Call Sign: K4CVI
James M Morris
1600 N Jefferson
Arlington VA 22205

Call Sign: WB2WIX
Jonathan E Kern
1820 N Jefferson St
Arlington VA 22205

Call Sign: N3NJM
George W Arthur
2017 N Jefferson St
Arlington VA 22205

Call Sign: WG1A
George W Arthur
2017 N Jefferson St
Arlington VA 22205

Call Sign: KI4WUL
Reinhard R Germ
2526 N Jefferson St
Arlington VA 22207

Call Sign: K4ADE
Robert W Ageton
2504 N Kenilworth St
Arlington VA 222071419

Call Sign: W4LMW
Thomas C Crabe
2517 N Kenilworth St
Arlington VA 22207

Call Sign: KE4CYF
Naoto Kada
2522 N Kenilworth St
Arlington VA 22207

Call Sign: N3JWK
Jason W Thayer
1506 N Kenilworth St
Arlington VA 22213

Call Sign: KJ4LQL
Florian Pfeiffer
308 N Kenmoore St
Arlington VA 22201

Call Sign: KG4VNC
Adam G Hahn
1811 N Kenmore St
Arlington VA 22207

Call Sign: AI4QB
Adam G Hahn
1811 N Kenmore St
Arlington VA 22207

Call Sign: N4GGO
John B Wood
1101 N Kensington 5
Arlington VA 22205

Call Sign: N4BYF
Thomas F Protz
3711 N Kensington St
Arlington VA 222071331

Call Sign: K1CCO
Bernal B Allen Jr
887A N Kensington St
Arlington VA 22205

Call Sign: KD4TAA
Michael J Scott
3319 N Kensington St
Arlington VA 22207

Call Sign: KB2HDP
Christopher T Rossi
1701 N Kent St
Arlington VA 22209

Call Sign: K1MHM
John P Retelle Jr
1701 N Kent St 608
Arlington VA 22209

Call Sign: N4ALN
Guy W Lovell
901 N Larrimore St
Arlington VA 222051410

Call Sign: K4KYO
Richard A Stalls
917 N Lexington St
Arlington VA 22205

Call Sign: K9PUP
Puppydog ARC
917 N Lexington St
Arlington VA 22205

Call Sign: W6VFM
American Radio Telegraphers
Society
917 N Lexington St
Arlington VA 22205

Call Sign: KB4UGF
Chester G Summitt
1634 N Lexington St
Arlington VA 22205

Call Sign: KC4ATV
Marian K Thompson
1634 N Lexington St
Arlington VA 22205

Call Sign: KG4KGA
Joseph P Angelone
2453 N Lexington St
Arlington VA 22207

Call Sign: AG4JW
Joseph P Angelone

2453 N Lexington St
Arlington VA 22207

Call Sign: KJ4NJF
Craig A Pennington
900 N Liberty St
Arlington VA 22205

Call Sign: NC4P
Craig A Pennington
900 N Liberty St
Arlington VA 22205

Call Sign: KA4LYY
Philip J Bassford
1013 N Liberty St
Arlington VA 22205

Call Sign: N2GJM
Michael J Badagliacca
511 N Lincoln St
Arlington VA 22201

Call Sign: W4NRO
Walter G Walker Jr
900 N Livingston St
Arlington VA 222051423

Call Sign: KI4YBP
Earl F Mellor
973 N Longfellow St
Arlington VA 222051637

Call Sign: KC2CAX
Kenneth L Briggs
1301 N Lynnbrook Dr
Arlington VA 22201

Call Sign: KK4CYY
Rene Bleiweiss
2218 N Madison St
Arlington VA 22205

Call Sign: KB4URT
Edward L Barrow
600 N Madison St Apt 435
Arlington VA 22203

Call Sign: KG4KAJ

Tiffany A Fetzner
3505 N Military Rd
Arlington VA 222074852

Call Sign: W4RV
Samuel K Brown Jr
3132 N Monroe
Arlington VA 22207

Call Sign: KE4IRS
Christina M Mac Donald
619 N Monroe St 4
Arlington VA 22201

Call Sign: KN4VV
John E Glover
901 N Monroe St 814
Arlington VA 22201

Call Sign: N7HRZ
Edward C Friday
801 N Monroe St Apt 413
Arlington VA 22201

Call Sign: KD4YI
John L Robuck
901 N Monroest 504
Arlington VA 222012355

Call Sign: KB4CBN
Harper B Atherton
10 N Montague St
Arlington VA 22203

Call Sign: KD4WGR
Rodrigo E Canadas
510 N Montana St
Arlington VA 22203

Call Sign: KB2WVG
Patrick J Pepe
1423 N Nash St Unit 11
Arlington VA 22209

Call Sign: KI4LSA
Aubrey L Mansfield
2724 N Nelson St
Arlington VA 22207

Call Sign: K4UDT
Aubrey L Mansfield
2724 N Nelson St
Arlington VA 22207

Call Sign: N3BM
Aubrey L Mansfield
2724 N Nelson St
Arlington VA 22207

Call Sign: KI4QCO
Landon T Densley
518 N Nelson St
Arlington VA 22203

Call Sign: WA4HIS
Eric W Nyman
1413 N Nicholas St
Arlington VA 22205

Call Sign: WA4RUQ
Barbara B Nyman
1413 N Nicholas St
Arlington VA 22205

Call Sign: WA1PGY
Mark J Schwartz
526 N Norwood St
Arlington VA 22203

Call Sign: K4KMU
Jack H Puerner
118 N Nottingham St
Arlington VA 22203

Call Sign: KA4WWT
John T Maurer
2220 N Nottingham St
Arlington VA 22205

Call Sign: W4MDT
Walter H Cheatham
1600 N Oak St 1612
Arlington VA 22209

Call Sign: KD5IQI
Susan L West
1600 N Oak St 1802
Arlington VA 22209

Call Sign: K8DM
David J Mitchell
1800 N Oak St 1802
Arlington VA 22209

Call Sign: KF4JGP
Andreas Peter
Skopec 1401 N Oak St 908
Arlington VA 22209

Call Sign: W2SMK
Stephen M Ketyer
1600 N Oak St Apt 1018
Arlington VA 222092765

Call Sign: KV4HZ
Stephen M Ketyer
1600 N Oak St Apt 1018
Arlington VA 222092765

Call Sign: N0CLT
David A Kohls
1600 N Oak St Apt 232
Arlington VA 22209

Call Sign: KC8YRA
Christopher J Khourey
1401 N Oak St Apt 303
Arlington VA 22209

Call Sign: N4FGJ
Vivian F Donahue
3080 N Oakland
Arlington VA 22207

Call Sign: KE4DBW
Susan M Diehl
3836 N Oakland St
Arlington VA 22207

Call Sign: KK4GOU
Martina E Sabo
1109 N Ohio St
Arlington VA 22205

Call Sign: KA3ZSG
Michael R Laidhold
1900 N Ohio St

Arlington VA 22205

Call Sign: KF4MUQ
Chris M Robbins
427 N Park Dr 1
Arlington VA 22203

Call Sign: AE4WO
Gilberto Cintron Molero
421 N Park Dr Apt 2
Arlington VA 222032308

Call Sign: W4KHZ
Anthony F Vogel
933 N Patrick Henry Dr
Arlington VA 22205

Call Sign: KI4FNF
George Putic
1519 N Patrick Henry Dr
Arlington VA 22205

Call Sign: KC4PQQ
Bart C Weller
3315 N Pershing Dr
Arlington VA 22201

Call Sign: KC4VCK
Bruce W Hunter
1203 N Pierce St 203
Arlington VA 22209

Call Sign: KI4WJW
Brendan B Meehan
1221 N Pierce St Apt 311
Arlington VA 22209

Call Sign: KJ4ZMR
Matt Howes
545 N Pollard
Arlington VA 22203

Call Sign: KB2SS
Kenneth P Kahn
820 N Pollard St Apt 604
Arlington VA 222031778

Call Sign: KE4DBX
Amanda C Mann

3514 N Potomac St
Arlington VA 22213

Call Sign: WD4DHW
Frederic W Bardsley Jr
1005 N Quantico St
Arlington VA 222051514

Call Sign: KF4OYC
Brendan D Mullen
979 N Quantico St
Arlington VA 22205

Call Sign: KN4RN
William J Powell
2520 N Quebec St
Arlington VA 22207

Call Sign: AC4BJ
Ronald C Clearwater
2520 N Quebec St
Arlington VA 222075005

Call Sign: KJ4HGZ
Marc I Schneider
1809 N Quesada St
Arlington VA 22205

Call Sign: N4NFH
Charles H Smith
1739 N Quincy St
Arlington VA 22207

Call Sign: W4UPM
Paul C Oscanyan
1020 N Quincy St 408
Arlington VA 22201

Call Sign: KB9ZUQ
Nathan P Lange
818 N Quincy St Apt 2008
Arlington VA 22203

Call Sign: KC4BGD
James C Oliver Jr
1820 N Quinn St 307
Arlington VA 22209

Call Sign: KJ4DFS

Brad A Bryant
1804 N Quinn St Apt 103
Arlington VA 222091333

Call Sign: KC4BGE
Marilyn J Oliver
1820 N Quinn St Apt 307
Arlington VA 22209

Call Sign: KB2FOS
Steven J Azzariti
1804 N Quinn St Apt 601
Arlington VA 22209

Call Sign: WB4LOH
Jonathan E Harmon
1316 N Quintana St
Arlington VA 22205

Call Sign: KC4GNC
Lisa S Fullarton
1026 N Randolph St
Arlington VA 22201

Call Sign: KJ4HXT
Timothy L Russer
1117 N Randolph St 204
Arlington VA 22201

Call Sign: N9IWD
Collier S Cook
1001 N Randolph St 409
Arlington VA 222015605

Call Sign: KC0OKN
Brent M Maxwell
850 N Randolph St Apt 1432
Arlington VA 22203

Call Sign: KK4CYX
Martin R Doczkat
1001 N Randolph St Apt 610
Arlington VA 22201

Call Sign: KI4MUO
Daniel K Guenther
850 N Randolph St Apt 903
Arlington VA 22203

Call Sign: KQ4EY
Louis N Luh
4143 N Richmond St
Arlington VA 22207

Call Sign: W7TRI
Alan E Schlank
4019 N River St
Arlington VA 22207

Call Sign: N9GFF
Scott L Parrish
1221 N Roosevelt St
Arlington VA 22205

Call Sign: KJ4IVE
Benjamin O Billings
1500 N Scott St
Arlington VA 22209

Call Sign: KI4RDI
Robert L Ryan Silva
2101 N Scott St Apt 93
Arlington VA 22209

Call Sign: KJ4UCC
Richard E Sweetland
2228 N Somerset
Arlington VA 22205

Call Sign: KB4USO
Andrew J Posch
2158 N Stafford St
Arlington VA 22207

Call Sign: KD4YXV
Priscilla A Posch
2158 N Stafford St
Arlington VA 22207

Call Sign: WA4FXN
Joseph E Posch
2158 N Stafford St
Arlington VA 22207

Call Sign: KG4RKL
Michael T Ingles
2313 N Stafford St
Arlington VA 22207

Call Sign: NV4K
Paul M Currer
1020 N Stafford St 308
Arlington VA 22201

Call Sign: KF3CJ
Douglas C Findlay
900 N Stafford St Apt 1017
Arlington VA 22203

Call Sign: WB2PCQ
Justin D Burrows
900 N Stafford St Apt 1706
Arlington VA 22203

Call Sign: KK4GOT
Evan M Benoit
900 N Stafford St Apt 2019
Arlington VA 22203

Call Sign: W4ESC
Russell M King Jr
900 N Stafford St No 1818
Arlington VA 22203

Call Sign: KK4DBE
Travis D Mathison
900 N Stafford St Unit 1410
Arlington VA 22203

Call Sign: W1EH
Charles C Schenck
900 N Stafford St Unit 911
Arlington VA 22203

Call Sign: KE4TOY
Kevin C Bell
1209 N Stuart St
Arlington VA 22201

Call Sign: KD4TLH
Elizabeth T Doggett
2607 N Stuart St
Arlington VA 22207

Call Sign: KE4OWH
Allen F Calvert
3031 N Stuart St

Arlington VA 222074118

Call Sign: AC0EV
Justin C Myers
900 N Stuart St Apt 1021
Arlington VA 22203

Call Sign: KJ4VTC
Daniel D Harbuck
2107 N Taft St 16
Arlington VA 22201

Call Sign: KA4PPM
George R Lufsey II
1545 N Taylor St
Arlington VA 22207

Call Sign: W3HQG
Irvin Hershowitz
900 N Taylor St Apt 408
Arlington VA 22203

Call Sign: W5FED
William J Galloway
900 N Taylor St Apt 723
Arlington VA 22203

Call Sign: N2GSV
Willis E Fox
900 N Taylor St Apt 826
Arlington VA 22203

Call Sign: KJ4HXS
Helen K Duval
3800 N Tazewell St
Arlington VA 22207

Call Sign: WB9SBK
Margaret A Cavanaugh
618A N Tazewell St
Arlington VA 22203

Call Sign: WB9SDW
Joseph C Cavanaugh
618A N Tazewell St
Arlington VA 22203

Call Sign: K4TOP
Joseph C Cavanaugh

618A N Tazewell St
Arlington VA 22203

Call Sign: KC8WTR
Philip J Sokolowski
229 N Thomas St
Arlington VA 22203

Call Sign: KG4ROC
Richard M Fox
2122 N Thomas St
Arlington VA 22207

Call Sign: W4PUJ
Richard L Daniels
3120 N Thomas St
Arlington VA 22207

Call Sign: N4YNI
William C Gurley
3207 N Trinidad St
Arlington VA 222131309

Call Sign: WD4RNR
John D Mc Clain
3307 N Trinidad St
Arlington VA 22213

Call Sign: KK4ARJ
Benjamin C Wilson
2533 N Upland St
Arlington VA 22207

Call Sign: WB7TOL
Clifford F Drown
3609 N Upland St
Arlington VA 22207

Call Sign: KI4THC
James L Olds
3810 N Upland St
Arlington VA 22207

Call Sign: KC8OXO
Robert G Layden
1939 N Upland St
Arlington VA 22207

Call Sign: W4KXC

Frank Toth
2607 N Upshur St
Arlington VA 22207

Call Sign: KJ4GZW
Raymond B Lombardi
2408 N Utah St
Arlington VA 22207

Call Sign: KI4SNG
William M Simmons
3545 N Utah St
Arlington VA 22207

Call Sign: WD4KXL
John M Pelkey
4301 N Vacation Ln
Arlington VA 22207

Call Sign: N1LSV
Arlene C Williams
1200 N Veitch St 1027
Arlington VA 22201

Call Sign: KC4YML
David W Stanley
2245 N Vermont St
Arlington VA 22207

Call Sign: WA4BFR
George Wolfhard
3818 N Wakefield St
Arlington VA 22207

Call Sign: KC4UHY
Nelson R Estrada
2512 N Washington Blvd
Arlington VA 22201

Call Sign: KC4GFX
Thomas J Crishock
2519 N Washington Blvd
Arlington VA 22201

Call Sign: KB9IVF
Shinichi Inoue
4600 N Washington Blvd 102
W
Arlington VA 22201

Call Sign: KB9OXF
Talin T Senner
4650 N Washington Blvd Apt 723
Arlington VA 22201

Call Sign: KJ4JNA
Jessica H Fillmore
114 N Wayne St 6
Arlington VA 22201

Call Sign: KJ4DZY
Benjamin T Zemek
113 N Wayne St Apt 6
Arlington VA 22201

Call Sign: KI4IPW
William B Mcgrath
3208 N Woodrow St
Arlington VA 22207

Call Sign: KE4JG
James A Hughes Jr
3734 N Woodrow St
Arlington VA 22207

Call Sign: KJ4VTB
Najib Kabbani
4849 Old Dominion Dr
Arlington VA 22207

Call Sign: KA2JGO
Steven J Lutgen
4300 Old Dominion Dr Apt 516
Arlington VA 22207

Call Sign: W0CBS
William G Calder Jr
1812 Queens Ln
Arlington VA 222013030

Call Sign: KC4QQB
Robert E Slye Jr
3601 Roberts Ln
Arlington VA 22207

Call Sign: K4EUX
Elmer D Jones

3918 S 12th St
Arlington VA 22204

Call Sign: KD4LJA
Scott A Taylor
5200 S 12th St
Arlington VA 22204

Call Sign: KJ4DFX
James M Cachine
601 S 12th St Freedom Center Annex
Arlington VA 22202

Call Sign: KK4CNC
Michael Birdseye
3007 S 13th St
Arlington VA 22204

Call Sign: K4DUM
Michael Birdseye
3007 S 13th St
Arlington VA 22204

Call Sign: KK4FFH
Producer D Drake
3007 S 13th St
Arlington VA 22204

Call Sign: K3DMR
Producer D Drake
3007 S 13th St
Arlington VA 22204

Call Sign: KD2GN
Peter A La Chance Jr
604A S 15th St
Arlington VA 22202

Call Sign: KB4KKD
Frances W Burgess
2404 S 1st Rd
Arlington VA 22204

Call Sign: K4GOR
Craig E Church
1612 S 22nd St
Arlington VA 22202

Call Sign: KD4NFF
Berkemeyer S Cuellar
5054 S 22nd St
Arlington VA 22206

Call Sign: KA0KLE
Ricky L De Graffenreid
Dmt 2300 S 24th Rd Apt 846
Arlington VA 22206

Call Sign: KT4EL
Walter H Parsons III
1307 S 24th St
Arlington VA 222021530

Call Sign: KJ4PUO
Nancy P Hemenway
5008 S 24th St
Arlington VA 22206

Call Sign: KJ4TTC
Nancy P Hemenway
5008 S 24th St
Arlington VA 22206

Call Sign: WB2DVX
Robert D Brown
4831A S 28th St
Arlington VA 22206

Call Sign: WB3BAR
David L Guthrie
4824 S 29th St C2
Arlington VA 22206

Call Sign: W4PLJ
John E Dorgan
3200 S 2nd St
Arlington VA 22204

Call Sign: KC4HZN
Susan L Toulmin
3312 S 2nd St
Arlington VA 22204

Call Sign: KC4HZO
Llewellyn M Toulmin
3312 S 2nd St
Arlington VA 22204

Call Sign: KJ4UCB
James S Adams
4316 S 34th St A2
Arlington VA 22206

Call Sign: N3EVT
Gerald R Greenwood
4233 S 36th St
Arlington VA 22206

Call Sign: N4JVM
Jaro Rykers
4233 S 36th St
Arlington VA 22206

Call Sign: N4AGB
Allen G Buckalew
5419 S 3rd St
Arlington VA 22204

Call Sign: KI4MNI
Allen G Buckalew
5419 S 3rd St
Arlington VA 22204

Call Sign: KJ4JMY
Donald R Bennett
5735 S 4th St
Arlington VA 22204

Call Sign: K1DRB
Donald R Bennett
5735 S 4th St
Arlington VA 22204

Call Sign: KD4VZM
Michael J Houston
5916 S 5th Rd
Arlington VA 22204

Call Sign: KG4YIW
Jon R Hansen
2915 S 6th St
Arlington VA 22204

Call Sign: N3USR
Jon R Hansen
2915 S 6th St

Arlington VA 22204

Call Sign: WB4MWF
David M Voigtsberger
3908 S 6th St
Arlington VA 22204

Call Sign: KI4YNP
Daniel D Voigtsberger
3908 S 6th St
Arlington VA 22204

Call Sign: WA6OJW
Peter R Renfree
3825 S 7th St
Arlington VA 22204

Call Sign: W1PRR
Peter R Renfree
3825 S 7th St
Arlington VA 22204

Call Sign: K1YC
Peter R Renfree
3825 S 7th St
Arlington VA 22204

Call Sign: KC4ZFL
Sharon M Renfree
3825 S 7th St
Arlington VA 222041519

Call Sign: KT4MV
Timothy R ONeill
2854 C1 S Abingdon
Arlington VA 22206

Call Sign: KG4DZA
Eric R Parker
417 S Abingdon St
Arlington VA 22204

Call Sign: WB2GBK
Neil I Title
2838 S Abingdon St
Arlington VA 22206

Call Sign: KK4ADO
Carolyn A Bainer

3081 S Abingdon St
Arlington VA 22206

Call Sign: W4ART
Arthur H Feller
2834 S Abingdon St Apt B1
Arlington VA 222061357

Call Sign: KI4QCP
Theodore R Hubbell
800 S Adams St
Arlington VA 22204

Call Sign: KC2PSZ
Kannan N Cangro
2710 S Adams St Apt 209
Arlington VA 22206

Call Sign: N3IV
Bradford A Cangro
2710 S Adams St Apt 209
Arlington VA 22206

Call Sign: KD4REF
Millard Peck III
2552B S Arlington Mill Dr
Arlington VA 22206

Call Sign: W1FAM
William H Von Alven
1101 S Arlington Ridge Rd
Arlington VA 22202

Call Sign: KC7YWL
Christine E Keys
2357 S Arlington Ridge Rd
Arlington VA 22202

Call Sign: KD4ITT
Erica M Frisbie
1301 S Arlington Ridge Rd 304
Arlington VA 22202

Call Sign: KG4EJR
Preston C Linson-Gentry
1101 S Arlington Ridge Rd 813
Arlington VA 22202

Call Sign: N4VIA

James L Gasch
622 S Barton St
Arlington VA 22204

Call Sign: KF4NML
Victor A Mortenson Jr
833 S Barton St
Arlington VA 22204

Call Sign: KJ4ZTQ
Stephen P Mccay
1400 S Barton St 419
Arlington VA 22204

Call Sign: KA1NKC
Paul C Brewer
1414 S Barton St 449
Arlington VA 22204

Call Sign: KG4QWE
Valerie H Meyer
2305 S Buchanan St
Arlington VA 222061014

Call Sign: W8VAL
Valerie H Meyer
2305 S Buchanan St
Arlington VA 222061014

Call Sign: KE4WGI
Brian B Stevenson
315 S Court House Rd
Arlington VA 222041947

Call Sign: KD4EMQ
Christopher P Johnson
1201 S Courthouse Rd Apt 709
Arlington VA 222044643

Call Sign: WB5VEG
Robert G Fiduk
2313 S Culpeper St
Arlington VA 22206

Call Sign: KI4NLT
Charles D Smith
750 S Dickerson 314
Arlington VA 22204

Call Sign: AI4OT
Charles D Smith
750 S Dickerson 314
Arlington VA 22204

Call Sign: WD4SDC
Stephen D Smith
2307 S Dinwiddie St
Arlington VA 22206

Call Sign: KK4GON
Kevin J Latman
1600 S Eads 1231N St
Arlington VA 22202

Call Sign: KI4GRV
Dancel G Dupont
1331 S Eads Apt 1602
Arlington VA 22202

Call Sign: N4UUW
Lee H Kyle
1600 S Eads St 1104 S
Arlington VA 22202

Call Sign: N1XXB
Stuart D Miller
1201 S Eads St 1908
Arlington VA 22202

Call Sign: KI4ZWS
Christopher M Antons
1201 S Eads St 419
Arlington VA 22202

Call Sign: KI4ZWT
Debra Yamanaka
1201 S Eads St 419
Arlington VA 22202

Call Sign: KD4FJR
Kenneth W Long Jr
1211 S Eads St 706
Arlington VA 22202

Call Sign: KC4TK
Charles J Spencer
1425 S Eads St Apt 1108
Arlington VA 22202

Call Sign: K6MXD
Max Kelly
1900 S Eads St Apt 1123
Arlington VA 22202

Call Sign: KG4UIO
Nick Corsaro
1425 S Eads St Apt 308
Arlington VA 22202

Call Sign: KG4PSC
Ayal I Sharon
1600 S Eads St Apt 701N
Arlington VA 22202

Call Sign: KG4IPP
William G Walsh
1600 S Eads St Apt 914 S
Arlington VA 22202

Call Sign: K4CBA
William G Walsh
1600 S Eads St Apt 914 S
Arlington VA 22202

Call Sign: KF4ZMP
Michael J Barnes
1211 S Eads St Ste 1608
Arlington VA 22202

Call Sign: KC0IWW
Michael D Sass
1330 S Fair St Apt 1607
Arlington VA 22202

Call Sign: N3CZL
Timothy R Willenbucher
2628 S Fern St
Arlington VA 222022512

Call Sign: WA3KZC
Arthur J Murray
203 S Fillmore St
Arlington VA 222042079

Call Sign: KI4DXK
Harold C Davis Jr
3531 S Four Mile Run Dr

Arlington VA 22206

Call Sign: KJ4QKJ
Matthew S Meagher
4081 S Four Mile Run Dr 102
Arlington VA 22204

Call Sign: KG4GSM
Ryan J Broughton
4193 S Four Mile Run Dr 103
Arlington VA 22204

Call Sign: KI4THL
Elizabeth C Davnie
4600 S Four Mile Run Dr 1030
Arlington VA 22204

Call Sign: KD6HVL
Megan L Mitchell
4141 S Four Mile Run Dr 303
Arlington VA 22204

Call Sign: KG4HTU
Michael F Stevenson
4500 S Four Mile Run Dr Apt
614
Arlington VA 22204

Call Sign: KF4JAA
David S Dill
1322 S Glebe Rd
Arlington VA 22204

Call Sign: WA4RFA
Bobby A Jones
2173 S Glebe Rd
Arlington VA 222045309

Call Sign: KC4KOV
Edwin L Williams
2929 S Glebe Rd
Arlington VA 222062745

Call Sign: KI4SNH
Benjamin L Bullough
3014 S Glebe Rd
Arlington VA 22206

Call Sign: KJ4ETJ

Dallen G Herzog
3018 S Glebe St
Arlington VA 22206

Call Sign: KE4HUB
David D Loveall
1808A S Grant St
Arlington VA 22202

Call Sign: W4KZI
Robert E Tachoir Jr
1416 S Greenbrier St
Arlington VA 22206

Call Sign: KB1EGA
Matthew S Munsey
2728 S Grove St
Arlington VA 222022424

Call Sign: WA4FNQ
Carl E Peake
641 S Harrison St
Arlington VA 22204

Call Sign: KE4SNW
Joshua Reiter
3110 S Hayes St
Arlington VA 222022336

Call Sign: WB4MJF
Randall C Kelly Sr
121 S Highland
Arlington VA 22204

Call Sign: KB4LRO
Ann M Kelly
121 S Highland St
Arlington VA 22204

Call Sign: KB4TYD
Sarah K Mansfield
121 S Highland St
Arlington VA 22204

Call Sign: KC4GFD
Kathryn A Kelly
121 S Highland St
Arlington VA 22204

Call Sign: KD4AXY
Randall C Kelly Jr
121 S Highland St
Arlington VA 22204

Call Sign: KG4DSJ
Richard J Kelly
121 S Highland St
Arlington VA 22204

Call Sign: KG4DYZ
Ginny M Kelly
121 S Highland St
Arlington VA 22204

Call Sign: N4DTF
Gus D Moshos
121 S Irving St
Arlington VA 22204

Call Sign: KB4EUE
Paul G Bailey
201 S Ivy St
Arlington VA 22204

Call Sign: WB4JQJ
Milton L Forrest
2111 S Jeff Dvs Hwy 410S
Arlington VA 22202

Call Sign: W5HVV
David B Rose
1600 S Joyce St 1201
Arlington VA 22202

Call Sign: W3HCS
Emanuel S Kemeny
1400 S Joyce St 602
Arlington VA 22202

Call Sign: W2DQR
George W Swenson
1600 S Joyce St Apt 125
Arlington VA 22202

Call Sign: WU4L
Stuart B Rosner
1400 S Joyce St Apt 1620
Arlington VA 22202

Call Sign: W4OOY
Harold W Cornelius
1400 S Joyce St Apt 1725
Arlington VA 222021867

Call Sign: KJ4FAH
Kelly J Eaton
1401 S Joyce St Apt 310
Arlington VA 22202

Call Sign: KC4ZCS
Emanuel S Kemeny
1400 S Joyce St Apt 602
Arlington VA 22202

Call Sign: KI4GS
James E Armstrong
1600 S Joyce St Apt 902
Arlington VA 22202

Call Sign: KB4KOE
Portia B Etheridge
3516 S Kemper Rd
Arlington VA 22206

Call Sign: WA6CCA
William H Trayfors
2401 S Lynn St
Arlington VA 22202

Call Sign: W4JJ
Jack W Parker Jr
839 S Monroe St
Arlington VA 222041537

Call Sign: KI4THI
Prentiss S De Jesus
1735 S Monroe St
Arlington VA 22204

Call Sign: K4PDJ
Prentiss S De Jesus
1735 S Monroe St
Arlington VA 22204

Call Sign: WD4RCA
Michael D Atherton
20 S Old Glebe Rd 204

Arlington VA 22204

Call Sign: KG4LON
Maximilian G Llea
24 S Old Glebe Rd Apt 204
Arlington VA 22204

Call Sign: WH6AKM
Ellen S Feldman
4415 S Pershing Ct
Arlington VA 22204

Call Sign: W4NDZ
Harold L Kassens
121 S Pershing Dr
Arlington VA 22204

Call Sign: WB4QKY
Ellen M Aaron
2100 S Pierce St
Arlington VA 22202

Call Sign: KA4NOT
Joseph J Marenick
815 S Quincy St
Arlington VA 22204

Call Sign: KJ4RNQ
Shrikant U Agashe
1125 S Quincy St 303
Arlington VA 22204

Call Sign: KB0YXM
Susan K Reinertson
3000 S Randolph St
Arlington VA 22206

Call Sign: KJ4DFY
Geraldine V Cox
2304 S Rolfe St
Arlington VA 22202

Call Sign: KJ4DZZ
Walter G Cox
2304 S Rolfe St
Arlington VA 22202

Call Sign: W4QY
George W Pickard

3125 S Stafford
Arlington VA 22206

Call Sign: KJ4VTD
Keith W Bryan
3301 S Stafford A 2
Arlington VA 22206

Call Sign: WA4FXX
Henry J Reed
637 S Stafford St
Arlington VA 22204

Call Sign: KG4KAG
Roland G Morrisette
1800 S Stafford St
Arlington VA 22204

Call Sign: AI4FN
Roland G Morrisette
1800 S Stafford St
Arlington VA 22204

Call Sign: N3WGJ
Benjamin A Herrick
3325 S Stafford St
Arlington VA 22206

Call Sign: KJ4BQC
Jeffrey L Henry
3525 A S Stafford St
Arlington VA 22206

Call Sign: KJ4ETI
James P Campbell
3569B S Stafford St
Arlington VA 22206

Call Sign: N5FC
Dennis A Coriell
3541 S Utah St
Arlington VA 22206

Call Sign: KI4YBM
Christian J Lewis
208 S Veitch St
Arlington VA 22204

Call Sign: KJ4PUP

Allen D Blume
2633 S Veitch St
Arlington VA 22206

Call Sign: KC4YSX
James E Barker III
2734 S Veitch St 2
Arlington VA 22206

Call Sign: KI4PYJ
David B Cole
2640 S Veitch St Apt 310
Arlington VA 222063037

Call Sign: KE4EID
James W Fox
3429 S Wakefield St
Arlington VA 22206

Call Sign: N1GSK
Nitin Natarajan
2841 A S Wakefield St
Arlington VA 22206

Call Sign: KE4QEK
Susanne M Hobson
1312 S Walter Reed Dr
Arlington VA 22204

Call Sign: KC4RXD
James T Mc Kenzie
811 S Walter Reed Dr Apt 162B
Arlington VA 22204

Call Sign: KD4ZLI
Jeffrey P Busse
607 S Walter Reed Dr Apt
642D
Arlington VA 222042274

Call Sign: KI4RSF
Christopher F Rosche
818 S Wayne St
Arlington VA 22204

Call Sign: W1RAI
Raymond W Rancourt
122 S Woodrow St
Arlington VA 22204

Call Sign: KI4DTP
Ian Sterne
2913 C S Woodstock St
Arlington VA 22206

Call Sign: KK4AGF
Charles E Lawson
6312 Seven Corners Center
Arlington VA 22044

Call Sign: KA1LKA
John P Duggan
4600 Washington Blvd
Arlington VA 22201

Call Sign: N4JKB
Herbert N Ries
5220 Washington Blvd
Arlington VA 22205

Call Sign: K3SRF
William T Doggette
5812 Washington Blvd
Arlington VA 22205

Call Sign: KB3GXR
Thomas B Doggette
5812 Washington Blvd
Arlington VA 22205

Call Sign: KB8UQI
Joseph E Mcdermott
6869 Washington Blvd
Arlington VA 222131120

Call Sign: WB2UPO
Edwin P Mcdermott
6869 Washington Blvd
Arlington VA 222131120

Call Sign: KJ4BRP
Adrian Blust
5016 Williamsburg Blvd
Arlington VA 22207

Call Sign: K4MKX
Edward B Beach
5112 Williamsburg Blvd

Arlington VA 22207

Call Sign: KJ4BVI
Patrick Sheehan
6001 Williamsburg Blvd
Arlington VA 22207

Call Sign: KE4TSN
Brian W Wells
1101 Wilson Blvd
Arlington VA 222099998

Call Sign: KE4WOV
Rodney Smith
1101 Wilson Blvd
Arlington VA 222099998

Call Sign: KE4WOW
Rachel A Cooper
1101 Wilson Blvd
Arlington VA 222099998

Call Sign: KE4WOX
Timothy C Cooper
1101 Wilson Blvd
Arlington VA 222099998

Call Sign: KE4WOY
Kenneth Lindsay
1101 Wilson Blvd
Arlington VA 222099998

Call Sign: KE4WOZ
Kenneth J Adams
1101 Wilson Blvd
Arlington VA 222099998

Call Sign: KE4WPA
Frederick C Allen
1101 Wilson Blvd
Arlington VA 222099998

Call Sign: KE4ZVM
Adrian T Buswell
1101 Wilson Blvd
Arlington VA 222099998

Call Sign: KS4WG
John C Hill

1101 Wilson Blvd
Arlington VA 222099998

Call Sign: W4HRL
Benjamin M Chambers
5910 Wilson Blvd
Arlington VA 22005

Call Sign: KB4YBU
John Metaxotos
6407 Wilson Blvd
Arlington VA 22205

Call Sign: WB4YBI
Paul B Baker
2200 Wilson Blvd 102 227
Arlington VA 22201

Call Sign: W4JE
Andrew W Clegg
4201 Wilson Blvd 1045
Arlington VA 22230

Call Sign: KF4TYR
Timothy P Chesser
4201 Wilson Blvd 110162
Arlington VA 22203

Call Sign: KD4YJS
Brendan G Hoar
2713 Wilson Blvd 2
Arlington VA 22201

Call Sign: KG4CGS
Shinichi Shikakubo
1101 Wilson Blvd 2000
Arlington VA 22209

Call Sign: KG4ZNE
National Science Foundation
ARC
4201 Wilson Blvd Rm 1045 11
Arlington VA 22230

Call Sign: KG4ZYW
National Science Foundation
ARC
4201 Wilson Blvd Rm 1045 11
Arlington VA 22230

Call Sign: K4NSF
National Science Foundation
ARC
4201 Wilson Blvd Rm 1045 11
Arlington VA 22230

Call Sign: AJ4ZF
Priya Gupta
1555 Wilson Blvd Ste 703
Arlington VA 22209

Call Sign: KJ4SSR
George Nimmer
1800 Wilson Blvd Unit 250
Arlington VA 22201

Call Sign: KR4MU
George L Saunders Jr
5125 Yorktown Blvd
Arlington VA 222071705

Call Sign: KF4PJW
J Christopher Ryan
5524 Yorktown Blvd
Arlington VA 22207

Call Sign: W4KIT
J Christopher Ryan
5524 Yorktown Blvd
Arlington VA 22207

Call Sign: KA6GLW
Peter A Hohenbrink
Arlington VA 22209

Call Sign: KA4OZI
Jay C Carpenter
Arlington VA 22210

Call Sign: KA1VLA
Anthony D Benedetto
Arlington VA 22215

Call Sign: W1SWH
Sean W Hall
Arlington VA 222070271

Call Sign: K4AF

Pentagon ARC
Arlington VA 22202

Call Sign: N3NSS
Joel A Starr
Arlington VA 22204

Call Sign: N4JJS
Randall A Watson
Arlington VA 22204

Call Sign: KG4MZT
Oleg Lazakovich
Arlington VA 22205

Call Sign: KG4WMS
Greg W Gutierrez
Arlington VA 22205

Call Sign: KI4YBE
John F Ackerson
Arlington VA 22205

Call Sign: KI4MWS
Ricardo A Roca
Arlington VA 22205

Call Sign: KJ4HXP
Paul Walczak
Arlington VA 22207

Call Sign: KK1MM
Michael N Elliott
Arlington VA 22207

Call Sign: KA9LSO
J O Albright
Arlington VA 22210

Call Sign: KF4FOQ
Allan R Feller
Arlington VA 22215

Call Sign: WB4GRW
William H Grigsby
Arlington VA 22215

Call Sign: KG6TUK
Sara L Jones

Arlington VA 22215

Call Sign: KD2RO
Joseph R Sylvester
Arlington VA 22215

Call Sign: WA9FMQ
Gary L Garriott
Arlington VA 22219

Call Sign: KC7FVP
Ian Swanson
Arlington VA 22219

Call Sign: KC5CW
Bennett Z Kobb
Arlington VA 222040749

Call Sign: AK4AV
Bennett Z Kobb
Arlington VA 222040749

Call Sign: N1VU
Sean W Hall
Arlington VA 222070271

Call Sign: W3KMK
Joel A Starr
Arlington VA 222103579

Call Sign: KI4IFU
James G Morris
Arlington VA 222156018

Call Sign: KI4TAO
James G Morris
Arlington VA 222156018

Call Sign: K4GEE
James G Morris
Arlington VA 222156108

Call Sign: KF6FFU
Ryan A Brown
Arlington VA 222191235

Call Sign: KC0UJA
Enrique Lara
Arlington VA 222192846

FCC Amateur Radio Licenses in Aroda

Call Sign: N4TWK
Eldon Hochstetler
Hc 5 Box 186
Aroda VA 22709

Call Sign: KA4VZE
David Hochstetler
3432 Orange Rd
Aroda VA 22709

Call Sign: WD4RGP
Harold K Carpenter Jr
552 Zeus Hunt Club Ln
Aroda VA 22709

FCC Amateur Radio Licenses in Arrington

Call Sign: KF4PHU
Michele A Pankey
Rt 1 Box 214 1B
Arrington VA 22922

Call Sign: KG4OFX
Sarah J Hawrysko
984 Lake Nelson Ln
Arrington VA 22922

Call Sign: KI4CMW
Shawn D Johnson
984 Lake Nelson Ln
Arrington VA 22922

Call Sign: W4ODH
David A James
3173 Phoenix Rd
Arrington VA 22922

FCC Amateur Radio Licenses in Arvonia

Call Sign: KG4FJC
John J Gnatowsky
25 Melita Rd
Arvonia VA 23004

FCC Amateur Radio Licenses in Ashburn

Call Sign: KG4WAG
John A Miller III
20588 12 Oaks Way
Ashburn VA 201475102

Call Sign: KC2BXE
Monica L Fitzgerald
44000 Aberdeen Ter
Ashburn VA 20147

Call Sign: NY2RN
Joseph J Fitzgerald II
44000 Aberdeen Ter
Ashburn VA 20147

Call Sign: N2CA
Jesse D Sheinwald
44280 Acushnet Ter
Ashburn VA 20147

Call Sign: KQ4CI
Evan Alford
42512 Alford Rd
Ashburn VA 201484509

Call Sign: KN4PK
Henry W Wessell
20811 Amberview Ct
Ashburn VA 20147

Call Sign: WA3NYF
William L Price Jr
21378 Applegrove Ct
Ashburn VA 20147

Call Sign: KJ4CJI
Matthew L Bell
21506 Arber Glen Ct
Ashburn VA 20148

Call Sign: KS4JM
Peter A Bowen
22567 Armstrong Ter Apt 313
Ashburn VA 20148

Call Sign: WT6M
John R Fulmer
43071 Autumnwood Sq
Ashburn VA 201485096

Call Sign: KK4HKC
Richard C Hersh III
22022 Avonworth Sq
Ashburn VA 20148

Call Sign: KI4UQO
Christine G Benonis
21570 Awbrey Pl
Ashburn VA 20148

Call Sign: KI4UQN
John T Benonis
21570 Awbrey Pl
Ashburn VA 20148

Call Sign: KJ4LAV
Thomas B Roisum
20157 Bandon Dunes Ct
Ashburn VA 20147

Call Sign: KD4ZKT
Joy L Ridgeway
21612 Bankbarn Ter
Ashburn VA 20148

Call Sign: KF4FOP
Harold T Buchanan
20303 Beechwood Ter 301
Ashburn VA 22011

Call Sign: KJ4HZJ
Luke F Therrien
43121 Belgreen Dr
Ashburn VA 20147

Call Sign: KI4QQI
Frank L Diroberto
22429 Belle Terra Dr
Ashburn VA 20148

Call Sign: AI4RM
Frank L Diroberto
22429 Belle Terra Dr
Ashburn VA 20148

Call Sign: N4OPN
Pamela J Bozzi
22687 Blue Elder Ter 203
Ashburn VA 20148

Call Sign: KF4VLQ
Jacob M Dawson
22687 Blue Elder Ter Unit 203
Ashburn VA 20148

Call Sign: W3AR
Anthony M Rutkowski
44441 Blueridge Meadows Dr
Ashburn VA 20147

Call Sign: KE4IBY
Allan D Witham
44100 Bristow Cir
Ashburn VA 20147

Call Sign: KB4UGI
James P Mc Kone
44137 Bristow Cir
Ashburn VA 22011

Call Sign: KG4ETV
James P Mc Kone
44137 Bristow Cir
Ashburn VA 201473310

Call Sign: KA8EFA
Terry A Lowe
21045 Cardinal Pond Ter 202
Ashburn VA 20147

Call Sign: KC4QYJ
Mildred B Fitch
21145 Cardinal Pond Ter Apt
113
Ashburn VA 201456130

Call Sign: N4ABM
Merritt W Olson
21125 Cardinal Ter Bb319
Ashburn VA 20147

Call Sign: KG4VNE
Thomas M Codella

43751 Carson Ct
Ashburn VA 20147

Call Sign: W2GP
Thomas M Codella
43751 Carson Ct
Ashburn VA 20147

Call Sign: KJ4GYK
Michael C Miller
21088 Carthagena Ct
Ashburn VA 20147

Call Sign: KE6LR
Paul T Gernhardt
21931 Castlehill Ct
Ashburn VA 20164

Call Sign: WB9TNA
Paul T Gernhardt
21931 Castlehill Ct
Ashburn VA 20164

Call Sign: N2YOZ
John W Lawson
20903 Cedarpost Sq 202
Ashburn VA 20147

Call Sign: KA2AJY
Scott F Nichols
43831 Chadwick Ter
Ashburn VA 20148

Call Sign: AA3XV
Kevin Jackson
42739 Chatelain Cir
Ashburn VA 20148

Call Sign: AI4IN
Gary W Strong
42845 Chesterton St
Ashburn VA 20147

Call Sign: KI4QCQ
Jeff D Strong
42845 Chesterton St
Ashburn VA 20147

Call Sign: N3LXR

John P Logsdon
21436 Chickacoan Trl Dr
Ashburn VA 20148

Call Sign: KK4HKF
Scott H Moffit
42649 Chisholm Dr
Ashburn VA 20148

Call Sign: N4GOU
James P Burke Jr
43902 Chloe Ter
Ashburn VA 201473806

Call Sign: KF4BTI
Matthew I Foote
20754 Citation Dr
Ashburn VA 20147

Call Sign: KF4BTJ
Janet R Foote
20754 Citation Dr
Ashburn VA 20147

Call Sign: KI4BYS
Benjamin T Foote
20754 Citation Dr
Ashburn VA 20147

Call Sign: W3GX
John I Foote
20754 Citation Dr
Ashburn VA 201474474

Call Sign: KB5TOU
David B Conrad
21011 Coburn Ter
Ashburn VA 20147

Call Sign: KF4BLT
Harlan D Worchel
20509 Comfort Ct
Ashburn VA 220113802

Call Sign: KJ4PVF
Spencer M Caesare
20658 Coppersmith Dr
Ashburn VA 20147

Call Sign: KF6NNR
Steven M Caesare
20658 Coppersmith Dr
Ashburn VA 20147

Call Sign: KE4QWI
Tekang Wang
44318 Cornish Ln
Ashburn VA 20147

Call Sign: W4HIH
Martin W Reagan
20667 Crescent Pointe Pl
Ashburn VA 20147

Call Sign: KD4DGO
Elizabeth Z Thevenet
20133 Crew Sq
Ashburn VA 20147

Call Sign: KD4DGQ
Jorge A Thevenet
20133 Crewe Sq
Ashburn VA 20147

Call Sign: KC4JI
Larry A Brown
43084 Croson Ln
Ashburn VA 20148

Call Sign: KC2AXF
Eric Ballance
21453 Deepwood Ter Apt314
Ashburn VA 20148

Call Sign: KJ4BSA
Daniel J Nagy
21806 Dragons Green Sq
Ashburn VA 20147

Call Sign: N4OTQ
Monica L Mellon
42824 Early Light Pl
Ashburn VA 20148

Call Sign: KJ4BXA
Harry L Harting Jr
20400 Elm Grove Ter
Ashburn VA 201473711

Call Sign: W9PK
Steven M Heidorn
21343 Fairhunt Dr
Ashburn VA 20148

Call Sign: KJ4ALJ
Peter D Quilty
43881 Felicity Pl
Ashburn VA 20147

Call Sign: KJ4WRK
Stephen R Jacobs
43885 Felicity Pl
Ashburn VA 20147

Call Sign: KI4OBR
Nathan E Watson
21374 Fernbrook Ct
Ashburn VA 20148

Call Sign: N1TCP
Nathan E Watson
21374 Fernbrook Ct
Ashburn VA 20148

Call Sign: KK4HBW
Michael R Hertrick
21490 Foche Ter
Ashburn VA 20148

Call Sign: KQ4HR
Steven J Perriello
22454 Forest Manor Dr
Ashburn VA 20148

Call Sign: KJ4VHV
Joanna Z Tumidajewicz
20935 Gardengate Av
Ashburn VA 20147

Call Sign: K3JB
James P Burke Jr
20902 Gardengate Cir
Ashburn VA 201474024

Call Sign: K4JB
James P Burke Jr
20902 Gardengate Cir

Ashburn VA 201474024

Call Sign: KJ4ISB
European Psk Club Us (Section 4)
20935 Gardengate Cir
Ashburn VA 20147

Call Sign: N4EPC
European Psk Club Us (Section 4)
20935 Gardengate Cir
Ashburn VA 20147

Call Sign: KI4WFV
Zbigniew Tyrlik
20935 Gardengate Cir
Ashburn VA 20147

Call Sign: KF4TGU
Matthew T Stickler
44992 George Washington Blvd
Ashburn VA 20147

Call Sign: KJ4VZN
David C Horn
43843 Glenhazel Dr
Ashburn VA 20147

Call Sign: N3USY
Constantine N Sofologis
43942 Glenhazel Dr
Ashburn VA 20147

Call Sign: KF4OGK
Farmwell Station Middle School
44281 Gloucester Pkwy
Ashburn VA 20147

Call Sign: KD0FUN
Christine M Bickmann
21798 Green Stable Sq 302
Ashburn VA 20147

Call Sign: KK4DBB
Nicholas M Schaff
42674 Gulicks Landing Ct
Ashburn VA 20148

Call Sign: W4POM
Nicholas M Schaff
42674 Gulicks Landing Ct
Ashburn VA 20148

Call Sign: W2ATF
Nicholas M Schaff
42674 Gulicks Landing Ct
Ashburn VA 20148

Call Sign: KJ4ULB
Afshin Sadeghi
21178 Hedgerow Ter
Ashburn VA 20147

Call Sign: KK4ERC
John T Beard
21286 Hedgerow Ter
Ashburn VA 20147

Call Sign: KJ4VTE
Asim Aziz
43883 Hibiscus Dr
Ashburn VA 20147

Call Sign: AA9BZ
Asim Aziz
43883 Hibiscus Dr
Ashburn VA 20147

Call Sign: KA2MXV
Scott N Hutchinson
21332 Hidden Pond Pl
Ashburn VA 20148

Call Sign: N3VMP
Victoria C Hutchinson
21332 Hidden Pond Pl
Ashburn VA 20148

Call Sign: N4GVM
Sarah H Nevins
21357 Hidden Pond Pl
Ashburn VA 201484022

Call Sign: WA4NTP
Arthur G Nevins
21357 Hidden Pond Pl
Ashburn VA 201484022

Call Sign: KI4VZA
Stephanie D Itchkawich
43100 Hillmont Ter
Ashburn VA 20148

Call Sign: WA4GLQ
James C Garrison
21428 Humbolt Sq
Ashburn VA 20147

Call Sign: KB9QQQ
Charles A Karrick
43108 Hunters Green Sq
Ashburn VA 20148

Call Sign: KD5CTJ
Erik Werner
43131 Huntsman Sq
Ashburn VA 20148

Call Sign: KG4EXW
Charles M Schlosser
21911 Hyde Park Dr
Ashburn VA 20147

Call Sign: N4CMS
Charles M Schlosser
21911 Hyde Park Dr
Ashburn VA 20147

Call Sign: KK4HVY
Veeranna C Valluri
21805 Iannis Spring Dr
Ashburn VA 20148

Call Sign: KH2UY
Kevin J Lecureux
21686 Kings Crossing Ter
Ashburn VA 20147

Call Sign: N1SML
John Brewer
42865 Kirkland St
Ashburn VA 20147

Call Sign: KJ4ZIG
Harry Runski
21624 Liverpool St

Ashburn VA 20147

Call Sign: KG4YIQ
Jaskaran Jamwal
21673 Liverpool St
Ashburn VA 20147

Call Sign: KK4CJJ
Andrew J Shank
43370 Livery Sq
Ashburn VA 20147

Call Sign: KG4IMX
Jerry O Sullivan
43419 Livery Sq
Ashburn VA 20147

Call Sign: KJ4PVH
Henry R Canciglia
20949 Lohengrin Ct
Ashburn VA 20147

Call Sign: N6CZG
Jirasak Visalsawat
43626 London Way
Ashburn VA 20147

Call Sign: KD4ZIF
Wayne R Walker
42461 Magellan Sq
Ashburn VA 20148

Call Sign: N1YQK
Marvin J Allred
42519 Magellan Sq
Ashburn VA 20148

Call Sign: KG4SEN
Michael R Pursifull
21518 Merion St
Ashburn VA 201474583

Call Sign: KF4PQK
Albert Shearer
44133 Merrywood Ct
Ashburn VA 20147

Call Sign: KC6EGF
Alan D Burkle

43064 Midvale Ct
Ashburn VA 201474453

Call Sign: KG4TVL
Michael D Gibat
44831 Milestone Sq 200
Ashburn VA 20147

Call Sign: WA5QWQ
Paul G Cariker
20818 Misty Meadow Ct
Ashburn VA 20147

Call Sign: WB6NOO
Joseph W Keifer III
44251 Mossy Brook Sq
Ashburn VA 20147

Call Sign: K4DBX
Sean W Hall
44084 Natalie Ter 102
Ashburn VA 20147

Call Sign: W4JAB
Joseph A Buttner
22821 Nichols Farm Way
Ashburn VA 20148

Call Sign: KD4PWV
Patrick N Macdonald
44344 Oldetowne Pl
Ashburn VA 20147

Call Sign: KD6JAT
Scott M Graham
21254 Olive Green Ct
Ashburn VA 20147

Call Sign: KG4RRO
Robert A Roncace
21217 Owls Nest Sq
Ashburn VA 20147

Call Sign: AC2H
Walter J Tolpa
19951 Palmer Classic Pkwy
Ashburn VA 20147

Call Sign: KA3TWV

Wendy J Tolpa
19951 Palmer Classic Pkwy
Ashburn VA 20147

Call Sign: KA3ICI
Ernest G Fine
44284 Panther Ridge Dr
Ashburn VA 201475518

Call Sign: KJ4BSD
Sandra A Monnette
43341 Parlor Sq
Ashburn VA 20147

Call Sign: KK4DLP
Christopher M Williamson
42975 Pascale Ter
Ashburn VA 20148

Call Sign: KI4OYM
Gerald M Ward
22454 Pine Ridge Ct
Ashburn VA 20148

Call Sign: W0ARD
Gerald M Ward
22454 Pine Ridge Ct
Ashburn VA 20148

Call Sign: KF4MHD
William J Clark
20906 Pioneer Ridge Ter
Ashburn VA 20147

Call Sign: KI4IIS
Tamara M Stoneburner
20683 Pomeroy Ct
Ashburn VA 20147

Call Sign: KI4IIT
Walter L Stoneburner II
20683 Pomeroy Ct
Ashburn VA 20147

Call Sign: KE8SF
Ramon J Hontanon
20686 Pomeroy Ct
Ashburn VA 201472855

Call Sign: KG4RRP
Benjamin H De Vore
43424 Postrail Sq
Ashburn VA 20147

Call Sign: W8AHM
John P Wittkoski
21022 Powderhorn Ct
Ashburn VA 20147

Call Sign: K8LF
Jerome S Svinicki
43294 Rachelle Ann Ct
Ashburn VA 20147

Call Sign: KF4CJQ
Theodosia M Svinicki
43294 Rachelle Ann Ct
Ashburn VA 20147

Call Sign: KJ4LAO
Alexander E Svinicki
43294 Rachelle Ann Ct
Ashburn VA 20147

Call Sign: KG4SUO
John T Singleton IV
43207 Ribboncrest Ter
Ashburn VA 20147

Call Sign: KR4DJ
Douglas R Lando
42993 Ridgeway Dr
Ashburn VA 20148

Call Sign: KK4HMW
Colton Ericksen
20282 River Ridge Ter 003
Ashburn VA 20147

Call Sign: KI4YND
Melody R Trainor
20280 River Ridge Ter 202
Ashburn VA 20147

Call Sign: N9MIP
Douglas A Tapp
44872 Rivermont Ter Apt 103
Ashburn VA 20147

Call Sign: N4OGL
Mark A Keiser
21035 Roaming Shores Ter
Ashburn VA 201473208

Call Sign: KA4RGN
Bernard E Massie Sr
42706 Ryan Rd
Ashburn VA 22011

Call Sign: AK4RA
Derek S Linden
43879 Sandburg Sq
Ashburn VA 20147

Call Sign: KF6JDC
Gus K Lott III
44435 Scientific Way
Ashburn VA 201472409

Call Sign: KJ4GYC
John T Hill
2081 Shy Beaver Ct
Ashburn VA 20147

Call Sign: KJ4GYD
John C Hill Jr
20831 Shy Beaver Ct
Ashburn VA 20147

Call Sign: N7OAS
Steven O Stansbury
20124 Silver Creek Tr Apt 303
Bdg 1
Ashburn VA 20147

Call Sign: WB4PFJ
Lawrence S Wilbur
22711 Simonet Blanc Ter
Ashburn VA 20148

Call Sign: W4QAW
Raymond E Spence Jr
19979 Smith Cir
Ashburn VA 20147

Call Sign: KK4DLV
Anthony C Williams Jr

20359 Snowpoint Pl
Ashburn VA 201472375

Call Sign: N6GON
Douglas P Hafen
20579 Snowshoe Sq 102
Ashburn VA 20147

Call Sign: KI4YCT
Nicholas Koopalethes
43615 Solheim Cup Ter
Ashburn VA 20147

Call Sign: K4RNT
Alexander P Smith
43300 116 Southern Walk Plaza
229
Ashburn VA 20148

Call Sign: KI4OWL
John F Breese III
42863 Spring Morning Ct
Ashburn VA 20148

Call Sign: KI4OWM
John F Breese Jr
42863 Spring Morning Ct
Ashburn VA 20148

Call Sign: KI4RIY
Evan C Dibona
42887 Spring Morning Ct
Ashburn VA 20148

Call Sign: KJ4GUM
Noel C Dibona
42887 Spring Morning Ct
Ashburn VA 20148

Call Sign: WA4LDA
Stevens R Miller
21646 Stillbrook Farm Dr
Ashburn VA 20148

Call Sign: KG4QFG
Elizabeth A Miller
21646 Stillbrook Farm Dr
Ashburn VA 201483612

Call Sign: KB3MK
Rodney A Hignite
21017 Strawrick Ter
Ashburn VA 201475323

Call Sign: KK4FFQ
Curt J Schwarz
43888 Stronghold Ct
Ashburn VA 20147

Call Sign: WZ3I
Robert P Beck
21417 Sturman Pl
Ashburn VA 20148

Call Sign: WN4RA
Richard W Allocca
43808 Sunset Ter
Ashburn VA 20147

Call Sign: KF4PBY
Craig W Hedges
20720 Sweetair Ct
Ashburn VA 20147

Call Sign: KF6BBS
Michael D Morningstar
43164 Tall Pines Ct
Ashburn VA 20147

Call Sign: KE4TCS
Randall J Hager
21001 Timber Ridge Ter 304
Ashburn VA 20147

Call Sign: KC4WFH
Terry L Valois
42453 Tourmaline Ln
Ashburn VA 201485664

Call Sign: W1FOX
Brian J Fox
42956 Val Aosta Dr
Ashburn VA 201487173

Call Sign: KG4GAZ
Edway R Johnson II
42756 Vestals Gap Dr
Ashburn VA 20148

Call Sign: W4ERJ
Edway R Johnson II
42756 Vestals Gap Dr
Ashburn VA 20148

Call Sign: KI4KXG
David Zabrosky
44477 Watertown Ter
Ashburn VA 20147

Call Sign: N4NMR
Michael F Bower
43304 Wayside Cir
Ashburn VA 20147

Call Sign: KD4WGU
Ruth E Bower
43304 Wayside Cir
Ashburn VA 201474621

Call Sign: K9PQI
Charles D Coyle
22571 Welborne Manor Sq
Ashburn VA 201483147

Call Sign: WA3THY
Scott J Shearer
21060 Willowbrook Dr
Ashburn VA 22011

Call Sign: KI4CTX
Charles A Gobs III
43752 Woodworth Ct
Ashburn VA 20147

Call Sign: W3TNC
Charles A Gobs III
43752 Woodworth Ct
Ashburn VA 20147

Call Sign: K4PSU
Thomas R Morgan
Ashburn VA 20146

Call Sign: KC4ZFM
James P Burke
Ashburn VA 20146

Call Sign: NL7MR
James L Cannon
Ashburn VA 20146

Call Sign: W4HFS
Richard T Senior
Ashburn VA 20146

Call Sign: WB6EFW
Scott J Morse
Ashburn VA 20146

Call Sign: KJ4MEZ
Michael Bohnett
Ashburn VA 20146

Call Sign: WR4L
Jan M Miller
Ashburn VA 201460190

Call Sign: WB8WKU
Eugene W May Jr
Ashburn VA 201462321

**FCC Amateur Radio Licenses
in Ashburn Farms**

Call Sign: KM4NR
Dennison D Gresham
43312 Dovetail Pl
Ashburn Farms VA 20147

Call Sign: KV4IJ
Dennison D Gresham
43312 Dovetail Pl
Ashburn Farms VA 20147

**FCC Amateur Radio Licenses
in Ashland**

Call Sign: KD4DRZ
Ellen S Bolton
12491 Ashcake Rd
Ashland VA 23005

Call Sign: WU4G
Ronnie A Bolton
12491 Ashcake Rd
Ashland VA 23005

Call Sign: N4EKD
Waddy E Bolton Jr
12491 Ashcake Rd
Ashland VA 23005

Call Sign: WA4OPW
Wilmer G Rogers
13132 Ashland Rd
Ashland VA 230059732

Call Sign: N4ZZR
Steven E Eddleton
Rt 1 Box 455
Ashland VA 23005

Call Sign: KF4YK
Charles H Frasher
14183 Broddies Trl
Ashland VA 230057217

Call Sign: KF4PDA
A Richard Turner II
11377 Cedar Ln
Ashland VA 23005

Call Sign: KI4WCG
Eric Rheinstein
9424 Charter Creek Dr Apt 2 E
Ashland VA 23005

Call Sign: N3NEX
Ruth I Campbell
12085 Cheroy Woods Ct
Ashland VA 23005

Call Sign: N4YMY
James A Campbell
12085 Cheroy Woods Ct
Ashland VA 230057934

Call Sign: KI4BET
Terry L Guthrie
416 Cornwallis Ct
Ashland VA 23005

Call Sign: KK4AIP
Frederick L Dye
12470 Cubs Ln

Ashland VA 23005

Call Sign: KB0MJG
Rose E Dickman
10110 Deer Ridge Pl
Ashland VA 230057933

Call Sign: N8ENT
Les C Widmyer
11202 Elmont Rd
Ashland VA 23005

Call Sign: KJ4NPL
William B Tyler
12134 Elmont Rd
Ashland VA 23005

Call Sign: KJ4BJC
William D Griffith
13353 Greenwood Church Rd
Ashland VA 23005

Call Sign: W4JHG
Frank H Howard
134 Hanover Ave
Ashland VA 23005

Call Sign: K4BAW
John E Owen
11382 Hanover Ave
Ashland VA 230057611

Call Sign: KD4RYT
James T Bailey
11370 Hanover Ave
Ashland VA 23005

Call Sign: K4CDS
Carl D Shaw
10405 Hiawatha Pathway
Ashland VA 23005

Call Sign: KI4RFT
Patricia J Osborne
10405 Hiawatha Pathway
Ashland VA 23005

Call Sign: KA4SBW
Steven W Harmon

14104 Hickory Oaks Ln
Ashland VA 23005

Call Sign: KK4ECN
Peter Geary
11139 Holly Berry Rd
Ashland VA 23005

Call Sign: N4MRV
Robert Grattan III
107 Howard St
Ashland VA 23005

Call Sign: KD4DSA
Gary A Belew
12018 Karen Dr
Ashland VA 23005

Call Sign: K4GLX
Dougald L Blue III
905 Kilby Station Rd
Ashland VA 23005

Call Sign: W4IOB
Frank A Penland
10283 Lakeridge Sq Ct Apt F
Ashland VA 23005

Call Sign: N4LZ
John T J Maceda
12275 Lees Ln
Ashland VA 23005

Call Sign: KD4BRE
William C Martin
805 Maple St
Ashland VA 23005

Call Sign: KC4ZIT
Charles A Felker
415 Mt Hermon Rd
Ashland VA 23005

Call Sign: KK4ESD
William T Gatewood
12261 Mt Hermon Rd
Ashland VA 23005

Call Sign: AC4DQ

Harry A Miller III
629 N James St
Ashland VA 23005

Call Sign: KI4BWH
Ronald J Nash Jr
515 N Washington Hwy
Ashland VA 23005

Call Sign: W4YLM
William A Wilson
517 N Washington Hwy
Ashland VA 23005

Call Sign: WA4VDA
Thomas W Foster
10493 Old Telegraph Rd
Ashland VA 230058102

Call Sign: KJ4WLJ
Michael L Patterson
13620 Peaceful Ln
Ashland VA 23005

Call Sign: WN4KJD
Michael L Patterson
13620 Peaceful Ln
Ashland VA 23005

Call Sign: N4YFB
Timothy E Rhodes
8445 Pheasant Rush Ct
Ashland VA 23005

Call Sign: N4TER
Timothy E Rhodes
8445 Pheasant Rush Ct
Ashland VA 23005

Call Sign: KK4IFE
Mary Frayser
10362 Rapidan Way
Ashland VA 23005

Call Sign: AB4U
Richard F Cook Jr
14288 Riverside Dr
Ashland VA 230053125

Call Sign: KC4PHZ
Gary D Szulczewski
11 Slash Ct
Ashland VA 23005

Call Sign: KD4RJN
Jamie A Stapleton
9237 Susquehanna Trl
Ashland VA 23005

Call Sign: KC4UTJ
Steve J Bowles
401 Thompson St
Ashland VA 23005

Call Sign: KC2WAU
Hinnerk Koepp
401 Thompson Str
Ashland VA 23005

Call Sign: N4ZCD
Lisa R Deaton
602 VA St
Ashland VA 23005

Call Sign: KO4OV
Nelson C Trinkle
12431 Whisana Ln
Ashland VA 23005

Call Sign: KF4IUE
Ford C Marquis
200 Winter Oak Dr
Ashland VA 23005

Call Sign: KG4EVN
Herman B Parrish
12342 Woodson Farm Ln
Ashland VA 23005

Call Sign: N4RUM
Linwood T Carwile
Ashland VA 23005

Call Sign: KA1DYI
Wayne E Williams Sr
Ashland VA 23005

Call Sign: KB4CUK

Margaret P Weiss
Ashland VA 23005

Call Sign: KF4SQA
James R Smith
Ashland VA 23005

Call Sign: KG4CHG
Harold L Hayhurst
Ashland VA 23005

Call Sign: KK4IFD
Vernon M Frayser
Ashland VA 23005

FCC Amateur Radio Licenses in Atkins

Call Sign: W4KOO
Henry S Atkins
Rt 1 Box 435
Atkins VA 24311

Call Sign: KE4TEC
James C Gardner
Atkins VA 24311

Call Sign: KE4TED
Cleo L Gardner
Atkins VA 24311

Call Sign: KF4GOK
Christopher L Brooks
Atkins VA 24311

FCC Amateur Radio Licenses in Atlantic

Call Sign: KL2IC
Matthew I Kruczek
10133 Atlantic Rd
Atlantic VA 23303

Call Sign: KE4MFK
David A Jagielski
33332 Wisharts Pt Rd
Atlantic VA 23303

Call Sign: KD4NVT

Wade G Moore
Atlantic VA 23303

Call Sign: KD4WTC
Herman E Chesser
Atlantic VA 23303

Call Sign: KE4MFL
Martin V Carver
Atlantic VA 23303

Call Sign: KK4HM
Norman J Marshall
Atlantic VA 23303

Call Sign: KJ4UYO
Mary V Hoffken
Atlantic VA 23303

Call Sign: KI4JEF
Michael S Waterfield
Atlantic VA 23303

Call Sign: N4LNX
Alula W Marshall
Atlantic VA 233030190

FCC Amateur Radio Licenses in Austinville

Call Sign: KF4BBE
Shannon D Austin
Rt 1 Box 160B
Austinville VA 24312

Call Sign: KI4OMR
Robert B Carter
65 Hide Away Rd
Austinville VA 24312

Call Sign: KI4JWH
Charles W Stone
139 Sunrise Dr
Austinville VA 24312

FCC Amateur Radio Licenses in Axton

Call Sign: W4AJJ

Troy L Davis
570 Country Pl Rd
Axton VA 24054

Call Sign: KI4PMP
Leonard B Bryan Jr
141 Gallery Rd
Axton VA 240542006

Call Sign: KG4SRJ
Jerry M Holbrook
4485 Hobson Rd
Axton VA 24054

Call Sign: N1PC
David C Eanes
1450 Old Liberty Dr
Axton VA 24054

Call Sign: WB4PAN
Charles W Davidson
1028 Plantation Dr
Axton VA 240542032

Call Sign: KJ4AMX
Hannah J Bennett
1345 Stillmeadow Rd
Axton VA 24054

Call Sign: KJ4AMV
Isaiah J Bennett
1345 Stillmeadow Rd
Axton VA 24054

Call Sign: KJ4AMU
Josiah J Bennett
1345 Stillmeadow Rd
Axton VA 24054

Call Sign: KJ4BZO
Rosannah J Bennett
1345 Stillmeadow Rd
Axton VA 24054

Call Sign: KJ4ADQ
Sherie J Bennett
1345 Stillmeadow Rd
Axton VA 24054

Call Sign: KJ4AMW
Susannah R Bennett
1345 Stillmeadow Rd
Axton VA 24054

Call Sign: KJ4ADN
William J Bennett
1345 Stillmeadow Rd
Axton VA 24054

Call Sign: KJ4AUW
Deannah J Bennett
1345 Stillmeadow Rd
Axton VA 24054

Call Sign: KI4KAS
Nancy B Smith
862 Sugar Barbour Rd
Axton VA 24054

Call Sign: W6ZJU
Vernon E Thompson
Axton VA 24054

FCC Amateur Radio Licenses in Aylett

Call Sign: WD4MOX
Stuart W Peace
132 Cherry Hill Cir W
Aylett VA 23009

Call Sign: KC2HPQ
David A Smith Sr
408 Courtney Ln
Aylett VA 23009

Call Sign: N4MXT
Raymond M Misseri
4467 Herring Creek Rd
Aylett VA 23009

Call Sign: KC4ZRH
James H Taylor
5511 Herring Creek Rd
Aylett VA 23009

Call Sign: AC4DK
Darrell G Toman

124 Hickory Woods Rd
Aylett VA 23009

Call Sign: KD4NIU
Jack G Barbour Jr
3108 Manfield Rd
Aylett VA 23009

Call Sign: WB4GXC
Jack G Barbour Jr
3108 Manfield Rd
Aylett VA 23009

Call Sign: KG4EOF
Kevin F Slater
115 Manqurn Ct
Aylett VA 23009

Call Sign: KG4TFP
William J De Doste
32 Mayfair Trace
Aylett VA 23009

Call Sign: KD4IGR
Elbert E George
121 McCauley Pkwy
Aylett VA 23009

Call Sign: KI4BML
Mark C Garnett
175 Newton Dr
Aylett VA 23009

Call Sign: KC4TDM
Christopher W Middleton
116 Parkwood Dr
Aylett VA 23009

Call Sign: N4CCV
Christopher W Middleton
116 Parkwood Dr
Aylett VA 23009

Call Sign: KJ4TRG
Glen P Hudson
260 Parkwood Dr
Aylett VA 23009

Call Sign: K4GWR

Glen P Hudson
260 Parkwood Dr
Aylett VA 23009

Call Sign: KC2AXM
Scott M Deshaies
68 Rosebud Run
Aylett VA 23009

Call Sign: KI4YGO
Jacqueline D Darnell
177 Smokey Rd
Aylett VA 23009

Call Sign: KI4EXX
Harry W Reed III
170 Upshaw Rd
Aylett VA 23009

Call Sign: KI4IEI
Robert W Mathias
9544 W River Rd
Aylett VA 23009

Call Sign: K2NUT
David A Smith Sr
Aylett VA 23009

FCC Amateur Radio Licenses in Baileys Crossroads

Call Sign: KI4SXO
Michael Whalan
6203 Lakeview Dr
Baileys Crossroads VA 22041

FCC Amateur Radio Licenses in Bandy

Call Sign: KD4KPA
Gary L Meadows
Hcr 63 Box 47
Bandy VA 24602

Call Sign: KA4IER
James W Meadows
676 Reynolds Ridge Rd
Bandy VA 24602

Call Sign: KF4TI
Ermil T Meadows
Star Rt Box 47
Bandy VA 24602

FCC Amateur Radio Licenses in Barboursville

Call Sign: KJ4MFN
Mike A Richardson
3140 Burnley Station Rd
Barboursville VA 22923

Call Sign: KJ4IGG
Jeffrey S Pixton
4474 Burnley Station Rd
Barboursville VA 22923

Call Sign: K4DND
David N Damon
4521 Burnley Station Rd
Barboursville VA 22923

Call Sign: KJ4CLX
Sean M Bryan
167 Cypress Cir
Barboursville VA 22923

Call Sign: KD4QBC
Robert E Dickerson
14077 Dickersons Ln
Barboursville VA 22923

Call Sign: KJ4BKX
Benjamin N M Guzzardi
15300 Dragon Hill Dr
Barboursville VA 22923

Call Sign: KD4CUL
James W Taylor Sr
3676 Gilbert Station Rd
Barboursville VA 22923

Call Sign: KC8LYQ
Timothy W Kisamore
16380 Hamm Farm Rd
Barboursville VA 22923

Call Sign: KC8MHB

Lisa D Kisamore
16380 Hamm Farm Rd
Barboursville VA 22923

Call Sign: KK4EDV
Susanne Zimmermann
76 Kieran Ln
Barboursville VA 22933

Call Sign: KB7ZWG
Bonnie J Colburn
45 Pine Tree Dr
Barboursville VA 22923

Call Sign: N4HRO
Michael T Colburn
45 Pine Tree Dr
Barboursville VA 22923

Call Sign: W4VST
Marlin V Wilson
4532 Stoney Point Rd
Barboursville VA 22923

Call Sign: WA4WQG
Herman A Dechent
856 Toms Rd
Barboursville VA 22923

Call Sign: N1NBM
Kim M Panagakos
123 White Cedar Rd
Barboursville VA 22923

Call Sign: KD4OCH
Norval F Fitzhugh Jr
Barboursville VA 22923

Call Sign: KE4WLL
Trevor S Varner
Barboursville VA 22923

Call Sign: WA4OVD
Charles F Varner
Barboursville VA 22923

FCC Amateur Radio Licenses in Barhamsville

Call Sign: WA4OVW
Raymond G Campbell
6501 Holly Fork Rd
Barhamsville VA 23011

Call Sign: KA3BCV
Larry S Hurst
Barhamsville VA 23011

FCC Amateur Radio Licenses in Barren Springs

Call Sign: KG4RTB
Sammy D Mcneely
393 Gardner Rd
Barren Springs VA 243133574

Call Sign: KA4WYI
William J Mc Neely
519 Gardner Rd
Barren Springs VA 24313

Call Sign: KI4KVQ
Chad N Hawks
927 Gardner Rd
Barren Springs VA 24313

Call Sign: KI4MTE
Michelle E Willis
927 Gardner Rd
Barren Springs VA 24313

Call Sign: KE4TEE
David L Frazier
St Rt 608
Barren Springs VA 24313

Call Sign: KE4UMJ
Matthew A Frazier
Barren Springs VA 24313

FCC Amateur Radio Licenses in Baskerville

Call Sign: KG4NUO
Chad L Carter
4187 Baskerville Rd
Baskerville VA 23915

Call Sign: NR4SS
Chad L Carter
4187 Baskerville Rd
Baskerville VA 23915

Call Sign: KJ4VJC
Patrick N Bradner
4187 Baskerville Rd
Baskerville VA 23915

Call Sign: KJ4VJH
Charles T Mooney Jr
18489 Hwy 47
Baskerville VA 23915

Call Sign: K4CTM
Charles T Mooney Jr
18489 Hwy 47
Baskerville VA 23915

FCC Amateur Radio Licenses in Bassett

Call Sign: KE4JAA
Wilbur D Utt
436 Applegate Ln
Bassett VA 24055

Call Sign: WB4SJC
Russell D Dunford
4516 Blackberry Rd
Bassett VA 24055

Call Sign: WA2NUQ
Robert C Strub
Rr2 Box 173
Bassett VA 24055

Call Sign: AE4BL
Robert D Snider
Rt 1 Box 293
Bassett VA 24055

Call Sign: KE4FBQ
Judy A Snider
Rt 1 Box 293
Bassett VA 24055

Call Sign: KF4FVV

Margaret I Wimmer
Rt 4 Box 396A
Bassett VA 24055

Call Sign: KF4FVW
William B Wimmer
Rt 4 Box 396A
Bassett VA 24055

Call Sign: KD4SQD
Oscar W Swaim Jr
Rt 6 Box 445
Bassett VA 24055

Call Sign: KI4SYT
Michael J Bush
41 Boxwood Ln
Bassett VA 24055

Call Sign: WB4WRD
Jesse S Bowles
2534 County Line Rd
Bassett VA 24055

Call Sign: WA4WRE
Kenneth M Bowles
2538 County Line Rd
Bassett VA 24055

Call Sign: N4GBO
Robert L Moore Sr
2056 Crestridge Rd
Bassett VA 240555219

Call Sign: N3FUT
Robert L Moore Sr
2056 Crestridge Rd
Bassett VA 240555219

Call Sign: WD4DUT
Peggy J Nunn
1822 Fork Mtn Rd
Bassett VA 24055

Call Sign: WD4DUU
Douglas W Nunn
1822 Fork Mtn Rd
Bassett VA 24055

Call Sign: KF4RMT
Brandon A Rakes
35 Harvest Ln
Bassett VA 24055

Call Sign: WD4NUT
Eugene H Aldridge
1233 Lacky Hill Rd
Bassett VA 24055

Call Sign: W5MWH
Marty W Hollandsworth
136 Mayberry Cir
Bassett VA 24055

Call Sign: KJ4IEL
Grady E Phillips
1517 Microfilm Rd
Bassett VA 24055

Call Sign: KG4NVR
Henry B Ingle
4985 Muddy Fork Rd
Bassett VA 24055

Call Sign: KJ4VMD
ARChie E Shelton Jr
155 Pinewood Ln
Bassett VA 24055

Call Sign: KB7TMX
Clarence G Hodnett
96 Riverside Dr
Bassett VA 240554247

Call Sign: N4YJK
Deborah P Snider
128 Sanville
Bassett VA 24055

Call Sign: N4FSZ
Elliott R Gee
239 Sanville Heights St
Bassett VA 24055

Call Sign: KE4YEW
Alicia N Gosline
128 Sanville Hgts
Bassett VA 24055

Call Sign: KF4WWZ
Silas G Sykes
241 Starcrest Ave
Bassett VA 240555060

Call Sign: W4RPS
Troy D Spencer
3196 Stones Dairy Rd
Bassett VA 240559741

Call Sign: N4RQZ
Edward Martinez
22 Tj Ct
Bassett VA 24055

Call Sign: AB2CF
Robert C Roseman
22 Tj Ct
Bassett VA 24055

Call Sign: KJ4NDV
Jerry L Spencer
381 Wilson Mill Rd
Bassett VA 24055

Call Sign: K4FWW
Albert W Harder
Bassett VA 24055

Call Sign: WA4WXL
Arlen C Doss
Bassett VA 24055

FCC Amateur Radio Licenses in Bastian

Call Sign: KG4HEO
Anthony T Kennedy
Rt 1 Box 1356
Bastian VA 24314

Call Sign: KD4WON
Robert M Shrader
Rt 1 Box 1475
Bastian VA 24314

Call Sign: KB8ANT
Kelli L Sarver

Rt 1 Box 55
Bastian VA 24314

Call Sign: K4ATK
Anthony T Kennedy
7474 Clear Fork Creek Rd
Bastian VA 24314

Call Sign: KE4EWX
Cherie D Stowers
8886 Clear Fork Creek Rd
Bastian VA 24314

Call Sign: KF4SMH
Gary E Akers
5977 Clearfork Creek Rd
Bastian VA 24314

Call Sign: KD4LMZ
Lorin B Hanshew
4531 N Scenic Hwy
Bastian VA 24314

FCC Amateur Radio Licenses in Bayse

Call Sign: K3CJU
Matthew Mitchell
164 Dale Dr
Basye VA 22810

Call Sign: N4JSN
Richard G D Antonio
268 Fritzel Way
Bayse VA 22810

Call Sign: N4ZKH
Marshall R Cooper Jr
Basye VA 22810

Call Sign: W4TXJ
Frank D Baxter
Basye VA 22810

Call Sign: KK4FKF
Kevin J Lipscomb Jr
Basye VA 22810

FCC Amateur Radio Licenses in Battery Park

Call Sign: KI4QOJ
Oscar K Kuhn
Battery Park VA 23304

FCC Amateur Radio Licenses in Bealeton

Call Sign: KJ4KTH
Hector J Rivera
11170 Ashley Brooke Dr
Bealeton VA 22712

Call Sign: KI4JH
Jonn A De Main Sr
6406 Beales Ct
Bealeton VA 22712

Call Sign: KA8JTJ
Deborah L Perrin
10831 Blakelane
Bealeton VA 22712

Call Sign: KJ4NVC
Jerry L Armstrong
7342 Botha Rd
Bealeton VA 22712

Call Sign: KD4MVK
Larry H Mc Kelvey
Rt 1 Box 94
Bealeton VA 22712

Call Sign: KJ4FZJ
Anthony W Weaver
10910 Bristol Pl
Bealeton VA 22712

Call Sign: N2GOS
Diane M Loree
6224 Buck Ct Lot 615
Bealeton VA 22712

Call Sign: KG4UCO
Robert W Pennell
7137 Catlett Rd
Bealeton VA 22712

Call Sign: KC4CVG
Robert L Taylor III
11123 Cedar Ln
Bealeton VA 22712

Call Sign: AD4DD
Perry L Olinger
11408 Cemetery Rd
Bealeton VA 227127707

Call Sign: KC0UIZ
Allen G Brandt
6683 Clarkes Meadow Dr
Bealeton VA 227126953

Call Sign: KF4POU
Dan C Sparks
4415 Courtneys Corner Rd
Bealeton VA 227127312

Call Sign: KE6IVQ
Kirk L Van Gorkom
7203 Covingtons Corner Rd
Bealeton VA 22712

Call Sign: KJ4ICV
Norman A Frizzle
11176 Crest Ln
Bealeton VA 22712

Call Sign: WD4FOV
Thomas R Young Jr
11180 Crest Ln
Bealeton VA 22712

Call Sign: KK4AWJ
Christopher D Phillips
11159 Eagle Ct
Bealeton VA 22712

Call Sign: KA9TTB
Joy L Chapman
13047 Elk Run Rd
Bealeton VA 227127325

Call Sign: W9JOP
Robert H Chapman
13047 Elk Run Rd

Bealeton VA 227127325

Call Sign: KB4BWM
Kennith V Moore
13328 Elk Run Rd
Bealeton VA 22712

Call Sign: W4BCK
Carl A Engh II
11301 Falling Creek Dr
Bealeton VA 227127731

Call Sign: K4AAH
Harold J Busse
4181 Granite St
Bealeton VA 22712

Call Sign: KI4JQE
Guy M Mengel
4527 Hurst Dr
Bealeton VA 22712

Call Sign: AI1G
Guy M Mengel
4527 Hurst Dr
Bealeton VA 22712

Call Sign: KB4CG
Jack A Jeffery
12530 Lake Coventry Dr
Bealeton VA 22712

Call Sign: KJ4GUU
Christopher W Wisehart
9703 Logan Jay Dr
Bealeton VA 22712

Call Sign: KD4CAI
James R Gildea
6862 Maplewood Dr
Bealeton VA 22712

Call Sign: KI4DME
Jerry L Hampton
6237 Marsh Run Dr
Bealeton VA 22712

Call Sign: KK4EAY
Scott L Schreiber

11108 N Windsor Ct
Bealeton VA 22712

Call Sign: N3AVY
William J Price
10686 Prairie View Ln
Bealeton VA 227126714

Call Sign: N4WVT
Micheal J Murray
6742 Schoolhouse Rd
Bealeton VA 22712

Call Sign: N4FV
James H Murray
6742 Schoolhouse Rd
Bealeton VA 22712

Call Sign: N5MYR
Jack B Walsmith
11242A Torrie Way
Bealeton VA 22712

Call Sign: KD4GKT
Hernando A Vera
10497 Weaversville Rd
Bealeton VA 22712

Call Sign: KI4FBJ
Cindy S Stokes
11164 G Willow Dr
Bealeton VA 22712

Call Sign: KI4DKZ
Steve D Legge
Bealeton VA 22712

FCC Amateur Radio Licenses in Beaverdam

Call Sign: KI4LAK
Jeffrey E Soderlund
19811 Anderson Mill Rd
Beaverdam VA 23015

Call Sign: N4CZJ
Willard T Mason
17076 Beaver Dam Rd
Beaverdam VA 23015

Call Sign: KI4AXX
Robert Mann Lowry
17477 Beaver Dam Rd
Beaverdam VA 23015

Call Sign: KD4IFU
John C Creger
Rt 2 Box 77D
Beaverdam VA 23015

Call Sign: KA4NYC
Alice A Boller
17022 Coatesville Rd
Beaverdam VA 23015

Call Sign: W8IRT
Paul Boller
17022 Coatesville Rd
Beaverdam VA 230151625

Call Sign: KC4PHW
James F Phillips
115 English Walnut Rd
Beaverdam VA 23015

Call Sign: W4OFS
Palmer T Mc Cormac
21175 Green Bay Rd
Beaverdam VA 23015

Call Sign: KE4CEP
Linda D Vitek
18682 Hollowing Creek Rd
Beaverdam VA 23015

Call Sign: KI4BWI
James R Grove Jr
17124 Katy Ln
Beaverdam VA 230151785

Call Sign: KF4PIV
Garland W Flournoy
12280 New Market Mill Rd
Beaverdam VA 23015

Call Sign: KA4NYB
Dina M Mayo
12650 Old Ridge Rd

Beaverdam VA 23015

Call Sign: WA4SFL
Douglas R Mayo
12650 Old Ridge Rd
Beaverdam VA 23015

Call Sign: KE5QIZ
Adrian C Ramirez
15436 Old Ridge Rd
Beaverdam VA 23015

Call Sign: W3FDC
Eynon T Rowland
14372 Scotchtown Rd
Beaverdam VA 23015

Call Sign: K4BMT
James A Revercomb
17148 Tulip Poplar Rd
Beaverdam VA 23015

Call Sign: KI4JLO
Joseph S Chandler
17168 Tulip Poplar Rd
Beaverdam VA 23015

Call Sign: KG4QWR
Jeffrey D Seay
16541 Tyler Station Rd
Beaverdam VA 23015

Call Sign: WA4CQX
Jerry L Jones
17438 Tyler Station Rd
Beaverdam VA 23015

Call Sign: W4ENG
Gregory J Williams
17093 White Pine Rd
Beaverdam VA 23015

Call Sign: KA4OKH
Bryan S Anderson
17182 White Pine Rd
Beaverdam VA 23015

**FCC Amateur Radio Licenses
in Bedford**

Call Sign: KC4VNF
Kenneth W Mac Donald
1726 3 Otters Rd
Bedford VA 24523

Call Sign: WB2DHW
Ernest Clark
608 3rd St Apt A11
Bedford VA 24523

Call Sign: KC4BUO
Thomas E Fitzgerald
612 3rd St Apt B6
Bedford VA 24523

Call Sign: AC4LK
Arthur N Ogden
931 Ashland Ave
Bedford VA 24523

Call Sign: KA5PDY
Thomas D Wilson
416 Avenel Ave
Bedford VA 24523

Call Sign: KG4VTA
Scott I Coles
3477 Big Island Hwy
Bedford VA 24523

Call Sign: NT9A
Herman Mack
718 Blue Ridge Ave Apt M121
Bedford VA 245232507

Call Sign: KD4YVK
Kathy S Profitt
1094 Bluegrass Ln
Bedford VA 245235648

Call Sign: KD4YVL
Alvin G Profitt
1094 Bluegrass Ln
Bedford VA 245235648

Call Sign: KC4WUL
Leo D Burnette Jr
Rt 3 Box 186

Bedford VA 24523

Call Sign: KF4FYH
Brian L Hawkins
Rt 4 Box 196 A
Bedford VA 24523

Call Sign: KC4SNM
Charlie B Per Dieu Sr
Rt 5 Box 234P
Bedford VA 24523

Call Sign: KC4UTD
Robert C Hudson
Rt 5 Box 252B
Bedford VA 24523

Call Sign: WB5DPZ
William L Brandt
Rt 1 Box 257W
Bedford VA 24523

Call Sign: KD4MGG
Jeffrey N Henderson
Rt 5 Box 261
Bedford VA 24523

Call Sign: N4LLY
Loren J Brown
Rt 4 Box 261D
Bedford VA 24523

Call Sign: N4MDX
Marlene M Ginsberg
Rt 4 Box 265
Bedford VA 24523

Call Sign: KC4BPC
Ohad Cohen
Rt 4 Box 265
Bedford VA 24523

Call Sign: N4NVB
Mikel B Davis
Rt 4 Box 265
Bedford VA 24523

Call Sign: KJ4BN
Allen P Larson

1207 Caravan Dr
Bedford VA 24523

Call Sign: W3HVE
Thomas C Freedom
1474 Central Manor Ln
Bedford VA 245234153

Call Sign: KJ4DQK
Lynne P Stebbins
5644 Chestnut Fork Rd
Bedford VA 24523

Call Sign: N4DRA
Daniel R Arthur
1172 Copperfield Rd
Bedford VA 24523

Call Sign: AD4ST
Charles L Beard
1518 Crowder Rd
Bedford VA 24523

Call Sign: KF6UTH
Richard L Diddams Jr
1069 Davis Mill Ln
Bedford VA 245236532

Call Sign: KJ4GVJ
James V Lewis
1175 Davis Mill Ln
Bedford VA 24523

Call Sign: KK4BSL
Derrick J Dinwiddie
1079 Dudes Dr
Bedford VA 24523

Call Sign: KK4BIU
Robert J Dinwiddie Jr
1079 Dudes Dr
Bedford VA 24523

Call Sign: KK4BIS
Carrie J Dinwiddie
1079 Dudes Dr
Bedford VA 24523

Call Sign: N4SLD

Addison L Mason Jr
1794 Fairfield Rd
Bedford VA 24523

Call Sign: N4XOO
Ivey J Whitehurst
1105 Fairview Dr
Bedford VA 24523

Call Sign: K4STE
Paul H Lilly Jr
6485 Falling Creek Rdr
Bedford VA 24523

Call Sign: KJ4APZ
Fierce Dreamer
1233 Forbes Mill Rd
Bedford VA 24523

Call Sign: KK4DPF
Iva H Daniels
1058 Glenwood Dr
Bedford VA 24523

Call Sign: K4OFQ
Robert D Woods
2450 Glenwood Dr
Bedford VA 24523

Call Sign: W2WDD
James D Rauscher
1125 Granite Dr
Bedford VA 24523

Call Sign: KM4GD
George A Stein IV
1189 Haven Heights Dr
Bedford VA 24523

Call Sign: KI4LYU
Frank T Marishak Jr
1201 Hobbs Mullins Ln
Bedford VA 245236474

Call Sign: KC4VOR
Richard K Michael
1206 Holland Forks Rd
Bedford VA 24523

Call Sign: WB2KID
Eugene H Thommen Jr
1076 Huntington Dr
Bedford VA 24523

Call Sign: KI4QYH
Billy R Jenkins
1042 Jay Bird Ln
Bedford VA 24523

Call Sign: K4BRJ
Billy R Jenkins
1042 Jay Bird Ln
Bedford VA 24523

Call Sign: AB4JY
Glen H De Long
1228 Knollwood Dr
Bedford VA 24523

Call Sign: KI4EQ
Jeffrey E Rash
1020 Legacy Dr
Bedford VA 24523

Call Sign: WV4B
Robert W Meadows
524 Longwood Ave
Bedford VA 24523

Call Sign: WD4POH
Robert W Meadows
524 Longwood Ave
Bedford VA 245233402

Call Sign: WA4QJF
Mary Ann M Hardy
607 Longwood Ave
Bedford VA 245233403

Call Sign: KC4VOQ
Eric C Allen
1113 Longwood Ave
Bedford VA 24523

Call Sign: KC4OEQ
Brian J Mitchell
1415 Longwood Ave
Bedford VA 24523

Call Sign: WA4YFJ
Lester C Robertson
950 Lyle St
Bedford VA 24523

Call Sign: KI4YWI
Joseph C Balsamo Jr
105 Mockingbird Cir
Bedford VA 24523

Call Sign: W2BAL
Joseph C Balsamo Jr
105 Mockingbird Cir
Bedford VA 24523

Call Sign: KJ4YQP
Hunter W Long
1966 Morgans Church Rd
Bedford VA 24523

Call Sign: KJ4KD
Donald G Yeargin
602 Mtn Ave
Bedford VA 245231945

Call Sign: W4JTB
John T Barrett
1900 N Hill Dr
Bedford VA 24523

Call Sign: N4JSK
Dennis L Kanode
1523 Newton Cir
Bedford VA 24523

Call Sign: KI4DL
Jack A Gross
1563 Newton Cir
Bedford VA 24523

Call Sign: KG4UJY
Joe Thompson
1421 Nicopolis Dr
Bedford VA 24523

Call Sign: KD4AZW
Robert A Fowler
1310 Oak Hill Ln

Bedford VA 245234347

Call Sign: K4UEK
O P Stancer
1509 Oakwood St
Bedford VA 245231617

Call Sign: K4HCC
Harlan C Cromer
1704 Oakwood St
Bedford VA 245231216

Call Sign: N2LNR
Eileen Narwid
1799 Otterhill Rd
Bedford VA 24523

Call Sign: W4OAF
Edwin J Narwid
1799 Otterhill Rd
Bedford VA 24523

Call Sign: KD4HVZ
Michael A Williams
1062 Overacre Dr
Bedford VA 24523

Call Sign: KD4PLZ
Brandy R Williams
1062 Overacre Dr
Bedford VA 24523

Call Sign: KG4JHW
Daniel C Terry
1114 Pawnee Rd
Bedford VA 24523

Call Sign: KF4ZBQ
Daniel R Martin
8255 Peaks Rd
Bedford VA 24523

Call Sign: WD4DUZ
Thomas C Wilmoth
708 Peaks St
Bedford VA 24523

Call Sign: KG4JHX
Jason Giglio

2486 Penicks Mill Rd
Bedford VA 24523

Call Sign: K4CQ
Lynchburg ARC Inc
1113 Pinecrest Ave
Bedford VA 24523

Call Sign: KC1BH
Gerald F Knowlton
1113 Pinecrest Ave
Bedford VA 24523

Call Sign: W1IE
Gerald F Knowlton
1113 Pinecrest Ave
Bedford VA 24523

Call Sign: KJ4CGK
Lloyd F Bible Jr
224 Pony Acres Rd
Bedford VA 24523

Call Sign: KN4TV
James L Blankenship
1578 Powell Ln
Bedford VA 24523

Call Sign: WB4CQ
James L Blankenship
1578 Powell Ln
Bedford VA 24523

Call Sign: KJ4ULJ
Eric S Fisher
1214 Rays Ln
Bedford VA 24523

Call Sign: KJ4ZZX
Roanoke Valley ARC
1214 Rays Ln 1
Bedford VA 24523

Call Sign: KI4FR
Meera C Behrens
1067 Rising Star Dr
Bedford VA 24523

Call Sign: KB4DTL

Harry L Carter
110 Riverbend Rd
Bedford VA 24523

Call Sign: KC4CFM
Elisabeth E Carter
110 Riverbend Rd
Bedford VA 24523

Call Sign: KE4CI
Roy L Carter
110 Riverbend Rd
Bedford VA 24523

Call Sign: KF4NCW
Norman E Crook
4488 Rock Cliff Rd
Bedford VA 24523

Call Sign: W4PY
Harvey C Bryant
1031 Shadow Ln
Bedford VA 245235393

Call Sign: KN4UI
Harvey C Bryant
1031 Shadow Ln
Bedford VA 245235393

Call Sign: KK4CB
Harvey C Bryant
1031 Shadow Ln
Bedford VA 245235393

Call Sign: N4KSV
Ruth M Fuller
121 Sheperd Ln
Bedford VA 24523

Call Sign: WA4RTX
Lawrence I Marcy
209 Sheperd Ln
Bedford VA 24523

Call Sign: KF4ZON
Anna P Profitt
4761 Shingle Block Rd
Bedford VA 24523

Call Sign: KK4BIY
Eric B Schrock
4761 Shingle Block Rd
Bedford VA 24523

Call Sign: WD4FMO
Richard A Kochendarfer
1014 Solaridge Dr
Bedford VA 24523

Call Sign: KG4PSE
Daniel R Arthur
4318 Timber Ridge Rd
Bedford VA 24523

Call Sign: N4PLV
Robert J Schnabl
1308 Tree Branch Rd
Bedford VA 245239502

Call Sign: K4LZJ
Homer M Bryant
545 Westview Ave
Bedford VA 24523

Call Sign: KJ4RWH
Jeff C Robertson
560 Westview Ave
Bedford VA 24523

Call Sign: WA8ALI
William C Seibert
616 Westview Ave
Bedford VA 24523

Call Sign: KC4VJH
Barry E Witt
1511 Wheatland Rd
Bedford VA 245231855

Call Sign: W4DUK
David A Houde
5257 Wheatland Rd
Bedford VA 24523

Call Sign: KD4QBF
James T Mc Govern
102 Woodcreek Rd
Bedford VA 24523

Call Sign: KC4EKO
David P Turpin
1120 Woodcrest Dr
Bedford VA 24523

Call Sign: KC4EKP
Pamela C Turpin
1120 Woodcrest Dr
Bedford VA 24523

Call Sign: K4JLP
Jeffrey L Parker
1276 Woods Edge Dr
Bedford VA 24523

Call Sign: WA4TCH
Robert E Mitchell Sr
1925 Woodside Ave
Bedford VA 24523

Call Sign: N4PLQ
Donald L Parks
Bedford VA 24523

Call Sign: KC4UAO
Martha D Beach
Bedford VA 24523

Call Sign: KF4VDK
Eric A Carlson
Bedford VA 24523

Call Sign: KI4FHX
Michelle C Ellinwood
Bedford VA 24523

Call Sign: KI4FHY
Robert S Ellinwood
Bedford VA 24523

Call Sign: WD4DER
John N Bradley
Bedford VA 245230147

**FCC Amateur Radio Licenses
in Belle Haven**

Call Sign: KC4AMZ

Mary Ann G Miles
2353 Belle Haven Rd
Belle Haven VA 23306

Call Sign: K4IHY
Douglas R Wehner
14283 Eastfield Dr
Belle Haven VA 23306

Call Sign: W0ADD
Alvy D Dunahoo
12358 Highland Dr
Belle Haven VA 23306

Call Sign: KC4AGH
Rhonda S Le Cato
36144 N Wainhouse Rd
Belle Haven VA 233060385

Call Sign: N3EHS
Larry D Doughty
35372 Occohannock Dr
Belle Haven VA 23306

Call Sign: KA3NXH
Linda Doughty
35372 Occohannock Dr
Belle Haven VA 23306

Call Sign: KC4YWM
Lucius J Kellam III
Rt 178
Belle Haven VA 23306

Call Sign: KD4PPH
Nancy M Mc Caleb
Belle Haven VA 23306

Call Sign: KD7AIJ
Eric L Dereng
Belle Haven VA 23306

Call Sign: KF4YH
Arthur C Miles
Belle Haven VA 23306

FCC Amateur Radio Licenses in Ben Hur

Call Sign: KC4AMX
Stephen Stewart
Ben Hur VA 24218

Call Sign: WA4NZT
Dillard L Graham
Ben Hur VA 24218

FCC Amateur Radio Licenses in Bena

Call Sign: K4IHQ
Edward E Roberts
Bena VA 23018

Call Sign: KE4WDV
William E Minnick
Bena VA 23018

FCC Amateur Radio Licenses in Bent Mountain

Call Sign: WA8SAK
Kenneth E Post
11364 Countyline Rd
Bent Mountain VA 24059

Call Sign: N8NUL
Sonya B Post
11364 Countyline Rd
Bent Mountain VA 240592272

Call Sign: KG4FWK
David A Witkege
639 Glendale Rd
Bent Mountain VA 24059

Call Sign: N2GZU
Thomas F Shevlin
10571 Ivy Ridge Rd
Bent Mountain VA 24059

Call Sign: N3BJ
Alan L Fryer
10651 Ivy Ridge Rd
Bent Mountain VA 240590111

Call Sign: WD4KZK
Charles E Lamb

10721 Sugar Camp Creek Rd
Bent Mountain VA 24059

Call Sign: W4KZK
Charles E Lamb
10721 Sugar Camp Creek Rd
Bent Mountain VA 24059

Call Sign: KF4RGH
Helen C Lamb
Bent Mountain VA 24059

FCC Amateur Radio Licenses in Bentonville

Call Sign: W3JSM
George W Hodgkiss
211 Lands Run Rd
Bentonville VA 22610

Call Sign: KE4TNA
Scott I Lurie
1089 Lands Run Rd
Bentonville VA 22610

Call Sign: KJ4ZTB
John D Carter
511 Seven Oaks Dr
Bentonville VA 22610

FCC Amateur Radio Licenses in Bergton

Call Sign: W3MMC
Robert T Niemeyer
20197 Arbuckle Rd
Bergton VA 22811

Call Sign: KG4GNJ
Warren D Dove Jr
19499 Brocks Gap Rd
Bergton VA 22811

Call Sign: KG4BLD
Austen D Strawderman
64153 Owl Hollow Ln
Bergton VA 22811

FCC Amateur Radio Licenses in Berryville

Call Sign: WB4FPD
Walter L Hughes
6 Academy Ct
Berryville VA 22611

Call Sign: KI4NAS
David W Gillenwater
1862 Allen Rd
Berryville VA 22611

Call Sign: KJ4ZVV
Zachariah D Zinman-Hillerson
11 Battletown Dr
Berryville VA 22611

Call Sign: N4ERZ
Zachariah D Zinman-Hillerson
11 Battletown Dr
Berryville VA 226119500

Call Sign: KE4JES
Peter H Kafitz
122 Battletown Dr
Berryville VA 22611

Call Sign: N7GHE
Richard L Greenwald
22 Battletown Dr
Berryville VA 226119612

Call Sign: KD7PUF
Michael F Murphy
125 Bittersweet Ln
Berryville VA 22611

Call Sign: W3IHZ
William B Linck
106 Blue Ridge St
Berryville VA 22611

Call Sign: K4KDY
Herbert T Blaker
Rte 1 Box 2425
Berryville VA 22611

Call Sign: KB4EAW

Sherman A Hetz
Rt 2 Box 3640
Berryville VA 22611

Call Sign: KE4SQY
Frederic B Underwood
Rr 2 Box 3865
Berryville VA 22611

Call Sign: KF4NQR
S A Owens
Rt 2 Box 4260
Berryville VA 22611

Call Sign: N3AIH
Richard E Davis
166 Cannon Ball Rd
Berryville VA 226112955

Call Sign: WD4KHP
Edward V Krom III
62 Country Ln
Berryville VA 226113131

Call Sign: KC4QYK
Marjorie G Krom
62 Country Ln Lot 19
Berryville VA 226113131

Call Sign: WA8YCK
Charles E Renner
217 Craigs Run Ct
Berryville VA 226111256

Call Sign: KJ4DOP
Jared L Bateman
711 Crums Church Rd
Berryville VA 22611

Call Sign: KD4ZUF
Luc A Gosselin
405 Hancock Ct
Berryville VA 22611

Call Sign: KG4WXC
Alfredo Ayuso
204 Henderson Ct
Berryville VA 22611

Call Sign: KD4GYT
Mark K Gribble
3087 Lord Fairfax Hwy
Berryville VA 22611

Call Sign: K4GYT
Mark K Gribble
3087 Lord Fairfax Hwy
Berryville VA 22611

Call Sign: N3MG
Mark K Gribble
3087 Lord Fairfax Hwy
Berryville VA 22611

Call Sign: KQ4WI
Anthony M Ashby
1001 Moose Rd
Berryville VA 22611

Call Sign: KF4TLX
Walter S Hall III
3000 Parshall Rd
Berryville VA 22611

Call Sign: K4GAO
Walter S Hall III
3000 Parshall Rd
Berryville VA 22611

Call Sign: KN4FH
Allen D Mc Corkle
317 Pierce Rd
Berryville VA 226112301

Call Sign: WA4NIW
Lee B Phillips
853 Russell Rd
Berryville VA 22611

Call Sign: K4USS
Lee B Phillips
853 Russell Rd
Berryville VA 22611

Call Sign: KD4IET
Margarette J Barb
2549 Senseny Rd
Berryville VA 22611

Call Sign: W4DHU
Irvin F Barb
2549 Senseny Rd
Berryville VA 22611

Call Sign: K4IET
Margarette J Barb
2549 Senseny Rd
Berryville VA 22611

Call Sign: KD4DFA
Valentin T Kruza
4754 Senseny Rd
Berryville VA 22611

Call Sign: KG4VBV
Joel B Evans
366 Shepherds Mill Rd
Berryville VA 22611

Call Sign: K9TTH
Joel B Evans
366 Shepherds Mill Rd
Berryville VA 22611

Call Sign: KJ4MFD
William K Shriver
6 Spring House Ln
Berryville VA 22611

Call Sign: KS4KZ
David M Waag
258 Spring House Ln
Berryville VA 226113141

Call Sign: KF4VLY
Ira T Lowe III
308 Treadwell St
Berryville VA 22611

Call Sign: KD4LSX
Samuel S James
27 W Main St Apt 3
Berryville VA 22611

Call Sign: KD4HRJ
Stanley A Monish
201 Walnut St

Berryville VA 22611

Call Sign: KE4NXQ
Laura J Monish
201 Walnut St
Berryville VA 22611

Call Sign: KA2IYS
Barbara A Boughton
2180 Withers Larue Rd
Berryville VA 22611

Call Sign: W8MHO
William H Martin Sr
Berryville VA 22611

FCC Amateur Radio Licenses in Big Island

Call Sign: KD4RMG
Barbara L Hensley
Rt 1 Box 324
Big Island VA 24526

Call Sign: K4LKV
Kenny L Kanode
1298 Churchill Rd
Big Island VA 24526

Call Sign: KD4RMH
Michael E Hensley
1075 Hensley Hollow Rd
Big Island VA 24526

Call Sign: W4MEH
Michael E Hensley
1075 Hensley Hollow Rd
Big Island VA 24526

Call Sign: KK4CSK
Jesse L Bryant
10750 Lee Jackson Hwy
Big Island VA 24526

Call Sign: KD4GQY
Herbert R Baty
11185 Lee Jackson Hwy
Big Island VA 24526

Call Sign: KG4FBW
David L Wray
11959 Lee Jackson Hwy
Big Island VA 24526

Call Sign: KJ4CHT
George C Wortley
1398 Tolley Meadow Rd
Big Island VA 24526

Call Sign: K4HBR
Larry T Frazier
1152 Tomlinson Dr
Big Island VA 24526

Call Sign: W4HMK
Horace R Hiner Jr
3977 Waugh Switch Rd
Big Island VA 24526

Call Sign: KD4RBW
Gary D Scott
Big Island VA 24526

Call Sign: KG4PUB
Benjamin S Fisher
Big Island VA 24526

FCC Amateur Radio Licenses in Big Laurel

Call Sign: KG4JZN
Mark A Adams Sr
7585 Big Laurel Rd
Big Laurel VA 24293

FCC Amateur Radio Licenses in Big Stone Gap

Call Sign: KE4JUN
John W Tate
2428 4th Ave
Big Stone Gap VA 24219

Call Sign: KG4ASW
James E Fields
2712 4th Ave
Big Stone Gap VA 24219

Call Sign: KR4KB
Joseph M Brummitt Sr
2339 4th Ave E
Big Stone Gap VA 24219

Call Sign: KF4AJA
Larry R Williams
2113 6th Ave E
Big Stone Gap VA 24219

Call Sign: KJ4HKG
Johnny Ramey
1720 Artesian Well Hollow Rd
Big Stone Gap VA 24219

Call Sign: KK4CMF
Christopher P Stapleton III
5040 Back Valley Rd
Big Stone Gap VA 24219

Call Sign: KF4SVK
David C Beasley
Rr 3 Box 1057
Big Stone Gap VA 24219

Call Sign: KE4YLN
Dennis K Ashley
Rt 3 Box 375
Big Stone Gap VA 24219

Call Sign: KF4GVZ
David R Coomer
Rt 3 Box 676
Big Stone Gap VA 24219

Call Sign: N4PIC
John L Lyons
Rt 1 Box 848
Big Stone Gap VA 24219

Call Sign: KG4VFO
Larry W Williams
603 Cherokee Ave
Big Stone Gap VA 24219

Call Sign: KG4WQX
Lou E Williams
603 Cherokee Ave W
Big Stone Gap VA 24219

Call Sign: KE4SCJ
Gary S Williams
2426 Clinch Haven Rd
Big Stone Gap VA 24219

Call Sign: KF4SKU
Vicki G Williams
2426 Clinch Haven Rd
Big Stone Gap VA 24219

Call Sign: KF4OGX
Wendy O Welch
404 Clinton Ave E
Big Stone Gap VA 242192930

Call Sign: KI4RYM
Richard C Jones
1724 Dawson Ave
Big Stone Gap VA 24219

Call Sign: W4FGT
Richard C Jones
1724 Dawson Ave
Big Stone Gap VA 24219

Call Sign: KE4KAA
Brian D Sturgill
220 E 24th St N
Big Stone Gap VA 24219

Call Sign: KF4SKV
Erin N Dalton
211 B E 25th St N
Big Stone Gap VA 242193659

Call Sign: K4YZY
Fred D Watkins
3517 E Stone Gap Rd
Big Stone Gap VA 24219

Call Sign: W4GDB
George F Watkins
3519 E Stone Gap Rd
Big Stone Gap VA 24219

Call Sign: KG4EBU
James F Taylor
1812 Egan Rd

Big Stone Gap VA 24219

Call Sign: KI4DPH
Larissa G Taylor
1812 Egan Rd
Big Stone Gap VA 24219

Call Sign: KG4IKL
Danny A Qualls
2132 Egan Rd
Big Stone Gap VA 24219

Call Sign: KK4CMG
Belinda J Reynolds
2497 Egan Rd
Big Stone Gap VA 24219

Call Sign: KB4DFK
James S Ringley
2641 Hillcrest Farms Rd
Big Stone Gap VA 24219

Call Sign: KE4YTS
Eddie L Carter
2559 Orr St
Big Stone Gap VA 24219

Call Sign: KT4QX
Billy R Coomer
1668 Seminary Church Loop
Big Stone Gap VA 24219

Call Sign: KE4MOR
Michael F Jones
1839 Swanson Rd
Big Stone Gap VA 24219

Call Sign: KE4SCK
Cynthia L Jones
302 W 5th St N
Big Stone Gap VA 24219

Call Sign: KS4OY
Jeffery D Jones
302 W 5th St N
Big Stone Gap VA 24219

Call Sign: AE4QB
Robert C Spears Sr

702 W 8th St N
Big Stone Gap VA 24219

Call Sign: AE4B
Robert C Spears Sr
702 W 8th St N
Big Stone Gap VA 242192212

Call Sign: KG4NAK
Thomas S Aistrop
807 W 8th St N
Big Stone Gap VA 24219

Call Sign: K4FYZ
James E Hensley
106 Wood Ave W
Big Stone Gap VA 24219

Call Sign: KK4BQU
Rickey L Hale
Big Stone Gap VA 24219

Call Sign: KC4NFW
Walter M Brummitt
Big Stone Gap VA 24219

Call Sign: KF4VDF
Charles G Elliott Sr
Big Stone Gap VA 24219

Call Sign: KG4PLC
Corey A Barker
Big Stone Gap VA 24219

Call Sign: KG4ONE
Davey L Horner
Big Stone Gap VA 24219

FCC Amateur Radio Licenses in Binghamton

Call Sign: KF4BJD
Ralph Arias
1372 Wov Ave Apt 214
Binghamton VA 23503

FCC Amateur Radio Licenses in Birdsnest

Call Sign: KC4UOD
Lucas Lewin
Birdsnest VA 23307

FCC Amateur Radio Licenses in Bishop

Call Sign: W4TOE
Albert O Sheets Jr
Bishop VA 24604

Call Sign: KR4DX
Clyde M Null Jr
Bishop VA 24604

FCC Amateur Radio Licenses in Blacksburg

Call Sign: KJ4WTB
Alex M Granata
3103 Alice Dr
Blacksburg VA 24060

Call Sign: KE5BVC
Joseph M Davis
302 Alleghany St 10
Blacksburg VA 24060

Call Sign: KJ4CGJ
Joseph A Shaw
302 Alleghany St Apt 4
Blacksburg VA 24060

Call Sign: KI4DMW
Mark Kaynor
803 Allendale Ct
Blacksburg VA 24060

Call Sign: KI4DMY
Julie Kaynor
803 Allendale Ct
Blacksburg VA 24060

Call Sign: KG4MFM
Richard D Taylor
700 11 Appalachian Dr
Blacksburg VA 24060

Call Sign: KI4RTC

Aydin S Akyurtlu
600 Appalachian Dr Apt 8
Blacksburg VA 24060

Call Sign: KJ4YQQ
Sudharsan Narayanan
702 Appalachian Dr Apt 8
Blacksburg VA 24060

Call Sign: KD4LQQ
Keith A Tyeryar
1110 Ascot Ln
Blacksburg VA 24060

Call Sign: KD4LQR
Kenneth L Blackard
1110 Ascot Ln
Blacksburg VA 24060

Call Sign: K3NGD
Felix G Sorrentino
1205 Ascot Ln
Blacksburg VA 24060

Call Sign: N4KEM
Robert A Schiek
3777 Bay Tree Pl
Blacksburg VA 24060

Call Sign: W2ZJJ
Charles E Nunnally Sr
2885 Big Falls Rd
Blacksburg VA 24060

Call Sign: KE4TJC
George R Stell
2101 Birch Leaf Ln
Blacksburg VA 24060

Call Sign: KK4FKA
Reese A Moore
10700 Blue Ridge Dr Apt L
Blacksburg VA 24060

Call Sign: KJ4DDR
Benjamin C Hilburn
10300 Blue Ridge Dr NW Apt B
Blacksburg VA 24060

Call Sign: KF4BDU
Preston L Hendricks
1495 Boxwood Dr
Blacksburg VA 24060

Call Sign: AG4WJ
Dan R Klemer
900 B7 Brightwood Manor
Blacksburg VA 24060

Call Sign: KB0UQS
Nathan Wang
607 Broce Dr
Blacksburg VA 24060

Call Sign: K8RLN
Don C Cox
802 Broce Dr
Blacksburg VA 24060

Call Sign: KK4BWO
Rebecca A Vizzi
500 Broce Dr Apt 57
Blacksburg VA 24060

Call Sign: KG4MYY
Karen L Everhardt
2101 Broken Oak Dr
Blacksburg VA 24060

Call Sign: KG4MYZ
Scott D Rapier
2101 Broken Oak Dr
Blacksburg VA 24060

Call Sign: WB8YRO
Margery A Davis
550 Brush Mtn Rd
Blacksburg VA 24060

Call Sign: W9KIC
William A Davis
550 Brush Mtn Rd
Blacksburg VA 240608528

Call Sign: N3AO
Carter W Craigie
570 Brush Mtn Rd

Blacksburg VA 24060

Call Sign: N3KN
Kay C Craigie
570 Brush Mtn Rd
Blacksburg VA 24060

Call Sign: KF4EVN
Gabriele Hilgert
102 Buckingham Pl
Blacksburg VA 24060

Call Sign: KF4HDU
T Keith Blankenship
409 Buckingham Pl
Blacksburg VA 24060

Call Sign: K4VVV
James A Overfelt
1250 Burley Ln
Blacksburg VA 24060

Call Sign: N4YEQ
William M Gentry
706 Burrus Dr
Blacksburg VA 24060

Call Sign: KK4DDD
Sean Shenton
702 Cambridge
Blacksburg VA 24060

Call Sign: KJ4NEC
Gerald B Pigford
113 Camelot Ct
Blacksburg VA 24060

Call Sign: KA4ZPT
David G Roberson
3550 Cameo Ln
Blacksburg VA 24060

Call Sign: W4DGR
David G Roberson
3550 Cameo Ln
Blacksburg VA 24060

Call Sign: N4QPH
Alan E Glick

2312 Capistrano St
Blacksburg VA 24060

Call Sign: KA8VRJ
Daniel W Arrington
2911 Cara Ct
Blacksburg VA 24060

Call Sign: KG4BGW
Thomas W Templeton
1503 Carlson Dr
Blacksburg VA 24060

Call Sign: KD4LQP
Bradley W Schilling
803 Cascade Ct
Blacksburg VA 24060

Call Sign: KD4VMK
Eric P Sivertson
822 Cascade Ct
Blacksburg VA 24060

Call Sign: K2PLL
Gary W Mason
1955 Cascades Rd
Blacksburg VA 24060

Call Sign: KI4OPK
Bradley S Absher
3829 Catawba Rd
Blacksburg VA 24060

Call Sign: KD4CUI
Richard Burns
130 Catnip Ln
Blacksburg VA 24060

Call Sign: KK4APR
Andrew S Kriz
509 Cedar Orchard Dr W
Blacksburg VA 24060

Call Sign: KE4FPK
Craig J Zolides
2835 Chelsea Ct
Blacksburg VA 24060

Call Sign: K4FCP

Richard J Beamish IV
712 Circle Dr
Blacksburg VA 24060

Call Sign: KJ4HRB
Frog Hollow ARC
712 Circle Dr
Blacksburg VA 24060

Call Sign: K4ZPA
Frog Hollow ARC
712 Circle Dr
Blacksburg VA 24060

Call Sign: K4BMS
Blacksburg Middle School ARC
712 Circle Dr
Blacksburg VA 24060

Call Sign: KG4ZYV
Richard J Beamish V
712 Circle Dr
Blacksburg VA 24060

Call Sign: K4ZYV
Richard J Beamish V
712 Circle Dr
Blacksburg VA 24060

Call Sign: KG4JRS
William N Gerig
886 Claytor S
Blacksburg VA 24060

Call Sign: KK4HVP
Charles C Blanchard
924 Conner Ln
Blacksburg VA 24060

Call Sign: KF7PLI
James V Clark III
13700 Copper Croft Run Apt E
Blacksburg VA 24060

Call Sign: KJ4LNG
John M Coggin
1056 Craig Creek Rd
Blacksburg VA 24060

Call Sign: KI4AWL
Noel Heiks
3291 Deer Run Rd
Blacksburg VA 24060

Call Sign: N1OYV
Donald J Braffitt
680 Deercroft Dr
Blacksburg VA 24060

Call Sign: KA4CSR
Vance E Miller
504 Dehart St
Blacksburg VA 24060

Call Sign: KK4BXF
David E Mellichamp
307 Dunton Dr
Blacksburg VA 24060

Call Sign: KD4OZF
Leslie R Mellichamp Jr
307 Dunton Dr SW
Blacksburg VA 24060

Call Sign: WA4SJT
Edward T Robinson
403 E Clay St
Blacksburg VA 24060

Call Sign: KJ4SYJ
Brian K Meadowcroft
201 Eakin St SE
Blacksburg VA 24060

Call Sign: N3SPG
Richard E Cobb
306 Eakin St SE
Blacksburg VA 24060

Call Sign: KI4KZW
David F Carroll
540 Edgewood Ln
Blacksburg VA 24060

Call Sign: KC4FNE
Robert P Schubert
906 Elliott Dr NE
Blacksburg VA 24060

Call Sign: KI4JPY
Thomas N Trump
1004 Emil Ct
Blacksburg VA 24060

Call Sign: KB4UOK
William D Miller
3575 Evergreen Trl
Blacksburg VA 24060

Call Sign: KF4SMI
Edward R Peltier
401 Fairfax Rd SE Apt 1433
Blacksburg VA 24060

Call Sign: KF4VCQ
Nathan A Croy
611 Fairview Ave
Blacksburg VA 24060

Call Sign: KF4CWM
Ward W Stevens III
1425 Falcon Ridge Rd
Blacksburg VA 24060

Call Sign: KJ4WSI
Thomas H Mills
205 Fincastle Dr
Blacksburg VA 24060

Call Sign: K4WEE
Thomas H Mills
205 Fincastle Dr
Blacksburg VA 24060

Call Sign: WX4RNK
Blacksburg Skywarn
1750 Forecast Dr
Blacksburg VA 24060

Call Sign: KK4GCW
Thomas W Weeks
4095 Fortress Dr
Blacksburg VA 24060

Call Sign: KF4UQQ
Eric P Lang
2700 Foxhunt Ln NW C

Blacksburg VA 24060

Call Sign: N4XQL
Kenneth W Meade Jr
7000L Foxridge
Blacksburg VA 24060

Call Sign: KC4WIC
James W La Pean Jr
800 J Foxridge Apts
Blacksburg VA 24060

Call Sign: KK4DKK
Samuel L Shiver
12300 Foxridge Ln NW Apt A
Blacksburg VA 24060

Call Sign: KA4FVW
Margaret L Bowen
417 Franklin Dr
Blacksburg VA 24060

Call Sign: KB3EBZ
Alexander B Miller
1229 Giles Rd
Blacksburg VA 24060

Call Sign: KJ4FWZ
Brandon J Lester
711 Giles Rd Apt 6
Blacksburg VA 24060

Call Sign: N4XWM
Jonathan L Dubovsky
212 Givens Ln
Blacksburg VA 24060

Call Sign: KE4JDE
Timothy C Towell
3109 Glade Rd
Blacksburg VA 24060

Call Sign: KA1RUD
William J Osborne
900 Glade Rd Apt 3
Blacksburg VA 240602656

Call Sign: N4TBD
Joe W Boling

2504 Gloucester Dr
Blacksburg VA 24060

Call Sign: AK4IS
Edward Lener
402 Grandview Dr
Blacksburg VA 24060

Call Sign: KG4HWN
Jeff M Lorrain
1832 1 Grayland St
Blacksburg VA 24060

Call Sign: KE4IMI
Ralph B Leland
1805 Grayland St Apt 2
Blacksburg VA 24060

Call Sign: KI4NHG
Leah M Potts
1901 Greenbrier Cir
Blacksburg VA 24060

Call Sign: K2UM
Gregory J Buhyoff
1302 Greendale Dr NW
Blacksburg VA 24060

Call Sign: N1SMM
Sharon D Davis
503 Hampton Ct
Blacksburg VA 24060

Call Sign: N4HY
Robert W Mc Gwier Jr
503 Hampton Ct
Blacksburg VA 24062

Call Sign: KJ4SYN
Joseph A Loferski
3230 Happy Hollow Rd
Blacksburg VA 24060

Call Sign: KG4LDW
Christopher S O Reilly
403 Hearthstone Dr
Blacksburg VA 24060

Call Sign: KA4BSA

Emily P Davis
406 Hearthstone Dr
Blacksburg VA 24060

Call Sign: KJ4DDS
Ravi M Mehra
4900 Heather Dr Apt J
Blacksburg VA 24060

Call Sign: N0XSU
Eric E Snyder
300 Hemlock Dr SE
Blacksburg VA 240605230

Call Sign: KF4BDT
Kostas C Giavis
750 Hethwood Blvd 1200 D
Blacksburg VA 24060

Call Sign: K4GWJ
Robert K Will
1104 Highland Cir
Blacksburg VA 24060

Call Sign: AG4KF
Denis Gracanin
1416 Highland Cir
Blacksburg VA 24060

Call Sign: KC4YFW
William Martin
1156 Hightop Rd Lot 65
Blacksburg VA 24060

Call Sign: KF4IZJ
Brett L Jackson
801 Horseshoe Ln
Blacksburg VA 24060

Call Sign: KB1QHL
Patrick A Cavanaugh
800 Houndschase Ln Apt A
Blacksburg VA 24060

Call Sign: KB3GTA
Brad M Smith
500 Houndschase Ln Apt E
Blacksburg VA 240604312

Call Sign: KI4WFD
Travis J Webb
410 Houston St Apt E
Blacksburg VA 24060

Call Sign: WD4EAR
Orville M Bragg
1170 Huff Ln
Blacksburg VA 24060

Call Sign: N2UX
Christopher L Mc Nabb
1338 Huff Ln
Blacksburg VA 24060

Call Sign: KG4VEU
Gaurav G Joshi
502 Hunt Club Rd 105
Blacksburg VA 24060

Call Sign: KG4OQS
Thurman S Deyerle IV
511 Hunt Club Rd 29C
Blacksburg VA 24060

Call Sign: KC4F
Bennie L Benton
101 Huntington Ln
Blacksburg VA 24060

Call Sign: KI4VME
Forest S Smith
121 Huntington Ln
Blacksburg VA 24060

Call Sign: WV4N
Stephen R Edwards
3409 Indian Meadow Dr
Blacksburg VA 24060

Call Sign: KJ4QLR
David A Henry
422 Janie Ln
Blacksburg VA 24060

Call Sign: KF4JFE
Shawn M Kekoa
439 Janie Ln
Blacksburg VA 24060

Call Sign: KI4MTG
Jerry W Gilley Jr
936 Jennelle Rd 8
Blacksburg VA 240600198

Call Sign: W4KEP
Charles W Bostian
1609 Kennedy St
Blacksburg VA 24060

Call Sign: KA4EPD
Michael H Harris
1902 Lacy Ln
Blacksburg VA 24060

Call Sign: KJ4VCX
Curren M Harris
1902 Lacy Ln
Blacksburg VA 24060

Call Sign: KF4VCT
Ralph D Badinelli
3385 Laurel Dr
Blacksburg VA 24060

Call Sign: KC4VMW
Jon E Fritsch
1904 Lindale Dr
Blacksburg VA 24060

Call Sign: N3MDG
Michael D Gale
502 Lucas Dr
Blacksburg VA 24060

Call Sign: KI4FOZ
Mark G Hounshell
1651 Lusters Gate Rd
Blacksburg VA 24060

Call Sign: KF4NVE
Andrew E Harper
2508 Manchester St
Blacksburg VA 24060

Call Sign: KB4GIW
Bruce B Harper
2508 Manchester St

Blacksburg VA 240608225

Call Sign: KD4YPL
Joseph G Falls
206 Maywood St
Blacksburg VA 24060

Call Sign: KE4TIR
Barbara H Falls
206 Maywood St
Blacksburg VA 24060

Call Sign: WA4NDH
Patricia A Baker
209 Maywood St
Blacksburg VA 24060

Call Sign: WB4WNI
Joseph A Baker
209 Maywood St
Blacksburg VA 24060

Call Sign: KS4XO
Richard W Armstrong Jr
908 McBryde Dr
Blacksburg VA 24060

Call Sign: KE4GIU
Maximilian Schuetz
933 McBryde Ln
Blacksburg VA 24060

Call Sign: K8TQS
Lindsay Coleman
612 McConkey St
Blacksburg VA 24060

Call Sign: KJ4BBJ
Dallas D Mcpeak
5800 McCoy Rd
Blacksburg VA 24060

Call Sign: KE4PIH
Mark H Salmon
1604 Meadowbrook Dr
Blacksburg VA 24060

Call Sign: KI4LJK
Leland S Williams

3510 Meadowbrook Dr
Blacksburg VA 24060

Call Sign: KI4PCC
Sarah J Hash
3510 Meadowbrook Dr
Blacksburg VA 24060

Call Sign: KF4YKF
George W Ratcliff
330 Merrimac Rd
Blacksburg VA 24060

Call Sign: KF4VNX
Stacy D Amburgey Sr
330 Merrimac Rd 95
Blacksburg VA 24060

Call Sign: WA4OFP
Mark W Sumner
2885 Mill Wood Ln
Blacksburg VA 24060

Call Sign: WA4JON
Henry S Pittard Jr
603 Montgomery
Blacksburg VA 24060

Call Sign: KD4QDL
Eric A Oicscn
610 Montgomery St
Blacksburg VA 24060

Call Sign: KB2FZO
David A Wert
1101 Mourning Dove Dr
Blacksburg VA 24060

Call Sign: KK4BWM
Michael S Lafon II
1613 Mt Tabor Rd
Blacksburg VA 24060

Call Sign: KI4AQJ
Rick W Fenrich
2344 Mt Tabor Rd
Blacksburg VA 24060

Call Sign: KG4MYW

Robert A Vaden
3904 Mt Tabor Rd
Blacksburg VA 24060

Call Sign: K4IUV
Donald A Prater
3120 Mt Tabor Rd
Blacksburg VA 24060

Call Sign: WA4SGX
Charlie W Smith
3702 Mt Zion Rd
Blacksburg VA 24060

Call Sign: KJ4OAP
Kevin T Sterne
200 N Knollwood Dr
Blacksburg VA 24060

Call Sign: W2NAF
Nathaniel A Frissell
1412 N Main St
Blacksburg VA 24060

Call Sign: KI4RIX
Michael J Benonis
1412 N Main St
Blacksburg VA 240602522

Call Sign: KI4TEQ
Phuriphat Dejsuphong
125 N Main St 255
Blacksburg VA 24060

Call Sign: KJ4PLG
Karen M Scott
315 New Kent Rd
Blacksburg VA 24060

Call Sign: KS4VPI
Karen M Scott
315 New Kent Rd
Blacksburg VA 24060

Call Sign: KB5SOY
Glenda S Von Dameck
2022 Northside Dr
Blacksburg VA 24060

Call Sign: K4GVD
Glenda S Von Dameck
2022 Northside Dr
Blacksburg VA 24060

Call Sign: KJ4SYK
Evan G Thomas
1734 October Glory Ct
Blacksburg VA 24060

Call Sign: KF4NLM
Craig A Ferguson
1518 Oriole Dr
Blacksburg VA 24060

Call Sign: KG4NIP
Katherine Ferguson
1518 Oriole Dr
Blacksburg VA 24060

Call Sign: KD4ZB
Henry B Henderson Jr
400 Owens St
Blacksburg VA 24060

Call Sign: KB4RKC
Greer W Elliott
304 Patrick Henry Dr
Blacksburg VA 24060

Call Sign: KJ4DES
Qian Liu
868 Patrick Henry Dr
Blacksburg VA 24060

Call Sign: KG4GLY
Carl W Craddock
1602 Patrick Henry Dr 103
Blacksburg VA 24060

Call Sign: WD4OVD
William L Conger
202 Pearman Rd
Blacksburg VA 24060

Call Sign: KI4JJN
Steven W Ellingson
4309 Pearman Rd
Blacksburg VA 24060

Call Sign: KI4KHR
Colin D Ellingson
4309 Pearman Rd
Blacksburg VA 24060

Call Sign: KI4UVB
Nathan J Ellingson
4309 Pearman Rd
Blacksburg VA 24060

Call Sign: KC4WXB
Bradley J Sullivan
604 Piedmont St
Blacksburg VA 24060

Call Sign: KE4FBR
Debora J Sullivan
604 Piedmont St
Blacksburg VA 24060

Call Sign: KI4PBY
S M S Hasan
303 Piedmont St Apt 8
Blacksburg VA 24060

Call Sign: KJ4QLQ
Jackson M Newton
4911 Preston Forest Dr
Blacksburg VA 24060

Call Sign: KD4VYM
Winston D Hawkins
211 Price St
Blacksburg VA 24060

Call Sign: K3ZT
Winston D Hawkins
211 Price St
Blacksburg VA 24060

Call Sign: K4VG
Winston D Hawkins
211 Price St
Blacksburg VA 24060

Call Sign: KI4GNE
Three Dog Repeater Group
4267 Prices Fork Rd

Blacksburg VA 24060

Call Sign: KC4Q
Michael N Knight
4267 Prices Fork Rd
Blacksburg VA 24060

Call Sign: KG4SLR
New River Wireless Association
4267 Prices Fork Rd
Blacksburg VA 24060

Call Sign: K4NRW
New River Wireless Association
4267 Prices Fork Rd
Blacksburg VA 24060

Call Sign: K4IJ
Michael N Knight
4267 Prices Fork Rd
Blacksburg VA 24060

Call Sign: KD4JEI
Kevin A Speed
702 Progress St Apt 3
Blacksburg VA 24060

Call Sign: KJ4DDQ
Paul H Masur
1207 Progress St NW Apt
7300A
Blacksburg VA 24060

Call Sign: KB8LNO
Keith W Holt
4530 Rhea Ridge Dr
Blacksburg VA 24060

Call Sign: KK4BWP
Kathryn A Prociv
3700 Richmond Ln Apt L
Blacksburg VA 24060

Call Sign: KK4BWS
Paul L Toffenetti
410 Ridgeview Dr
Blacksburg VA 24060

Call Sign: W4WYT

Ranson J Pelt Jr
310 Rucker Rd
Blacksburg VA 24060

Call Sign: KF4VCP
Theodore L Ellmore
805 S Main St
Blacksburg VA 24060

Call Sign: NB4P
Theodore L Ellmore
805 S Main St
Blacksburg VA 24060

Call Sign: KK4EDI
Alexandru Turcu
1100 S Main St Apt 3
Blacksburg VA 24060

Call Sign: KB4DOG
Kara M Baumann
308 Seminole Dr
Blacksburg VA 24060

Call Sign: KF4RGF
William T Baumann
308 Seminole Dr
Blacksburg VA 24060

Call Sign: KF4VCR
William P Baumann
308 Seminole Dr
Blacksburg VA 24060

Call Sign: KE4NFE
Dong S Ha
407 Seminole Dr
Blacksburg VA 24060

Call Sign: NI1N
Thomas J Mc Alee Jr
4242 Shady Grove Ln
Blacksburg VA 24060

Call Sign: KJ4OAQ
John M Oliver
1902 Shelor Ln
Blacksburg VA 24060

Call Sign: KJ4PMT
Christopher G Evans
1206 Snyder Ln Apt 1800E
Blacksburg VA 24060

Call Sign: KI4PJI
Richard C Furr
708 Southgate Dr
Blacksburg VA 24060

Call Sign: KQ4JG
George B Garrott
207 Spickard St
Blacksburg VA 24060

Call Sign: W4PZW
George B Garrott
207 Spickard St
Blacksburg VA 24060

Call Sign: K4KDJ
VA Tech ARA
347 Squires Student Center
Blacksburg VA 24061

Call Sign: KJ4JRB
John M Mcintosh
14506 Stroubles Creek
Blacksburg VA 24060

Call Sign: WD8NKA
Brian G Burgess
14408 Stroubles Creek Rd
Blacksburg VA 24060

Call Sign: KG4TPR
Daniel B Burgess
14408 Stroubles Creek Rd
Blacksburg VA 24060

Call Sign: KB2SVG
Edmund A Holohan III
14607 Stroubles Creek Rd
Blacksburg VA 24060

Call Sign: KI4NYS
Ashton R Snelgrove
316 1 Sunset Blvd
Blacksburg VA 24060

Call Sign: KI4RTD
Nolan J Snelgrove
316 Sunset Blvd 1
Blacksburg VA 24060

Call Sign: WB2PVF
Dale M Pokorski
680 Sunshine Farm Ln
Blacksburg VA 240608900

Call Sign: KG4ZEV
Wesley R Ferrell
1297 Sweeny Rd
Blacksburg VA 24060

Call Sign: KG4YVM
Angela M Dautartas
2006 Sycamore Trl
Blacksburg VA 24060

Call Sign: KA1WXI
Zachary J Bortolot
209 Tee St 8
Blacksburg VA 24060

Call Sign: KI4NYT
Andrew J Mike
209 Tee St Apt 10
Blacksburg VA 24060

Call Sign: KF4BDV
Jin Xu
Terrace View 800A
Blacksburg VA 24060

Call Sign: KD4LQU
Jyothikumar Jagannathan
1200C Terrace View Apts
Blacksburg VA 24060

Call Sign: KF4BDW
Jonathan P Martin
1215 Thomas Ln
Blacksburg VA 24060

Call Sign: KF4PSI
Ronnie W Kitts
1295 Thomas Ln

Blacksburg VA 24060

Call Sign: KU4AG
Kenneth W Lewis
701 Toms Creek Rd
Blacksburg VA 24060

Call Sign: K4DCP
Eldridge E Rowe Sr
901 Toms Creek Rd
Blacksburg VA 24060

Call Sign: N8IRZ
Emily H Lewis
701 Tows Creek Rd
Blacksburg VA 24060

Call Sign: KJ4SYH
Thomas C Bond
3242 Tucker Rd
Blacksburg VA 24060

Call Sign: KG4KCN
Mark H Eisenbies
501 Turner St
Blacksburg VA 24060

Call Sign: KJ4SYI
Patrick V Butler
306 Turner St NE
Blacksburg VA 24060

Call Sign: KG4FKI
David J Roesler
913 University Blvd Apt B 13
Blacksburg VA 24060

Call Sign: KK4EAB
Matthew T Via
917 University Blvd Apt D7
Blacksburg VA 24060

Call Sign: KJ4FGC
Bin Li
1214 University City Blvd Apt 95
Blacksburg VA 24060

Call Sign: KG4MKO

Maneesh Soni
1009 University City Blvd Apt
H 13
Blacksburg VA 24060

Call Sign: KK4EAA
Brian W Roper
1221 University City Blvd Apt
U207
Blacksburg VA 24060

Call Sign: KJ4WKZ
Kyung Eun Yoon
1216 University City Blvd C31
Blacksburg VA 24060

Call Sign: KJ4WKY
Soonkie Nam
1216 University City Blvd C31
Blacksburg VA 24060

Call Sign: WB4ONS
David A Danello
1210 University City Blvd J 118
Blacksburg VA 24060

Call Sign: KE4IMK
Steven M Henry
1207L University Ter
Blacksburg VA 24060

Call Sign: KE4IML
Jeffrey A Gaston
1207L University Ter
Blacksburg VA 24060

Call Sign: KE4IMM
Robert S Vachalek
1207L University Ter
Blacksburg VA 24060

Call Sign: KJ4LNC
Benjamin T Rice
1208 D University Ter
Blacksburg VA 24060

Call Sign: KK4DZY
Bharat Kunduri
1209 University Ter Apt G

Blacksburg VA 24060

Call Sign: KB4EMZ
Miguel A Despian Jr
University Village 22
Blacksburg VA 24060

Call Sign: KD4DPX
John D Nichols
303 Upland Rd
Blacksburg VA 24060

Call Sign: KD4DPY
Michael A Nichols
303 Upland Rd
Blacksburg VA 24060

Call Sign: KE4YNS
Melanie J Adkins
1872 Wake Forest Rd
Blacksburg VA 24060

Call Sign: N3GAI
Elizabeth A Chisholm
703 Washington St Apt 4
Blacksburg VA 24060

Call Sign: KG4GLX
Stephen D Lepera
105 B Watson
Blacksburg VA 24060

Call Sign: K8HI
George W Gorsline Jr
624 Watson Ln NW
Blacksburg VA 24060

Call Sign: KF4NVC
James M Davis
307 K Webb St
Blacksburg VA 24060

Call Sign: KE4ZQA
Robert A Simonds
2540 Welcome Rd
Blacksburg VA 24060

Call Sign: KD4OXM
Elizabeth B Strader Sweeney

1206 Westover Dr
Blacksburg VA 24060

Call Sign: WA4LPR
Dennis G Sweeney
1206 Westover Dr
Blacksburg VA 24060

Call Sign: KJ4NDZ
Maribeth B Coluni
1305 Westover Dr
Blacksburg VA 24060

Call Sign: W4MSD
Robert E Tatum
1401 Westover Dr NW
Blacksburg VA 24060

Call Sign: KE4IMH
Arief B Suharko
1711 Whipple Dr 16
Blacksburg VA 24060

Call Sign: KJ4BKW
Claudio Da Silva
302 Whittemore 0111
Blacksburg VA 24061

Call Sign: KB5YY
Theodore C Von Dameck
414 Wildflower Ln NW
Blacksburg VA 24060

Call Sign: KG4FPC
Brian D Ekey
206 Wilson Ave
Blacksburg VA 24060

Call Sign: KJ4OOE
David W Rettig
302 Woodbine Dr
Blacksburg VA 240601442

Call Sign: KE4GVG
Alvin P Schmitt
312 Woodbine Dr
Blacksburg VA 24060

Call Sign: KJ4WTC

Jan Helge Bohn
2360 Woodland Hills Dr
Blacksburg VA 24060

Call Sign: KD4CIY
William O Plymale
110 Yorkshire Ct
Blacksburg VA 24060

Call Sign: KE4TIU
Vicki J Plymale
110 Yorkshire Ct
Blacksburg VA 24060

Call Sign: K4EP
Philip J Balister
Blacksburg VA 24062

Call Sign: KE4FPN
Joseph T Reid
Blacksburg VA 24062

Call Sign: N3PB
Phillip E Benchoff
Blacksburg VA 24062

Call Sign: W4LVS
Elvis Grotto RC
Blacksburg VA 24062

Call Sign: KE4GTS
Lyle M Evans
Blacksburg VA 24063

Call Sign: N4UOY
Robert S Smith
Blacksburg VA 24063

Call Sign: KA8UDZ
Bruce E Kemp
Blacksburg VA 24062

Call Sign: N8ZIK
Michael R Fleming
Blacksburg VA 24062

Call Sign: W4IQ
Randall Nealy
Blacksburg VA 24062

Call Sign: KE4TIS
Laine V Buckwalter
Blacksburg VA 24063

Call Sign: KF4LLU
Sandra M Knapp
Blacksburg VA 24063

Call Sign: KF4VNY
Steven Q Croy
Blacksburg VA 24063

Call Sign: KJ4EIT
Richard B Tilley
Blacksburg VA 24063

Call Sign: N6QDO
James W Marchant
Blacksburg VA 240620995

Call Sign: KG4OOM
Christian W Hearn
Blacksburg VA 240621251

Call Sign: WB6CWE
Karl R Precoda
Blacksburg VA 240630650

Call Sign: K4TRT
Karl R Precoda
Blacksburg VA 240630650

FCC Amateur Radio Licenses in Blackstone

Call Sign: KE4PWG
Jonathan M Matthews
407 2nd St
Blackstone VA 23824

Call Sign: N4OQD
Alan R Dyck
Rt 2 Box 209 E
Blackstone VA 23824

Call Sign: KE4WZJ
John M Kundman
1472 Cox Rd

Blackstone VA 23824

Call Sign: K4BKT
Richard G Patterson Jr
2036 Cox Rd
Blackstone VA 238243016

Call Sign: KG4TMQ
Carroll L Rion
204 Forest Dr
Blackstone VA 23824

Call Sign: KF4NEA
Robert W Price
720 N Main St
Blackstone VA 23824

Call Sign: KI4GEL
Scott C Matthew
3275 The Grove Rd
Blackstone VA 23824

Call Sign: KA4DAU
David C Matthew
3275 The Grove Rd
Blackstone VA 238243927

Call Sign: KF4JKD
Delilah M Matthew
3275 The Grove Rd
Blackstone VA 238243927

Call Sign: KG4NFW
Richard G Patterson Jr
2115 Yellowbird Rd
Blackstone VA 238244355

Call Sign: KG4NFX
Elizabeth M Patterson
2115 Yellowbird Rd
Blackstone VA 238244355

Call Sign: K4ENP
Elizabeth M Patterson
2115 Yellowbird Rd
Blackstone VA 238244355

Call Sign: KE4VOQ
Nicholas Ballano

Blackstone VA 23824

**FCC Amateur Radio Licenses
in Blairs**

Call Sign: KB4FLY
James W Hicks
Rt 1 Box 250H
Blairs VA 24527

Call Sign: KE4DJQ
John W Mc Call Sr
2007 Dale Dr
Blairs VA 24527

Call Sign: K4DJQ
John W Mc Call Sr
2007 Dale Dr
Blairs VA 24527

Call Sign: KD4SSE
Edward E Caviness Jr
326 Deerwood Dr
Blairs VA 24527

Call Sign: W4PGY
Edward E Rash
248 Woodcreek Pl
Blairs VA 24527

Call Sign: K4HUD
Austin E Jones Jr
Blairs VA 24527

Call Sign: KS4OU
Lyle C Motley
Blairs VA 24527

**FCC Amateur Radio Licenses
in Bland**

Call Sign: KE4TIY
Ina K Miller
Rt 1 Box 164
Bland VA 24315

Call Sign: KF4JBS
Larry H Stowers
Rt 1 Box 244

Bland VA 24315

Call Sign: KD4JWK
Loay D Ball
Rr 1 Box 34 1B
Bland VA 24315

Call Sign: KD4IFE
Gay N Riddle
Rt 2 Box 458
Bland VA 24315

Call Sign: KD4IYJ
George T Riddle
Rt 2 Box 458
Bland VA 24315

Call Sign: KI4TYM
Randolph B Townley II
11077 E Blue Grass Trl
Bland VA 24315

Call Sign: N4AZJ
Thomas E Mallory Jr
1732 Main St
Bland VA 24315

Call Sign: KD4JOH
Robert H Sadler
126 Valley View Ln Rr 1 Box
257 D
Bland VA 24315

Call Sign: KI4AZB
Cecil W Nelson
770 Walkerscreek Rd
Bland VA 24315

Call Sign: K4AEX
Cecil W Nelson
770 Walkerscreek Rd
Bland VA 24315

Call Sign: KD4VYN
Betty M Ball
Bland VA 24315

Call Sign: KE4LYJ
Harold W Ramsey

Bland VA 24315

Call Sign: N4LVH
James B Walls
Bland VA 24315

**FCC Amateur Radio Licenses
in Bloxom**

Call Sign: KK4EYM
Robin A Armstrong
24087 Anns Cove Rd
Bloxom VA 23308

Call Sign: KJ4COV
Wayne H Lewis
14600 Bethel Church Rd
Bloxom VA 23308

Call Sign: KI4UGU
Jacqueline C Henshaw-
Anderson
15095 Bethel Church Rd
Bloxom VA 23308

Call Sign: KI4JSL
Matthew Anderson
15095 Bethel Church Rd
Bloxom VA 23308

Call Sign: KD4NFI
Robert J Reynolds
17373 Big Rd
Bloxom VA 23308

Call Sign: KD4NVF
Jonathan I Barrett
25316 Lewis Dr
Bloxom VA 23308

Call Sign: KE4AKR
Patricia L Brough
26491 Mason Rd
Bloxom VA 23308

**FCC Amateur Radio Licenses
in Blue Ridge**

Call Sign: KF4CRA

Thomas E Smith
1496 Archway Rd
Blue Ridge VA 24064

Call Sign: KI4CJD
Gerald L Mclouth
1441 Audrey Ln
Blue Ridge VA 24064

Call Sign: WA6CRA
Phillip A Wilson Jr
1355 Big Otter Dr
Blue Ridge VA 240643084

Call Sign: K6CRA
Phillip A Wilson Jr
1355 Big Otter Dr
Blue Ridge VA 240643084

Call Sign: KA3NIR
Roy E Heinlen Jr
5488 Blue Ridge Blvd
Blue Ridge VA 24064

Call Sign: W8PJB
Roy E Heinlen Jr
517 Blue Ridge Dr
Blue Ridge VA 24064

Call Sign: KJ4PHQ
Brandon M Kincer
3835 Blueridge Blvd
Blue Ridge VA 24064

Call Sign: K4HGJ
Edward W Clark Jr
5426 Bore Auger Rd
Blue Ridge VA 24064

Call Sign: KC4CIB
Robert W Wilson
Rt 1 Box 672
Blue Ridge VA 24064

Call Sign: KC4NBC
Jayson T Firebaugh
74 Chesney Pl
Blue Ridge VA 24064

Call Sign: KG4TDI
Laurie A Beiswenger
58 Foxcroft Ln
Blue Ridge VA 24064

Call Sign: AI4AP
Laurie A Beiswenger
58 Foxcroft Ln
Blue Ridge VA 24064

Call Sign: WD4BHL
Earl M Frazier
86 Makayla Dr
Blue Ridge VA 24064

Call Sign: KG4LLU
James V Bradshaw
1875 Mtn View Church Rd
Blue Ridge VA 24064

Call Sign: KG4LLV
Amy T Bradshaw
1875 Mtn View Church Rd
Blue Ridge VA 24064

Call Sign: WC4A
Mary A Waddell
233 Oak Dr
Blue Ridge VA 24064

Call Sign: WA4V
Jack H Waddell
233 Oak Dr
Blue Ridge VA 24064

Call Sign: W4DRR
Robert A Grevillius
376 Poplar Dr
Blue Ridge VA 24064

Call Sign: KJ4PZX
Christopher D Bateson
436 Scalybark Dr
Blue Ridge VA 24064

Call Sign: KC4WMK
Glen M Johnson
160 Silverbirch Dr
Blue Ridge VA 24064

Call Sign: KC4WMI
David R Schroeder
1118 Tomahawk Ln
Blue Ridge VA 240643609

Call Sign: KF4WWY
David K Deel
2836 Webster Rd
Blue Ridge VA 240641916

Call Sign: WA4YHA
Norman A Jones
55 Willow Cir
Blue Ridge VA 24064

Call Sign: KC2GLL
Edward J Zaleski
406 Woodlawn Ave
Blue Ridge VA 24064

Call Sign: KB4NNE
David E Frame
645 Woodlawn Ave
Blue Ridge VA 24064

Call Sign: N4LVQ
Steve L Hurt
1695 Wooldridge Rd
Bluc Ridge VA 24064

Call Sign: KA4QYN
Emerson N Lamb
Blue Ridge VA 24064

Call Sign: KC4VAY
Keith A Freeman
Blue Ridge VA 24064

Call Sign: KI4RVW
Aimee Stultz
Blue Ridge VA 24064

Call Sign: KI4LAW
Darian G Stultz
Blue Ridge VA 24064

Call Sign: KI4MPR
Diane L Stultz

Blue Ridge VA 24064

Call Sign: K1QIJ
Daniel D Davison
Blue Ridge VA 24077

FCC Amateur Radio Licenses in Bluefield

Call Sign: K8HZM
Albert J Allen
105 Allendale St
Bluefield VA 24605

Call Sign: KI4DZV
William P Sherman
457 Andrea Ln
Bluefield VA 24605

Call Sign: KD4LNE
Betsy A Breedlove
118 Arizona Dr
Bluefield VA 24605

Call Sign: KD4LNF
Jerry A Breedlove
118 Arizona Dr
Bluefield VA 246058913

Call Sign: KI4NWV
Keith Akers
387 Ashworth Ln
Bluefield VA 24605

Call Sign: KI4DZR
Richard L Bryant
276 Big Branch Rd
Bluefield VA 24605

Call Sign: KE4IVD
Douglas M Mitchem Jr
1323 Big Branch Rd
Bluefield VA 24605

Call Sign: KD4IFC
Sheila B Mc Carty
1764 Big Branch Rd
Bluefield VA 24605

Call Sign: KD4IFD
Dale A Mc Carty
1764 Big Branch Rd
Bluefield VA 24605

Call Sign: KA4YDN
Donald R Harris
630 Blue Jay Ln
Bluefield VA 24605

Call Sign: KG4AYM
Patricia A Dietrich
Rr 2 Box 212
Bluefield VA 24605

Call Sign: KF4YGL
George W Dietrich
Rt 2 Box 212
Bluefield VA 24605

Call Sign: KE4LBV
Donna G Roten
Rt 2 Box 272D
Bluefield VA 24605

Call Sign: KE4CWX
Betty H Chambers
Rt 2 Box 294
Bluefield VA 24605

Call Sign: KF4GWZ
Christopher A Porshia
Rt 2 Box 366 B
Bluefield VA 24605

Call Sign: KG4MCC
David B Cox
Rt 2 Box 367 M
Bluefield VA 24605

Call Sign: KD4JVU
Richard A Hancock Jr
Rt 3 Box 374
Bluefield VA 24605

Call Sign: WA4DFD
James F Safewright Jr
Rt 1 Box 394A
Bluefield VA 24605

Call Sign: KE4IVE
Robert E Matney
Rt 1 Box 469
Bluefield VA 24605

Call Sign: KD4MSO
Ronald L Bennett
406 Calvin St
Bluefield VA 24605

Call Sign: KD4ARO
Debra J Stacy
322 Circle Dr
Bluefield VA 24605

Call Sign: KI4URO
Brian S Leedy
331 Circle Dr
Bluefield VA 24605

Call Sign: KG4UQT
Charles E Presley
40 College Dr
Bluefield VA 24605

Call Sign: N4ZCB
David A Brooks
105 East St
Bluefield VA 24605

Call Sign: KA4CGP
Lewis C Hartsock
102 Edgewood Rd
Bluefield VA 24605

Call Sign: KD4ARY
Doug R Hash
302 Edgewood Rd
Bluefield VA 24605

Call Sign: N8OMA
Mark D Turner
305 Edgewood Rd
Bluefield VA 24605

Call Sign: WD4DZS
Johnnie E Turner
316 Edgewood Rd

Bluefield VA 24605

Call Sign: KD4ARW
David A Wohlford
631 Fairway St
Bluefield VA 24605

Call Sign: WD4HTI
Thurman W Williams
107 Fincastle Ln
Bluefield VA 24605

Call Sign: KD4ZUA
George E Fisher III
213 Fincastle Ln
Bluefield VA 246059696

Call Sign: KF4PCC
George E Fisher IV
213 Fincastle Ln
Bluefield VA 246059696

Call Sign: KF4YBU
VA K Fisher
213 Fincastle Ln
Bluefield VA 246059696

Call Sign: W4OF
George E Fisher III
213 Fincastle Ln
Bluefield VA 246059696

Call Sign: KC4GIT
David W Brewster
214 Fincastle Ln
Bluefield VA 24605

Call Sign: KC4GIV
Tresha F Brewster
214 Fincastle Ln
Bluefield VA 24605

Call Sign: KD4ART
John H Hawkins
302 Fincastle Ln
Bluefield VA 24605

Call Sign: WM8M
James S Leedy

1014 Greever Ave
Bluefield VA 24605

Call Sign: KI4DZP
Larry E Carbaugh
112 Highland Ave
Bluefield VA 24605

Call Sign: WD4EVS
Albert K Ruble
218 Highland Ave
Bluefield VA 24605

Call Sign: N4ZMB
Reece W Nienstadt
100 Hillcrest Dr
Bluefield VA 24605

Call Sign: KD4MJT
Brenda C Scott
303 Hockman Pike
Bluefield VA 24605

Call Sign: N4QQM
George R Scott
303 Hockman Pike
Bluefield VA 24605

Call Sign: KD4ARQ
Larry W Lambert
2024 Lee Ave
Bluefield VA 24605

Call Sign: KF4NYB
Kenneth E Boone
211 Logan St
Bluefield VA 24605

Call Sign: KC4CAE
Deborah A Hash
212 Long St
Bluefield VA 24605

Call Sign: WB4BBF
Larry R Hash
212 Long St
Bluefield VA 24605

Call Sign: KJ4YTR

Bruce A Puckett
112 Meadow Ln
Bluefield VA 24605

Call Sign: KE4MFM
Timothy G Honaker
405 Mtn Ln
Bluefield VA 24605

Call Sign: KJ4BXS
George D Leedy
1002 Mtn Ln
Bluefield VA 24605

Call Sign: KI4EPR
Johnny T Matusevich Jr
401 Mtn View Dr
Bluefield VA 24605

Call Sign: KI4SZA
Roger E Nesselrodt
4667 Mud Fork Rd
Bluefield VA 24605

Call Sign: KG4AUJ
Edward B Chafin Jr
160 Murphy Ave
Bluefield VA 24605

Call Sign: KD4WOQ
Joseph W Akers
112 Reynolds Ave
Bluefield VA 24605

Call Sign: KE4RYG
Patricia M Akers
112 Reynolds Ave
Bluefield VA 24605

Call Sign: N4DBC
David B Cox
173 Ridgecrest St
Bluefield VA 24605

Call Sign: KQ4Q
Mark L Williams
410 Ridgeway Dr
Bluefield VA 246051630

Call Sign: W4VT
Donald L Williams Jr
412 Ridgeway Dr
Bluefield VA 246051630

Call Sign: KA8AWS
Robert L Rounion
307 Riverview Dr
Bluefield VA 24605

Call Sign: N4NRF
Bill Mays
612 Robin St
Bluefield VA 24605

Call Sign: KA8DRY
Vona L Arbogast
618 Robin St
Bluefield VA 246059416

Call Sign: KA8DSQ
Derek D Arbogast
618 Robin St
Bluefield VA 246059416

Call Sign: KD4IFF
Ronald J Chambers
433 Ruble Hill Rd
Bluefield VA 24605

Call Sign: KG4CTJ
Danny J Neely
631 Sedgewren
Bluefield VA 24605

Call Sign: KD4ARP
Gregg J Parris
670 Summit St
Bluefield VA 24605

Call Sign: N4ZES
Buddy E Melvin
1911 Tazewell Ave
Bluefield VA 24605

Call Sign: KD4WOM
Kimber A Hayes
1938 Tazewell Ave
Bluefield VA 24605

Call Sign: N4KAE
Gary L Dalton
229 VA Ave
Bluefield VA 24605

Call Sign: WB4KUO
James B Hayes Sr
2039 VA Ave
Bluefield VA 24605

Call Sign: KD4ZTV
Bill N Shotto
2041 VA Ave
Bluefield VA 24605

Call Sign: KD4ARU
Richard H French
2088 VA Ave
Bluefield VA 24605

Call Sign: KE4HQD
John J West
2019 VA Hgts Dr Ap 2B
Bluefield VA 24605

Call Sign: KF4KNX
Debra A Hornbarger
101 View Ct
Bluefield VA 24605

Call Sign: KI4DZO
Charles J Carbaugh
Bluefield VA 24605

Call Sign: W4DZO
Charles J Carbaugh
Bluefield VA 24605

FCC Amateur Radio Licenses in Bluemont

Call Sign: KG4YQP
James E Holdeman
33900 Austin Grove Rd
Bluemont VA 20135

Call Sign: WA3NDO
Henry L Ciotti

413 Barker Ln
Bluemont VA 20135

Call Sign: W3NDO
Henry L Ciotti
413 Barker Ln
Bluemont VA 20135

Call Sign: W3DIY
Henry L Ciotti
413 Barker Ln
Bluemont VA 20135

Call Sign: K5YDR
Stanley R Marks II
19575 Blueridge Mtn Rd
Bluemont VA 20135

Call Sign: N8NCC
Ann Marie Macionski
Rt 2 Box 255G
Bluemont VA 22012

Call Sign: KR4ZE
Ken E Haltenhoff
Rt 1 Box 300
Bluemont VA 22012

Call Sign: KC4BOL
Randolph W Cabell
Rt 1 Box 448A
Bluemont VA 22012

Call Sign: N3TXJ
Robert R Lines
138 Cedar Ln
Bluemont VA 20135

Call Sign: KK4BWU
Daniel W Youngstrom
19261 Foggy Bottom Rd
Bluemont VA 20135

Call Sign: KB4YMF
Leslie M Rinehart
479 Hemlock Ln
Bluemont VA 20135

Call Sign: KA8BHN

Edward M Leonard Sr
32638 Mt Weather Rd
Bluemont VA 20135

Call Sign: N4OHE
Craig W Saverine
32700 Mt Weather Rd
Bluemont VA 20135

Call Sign: KE4GSX
Tyler K Schefter
179 Pine Grove Rd
Bluemont VA 20135

Call Sign: KA2TPK
Peter T Harding
136 Poston Ln
Bluemont VA 20135

Call Sign: KM4RM
William V Perry Sr
17429 Raven Rocks Rd
Bluemont VA 20135

Call Sign: W4AAU
Anthony K Carbone
17534 Raven Rocks Rd
Bluemont VA 20135

Call Sign: N4KQH
Roger W Rinehart
456 Redbud Ln
Bluemont VA 20135

Call Sign: W4YQ
Robert F Johnson Sr
19606 Ridgeside Rd
Bluemont VA 20135

Call Sign: W4YZ
William L Johnson
19606 Ridgeside Rd
Bluemont VA 20135

Call Sign: KJ4SYL
Kevin P Burns
524 River Park Ln
Bluemont VA 20135

Call Sign: WA4EJH
Vernon O Mann
3295 River Rd
Bluemont VA 201359512

Call Sign: KB3MIY
Andrew R Hower
Bluemont VA 20135

Call Sign: KG4WHP
Joseph A Hewlett
Bluemont VA 20135

Call Sign: KJ4WRI
Robert D Barnhill
Bluemont VA 20135

Call Sign: WA3URA
Jerald M Peterson
Bluemont VA 201350223

FCC Amateur Radio Licenses in Bohannon

Call Sign: KJ4TJL
David N Montgomery
163 Mill Rd
Bohannon VA 23021

FCC Amateur Radio Licenses in Boissevain

Call Sign: WB4ZNA
Paul E Baker
Boissevain VA 24606

FCC Amateur Radio Licenses in Bon Air

Call Sign: KG4QIU
Evan L Davies Jr
1023 Buford Rd
Bon Air VA 23235

Call Sign: KD4YVP
Margaret A Norman
10008 Old Bon Air Pl
Bon Air VA 23235

Call Sign: KA4MDB
Thomas S Adkins
8425 W Bon View Dr
Bon Air VA 23235

FCC Amateur Radio Licenses in Boones Mill

Call Sign: KC4WMH
Michael D Bishop Jr
6351 Back Creek Rd
Boones Mill VA 24065

Call Sign: KE4EAA
Paul H Daneils
2455 Bethany Rd
Boones Mill VA 24065

Call Sign: KF4BGE
Dina G Daniels
2455 Bethany Rd
Boones Mill VA 24065

Call Sign: W4ZSM
Michael F Kavanaugh
8261 Boones Chapel Rd
Boones Mill VA 24065

Call Sign: N4AVY
Robert N Harden
870 Boones Mill Rd
Boones Mill VA 24065

Call Sign: KB4SNK
Robbie J Leffue
Rt 2 Box 140 B
Boones Mill VA 24065

Call Sign: KC4VJC
Doug K Finnigan
Rt 3 Box 1867
Boones Mill VA 24065

Call Sign: KC4YAJ
Roger L Clark
Rt 1 Box 522
Boones Mill VA 24065

Call Sign: KC4KQK

Michael T Mc Guire
Rt 3 Box 750
Boones Mill VA 24065

Call Sign: AD4AV
Carlos W Garrett
370 Cahas Ln
Boones Mill VA 24065

Call Sign: KF4PHW
Michael W Hevener
240 Crestridge Dr
Boones Mill VA 24065

Call Sign: WB4OXM
James R Davidson III
7225 Franklin Rd
Boones Mill VA 24065

Call Sign: KG4WDV
Robert A House
7439 Franklin Rd
Boones Mill VA 24065

Call Sign: KG4GBZ
Daniel E Vaught
1729 Green Level Rd
Boones Mill VA 24065

Call Sign: K4DEV
Daniel E Vaught
1729 Green Level Rd
Boones Mill VA 24065

Call Sign: K1WAK
William A Keller
175 Hayfield Dr
Boones Mill VA 24065

Call Sign: K9PJ
Philip G Jung
180 Hayfield Dr
Boones Mill VA 24065

Call Sign: KA4NEF
Edward L Wimmer
500 Heatherwood Dr Apt 201
Boones Mill VA 24065

Call Sign: KF4RZN
David M Garst
43 Hemlock Dr
Boones Mill VA 24065

Call Sign: KF4SHR
Jesse N Jones Jr
570 Mirey Branch Rd
Boones Mill VA 24065

Call Sign: KB4HEK
Bernie F Ferrell Jr
1406 Naff Rd
Boones Mill VA 240654014

Call Sign: KM4XB
Gary W Martin
3813 Naff Rd
Boones Mill VA 24065

Call Sign: N4FXA
Norma Kay S Martin
3813 Naff Rd
Boones Mill VA 24065

Call Sign: WA4GW
Gary W Martin
3813 Naff Rd
Boones Mill VA 24065

Call Sign: KG4JSO
William A Keller
1974 Red Valley Rd
Boones Mill VA 24065

Call Sign: KC4OVI
Frank O Brien
7924 Spotswood
Boones Mill VA 24065

Call Sign: KI4FGY
Carla B Hosmer
205 Summerbreeze Dr
Boones Mill VA 24065

Call Sign: KI4CSW
Kenneth W Hosmer
205 Summerbreeze Dr
Boones Mill VA 24065

Call Sign: KI4ILV
Barry G Hall
3085 Taylors Rd
Boones Mill VA 24065

Call Sign: N5MR
Barry G Hall
3085 Taylors Rd
Boones Mill VA 24065

Call Sign: KG4UAU
Andrew B Kniowski
2261 White Oak Rd
Boones Mill VA 24065

Call Sign: KF4OOS
Malcolm D Dunahoo
Boones Mill VA 24065

Call Sign: K4PQV
Frank E Dawson
Boones Mill VA 24065

Call Sign: KB2ZUY
Thomas M Boylan
Boones Mill VA 24065

Call Sign: KB4ZUK
Edward C Ware
Boones Mill VA 24065

Call Sign: KJ4FTR
James D Dearing Jr
Boones Mill VA 24065

FCC Amateur Radio Licenses in Boston

Call Sign: KB2WTG
Wesley M D Frost
11247 Boston Dr
Boston VA 22713

Call Sign: AJ4XC
Rene D Mock
4412 Deer Ln
Boston VA 22713

Call Sign: KI4EEK
Richard E Becker
11759 Obannons Mill Rd
Boston VA 22713

Call Sign: W6LWG
Richard E Becker
11759 Obannons Mill Rd
Boston VA 22713

Call Sign: KD4VNO
Kevin J O Brien
10521 Old Stillhouse Rd
Boston VA 22713

Call Sign: N4JI
William R Mc Neil
10551 Old Stillhouse Rd
Boston VA 227134042

Call Sign: W4FIA
Donald L Haas
5607 Sperryville Pike
Boston VA 22713

Call Sign: KJ4RJE
Eric W Hohman
Boston VA 22713

FCC Amateur Radio Licenses in Bowling Green

Call Sign: KI4CQB
Richard L Lesh
150 Courthouse Ln Apt 19
Bowling Green VA 22427

Call Sign: N4BIC
Richard L Lesh
150 Courthouse Ln Apt 19
Bowling Green VA 22427

Call Sign: KG4YLW
William R Taylor III
163 Lee St
Bowling Green VA 22427

Call Sign: KB4CKZ
Arthur Cherry

229 Maury Avae
Bowling Green VA 22427

Call Sign: KC4BRT
Leslie B Moore
17450 Mill Run Ln
Bowling Green VA 224272124

Call Sign: KK4AJS
Alan T Richardson
280 Roper Dr
Bowling Green VA 22427

Call Sign: KH6GDE
Carlos J Jimenez
17092 Sarah St
Bowling Green VA 22427

Call Sign: KD4KNR
Steven T Lynd
16044 Tyler Ct
Bowling Green VA 22427

Call Sign: KB8YIQ
Steven M Walter
17247 White Meadows Dr
Bowling Green VA 22427

Call Sign: KE4BSU
IIenry G Lynd
Bowling Green VA 22427

FCC Amateur Radio Licenses in Boyce

Call Sign: KF4FWK
James M Brock III
Rt 1 Box 178 Aa
Boyce VA 22620

Call Sign: KE4JJV
Zachariah D Zinman Hillerson
Rt 1 Box 73
Boyce VA 22620

Call Sign: N3QPM
William L Rodgers III
679 Carefree Ln
Boyce VA 22620

Call Sign: KC4CK
Christine E Kestner
21 E Sharon Dr
Boyce VA 22620

Call Sign: WA6BGG
Tracy N Sturchio
100 Meadow View Dr
Boyce VA 22622

Call Sign: K4MMM
Clarke County ARC
1741 Old Chapel Rd
Boyce VA 22620

Call Sign: NS4DX
North Shenandoah Dx
Association
1741 Old Chapel Rd
Boyce VA 22620

Call Sign: W4WSF
Inter Circle Dx Association
1741 Old Chapel Rd
Boyce VA 22620

Call Sign: N4MM
John C Kanode
1741 Old Chapel Rd
Boyce VA 226209718

Call Sign: W4ZHE
Arthur H Clarke
125 W Main St
Boyce VA 22620

Call Sign: WZ4Q
Raymond V Burton
Boyce VA 22620

FCC Amateur Radio Licenses in Boydton

Call Sign: KJ4BMS
Richard B Puryear
3441 Alexander Ferry Rd
Boydton VA 23917

Call Sign: KC4RXL
Dennis W Price
Rt 1 Box 14
Boydton VA 23917

Call Sign: KC4ITK
Richard D Simmons
Rte 1 Box 51 1A
Boydton VA 23917

Call Sign: KC4ITM
Vincent E Williams
Rt 1 Box 99
Boydton VA 23917

Call Sign: NL7LR
Alan W Champagne
547 Chinia Grove Rd
Boydton VA 23917

Call Sign: KD4ZTK
Douglas L Shrimplin
20 Elm Hill Dr
Boydton VA 23917

Call Sign: KE4IWV
Adele M Shrimplin
20 Elm Hill Dr
Boydton VA 23917

Call Sign: K7KFC
Michael Farrow
98 Finch Ln
Boydton VA 23917

Call Sign: KC4CGI
Roger C Comer
1588 Keats Point Rd
Boydton VA 23917

Call Sign: KJ4VJE
Jimmy L Clark
49 Mineral Springs Rd
Boydton VA 23917

Call Sign: K4PSV
Jimmy L Clark
49 Mineral Springs Rd
Boydton VA 23917

Call Sign: KJ4VJI
Ricardo N Pina
81 St Leon Rd
Boydton VA 23917

Call Sign: KC4RXM
John L Fowler Jr
Boydton VA 23917

FCC Amateur Radio Licenses in Boykins

Call Sign: AE4EG
James T Gray
18199 Old Branchville Rd
Boykins VA 23827

FCC Amateur Radio Licenses in Bracey

Call Sign: KE4APE
Thomas A Nichols
422 Boardman Dr
Bracey VA 23919

Call Sign: KE4SGB
Sarah J Nichols
422 Boardman Dr
Bracey VA 23919

Call Sign: N4ZBA
Alice H Rozenbroek
36 Clai Ct
Bracey VA 239191868

Call Sign: N0LA
Peter H La Fosse
169 Hawks Nest Dr
Bracey VA 23919

Call Sign: N4OKH
Harry H Allman
258 Lakeview Dr
Bracey VA 23919

Call Sign: KF4ENC
Martin J Stack
288 Lucky Ln

Bracey VA 23919

Call Sign: KI4KES
Rebecca L Clary
799 Nellie Jones Rd
Bracey VA 23919

Call Sign: K4SDC
Stephen D Clary
799 Nellie Jones Rd
Bracey VA 23919

Call Sign: K4SDC
Stephen D Clary
799 Nellie Jones Rd
Bracey VA 23950

Call Sign: AI4JR
Stephen D Clary
799 Nellie Jones Rd
Bracey VA 23950

Call Sign: KC5HOS
James R Goode II
518 Tanglewood Dr
Bracey VA 239190669

FCC Amateur Radio Licenses in Brandy Station

Call Sign: KB2OM
William M Gross
11018 Mt Zion Chruch Rd
Brandy Station VA 22714

FCC Amateur Radio Licenses in Breaks

Call Sign: KD4SUN
Jeffery R Raines
Rt 693 Box 209
Breaks VA 24607

Call Sign: KE4SCM
Crystal R Raines
Rt 693
Breaks VA 24607

Call Sign: N4HBH

John P Raines
Breaks VA 24607

Call Sign: KE4MOP
Rebecca L Wallace
Breaks VA 24607

Call Sign: KE4MOQ
Christopher B Wallace
Breaks VA 24607

Call Sign: KF4VOZ
Bryan K Clevenger
Breaks VA 24607

Call Sign: KD4VRA
Connie Raines
Breaks VA 24607

FCC Amateur Radio Licenses in Bremo Bluff

Call Sign: KE4SAM
Samuel E Smith
373 Dixie Winds Dr
Bremo Bluff VA 23022

FCC Amateur Radio Licenses in Bridgewater

Call Sign: KI4NAQ
Julie F Briden
1402 Airport Rd
Bridgewater VA 22812

Call Sign: KF4OWB
Ken Briden
1402 Airport Rd
Bridgewater VA 22812

Call Sign: KU4XN
Gayle L Shull
2458 Airport Rd
Bridgewater VA 22812

Call Sign: KG4JBF
Gail E Shull
2458 Airport Rd
Bridgewater VA 22812

Call Sign: KG4KKT
Keith A Lambert
2697 Airport Rd
Bridgewater VA 22812

Call Sign: KA4EEI
Robert A Smith
410 Barbee St
Bridgewater VA 22812

Call Sign: N4NSB
Douglas L Dailey
423 Barbee St Apt 10
Bridgewater VA 22812

Call Sign: KD4AGN
Michael C Plaugher
Rt 1 Box 384
Bridgewater VA 22812

Call Sign: KD4ATR
Randall S Knicely
Rt 1 Box 430
Bridgewater VA 22812

Call Sign: WD4HVO
Curtis W Heisey
Rt 1 Box 6
Bridgewater VA 22812

Call Sign: KE4GIE
Terry L Stockner
102 Bridgeport Dr
Bridgewater VA 22812

Call Sign: KI4JRQ
Frank D Aigner
7101 Cam Bell Rd
Bridgewater VA 22812

Call Sign: K4FDA
Frank D Aigner
7101 Cam Bell Rd
Bridgewater VA 22812

Call Sign: KI4CQS
Neil K Cupp
7499 Community Center Rd

Bridgewater VA 22812

Call Sign: KI4DMD
Richard E Knupp
309 Dry River Rd
Bridgewater VA 22812

Call Sign: N4REK
Richard E Knupp
309 Dry River Rd
Bridgewater VA 22812

Call Sign: KG4BLE
James L Rodeffer
75 Grindstone Rd
Bridgewater VA 22812

Call Sign: KG4DXF
Patricia L Rodeffer
75 Grindstone Rd
Bridgewater VA 22812

Call Sign: KG4YLG
Jason L Miller
6607 Hemlock Cove Ln
Bridgewater VA 22812

Call Sign: N4RCE
Andrew L Pearson
105 Hickory Ln
Bridgewater VA 22812

Call Sign: KE4FKJ
Cathy H Payne
200 Holly Hill Dr
Bridgewater VA 22812

Call Sign: WA4E
Mark L Payne
200 Holly Hill Dr
Bridgewater VA 22812

Call Sign: KF4OCF
Peter L Gillerstedt
Ksk Aircraft Inc
Bridgewater VA 22812

Call Sign: KF4OCG
Catrina E L Ingemarsson

Ksk Aircraft Inc
Bridgewater VA 22812

Call Sign: K4NE
Charles P Harder
3557 Mallard Dr
Bridgewater VA 22812

Call Sign: KF4LRQ
Wanda B Harder
3557 Mallard Dr
Bridgewater VA 22812

Call Sign: W4RBC
Eastern Mennonite University
ARC
3557 Mallard Dr
Bridgewater VA 22812

Call Sign: K1MEF
Michael D Meffert
1586 Mossy Creek Rd
Bridgewater VA 22812

Call Sign: KA1USY
Sallie S Meffert
1586 Mossy Creek Rd
Bridgewater VA 22812

Call Sign: W4MEF
Michael D Meffert
1586 Mossy Creek Rd
Bridgewater VA 22812

Call Sign: KI4RTQ
Harold L Knicely
765 N Main
Bridgewater VA 22812

Call Sign: KG4DEX
Anna M Keller
302 N River Rd
Bridgewater VA 22812

Call Sign: N4XHE
Herman E Wing
232 Paradise Ln
Bridgewater VA 22812

Call Sign: KD4OXP
William F Hohenstein
306 Pope St
Bridgewater VA 22812

Call Sign: KG4JOC
Ralph E Shull II
29 Pops Ln
Bridgewater VA 22812

Call Sign: KG4JOD
Diana M Shull
29 Pops Ln
Bridgewater VA 22812

Call Sign: KG4KKW
Ralph E Shull
47 Pops Ln
Bridgewater VA 22812

Call Sign: KF4ZWK
Steven F Tennyson
107 S Sandstone Ln
Bridgewater VA 228120212

Call Sign: KJ4MWU
Thomas F Endress
117 Sunbright Dr
Bridgewater VA 22812

Call Sign: KJ4TOM
Thomas F Endress
117 Sunbright Dr
Bridgewater VA 22812

Call Sign: KE4HVO
Joseph M Mc Intyre
105 W College St
Bridgewater VA 22812

Call Sign: KB4DJN
Elwood A Shrader
126 W Rainbow Dr
Bridgewater VA 228121736

Call Sign: KD4JBZ
Thomas A Danisavich
109B Weeping Willow Ln
Bridgewater VA 22812

Call Sign: W4BHD
Nelson M Seese
9 Will Ln
Bridgewater VA 22812

Call Sign: KJ4SIT
Scott A Long
6513 Windy Cove Rd
Bridgewater VA 22812

Call Sign: K4RHQ
Clayton N Towers
209 Wynant Pl
Bridgewater VA 22812

Call Sign: KF4JDA
Marion D Long
Bridgewater VA 22812

Call Sign: KG4CHL
Robert J Tennyson
Bridgewater VA 22812

Call Sign: WA4HER
Kenneth D Slagell
Bridgewater VA 22812

Call Sign: WA4UVA
Robert O Ham III
Bridgewater VA 22812

**FCC Amateur Radio Licenses
in Brightwood**

Call Sign: AB8GX
John E Simons
6108 N Seminole Trl
Brightwood VA 22715

Call Sign: KI4SLP
James H Smith
741 Ridgeview Rd
Brightwood VA 22715

Call Sign: KI4SLO
Kimberly A Johnson-Smith
741 Ridgeview Rd
Brightwood VA 227151580

Call Sign: KD4MVQ
Curtis L Hanson
Brightwood VA 22715

FCC Amateur Radio Licenses in Bristol

Call Sign: W4LGY
Bernard H Leonard Sr
22413 Apache Ln
Bristol VA 242021643

Call Sign: KI4FGG
Claude A Hollaway Jr
Archery Range Rd Box 23658
Bristol VA 24202

Call Sign: WD4GXS
Douglas R Weberling
455 Arlington Ave
Bristol VA 24201

Call Sign: K4FVJ
Richard M Puckett
805 Arlington Ave
Bristol VA 24201

Call Sign: KI4RYO
James C Bundy
33 Aspen Cir
Bristol VA 242018710

Call Sign: KI4VBE
Jason C Dye
15334 Bordwine Rd
Bristol VA 24202

Call Sign: KN4SX
Gilbert M Johnson
113 Bristol View Dr
Bristol VA 24201

Call Sign: WA4MBS
Sidney B Anderson
14351 Brynwood Dr
Bristol VA 24202

Call Sign: N4YHV

Stephen B Canter
18144 Buffalo Pond Rd
Bristol VA 24202

Call Sign: KJ4SLJ
Beth E Pullon
21119 Campground Rd
Bristol VA 24202

Call Sign: KJ4SLI
Robert K Swiney
21119 Campground Rd
Bristol VA 24202

Call Sign: WE4AWJ
Emmit B Wilson
2240 Catherine St
Bristol VA 24201

Call Sign: KE4YSG
Robert C Weaver
325 Cherokee Rd
Bristol VA 24201

Call Sign: WD4BJD
William C Huber Jr
408 Clinton Ave
Bristol VA 24201

Call Sign: KE4OUY
James M Woodrum
54 Deertrack Ln
Bristol VA 242011934

Call Sign: KB4DXP
Phillip R Martin Sr
60 Deertrack Ln
Bristol VA 24201

Call Sign: KE4SAB
Michael K Jones
102 Dew Drop Pl
Bristol VA 24201

Call Sign: W4MAR
Michael K Jones
102 Dew Drop Pl
Bristol VA 24201

Call Sign: KG4ZXL
Steven M Jones
102 Dew Drop Pl
Bristol VA 24201

Call Sign: WA4LKI
Robie M Parks
432 E Valley Dr
Bristol VA 24201

Call Sign: KJ4CFQ
Alan M Mcfarlane
717 E Valley Dr
Bristol VA 24201

Call Sign: K4CYY
Phillip J Diltz
420 Floyd St
Bristol VA 24201

Call Sign: ND4M
Franklin G Mc New
1113 Foxcroft Rd
Bristol VA 24201

Call Sign: WB4FEJ
Walter L Hale
199 Freedom Rd
Bristol VA 24201

Call Sign: KF4AQJ
Herman L Wheeler
549 Garden Ln
Bristol VA 24201

Call Sign: KF4AQK
Noah B Holbrook
601 Garden Ln
Bristol VA 24201

Call Sign: W4MC
Edgar D Mc Farlane
638 Garden Ln
Bristol VA 24201

Call Sign: W4UZ
David E Mc Farlane
638 Garden Ln
Bristol VA 24201

Call Sign: KD4DMM
Maurice D Miller III
4517 Gate City Hwy
Bristol VA 24202

Call Sign: KK4CSF
Robert H Johnson
11192 Goose Creek Rd
Bristol VA 24202

Call Sign: WC4L
Allen W Shepherd
160 Grable Rd
Bristol VA 24201

Call Sign: KF4ZTN
Cathy D Stephenson
47 Green Valley Rd
Bristol VA 24202

Call Sign: WA4EHV
Sam N Stephenson
47 Green Valley Rd
Bristol VA 24202

Call Sign: N4YZN
Ronald M Mann
184 Greenbriar Ln
Bristol VA 24201

Call Sign: K4OBY
James G Hall Jr
23160 Hamlet Ln
Bristol VA 24202

Call Sign: KE4WGV
Jeffery L Branham
15253 Hearst Rd
Bristol VA 24202

Call Sign: KE4EJW
George A Tipton Jr
414 Hill Dr
Bristol VA 242012565

Call Sign: N4QGM
Fredrick W Smith
21 Hilltop Dr

Bristol VA 24201

Call Sign: KA4PYG
Tivis A Fields
150 Hilltop Dr
Bristol VA 24201

Call Sign: N4TIV
Tivis A Fields
Hilltop Dr
Bristol VA 24201

Call Sign: KI4TDW
Gas Line Groovies ARC
13353 Holbrook St
Bristol VA 24202

Call Sign: NG4I
Gas Line Groovies ARC
13353 Holbrook St
Bristol VA 24202

Call Sign: KE4MOB
Steven E Matda
13353 Holbrook St
Bristol VA 24202

Call Sign: WD4DNE
Cecil O Parsons
41 Homestead Dr
Bristol VA 24201

Call Sign: KB4WLW
Claude G Wilson
61 Homestead Dr
Bristol VA 24201

Call Sign: N4UOR
Curtis A Murray
134 Independence Dr
Bristol VA 242011948

Call Sign: WA4JMT
William A Johnson
1726 Island Rd
Bristol VA 24201

Call Sign: KC4YSW
Ernest C Layell

1790 Island Rd
Bristol VA 24201

Call Sign: KD4CCO
Dallas B Cassell Jr
10165 Island Rd
Bristol VA 24202

Call Sign: N4XFB
Michael D Litz
96 Jane Ln
Bristol VA 24201

Call Sign: WE4T
Leland C Waterman
2134 Kings Mill Pike
Bristol VA 24201

Call Sign: NP4EM
Charles R Shupe Jr
20 Kriswood Dr
Bristol VA 24201

Call Sign: KA4ZDY
Louise S Anderson
408 Laurel Dr
Bristol VA 24201

Call Sign: KF4FHY
Kevin W Wheeler
1724 Lee Hwy
Bristol VA 24201

Call Sign: WD4SDW
Carl F Hearl
14375 Lee Hwy
Bristol VA 24202

Call Sign: N8LGQ
Kenneth M Drushal
16114 Lee Hwy
Bristol VA 24201

Call Sign: KD4WMX
Kenneth W Merrill
15255 Lee Hwy Apt 1
Bristol VA 24202

Call Sign: KF4LNE

Daniel E Buchanan Jr
1971 Lee Hwy Ste 4
Bristol VA 24201

Call Sign: KD4QBY
Sandra L Hutchison
917 Lewis St
Bristol VA 24201

Call Sign: W3FOO
Frank P Hutchison
917 Lewis St
Bristol VA 24201

Call Sign: W4SL
David J Caldwell
1 Liberty Pl Apt 137
Bristol VA 24201

Call Sign: W4CEI
Roy K Hill
5519 Livingston Creek Rd
Bristol VA 242022213

Call Sign: KB5YGL
Robert L Puckett Jr
23031 Lone Eagle Dr
Bristol VA 24202

Call Sign: KJ4NAU
Jeffrey L Wilson
1736 Long Crescent Dr
Bristol VA 24201

Call Sign: W9AWR
Jack A Aaron
15 Long Crescent Rd
Bristol VA 242013521

Call Sign: KG4EIT
Christy S Harris
15509 Lookout Ridge
Bristol VA 24202

Call Sign: KF4FHU
Rick L Schultz
392 Lynnwood Dr
Bristol VA 24201

Call Sign: KE4FEQ
Andrew Dannhardt
394 Lynwood Dr
Bristol VA 24201

Call Sign: KJ4WAH
Paticia S Brown
13150 Marietta Dr
Bristol VA 24202

Call Sign: KF4SMD
Marice L Rose
1215 Massachusetts Ave
Bristol VA 24201

Call Sign: KI4YYW
Jack C Lee Jr
208 Meadowcrest Dr
Bristol VA 24201

Call Sign: KD4IOK
Tim J Sturgill
237 Meadowcrest Dr
Bristol VA 24201

Call Sign: KD4IOL
Margaret J Sturgill
237 Meadowcrest Dr
Bristol VA 24201

Call Sign: WD4AGO
Wendell B Jones III
404 Meadowcrest Dr
Bristol VA 24201

Call Sign: N4AKZ
Phil M Berry
356 Monticello Dr
Bristol VA 24201

Call Sign: KD4NGI
Robert L Hobbs
15286 Monticello Dr
Bristol VA 24202

Call Sign: W4EIH
Scott A Bullock
15456 Monticello Dr
Bristol VA 24202

Call Sign: KC4CMA
William K Hagy Jr
15528 Monticello Dr
Bristol VA 24202

Call Sign: WD4BXV
Patricia A Berry
15538 Monticello Dr
Bristol VA 24202

Call Sign: WD4CYZ
Richard C Perry
110 New York St
Bristol VA 24201

Call Sign: KB4KGL
Doug E Maiden
9143 Nininger Rd
Bristol VA 24202

Call Sign: KD4ION
Jack B King
229 Oakview Dr
Bristol VA 24201

Call Sign: W4FTP
Tim E Johnston II
10227 Oakwinds Cir
Bristol VA 24201

Call Sign: KE4RDQ
Bobby R Rachel
9424 Patrick Ln
Bristol VA 24202

Call Sign: KK4HEU
Larry E Ball
21434 Plantation Rd
Bristol VA 24202

Call Sign: KC4WDB
Allen W Ford
727 Portsmouth Ave
Bristol VA 24201

Call Sign: N4NNZ
Walter C Ford
100 Raintree Cir

Bristol VA 24201

Call Sign: KD4BNB
Mark K Draper
1229 Reedy Creek Rd
Bristol VA 24201

Call Sign: KJ4WJK
Charles E Taylor
5006 Reedy Creek Rd
Bristol VA 24202

Call Sign: KG4FBK
Johny C Pilkenton Sr
12037 Reedy Creek Rd
Bristol VA 24202

Call Sign: KC4VMM
Randy M Minton
8409 Rich Valley Rd
Bristol VA 24201

Call Sign: KG4CPK
Wesley D Guinn
10279 Rich Valley Rd
Bristol VA 24202

Call Sign: KB4ROW
Stephen T Monroe
97 Robin Cir
Bristol VA 24201

Call Sign: KE4ZRK
Peter J Mursak
243 Robin Cir
Bristol VA 242025923

Call Sign: KG4UBO
Angela H Dannhardt
409 Santa Monica Dr
Bristol VA 24201

Call Sign: KA4CUE
Richard H Dannhardt
815 Santa Monica Dr
Bristol VA 24201

Call Sign: KJ4CBW
Betty B Schoenhardt

425 Seminole Rd
Bristol VA 24201

Call Sign: KF4DVZ
Neil A Ashley
2445 Shakesville Rd
Bristol VA 24201

Call Sign: K4FJW
George T Shutters
305 Shipley Dr
Bristol VA 24201

Call Sign: K4PAP
Daniel R Higgins
228 Sioux Rd
Bristol VA 24201

Call Sign: KA4JMA
Nina R Higgins
228 Sioux Rd
Bristol VA 24201

Call Sign: WD4LMC
Harold E Higgins
228 Sioux Rd
Bristol VA 24201

Call Sign: KG4WZD
Cheryl L Olinger
228 Sioux Rd
Bristol VA 24201

Call Sign: K4CLO
Cheryl L Olinger
228 Sioux Rd
Bristol VA 24201

Call Sign: KJ4JSF
James E Melvin II
15314 Skyland Ave
Bristol VA 24202

Call Sign: KJ4SKV
Kimberly A Melvin
15314 Skyland Ave
Bristol VA 24202

Call Sign: KI4YYK

Charles E Rhoton
107 St Andrews Dr
Bristol VA 24202

Call Sign: AC0QX
Daniel E Dayton
517 5 State St 3rd Floor Room 7
Bristol VA 24201

Call Sign: AK4RK
Daniel E Dayton
517 5 State St 3rd Floor Room 7
Bristol VA 24201

Call Sign: KC4HUH
Gary M Shell
13422 Stone Dr
Bristol VA 24202

Call Sign: KG4MGV
William M Shell
13422 Stone Dr
Bristol VA 24202

Call Sign: K4ITV
Charles R Whicker
420 Terry Dr
Bristol VA 24201

Call Sign: KJ4UXV
Linda K Smith
1201 Texas Ae
Bristol VA 24201

Call Sign: KK4DFW
Michael D Lester
114 Texas Ave
Bristol VA 24201

Call Sign: K4EAZ
Mark W Smith
1201 Texas Ave
Bristol VA 24201

Call Sign: N4EZ
Mark W Smith
1201 Texas Ave
Bristol VA 24201

Call Sign: WD4FGX
Terry L Webb
118 Timber Oak Dr
Bristol VA 242013064

Call Sign: N8FJQ
Elmer F Jordan
330 Vance St
Bristol VA 24201

Call Sign: N4YK
Edwin A Blevins
539 Ventura Dr
Bristol VA 24201

Call Sign: WA4CDC
William R Shearin
547 Ventura Dr
Bristol VA 24201

Call Sign: KG4SAL
Kevin C Schurtz
117 W Valley Dr
Bristol VA 24201

Call Sign: WB4BHF
James G Hall
7327 White Pine Cir
Bristol VA 24202

Call Sign: AC4JD
Michael L Terry
7795 Wolf Run Rd
Bristol VA 24202

Call Sign: KU4MF
Earnest L Leonard
7373 Wolfrun Rd
Bristol VA 24202

Call Sign: K4TEN
Frankie J Hunt Jr
175 Woodland Cir
Bristol VA 24201

Call Sign: KI4EHF
Benjamin C Hunt
175 Woodland Cir
Bristol VA 24201

Call Sign: KI4CAD
Rebecca A Hunt
175 Woodland Cir
Bristol VA 24201

Call Sign: W4TEN
Rebecca A Hunt
175 Woodland Cir
Bristol VA 24201

Call Sign: KA4PRV
Alice E Barker
25 Woodstock Ln
Bristol VA 24201

Call Sign: W4KQH
William B Barker Jr
25 Woodstock Ln
Bristol VA 24201

Call Sign: KF4EKM
Christopher L Barry
Bristol VA 24203

Call Sign: N4PQM
Curtis J Malcolm Jr
Bristol VA 242030503

FCC Amateur Radio Licenses in Bristow

Call Sign: NG3L
Michael C Joos
9897 Airedale Ct
Bristow VA 20136

Call Sign: KJ4ETH
Joe C Birkhead IV
11804 Alexander Hays Rd
Bristow VA 20136

Call Sign: WA4YGI
Charles J Dale Jr
12844 Arnot Ln
Bristow VA 20136

Call Sign: N0HOF
James D Nickum

12947 Brigstock Ct
Bristow VA 201363118

Call Sign: WQ0U
James D Nickum
12947 Brigstock Ct
Bristow VA 201363118

Call Sign: KC4UEB
Richard C Keller
12124 Bristow Rd
Bristow VA 20136

Call Sign: KG4YIT
Sastry V Daita
10624 Bristow Station Dr
Bristow VA 20136

Call Sign: KF4KKI
John D Jester
9153 Cascade Falls Dr
Bristow VA 20136

Call Sign: KG4KZX
Kevin M Davis
10892 Clara Barton Dr
Bristow VA 20136

Call Sign: KJ4MTO
Christopher J Thornburg
12605 Crabtreefalls Dr
Bristow VA 20136

Call Sign: KI4BXS
W Alman Reames Jr
9635 Craighill Dr
Bristow VA 201362573

Call Sign: KJ4EOY
Burnett L Deyerle III
9737 Craighill Dr
Bristow VA 20136

Call Sign: KI4AZX
David Meola
10033 Darnaway Ct
Bristow VA 201363039

Call Sign: WA0VYJ

Kenneth D Aldridge
10039 Dragoon Guards Ct
Bristow VA 20136

Call Sign: K1KDA
Kenneth D Aldridge
10039 Dragoon Guards Ct
Bristow VA 20136

Call Sign: KG4JOV
Dorothy L Jordon
12925 Dunbarton Dr
Bristow VA 20136

Call Sign: KJ4MTN
Theodore W Hollabaugh
8754 Dunstable Loop
Bristow VA 20136

Call Sign: KJ4ICW
Marlee C Foster
10137 Elliston Ct
Bristow VA 20136

Call Sign: KJ4MTT
Laura D Burget
10841 General Kirkland Dr
Bristow VA 20136

Call Sign: KJ4FDG
Alan K Gideon
8754 Grantham Ct
Bristow VA 20136

Call Sign: K5AKG
Alan K Gideon
8754 Grantham Ct
Bristow VA 20136

Call Sign: N4MWX
Jerry E Carter
12271 Grimsby Ln
Bristow VA 20136

Call Sign: KF4TTM
Douglas W Baldwin
12279 Grimsby Ln
Bristow VA 20136

Call Sign: N6JFG
Ahmad Mobarak
13512 Grouserun Ln
Bristow VA 20136

Call Sign: KK4DCZ
Ronald K Mcnuss
12081 Hartwood Meadow Pl
Bristow VA 20136

Call Sign: KO4ZL
Jeffrey L Innes
13270 Lawrence Ln
Bristow VA 20136

Call Sign: KC4OLE
Aaron P Steketee
12326 Malvern Way
Bristow VA 20136

Call Sign: KJ4RNO
Kimberly A Steffen
12600 Moray Firth Way
Bristow VA 20136

Call Sign: KI4YCR
Robert A Steffen
12600 Moray Firth Way
Bristow VA 20136

Call Sign: KI4AWA
Jessica L Gausmann
9124 Mossy Rock Ct
Bristow VA 20136

Call Sign: KI4QFA
Bay ARC
12215 Murdo Ct
Bristow VA 20136

Call Sign: KG6ZR
Leonard A Hook
12215 Murdo Ct
Bristow VA 201361942

Call Sign: KD4KBX
Richard A Massie
13649 Newtonmore Pl
Bristow VA 20136

Call Sign: WB7TPJ
David A Carroll
11924 Ricketts Battery Dr
Bristow VA 20136

Call Sign: KB7NTF
Daniel P Shellman
8564 Rothbury Dr
Bristow VA 20136

Call Sign: N0PVP
Patricia A Odell
8671 Ruby Rise Pl
Bristow VA 20136

Call Sign: N0PVQ
Chauncey A Odell
8671 Ruby Rise Pl
Bristow VA 20136

Call Sign: N3MA
Michael G Jacoby
9778 Runner Stone Pl
Bristow VA 20136

Call Sign: WH6KT
Charles M Smedley
10106 Sir Reynard Ln
Bristow VA 201362549

Call Sign: KU4BN
Mark A St Germain
9720 Snare Drum Ct
Bristow VA 22013

Call Sign: KQ4TA
Daniel W Deibel
9886 Sounding Shore Ln
Bristow VA 20136

Call Sign: KD6DBX
Kendall L Carpenter
10048 Spindle Foot Ct
Bristow VA 201361934

Call Sign: KC4TVN
George P Moss Jr
9438 Struthers Glen Ct

Bristow VA 20136

Call Sign: N3QQA
John A Crupi
8913 Telford Ct
Bristow VA 20136

Call Sign: KG4CFQ
Daniel A Herschler
12004 Thornbrooke Ct
Bristow VA 20136

Call Sign: K9POO
Daniel A Herschler
12004 Thornbrooke Ct
Bristow VA 20136

Call Sign: N7QLK
Wayne D Phillips
10046 Tummel Falls Dr
Bristow VA 20136

Call Sign: K1TJR
Thomas J Rowland Jr
12023 Underwood Ct
Bristow VA 20136

Call Sign: KC7ZN
Matthew D Crosman
12004 Vantagc Point Ct
Bristow VA 20136

Call Sign: KJ4IDA
Ami Abramson
12009 Vantage Point Ct
Bristow VA 20136

Call Sign: N4MWU
Warren G Bain
9290 Weathersfield Dr
Bristow VA 201361712

Call Sign: AG4EQ
Warren G Bain
9290 Weathersfield Dr
Bristow VA 201361712

FCC Amateur Radio Licenses in Broad Run

Call Sign: AI4LT
David A Hendricks
5625 Beverleys Mill Rd
Broad Run VA 20137

Call Sign: KD4QHR
David K Schubel
Rt 1 Box 53A
Broad Run VA 22014

Call Sign: WD8CTJ
Gregory L D Brown
6108 Browning Ln
Broad Run VA 20137

Call Sign: N3BML
Susan L Stout
6188 Evergreen Mtn Rd
Broad Run VA 20137

Call Sign: KJ4EOO
Jason A Donnelly
5391 Farrington Ln
Broad Run VA 20137

Call Sign: NZ4N
Ansel N Page
6013 Fieldcrest Ln
Broad Run VA 20137

Call Sign: N4MFP
Michael R Neal
17005 Gaines Rd
Broad Run VA 22014

Call Sign: KG4PIW
Stephen J Macmahon
6101 General Huntun Rd
Broad Run VA 20137

Call Sign: KG4RRQ
William M Weber
5138 Laurel Ln
Broad Run VA 20137

Call Sign: WD4EQF
Marcia F Newell
5506 Mtn Rd

Broad Run VA 22014

Call Sign: KN4CY
Peter A Popovich
4959 Old Buckland Rd
Broad Run VA 20137

Call Sign: KE4DFH
Gary E Morin
5723 Turner Rd
Broad Run VA 20137

Call Sign: KG4EHI
Richard F Webster Jr
Broad Run VA 20137

FCC Amateur Radio Licenses in Broadlands

Call Sign: WB4PKP
Neil J Sommerfield
21381 Glebe View Dr
Broadlands VA 20148

Call Sign: KJ4BRW
Patrick L Howard
43095 Hunters Green Sq
Broadlands VA 20148

FCC Amateur Radio Licenses in Broadway

Call Sign: KD4IKW
William E Killen Sr
192 Atlantic Ave
Broadway VA 22815

Call Sign: KA1LSK
Anne L Underwood
120 D Atlantic Ave
Broadway VA 22815

Call Sign: KE4LKQ
Victor E Alger
500 Bird Song Ln
Broadway VA 22815

Call Sign: K4XTT
Victor E Alger

500 Bird Song Ln
Broadway VA 22815

Call Sign: KC4YAR
Marshall R Cooper
Rt 2 Box 109A1
Broadway VA 22815

Call Sign: KC4RKG
Hollen G Helbert
Rt 3 Box 97
Broadway VA 22815

Call Sign: KJ4NPU
Michael E Turner
5381 Brocks Gap Rd
Broadway VA 22815

Call Sign: K4MIC
Michael E Turner
5381 Brocks Gap Rd
Broadway VA 22815

Call Sign: KJ4DOB
Alan C Nicol
179 Buchanan Dr
Broadway VA 22815

Call Sign: WA4KKL
Fredric N Buckingham
11393 Daphna Rd
Broadway VA 22815

Call Sign: W4KKL
Fredric N Buckingham
11393 Daphna Rd
Broadway VA 22815

Call Sign: N4DAI
Dale A Showalter
258 Dogwood Dr
Broadway VA 22815

Call Sign: K3NLT
Russell A Mumaw
540 Freemont Cir
Broadway VA 22815

Call Sign: KG4PRR

Daryl M Coffman
2684 Hillyard Dr
Broadway VA 22815

Call Sign: KF4BFL
Wilton B Thomas
12899 Hisers Ln
Broadway VA 228152722

Call Sign: KF4SVR
David A Hughes
14780 Justice Crossing
Broadway VA 22815

Call Sign: KG4GWM
Robert E Waggy
2584 Mayland Rd
Broadway VA 22815

Call Sign: KG4GNG
Michael A Funkhouser
15809 Mt Valley Rd
Broadway VA 22815

Call Sign: KG4FQV
Oren K Foster
15809 Mtn Valley Rd
Broadway VA 22815

Call Sign: KG4FYG
Tammy S Foster
15809 Mtn Valley Rd
Broadway VA 22815

Call Sign: KJ4TPA
Michael J Turner
17383 N Mtn Rd
Broadway VA 22815

Call Sign: K4MKT
Michael J Turner
17383 N Mtn Rd
Broadway VA 22815

Call Sign: KC8JPK
Michael R Wagoner
11876 N Valley Pike
Broadway VA 22815

Call Sign: WV3J
Paul M Helbert
12558 N Valley Pike
Broadway VA 22815

Call Sign: KF4WWM
Kevin W Barb
9161 Phillips Store Rd
Broadway VA 22815

Call Sign: N9AHQ
Howard J Zehr
168 S Sunset Dr
Broadway VA 22815

Call Sign: KC4TTS
Phillip W Thompson
13282 Timber Way
Broadway VA 22815

Call Sign: KJ4EVZ
James L Junkins
256 W Springbrook Rd
Broadway VA 22815

Call Sign: W4JLJ
James L Junkins
256 W Springbrook Rd
Broadway VA 22815

Call Sign: W8GVE
Howard L Reichle
197 Walnut Dr
Broadway VA 22815

Call Sign: KE4CKD
Shannon M Mongold
186 Walnut Dr
Broadway VA 22815

Call Sign: N4AZK
Janet M Shank
Broadway VA 22815

Call Sign: WD4KMU
Randall E Shank
Broadway VA 22815

FCC Amateur Radio Licenses in Brodnax

Call Sign: KJ4BMK
Kody L Cross
630 Dixie Bridge Rd
Brodnax VA 23920

Call Sign: KI4SHC
Jason R Hawkins
548 Main St
Brodnax VA 23920

Call Sign: KI4VAS
Tony J Preston
743 Oak Rd
Brodnax VA 23920

Call Sign: KI4RNM
Lake County ARS
Brodnax VA 23920

Call Sign: W4LCA
Lake County ARS
Brodnax VA 23920

Call Sign: W4WCT
Charles E Davidson III
Brodnax VA 23920

FCC Amateur Radio Licenses in Brookneal

Call Sign: N4ZCJ
Oliver F Bowe III
132 B Carson St
Brookneal VA 245283128

Call Sign: KJ4IGE
Gregory A Davis
528 Down Creek Rd
Brookneal VA 24528

Call Sign: KB4WHW
Benjamin L Ginther
107 Falling Hill Rd
Brookneal VA 24528

Call Sign: N2AAM

David L Marthouse
225 Hunter Rd
Brookneal VA 24528

Call Sign: KD4AWB
Johnie C Kilgore
3506 Lewis Ford Rd
Brookneal VA 24528

Call Sign: W4BGS
Baxter G Shutt Jr
708 Lynchburg Ave
Brookneal VA 245282808

Call Sign: WB4FCU
Larry K Martin
1264 Lynchburg Ave
Brookneal VA 24528

Call Sign: KB4TPV
Kenneth E Conner Jr
308 VA Ave
Brookneal VA 24528

Call Sign: KD4CRO
Sandra J Rice
Brookneal VA 24528

Call Sign: KC4EAD
Paul D Irby
Brookneal VA 24528

Call Sign: KG4DDS
Vernon D Angel
Brookneal VA 24528

Call Sign: KI4CZT
Robert W Millner
Brookneal VA 24528

FCC Amateur Radio Licenses in Buchanan

Call Sign: KE4CHY
Darryl L Newcomb
Rt 2 Box 17D
Buchanan VA 24066

Call Sign: K4VBZ

Thurman E Ayers
Rt 1 Box 190
Buchanan VA 24066

Call Sign: KE4CHX
Lewis D Newcomb
Rt 1 Box 191C
Buchanan VA 24066

Call Sign: KJ4QOF
E Drake Breeden
292 Culpepper Ave
Buchanan VA 24066

Call Sign: K4SAP
E Drake Breeden
292 Culpepper Ave
Buchanan VA 24066

Call Sign: KJ4QLO
Rachel K Higginbotham
184 Lake Catherine Dr
Buchanan VA 24066

Call Sign: KJ4CGR
Myra K Roach
2597 Lithia Rd
Buchanan VA 24066

Call Sign: KJ4CGO
Philip E Roach
2597 Lithia Rd
Buchanan VA 24066

Call Sign: KG4WLP
Fred W Haxton
1507 Oak Ridge Rd
Buchanan VA 24066

Call Sign: KQ4NW
Heyward C Thompson Jr
1060 Old Hollow Rd
Buchanan VA 24066

Call Sign: W4TU
Heyward C Thompson Jr
1060 Old Hollow Rd
Buchanan VA 24066

Call Sign: WB4VVH
Carlton F Ayers
1252 Wheatland Rd
Buchanan VA 24066

Call Sign: K4AUU
Janice M Coffey
Buchanan VA 24066

FCC Amateur Radio Licenses in Buckingham

Call Sign: KE4NGZ
Jamie C Mc Kaig
Rt 1 Box 2505
Buckingham VA 23921

Call Sign: KE4IBE
Melvin J Gregory Jr
Hc 02 Box 329
Buckingham VA 23921

Call Sign: KC4ZLZ
Reese E Carroll Jr
Rt 1 Box 760
Buckingham VA 23921

Call Sign: N3ENW
Martin B Wangberg
1698 Manteo Rd
Buckingham VA 23921

Call Sign: KE4IBD
John C Myers
Rt 640
Buckingham VA 23921

Call Sign: KA2IKN
Donald E Moore
12977 W James Anderson Rd
Buckingham VA 23921

Call Sign: N3XNB
James L Rosser
424 Watoga Rd
Buckingham VA 23921

FCC Amateur Radio Licenses in Buena Vista

Call Sign: N4CAD
Ralph T Henson Sr
1121 12th Maple Ave
Buena Vista VA 24416

Call Sign: KC4NWV
Rachel L Mc Callister
810 13th St
Buena Vista VA 24416

Call Sign: KC4NWW
William R Mc Callister Jr
810 13th St
Buena Vista VA 24416

Call Sign: KC4UUJ
Joan D Mc Callister
810 13th St
Buena Vista VA 24416

Call Sign: WB2RNF
Christopher A Camuto
Rt 1 Box 160A
Buena Vista VA 24416

Call Sign: KC4CSY
Siegfried W Roscher
Rte 1 Box 164
Buena Vista VA 24416

Call Sign: KD4VRW
Lon J Mc Callister
Rt 1 Box 205
Buena Vista VA 24416

Call Sign: KE4RWZ
Charles W Flint
Rt 1 Box 425
Buena Vista VA 24416

Call Sign: WB4HNJ
William H Byles
2275 Cedar Ave
Buena Vista VA 24416

Call Sign: KA8URT
Constance B Miller
2275 Cedar Ave

Buena Vista VA 244161913

Call Sign: KF4IZK
Robert D Gay
2355 Cedar Ave
Buena Vista VA 244161811

Call Sign: KE4BOB
Robert D Gay
2355 Cedar Ave
Buena Vista VA 244161811

Call Sign: KC4UUK
Paul F Davis Jr
1153 Cherry Ave
Buena Vista VA 24416

Call Sign: KJ4KWB
Alan J Porter
944 E 22nd St
Buena Vista VA 24416

Call Sign: KJ4KYL
Elaine H Porter
944 E 22nd St
Buena Vista VA 24416

Call Sign: KJ4KWA
John F Porter
944 E 22nd St
Buena Vista VA 24416

Call Sign: KJ4KWC
Samuel T Porter
944 E 22nd St
Buena Vista VA 24416

Call Sign: KJ4KVZ
Thomas R Porter
944 E 22nd St
Buena Vista VA 24416

Call Sign: KJ4EXX
Dean S Slough
208 E 29 St
Buena Vista VA 24416

Call Sign: KC6QGS
Randall Cluff

2636 Edgewood Rd
Buena Vista VA 24416

Call Sign: KJ4KVT
Dana R Dwyer
1944 Forest Ave
Buena Vista VA 24416

Call Sign: KC4UIN
Robert M Davis
2070 Forest Ave
Buena Vista VA 24416

Call Sign: KG4RUJ
Rose M Fix
2764 Glasgow Hwy
Buena Vista VA 24416

Call Sign: KG4LKJ
Thomas L Fix
2764 Glasgow Hwy
Buena Vista VA 244164909

Call Sign: WE1FIX
Thomas L Fix
2764 Glasgow Hwy
Buena Vista VA 244164909

Call Sign: KB4MDF
Ernest L King Jr
494 Hemlock Ave
Buena Vista VA 24416

Call Sign: WL7GY
Michael S Patterson
268 Jorden Rd
Buena Vista VA 24416

Call Sign: KB4WHR
Wesley L Robinson
70 Lemon Dr
Buena Vista VA 24416

Call Sign: KC4OKJ
Raymond L Henson
2936 Lombardy Ave
Buena Vista VA 24416

Call Sign: KI4QMH

Lisa M Davis
345 Long Hollow Rd
Buena Vista VA 24416

Call Sign: N3GEI
Preston L Fitzberger
2252 Maple Ave
Buena Vista VA 24416

Call Sign: KG4PUA
Keith E Gibson Sr
2252 Maple Ave
Buena Vista VA 24416

Call Sign: KD5DBA
Warren W Ward Jr
2464 Maple Ave
Buena Vista VA 24416

Call Sign: K4IEA
William R Mc Callister Sr
2047 Mt View Rd
Buena Vista VA 24416

Call Sign: KK4CUZ
Michael D Hall
2227 Oak Ave
Buena Vista VA 24416

Call Sign: KJ4KVY
Robert E Huch
55 Paxton House Dr
Buena Vista VA 24416

Call Sign: KE4PHS
Carroll A Coffey
2460 Pine Ave
Buena Vista VA 24416

Call Sign: WB4WC
William E Coffey
2460 Pine Ave
Buena Vista VA 24416

Call Sign: KC4WRC
Fred C Vaughan Jr
2364 Spruce Ave
Buena Vista VA 24416

Call Sign: KA4TGK
Claude D Sanderson Sr
2519 Sycamore
Buena Vista VA 24416

Call Sign: KE4NRD
Timothy D Clarkson
321 W 29th St
Buena Vista VA 24416

Call Sign: W4SVP
Stephen A Presti
240 Weavers Way
Buena Vista VA 24416

Call Sign: KK4AIJ
James R Youngblood
24 Wing Walker Way
Buena Vista VA 244164031

Call Sign: AK4JS
James R Youngblood
24 Wing Walker Way
Buena Vista VA 244164031

Call Sign: WA3HJJ
Mike E Bailey
Buena Vista VA 244160847

FCC Amateur Radio Licenses in Buffalo Junction

Call Sign: KC4QAZ
Barnabas Willoby
Rt 1 Box 154
Buffalo Junction VA 24529

Call Sign: N4NQF
Robert W Pettit
400 Dogwood Rd
Buffalo Junction VA 24529

Call Sign: KC7JVE
Rodney A Goodacre
1178 Gravel Hill Rd
Buffalo Junction VA 24529

Call Sign: N4OAM
Robert J Mc Kay

244 Palomino Rd
Buffalo Junction VA 24529

Call Sign: KM4F
Bernard C Rodenhizer III
368 Wynde Pointe Ln
Buffalo Junction VA 24529

Call Sign: KC4RXQ
Gary L Jones
Buffalo Junction VA 24529

FCC Amateur Radio Licenses in Bumpass

Call Sign: K2DJL
Arthur A Mc Comas
2318 Belle Meade Rd
Bumpass VA 23024

Call Sign: KJ4BYE
Patrick J Reitelbach
3346 Belle Meade Rd
Bumpass VA 23024

Call Sign: W4YOO
Patrick J Reitelbach
3346 Belle Meade Rd
Bumpass VA 23024

Call Sign: KJ4WED
Barry W Powell
469 Belsches Rd
Bumpass VA 23024

Call Sign: NB4W
Steven C Marrs
188 Bethany Church Rd
Bumpass VA 23024

Call Sign: KE4FSL
Ed W Winfree
1467 Bethany Church Rd
Bumpass VA 230243506

Call Sign: KM4OO
Steve D Shergold
Rt 4 Box 1130
Bumpass VA 23024

Call Sign: N4HYR
Lewis E Daniel
Rt 2 Box 2556
Bumpass VA 23024

Call Sign: KE4MJU
William H Mc Kinney
Rt 2 Box 3785
Bumpass VA 23024

Call Sign: AB8ER
Casey D Jones
3836 Breaknock Rd
Bumpass VA 23024

Call Sign: KI4ITU
Tami J Ludwig
66 Cedar Post Ranch Rd
Bumpass VA 23024

Call Sign: WB2INP
Richard F Lindmeier
280 Cooke Ln
Bumpass VA 23024

Call Sign: KE4UVD
Scott F Miller
104 Copper Line Rd
Bumpass VA 23024

Call Sign: N1WNA
John R Scanlon
415 Johnsons Mill Farm
Bumpass VA 23024

Call Sign: KG4PSA
Richard C Upshur
516 Lewis Hill Ln
Bumpass VA 23024

Call Sign: KG4QJB
Mary C Upshur
516 Lewis Hill Ln
Bumpass VA 23024

Call Sign: KD4PKP
Ann L Heidig
5513 Lewiston Rd

Bumpass VA 23024

Call Sign: W2KM
Willard R Heidig
5513 Lewiston Rd
Bumpass VA 230248818

Call Sign: K4BZK
William L King Jr
136 Little River Farm Rd
Bumpass VA 23024

Call Sign: N3CLL
James H Lehnert
11101 Lucks Rd
Bumpass VA 230249623

Call Sign: KE2YR
Victor J Mirota
2723 Moody Town Rd
Bumpass VA 23024

Call Sign: KG6GCQ
Debra L Grys
27 Oak Knoll Pl
Bumpass VA 23024

Call Sign: KF6CUE
Casimir W Grys
27 Oak Knoll Pl
Bumpass VA 230243314

Call Sign: W9HLV
Leland W Miller
631 Oak Rd
Bumpass VA 23024

Call Sign: KI4YGN
Michael A Carioscia
707 Point Dr
Bumpass VA 23024

Call Sign: W4FZ
Wade W Frazee Jr
741 Point Dr
Bumpass VA 23024

Call Sign: KF4NZO
Frank A Bryant Jr

25 Rivers Bend Ln
Bumpass VA 23024

Call Sign: KG4KGS
Kenneth G Sutton
1738 Signboard Rd
Bumpass VA 230243645

Call Sign: WD4GEE
David M Walker
60 Turners Mill Rd
Bumpass VA 23024

Call Sign: KD4EJD
Patricia A Gibson
410 Tyler Point Ln
Bumpass VA 230244644

Call Sign: W4NSU
Andrew L Gibson
410 Tyler Point Ln
Bumpass VA 230244644

Call Sign: KC8OCJ
Mathew J Lyons
367 Wickham Rd
Bumpass VA 23024

FCC Amateur Radio Licenses in Burgess

Call Sign: N8JNK
John F Witschey
70 Betts View Ln
Burgess VA 22432

Call Sign: W3AOH
Anthony F Susen
193 Old Gledge Point Rd
Burgess VA 22432

Call Sign: KS4YC
John N Dingley
St Rt 811
Burgess VA 22432

Call Sign: W1UXK
Arthur W Rogerson
Burgess VA 22432

Call Sign: AB4LJ
James M Thompson
Burgess VA 22432

Call Sign: KI4UWE
Lael R Easterling
Burgess VA 22432

Call Sign: KJ4KCD
Martin T Heacock
Burgess VA 22432

Call Sign: KJ4KCE
Cathy V Heacock
Burgess VA 224320276

Call Sign: KJ4TYR
James W Smith
Burgess VA 224320575

FCC Amateur Radio Licenses in Burke

Call Sign: KB4NQN
Frederick S Thompson
9106 Andromeda Dr
Burke VA 22015

Call Sign: KD4CTO
Marie Luise Giese
5113 Arrit Ct
Burke VA 22015

Call Sign: N5JBY
Richard Giese
5113 Arrit Ct
Burke VA 22015

Call Sign: KD4STC
Thomas S Nelson
9518 Ashbourn Dr
Burke VA 22015

Call Sign: WA4LYM
John F Osborne
6203 Atherstone Ct
Burke VA 22015

Call Sign: KG4MGB
David L Beadner
10735 Basket Oak Ct
Burke VA 220152402

Call Sign: KB9SPC
Jesse W Wright
5534 Beaconsfield Ct
Burke VA 22015

Call Sign: KE4JHN
Albert Sachs
9160 Bloom Ct
Burke VA 22015

Call Sign: KD4SZY
David L Kelly
9002 Bluffwood Ct
Burke VA 22015

Call Sign: KG4GKC
Paul C Christie
10325 Bridgetown Pl
Burke VA 22015

Call Sign: KI4YNC
Eric S Harmon
9687 Britford Dr
Burke VA 22015

Call Sign: KJ4LAU
Stephen E Belisle
5418 Brixham Ct
Burke VA 22015

Call Sign: WA4CFT
Melvin J Murray
9038 Brook Ford Rd
Burke VA 22015

Call Sign: KI4RBR
Michael L Mcminn
5765 Burke Center Pkwy 200
Burke VA 22015

Call Sign: KI4JSV
Lake Braddock Secondary
School ARC
9200 Burke Lake Rd

Burke VA 22015

Call Sign: WB4NBI
Stephen W Gibson
9642 Burke Lake Rd
Burke VA 22015

Call Sign: K4DUQ
James F Glennon
9642 Burke Lk Rd 303
Burke VA 22015

Call Sign: KD4GBX
Dean T Mcintyre
5801 Burke Manor Ct
Burke VA 22015

Call Sign: KF4MDI
Thomas A Tullia
9872 Burke Pond Ct
Burke VA 220152940

Call Sign: KA4BOA
Clyde L Luther
9732 Burke View Ct
Burke VA 22015

Call Sign: KF4WZB
Matthew G Sherburne
5975 Burnside Landing Dr
Burke VA 22015

Call Sign: W4NLT
Michael A Kubishen
6052 Burnside Landing Dr
Burke VA 220152521

Call Sign: N4WWL
David J Trachtenberg
9233 Byron Ter
Burke VA 22015

Call Sign: N4GJJ
David G Page
5400 Calstock Ct
Burke VA 22015

Call Sign: KJ4EPA
Vincent S Chernesky

5226 Capon Hill Pl
Burke VA 22015

Call Sign: KS4E
John W Ailes V
6010 Carrindale Ct
Burke VA 22015

Call Sign: N1LRQ
Luanne C Ailes
6010 Carrindale Ct
Burke VA 22015

Call Sign: WA3TOL
Edward W Morthimer
10933 Carters Oak Way
Burke VA 22015

Call Sign: WM5C
Robert D Edsall
10116 Chestnut Wood Ln
Burke VA 22015

Call Sign: K1NME
John E Acton
9715 Church Way
Burke VA 22015

Call Sign: KB8UZW
Charlene H Conaway
6074 Clerkenwell Ct
Burke VA 22015

Call Sign: W8HNT
William H Conaway
6074 Clerkenwell Ct
Burke VA 220153225

Call Sign: KK4EAU
Edward Kirkley
9204 Cork Pl
Burke VA 22015

Call Sign: W5NMK
Charles J Stockstill
7102 Counter Pl
Burke VA 22015

Call Sign: WD4CJW

William A Wampler
6112 Covered Bridge Rd
Burke VA 22015

Call Sign: KI4UGA
OBrian G Mckinley
6243 Covered Bridge Rd
Burke VA 22015

Call Sign: KJ4IVF
Diego J Blengio
5436 Crossrail Dr
Burke VA 22015

Call Sign: KA1TUL
Marcos Melendez
5831 Crowfoot Dr
Burke VA 220153321

Call Sign: KG4YEE
Ekaterina T Chelpon
9733 Dellford Ct
Burke VA 22015

Call Sign: KG4URY
Harry T Chelpon
9733 Dellford Ct
Burke VA 22015

Call Sign: KG4QHQ
Christine P Starr
6118 Dory Landing Ct
Burke VA 22015

Call Sign: WA4RDG
John R Hebert
5303 Dunleer Ln
Burke VA 22015

Call Sign: WA3USX
Robert D Roesler
5216 Dunleigh Dr
Burke VA 22015

Call Sign: KA8VZB
Joe W Alvis
5254 Dunleigh Dr
Burke VA 22015

Call Sign: K3EUE
Patrick H Roth
10214 Eagle Landing Ct
Burke VA 22015

Call Sign: KF4IRU
Grace M Parker
10211 Faire Commons Ct
Burke VA 22015

Call Sign: KF4BPK
Robert L Parker
10211 Faire Commons Ct
Burke VA 220152858

Call Sign: N4QZS
Leonard L Bednar
5427 Flint Tavern Pl
Burke VA 22015

Call Sign: KI4JPZ
Heather F Carter
9018 Fox Lair Dr
Burke VA 22015

Call Sign: WA7ZQV
Linda L Welch
6210 Fushsimi Ct
Burke VA 220153451

Call Sign: WB7VUM
Dennis E Welch
6210 Fushsimi Ct
Burke VA 220153451

Call Sign: WB4GTH
William J Minor Jr
5304 Greenough Pl
Burke VA 22015

Call Sign: KB4VLP
Norman S Rosenthal
6157 Hatches Ct
Burke VA 22015

Call Sign: KI4IJJ
Casey B Hammond
6011 Heathwick Ct
Burke VA 22015

Call Sign: KK4HKG
Richard A Gorbutt
9968 Hemlock Woods Ln
Burke VA 22015

Call Sign: W8XPK
Richard A Gorbutt
9968 Hemlock Woods Ln
Burke VA 22015

Call Sign: KG4RKM
Diana G Earp
9983 Hemlock Woods Ln
Burke VA 22015

Call Sign: KF4CNJ
Kim U Maxwell
5621 Herberts Crossing Dr
Burke VA 22015

Call Sign: KI4MUF
Charles C Yeh
10421 Heritage Landing Rd
Burke VA 22015

Call Sign: N6YKB
William C Glidden
5900 Hollow Oak Ct
Burkc VA 22015

Call Sign: KI4RCX
Janet L Glidden
5900 Hollow Oak Ct
Burke VA 22015

Call Sign: K3GS
Gary N Skillicorn
9107 Home Guard Dr
Burke VA 22015

Call Sign: KI4NOE
Frank J Kaleba
6446 Honey Tree Ct
Burke VA 22015

Call Sign: KQ8W
Frank J Kaleba
6446 Honey Tree Ct

Burke VA 22015

Call Sign: N3FK
Frank J Kaleba
6446 Honey Tree Ct
Burke VA 22015

Call Sign: KD4LSQ
Arlene G Forbes
6454 Honey Tree Ct
Burke VA 22015

Call Sign: KE0GP
Carl E Gluck
9640 Ironmaster Dr
Burke VA 22015

Call Sign: KE4EFQ
Theodore Freeman
5823 Jacksons Oak Ct
Burke VA 22015

Call Sign: WB2YRL
Jeffrey H Siegell
8919 Kenilworth Dr
Burke VA 22015

Call Sign: KJ4OXO
Antwong L Berkley
6023 Kerrwood St
Burke VA 22015

Call Sign: KF4GDF
Richard A Taschler
6209 Kersey Ct
Burke VA 22015

Call Sign: KD4SZZ
Walton T Sauerbier
5829 Kestrell Ct
Burke VA 22015

Call Sign: KB3GOQ
Emily A Kenealy
9517 Kirkfield Rd
Burke VA 22015

Call Sign: K1DOS
Henry D Kenealy

9517 Kirkfield Rd
Burke VA 22015

Call Sign: WA4RQA
Leroy L Reay Jr
9526 Kirkfield Rd
Burke VA 22015

Call Sign: W4ITU
Us Itu Delegates Club
10120 Lake Haven Ct
Burke VA 22015

Call Sign: W4RI
Paul L Rinaldo
10120 Lake Haven Ct
Burke VA 22015

Call Sign: N4QFZ
John F Hume Jr
9925 Lakepointe Ct
Burke VA 220151818

Call Sign: KA3WHB
Larry M Spence
5414 Lighthouse Ln
Burke VA 22015

Call Sign: KI4JPW
Joseph C Kempin
5498 Lighthouse Ln
Burke VA 22015

Call Sign: KA6RTZ
James J Hastings
6004 Lincolnwood Ct
Burke VA 22015

Call Sign: WB4NGR
Joel M Schnur
6009 Lincolnwood Ct
Burke VA 22015

Call Sign: KB3NG
Richard D Battle
9808 Longmead Ct
Burke VA 22015

Call Sign: KD4HIX

David J Whalen
6106 Lundy Pl
Burke VA 22015

Call Sign: KD4ILN
George W M Brown Jr
9336 Mainsail Dr
Burke VA 22015

Call Sign: KF4KFJ
Michael S Fantin
10140 Marshall Pond Rd
Burke VA 22015

Call Sign: KK4CBL
Larry D Walker
10160 Marshall Pond Rd
Burke VA 22015

Call Sign: KI4JQA
Brian L Chang
5733 Mason Bluff Dr
Burke VA 22015

Call Sign: AJ4FP
Philip E Beheler
10207 Merridith Cir Apt 103
Burke VA 22015

Call Sign: N8QI
Philip E Beheler
10207 Merridith Cir Apt 103
Burke VA 22015

Call Sign: KF4PQD
David E Dillard
5462 Midship Ct
Burke VA 22015

Call Sign: WA4LSE
James A Thomas
7304 Mizzen Pl
Burke VA 22015

Call Sign: KF4OSM
Mark W Barnes
7315 Mizzen Pl
Burke VA 22015

Call Sign: KI4PRJ
Sandra E Lennon
5446 Mt Corcoran Pl
Burke VA 220152147

Call Sign: W4NNP
Sandra E Lennon
5446 Mt Corcoran Pl
Burke VA 220152147

Call Sign: KG4SEK
George A Bonina
5801 New England Woods Dr
Burke VA 22015

Call Sign: K3ROO
George A Bonina
5801 New England Woods Dr
Burke VA 22015

Call Sign: KE4DXD
Peter H Bahniuk
5801 Oak Bucket Ct
Burke VA 22015

Call Sign: KE4RWF
James J Wieboldt
5934 Oak Leather Dr
Burke VA 22015

Call Sign: KC4SUY
Charlotte Laqui
5909 Oak Ridge Ct
Burke VA 22015

Call Sign: KE6FQP
Scott R Sizemore
5908 Oakland Park Dr
Burke VA 22015

Call Sign: KJ4FUV
Janet L Josten
9451 Onion Patch Dr
Burke VA 22015

Call Sign: KG4JNE
Justin D Kirker
10004 Park Woods Ln
Burke VA 22015

Call Sign: KB1FVZ
Rebecca A Kirker
10004 Park Woods Ln
Burke VA 22015

Call Sign: N4YZU
Robert C Bonn Jr
10024 Park Woods Ln
Burke VA 22015

Call Sign: N4WUV
Craig R Feinberg
6714 Passageway Pl
Burke VA 220154239

Call Sign: WD9AWJ
Keith A King
5546 Peppercorn Dr
Burke VA 22015

Call Sign: KE4UVF
Andrea L Van Ness
10336 Pond Spice Ter
Burke VA 22015

Call Sign: KJ4LYD
Gregory Josephs
5980 Powells Landing Rd
Burke VA 22015

Call Sign: AJ4QZ
Gregory Josephs
5980 Powells Landing Rd
Burke VA 22015

Call Sign: KB4WHO
Charles M Palmer
5907 Quintana Ct
Burke VA 22015

Call Sign: WB2GVZ
Gary M Graceffo
6518 Raftelis Rd
Burke VA 22015

Call Sign: KI4BYJ
Stephen J Graceffo
6518 Raftelis Rd

Burke VA 22015

Call Sign: KI4NFG
Curt M Shaffer
9305 Raintree Rd
Burke VA 22015

Call Sign: KJ4BQD
Norbert C Tagge
9906 Rand Dr
Burke VA 22015

Call Sign: KF4PSX
Linda M Le Annais
5638 Rapid Run Ct
Burke VA 22015

Call Sign: KA3CPT
James J Yven
10512 Reeds Landing Cir
Burke VA 22015

Call Sign: KF4OSG
Noah J Misch
9756 Rehanek Ct
Burke VA 22015

Call Sign: WB7TZZ
Jon T Asai
9511 Retriever Rd
Burke VA 22015

Call Sign: N4TVC
Charles R Allen
5910 Ridge Ford Dr
Burke VA 22015

Call Sign: KJ4WCN
Joel R Dobles
5910 Roberts Common Ct
Burke VA 22015

Call Sign: KG4JBB
Janet M Shadle
5720 Round Top Ln
Burke VA 22015

Call Sign: KK4FYT
Laura A Lukes

9606 Scorpio Ct
Burke VA 22015

Call Sign: KC4YFM
Edward C Van Reuth
10722 Shingle Oak Ct
Burke VA 22015

Call Sign: KI4LJE
Amy C Diluccio
10724 Shingle Oak Ct
Burke VA 22015

Call Sign: KC4YMI
John Diluccio
10724 Shingle Oak Ct
Burke VA 22015

Call Sign: KD4LSP
Susana C Di Luccio
10724 Shingle Oak Ct
Burke VA 22015

Call Sign: KJ4BII
Mike J Diluccio
10724 Shingle Oak Ct
Burke VA 22015

Call Sign: KA4UAW
Glen A Davis
9518 Sloop Ct
Burke VA 22015

Call Sign: KG4ZYZ
Laurence B Toyer
10304 Steamboat Landing Ln
Burke VA 220152542

Call Sign: KB2PG
Mark A Wagner
10354 Steamboat Landing Ln
Burke VA 22015

Call Sign: KG6BIV
Mark T Kaminsky
6702 Sunset Woods Ct
Burke VA 22015

Call Sign: KJ4JWN

David R Concepcion
5511 Swift Current Ct
Burke VA 22015

Call Sign: W4AWM
John H Bauer
5612 Tilia Ct
Burke VA 220152033

Call Sign: KD4ZLH
Tong Q Tran
9368 Tucker Woods Ct
Burke VA 22015

Call Sign: W4EGF
Edward G Finn
9511 Vandola Ct
Burke VA 22015

Call Sign: N3BHH
Charles P Hurley
7027 Veering Ln
Burke VA 22015

Call Sign: W6CPH
Charles P Hurley
7027 Veering Ln
Burke VA 22015

Call Sign: KC4OKM
Michael S Montemerlo
9619 Villagesmith Way
Burke VA 22015

Call Sign: N4YOA
Melvin D Montemerlo
9619 Villagesmith Way
Burke VA 22015

Call Sign: AB4GM
William P Kinsella
5300 Weetman St
Burke VA 22015

Call Sign: KK4FRG
Stephen J Cirelli
9637 Westport Ln
Burke VA 22015

Call Sign: WB4UKD
Craig M Masterson
6229 Wilmette Dr
Burke VA 22015

Call Sign: WB7RBX
Raymond R Hitchcock
6207 Wilmington Dr
Burke VA 22015

Call Sign: KA4OZJ
Sanford I Kantor
6216 Wilmington Dr
Burke VA 22015

Call Sign: N4GOO
Mary Lu Bednarsky
9415 Windsor Way
Burke VA 22015

Call Sign: NW4H
Raymond H Bednarsky
9415 Windsor Way
Burke VA 22015

Call Sign: WA4KEB
Ross L Amico
6013 Windward Dr
Burke VA 220153829

Call Sign: KS4LP
Wesley A Ballenger Jr
6015 Windward Dr
Burke VA 220153829

Call Sign: KB1JTT
Justin W Katsuki
5886 Wood Flower Ct
Burke VA 22015

Call Sign: KC4RVM
Barbara H Kaplan
5806 Wood Laurel Ct
Burke VA 22015

Call Sign: KG4UHR
Alexander M Golden
9437 Wooded Glen Ave
Burke VA 22015

Call Sign: K6HSK
Matij Mirko
5859 Wye Oak Commons Ct
Burke VA 220152871

Call Sign: KJ4VTO
Scott F Downey
Burke VA 220090272

Call Sign: KF4OSS
Charles W Ross
Burke VA 220091281

FCC Amateur Radio Licenses in Burkeville

Call Sign: KC4ALL
Grover E Reeves
Rt 1 Box 55
Burkeville VA 23922

Call Sign: W2CPB
Carl P Biggs III
117 Deems St
Burkeville VA 23922

Call Sign: N4XQG
Luther T Goldsmith
4901 E Patrick Henry Hwy
Burkeville VA 23922

Call Sign: KC0GBQ
William C Thompson III
308 Harris Spring Rd
Burkeville VA 23922

Call Sign: KG4BGP
Edward B Graham
311 Harris Spring Rd
Burkeville VA 23922

Call Sign: KG4BGQ
Thomas D Graham
311 Harris Spring Rd
Burkeville VA 23922

Call Sign: KG4HLE
Benjamin B Graham

311 Harris Spring Rd
Burkeville VA 23922

Call Sign: KI4WCH
Stirel M Paxton Jr
561 Quail Crossing Rd
Burkeville VA 23922

Call Sign: W5PAX
Stirgel M Paxton Jr
561 Quail Crossing Rd
Burkeville VA 23922

Call Sign: KJ4CWG
Horace L Ellett
7972 W Courthouse Rd
Burkeville VA 23922

FCC Amateur Radio Licenses in Burnsville

Call Sign: KC4JWH
Joyce A Hevener
9422 Dry Run Rd
Burnsville VA 24487

Call Sign: KC4JWI
Dempsie L Hevener
9422 Dry Run Rd
Burnsville VA 24487

Call Sign: KD4WPN
John A C Hillegass Jr
29147 Raccoon Ford Rd
Burr Hill VA 22433

Call Sign: KJ4HKK
Anette E Hillegass
29147 Raccoon Ford Rd
Burr Hill VA 22433

Call Sign: K4GTI
John A C Hillegass Jr
29147 Raccoon Ford Rd
Burr Hill VA 22433

FCC Amateur Radio Licenses in Callands

Call Sign: KI4PMQ
Ruby D Marks
126 Sago Rd
Callands VA 24530

Call Sign: KM4AW
Wade W Walton Sr
2672 Water Oak Rd
Callands VA 24530

FCC Amateur Radio Licenses in Callao

Call Sign: KD4SAE
Gayle F Davis
Rt 1 Box 429A
Callao VA 22435

Call Sign: W3HDW
Karl D Toll
2918 Hampton Hall Rd
Callao VA 22435

Call Sign: KG4IPT
Northern Neck Contest Club
2540 Hampton Hall Rd Rt 202
Callao VA 22435

Call Sign: K4DCA
Carl L Vogt
Callao VA 22435

Call Sign: KC4RBO
Phillip B Beauchamp Jr
Callao VA 22435

Call Sign: KC4RBQ
Phillip B Beauchamp Sr
Callao VA 22435

Call Sign: KC4RBR
John A Beauchamp
Callao VA 22435

Call Sign: W4HBT
John A Hawn Jr
Callao VA 22435

Call Sign: KB4TRJ

Marbury M Hutchison
Callao VA 22435

Call Sign: KD3PC
David M Dabay
Callao VA 22435

Call Sign: KD4CAZ
Gladys A Beaulieu
Callao VA 22435

Call Sign: N4CX
Andrew J Beaulieu
Callao VA 22435

Call Sign: KB4KOQ
James L Prillaman
Callao VA 22435

Call Sign: KB4KOR
Patricia A Prillaman
Callao VA 22435

FCC Amateur Radio Licenses in Callaway

Call Sign: KA9PDD
James E Dunn
1115 6 Mi Post Rd
Callaway VA 240674803

Call Sign: NB8B
Suzanne E Novak
765 Algoma Rd
Callaway VA 24067

Call Sign: KE4OAL
Jack L Blake
8061 Callaway Rd
Callaway VA 24067

Call Sign: AI4LL
Jack L Blake
8061 Callaway Rd
Callaway VA 24067

Call Sign: KB4WNT
Edwin R Durham
1601 Dugspur Rd

Callaway VA 24067

Call Sign: KI4NOA
Keith J Duvall
2365 Dugspur Rd
Callaway VA 240673015

Call Sign: KF4PGR
Edward B Dillon
250 Isolane Rd
Callaway VA 24067

Call Sign: KI4VJ
John W Kinsey
940 Rockridge Rd
Callaway VA 24067

Call Sign: KI4ZND
Francine W Arrington
14 Walnut Grove Dr
Callaway VA 24067

Call Sign: KG6AR
Christy Williams
220 Woods Landing Ln
Callaway VA 24067

FCC Amateur Radio Licenses in Cana

Call Sign: N2CVU
Joseph A De Clerico
400 Backwoods Ln
Cana VA 24317

Call Sign: N4MBX
Mabel M Utt
Rt 1 Box 383
Cana VA 24317

Call Sign: KE4AAN
Mitchell R Hawks
1212 Brushy Fork Rd
Cana VA 24317

Call Sign: KK4CWL
Edward M Easter
149 Farmbrook Rd
Cana VA 24317

Call Sign: KD4KMJ
Howard D Stockner
1800 Flint Hill Rd
Cana VA 24317

Call Sign: AE4ZM
Robert L Vernon
4058 Flower Gap Rd
Cana VA 24317

Call Sign: KF4WAL
Darrell I Gwyn
21 L Js Ln
Cana VA 243170218

Call Sign: KG4HEN
Pauline D Hawks
1620 Pauls Creek Church Rd
Cana VA 24317

Call Sign: WB4ZTY
Clarence E Hawks
1620 Pauls Creek Curch Rd
Cana VA 24317

Call Sign: K4XME
Marvin C Edwards
1388 Sandy Ridge Rd
Cana VA 24317

Call Sign: KF4ZBC
Gerald Rw Clemons
120 Speas Mill Rd
Cana VA 24317

Call Sign: KF4WMW
Berlie F Richardson
522 Sunset Dr
Cana VA 24317

Call Sign: KG4INI
Jessica L Richardson
522 Sunset Dr
Cana VA 24317

Call Sign: WA4SFT
Luke F Dawson
3255 Wards Gap Rd

Cana VA 24317

Call Sign: W4FNH
Lonnie M Utt
4124 Wards Gap Rd
Cana VA 24317

Call Sign: KJ4LIO
Jerry D Mc Millian
5781 Wards Gap Rd
Cana VA 24317

Call Sign: KJ4LIN
Donnie R Mc Millian
5787 Wards Gap Rd
Cana VA 24317

Call Sign: KK4CWJ
Charles M Easter
354 Woodcreek Dr
Cana VA 24317

Call Sign: KF4MBL
Jerry G Nichols
Cana VA 24317

Call Sign: KF4VLW
Robert C Easter
Cana VA 24317

Call Sign: KF4WAM
Kathy M Easter
Cana VA 24317

FCC Amateur Radio Licenses in Cape Charles

Call Sign: KJ4QYX
Sheree E Terry
15 Nectarine St
Cape Charles VA 23310

Call Sign: KJ4AG
Austin C Davis
5 Randolph Ave
Cape Charles VA 23310

Call Sign: KB2BBK
Douglas C Charlton

6221 Riverside Farm Ln
Cape Charles VA 23310

FCC Amateur Radio Licenses in Cardinal

Call Sign: N4ISO
Nanci W Reaves
Heron Point Box 100
Cardinal VA 23025

Call Sign: KE4VPG
Susan L Jennette
280 Long Point Ln
Cardinal VA 23025

FCC Amateur Radio Licenses in Carrollton

Call Sign: WB4ETD
Michael J Stuart
14447 Bayview Dr
Carrollton VA 23314

Call Sign: K4IWA
Kirsten B Roth
404 Blue Heron Trl
Carrollton VA 233143534

Call Sign: N4WHE
Kenneth W Bunch
Rt 1 Box 232B
Carrollton VA 23314

Call Sign: N4VEA
Phillip M Gillihan
Rt 2 Box 98
Carrollton VA 23314

Call Sign: KF4NAE
Clifford L Halterman II
15317 Bro Gain Ln
Carrollton VA 23314

Call Sign: KF4URU
David L Reynolds Sr
22448 Doris Ct
Carrollton VA 23314

Call Sign: W4WER
William M Fulcher Jr
12 Merritt Cove Rd
Carrollton VA 23314

Call Sign: KI4PS
Jerry C Rogers
6 Nelson Maine
Carrollton VA 23314

Call Sign: KE4TYE
Jimmy L Norville
12735 Nike Park Rd
Carrollton VA 23314

Call Sign: WB4KZI
Randolph W Grigg
14038 Osborne Ln
Carrollton VA 23314

Call Sign: KB9CUM
Philip D Wise
14062 Ponderosa Ln
Carrollton VA 23314

Call Sign: KI4BIO
Paul A Vasilauskis
23080 Quail Covey Ct
Carrollton VA 233142255

Call Sign: KE4WLV
Elliot A Pagano
22317 Riverpoint Tr
Carrollton VA 23314

Call Sign: KJ4WCJ
Nathan W Greene
529 Shoreline Rd
Carrollton VA 23314

Call Sign: KI4UWF
Thornton A Cutchin
11021 Smith Neck Rd
Carrollton VA 23314

Call Sign: KI4UNP
Michael J Parker
13120 Smiths Neck Rd
Carrollton VA 23314

Call Sign: KI4YLW
Scott M Parker
13120 Smiths Neck Rd
Carrollton VA 23314

Call Sign: KF4NMC
Judith L Bander
24530 Sugar Hill Rd
Carrollton VA 23314

Call Sign: WA4WEF
Morris A Bander
24530 Sugar Hill Rd
Carrollton VA 23314

Call Sign: KC4WNV
Julian E Meredith Sr
24694 Sugar Hill Rd
Carrollton VA 23314

Call Sign: KJ4PGF
Steven A Johnston
15091 Sundew Dr
Carrollton VA 23314

Call Sign: KE4BZO
Jason M Carlton
22438 Sundown Dr
Carrollton VA 23314

Call Sign: K1OB
Russell J Ouellette
22438 Sundown Dr
Carrollton VA 23314

Call Sign: KC4YRN
William C Wallace Jr
23261 Tara Ct
Carrollton VA 23314

Call Sign: KF4NMD
Paula Q Wallace
23261 Tara Ct
Carrollton VA 23314

Call Sign: K4WCW
William C Wallace Jr
23261 Tara Ct

Carrollton VA 23314

Call Sign: W4RGN
Jarvis M Hearn
12223 Teal Ct
Carrollton VA 23314

Call Sign: N3YIK
Kurt F Kappen
22306 Tradewinds Dr
Carrollton VA 23314

Call Sign: WA4LNM
James F Chapman
21445 Twin Hill Rd
Carrollton VA 23314

Call Sign: K2VXO
David W Utter
Carrollton VA 23314

Call Sign: KK4BWK
Steven J Williams II
29032 Holly Run Dr
Carrsville VA 23315

Call Sign: KF4ZPH
Thomas M Hoernig
4490 Stevens Dr
Carrsville VA 23315

Call Sign: KD4FLJ
Elizabeth J Scott
29187 Walters Hwy
Carrsville VA 23315

Call Sign: KC4ZLM
Sharon F Veazey
14754 Cabin Point Rd
Carson VA 23830

Call Sign: WD4OIM
Page K Veazey

14754 Cabin Point Rd
Carson VA 23830

Call Sign: KI4SSP
Field Comm Association
Carson VA 238300071

Call Sign: KQ4RG
John B Hudgins
Carson VA 238300071

Call Sign: KC4LEO
Leo Henderson
87 Boston Hill Rd
Cartersville VA 23027

Call Sign: W4CNY
Edward Sams
33 Highpockets Rd
Cartersville VA 23027

Call Sign: KJ4YEH
Azaryah G Baggott
49 Jefferson Rd
Cartersville VA 23027

Call Sign: KJ4YDB
Hananyah D Baggott
49 Jefferson Rd
Cartersville VA 23027

Call Sign: KJ4YDC
Kelaiah A Baggott
49 Jefferson Rd
Cartersville VA 23027

Call Sign: KJ4YDD
Rosemary Baggott
49 Jefferson Rd
Cartersville VA 23027

Call Sign: KJ4YEF
Shaun L Baggett
49 Jefferson Rd
Cartersville VA 23027

Call Sign: KJ4YEG
Yehoshua M Baggott
49 Jefferson Rd
Cartersville VA 23027

Call Sign: WB4ZRG
John C Schalestock
5053 Weston Rd Box 21
Casanova VA 20139

Call Sign: KD6RNE
Marvin B Hearrell Jr
Casanova VA 20139

Call Sign: KD6WRY
Steven N Hearrell
Casanova VA 20139

Call Sign: AD4VA
Marvin B Hearrell Jr
Casanova VA 20139

Call Sign: KE4GCW
Angela E Addario
Casanova VA 22017

Call Sign: KG4DGG
Brenda G Hearrell
Casanova VA 201390282

Call Sign: KC3RE
Martin Berkofsky
Casanova VA 201390288

Call Sign: KD4SDV
Pete M Wilson
Rt 1 Box 1066
Cascade VA 24069

Call Sign: KI4EJV
Christopher S Mitchell
4969 Cascade Mill Rd
Cascade VA 24069

Call Sign: KJ4AMY
Kathy S Jones
1440 Hunnington Trl
Cascade VA 24069

Call Sign: KJ4ACP
Southside ARC
1440 Huntington Trl
Cascade VA 24069

Call Sign: KI4PMM
Dewey L Jones
1440 Huntington Trl
Cascade VA 24069

Call Sign: KI4EJW
William B Pearce
217 Loblolly Dr
Cascade VA 24069

Call Sign: W4WBP
William B Pearce
217 Loblolly Dr
Cascade VA 24069

Call Sign: KF4WKC
William J Shelton
13184 Martinsville Hwy
Cascade VA 24069

Call Sign: KM4BJ
Francis A Gard Jr
5757 Whispering Pines Rd
Cascade VA 240693829

FCC Amateur Radio Licenses in Castleton

Call Sign: KE7HXJ
Brett S Blackham
353 Aaron Mtn Rd
Castleton VA 22716

Call Sign: KF4YKP
Marcia Murray
29 Alta Vista
Castleton VA 22716

Call Sign: KF4YKQ
Wayne T Murray
29 Alta Vista Ln
Castleton VA 22716

Call Sign: KC4RLF
Joseph W O Leary
Rt 1 Box 120
Castleton VA 22716

Call Sign: KC4KPS
Jason L Fox
Rt 1 Box 199
Castleton VA 22716

FCC Amateur Radio Licenses in Castlewood

Call Sign: KI4FRL
Harold A Mcdaniel Jr
Rt 2 Box 127
Castlewood VA 242249760

Call Sign: K4CBE
Cecil B Ennis
Rt 1 Box 144
Castlewood VA 24224

Call Sign: KE4ONN
Eddie L Fields
Rr 1 Box 366
Castlewood VA 24224

Call Sign: KF4FEL
Elizabeth A Newberry
Rt 1 Box 377 R
Castlewood VA 24224

Call Sign: KF4KTI
Matthew W Sutherland
Rt 1 Box 377 V
Castlewood VA 24224

Call Sign: WA4OFO
David L Simmerly
Rt 1 Box 435
Castlewood VA 24224

Call Sign: KB4WCS

Linda A Simmerly
Rt 1 Box 464 A
Castlewood VA 24224

Call Sign: KF4MNX
Marvin L Patrick
Rt 1 Box 78
Castlewood VA 24224

Call Sign: KF4BWF
Kenneth B Newberry
446 Clairmont Cir
Castlewood VA 24224

Call Sign: KI4YYC
Ben M Hale
1763 Copper Ridge Rd
Castlewood VA 24224

Call Sign: KI4UAO
Ricky E Hale
1763 Copper Ridge Rd
Castlewood VA 24224

Call Sign: KI4ZJT
VA Defense Force Highlands
Brigade ARC
205 Heralds Valley Rd
Castlewood VA 24224

Call Sign: K4VDF
VA Defense Force Highland
Bde 34th Bn
205 Heralds Valley Rd
Castlewood VA 24224

Call Sign: KD4DRJ
Robert P Bratton
Castlewood VA 24224

Call Sign: KC4WQR
Karen L Powers
Castlewood VA 24224

Call Sign: KE4PXQ
David L Phillips
Castlewood VA 24224

Call Sign: KE4ZAM

Randy W Sluss
Castlewood VA 24224

Call Sign: KF4YTF
Kitty S Phillips
Castlewood VA 24224

Call Sign: KJ4VQX
Dustin S Blackson
Castlewood VA 24224

FCC Amateur Radio Licenses in Catawba

Call Sign: KF4LBE
David A Hewitt
7020 Blacksburg Rd
Catawba VA 24070

Call Sign: KF4MUA
Courtney K Hewitt
7020 Blacksburg Rd
Catawba VA 24070

Call Sign: KI4FZU
John K Anderson
9089 Blacksburg Rd
Catawba VA 24070

Call Sign: K4JKA
John K Anderson
9089 Blacksburg Rd
Catawba VA 24070

Call Sign: KI4GOT
Karen L Anderson
9089 Blacksburg Rd
Catawba VA 24070

Call Sign: KB4IPR
Raymond G Hendrick
Rt 620 Box 387A
Catawba VA 24070

Call Sign: KD4OBH
Ruth Z Hendrick
Rt 620 Box 387A
Catawba VA 24070

Call Sign: WA4NMK
Ronald J Morgan
Rt 1 Box 474
Catawba VA 24070

Call Sign: KI4MUR
Christopher N Short
Rt 1 Box 593 A
Catawba VA 24070

Call Sign: WA4NDI
James F Light
8418 Gravel Hill Rd
Catawba VA 24070

Call Sign: KA4EIQ
Catherine W Light
8418 Gravelhill Rd
Catawba VA 240702113

Call Sign: KG4ALI
Kevin A Shinpaugh
395 McAfee Branch Ln
Catawba VA 24070

Call Sign: KF4YLM
Joshua M Arritt
8841 Newport Rd
Catawba VA 24070

Call Sign: K4IQ
John B Mitchell
Catawba VA 24070

FCC Amateur Radio Licenses in Catersville

Call Sign: KI4ITS
Harold L Converse
1096 Ampthill Rd
Catersville VA 23027

FCC Amateur Radio Licenses in Catharpin

Call Sign: AJ4JO
Samuel H Fowler Jr
12143 Richland Dr
Catharpin VA 20143

Call Sign: W4AEV
Samuel H Fowler Jr
12143 Richland Dr
Catharpin VA 20143

Call Sign: KE4RTL
Brian K Richter
12002 Robin Dr
Catharpin VA 22018

Call Sign: N9BGQ
Bruce D Myrehn
3480 Sanders Ln
Catharpin VA 20143

Call Sign: KK4FYX
Beth A Waller
3803 Sanders Ln
Catharpin VA 20143

Call Sign: AK4PK
Richard W Waller
3803 Sanders Ln
Catharpin VA 20143

Call Sign: N4EDE
Dale T Smith
4413 Shari Ct
Catharpin VA 201431004

Call Sign: W4PJP
Herbert M Plummer
4827 Sudley Rd
Catharpin VA 22018

Call Sign: KK4FL
David P Bannister
Catharpin VA 20143

Call Sign: W4ZB
Paul S Richter
Catharpin VA 20143

FCC Amateur Radio Licenses in Catlett

Call Sign: KD4QIW
Joseph G Benfit

4196 Brookfield Dr
Catlett VA 22019

Call Sign: AJ4LL
Ross L Primrose
3537 Days Ln
Catlett VA 20119

Call Sign: N4RP
Ross L Primrose
3537 Days Ln
Catlett VA 20119

Call Sign: WB8VUW
Thomas B Noble
11887 Elk Run Rd
Catlett VA 20119

Call Sign: KA4RRU
Michael Trowbridge
11325 Eskridges Ln
Catlett VA 20119

Call Sign: KR4TTY
Gar Field High School ARC
11325 Eskridges Ln
Catlett VA 22019

Call Sign: KF4AGR
Gar Field High School ARC
11325 Eskridges Ln
Catlett VA 22019

Call Sign: WA3AJC
Charles N Fellows
8383 Greenwich Rd
Catlett VA 201191924

Call Sign: KI4VEO
Howard L Walker
8030 Kettle Run Ct
Catlett VA 20119

Call Sign: WA0CIE
Julius B Wlaschin
7742 Overbrook Dr
Catlett VA 201191761

Call Sign: KG4MCL

Victoria B Kelley
2572 Partridge Run Way
Catlett VA 20119

Call Sign: AB4DL
David R Kelley
2572 Partridge Run Way
Catlett VA 201192556

Call Sign: AE4HS
James M Daniel
9212 Prospect Ave
Catlett VA 20119

Call Sign: KD4QIU
Peter E Rawlings
Quail Run Box 357 Rr 2
Catlett VA 22019

Call Sign: KG4CYN
Elmer Robertson
10826 Shenandoah Path
Catlett VA 201192153

Call Sign: KC7UQL
Steven D Graubard
4202 St Stephens Ct
Catlett VA 20119

Call Sign: KF4UQT
Lisa M Graham
Catlett VA 20119

Call Sign: KI4ZKJ
Greg Moyers
Catlett VA 20119

Call Sign: KI4ZKI
Henry Moyers
Catlett VA 20119

FCC Amateur Radio Licenses in Cauthornville

Call Sign: KI4AXZ
Dolores A Bogetti
Hc 1 Box 129A
Cauthornville VA 23148

FCC Amateur Radio Licenses in Cctlett

Call Sign: WA1FAZ
Victor J Moretti
8012 Taylor Rd
Cctlett VA 201191749

FCC Amateur Radio Licenses in Cedar Bluff

Call Sign: KI4TYK
Danny W Starling
2262 Bandy Rd
Cedar Bluff VA 24609

Call Sign: KE4YNT
Charles T Shinall
335 Birmingham Rd
Cedar Bluff VA 24609

Call Sign: KB4TAJ
Michael D Luttrell
Rt 2 Box 100
Cedar Bluff VA 24609

Call Sign: KA4PGC
Jay R Mc Coy
Rr 3 Box 2390
Cedar Bluff VA 246098996

Call Sign: KC4KTM
Mary A Mc Coy
Rr 3 Box 2390
Cedar Bluff VA 246098996

Call Sign: KE4CXC
Keith W Rife
Rt 2 Box 7125
Cedar Bluff VA 246099004

Call Sign: KI4EPS
Roger L Keen
254 Lick Branch Rd
Cedar Bluff VA 24609

Call Sign: NO4H
Lloyd D Worley
170 Mockingbird Dr

Cedar Bluff VA 246098229

Call Sign: KK4UB
Diana J Worley
170 Mockingbird Dr
Cedar Bluff VA 246098229

Call Sign: KI4TYL
Terry L Johnson
2516 Old Hwy 19
Cedar Bluff VA 24609

Call Sign: KD4TC
Lawrence L Hagy
367 Ponderosa Heights Rd
Cedar Bluff VA 24609

Call Sign: N4NP
Ronald D Keene
791 Spring Hill Rd
Cedar Bluff VA 24609

Call Sign: KD4KPB
James M Hutchinson III
1588 Wardell Rd
Cedar Bluff VA 24609

Call Sign: N4TCA
Tri-County ARC
194 White Dr
Cedar Bluff VA 24609

Call Sign: KG4SWQ
Tri-County ARC
194 White Dr
Cedar Bluff VA 24609

Call Sign: KI4HYP
Amanda D Shelton
1061 Willow Springs Rd
Cedar Bluff VA 24609

Call Sign: KE4THM
Steven H Beavers
122 Wingo Ln
Cedar Bluff VA 24609

Call Sign: KC4IFG
Jane W Crawford

Cedar Bluff VA 24609

Call Sign: KM4FY
George D Crawford
Cedar Bluff VA 24609

Call Sign: N4TBZ
Ronald K James
Cedar Bluff VA 24609

Call Sign: N4ZZQ
Alfred L Keen Jr
Cedar Bluff VA 24609

Call Sign: N8QJG
Thomas B Cortellesi
Cedar Bluff VA 24609

Call Sign: KI4YRC
David B Mahone
Cedar Bluff VA 24609

Call Sign: K4YNW
Wilbert G Thomas
Cedar Bluff VA 246090948

Call Sign: KG4BTL
Hazel V Thomas
Cedar Bluff VA 246090948

FCC Amateur Radio Licenses in Center Cross

Call Sign: KJ4DMK
Steven G Beasley
10073 Howerton Rd
Center Cross VA 22437

Call Sign: KI4NJT
Herman D Sears
Center Cross VA 22437

Call Sign: KI4NJS
Jacqueline L Sears
Center Cross VA 22437

FCC Amateur Radio Licenses in Centreville

Call Sign: KJ4QKO
Mary Joanne A Allmond
14509 4 Chimney Dr
Centreville VA 20120

Call Sign: AI4QC
William G Allmond
14509 4 Chimney Dr
Centreville VA 20120

Call Sign: KG4JAL
Joseph E Bertoni
14606 Algretus Dr
Centreville VA 20120

Call Sign: KF4PQM
Decha Lee
13985 Antonia Ford Ct
Centreville VA 20120

Call Sign: KG4BMW
Michael R Conner
14204 Asher View
Centreville VA 201215316

Call Sign: WV4V
Brian W Treadwell
6258 Astrid Cove
Centreville VA 201201853

Call Sign: KF4CWH
Douglas S Hudson
13905 Barnsley Pl
Centreville VA 201205209

Call Sign: KC4EZW
Mark W Underwood
13646 Barren Springs Ct
Centreville VA 22020

Call Sign: KF4WLD
James T Palmer
14664 Basingstoke Loop
Centreville VA 20120

Call Sign: KG4SFT
Jason T Luttgens
14698 Basingstoke Loop
Centreville VA 20120

Call Sign: KI4OBQ
John K Murray
6212 Battalion St
Centreville VA 20121

Call Sign: KJ4LBA
Christopher L Smith
14506 Battery Ridge Ln
Centreville VA 20120

Call Sign: KG4DVB
Joseph M O Brien
14538 Battery Ridge Ln
Centreville VA 201202877

Call Sign: KA3SBX
Leslie Vandivere
13825 Baywood Ct
Centreville VA 22020

Call Sign: KI4ZZW
Suresh Marella
5709 Bent Tree Ln Apt 201
Centreville VA 20121

Call Sign: KI2SRW
Suresh Marella
5709 Bent Tree Ln Apt 201
Centreville VA 20121

Call Sign: KE4QND
Edwin S Summers
5719 Bent Tree Ln Apt 303
Centreville VA 20121

Call Sign: KG4QXM
John D Hagarty
13902 Big Yankee Ln
Centreville VA 20121

Call Sign: N4XTH
Christine C Anderson
14922 Boydell Dr
Centreville VA 20120

Call Sign: AB4TF
Alan L Anderson
14922 Boydell Dr

Centreville VA 201201534

Call Sign: KJ4WKF
Martin A Rothwell
5483 Braddock Ridge Dr
Centreville VA 20120

Call Sign: KC4WES
Judith A Lewis
5485 Braddock Ridge Dr
Centreville VA 20120

Call Sign: N4SCK
Robert V Lewis
5485 Braddock Ridge Dr
Centreville VA 20120

Call Sign: KA3OIP
Sean P Mc Closkey
13847 F Braddock Springs Rd
Centreville VA 20121

Call Sign: W2HRK
Jay R Hern
5214 Braywood Dr
Centreville VA 220204101

Call Sign: KG4VJL
Kenneth C Cowan
5235 Braywood Dr
Centreville VA 20120

Call Sign: AI4UY
Kenneth C Cowan
5235 Braywood Dr
Centreville VA 20120

Call Sign: KJ4ZLC
Syrus Mesdaghi
5124 Brittney Elyse Cir Apt K
Centreville VA 20120

Call Sign: WB4GDB
Stephen C Foster
6755 Bronze Post Rd
Centreville VA 220212189

Call Sign: WA4KFZ
Mark D Braunstein

14345 Brookmere Dr
Centreville VA 201204106

Call Sign: K4CGC
Roy B Shrout Jr
7514 Bull Run Dr
Centreville VA 220202501

Call Sign: KA4SMY
Roberta M Pala
6606 Bull Run Post Office Rd
Centreville VA 201201005

Call Sign: WB4NFB
William P Pala Jr
6606 Bull Run Post Office Rd
Centreville VA 201201005

Call Sign: KC4VXH
William E Kamm
6638 Bull Run Post Office Rd
Centreville VA 201201005

Call Sign: KG4NSZ
Carl C Crown
13805 Cabells Mill Dr
Centreville VA 20120

Call Sign: W0STY
Carl C Crown
13805 Cabells Mill Dr
Centreville VA 20120

Call Sign: KE4UYF
Carl C Crown
13805 Cabells Mill Dr
Centreville VA 20120

Call Sign: KI4DTL
Paul S Bassett III
13987 Cabells Mill Dr
Centreville VA 20120

Call Sign: KE4EUB
David S Smail
6022 Callaway Ct
Centreville VA 20121

Call Sign: AC4JV

Jerry A Moore
14710 Carlbern Dr
Centreville VA 20120

Call Sign: KD4ITO
Judith A Moore
14710 Carlbern Dr
Centreville VA 20120

Call Sign: K4HFE
William F Kirlin
14912 Carlbern Dr
Centreville VA 220201509

Call Sign: KC4OBU
Linn C Klitzkie
15015 Carlbern Dr
Centreville VA 22020

Call Sign: AG4DI
Eric P Lang
5119 Castle Harbor Way
Centreville VA 20120

Call Sign: N4NTW
Karl L Hoffman
14606 Cedar Knoll Dr
Centreville VA 201202895

Call Sign: KI4JLJ
Gerald R Taylor III
5727 Cedar Walk 203
Centreville VA 201214543

Call Sign: AG4FI
Edwin S Summers
5727 Cedar Walk Apt 104
Centreville VA 20121

Call Sign: KE4TMY
Judith A Sutto
13650 Clarendon Spgs Ct
Centreville VA 22020

Call Sign: KG4SHB
Stephen C Schreppler
5872 Clarendon Springs Pl
Centreville VA 20121

Call Sign: KE4ULV
Robert W Hall Jr
14317 Climbing Rose Way 106
Centreville VA 22020

Call Sign: KJ4UYB
Christopher M Flynn
14405 Coachway Dr
Centreville VA 20120

Call Sign: KK4GSF
John A Garman
14414 Coachway Dr
Centreville VA 20120

Call Sign: N3MBL
Garcia F Doores
14749 Compton Rd
Centreville VA 20121

Call Sign: KT4DZ
Ivan A Reeder
14107 Compton Valley Way
Centreville VA 201215001

Call Sign: NN4IR
Ivan A Reeder
14107 Compton Valley Way
Centreville VA 201215001

Call Sign: KI4IPL
Andy R Pethiel
6902 Confederate Ridge Ln
Centreville VA 20121

Call Sign: N5EXX
Kenneth R Brooke
14708 Cranoke St
Centreville VA 20120

Call Sign: WB3CBA
Lester C Bond Jr
14547 Creek Branch Ct
Centreville VA 20120

Call Sign: KD4WGN
Dennis J Wilson
14581 Creek Branch Ct
Centreville VA 20120

Call Sign: KB3MUS
Stephen B Chiama
13905 Cristo Ct
Centreville VA 20120

Call Sign: KC4ONX
John A Tucker
5708 Croatan Ct
Centreville VA 20120

Call Sign: K5MBP
Jon H Bryson
14901 Cub Run Park Dr
Centreville VA 22020

Call Sign: KD4HAS
Larry T Wiggins
6062 Deer Hill Ct
Centreville VA 22020

Call Sign: KF4RUU
Peter M Schumann
13916 Deviar Dr
Centreville VA 20120

Call Sign: N0UID
Linda D Hart
5863 E Post Corners Trl
Centreville VA 20120

Call Sign: N4KRC
David J Francis
14818 Edman Rd
Centreville VA 20121

Call Sign: KD5KJN
Laura L Raderman
5221 Ellicott Ct
Centreville VA 20120

Call Sign: W2CMF
Christopher M Flynn
6503 Fawn Hollow Pl
Centreville VA 201201050

Call Sign: KC5BMR
Charles M Holt
6301 Field Flower Trl

Centreville VA 20121

Call Sign: KJ4ZTO
Thomas E Shinn
14401 Filly Ct
Centreville VA 20120

Call Sign: K4SWK
Thomas E Shinn
14401 Filly Ct
Centreville VA 20120

Call Sign: WA4ARP
Robert T Beisgen Jr
13615 Forest Pond Ct
Centreville VA 20121

Call Sign: KD4KLK
William J Van Der Vossen
13634 Forest Pond Ct
Centreville VA 201213011

Call Sign: KO4UJ
Peter W Franck
6354 Generals Ct
Centreville VA 20121

Call Sign: WB4UNB
Charles D Collier
14225 Glade Spring Dr
Centreville VA 201215603

Call Sign: ND3A
Robert N Shapiro
14229 Glade Spring Dr
Centreville VA 201215607

Call Sign: KD4KLI
William P Shealy
5409 Gladewright Dr
Centreville VA 20120

Call Sign: KJ4EAW
Thomas H Williams
5444 Gladewright Dr
Centreville VA 201203333

Call Sign: KA8UOV
David W Wiley

14473 Glencrest Cir
Centreville VA 22020

Call Sign: KB4LFQ
Lisa A Floyd
14984 Gold Post Ct
Centreville VA 22020

Call Sign: KD4LOM
Charles K Mc Craw
14457 Golden Oak Rd
Centreville VA 22020

Call Sign: KA4BAQ
Michael W Comeau
14533 Golden Oak Rd
Centreville VA 22020

Call Sign: KE4NFH
Brian D Easter
14559 Golden Oak Rd
Centreville VA 22020

Call Sign: KB0KCZ
Bryan E Laird
14552 Granville Ln
Centreville VA 20120

Call Sign: KJ4GUN
Joseph Y Yoon
13456 Gray Valley Ct
Centreville VA 20120

Call Sign: WA0LMI
Henry H Allen
14795 Green Park Way
Centreville VA 20120

Call Sign: N3KRA
Fee H Lee
5608 Gresham Ln
Centreville VA 20120

Call Sign: KF4MZX
Valentina Chegai
15029 Greymont Dr
Centreville VA 20120

Call Sign: KF4MZY

Gianluca Chegai
15029 Greymont Dr
Centreville VA 20120

Call Sign: KG4UPP
Karl W Berger
6491 Gristmill Sq Ln
Centreville VA 201203725

Call Sign: W4KRL
Karl W Berger
6491 Gristmill Sq Ln
Centreville VA 201203725

Call Sign: KG4UNL
Matthew Berger
6491 Gritmill Sq Ln
Centreville VA 20120

Call Sign: WA4CSV
Karen M Schweikart
14020B Grumble Jones Ct
Centreville VA 22020

Call Sign: KD4UNV
Frances S Pike
15306 Harmony Hill Ct
Centreville VA 22020

Call Sign: KC4VMV
Thomas W Pike
15306 Harmony Hill Ct
Centreville VA 20120

Call Sign: KC2TGR
Michael A Nicoletti
5712 Hollow Oak Ln Apt 204
Centreville VA 20121

Call Sign: N4CG
F Clark Gesswein
15120 Honsena Dr
Centreville VA 201201418

Call Sign: KF4ZJR
Andreas Palmer
14801 Hunting Path Pl
Centreville VA 20120

Call Sign: KG4CKI
Lanny L De Camp
5312 Indian Rock Rd
Centreville VA 20120

Call Sign: KD4ZTT
Harry W Gray
6511 Insignia Ct
Centreville VA 20121

Call Sign: KD4LSY
Jeffrey N Lindamood
6719 Jade Post Ln
Centreville VA 22020

Call Sign: N3DBL
Charles W Meeks
14705 Jarnigan St
Centreville VA 22020

Call Sign: W5GMO
Mark D Delcambre
14735 Jarnigan St
Centreville VA 20120

Call Sign: KA2TXX
William H Ackerman Jr
14927 Jaslow St
Centreville VA 201201538

Call Sign: KK4GOW
Mary R Moon
15326 Jordans Journey Dr
Centreville VA 20120

Call Sign: K3OXL
Charles H John Jr
14913 Kamputa Dr
Centreville VA 20120

Call Sign: K4FHK
Thomas F Lindsley
13800 Leland Rd
Centreville VA 201202042

Call Sign: KB4IKU
Margarete W Lindsley
13800 Leland Rd
Centreville VA 201202042

Call Sign: K2DPG
Thomas F Lindsley
13800 Leland Rd
Centreville VA 201202042

Call Sign: W4ZQD
Leslie J Benton Jr
14610 Lilva Dr
Centreville VA 22020

Call Sign: KC4CBH
Michael A Cross
14315 Little Rocky Mt Ct
Centreville VA 20120

Call Sign: KC5MTL
Joseph E Bajin
6327 Littlefield Ct
Centreville VA 20121

Call Sign: KC4EDY
Bruce J Lambert
14073 Lotus Ln Apt 935
Centreville VA 20120

Call Sign: WD5CYD
Anthony F Bracewell
6811 Malton Ct
Centreville VA 22020

Call Sign: KG4OAW
Douglas E Coulter
6867 Malton Ct
Centreville VA 20121

Call Sign: KB3GFI
Craig A Janus
6504 Marston Cluster
Centreville VA 20120

Call Sign: KC8SHE
James E Plymyer
15406 Martins Hundred Dr
Centreville VA 201201197

Call Sign: KF4CKF
Allen M Gilcrest
14507 Meeting Camp Rd

Centreville VA 201212595

Call Sign: KI4AFS
Susan R Geis
13929 Middle Creek Pl
Centreville VA 20121

Call Sign: AB4RV
Mark A Goldberg
6855 Muskett Way
Centreville VA 20121

Call Sign: N4VOD
Klaus B Bartels
14370 Nandina Ct
Centreville VA 22020

Call Sign: KG4TLT
Mark J Wiseman
13988 New Braddock Rd
Centreville VA 20121

Call Sign: KE4POJ
Byong K Cho
13564 Northbourne Dr
Centreville VA 20120

Call Sign: N4VYW
Glenn W Schumaker
5608 Ottawa Rd
Centreville VA 20120

Call Sign: N4ZQA
Conrad A Johnson
6329 Paddington Ln
Centreville VA 22020

Call Sign: N4APP
Steven E Carroll
6526 Palisades Dr
Centreville VA 201213808

Call Sign: KJ4IDZ
Jim Yen
14734 Pickets Post Rd
Centreville VA 20121

Call Sign: W4DKS
Daniel K Sullivan

14737 Pickets Post Rd
Centreville VA 20121

Call Sign: WD4SGR
Herbert E Hunter
5641 Pickwick Rd
Centreville VA 201202058

Call Sign: WA9JCL
Ronald R Rifenberg
6201 Point Cir
Centreville VA 201201161

Call Sign: KC4SVB
Kenneth J Daniels
15003 Ponderlay Dr
Centreville VA 22020

Call Sign: KE4ET
Gerald R Taylor III
5815 F Post Corners Trl
Centreville VA 20120

Call Sign: KC2FE
Elliott S Kohn
5817 G Post Corners Trl
Centreville VA 20120

Call Sign: KE6CXG
Ren H Broyles
5833 B Post Corners Trl
Centreville VA 20120

Call Sign: KJ4RDI
Richard S Bordelon
5822 Post Corners Trl Apt D
Centreville VA 20120

Call Sign: KI4THG
Meghan A Nelson
14705 Rabbit Run Ct
Centreville VA 20120

Call Sign: N3KBO
Melvin G Seyle III
13830 Rampant Lion Ct
Centreville VA 20120

Call Sign: KF4YGR

Mark W Maier
14115 Rock Canyon Dr
Centreville VA 20121

Call Sign: KI4EAZ
Sean P Mayo
5806 Rock Forest Ct
Centreville VA 20121

Call Sign: KG4WAQ
Peter S Jensen
5638 Rocky Run Dr
Centreville VA 20120

Call Sign: KG4HAM
Lisa G Geberth
14405 Round Lick Ln
Centreville VA 20120

Call Sign: KG4GSQ
Paul H Geberth
14405 Round Lick Ln
Centreville VA 20120

Call Sign: KF4TOK
Juliet N Bui
14181 Royal Oak Ln
Centreville VA 20120

Call Sign: KC4QAT
James E Grant
14195 Royal Oak Ln
Centreville VA 22020

Call Sign: KB3EDH
Brendan L Malone
14803 Rydell Rd Apt 104
Centreville VA 20121

Call Sign: WD4DAM
William A Dize Jr
14406 Saguaro Pl
Centreville VA 22020

Call Sign: AE4ZF
Ted W Warnock
13990 Sawteeth Way
Centreville VA 20121

Call Sign: KJ4GYB
Larry L Janeshek
5602 Schoolfield Ct
Centreville VA 20120

Call Sign: KJ4LAX
Michael A Ihde
6155 Singletons Way
Centreville VA 20121

Call Sign: KJ4CNL
David R Arllen
6596 Skylemar Trl
Centreville VA 20121

Call Sign: AJ4JC
David R Arllen
6596 Skylemar Trl
Centreville VA 20121

Call Sign: KD4ITQ
Aryan Razeghi
15174 Stillfield Pl
Centreville VA 20120

Call Sign: KJ4UBZ
Brian D Knobbs
6129 Stonepath Cir
Centreville VA 20120

Call Sign: KB4LOJ
Jerald B Sussman
6153 Stonepath Cir
Centreville VA 22020

Call Sign: N3KDC
Robert J Carroll III
14615 Store House Dr
Centreville VA 20121

Call Sign: KF4ZOU
Frederick C Sanner
6203 Summer Pond Dr I
Centreville VA 20121

Call Sign: KE5HDY
William A Meyers
14347D Summer Tree Rd
Centreville VA 20121

Call Sign: N4COV
Henry L Maurer
14300 Summer Tree Rd Apt F
Centreville VA 22020

Call Sign: WN3T
Richard E Dessel
5441 Summit St
Centreville VA 20120

Call Sign: KK4DPT
Jeffrey B Mitchell
15260 Surrey House Way
Centreville VA 20120

Call Sign: KK4HKE
Stephen C Beuttel
5662 Thorndyke Ct
Centreville VA 20120

Call Sign: KI4LR
Michael F Mc Nea
5441 Treeline Dr
Centreville VA 201201651

Call Sign: KE6BVM
Stephen P Huneke
6502 Trillium House Ln
Centreville VA 201203756

Call Sign: KK4AWH
Matthew G Zackschewski
6517 Trillium House Ln
Centreville VA 20120

Call Sign: WB4KLC
William D Roberts
6520 Trillium House Ln
Centreville VA 20120

Call Sign: KJ4LAW
Matthew R Astley
6407 VA Pine Ct
Centreville VA 20121

Call Sign: KG4ZAQ
Carroll M Barrett
13819 Wakley Ct

Centreville VA 20121

Call Sign: KF4AZY
J Kevin Nelson
14347 Watery Mtn Ct
Centreville VA 201202818

Call Sign: KG4FSO
Bennett A Cohen
13624 Weinstein Ct
Centreville VA 20120

Call Sign: KG4URV
Melissa N Wagner
15303 Whispering Glen Ct
Centreville VA 20120

Call Sign: KJ4CNQ
Peter E Sielinski
15055 White Post Ct
Centreville VA 20121

Call Sign: WN7S
Richard C Kwiatkowski
14415 William Carr Ln
Centreville VA 20120

Call Sign: KG4OFD
David A Rothrock
14607 Willow Creek Dr
Centreville VA 20120

Call Sign: WS1B
Ronald J Perry
14134 Wood Rock Way
Centreville VA 22020

Call Sign: W4KFC
Kenneth N Clark
14575 Woodland Ridge Dr
Centreville VA 22020

Call Sign: WA4PRF
Andrew V Clark
14575 Woodland Ridge Dr
Centreville VA 22020

Call Sign: WA2HVD
Lester C Burgwardt

5107 Woodmere Dr 304
Centreville VA 20120

Call Sign: KD4BXT
Michael S Kelsen
Centreville VA 20120

Call Sign: KF4TSH
Sean P Regan
Centreville VA 20122

Call Sign: KJ4TQR
Keith G Walters
Centreville VA 20122

Call Sign: WP4IJ
Juan C Torres
Centreville VA 201220011

Call Sign: WH7Q
North Shore RC
Centreville VA 201222053

FCC Amateur Radio Licenses in Ceres

Call Sign: KD4JOE
Jason W Groseclose
Rt 1 Box 113
Ceres VA 24318

Call Sign: N4TWR
John A Brewster
Rt 1 Box 185
Ceres VA 243189713

Call Sign: WA4HIK
Richard G Earls
2467 Foglesong Valley Rd
Ceres VA 24318

Call Sign: KD4ZTW
William E Mills
44 Red Diamond Ln
Ceres VA 24318

Call Sign: KA4UFF
Randolph L Moler
126 Willow Springs Rd

Ceres VA 24318

FCC Amateur Radio Licenses in Cester

Call Sign: WB2ZMZ
Walter R Wend
4317 Village Creek Dr
Cester VA 23831

Call Sign: KI4SCP
Walter R Wend
4317 Village Creek Dr
Cester VA 23831

FCC Amateur Radio Licenses in Champlain

Call Sign: K3GDU
Jasper C Battle
Rr 3 Box 7 B
Champlain VA 22438

Call Sign: KJ4IET
George F Hester II
1916 Lloyds Rd
Champlain VA 22438

Call Sign: KD4MCR
VA J Williams
Champlain VA 22438

FCC Amateur Radio Licenses in Chantilly

Call Sign: KK4DOU
Ryan M Miles
14434 Albemarle Point Pl Ste
10
Chantilly VA 20151

Call Sign: WB0POH
Kevin M Gaukel
25650 America Sq
Chantilly VA 20152

Call Sign: KG4FYW
Scott T Shaw
13625 Bare Island Dr

Chantilly VA 201514113

Call Sign: KI4EKK
VA L Wright
3857 Beech Down Dr
Chantilly VA 20151

Call Sign: KI4FNL
Vortex Of Chaos
3857 Beech Down Dr
Chantilly VA 201513348

Call Sign: KG4VER
Jason L Wright
3857 Beech Down Dr
Chantilly VA 201513348

Call Sign: KI6NNM
Dewitt T Latimer IV
15117 Bernadette Ct
Chantilly VA 20151

Call Sign: KJ4TAW
Dewitt T Latimer IV
15117 Bernadette Ct
Chantilly VA 20151

Call Sign: KJ4TAV
Jennifer R Latimer
15117 Bernadette Ct
Chantilly VA 20151

Call Sign: KD4HBO
Ivan J Galysh
3916 Bokel Dr
Chantilly VA 20151

Call Sign: KG4BSY
Ricky L Hill
14511 Braniff Cir
Chantilly VA 20151

Call Sign: KG4JWH
Scott S Szachara
13445 Brookfield Dr
Chantilly VA 20151

Call Sign: W4OKF
Scott S Szachara

13445 Brookfield Dr
Chantilly VA 20151

Call Sign: WB3CIG
Michael P Walgren
25654 Cabin Point Ct
Chantilly VA 20152

Call Sign: KK4HDH
Jason C Beloncik
43182 Center St
Chantilly VA 20152

Call Sign: W3CUM
Christopher M Patton
14408 Chantilly Crossing Ln
109
Chantilly VA 20151

Call Sign: WB5CIP
Daniel R Adams
13613 Chevy Chase Ln
Chantilly VA 201513374

Call Sign: WA2JHK
Joseph W Keifer III
13823 Claret Ct
Chantilly VA 22021

Call Sign: KK4GEG
Chantilly Aerospace Employees
Radio Organization
15049 Conference Center Dr
Ch1 120
Chantilly VA 20151

Call Sign: KA4HLG
Raymond A Pfaff
4333 Cub Run Rd
Chantilly VA 20151

Call Sign: KF4BPJ
Christopher L Sterritt
4359 Cub Run Rd
Chantilly VA 22021

Call Sign: N2YO
Ciprian Sufitchi
4519 Cub Run Rd

Chantilly VA 20151

Call Sign: KI4QNK
Filip Sufitchi
4519 Cub Run Rd
Chantilly VA 20151

Call Sign: KP4ENU
Salvador Suau
13491 Edgerock Ct
Chantilly VA 20151

Call Sign: N4PKL
John M Weinstein
43401 Edgewater St
Chantilly VA 20152

Call Sign: W4AWL
Milton L Snyder
4410 Fallen Oak Dr
Chantilly VA 20151

Call Sign: W8ZG
David L Windom
4625 Fillingame Dr
Chantilly VA 22021

Call Sign: WS6W
David D Bailey
13773 Flowing Brook Ct
Chantilly VA 20151

Call Sign: KD4SJK
Denise L Bailey
4292 Galesbury Ln
Chantilly VA 22021

Call Sign: WB6WNW
William M Jackson
4307 General Kearny Ct
Chantilly VA 20151

Call Sign: KJ4SZL
Parrish B Payne
4520 Hazelnut Ct
Chantilly VA 20151

Call Sign: KD4ITS
David C Kochendarfer Jr

15407 Herndon Ave
Chantilly VA 20151

Call Sign: N4SOP
Steven C Dickson
26160 Iverson Dr
Chantilly VA 201523665

Call Sign: KB0VQF
John W Howe
13944 James Cross St
Chantilly VA 20151

Call Sign: AC7FE
Dwayne E Block
13812 Leighfield St
Chantilly VA 201512503

Call Sign: KD7JGO
Sharon J Block
13812 Leighfield St
Chantilly VA 201512503

Call Sign: KI4JFL
Thomas W Henderson
4712 Lewis Woods Ct
Chantilly VA 20151

Call Sign: KI4YD
Andrew T Shelton
42762 Locklear Ter
Chantilly VA 20152

Call Sign: K5BWI
William Gavin
15227 Louis Mill Dr
Chantilly VA 20151

Call Sign: KF4LWX
William B Marsh
13817 Lowry Dr
Chantilly VA 20151

Call Sign: AC4CC
Gary N Ross
14601 Lufthansa Cir
Chantilly VA 20151

Call Sign: AB4UN

Loren L Leeper Jr
14603 Lufthansa Cir
Chantilly VA 22021

Call Sign: KB5LA
Louis E Marble
13401 Melville Ln
Chantilly VA 22021

Call Sign: WD4GUG
Walter R Porter
4023 Novar Dr
Chantilly VA 22021

Call Sign: KC3NI
Russell H Jack
14721 Pan Am Ave
Chantilly VA 20151

Call Sign: KF4QLD
Jon C Caswell
5160 Parkstone Dr 205
Chantilly VA 201513813

Call Sign: K4EGL
Andrew Sweder Jr
4234 Pennsboro Ct
Chantilly VA 22021

Call Sign: KF4WAW
Lam T Nguyen
13724 Penwith Ct
Chantilly VA 20151

Call Sign: W6MFF
James C Rill
13419 Pitch Pine Ct
Chantilly VA 22021

Call Sign: WB4LRB
David R Altman
13449 Point Pleasant Dr
Chantilly VA 201512447

Call Sign: K4NOR
David R Altman
13449 Point Pleasant Dr
Chantilly VA 201512447

Call Sign: N3AYL
Mitchell J Corriel
25928 Poland Rd
Chantilly VA 20152

Call Sign: N5ADO
Kevin J Barry
13406 Sand Rock Ct
Chantilly VA 22021

Call Sign: KI4QNH
Felipe Morales Jr
4613 Sand Rock Ln
Chantilly VA 20151

Call Sign: KI4FBI
Thomas D Bamford
4630 Sand Rock Ln
Chantilly VA 20151

Call Sign: KG4FFA
Donald L Bamford
4630 Sand Rock Ln
Chantilly VA 201512470

Call Sign: N7XCO
Clint A Mundinger
25938 Sarazen Dr
Chantilly VA 20152

Call Sign: KD0FPG
Charles B Roberts
4351 Silas Hutchinson Dr
Chantilly VA 20151

Call Sign: KJ4SFB
Abraham Drier
4518 Silas Hutchinson Dr
Chantilly VA 20151

Call Sign: AB4CW
Abraham Drier
4518 Silas Hutchinson Dr
Chantilly VA 20151

Call Sign: N4GCG
Edward L Collins
4620 Star Flower Dr
Chantilly VA 22021

Call Sign: KB2OAY
Michael E Brooks
4636 Star Flower Dr
Chantilly VA 20151

Call Sign: KI4BNS
Howard B Ellis
13653 Stepney Ln
Chantilly VA 20151

Call Sign: N3QYJ
Eliud Bonilla
4805 Stonecroft Blvd
Chantilly VA 20151

Call Sign: KM4CO
Peter A Barthelson
14120 K Sullyfield Cir
Chantilly VA 20151

Call Sign: K3DKR
Cyril J Fedor
13515 Tabscott Dr
Chantilly VA 201512746

Call Sign: KA3WUT
Ryan P Stapleton
13624 Tabscott Dr
Chantilly VA 20151

Call Sign: WB9UBQ
Robert F Oberle
14503 United Dr
Chantilly VA 20151

Call Sign: WX1H
Paul J Marciello
13923 Valley Country Dr
Chantilly VA 20151

Call Sign: KC4RSY
Melvin M Mc Ghee
4516 Waverly Crossing Ln
Chantilly VA 20151

Call Sign: KK4DOY
Marshall R Wilder
Chantilly VA 20153

Call Sign: W6HGF
Allan F Danis
Chantilly VA 201530164

Call Sign: KD4DXF
Manuel A Ojeda
Chantilly VA 201530824

Call Sign: WB4QVA
Ronald E Brents
Chantilly VA 201531063

Call Sign: N3KL
Kevin M Loch
Chantilly VA 201532081

Call Sign: KC4KCT
Michael D May
4169 Meadow Land Ct
Chantily VA 22021

FCC Amateur Radio Licenses in Charles City

Call Sign: KJ4MGT
Simon A Mckenzie
5470 Bella Rosa Way
Charles City VA 23030

Call Sign: W9NNK
David W Caywood
6530 Cattail Rd
Charles City VA 23030

Call Sign: N4ZQH
Ozell E Ard Jr
5820 Monguy Rd
Charles City VA 23030

Call Sign: KF4EVJ
John R Tonnesen III
6250 Old Union Rd
Charles City VA 23030

Call Sign: KK4AIV
Richard S Hedgepeth
4712 Roxbury Rd
Charles City VA 23030

Call Sign: W4RSH
Richard S Hedgepeth
4712 Roxbury Rd
Charles City VA 23030

Call Sign: NE3Q
George W Fear
5140 Ruth S Ct
Charles City VA 23030

Call Sign: KI4YTT
Patricia F Davis
5140 Ruths Ct
Charles City VA 23030

Call Sign: AK4NJ
Douglas B Payne
12401 Wilcox Neck Rd
Charles City VA 23030

FCC Amateur Radio Licenses in Charlotte Courthouse

Call Sign: KI4EAS
Jacqueline D Gray
705 Abilene Rd
Charlotte Courthouse VA 23923

Call Sign: KI4BJS
John A Gray Jr
705 Abilene Rd
Charlotte Courthouse VA 23923

Call Sign: N2VOR
Jack H Zorn
5820 Bethlehem Rd
Charlotte Courthouse VA 23923

Call Sign: KF4DPC
Daniel A Mitchell
Rt 1 Box 534
Charlotte Courthouse VA 23923

Call Sign: N2AJN
James L Killip
Rt 2 Box 85
Charlotte Courthouse VA 23923

Call Sign: N2BDA
Inez L Killip
Rt 2 Box 85
Charlotte Courthouse VA 23923

Call Sign: KK4FPO
Gerald E Ritacco
250 Datt Rd
Charlotte Courthouse VA 23923

Call Sign: KK4GER
Gerald E Ritacco
250 Datt Rd
Charlotte Courthouse VA 23923

Call Sign: KE4RWN
Lawrence J Mc Glynn
770 Fearstown Rd
Charlotte Courthouse VA 23923

Call Sign: KF4TCE
Theresa K Dunbar
2159 Vincent Store Rd
Charlotte Courthouse VA 23923

Call Sign: KF4TFZ
Roger C Martin Sr
2159 Vincent Store Rd
Charlotte Courthouse VA 23923

Call Sign: W2DSI
John F Mingle
1260 Waddell Nelson Rd
Charlotte Courthouse VA 23923

FCC Amateur Radio Licenses in Charlottesville

Call Sign: KO4WQ
Richard Berman
205A 2nd St NW
Charlottesville VA 22902

Call Sign: W4EDO
Carl D Brewer
3578 Airport Acres Rd
Charlottesville VA 22911

Call Sign: W2IDN

William A Coughlin
1005 Allendale Dr
Charlottesville VA 22901

Call Sign: KJ4KCF
Christopher V Halstead
415 Altamont St
Charlottesville VA 22902

Call Sign: KI4LWC
Carson I Herndon
805 Altavista Ave
Charlottesville VA 22902

Call Sign: WD6CVB
Leo J Bourne
1893 Amberfield Dr
Charlottesville VA 22911

Call Sign: KB4JWK
Frederick E Butler
2560 Andrew Ln
Charlottesville VA 22901

Call Sign: KE4AMI
Brent F Vickery
103 A Antoinette Ct
Charlottesville VA 22903

Call Sign: W2BR
Robert A Ross
135 Apple Ln
Charlottesville VA 22903

Call Sign: KA4BMT
Glen C Henderson
3326 Arbor Ter
Charlottesville VA 22911

Call Sign: WB5BNT
Tommy L Moore Sr
1455 Ashland Dr
Charlottesville VA 22911

Call Sign: AB4AT
Edward B Dean
613 Avon St
Charlottesville VA 22902

Call Sign: KB4TKE
Edward B Dean
613 Avon St
Charlottesville VA 22902

Call Sign: KD6WJK
Kimberley T Irons
1119 Avon St
Charlottesville VA 22902

Call Sign: N7RI
Ralph L Irons
1119 Avon St
Charlottesville VA 22902

Call Sign: KG4YYL
Kimberley T Irons
1119 Avon St
Charlottesville VA 22902

Call Sign: KG4FOL
Donna M Jordan
1775 Avon St Ext
Charlottesville VA 22902

Call Sign: W4AVU
Thomas W Hopkinson
2600 Baeeacks Rd C28
Charlottesville VA 22901

Call Sign: AA4D
George C Grotz
2212 Banbury St
Charlottesville VA 22901

Call Sign: KC2LVK
Brian R Kent
61E Barclay Pl Ct
Charlottesville VA 22901

Call Sign: W3ANS
Dale H Levisay
2600 Barracks Rd Apt C22
Charlottesville VA 22901

Call Sign: N6MEH
Robert J Cahill
2600 Barracks Rd C11
Charlottesville VA 229012197

Call Sign: WB3BJZ
John E Effland III
2801 Barracksdale Ln
Charlottesville VA 22901

Call Sign: KF4RKR
Charles M Grisham
3390 Bear Den Ct
Charlottesville VA 22903

Call Sign: KF4JHD
Charles P Owen
111 Bennington Rd
Charlottesville VA 22903

Call Sign: W2HD
Harry J Dannals
1800 Bentivar Dr
Charlottesville VA 229118229

Call Sign: KG9HP
Dwight Williams III
906 Bing Ln
Charlottesville VA 22903

Call Sign: W3KDR
John R Oliver
1428 Birchcrest Ln
Charlottesville VA 22911

Call Sign: KG4ZWE
Andrea D Oliver
1428 Birchcrest Ln
Charlottesville VA 22911

Call Sign: KG4ZWD
John R Oliver
1428 Birchcrest Ln
Charlottesville VA 22911

Call Sign: KI4DLA
Jerome A Ix Jr
1571 Birnam Dr
Charlottesville VA 22901

Call Sign: K9MBQ
Alan W Swinger
3205 Blandemar Dr

Charlottesville VA 229037424

Call Sign: KJ4RPT
Dawn E Sprouse
3852 Blenheim Rd
Charlottesville VA 22902

Call Sign: N4HRV
Harry R Villwock
4234 Blenheim Rd
Charlottesville VA 22902

Call Sign: WD4KWY
Douglas W Webbink
118 Blueberry Rd
Charlottesville VA 22911

Call Sign: KA4RKF
Michael C Sutphin
Rt 9 Box 158A
Charlottesville VA 22901

Call Sign: KE4DDR
Donald E Bush
Rt 4 Box 209
Charlottesville VA 22901

Call Sign: KD4KWE
Richard L Noel
Rt 9 Box 258B
Charlottesville VA 22902

Call Sign: KI4GQJ
Matthew L Modic
2506 Brandermill Pl
Charlottesville VA 22911

Call Sign: N9GTO
Victor M Modic
2506 Brandermill Pl
Charlottesville VA 22911

Call Sign: N4EGM
Gunther A Vogt
1628 Brandywine Dr
Charlottesville VA 22901

Call Sign: KG4TCO
Brian W Bills

815 Broomley Rd
Charlottesville VA 22901

Call Sign: W2PBJ
Brian T Fovel
2289 Browns Gap Tpke
Charlottesville VA 22901

Call Sign: AB3BB
Bruce D Budinger
1620 Bruce Ave
Charlottesville VA 22903

Call Sign: KB3JSI
Cheryl-Lynn J Budinger
1620 Bruce Ave
Charlottesville VA 22903

Call Sign: W4OZJ
Frederic R Schwab
148 Buckingham Cir
Charlottesville VA 22903

Call Sign: KD4CQX
Henry P Fuller
1503 Bunker Hill Dr
Charlottesville VA 22901

Call Sign: AA4CN
Bruce H Collins
1046 Burchs Creek Rd
Charlottesville VA 22903

Call Sign: KF4JHE
Deborah L B Owen
803 Cabell Ave
Charlottesville VA 22903

Call Sign: K4QKH
ARChibald D Owen Sr
45 Canterbury Rd
Charlottesville VA 229034700

Call Sign: WA6MMR
Michael J Di Girolamo
2685 Cardinal Ridge Rd
Charlottesville VA 22901

Call Sign: K4MMR

Michael J Di Girolamo
2685 Cardinal Ridge Rd
Charlottesville VA 22901

Call Sign: KG4SSN
Melanie J Di Girolamo
2685 Cardinal Ridge Rd
Charlottesville VA 22901

Call Sign: W4XN
Michael J Di Girolamo
2685 Cardinal Ridge Rd
Charlottesville VA 22901

Call Sign: KG4AZP
Jonathan S Kennison
1500 Carlton Ave 17
Charlottesville VA 229025883

Call Sign: KK4HUL
Glen E Miller
530 Caroline Ave
Charlottesville VA 22902

Call Sign: W6UZ
John D Gray
110 Carrsbrook Ct
Charlottesville VA 22901

Call Sign: KG4EUH
Melissa A Dennig
776 Castle Ct
Charlottesville VA 22901

Call Sign: KC4TTZ
Avery Catlin
1898 Catlin Rd
Charlottesville VA 22901

Call Sign: W3DX
Robert S Capon
107 Cavalier Dr
Charlottesville VA 22901

Call Sign: W3DXX
Howard J Capon
107 Cavalier Dr
Charlottesville VA 22901

Call Sign: N1QWM
Philip H Dickinson
330 Cedar Bluff Rd
Charlottesville VA 22901

Call Sign: KI4RQI
Philip H Dickinson
330 Cedar Bluff Rd
Charlottesville VA 22901

Call Sign: WB4FZV
Reuben E Maine
770 Chapel Hill Rd
Charlottesville VA 22901

Call Sign: W4DO
William H Faulkner Jr
810 Chapel Hill Rd
Charlottesville VA 22901

Call Sign: K3ZM
Peter H Briggs
876 Chapel Hill Rd
Charlottesville VA 22901

Call Sign: K2ULW
Raymond R La Falce
1266 Chatham Rdg
Charlottesville VA 22901

Call Sign: N2QBQ
Mary Ann B La Falce
1266 Chatham Ridge Rd
Charlottesville VA 22901

Call Sign: KK4DFU
Francisco Velez V
1810 Chelsea Dr
Charlottesville VA 22903

Call Sign: KE4CFQ
Mark A Crumley
1511 Chesapeake St
Charlottesville VA 22902

Call Sign: KF4JNC
Jeremy C Clark
1030 Cheshire Ct
Charlottesville VA 22902

Call Sign: KF4MEF
Nancy D Holliday
3002 Colonial Dr
Charlottesville VA 22911

Call Sign: KC4UAV
George O Carroll Jr
3008 Colonial Dr
Charlottesville VA 22901

Call Sign: KI4PXT
Brian S Weidman
3030 Colonial Dr
Charlottesville VA 22911

Call Sign: KD4MML
Jason G Zeibel
270 17 Colonnade Dr
Charlottesville VA 229034961

Call Sign: KD7YDG
Hirofumi Kawakubo
244 Colonnade Dr Apt 35
Charlottesville VA 22903

Call Sign: KK4HUN
Aaron M Boggs
320 Commanwealth Ct Apt C
Charlottesville VA 22901

Call Sign: KA4VHR
Erik E Swanson
124 Commonwealth Cir
Charlottesville VA 22901

Call Sign: KG4WGR
Mark D Carroll
326 Commonwealth Ct Apt G
Charlottesville VA 22901

Call Sign: KI4BFM
Dennis N Mennerich
2403 Commonwealth Dr
Charlottesville VA 229011621

Call Sign: K4THE
Dennis N Mennerich
2403 Commonwealth Dr

Charlottesville VA 229011621

Call Sign: N1RHT
Douglas M Michon
2251 F Commonwealth Dr
Charlottesville VA 229011516

Call Sign: KE4JYV
Benjamin W Mosby III
117 Commonweath Cir
Charlottesville VA 22901

Call Sign: KK4EDX
Ignac Jakovac
1567 Cool Spring Rd
Charlottesville VA 22901

Call Sign: WD4DDV
Steven W Yates
3029 Copper Knoll Rd
Charlottesville VA 22901

Call Sign: KC5QIA
Joanne D Hess
2645 Coralberry Pl
Charlottesville VA 22911

Call Sign: KB4MUF
Ernest F Dukes Jr
2645 Coralberry Pl
Charlottesville VA 229118276

Call Sign: W4MOG
Doss C Cooper
1147 Court Yard Dr
Charlottesville VA 22903

Call Sign: KG4DIA
Colin T Rae Sr
305 Crestfield Ct
Charlottesville VA 22911

Call Sign: W4RAE
Colin T Rae Sr
305 Crestfield Ct
Charlottesville VA 22911

Call Sign: KG4VWQ
Regina L Rae

305 Crestfield Ct
Charlottesville VA 22911

Call Sign: KJ4JEF
Samuel H Barry
2320 Crestmont Ave
Charlottesville VA 22903

Call Sign: KD4ANA
David C Carter
2327 Crestmont Ave
Charlottesville VA 22903

Call Sign: KD4SOC
William P Snavely Sr
1551 Dairy Rd
Charlottesville VA 22903

Call Sign: KC9INE
Benjamin R Lechlitner
2588 Dick Woods Rd
Charlottesville VA 22903

Call Sign: KJ4RPR
Eugene W Mcclurken Jr
120 Dorset Ct
Charlottesville VA 229118336

Call Sign: WA4ZZB
William L Harris Jr
1578 Dudley Mtn Rd
Charlottesville VA 22903

Call Sign: KF4APO
Marlene R Hopkins
319 Eastbrook Dr
Charlottesville VA 22901

Call Sign: KC5CI
Gerald B Petencin
508 Eastbrook Dr
Charlottesville VA 22901

Call Sign: KD8ARI
Ronald F Duplain
520 Edgemont Rd
Charlottesville VA 229032454

Call Sign: KI6LU

Donn V Campbell
3109 Edgewater Dr
Charlottesville VA 22911

Call Sign: KF4AGV
Ruth L Stornetta
19 Elliewood Ave
Charlottesville VA 22903

Call Sign: KD4ASI
Richard C Lang
803 Elliott Ave
Charlottesville VA 22902

Call Sign: KI4AZY
Michael W Lowry Jr
1109 Elliott Ave
Charlottesville VA 22901

Call Sign: K4AZY
Michael W Lowry Jr
1109 Elliott Ave
Charlottesville VA 22901

Call Sign: KD4GRZ
Charles A Eastwood
746 Exton Ct
Charlottesville VA 22901

Call Sign: KC4LMA
Roy S Fair
433 Fairway
Charlottesville VA 22901

Call Sign: KJ4EYO
John C Gallant Jr
433 Fairway Ave
Charlottesville VA 22902

Call Sign: AJ4UN
John C Gallant Jr
433 Fairway Ave
Charlottesville VA 22902

Call Sign: K2JQE
Carl D Moje
1615 Far Hills Rd
Charlottesville VA 229019406

Call Sign: KA3NXN
Jaime Bernate
114 Fielding Dr
Charlottesville VA 229026458

Call Sign: KD4IDU
Megan E Bernate
114 Fielding Dr
Charlottesville VA 229026458

Call Sign: KI4UQU
Mario Gubo
2310 Finch Ct
Charlottesville VA 22911

Call Sign: K4MDX
Mario Gubo
2310 Finch Ct
Charlottesville VA 22911

Call Sign: W9MAX
Max Wild
2310 Finch Ct
Charlottesville VA 22911

Call Sign: W4MBW
Martin B Wangberg
2330 Finch Ct
Charlottesville VA 22911

Call Sign: WD4EUY
Max Berman
2035 Foal Ln
Charlottesville VA 22901

Call Sign: KG4ZWF
Mark A Kirk
135 Fontana Ct
Charlottesville VA 22911

Call Sign: KB3RHO
David C Cauffield
865 Fountain Ct Apt B
Charlottesville VA 22901

Call Sign: KG4ZWC
Kishore V Persaud
2712 Gatewood Cir
Charlottesville VA 229117403

Call Sign: KA2NMD
Robert F Hassenfratz
61 Georgetown Green
Charlottesville VA 229012141

Call Sign: KI4JNA
Ragdad National ARC
147 Georgetown Green
Charlottesville VA 22901

Call Sign: KC5BGQ
Brian C O Rourke
147 Georgetown Green
Charlottesville VA 22901

Call Sign: N3OI
Brian C O Rourke
147 Georgetown Green
Charlottesville VA 22901

Call Sign: KD4WFX
Anthony A Valente
210 Georgetown Rd
Charlottesville VA 22901

Call Sign: KD4USX
Tammy L Barboza
162 Georgetown Rd 2
Charlottesville VA 22901

Call Sign: WB6ZUI
David S Cafiso
819 Gilliams Mtn Rd
Charlottesville VA 229039757

Call Sign: KJ4QHG
Gregg A Korbon
350 Gillums Ridge Rd
Charlottesville VA 229037653

Call Sign: NO1U
Gregg A Korbon
350 Gillums Ridge Rd
Charlottesville VA 229037653

Call Sign: KC4WMY
Jeremy P Jannotta
1695 Goldentree Pl

Charlottesville VA 22901

Call Sign: W3WAC
James A Copony
1705 Goldentree Pl
Charlottesville VA 22911

Call Sign: KG4IJB
Charles R Byam Jr
1730 Goldentree Pl
Charlottesville VA 22911

Call Sign: KC4ZDX
Dale W Harris
1702 Gordon Ave
Charlottesville VA 22903

Call Sign: WB3DZC
Richard F Bradley
4509 Grand View Dr
Charlottesville VA 22901

Call Sign: KG4AKD
Klaus H Kudielka
3917 Greenville Dr
Charlottesville VA 229037672

Call Sign: K4EMM
Elizabeth M Kirby
3917 Grenville Dr
Charlottesville VA 229037672

Call Sign: K4UHW
Anne M Mills
3917 Grenville Dr
Charlottesville VA 229037672

Call Sign: K4APM
Linda M Mills
3917 Grenville Dr
Charlottesville VA 229039723

Call Sign: W4SM
Stacey E Mills
3917 Grenville Dr
Charlottesville VA 229039723

Call Sign: N1DKY
Bruce P Dembling Phd

608 Grove Ave
Charlottesville VA 22902

Call Sign: WA4TTE
David L Rae
1419 Grove Rd
Charlottesville VA 22901

Call Sign: K4FRV
Don C Hendrix
104 Grover Ct
Charlottesville VA 22901

Call Sign: KI4NTO
Jon B Hunter II
108 Hartmans Mill Rd
Charlottesville VA 22902

Call Sign: WA4LNY
Richard T Eppink
212 Harvest Dr
Charlottesville VA 229034849

Call Sign: KC4ZIG
John M Deegan
1029 Hazel St
Charlottesville VA 22902

Call Sign: KK4EDS
Ronald D Williams
1715 Hearthglow Ln
Charlottesville VA 22901

Call Sign: KF4CRI
Robert K Starling III
1778 Hearthglow Ln
Charlottesville VA 22901

Call Sign: KF4CRJ
Robert K Starling Jr
1778 Heathglow Ln
Charlottesville VA 22901

Call Sign: KC0NQV
John B Hurst
139 Hessian Hills Cir Apt 3
Charlottesville VA 22901

Call Sign: KJ4HGQ

Donald L Lepsch
432 Hidden Ridge Rd
Charlottesville VA 22902

Call Sign: KJ4HGP
Priscilla C Lepsch
432 Hidden Ridge Rd
Charlottesville VA 22902

Call Sign: W2PVY
Joseph A Giovanelli
751 Hillsdale Dr Apt 215
Charlottesville VA 22901

Call Sign: KE4PIQ
Owen N Wells
2411 Hillwood Pl
Charlottesville VA 22901

Call Sign: AA1RU
Jeremy Waters
2611 Holkham Dr
Charlottesville VA 22901

Call Sign: AA1RN
Veronica C Waters
2611 Holkham Dr
Charlottesville VA 22901

Call Sign: KJ4PE
Joseph H Greenberg
255 Homestead Ln
Charlottesville VA 22902

Call Sign: KG4NGV
Joshua B Malone
2527 Hydraulic Rd Apt 57
Charlottesville VA 22903

Call Sign: W4YRA
VA Young Radio Amateurs
Assn
3000 Idlewood Dr
Charlottesville VA 22901

Call Sign: K4VPI
Vpi Alumni RC
3000 Idlewood Dr
Charlottesville VA 22901

Call Sign: KG4UKC
VA Young Radio Amateurs
Assn
3000 Idlewood Dr
Charlottesville VA 22901

Call Sign: KG4SYS
Dennis L Mills
3000 Idlewood Dr
Charlottesville VA 229011126

Call Sign: KG4QVP
Benjamin L Mills
3000 Idlewood Dr
Charlottesville VA 229011126

Call Sign: N4CV
Benjamin L Mills
3000 Idlewood Dr
Charlottesville VA 229011126

Call Sign: KB9WCW
Esther A Fuchs
365 Ivy Vista Dr
Charlottesville VA 22903

Call Sign: KI4GQH
John E Gersbach Jr
2728 Jasmine Ter
Charlottesville VA 22911

Call Sign: KD4IGV
Ravi Gadiraju
1800 Jefferson Park Ave 92
Charlottesville VA 22903

Call Sign: KD4GSA
Peter R Molnar
1900 Jefferson Park Ave Apt 2
Charlottesville VA 22903

Call Sign: AK4CX
Joseph B Burch
2653 Jefferson Park Cir
Charlottesville VA 22903

Call Sign: KD4OXN
Roger L Ritenour

510 Jester Ln
Charlottesville VA 22901

Call Sign: KE4LKT
Edward W Shaver
769 Joy Ct
Charlottesville VA 22902

Call Sign: KD4QBA
Donald L Reid
1843 Keiser Ridge
Charlottesville VA 22911

Call Sign: KX4P
John H Green
2593 Kendalwood Ln
Charlottesville VA 22911

Call Sign: WB3IYQ
Andrew W Dillaway
2635 Kendalwood Ln
Charlottesville VA 22911

Call Sign: KA4UPY
Roy G Edmonds
1279 Kenwood Ln
Charlottesville VA 22901

Call Sign: KI4PXX
Robert R Cardell III
1302 Kenwood Ln
Charlottesville VA 22901

Call Sign: K4MTX
Casimir E Norrisey
1319 Kenwood Ln
Charlottesville VA 22901

Call Sign: W4SXH
Benjamin L Atkins
110 Kerry Ln
Charlottesville VA 22901

Call Sign: WB2RNG
Anthony J Camuto
2560 Kimbrough Cir
Charlottesville VA 22901

Call Sign: KB4EPK

Lawrence R Eicher
808 King William Dr
Charlottesville VA 22901

Call Sign: WA4LAB
Charles M Ward
2486 Lake Albemarle Rd
Charlottesville VA 22901

Call Sign: WD4KUW
Louise C Ward
2486 Lake Albemarle Rd
Charlottesville VA 22901

Call Sign: KE4DDO
Peter R Thorsen Jr
58 Lake Forest Dr
Charlottesville VA 22901

Call Sign: AA6O
Edward M Schneider
1521 Lake Forest Dr
Charlottesville VA 22901

Call Sign: WB4GWH
James T Diffin
1905 Lambs Rd
Charlottesville VA 229018977

Call Sign: N4FWA
Hein B Hvatum
104 Lancaster Ct
Charlottesville VA 22901

Call Sign: N4PGS
Gregory H Faust
2624 Lawrence Rd
Charlottesville VA 22901

Call Sign: KC4TAC
Elizabeth L Arthur
2735 Leeds Ln
Charlottesville VA 22901

Call Sign: KA4FOX
Steven R Fox
530 Lego Dr
Charlottesville VA 22911

Call Sign: KA4MCA
Donald P Firer
1414 Lester Dr
Charlottesville VA 22901

Call Sign: KF4FRN
Rosemary K Firer
1414 Lester Dr
Charlottesville VA 22901

Call Sign: KJ4ITA
Russell D Roberts
1013 Linden Ave Apt I
Charlottesville VA 22902

Call Sign: KF4UTD
Edward J Deasy Jr
945 Locust Ave
Charlottesville VA 22901

Call Sign: KD4ATF
Diane R Mitchell
1112 Locust Ave
Charlottesville VA 22901

Call Sign: KE4VJW
Robert O Mitchell Sr
1112 Locust Ave
Charlottesville VA 22901

Call Sign: KE4QDP
Robert O Mitchell Jr
1112 Locust Ave
Charlottesville VA 229014051

Call Sign: K3NDH
Peter E Rosden
1505 London Rd
Charlottesville VA 229018881

Call Sign: KJ4ZIL
Hugh C Garrison Jr
3259 Lonesome Mtn Rd
Charlottesville VA 22911

Call Sign: WA3WRV
Forrest D Workman
3520 Lonesome Mtn Rd
Charlottesville VA 229116014

Call Sign: KN4ZA
Heinz Schnait
133A Longwood Dr
Charlottesville VA 22903

Call Sign: N4AOP
William Day Jr
1807 Lonicera Way
Charlottesville VA 229119030

Call Sign: N4OQK
Mark A Day
1807 Lonicera Way
Charlottesville VA 229119030

Call Sign: W4NPX
Robert H Blodinger
5003 Madison Ct
Charlottesville VA 22901

Call Sign: WB4KPW
Lisa S Beazell
926 Marshall St
Charlottesville VA 22901

Call Sign: KG4DRK
Mervel E Runion
287 Martin Kings Rd
Charlottesville VA 22902

Call Sign: KJ4YHE
Daniel Milner
98 Meadowbrook Ct
Charlottesville VA 22901

Call Sign: KI4OMA
Shirley S Robinson
2007 Meadowbrook Rd
Charlottesville VA 22903

Call Sign: AD4GK
David L Brown
2700 Meriwether Dr
Charlottesville VA 22901

Call Sign: KD4CUJ
Kay D Brown
2700 Meriwether Dr

Charlottesville VA 22901

Call Sign: AA4B
Stephen E Bach
1208 Meriwether St
Charlottesville VA 229025421

Call Sign: AI4ZG
Philip J Stenger
124 Mill Creek Dr
Charlottesville VA 22902

Call Sign: K8OG
Philip J Stenger
124 Mill Creek Dr
Charlottesville VA 22902

Call Sign: KJ4XZ
Wilfred M Seay
456 Miller School Rd
Charlottesville VA 22903

Call Sign: KG4NXW
Benjamin S Lang
1611 Milton Rd
Charlottesville VA 22902

Call Sign: KA4TTP
Robert E Miller Sr
1685 Milton Rd
Charlottesville VA 22902

Call Sign: KK4EDW
Travis J Koshko
13 Mobile Ln
Charlottesville VA 22903

Call Sign: KD4HBX
Steve D Clements
1556 Monacan Trl Rd
Charlottesville VA 22903

Call Sign: KK4HKH
Lijun Li
112 Montebello Cir Apt 4
Charlottesville VA 22903

Call Sign: KA4YCM
George A Woods

4 Monterey Dr
Charlottesville VA 22901

Call Sign: KD4EEX
Helen I Johnson
12 Monterey Dr
Charlottesville VA 22901

Call Sign: KJ4RPQ
Robert D Templeman Jr
2506 Montgomery Ridge Rd
Charlottesville VA 22911

Call Sign: KF4FYI
Grayson P Dowell
1411 Monticello Rd
Charlottesville VA 22902

Call Sign: WB2PJT
Brent E Lunnen
1327 Mosbys Reach
Charlottesville VA 22901

Call Sign: KI4HWE
Charles M Winkler
603 Moseley Dr
Charlottesville VA 229034219

Call Sign: WB4YRG
Earle M Welch Jr
1111 Mtn Rd
Charlottesville VA 22901

Call Sign: KG4EWV
Christine M Winner
108 N Baker St Apt B
Charlottesville VA 22903

Call Sign: AB4XT
John C Knight
2120 N Pantops Dr
Charlottesville VA 22901

Call Sign: N4ZSC
VA G Knight
2120 N Pantops Dr
Charlottesville VA 22901

Call Sign: K4SDS

Earl R Savage
2409 Northfield Rd
Charlottesville VA 22901

Call Sign: KF4UCI
Elmer F Scott Jr
2079 Northwood Park Rd
Charlottesville VA 22911

Call Sign: KJ4RPW
Jonathan A Scott
2079 Northwood Park Rd
Charlottesville VA 22911

Call Sign: KF4APN
John S Darrell
1 Oak Cir
Charlottesville VA 22901

Call Sign: WB2KJY
Elizabeth A Fuchs
105 Obsesrvatory Ave
Charlottesville VA 229033002

Call Sign: KJ4ZWD
Stephen C Merrell
143 Old 5th Cir
Charlottesville VA 22903

Call Sign: KD4MAB
Joseph W Crockett Jr
1786 Old Brook Rd
Charlottesville VA 22901

Call Sign: KB1HMF
Edward B Elron
1125 Old Garth Rd
Charlottesville VA 22901

Call Sign: WA4IUN
John H Chappell Sr
21 Orchard Rd
Charlottesville VA 22903

Call Sign: KE4BVR
Dale W Jessen
114 Overlook Dr
Charlottesville VA 22903

Call Sign: KE4BVS
Bethany S Jessen
114 Overlook Dr
Charlottesville VA 22903

Call Sign: WA4YFV
Dennis F Wilson Jr
1155 Owensville Rd
Charlottesville VA 22901

Call Sign: KG4AZN
Michael C Wyatt
1464 Oxford Rd
Charlottesville VA 22903

Call Sign: KJ4HKJ
Christopher W Green
536 Pantops Ctr 327
Charlottesville VA 22911

Call Sign: AG4DN
Martin B Mait
250 Pantops Mt Rd 5208
Charlottesville VA 22911

Call Sign: KG4FOM
Lair D Haugh
435 Park St
Charlottesville VA 22902

Call Sign: AA4DH
Lair D Haugh
435 Park St
Charlottesville VA 22902

Call Sign: KC0EAV
Mary X Hanna
308 Parkwood Pl
Charlottesville VA 22901

Call Sign: KD4PVP
Andrew G Lefko
1234 Pebble Brook Ln Apt 108
Charlottesville VA 22902

Call Sign: KD4EJC
Barbara A Heise
113 Pepper Pl
Charlottesville VA 22902

Call Sign: KJ4YWP
Alexander N Olihovik
145 Peters
Charlottesville VA 22904

Call Sign: KT4UO
Terry L Henderson
107A Piedmont Ave S
Charlottesville VA 22903

Call Sign: KI4BSZ
Mark R Whitis
107A Piedmont Ave S
Charlottesville VA 229032945

Call Sign: AK4OL
Mark R Whitis
107A Piedmont Ave S
Charlottesville VA 229032945

Call Sign: WD4AYS
Earl C Elliott
1460 Pinedale Rd
Charlottesville VA 229019418

Call Sign: WD4PKS
Lewis D Wenger
1117 Pinehurst Ct
Charlottesville VA 22901

Call Sign: K4JMY
James E Walker Sr
5135 Piney Mtn Rd Private
Charlottesville VA 229116110

Call Sign: KG4QHZ
Kenneth W Smith Jr
163 Pleasant Ridge Rd
Charlottesville VA 22911

Call Sign: KE4AQC
James B Nelson
1570 Poes Ln
Charlottesville VA 22901

Call Sign: KE4AQD
Robert H Nelson
1570 Poes Ln

Charlottesville VA 22901

Call Sign: KJ4GSV
Richard A Prestiy
1650 Poes Ln
Charlottesville VA 22911

Call Sign: KJ4RAP
Richard A Prestiy
1650 Poes Ln
Charlottesville VA 22911

Call Sign: KE4CKI
Pat Haden
1293 Pounding Creek Rd
Charlottesville VA 22903

Call Sign: KE4ZXD
Warren D Blatz III
1894 Powell Creek Ct
Charlottesville VA 22911

Call Sign: KG4ASF
Sutherland Middle School ARC
2801 Powell Creek Dr
Charlottesville VA 22901

Call Sign: KE4DDQ
John A Toms
3568 Pritchett Ln
Charlottesville VA 22911

Call Sign: AG4N
Edson S Hineline Jr
2990 Proffit Rd
Charlottesville VA 22911

Call Sign: AK4OH
Paul M Mckee
3141 Proffit Rd
Charlottesville VA 22911

Call Sign: KB4TMB
William A Faust
145 Quince Ln
Charlottesville VA 22902

Call Sign: KJ4PJI
Ioan Miftode

709 Rainier Rd
Charlottesville VA 22903

Call Sign: KI4NTM
Andre G Berkin
1670 Ravens Pl
Charlottesville VA 229117527

Call Sign: KD4CQY
Jon Gefaell
212 B Raymond Ave
Charlottesville VA 22901

Call Sign: K4CQY
Jon Gefaell
212 B Raymond Ave
Charlottesville VA 229033641

Call Sign: W4OJ
Jon Gefaell
212B Raymond Ave
Charlottesville VA 229033641

Call Sign: KK4AMI
Michael J Wolfe
2136 Red Hill Rd
Charlottesville VA 22903

Call Sign: AA4KH
Albert M Bottoms
104 Reynard Dr
Charlottesville VA 229012024

Call Sign: K4RK
Robert L Kelsey
105 Reynard Dr
Charlottesville VA 22901

Call Sign: KI4SQW
Keith C Fuller
1900 Rio Hill Center 103
Charlottesville VA 22901

Call Sign: N1NZG
Jonathan A Velez
1649 Rio Hill Dr Apt 302
Charlottesville VA 22901

Call Sign: KT0P

Scott W Hooper
1104 River Oaks Ln
Charlottesville VA 22901

Call Sign: KD4BTP
Dolores J Deegan
320 Riverbend Dr Apt 2D
Charlottesville VA 22911

Call Sign: KI4PXS
James L Hall
984 Rock Creek Rd
Charlottesville VA 22903

Call Sign: KC4ZKA
Boris Starosta
802 Rockland Ave
Charlottesville VA 22901

Call Sign: WA4CYQ
Garland E Honaker
919 Rockland Ave
Charlottesville VA 22902

Call Sign: KD4BZJ
Gussie L Abrahamse
387 Rocky Hollow Rd
Charlottesville VA 22901

Call Sign: KD4BZK
Dale A Abrahamse
387 Rocky Hollow Rd
Charlottesville VA 22901

Call Sign: N2YDW
Alfred Shapero
401 Rocky Hollow Rd
Charlottesville VA 229118563

Call Sign: WA6HRY
Alfred C Kilham
753 Rocky Hollow Rd
Charlottesville VA 22901

Call Sign: KG4NMG
Rolf A Braun
2355 Rocky Run
Charlottesville VA 22901

Call Sign: KD4AZR
Leila S Shenkir
420 Rookwood Dr
Charlottesville VA 229034732

Call Sign: KG4TWN
William T Ross
517 Rookwood Pl
Charlottesville VA 22903

Call Sign: W4CHO
William T Ross
517 Rookwood Pl
Charlottesville VA 22903

Call Sign: KA7PCM
James R Quartz
1512 Rose Hill Dr
Charlottesville VA 22903

Call Sign: KI4YTS
Theodore E Reuter
475 Rosemont Dr
Charlottesville VA 22901

Call Sign: KE4EXD
John R Melton
1620 Rugby Ave Apt D
Charlottesville VA 22903

Call Sign: K2SSB
Stanley S Hazen
1334 Rugby Rd
Charlottesville VA 229031248

Call Sign: K4EBL
Richard S Hildebrand
1106 Rustic Willow Ln
Charlottesville VA 22911

Call Sign: KD5FPJ
Carlton Barnes
924 A S 1st
Charlottesville VA 22902

Call Sign: K3AA
Brass
1562 Secretarys Rd
Charlottesville VA 22902

Call Sign: K4CGY
James C Owen III
1562 Secretarys Rd
Charlottesville VA 22902

Call Sign: W3PWN
Finnian Cornelison
3445 Seminole Trl
Charlottesville VA 22911

Call Sign: KE4WDL
Richard A Sprenkle
100 Shale Pl
Charlottesville VA 22902

Call Sign: KG4ZWB
Douglas E Steele
243 Shamrock Rd
Charlottesville VA 22903

Call Sign: KC4FPW
John M Hopkinson
101 Shawnee Ct
Charlottesville VA 22901

Call Sign: K4LTY
John J Vlasis
2208 Shelby Dr
Charlottesville VA 22901

Call Sign: KI4NTL
Christopher T S Covington
2306 A Shelby Dr
Charlottesville VA 22901

Call Sign: N1COV
Christopher T S Covington
2306 A Shelby Dr
Charlottesville VA 22901

Call Sign: WA4QFL
James C Pruett Jr
2400 Simeon Ct
Charlottesville VA 22902

Call Sign: N4KZP
Douglas E Steele
1226D Smith St

Charlottesville VA 22901

Call Sign: K2AOE
Kenneth I Kellermann
102 Smithfield Ct
Charlottesville VA 22901

Call Sign: KG4WJH
Ephraim C Ewing
166 Spring Mtn Rd
Charlottesville VA 22902

Call Sign: WD4BAV
Lee F Groller
580 Stagecoach Rd
Charlottesville VA 22902

Call Sign: KJ4WGA
Jeffrey A Bush
3791 Stony Point Rd
Charlottesville VA 22911

Call Sign: KA4JJD
Michael F Rein
109 Sturbridge Rd
Charlottesville VA 22901

Call Sign: KG4FON
David B Corzilius
218 A Sunset Ave
Charlottesville VA 22903

Call Sign: KE4JSU
William K Mc Coy
206 Surrey Rd
Charlottesville VA 22901

Call Sign: KJ4ECE
Joshua R Bush
1214 Swan Lake Dr Apt 301
Charlottesville VA 22902

Call Sign: KD4HOA
Donna C Hancock
1920 Swanson Dr Apt 11
Charlottesville VA 22901

Call Sign: KE4UKY
Matthew J Dean

4300 Sylvan Ln
Charlottesville VA 22911

Call Sign: KE4UKZ
Jonathan L Dean
4300 Sylvan Ln
Charlottesville VA 22911

Call Sign: WB9HGZ
Paul K Dean
4300 Sylvan Ln
Charlottesville VA 22911

Call Sign: WD9EIA
Eileen M Dean
4300 Sylvan Ln
Charlottesville VA 22911

Call Sign: K4TFS
Tandem Friends School
279 Tandem Ln
Charlottesville VA 22901

Call Sign: K4RKA
Ronald K Richey
2318 Tarleton Dr
Charlottesville VA 22901

Call Sign: WB4RBW
Nancy L Richey
2318 Tarleton Dr
Charlottesville VA 229011827

Call Sign: KJ4SIS
Timothy D Ray
1084 Taylors Gap Rd
Charlottesville VA 22903

Call Sign: KC4TIM
Timothy D Ray
1084 Taylors Gap Rd
Charlottesville VA 22903

Call Sign: W2HHG
Stephen K Stearns
220 Terrell Rd W
Charlottesville VA 22901

Call Sign: W4KSH

Veryl W Rupp
103 Terrybrook Dr
Charlottesville VA 229119130

Call Sign: K4ISW
Le Roy D Moyer
1863 Thomas Jeff Pky
Charlottesville VA 229027520

Call Sign: KI4RIV
Elizabeth D Phillips
1048 Tilman Rd
Charlottesville VA 22901

Call Sign: AD6JV
William Phillips
1048 Tilman Rd
Charlottesville VA 22901

Call Sign: KK4EDR
James S Arthur
1053 Tilman Rd
Charlottesville VA 22901

Call Sign: KB2XX
Paul H Schwartz
1080 Tilman Rd
Charlottesville VA 22901

Call Sign: KJ4RPP
John L Ball Jr
1098 Tilman Rd
Charlottesville VA 22901

Call Sign: KU4KAE
John L Ball Jr
1098 Tilman Rd
Charlottesville VA 22901

Call Sign: KQ4MZ
Theodore J Bittner Jr
1261 Timberbranch Ct
Charlottesville VA 22902

Call Sign: KA1HJB
William M Merone
3249 Timberwood Pkwy
Charlottesville VA 22911

Call Sign: AC4ZQ
Michael J Duvall
1775 Tinkers Cove
Charlottesville VA 22901

Call Sign: KO4OC
Sharon S Duvall
1775 Tinkers Cove Rd
Charlottesville VA 22901

Call Sign: KF4NOO
Francis M O Leary
4003 Tompkins Dr
Charlottesville VA 229119110

Call Sign: WB1BSD
Brian A Boyter
4008 Tompkins Dr
Charlottesville VA 22901

Call Sign: KJ4WMS
Jill L Laplante
102 Turtle Creek Rd Apt 10
Charlottesville VA 22901

Call Sign: WA4UPI
Edwin J Bernet
2104 Twyman Rd
Charlottesville VA 22903

Call Sign: K4IRL
Ide R Lane Jr
1711 Vermira Pl
Charlottesville VA 229012939

Call Sign: K1IL
Ide R Lane Jr
1711 Vermira Pl
Charlottesville VA 229012939

Call Sign: W6RL
Ide R Lane Jr
1711 Vermira Pl
Charlottesville VA 229012939

Call Sign: KG4DCY
Debra J Hawrysko
1244 Villa Ln
Charlottesville VA 22903

Call Sign: KD4NRE
Allen E Green
660 W Rio Rd
Charlottesville VA 22901

Call Sign: KJ4OK
Harry O Martin Jr
2413 Wakefield Rd
Charlottesville VA 22901

Call Sign: N4RDC
Scott A Martin
2413 Wakefield Rd
Charlottesville VA 22901

Call Sign: N4LBS
George E Hall
2925 Watts Passage Rd
Charlottesville VA 22901

Call Sign: N4LBT
Kathryn R Hall
2925 Watts Passage Rd
Charlottesville VA 22901

Call Sign: KI4DSQ
L Paul Harnois
402 Wellington Dr
Charlottesville VA 22903

Call Sign: KG4DIB
Herbert I Moss
411 Westmoreland Ct
Charlottesville VA 229011242

Call Sign: N1LOJ
Ira Kreisman
413 Westmoreland Ct
Charlottesville VA 22901

Call Sign: KJ4JEE
Jared M Deane
122 Westwood Cir
Charlottesville VA 22903

Call Sign: WA4EMP
John B Heltzel
1527 Westwood Rd

Charlottesville VA 229035153

Call Sign: KD4TOR
William P Arnold III
106 Whetstone Pl
Charlottesville VA 229012118

Call Sign: K4IB
William P Arnold III
106 Whetstone Pl
Charlottesville VA 229012118

Call Sign: KG4IHO
Douglas L Whitman
2285 Whippoorwill Rd
Charlottesville VA 22901

Call Sign: KD4QBD
Robert F Alexander
55 Whitcover Cir
Charlottesville VA 22901

Call Sign: KG4MFN
Nancy K Forsberg
804 White Rock Rd
Charlottesville VA 22902

Call Sign: WB2MVA
Robert N Lindsay
107 Wild Flower Dr
Charlottesville VA 22901

Call Sign: KD4RWX
Joseph D Fritz
2306 Williamsburg Rd
Charlottesville VA 22901

Call Sign: W2BNX
William C Uzzell
102 Wilson Ct
Charlottesville VA 22901

Call Sign: KA9DEB
Edward M Murphy
1063 Wintergreen Ln
Charlottesville VA 22903

Call Sign: KJ4VCY
Whitney L Richardson

694 Woodburn Ct
Charlottesville VA 22901

Call Sign: KF4EFY
William A Poindexter
1882 Woodburn Rd
Charlottesville VA 22901

Call Sign: W4IWW
Eugene V Bossieux Jr
2529 Woodland Rd
Charlottesville VA 22903

Call Sign: K4VI
Walter E Taylor
803 Woodlands Rd
Charlottesville VA 22901

Call Sign: KI4KNK
Jared Cooper
396 Wynridge Ln
Charlottesville VA 22901

Call Sign: KI4ZMO
Kyle M Ringgenberg
157 Yellowstone Dr 208
Charlottesville VA 22903

Call Sign: KG4AFB
Joshua A Humphries
235 Yellowstone Dr Apt 101
Charlottesville VA 22903

Call Sign: KI4ZMN
Kevin G Bender
157 Yellowstone Dr Apt 20B
Charlottesville VA 22903

Call Sign: N4MKW
Bruce E Martin
1721 Yorktown Dr
Charlottesville VA 22901

Call Sign: KE4CVW
Erwin A Villiger
Charlottesville VA 22903

Call Sign: KE4KLC
Mary C Pleasants

Charlottesville VA 22903

Call Sign: K4DU
Robert E Pattison
Charlottesville VA 22906

Call Sign: KD4WXY
Shawn M Pattison
Charlottesville VA 22906

Call Sign: K4MW
Peter D Wildman
Charlottesville VA 229067372

Call Sign: K6BC
Charles G Battig
Charlottesville VA 229068185

Call Sign: KB6RM
Rose Marie B Battig
Charlottesville VA 229068185

Call Sign: KC4RGY
Patricia M Huey
Charlottesville VA 22902

Call Sign: W4UVA
University Of VA ARC
Charlottesville VA 22904

Call Sign: KJ4KIH
Kenneth S Kang
Charlottesville VA 22905

Call Sign: KE4BRH
Alisa C Wildman
Charlottesville VA 22906

Call Sign: KE4OCK
Charles L Wildman
Charlottesville VA 22906

Call Sign: WA4TFZ
Albemarle ARC Inc
Charlottesville VA 22906

Call Sign: KG4TWO
Pamela H Brownfield
Charlottesville VA 22906

Call Sign: KI4GQI
Hal Brownfield
Charlottesville VA 22906

Call Sign: K4IHB
Hal Brownfield
Charlottesville VA 22906

Call Sign: KK4FJZ
Benjamin R Kreuter
Charlottesville VA 229022252

Call Sign: KI4HWG
Jens W Clark
Charlottesville VA 229030517

Call Sign: W4PRT
Peter R Thorsen Jr
Charlottesville VA 229054491

Call Sign: KI4JVO
Albemarle ARC
Charlottesville VA 229066833

Call Sign: W4DO
Albemarle ARC
Charlottesville VA 229066833

Call Sign: KG4OVD
Matthew C Brownfield
Charlottesville VA 229067861

Call Sign: KH6NC
Gary H Nakata
Charlottesville VA 229067943

Call Sign: K4TY
Charles G Battig
Charlottesville VA 229068185

Call Sign: KB4RM
Rose Marie B Battig
Charlottesville VA 229068185

FCC Amateur Radio Licenses in Chase City

Call Sign: KA2RAF

C J Crosby
Rt 1 Box 1745
Chase City VA 239245213

Call Sign: K4RAF
C J Crosby
Rt 1 Box 1745
Chase City VA 239245213

Call Sign: KC4RXN
Charles B Yancey
Rt 1 Box 190
Chase City VA 23924

Call Sign: KC4RXO
Anthony L Rickman
Rt 1 Box 1929
Chase City VA 23924

Call Sign: KC4ITJ
Gary A Brown
Rt 2 Box 250
Chase City VA 23924

Call Sign: KB2AHX
Eileen Partusch
1371 Courthouse Rd
Chase City VA 23924

Call Sign: KB2AHY
Richard D Partusch
1371 Courthouse Rd
Chase City VA 23924

Call Sign: WD4KTO
Linard S Bayne
5501 Fort Mitchell Dr
Chase City VA 23924

Call Sign: KE4SN
Frank A Palacky
26247 Hwy Forty Nine
Chase City VA 239244309

Call Sign: KJ4BMR
Richard A Magann
611 N Marshall St
Chase City VA 23924

Call Sign: KB2AHZ
Charles J Kubasek III
3608 Old Cox Rd
Chase City VA 23924

Call Sign: KJ4BMQ
Leslie A Kubasek
3608 Old Cox Rd
Chase City VA 23924

Call Sign: KC4ITI
Milton C Watkins
Rt 49
Chase City VA 23924

Call Sign: KC4ITL
Joey H Grube
116 S Madison St
Chase City VA 23924

Call Sign: AC4EC
Wallace L Icenhour
310 W Sycamore St
Chase City VA 23924

Call Sign: KD4DVS
Linda C Icenhour
310 W Sycamore St
Chase City VA 23924

Call Sign: KJ4LJQ
William T Cowan
1679 Watkins Forest Rd
Chase City VA 23924

Call Sign: AJ4RD
William T Cowan
1679 Watkins Forest Rd
Chase City VA 23924

Call Sign: KC4ITF
Charles B Petersen
Chase City VA 23924

Call Sign: WA2SSV
Clifford M Mosby
Chase City VA 23924

Call Sign: KJ4DWH
Jesse C Adkins
441 Anderson Rd
Chatham VA 24531

Call Sign: KJ4DWG
Linda G Adkins
441 Anderson Rd
Chatham VA 24531

Call Sign: KF4JDX
David C Prather
1989 Climax Rd
Chatham VA 24531

Call Sign: KE4EWZ
David L Adams
4117 Fairview Rd
Chatham VA 24531

Call Sign: KG4PGI
Merriwell Q Motley III
386 Greenbay Rd
Chatham VA 24531

Call Sign: N1WG
Walter W Gowen
5262 Irish Rd
Chatham VA 24531

Call Sign: KB9NLP
Jason R Ince
597 Meaddock Ln
Chatham VA 24531

Call Sign: K4KWX
Landon R Worsham
111 Military Dr
Chatham VA 24531

Call Sign: WB4PCK
Francis C Taylor
312 Military Dr
Chatham VA 24531

Call Sign: KD4TBC

Stuart D Roach
2060 Riddle Rd
Chatham VA 24531

Call Sign: KG4QLU
David C Collins
2260 Riddle Rd
Chatham VA 245314698

Call Sign: KE4FZH
Tina R Roach
2060 Riddle Rd
Chatham VA 24531

Call Sign: N4UPC
Rondie G Grant
560 Samuel Harris Ln
Chatham VA 24531

Call Sign: KI4HDC
Jeremy S Hood
582 Sheva Rd
Chatham VA 24531

Call Sign: KI4HYZ
David J Powers
4688 Spring Garden Rd
Chatham VA 24531

Call Sign: KG4IXS
Richard A Vaughan
316 Spruce Hill
Chatham VA 24531

Call Sign: K2QWZ
Stephen B Ignacki
1425 Tightsqueeze Rd
Chatham VA 24531

Call Sign: KI4OON
Odell S Cheek
3017 Union Hall School Rd
Chatham VA 24531

Call Sign: AJ4BQ
Odell S Cheek
3017 Union Hall School Rd
Chatham VA 24531

Call Sign: KJ4CAL
Thomas A Nicholson
612 Woodlawn Academy Rd
Chatham VA 24531

Call Sign: KJ4CAK
Thomas L Nicholson
612 Woodlawn Academy Rd
Chatham VA 24531

Call Sign: KI4OTS
Pittsylvania County Emergency
Management
Chatham VA 24531

Call Sign: WB4KJR
Pittsylvania County Emergency
Management
Chatham VA 24531

Call Sign: N4UTN
Calvin C Burnette
Chatham VA 24531

Call Sign: KI4KAM
Averett G Motley
Chatham VA 24531

Call Sign: KI4KAL
Billie J Roach
Chatham VA 24531

Call Sign: KI4KOP
Donna M Motley
Chatham VA 24531

Call Sign: KJ4ANB
Natalie D Motley
Chatham VA 24531

Call Sign: KC4HRE
Susan R Burnette
Chatham VA 245310951

FCC Amateur Radio Licenses in Check

Call Sign: KF4GVK
Robert F Mc Nabb Jr

171 Cana Rd
Check VA 24072

Call Sign: KF4GUS
Alexander J Mc Nabb
171 Cana Rd
Check VA 24072

Call Sign: KG4MAV
Russell F Abbey F
1090 Hale Rd NE
Check VA 240723220

Call Sign: KB4TVB
Wanda G Lineberry
851 Level Bottom Rd
Check VA 24072

Call Sign: WB4TGT
William B Lineberry
851 Level Bottom Rd
Check VA 24072

Call Sign: KI4KEJ
Thomas Z Jefferies
614 Shawsville Pike
Check VA 24072

FCC Amateur Radio Licenses in Cheriton

Call Sign: KD4NWD
Mary L Wood
21342 Wilkins Dr
Cheriton VA 233160205

Call Sign: N4WAO
Denis P Wood
21342 Wilkins Dr
Cheriton VA 233160205

Call Sign: KJ4QZH
Kentrell A Brown
Cheriton VA 23316

Call Sign: KC4DWI
Belford D Kellam
Cheriton VA 23316

FCC Amateur Radio Licenses in Chesapeake

Call Sign: KC2COT
Mark K Bowden
701 Abilene Ct
Chesapeake VA 23322

Call Sign: KI4KNX
William T Swartz
504 Aguila Ct
Chesapeake VA 233227142

Call Sign: KG4VWV
Ralph W Gibson Jr
121 Alamoot Dr
Chesapeake VA 23322

Call Sign: KK4GKB
Raquel M Toro
121 Allen Dr
Chesapeake VA 23322

Call Sign: N4FER
Robert L Walker
1884 Ames Cir W
Chesapeake VA 23321

Call Sign: KF4EPI
William C Dekker
816 Amy Marie Ln
Chesapeake VA 23320

Call Sign: N4GFA
Donnie B Jones
3312 Andrews Dr
Chesapeake VA 233231943

Call Sign: KK4GJZ
Raymon J Johnson
901 Angel Ct
Chesapeake VA 23320

Call Sign: KE4EML
Wesley R Conn Jr
1413 Anne Ave
Chesapeake VA 23324

Call Sign: KJ4KEB

Zachary E Newhart
612 Appaloosa Trl
Chesapeake VA 23323

Call Sign: K4WYS
Walton R Hood
2129 Arbutus Cir
Chesapeake VA 233235038

Call Sign: KC4TZP
Kerry E Cottingham
816 Arcadia Rd
Chesapeake VA 23320

Call Sign: KJ4AVN
Al T Nesmith Sr
1020 Artisan Ave
Chesapeake VA 23323

Call Sign: W9DKR
Jerauld S Peacock
1029 Artisan Ave
Chesapeake VA 233236801

Call Sign: N4CRV
Carl A Coppersmith
5209 Askew Rd
Chesapeake VA 23321

Call Sign: AA4MB
Herbert E Boomhower
1900 Athens Ct
Chesapeake VA 23323

Call Sign: WD4LGE
Oswald L Bonney III
1020 Austin Dr
Chesapeake VA 23320

Call Sign: W1JH
Robert E Sulouff Jr
1408 Baffy Loop
Chesapeake VA 23320

Call Sign: KF4RFL
Brian M Eads
2705 Bainbridge Blvd
Chesapeake VA 23324

Call Sign: KC4QNB
Martin D Begley
3000 Bainbridge Blvd
Chesapeake VA 23324

Call Sign: KD4GIU
Charles S Maphis
4535 Bainbridge Blvd Lot 27
Chesapeake VA 23320

Call Sign: KE4Z
Sanford R Smith
912 Balford Ln
Chesapeake VA 23320

Call Sign: KM4ZW
Andrew D Smith
912 Balford Ln
Chesapeake VA 23320

Call Sign: N0RVF
Eulalia T Fisher
1328 Ballahack Rd
Chesapeake VA 233222441

Call Sign: KK4CJY
Victoria E Scott
2012 Ballahack Rd
Chesapeake VA 23322

Call Sign: KF4UCC
George H Tibbetts
4121 Ballahack Rd
Chesapeake VA 23322

Call Sign: KQ4IX
Bradley B Garrett
3108 Bangor Dr
Chesapeake VA 23321

Call Sign: KE4RZP
Scott A Alvey
4027 Barn Owl Ln
Chesapeake VA 23321

Call Sign: KF4MFR
Michael D Qualls
4809 Barn Swallow Dr
Chesapeake VA 23321

Call Sign: N4ZDL
William B Qualls
4809 Barn Swallow Dr
Chesapeake VA 23321

Call Sign: N4VWP
Michael J Dunleavy
309 Bartell Ct
Chesapeake VA 23320

Call Sign: K4FVB
Lawrence D Davis
336 Bartell Dr
Chesapeake VA 23320

Call Sign: KD4OGL
Maynard L Inman Jr
2117 Battery Park Rd
Chesapeake VA 23323

Call Sign: N4CUT
Claire S Mundy
3116 Battlefield Blvd S
Chesapeake VA 23322

Call Sign: KI4RUH
Geoffrey B Runyon
1026 Baugher Ave
Chesapeake VA 23323

Call Sign: KD4GJF
John R Czarny Jr
536 Bay Oak Dr
Chesapeake VA 23323

Call Sign: WA9IWS
Alan L Stubbe
713 Baywood Trl
Chesapeake VA 23323

Call Sign: KG4SJA
Kenneth F Royse
717 Baywood Trl
Chesapeake VA 23323

Call Sign: N3GX
Alejandro Gonzalez
100 Beau Landing

Chesapeake VA 23322

Call Sign: W9UDI
George Wucivic
104 Beau Landing
Chesapeake VA 23320

Call Sign: KI4LHM
Kevin C Duryea
808 Beaver Creek Ct
Chesapeake VA 23322

Call Sign: KF4ZEN
Rick G Young
1348 Beaver Dam Rd
Chesapeake VA 23322

Call Sign: WB4ZSQ
Warren W Woessner Sr
1524 Beaver Dam Rd
Chesapeake VA 23322

Call Sign: KF4DAT
Andrew B Menefee
2524 Bellechase Ct
Chesapeake VA 23321

Call Sign: KE4LZU
John H Foreman III
825 Bellingham Dr
Chesapeake VA 23322

Call Sign: N7ROR
Lawrence P Whiting
1528 Benefit Rd
Chesapeake VA 23322

Call Sign: WD9IME
Arthur W Bradley
323 Big Pond Ln
Chesapeake VA 23323

Call Sign: KC4UTG
James T Dillon
1709H Birchtrail Cir
Chesapeake VA 23320

Call Sign: KK7XB
Douglas A Cammel

4601 Birsay Ct
Chesapeake VA 23321

Call Sign: KJ4UII
Michael A Hayden
400 Bishop St
Chesapeake VA 23323

Call Sign: WB2ZDL
George R Schuchman
809 Blackthorne Dr
Chesapeake VA 23322

Call Sign: KV4GR
George R Schuchman
809 Blackthorne Dr
Chesapeake VA 23322

Call Sign: N4YBM
Joseph W Rotz
445 Blanche Dr
Chesapeake VA 23323

Call Sign: KG4FOP
Sean R Poole
449 Blanche Dr S
Chesapeake VA 23323

Call Sign: KG4UKT
Gary L Waldrop
913 Bowling Green Trl
Chesapeake VA 233203111

Call Sign: KR4IM
Donald W Bennett
926 Bowling Green Trl
Chesapeake VA 23320

Call Sign: KD4SVO
Nancy L Bennett
926 Bowling Green Trl
Chesapeake VA 23320

Call Sign: N4POE
James A Brooks
Mou 1 Box 548
Chesapeake VA 23322

Call Sign: KD4FSR

William C Place
Mou 1 Box 623
Chesapeake VA 23322

Call Sign: KD4MVM
Ronald B Prewitt Jr
Mou 1 Box 771
Chesapeake VA 23322

Call Sign: KF4RQN
Chester J Quehl
1509 Boxwood Dr
Chesapeake VA 23323

Call Sign: KI4MNF
Leo B Henderson
2249 Branch Dr
Chesapeake VA 23321

Call Sign: WA4HPJ
Jerry C Dell
924 Brandermill Dr
Chesapeake VA 23322

Call Sign: KG4VWW
Perry B Ehle
426 Brandon Way
Chesapeake VA 23320

Call Sign: KJ4AVL
Felicia Y Baker-Davis
512 Brandon Way
Chesapeake VA 23320

Call Sign: KD4GJK
Terri L Bishop
3352 Brandywine Dr
Chesapeake VA 23321

Call Sign: WA4MAV
R J Bishop
3352 Brandywine Dr
Chesapeake VA 23321

Call Sign: NV6T
Lawrence E Weed
3312 Brandywine Dr
Chesapeake VA 233214909

Call Sign: KE4MIL
Stuart L Spatz
1017 Breckenridge Ct
Chesapeake VA 23320

Call Sign: K4MIL
Stuart L Spatz
1017 Breckenridge Ct
Chesapeake VA 23320

Call Sign: KM4WW
George R King
600 Briarwood Dr
Chesapeake VA 23320

Call Sign: W8PBR
Maurice L Lindsay
1224 Brigade Dr
Chesapeake VA 233224315

Call Sign: KD4RXD
John J Mack
429 Brisa Dr
Chesapeake VA 23320

Call Sign: W2VVJ
James W Childs Sr
233 Britwell Dr
Chesapeake VA 23322

Call Sign: KJ4YTE
Steven R Yewcic
2452 Broadnax Cir
Chesapeake VA 23323

Call Sign: N0OJQ
Petra Schuchardt
611 Broadwinsor Crescent
Chesapeake VA 23322

Call Sign: N0EZH
Gary O Schuchardt
611 Broadwinsor Crescent
Chesapeake VA 23322

Call Sign: WH6AQ
Kevin A Schafer
616 Broadwinsor Crescent
Chesapeake VA 23322

Call Sign: KD4JMB
James A Gross
1226 Brookside Landing
Chesapeake VA 23320

Call Sign: KG4ZHP
Henry S Hughes III
1104 Buford Ct
Chesapeake VA 23320

Call Sign: AJ4YN
Ray B Kauffman
3140 Bunch Walnut Rd
Chesapeake VA 23322

Call Sign: KE4KEE
Grant J Francis
2707 Buskey Rd
Chesapeake VA 23322

Call Sign: KD4GSI
Della J Ipock
1026 Calloway Ave
Chesapeake VA 23324

Call Sign: N4SHI
Preston P Ipock
1026 Calloway Ave
Chesapeake VA 23324

Call Sign: KA2IFH
David M Gianquitto
2500 Calonia Arch
Chesapeake VA 23323

Call Sign: KN4OH
Carl W Volz
809 Calvert Ct
Chesapeake VA 23320

Call Sign: KA3GAO
Lorena L Pearce
3520 Calverton Way
Chesapeake VA 23321

Call Sign: WD4HNO
Jacob H King Sr
3041 Camelot Blvd

Chesapeake VA 23323

Call Sign: KE4LPM
Thomas A Baker
1561 Campostella Rd Lot 22C
Chesapeake VA 23320

Call Sign: KE4HUA
Donald J Murdock
729 Canal Dr
Chesapeake VA 23323

Call Sign: KB4FXV
Cecil K Dillon
1104 Canal Dr
Chesapeake VA 23323

Call Sign: KD4ARJ
James C Laratta
2806 Canton Ave
Chesapeake VA 23325

Call Sign: KA4WXC
Frank M Dendis
708 Caravelle Dr
Chesapeake VA 23320

Call Sign: KJ4LER
Gil P Davis
284 Carawan Ln
Chesapeake VA 23322

Call Sign: KO4SC
Charles A Mc Lellan
353 Carawan Ln
Chesapeake VA 23322

Call Sign: KK4CKG
Carl N Wood
1018 Cardinal St
Chesapeake VA 23322

Call Sign: KB8SNA
Justin M Kusterer
2444 Carnation Ln
Chesapeake VA 23325

Call Sign: KJ4UIK
Caleb W Brewer

2004 Carolina Rd
Chesapeake VA 23322

Call Sign: KJ4IWX
Jason S Harris
2024 Carolina Rd
Chesapeake VA 23322

Call Sign: KJ4IWY
Norman D Harris
2024 Carolina Rd
Chesapeake VA 23322

Call Sign: K4NDH
Norman D Harris
2024 Carolina Rd
Chesapeake VA 23322

Call Sign: KE6BQW
Michaelangelo T Tungol
2228 Carolina Rd
Chesapeake VA 23322

Call Sign: KK4HLL
Judith P Tungol
2228 Carolina Rd
Chesapeake VA 23322

Call Sign: N4GDX
Michaelangelo T Tungol
2228 Carolina Rd
Chesapeake VA 23322

Call Sign: KC4ESJ
Shel J Sacks
1814 Carrollwood Cmn
Chesapeake VA 23320

Call Sign: KJ4WDW
Maurice R Mckenney
109 Causeway Dr
Chesapeake VA 23322

Call Sign: KA2DIQ
David R Peters
1245 Cedar Mill Sq
Chesapeake VA 233202747

Call Sign: KA4AQM

Randall D Melton
436 Cedar Pointe Ln
Chesapeake VA 23323

Call Sign: KD4GIH
Kristina M Melton
436 Cedar Pointe Ln
Chesapeake VA 23323

Call Sign: KG4TAW
Herbert F Poindexter Jr
201 Cedar Rd
Chesapeake VA 23322

Call Sign: KD4KJI
Willard C Meiggs Jr
309 Cedar Rd
Chesapeake VA 23320

Call Sign: KJ4PGJ
Chesapeake Center For Science
And Technology Hs ARC
1617 Cedar Rd
Chesapeake VA 23322

Call Sign: W4FOS
Chesapeake Center For Science
And Technology Hs ARC
1617 Cedar Rd
Chesapeake VA 23322

Call Sign: KB1BBS
John C Maheu
2427 Cedarville Rd
Chesapeake VA 233221567

Call Sign: KT4RK
John S Parsons
1823 Centerville Tpk S
Chesapeake VA 23322

Call Sign: KF0FA
Laurina M Spolidoro
1808 Charlotte Ann Ct
Chesapeake VA 23321

Call Sign: KA4CHY
Calvin M Brown
5112 Charlotte St

Chesapeake VA 23321

Call Sign: KJ4YKJ
Michael E Mccormick
2004 Cherry Ln
Chesapeake VA 23323

Call Sign: KK4HLK
Rey-Quintin M Martin
1221 Cherrytree Ln
Chesapeake VA 23320

Call Sign: KG4YEV
Bruce H Snyder
1305 Chestnut Ave
Chesapeake VA 23325

Call Sign: N2XRY
Clarence H Mosley
3148 Churchland Blvd Apt F2
Chesapeake VA 23321

Call Sign: KC7SDQ
David H Dillard
4943 Clifton St
Chesapeake VA 23321

Call Sign: KG4SJC
Barry I Marsh
3418 Clover Rd E
Chesapeake VA 233214417

Call Sign: W4GFO
Matthew G Rawlings
401 Cobblewood Arch
Chesapeake VA 23320

Call Sign: KK4DWQ
Gary A Payne Jr
1228 Cool Brook Trl
Chesapeake VA 23320

Call Sign: KI4TCI
F Sean Gorman
1340 Copper Stone Cir
Chesapeake VA 23320

Call Sign: W5CDR
F Sean Gorman

1340 Copper Stone Cir
Chesapeake VA 23320

Call Sign: KJ4AVJ
Joan Gorman
1340 Copperstone Cir
Chesapeake VA 23320

Call Sign: WJ4OAN
Joan Gorman
1340 Copperstone Cir
Chesapeake VA 23320

Call Sign: KA4FCC
Marvin R Eley
1 Corby Cir
Chesapeake VA 23320

Call Sign: KJ4UEJ
Art Thiemans Memorial Club
2712 Cornet St
Chesapeake VA 23321

Call Sign: AA4AT
Art Thiemens Memorial Club
2712 Cornet St
Chesapeake VA 23321

Call Sign: K0IBS
John D Johnson
2712 Cornet St
Chesapeake VA 23321

Call Sign: KF4HJL
Mary C Johnson
2712 Cornet St
Chesapeake VA 23321

Call Sign: WD5GHA
Robert L Cerquoz
301 Cotton Mill Ct
Chesapeake VA 23323

Call Sign: N8YDQ
Paul S Nowak
104 Country Club Blvd
Chesapeake VA 23322

Call Sign: KJ4NFL

Adam C Nowak
104 Country Club Blvd
Chesapeake VA 23322

Call Sign: KE8YN
Stephen F Nowak
104 Country Club Blvd
Chesapeake VA 233222136

Call Sign: KA4AUA
Major L Swindell Jr
401 Country Trl Rd
Chesapeake VA 23320

Call Sign: KB4YQ
Joseph S Crowling
3451 Cricket Hallow Ln
Chesapeake VA 23321

Call Sign: KA3HMQ
Douglas H Jones
1309 Croatan Ct
Chesapeake VA 23320

Call Sign: KJ4GDE
Clayton J Carriker
401 Crosstie Ct
Chesapeake VA 23323

Call Sign: KE4KIK
Eric W Jones
209 Crosswinds Dr Apt 101
Chesapeake VA 23320

Call Sign: K4HVR
Floyd H Miller Jr
537 Crown Crescent
Chesapeake VA 23325

Call Sign: WA4N
Earl J Nelson
1145 Crystalwood Cir
Chesapeake VA 23320

Call Sign: KK4BNR
John L Monroe
1108 Cutspring Rd
Chesapeake VA 23322

Call Sign: KK4BNS
Courtney M Fairing
3701 Cypress Mill Ct
Chesapeake VA 23322

Call Sign: KI4ZUX
William H Fairing
3701 Cypress Mill Ct
Chesapeake VA 23322

Call Sign: W1ATA
William H J Fairing
3701 Cypress Mill Ct
Chesapeake VA 23322

Call Sign: W8JSA
Jeffrey S Austin
1365 Cypress Pl
Chesapeake VA 233202707

Call Sign: KJ4LEU
Daizsa R Holland
1284 Damyien Arch
Chesapeake VA 23320

Call Sign: KG4NUG
Bradley S Garner
4509 Davids Mill Dr
Chesapeake VA 23321

Call Sign: KE4GPA
John E Garner
4509 Davids Mill Dr
Chesapeake VA 23321

Call Sign: WD4RPP
Haydn Rubelmann
1222 Davis Ave
Chesapeake VA 23325

Call Sign: KZ4CMB
Charles M Beeson
1501 Debreck Way
Chesapeake VA 23320

Call Sign: KF4DUH
Ronnie H Trager
912 Deep Creek Blvd
Chesapeake VA 23323

Call Sign: KC4JIK
Richard J Cosendine
1401 Deep Creek Blvd 127
Chesapeake VA 23323

Call Sign: KD4EAT
Charles A Felton
2401 Deerfield Crescent
Chesapeake VA 233212414

Call Sign: KD4CXI
Robert F Castellow
507 Dent Pl
Chesapeake VA 23325

Call Sign: KB2QWF
Christopher P Mc Kelvey
2408 Devonshire Dr
Chesapeake VA 23323

Call Sign: WT4R
James R Allen
240 Dexter St E
Chesapeake VA 23324

Call Sign: KC4SMC
Michael V Seimetz
805 Doe Run Dr
Chesapeake VA 23320

Call Sign: WA4UJT
Joseph L Rowe
3000 Dogwood Ter
Chesapeake VA 23321

Call Sign: KI4TCD
Gayle D Rowe
3000 Dogwood Ter
Chesapeake VA 23321

Call Sign: WA4GDR
Gayle D Rowe
3000 Dogwood Ter
Chesapeake VA 23321

Call Sign: KB4ONR
James R Laprade
408 Dorchester Ct

Chesapeake VA 233228892

Call Sign: KE4YQ
Lynde D Blair
237 Downing Dr
Chesapeake VA 233228746

Call Sign: KA4RKJ
Lisa A Griffith
180 Driftwood Dr
Chesapeake VA 23320

Call Sign: KJ4NGD
Brandon K Raiford
4108 Duke Of Gloucester Dr
Chesapeake VA 23321

Call Sign: NI4Y
William K Raiford
4108 Duke Of Gloucester Dr
Chesapeake VA 23321

Call Sign: K4JV
Chesapeake Dx Association
2200 F Dunbarton Dr
Chesapeake VA 23325

Call Sign: W4WV
William M Verebely Jr
2200 Dunbarton Dr Ste F
Chesapeake VA 23325

Call Sign: W4MDR
John E Volkstorf Sr
3551 Dunedin Dr 102
Chesapeake VA 23321

Call Sign: WB4MRW
Richard R Smith Jr
3543 Dunedin Dr Apt 201
Chesapeake VA 23321

Call Sign: KF4RYM
Anthony D Hartwell
3228 Dunworken Dr
Chesapeake VA 23321

Call Sign: KE4NBU
Paul K Paulk

2148 E Armada Dr
Chesapeake VA 23321

Call Sign: KC4UXU
Robert J Mc Cracken III
100 E Royce Dr
Chesapeake VA 23320

Call Sign: KA4VBD
Laura J Harrell
303 E St Brides Rd
Chesapeake VA 23322

Call Sign: K4DQS
Clarence D Hickman
1617 Eagle Hill Dr
Chesapeake VA 23321

Call Sign: K4BIY
Alfred V La Rue
1704 Eagle Hill Dr
Chesapeake VA 23321

Call Sign: N9UND
Sandra B Wright
1409 Eaglestone Arch
Chesapeake VA 23322

Call Sign: ND1V
Robert R Wright
1409 Eaglestone Arch
Chesapeake VA 23322

Call Sign: KI4HNC
Timothy L Dodge Sr
1226 Edgewood Ave
Chesapeake VA 23324

Call Sign: N4WVM
Michael J Tincher
117B Edna St
Chesapeake VA 23320

Call Sign: AF4C
Dale L Mc Pherson
2029 Elbow Rd
Chesapeake VA 23320

Call Sign: WA4WPN

Stella L Mc Pherson
2029 Elbow Rd
Chesapeake VA 23320

Call Sign: KK4CJV
Benjamin J Hobbs
1130 Elder Ave
Chesapeake VA 23325

Call Sign: KB8MUS
Robert O Daniels
1328 Elder Ave
Chesapeake VA 23325

Call Sign: K4BDW
Byron D Ward Jr
3536 Elkton Dr
Chesapeake VA 233214434

Call Sign: WA7YHV
James H Radford
3637 Elkton Dr
Chesapeake VA 23321

Call Sign: KG6WVY
Todd E Smith
721 Elm Forest Ct
Chesapeake VA 23322

Call Sign: KA4UQX
Brian M Howard
4109 Ember Hill Ln
Chesapeake VA 23321

Call Sign: W6RHS
Robbie H Scott Jr
1801 Emerald Sea Dr
Chesapeake VA 23323

Call Sign: WD4JGF
Willie J Cahoon
2036 English Ave
Chesapeake VA 23320

Call Sign: KI4SWI
Ralph M Lavender
700 Erik Paul Dr
Chesapeake VA 23322

Call Sign: KK4ML
Ralph M Lavender
700 Erik Paul Dr
Chesapeake VA 23322

Call Sign: KE3SY
Domenick M Iafrato Jr
113 Esplanade Pl
Chesapeake VA 233202085

Call Sign: KB4CPT
Lawrence L Carlson
343 Esplanade Pl
Chesapeake VA 23320

Call Sign: KC4NJM
Thomas F Powers
209 Essex Dr
Chesapeake VA 23320

Call Sign: KB8UQW
Gwendolyn R Keller
3504 Executive Center Dr 310
Chesapeake VA 23321

Call Sign: N3MH
Marie T Harvey
609 Fairfield Dr
Chesapeake VA 23320

Call Sign: N4JH
Julian T Harvey
609 Fairfield Dr
Chesapeake VA 23320

Call Sign: KF4PWV
Davis L Main
1107 Fairway Dr
Chesapeake VA 23320

Call Sign: AG4OK
Davis L Main
1107 Fairway Dr
Chesapeake VA 23320

Call Sign: KJ4KEC
Spencer P Petersen
3429 Faxfield Dr
Chesapeake VA 23323

Call Sign: KB1DKI
Jeanne L Oldrich
1140 Ferebee Ave
Chesapeake VA 23324

Call Sign: N1ZZW
Glenn J Oldrich
1140 Ferebee Ave
Chesapeake VA 23324

Call Sign: KH6HHS
Talley V George III
709 Fern Quay
Chesapeake VA 23320

Call Sign: W4TVG
Talley V George III
709 Fern Quay
Chesapeake VA 23320

Call Sign: N4BJB
Brian J Bodnar
2229 Ferndale Rd
Chesapeake VA 23323

Call Sign: KG4IDJ
Inez P Brittingham
2237 Ferndale Rd
Chesapeake VA 23323

Call Sign: W4ZDZ
William V Lundy
2309 Firman St
Chesapeake VA 23323

Call Sign: KJ4YKH
Joshua L Horton
4328 Fontana Ave
Chesapeake VA 23325

Call Sign: W4LPF
Earl H Selover
1200 Fordyce Dr
Chesapeake VA 23322

Call Sign: KC4UWG
David L Desler Sr
957 Forest Lakes Dr

Chesapeake VA 23322

Call Sign: KJ4JIJ
Phillip C Petersen
3429 Foxfield Dr
Chesapeake VA 23323

Call Sign: K4KUJ
Richard T Tillett
4209 Foxxglen Run
Chesapeake VA 23321

Call Sign: KK4GKD
Hartley J Moon III
233A Frank Dr
Chesapeake VA 23322

Call Sign: KD4MBA
Kent W Wells
408 Gallbush Rd
Chesapeake VA 23322

Call Sign: KI4SAX
Daniel J Reeves
305 Gallenway Ter
Chesapeake VA 23322

Call Sign: KD4OCL
Norman L Sehen
1400C Garden Ct
Chesapeake VA 23322

Call Sign: KJ4AHU
Matthew Carey
316 George Washington Hwy N
Chesapeake VA 23323

Call Sign: KC4FLA
Michael S Carey
316 George Washington Hwy N
Chesapeake VA 23323

Call Sign: KI4SPJ
William S Mayeux
345 George Washington Hwy N
Chesapeake VA 23323

Call Sign: W4ZPV
Allen J Earnhardt

1041 George Washington Hwy
N
Chesapeake VA 23323

Call Sign: KI4ZPV
Joseph B Hand
2629 Gilmerton Rd
Chesapeake VA 23323

Call Sign: KI4ZPW
Samantha L Hand
2629 Gilmerton Rd
Chesapeake VA 23323

Call Sign: W4YOO
John J Reitelbach Jr
2025 Girard Ave
Chesapeake VA 23323

Call Sign: KI4KSN
Jeffrey A Smith
604 Gladesdale Dr
Chesapeake VA 23322

Call Sign: KA3ANF
Kenneth A Schultz
604 Gladesdale Dr
Chesapeake VA 233203451

Call Sign: KI4ODG
John W Moody
1432 Glendale Ave
Chesapeake VA 23323

Call Sign: KC7BFI
David R Robison
701 Gloria Dr
Chesapeake VA 23322

Call Sign: KD7ETU
David R Robison
701 Gloria Dr
Chesapeake VA 23322

Call Sign: WB5WKA
Shirley E Willis
1920 Goldeneye Dr
Chesapeake VA 23320

Call Sign: KI4FNR
Karon P Hardy
348 Gracie Rd
Chesapeake VA 23325

Call Sign: KI4EIW
Karon P Hardy
348 Gracie Rd
Chesapeake VA 23375

Call Sign: KC4FKY
Mary M Howie
357 Gracie Rd
Chesapeake VA 23325

Call Sign: KD4JMC
Joseph C Landin Jr
812 Grantham Ln
Chesapeake VA 23322

Call Sign: AE6QE
Richard W Clement
911 Grantham Ln
Chesapeake VA 23322

Call Sign: KM4DH
Calvert W Tazewell
704 Green Tree Cir 103
Chesapeake VA 23320

Call Sign: WB3KOF
Brian J Tate
703 Green Tree Cir 203
Chesapeake VA 23320

Call Sign: KB4DYE
John G Humphrey
4329 Greendell Rd
Chesapeake VA 23321

Call Sign: WD4GVU
Bernhard A Seitz
4252 Greenleaf Dr
Chesapeake VA 233214215

Call Sign: KC4PSR
S Allen Grimsley
4312 Greenleaf Dr
Chesapeake VA 23321

Call Sign: K4BVN
Forrest E Murray
417 Guynn Ave
Chesapeake VA 233233105

Call Sign: KJ4URT
Michael X Lauzon
430 Habour N Dr
Chesapeake VA 23320

Call Sign: KE4JFN
Joseph M Donahue
236 Haledon Rd
Chesapeake VA 23320

Call Sign: KF4PAW
Edward A Turner
2716 Halsey St
Chesapeake VA 23324

Call Sign: W3GAQ
Raymond L Thomas
2332 Halyard Ln
Chesapeake VA 233234044

Call Sign: K4VWU
Joe C Phibbs
168 Harbor Watch Dr
Chesapeake VA 23320

Call Sign: KA4BFT
Stephen D Buell
3134 Harvesttime Crescent
Chesapeake VA 233215902

Call Sign: KI4GAO
Edward L Kerlin III
228 Haviland Rd
Chesapeake VA 23320

Call Sign: KI4RUI
Kenneth H Jensen
734 Hawkhurst Dr
Chesapeake VA 23322

Call Sign: WA4LPM
Harvey L Bryant Jr
4012 Hawksley Dr
Chesapeake VA 23321

Call Sign: KA4BFS
Eloise B Bryant
4012 Hawksley Dr
Chesapeake VA 233215424

Call Sign: AI4XT
Boyd D Yarbrough
4224 Hawksley Dr
Chesapeake VA 233215428

Call Sign: W9BD
Boyd D Yarbrough
4224 Hawksley Dr
Chesapeake VA 233215428

Call Sign: KF4IYU
Thomas W Englert
1211 Hawthorne Dr
Chesapeake VA 23325

Call Sign: KF4KLY
Thomas W Englert
1211 Hawthorne Dr
Chesapeake VA 23325

Call Sign: KJ4PPK
Thomas W Englert IV
1211 Hawthorne Dr
Chesapeake VA 23325

Call Sign: W9OCT
Michael G Duckworth
1219A Hazel Ave
Chesapeake VA 23325

Call Sign: KF4KLZ
Sean T Gable
1765 Head Of River Rd
Chesapeake VA 23322

Call Sign: KJ4URU
Dominik S Rodriguez
1106 Hearthstone Landing
Chesapeake VA 23320

Call Sign: KK4CKB
Logan M Rice

304 Heritage Cir
Chesapeake VA 23322

Call Sign: WA4HHG
Robert C Rippel
2341 Herring Ditch Rd
Chesapeake VA 233236419

Call Sign: KG4CNJ
Johnny O Hall
309 Hickory Rd E
Chesapeake VA 23322

Call Sign: N4GSP
Arthur D Cahoon Jr
861 Hill Well Rd
Chesapeake VA 23322

Call Sign: KD4OSP
Donald R Burke
945 Hollywood Dr
Chesapeake VA 23320

Call Sign: KG4UKV
Richard L Smith
509 Homestead Rd
Chesapeake VA 23321

Call Sign: KC4USH
Richard L Smith
509 Homestead Rd
Chesapeake VA 23321

Call Sign: KC4RIC
Richard L Smith
509 Homestead Rd
Chesapeake VA 23321

Call Sign: KU4LN
Chester A Leibrand
605 Homestead Rd
Chesapeake VA 23321

Call Sign: KD7JJB
Courtney A Kerr
445 Honey Locust Way
Chesapeake VA 23320

Call Sign: KE7BDF

Machelle Kerr
445 Honey Locust Way
Chesapeake VA 23320

Call Sign: KJ4EOJ
Regina R Taylor
1813 Hoover Ave
Chesapeake VA 23324

Call Sign: KF4YQK
Mark A Robertson
2717 Horseshoe Dr
Chesapeake VA 23322

Call Sign: KF4IYR
Robert A Pond Jr
1625 Hydenwood Cres
Chesapeake VA 23321

Call Sign: KE4GOX
Wesley R Conn Sr
2710 Ike St Lot 90
Chesapeake VA 23324

Call Sign: KD6FIG
Richard E Stanley
3303 Indian River Rd
Chesapeake VA 23325

Call Sign: KE6WWD
Eileen M Stanley
3303 Indian River Rd
Chesapeake VA 23325

Call Sign: N4NZZ
William L Holmes III
3307 Indigo Rd
Chesapeake VA 23325

Call Sign: KD4AYL
Michael D Baxter
1146 Inland Rd
Chesapeake VA 23320

Call Sign: KG4PMK
Scott D Harvey
725 B Inlet Quay
Chesapeake VA 23320

Call Sign: KC6BIW
James H Donnelly
805 Iverness Ct
Chesapeake VA 23320

Call Sign: NE4D
Ian D Howard
832 Jo Anne Cir
Chesapeake VA 233223835

Call Sign: AL7HW
Thomas F Sherwood
2200 Jolliff Rd
Chesapeake VA 23321

Call Sign: KE4NAX
Denise L Mc Nelly
1219 Kay Ave
Chesapeake VA 23324

Call Sign: N4KQC
Tony W Thomas
152 Kempsville Rd
Chesapeake VA 23320

Call Sign: KJ4ZSH
James E Morgan
384 Kempsville Rd
Chesapeake VA 23320

Call Sign: NA3Z
James E Morgan
384 Kempsville Rd
Chesapeake VA 23320

Call Sign: KM4BO
Michael L Cottingham
60 King George Quay
Chesapeake VA 23325

Call Sign: KD4NOU
Mark A Stevens
13C Kingsbridge Way S
Chesapeake VA 23320

Call Sign: KD4HEG
Sharon E Moore
1276 Kingsway Dr
Chesapeake VA 23320

Call Sign: N6ZO
Chester H Moore
1276 Kingsway Dr
Chesapeake VA 23320

Call Sign: N4FX
Chester H Moore
1276 Kingsway Dr
Chesapeake VA 23320

Call Sign: NX4XX
Sharon E Moore
1276 Kingsway Dr
Chesapeake VA 23320

Call Sign: KK4GKA
Devonte Thomas
3041 Knight Rd
Chesapeake VA 23323

Call Sign: WA4ATZ
Robert H Hill
2325 Lakewood Ln
Chesapeake VA 23321

Call Sign: W2RCG
Frank J Gryniak
2516 Lakewood Ln
Chesapeake VA 233213704

Call Sign: KI4LDV
Gerald R Hall
2858 Lambert Tr
Chesapeake VA 23323

Call Sign: KI4SOL
Thomas P Larsen
2532 Lanier St
Chesapeake VA 23324

Call Sign: W4NDS
Stephen A Dekrone
201 Larkspur Ct
Chesapeake VA 23322

Call Sign: N4NIG
Charles V Reynolds
829 Larkspur Ln

Chesapeake VA 23320

Call Sign: N4TOZ
Linda L Reynolds
829 Larkspur Ln
Chesapeake VA 23320

Call Sign: KI4EUM
Richard A Graham
104 Las Gaviotas Lndg
Chesapeake VA 23322

Call Sign: N4YNS
Weston W King
1329 Laurel Ave
Chesapeake VA 23325

Call Sign: N3CHW
James T Hopkins
204 Lee Ct
Chesapeake VA 23320

Call Sign: WA4OTB
Robert M Hodges Sr
112 Lenore Trl
Chesapeake VA 23320

Call Sign: W4WRP
Willard C Stewart Sr
4102 Leyte Ave
Chesapeake VA 23324

Call Sign: KB4NEX
John S Alexander III
2425 Lindbergh Ave
Chesapeake VA 23325

Call Sign: KF4RVW
Robert T Jordan Jr
4123 Lindenwood Dr
Chesapeake VA 23321

Call Sign: KC4FEO
Pat L Hough
208 Lindsey Ave
Chesapeake VA 23320

Call Sign: KI4HPG
Michael E Haas

435 Linkenborough Dr
Chesapeake VA 23322

Call Sign: WB4KJF
Gerald E Priest
1924 Lisbon Rd
Chesapeake VA 23321

Call Sign: KC4KMZ
Steve R Moore
2041 Lockard Ave
Chesapeake VA 23320

Call Sign: KJ4AVM
Suzanne C Snowden
112 Locks Ln
Chesapeake VA 23320

Call Sign: KJ4SNO
Suzanne C Snowden
112 Locks Ln
Chesapeake VA 23320

Call Sign: KI4LWR
Paul T Biecker
2126 Logans Mill Trl
Chesapeake VA 23320

Call Sign: KJ4LET
Famous E Spellman Jr
2220 Logans Mill Trl
Chesapeake VA 23320

Call Sign: KJ4UIM
Michael C Hogan
1220 Long Ridge Rd
Chesapeake VA 23322

Call Sign: KE4SCQ
John P Stanley
3717 Ludgate Dr
Chesapeake VA 23321

Call Sign: KE4SCR
Ann Marie Stanley
3717 Ludgate Dr
Chesapeake VA 23321

Call Sign: N4DLD

Philip T Stanley
3717 Ludgate Dr
Chesapeake VA 23321

Call Sign: WB4WPH
Edward S Hardin
3233 Lynnhurst Blvd
Chesapeake VA 233214427

Call Sign: KJ4LFV
Shaquita M White
1332 Macdonald Rd Apt F
Chesapeake VA 23325

Call Sign: WA4RGU
Lavin Williams
857 Main Creek Rd
Chesapeake VA 23320

Call Sign: KB4IQC
David W Peters
209 Mann Dr
Chesapeake VA 23320

Call Sign: KJ4RYK
The Brothers Net
4913 Manning Ct
Chesapeake VA 23321

Call Sign: W9BRO
The Brothers Net
4913 Manning Ct
Chesapeake VA 23321

Call Sign: KI4ZAC
Philip E Henline
4913 Manning Ct
Chesapeake VA 23321

Call Sign: WA9KFB
Philip E Henline
4913 Manning Ct
Chesapeake VA 23321

Call Sign: KF4OLX
Michael P Schuelke
3452 Maori Dr
Chesapeake VA 233214804

Call Sign: KE4OMK
Clifford L Monroe
3504 Maori Dr
Chesapeake VA 23321

Call Sign: WA9USE
Sherman E Foster
4072 Maple Dr
Chesapeake VA 23321

Call Sign: W4MGU
Raymond D Blakeslee Jr
4129 Maple Dr
Chesapeake VA 23321

Call Sign: KC4MYI
Linda R Black
3524 Mardean Dr
Chesapeake VA 233214478

Call Sign: KF4MFL
James T Black
3524 Mardean Dr
Chesapeake VA 233214478

Call Sign: KG4YEW
Gregory D Peck
2704 Mark St
Chesapeake VA 23324

Call Sign: KB4HPH
Floyd H Blythe Jr
2802 Mark St
Chesapeake VA 233242948

Call Sign: N4BZI
Felton L Ausley Jr
208 Marsh Wren Ct
Chesapeake VA 23320

Call Sign: KJ4DWI
Charles R Barefield
709 Marston Ave
Chesapeake VA 23322

Call Sign: KF4GIW
William J Morgan Jr
3512 Martin Johnson Rd
Chesapeake VA 23323

Call Sign: KK4GKC
Tychina S King
2908 Mattox Dr
Chesapeake VA 23325

Call Sign: KI4DNN
Deborah D Hunter
1006 Mayfield Ave
Chesapeake VA 23324

Call Sign: KI4FNN
Ronald O Hunter
1006 Mayfield Ave
Chesapeake VA 23324

Call Sign: WD4GVE
Francis W Campbell
2804 Meadow Wood Crt W
Chesapeake VA 23321

Call Sign: W4GEO
George B Hartsell Jr
4223 Meadow Wood Dr
Chesapeake VA 23321

Call Sign: KD4IEI
Kathy C Fatico
4261 Meadow Wood Dr
Chesapeake VA 23321

Call Sign: KS4DO
Frank A Fatico
4261 Meadow Wood Dr
Chesapeake VA 23321

Call Sign: KF4DAV
Gerard Merbler
4204 Meadowgate Ct
Chesapeake VA 23321

Call Sign: KC4GSO
Heather M Shields
4200A Meadowlark St
Chesapeake VA 23322

Call Sign: KA4FXW
Carl J Meyer
4244 Meadowridge Dr

Chesapeake VA 23321

Call Sign: KI4RUL
Anthony F Guida
2304 Meiggs Rd
Chesapeake VA 23323

Call Sign: KC4FLA
Michael S Carey
2524 Meiggs Rd
Chesapeake VA 23323

Call Sign: N4ABR
George A Estes
308 Melonie Ct
Chesapeake VA 233226714

Call Sign: KE4RBN
Gary N Guillory
1140 Merchants Ct Apt 2C
Chesapeake VA 23320

Call Sign: KG4SPF
Scott D Abbey
1103 Merchants Ct Apt 3A
Chesapeake VA 23320

Call Sign: WA5TXQ
Earl C Webre
3400 Miars Farm Cir
Chesapeake VA 23434

Call Sign: KJ4EOH
James L Underwood
309 Middle Oaks Dr
Chesapeake VA 23322

Call Sign: KJ4VIH
Eva L Midgette
2041 Miller Ave
Chesapeake VA 23320

Call Sign: K4UX
Albert P Bianchi
500 Millstone Rd
Chesapeake VA 233224367

Call Sign: KD0DV
Frederick A Balster Jr

220 Millwood Ave
Chesapeake VA 23322

Call Sign: N0EWL
Norma F Balster
220 Millwood Ave
Chesapeake VA 23322

Call Sign: KB4LRZ
William C Hoffman
4101 Mingo Trl
Chesapeake VA 23325

Call Sign: KI4ODF
Matthew M Johnson
912 Mocking Bird Ct
Chesapeake VA 23322

Call Sign: WD8QAL
John L Sparks
1507B Mockingbird Ct
Chesapeake VA 23322

Call Sign: KG4TMW
Charles M Beeson
1328 Monarch Reach
Chesapeake VA 23320

Call Sign: KI4DEX
Charles M Beeson
1328 Monarch Reach
Chesapeake VA 23320

Call Sign: KC4UPH
Zane A Bedient
520 Montevale Dr
Chesapeake VA 23320

Call Sign: KG4ZGA
Jeffrey W Spyker
444 Mt Pleasant Rd
Chesapeake VA 233223542

Call Sign: WA4BUK
Lemuel L Murden
1800 Mt Pleasant Rd
Chesapeake VA 233221217

Call Sign: KJ4TJX

Frank J Lawsky
1329 Myrtle Ave
Chesapeake VA 23325

Call Sign: KK4SN
Jeffrey D Koke
928 N Haven Cir
Chesapeake VA 233227534

Call Sign: KG4ZFZ
Jason A Kennedy
216 N Sparrow Rd
Chesapeake VA 23325

Call Sign: K4WZK
Edward J Brooks
800 Needlerush Ct
Chesapeake VA 23320

Call Sign: KJ4EOI
Maurice A Grandberry
11 Newstead Cir
Chesapeake VA 23320

Call Sign: KD4WRF
George A Peele III
308 Ninton Ave
Chesapeake VA 23323

Call Sign: KF4KME
Neal L Smith
616 Norcova Dr
Chesapeake VA 23320

Call Sign: KI4KNY
Mark A Drew Sr
732 Norcova Sr
Chesapeake VA 23320

Call Sign: KI4RUK
Eugene V Wilson
1429 Norlina Dr
Chesapeake VA 23322

Call Sign: K4NDH
Nsga Northwest Recreation
Services
Commanding Officer Code 01
Nsga NW

Chesapeake VA 23322

Call Sign: AH6JH
Peter D Dennant Jr
804 Nugent Dr
Chesapeake VA 233223720

Call Sign: KA4EAK
Craig J Schneider
911 Nugent Dr
Chesapeake VA 23320

Call Sign: WB4CZP
Charlie L Hurt Jr
4065 Oak Dr
Chesapeake VA 23321

Call Sign: KF4EBE
Jean S Walker
317 Oak Hill Way
Chesapeake VA 23320

Call Sign: KI4RUD
Douglas J Kent
603 Oak Mears Cove
Chesapeake VA 23323

Call Sign: AG4MQ
Bernard M Lavezza
411 Oaklette Dr
Chesapeake VA 23325

Call Sign: AA4BL
Bernard M Lavezza
411 Oaklette Dr
Chesapeake VA 23325

Call Sign: KC4ZWF
La Nette G Desler
313 Old Dr
Chesapeake VA 23320

Call Sign: KB4VMB
Carter G Culpepper
3044 Old Mill Rd
Chesapeake VA 23323

Call Sign: KK4FXV
Christopher B Zatezalo

2807 Omar St
Chesapeake VA 23324

Call Sign: KG4EUG
Robert M Pope Jr
1534 Orchard Grove Dr
Chesapeake VA 23320

Call Sign: KB0TDY
David M Graham
1313 Oregon Crossing
Chesapeake VA 23322

Call Sign: KC4UFO
Gladys M Smith
1300 Ormer Rd
Chesapeake VA 23325

Call Sign: KC4UFP
Jesse L Hill
1300 Ormer Rd
Chesapeake VA 23325

Call Sign: KC4UFO
Jesse L Hill
1300 Ormer Rd
Chesapeake VA 23325

Call Sign: KD4VNL
Wayne D Masnick
1502A Osprey Ct
Chesapeake VA 23322

Call Sign: KD4MCV
Denise J Bulone
1506B Osprey Ct
Chesapeake VA 23322

Call Sign: KI4PPN
Michael W Sheeley
513 Owens Ter
Chesapeake VA 23323

Call Sign: N4LZC
Henry C Cahoon Sr
428 Parker Rd
Chesapeake VA 23320

Call Sign: KF4GIX

Donavan D Moorman
712 Paula Dr
Chesapeake VA 23322

Call Sign: WF7B
John K Culliton
1043 Paxson Ave
Chesapeake VA 23324

Call Sign: K5VIP
Nathern B Priddy
723 Peachtree Dr
Chesapeake VA 233227732

Call Sign: K3MLH
Jack R Alberts Jr
3125 Pelham St
Chesapeake VA 23324

Call Sign: KB4AXU
Vernon L Marshall III
4425 Pepper Ridge Ct
Chesapeake VA 23321

Call Sign: KI4ORD
Jason M Helwig
3902 Pine Grove Landing
Chesapeake VA 23322

Call Sign: W2PGM
Frank J Di Lustro
3212 Pineridge Dr
Chesapeake VA 233215404

Call Sign: N4HBB
Wilbur G Carawan
3317 Pineridge Dr
Chesapeake VA 23321

Call Sign: KE4SAZ
Joseph M Sammon
614 Pintail Ln
Chesapeake VA 23323

Call Sign: WD4DWA
Thomas C Jones
1321 Placid Way
Chesapeake VA 23320

Call Sign: KG4EGG
Jeremy E Chojnacki
456 Plummer Dr
Chesapeake VA 23323

Call Sign: KB4JND
Amorella M Davis
2316 Pocaty Rd
Chesapeake VA 23322

Call Sign: KG4CAT
Edmond E Maitland
2420 Pocaty Rd
Chesapeake VA 23322

Call Sign: KA3RPF
Michael A Vesco Sr
3917 Point Elizabeth Dr
Chesapeake VA 23321

Call Sign: KI4MND
Oscar T Macapobre
804 Pompano Arch
Chesapeake VA 23322

Call Sign: WD4NKU
Ernest R Scherger Sr
703 Pond Ln
Chesapeake VA 23325

Call Sign: W4MVB
Jesse H Morris
804 Poplar Ridge Dr
Chesapeake VA 233223423

Call Sign: WB4UVH
James T Hardee
2624 Powell Cir
Chesapeake VA 23323

Call Sign: KI4VMC
Florence H Hardee
2624 Powell Cir
Chesapeake VA 23323

Call Sign: WB4UVG
Florence H Hardee
2624 Powell Cir
Chesapeake VA 23323

Call Sign: KF4DAZ
Cecil E Tarkenton
2901 Princess Anne Cres
Chesapeake VA 23321

Call Sign: KF4LZB
William L Ripley
2936 Princess Anne Crs
Chesapeake VA 23321

Call Sign: KD4UFG
Rita M Ferguson
4161 Prindle Ct Apt 304
Chesapeake VA 23321

Call Sign: KS4NO
Michael S Kimbrel
2520 Prudden Trace
Chesapeake VA 23323

Call Sign: KJ4EOK
Brendan M Mccarty
543 Queenswood Ter
Chesapeake VA 23322

Call Sign: KF4RXM
John P Higgins
3001 Radcliffe Ln
Chesapeake VA 23321

Call Sign: KA4AAC
Dorsey W Bull
301B Rainbow Ln
Chesapeake VA 23320

Call Sign: KD7BHS
Thomas M Harrison Jr
816 Rainbow Run
Chesapeake VA 23320

Call Sign: WB4HJM
John W Cramer
4283 Raleigh Rd
Chesapeake VA 23321

Call Sign: N1HJI
Philomena L Hoar
1025 Ramsgate Ln

Chesapeake VA 23322

Call Sign: N1VTA
Philomena T Hoar
1025 Ramsgate Ln
Chesapeake VA 23322

Call Sign: WA1C
Gary L Hoar
1025 Ramsgate Ln
Chesapeake VA 23322

Call Sign: KJ4CVS
Mark S Stanley
600 Ravenwoods Dr
Chesapeake VA 23322

Call Sign: KJ4EZH
Robert C Smith
633 Ravenwoods Dr
Chesapeake VA 23322

Call Sign: KG4IST
Leland C Martin
907 Red Bay Ln
Chesapeake VA 23322

Call Sign: KC0JZO
Logan T Beebe
238 Red Cedar Ct Apt 3C
Chesapeake VA 23320

Call Sign: NA4Z
Gerald S Johnson
1016 Redstart Ave
Chesapeake VA 23324

Call Sign: N4ZGT
Floyd D Whitehurst
4709 Regal Ct
Chesapeake VA 23321

Call Sign: KG4BGZ
Alan W Richards
505 Renaissance Ct
Chesapeake VA 23320

Call Sign: KA4VYT
William B Pringle

146 Ridgewood Rd
Chesapeake VA 233252250

Call Sign: KK4CJW
Duawana J Robinson
4028 River Breeze Cir
Chesapeake VA 23321

Call Sign: K4GEM
Samantha C Collins
2025 River Pearl Way
Chesapeake VA 23321

Call Sign: KB4TFY
Marion F Carter
2061 River Pearl Way
Chesapeake VA 23321

Call Sign: KK4CJZ
Corey R Parker
1417 Rivers Edge Trace
Chesapeake VA 23323

Call Sign: KB0WOX
Patrick A Hillmeyer
1451 Rivers Edge Trace
Chesapeake VA 23323

Call Sign: KD4ARM
Alan G Franza
216 Robert St
Chesapeake VA 23320

Call Sign: KK4EJQ
Harold K Godwin
904 Robert Welch Ct
Chesapeake VA 23320

Call Sign: K7FSU
Harold K Godwin
904 Robert Welch Ct
Chesapeake VA 23320

Call Sign: KF4LOE
Hampton Roads Radio
Association
640 Rock Dr
Chesapeake VA 233234214

Call Sign: WF4R
William B Runyon Sr
640 Rock Dr
Chesapeake VA 233234214

Call Sign: K4HRR
Hampton Roads Radio
Association
640 Rock Dr
Chesapeake VA 233234214

Call Sign: KD4FUW
Al L Edwards
1900B Rodgers St
Chesapeake VA 23324

Call Sign: KB4YY
Ralph E Chamberlain
1203 Rosemont Ave
Chesapeake VA 233241655

Call Sign: KI4QAV
Paul V Waters
2532 Roundtree Cir
Chesapeake VA 23323

Call Sign: N4SFH
Robert M Holt
2539 Roundtree Cir
Chesapeake VA 23323

Call Sign: KI4BQH
Stargel R Doane
2633 Roundtree Cir
Chesapeake VA 23323

Call Sign: KF4KLM
Gregory A Mccoy
2609 Roungtree Cir
Chesapeake VA 23323

Call Sign: WA2HMT
Robert W Ryan
232 Royal Oak Dr
Chesapeake VA 23322

Call Sign: KA4PFU
Jerry Locklear
2333 S Centerville Tpke

Chesapeake VA 23322

Call Sign: WA1YCP
Harvey M Hoffman
200 Sabal Palm Ln 303
Chesapeake VA 233201736

Call Sign: KC4NRW
Amy M Byrd
548 Saddlehorn Dr
Chesapeake VA 23322

Call Sign: WA4YSE
Lyman E Byrd
548 Saddlehorn Dr
Chesapeake VA 23322

Call Sign: KD4CXQ
Robert E Copeland Jr
636 Saddlehorn Dr
Chesapeake VA 233221304

Call Sign: N2EDQ
James J Westerhold
808 Sagebrook Run
Chesapeake VA 23322

Call Sign: KB6SFS
Brian K Gansz
321 San Roman Dr
Chesapeake VA 23322

Call Sign: WA3QWA
Marc J Fink
635 Sandcastle Way
Chesapeake VA 23320

Call Sign: KA7ESX
William J Galvin
1201 Sanderson Rd
Chesapeake VA 23322

Call Sign: K4QVW
William J Galvin
1201 Sanderson Rd
Chesapeake VA 23322

Call Sign: KJ4URQ
Madison T Weatherly

2028 Sanderson Rd
Chesapeake VA 23322

Call Sign: KA2AFN
Scott J Lewis
1107 Santeetlah Ave
Chesapeake VA 23325

Call Sign: KK4CKA
Moriah N Felder
101 Scarlett Dr
Chesapeake VA 23322

Call Sign: KE4DQX
Richard A Woodman Jr
1000 Scenic Blvd
Chesapeake VA 23320

Call Sign: WA4KAQ
Dolive T Durant
4025 Scotfield Dr
Chesapeake VA 23321

Call Sign: KI4HND
Jason R Bunty
1239 Seaboard Ave
Chesapeake VA 23324

Call Sign: KG4JUX
David R Jenkins
715 Shadowfield Ct
Chesapeake VA 23322

Call Sign: KD4NBT
Peter P Parrie
712 Shadowfield Ct
Chesapeake VA 23322

Call Sign: KG4RHO
Michael A Monteith
3221 Shadyside Ln
Chesapeake VA 23321

Call Sign: N4BBV
Francis E Nugent
1041 Sharon Dr
Chesapeake VA 23320

Call Sign: W2HM

Robert J Mapp
4130 Shawnee Dr
Chesapeake VA 23325

Call Sign: K1JR
John J Rozich
748 Shell Rd
Chesapeake VA 23323

Call Sign: AC5ST
Robert E Chilldres
805 Shell Rd
Chesapeake VA 233234117

Call Sign: N4BRA
Eugene R Taylor
805 Shetland Dr
Chesapeake VA 23322

Call Sign: KC4URB
David M Stephens
1717 Shipyard Rd
Chesapeake VA 23323

Call Sign: KJ4JIK
Michael C Wilkinson
425 Shorebird Ln
Chesapeake VA 23323

Call Sign: KJ4KED
Michael C Wilkinson II
425 Shorebird Ln
Chesapeake VA 23323

Call Sign: KA4TWI
Aubrey W Parsons
237 Sierra Dr
Chesapeake VA 23322

Call Sign: KA4IRG
Gary R Woolard
541 Sign Pine Rd
Chesapeake VA 23322

Call Sign: KJ4WDV
James E Manley
1320 Simon Dr
Chesapeake VA 23320

Call Sign: K2MAN
James E Manley
1320 Simon Dr
Chesapeake VA 23320

Call Sign: KD4KJO
Richard E Harris
2633 Smithson Dr
Chesapeake VA 23322

Call Sign: KD4OGK
Caredwyn T Harris
2633 Smithson Dr
Chesapeake VA 23322

Call Sign: KJ4WDT
Richard E Harris
2633 Smithson Dr
Chesapeake VA 233222228

Call Sign: KI4ORF
Dennis A Walker
1216 Smokey Mtn Trl
Chesapeake VA 23320

Call Sign: KQ4TJ
Robert F Morris Jr
8 Sol Thorpe Ln
Chesapeake VA 23325

Call Sign: KE4IHQ
Bart C Bennick
2521 Southern Pines Dr
Chesapeake VA 23323

Call Sign: KI4FJG
Bart C Bennick
2521 Southern Pines Dr
Chesapeake VA 23323

Call Sign: W4BCB
Bart C Bennick
2521 Southern Pines Dr
Chesapeake VA 23323

Call Sign: KB0LFY
Andrew R Casiello
704 Southwood Dr
Chesapeake VA 23322

Call Sign: KG4YEU
Nathan M Casiello
704 Southwood Dr
Chesapeake VA 23322

Call Sign: KF4WBO
Kim J Habit
310 Sparrow Rd
Chesapeake VA 23325

Call Sign: W4IPA
Dexter E Phibbs
700 Sparrow Rd
Chesapeake VA 23325

Call Sign: WA4DHV
Emerson E Henry
1923 Sparrow Rd
Chesapeake VA 23320

Call Sign: KE4NXS
Pamela D Jones
1723 Speedy Ave
Chesapeake VA 23320

Call Sign: KE4NXT
Cody L Jones
1723 Speedy Ave
Chesapeake VA 23320

Call Sign: KH2XN
Barbara W Girardin
916 Speight Lyons Loop
Chesapeake VA 23322

Call Sign: KH2YG
David J Girardin
916 Speight Lyons Loop
Chesapeake VA 23322

Call Sign: KH2XM
David W Girardin
916 Speight Lyons Loop
Chesapeake VA 23322

Call Sign: KH2XT
Emily G Girardin
916 Speight Lyons Loop

Chesapeake VA 23322

Call Sign: WH2AAQ
Kenneth E North
330 Spice Bush Ct
Chesapeake VA 23320

Call Sign: N2KEN
Kenneth E North
330 Spice Bush Ct
Chesapeake VA 23320

Call Sign: KJ4EOL
Matthew R Vaugh
2700 Spinners Way
Chesapeake VA 23323

Call Sign: KD4ILS
Rose Armstrong
428 Spurlane Cir
Chesapeake VA 23320

Call Sign: KJ4EWW
Chesapeake Community
Communications Club
428 Spurlane Cir
Chesapeake VA 23322

Call Sign: KJ4EXH
Chesapeake Community
Emergency Response
Communications Team
428 Spurlane Cir
Chesapeake VA 23322

Call Sign: KB4LIF
Ruth A Bigio
428 Spurlane Cir
Chesapeake VA 23322

Call Sign: WA4SQL
Robert Armstrong
428 Spurlane Cir
Chesapeake VA 233205463

Call Sign: KG4DTC
Mary A Gahagan
3321 St Lawrence Dr
Chesapeake VA 23325

Call Sign: AF4CD
Lynn E Gahagan
3321 St Lawrence Dr
Chesapeake VA 233252819

Call Sign: KE4EMJ
Leonardus J Dendekker
908 Staffordshire Ct
Chesapeake VA 23322

Call Sign: KD4VRH
William H Reuter
302 Stalham Rd
Chesapeake VA 23325

Call Sign: N4QYZ
Jane M Reuter
302 Stalham Rd
Chesapeake VA 23325

Call Sign: KJ4YKG
Duane D Ettwein
800 Stardale Dr
Chesapeake VA 23322

Call Sign: KE4PUG
Richard K Myers
1008 Stillmeadow Ct
Chesapeake VA 23320

Call Sign: KE4PUH
Barbara H Myers
1008 Stillmeadow Ct
Chesapeake VA 23320

Call Sign: W4ADM
John E Adams
701 Stockleybridge Dr
Chesapeake VA 23320

Call Sign: AB4XQ
Patricia M Raiford
3904 Stonebridge Ct
Chesapeake VA 23321

Call Sign: KA4GEU
Elisa K Kay
3089 Stratford Ct

Chesapeake VA 23321

Call Sign: KJ4RHN
Clyde D Campbell
2912 Stratford Dr
Chesapeake VA 23321

Call Sign: W4MIK
Michael L Hodges
816 Sugar Maple Ln
Chesapeake VA 23320

Call Sign: W4WDP
William D Pleban
820 Sugar Maple Ln
Chesapeake VA 23322

Call Sign: KG4RMM
Andrew W Ejma
548 Summit Ridge Dr
Chesapeake VA 23322

Call Sign: W4NDN
Billy R Payne Jr
517 Sunderland Ter
Chesapeake VA 23322

Call Sign: KG4TAV
Steven E Lewis
4533 Sunray Ave
Chesapeake VA 233212629

Call Sign: K9SEL
Steven E Lewis
4533 Sunray Ave
Chesapeake VA 233212629

Call Sign: KA4FYA
John G Patterson
2921 Sunrise Ave
Chesapeake VA 23324

Call Sign: KJ4LEV
Annalisa E Murden
4207 Surf Ave
Chesapeake VA 23325

Call Sign: KJ4SYM
Travis L Cochran

620 Sydenham Blvd
Chesapeake VA 23322

Call Sign: KI4JLS
Daniel W Carlson
4405 Tartan Arch
Chesapeake VA 233214281

Call Sign: AI4KJ
Daniel W Carlson
4405 Tartan Arch
Chesapeake VA 233214281

Call Sign: K4HXM
George W Singleback
4105 Taylor Rd
Chesapeake VA 23321

Call Sign: K4DXB
Edward D Eachus
4109 Taylor Rd
Chesapeake VA 23321

Call Sign: KB4RLB
Harry A Clark
4113 Taylor Rd
Chesapeake VA 23321

Call Sign: KF4PAU
Eugene V Primm
4141 Terry Dr
Chesapeake VA 23321

Call Sign: KD4QOC
Carl S Kusky Jr
4205 Terry Dr
Chesapeake VA 23321

Call Sign: KG4KQN
Samantha C Collins
4323 Terry Dr
Chesapeake VA 23321

Call Sign: KG4OIK
Teresa A Collins
4323 Terry Dr
Chesapeake VA 23321

Call Sign: KG4JVY

John J Collins
4323 Terry Dr
Chesapeake VA 233214547

Call Sign: AC7SG
Robert H Creigh
4321 Terry Dr
Chesapeake VA 23321

Call Sign: KK4CWM
Daniel M Barlow
1205 Timberlake Ct
Chesapeake VA 23320

Call Sign: KJ4RHO
William B Quella Jr
4308 Towanda Rd
Chesapeake VA 23325

Call Sign: KC4EHO
Herman M Quattlebaum
3109 Trumpet Rd
Chesapeake VA 23321

Call Sign: WD4SEL
Stuart E Beaber Jr
3033 Tyre Neck Rd
Chesapeake VA 23321

Call Sign: N4WQH
Michael D Clark
940 Unicorn Trl
Chesapeake VA 23320

Call Sign: N4HBP
Francis J Bolshazy
812 Union Forge Ln
Chesapeake VA 233201813

Call Sign: W4VAS
William B Plummer
1118 VA Ave
Chesapeake VA 23324

Call Sign: N2WCR
John R Hockler
1129 Valmire Dr
Chesapeake VA 23320

Call Sign: WA4HZQ
Howard L Damask
1152 Valmire Dr
Chesapeake VA 23320

Call Sign: WD4NLV
Walter D Johnson
106 Van Luik Ct
Chesapeake VA 23325

Call Sign: KE4URE
Timothy D Sutton
1069 Vanderploeg Dr
Chesapeake VA 23320

Call Sign: KJ4VKU
M Porter Mcneill
436 Vanette Dr
Chesapeake VA 23322

Call Sign: KD4VRL
Catherine L Kowalsky
337 Velva Dr
Chesapeake VA 23325

Call Sign: KJ4AGF
Adam C Escobar
423 Vesparian Cir
Chesapeake VA 23322

Call Sign: WB7OJV
Darrell R Buxton
401 Vespasian Cir
Chesapeake VA 23322

Call Sign: KD4YPY
William H Oyster
524 Vicksdell Cres
Chesapeake VA 23320

Call Sign: N4KED
Janice M Oyster
524 Vicksdell Cres
Chesapeake VA 23320

Call Sign: KD4ARF
Richard S Haynes
3408 W Landing Dr
Chesapeake VA 23322

Call Sign: W4ARF
Richard S Haynes
3408 W Landing Dr
Chesapeake VA 23322

Call Sign: K4CWC
Richard J Halstead
2703 W Meadow Dr
Chesapeake VA 23321

Call Sign: KT4KR
Robin D Orr
2706 W Meadow Dr
Chesapeake VA 23321

Call Sign: K4PRR
Frank W Duvall Sr
133 W Royce Dr
Chesapeake VA 23320

Call Sign: KE4ZHW
Richard C Schrader
1409 Walnut Ave
Chesapeake VA 23325

Call Sign: KI4KRF
Robert G Rensch Jr
1506 Walnut Ave
Chesapeake VA 233253732

Call Sign: KK4BNT
T Jeffrey Salb
809 Walnut Forest Ct
Chesapeake VA 23322

Call Sign: WA3ZXN
Frederick R Flach
552 Warren Ave
Chesapeake VA 23322

Call Sign: N2IJ
Raymond Garraud
10 Warwick Cir
Chesapeake VA 23320

Call Sign: KG4WOJ
James D Rogers
625 Washington Dr

Chesapeake VA 23322

Call Sign: KF4NHM
Michael E Conte
1096 Washington Dr
Chesapeake VA 23456

Call Sign: W2MLC
Michael L Conte
1096 Washington Dr
Chesapeake VA 233227548

Call Sign: KD4UHE
William L Oelrich
701 Watch Island Reach
Chesapeake VA 23320

Call Sign: KJ4KZJ
Charles V Reynolds
709 Water Hickory Ct
Chesapeake VA 23320

Call Sign: N4NIG
Charles V Reynolds
709 Water Hickory Ct
Chesapeake VA 23320

Call Sign: WY7C
Curtis J Commander
605 Water Oak Ct
Chesapeake VA 23322

Call Sign: KI4LVP
Richard M Meserve III
912 Waterford Dr
Chesapeake VA 23322

Call Sign: K4AV
Melvin D Gaskins
1053 Waters Rd
Chesapeake VA 23322

Call Sign: WB4FKN
Alan L Ives
1130 Waters Rd
Chesapeake VA 23320

Call Sign: KC4WOU
William S Grant

1205 Waters Rd
Chesapeake VA 23322

Call Sign: KD4BJJ
Marilyn R Presley
1301 Waters Rd
Chesapeake VA 23320

Call Sign: W1SKY
George Zultanky
1307 Waters Rd
Chesapeake VA 233228807

Call Sign: KC4UXV
Brent A Paluszka
1561 Waterside Dr
Chesapeake VA 23320

Call Sign: N3HGK
Paul D Paluszka
1561 Waterside Dr N
Chesapeake VA 23320

Call Sign: KI4VCU
Anthony F Germanotta Jr
1601 Waterway Cir
Chesapeake VA 23322

Call Sign: KJ4AVK
Mark A Burns
1027 Weeping Willow Dr
Chesapeake VA 23322

Call Sign: KE4GPD
David W Ryan
1039 Weeping Willow Dr
Chesapeake VA 23322

Call Sign: KJ4EOG
Anthony W Roth
1040 Weeping Willow Dr
Chesapeake VA 23322

Call Sign: KC9HTX
Marcus W Daniels
917 Whisper Hollow Dr
Chesapeake VA 233229516

Call Sign: WB9PGV

Philip K Bess
508 Whistle Town Rd
Chesapeake VA 23322

Call Sign: WD9COV
Ellyn E Bess
508 Whistle Town Rd
Chesapeake VA 23322

Call Sign: KI4ZNO
William A OConnor Jr
520 Whistle Town Rd
Chesapeake VA 23322

Call Sign: K1QAD
William A OConnor Jr
520 Whistle Town Rd
Chesapeake VA 23322

Call Sign: KJ4URS
Lee W Foster
3709 White Chapel Arch
Chesapeake VA 23321

Call Sign: KJ4ZYS
Rebecca M Kurgan
220 White Dogwood Dr
Chesapeake VA 23322

Call Sign: W4BOO
Rebecca M Kurgan
220 White Dogwood Dr
Chesapeake VA 23322

Call Sign: W4UWS
William H Bass Jr
313 White Dogwood Dr
Chesapeake VA 233224165

Call Sign: KG4TNW
Paul S Frank
3116 Whitetail Ct
Chesapeake VA 23323

Call Sign: KB4UQE
Steven P Shils
844 Wickford Dr
Chesapeake VA 233206659

Call Sign: KC4OSS
Daniel R Campbell
1605 Widgeon Ct
Chesapeake VA 23320

Call Sign: KG4EQT
Leonard W King Jr
1213 Wilbur Ave
Chesapeake VA 23324

Call Sign: KE4RBH
Ronald J Welner
1223 Wilbur Ave
Chesapeake VA 23324

Call Sign: W4NKU
James E Minchew Jr
1709 Wild Duck Crossing
Chesapeake VA 23321

Call Sign: KJ4JAV
Edwin S Renegar
2525 Wild Horse Ridge
Chesapeake VA 23322

Call Sign: KJ4HNO
Jackson R Renegar
2525 Wild Horse Ridge
Chesapeake VA 23322

Call Sign: KU4YW
David J Parks
505 William Crest
Chesapeake VA 23323

Call Sign: N7OZE
Marilyn A Burch
505 William Crest
Chesapeake VA 23323

Call Sign: KI4VMF
Johnnie E Everette
821 Williams Ave
Chesapeake VA 23323

Call Sign: KD4HUN
Peggy J Setzer
1304 Willow Ave
Chesapeake VA 23325

Call Sign: KQ4BA
James H Setzer
1304 Willow Ave
Chesapeake VA 23325

Call Sign: KD4HUM
Alex A Setzer
1310 Willow Ave
Chesapeake VA 23325

Call Sign: N4XAK
Daniel P Hunt
317 Willow Bend Ct
Chesapeake VA 23323

Call Sign: N4XAM
Patricia J Hunt
317 Willow Bend Ct
Chesapeake VA 23323

Call Sign: WA4TDS
James R Mc Fadden
514 Willow Bend Dr
Chesapeake VA 23323

Call Sign: KM4WZ
Matthew P Ipock
646 Willow Bend Dr
Chesapeake VA 23323

Call Sign: KA3CPB
F Peter Rohrmayer III
736 Willow Brook Rd
Chesapeake VA 23320

Call Sign: KA3CPC
Phyllis A Rohrmayer
736 Willow Brook Rd
Chesapeake VA 23320

Call Sign: KB8GGB
John J Walker III
1204 Willow Creek Ct
Chesapeake VA 23321

Call Sign: WB4GXE
Jack G Starr
728 Willow Oak Dr

Chesapeake VA 23320

Call Sign: KA4MPT
Martin R Hager Sr
2860 Willowwood Dr
Chesapeake VA 23323

Call Sign: KF4LJO
Phillip Knight
1037 Windswept Cir
Chesapeake VA 23320

Call Sign: KO4CU
Lawrence W Pike
925 Wingfield Ave
Chesapeake VA 23325

Call Sign: KJ4URR
Ryan Rains
1204 Wingfield Ave
Chesapeake VA 23325

Call Sign: KJ4URP
Brittany O Gordon
1418 Wingfield Ave
Chesapeake VA 23325

Call Sign: WA4JRC
Justin R Cahoon
2100 Wintergreen Dr
Chesapeake VA 23323

Call Sign: KF4QGM
Russell S Cravens
512 Winwood Dr
Chesapeake VA 23323

Call Sign: KD4AJD
Andrew M Cooper
424 Wittington Dr
Chesapeake VA 23322

Call Sign: KC4UJX
William D Jones
1515 Wood Ave
Chesapeake VA 23325

Call Sign: KC4NMZ
Annalisa E Murden

1516 Wood Ave
Chesapeake VA 23325

Call Sign: KJ4EBT
K4Amg Memorial ARC
721 Wood Buck Ln
Chesapeake VA 23323

Call Sign: K4AMG
K4Amg Memorial ARC
721 Wood Buck Ln
Chesapeake VA 23323

Call Sign: KE4ACK
Melody L Siff
721 Wood Duck Ln
Chesapeake VA 23323

Call Sign: WA4BUE
Richard L Siff
721 Wood Duck Ln
Chesapeake VA 23323

Call Sign: W4BUE
Richard L Siff
721 Wood Duck Ln
Chesapeake VA 23323

Call Sign: KE4HGN
Victor L Vanderberg
904 Woodcott
Chesapeake VA 23320

Call Sign: KI4IRN
Thomas F Gaine
917 Woodcott Dr
Chesapeake VA 23322

Call Sign: WA4ACU
Wayne T Blythe
4120 Woodcroft Ln
Chesapeake VA 23321

Call Sign: N4PR
Clarence H Stegall
4209 Woodland Dr
Chesapeake VA 23321

Call Sign: KA4MPS

Aubrey E Hartman
4242 Woodland Dr
Chesapeake VA 23321

Call Sign: KK4CJX
Katelyn V Tisdel
4329M Woodland Dr
Chesapeake VA 23321

Call Sign: KA4BLY
Angelia G Setliff
836 Woodrow Ct
Chesapeake VA 23320

Call Sign: WD4PKF
Michael S Setliff
836 Woodrow Ct
Chesapeake VA 23320

Call Sign: AA0EI
Scott A Novotny
405 Woodspring Arch
Chesapeake VA 23320

Call Sign: KI4KTQ
Alysha B Alexander
508 Woodstream Way
Chesapeake VA 23322

Call Sign: KG4OIL
VA R Romero
805 Wright Ave
Chesapeake VA 23324

Call Sign: KD4KJJ
VA M Galvin
3014 Yakima Rd
Chesapeake VA 23325

Call Sign: N1DYU
William J Bergin
833 Yorkshire Trl
Chesapeake VA 23322

Call Sign: KE4EBJ
James A Bell
Chesapeake VA 23322

Call Sign: N4RMZ

Ila J Culliton
Chesapeake VA 23324

Call Sign: KE4LZT
Niles W Berry
Chesapeake VA 23325

Call Sign: KA4EDI
James G Gwaltney
Chesapeake VA 23321

Call Sign: KI4ZNQ
Ralph Andrews
Chesapeake VA 23327

Call Sign: KG4BNX
Chesapeake Contest Club
Chesapeake VA 23328

Call Sign: KJ4DSF
Brian D Hughes
Chesapeake VA 23328

Call Sign: W1BDH
Brian D Hughes
Chesapeake VA 23328

Call Sign: KJ4KTV
Cindy L Pesente
Chesapeake VA 23328

Call Sign: KI4TPD
Franklin H Kennedy
Chesapeake VA 23328

Call Sign: KJ4HXI
Richard W Durstine
Chesapeake VA 23328

Call Sign: W4CAR
Chesapeake ARS Inc
Chesapeake VA 233230867

Call Sign: KJ4YWM
Tadaaki Sotodate
Chesapeake VA 233272681

Call Sign: K7UO
Tracy K Wood

Chesapeake VA 233286829

FCC Amateur Radio Licenses in Chester

Call Sign: N4LLJ
William G Martin
4020 Angarde Dr
Chester VA 23831

Call Sign: KI4YGQ
Scott A Schumann
13406 Back Stretch Ct
Chester VA 23836

Call Sign: W4TNX
John R Youell
3910 Baldwin Rd
Chester VA 23831

Call Sign: KF4AUZ
Dwight S Durmon
5279 Beachmere Ter
Chester VA 23831

Call Sign: WB4HUL
Sidney B Scott
500 Bermuda Hundred Rd
Chester VA 23836

Call Sign: KC4JYL
Jason B Scott
500 Bermuda Hundred Rd
Chester VA 23836

Call Sign: KE4ESR
Jerry L Norwood
14216 Bermuda Point Ct
Chester VA 23831

Call Sign: W4REC
Vincent A Pacelli
3010 Blithe Dr
Chester VA 23831

Call Sign: WD4NYO
Bernard W Harrell
14120 Bolling Ave
Chester VA 238366009

Call Sign: KD4MUR
Lois G Comer
16901 Branders Bridge Rd
Chester VA 23831

Call Sign: KJ4ZIN
Justin D George
1110 Cameron Ave
Chester VA 23836

Call Sign: N4CXZ
David N Williams
3512 Castlebury Dr
Chester VA 23831

Call Sign: KD4UFQ
Andrew D Crews
3559 Castlebury Dr
Chester VA 23831

Call Sign: W4BTF
Charles T Draper
3570 Castlebury Dr
Chester VA 238311861

Call Sign: KG4GCA
Paul G Ruppert
3537 Castlebury Dr
Chester VA 23831

Call Sign: KF4ADG
William E Davis
14512 Central Ave
Chester VA 23831

Call Sign: WJ4I
Millard F Edwards
14609 Central Ave
Chester VA 23831

Call Sign: KF4MEE
Thomas H Jones Jr
12245 Chestertowne Rd
Chester VA 23831

Call Sign: KA4EHP
Jerry Hendrick Jr
4281 Daniel St

Chester VA 23831

Call Sign: N4NNC
Michael T Robbins
14104 Donnaford Dr
Chester VA 23831

Call Sign: WB4YFT
Michael T Robbins
14104 Donnaford Dr
Chester VA 23831

Call Sign: KE4AUI
Aston G Abbott Jr
14204 Drumvale Dr
Chester VA 23831

Call Sign: K3KE
Edward T Land
4600 Dunkirk Dr
Chester VA 23831

Call Sign: N3YPE
Mary K Land
4600 Dunkirk Dr
Chester VA 238316813

Call Sign: KF4GFW
Raymond W Earley Jr
11220 Eagle Point
Chester VA 23831

Call Sign: KF4YHD
Brenda G Earley
11220 Eagle Point Rd
Chester VA 23831

Call Sign: WD4BAT
Arthur W Earley
4825 Ecoff Ave
Chester VA 238311608

Call Sign: K4TX
Charles R Stigberg
220 Enon Church Rd
Chester VA 23836

Call Sign: KE4RTQ
Robert S De Freitas

230 Enon Church Rd
Chester VA 23836

Call Sign: KA2UAL
Frank Pectal
10821 Erin Green Ct
Chester VA 23831

Call Sign: KC4TJD
Joe T Kaufhold
3800 Festival Park Plz Apt
211E
Chester VA 23831

Call Sign: KD4IFV
Anson W Garrett Jr
1649 Forest Glenn Cir
Chester VA 23836

Call Sign: W3NS
Anson W Garrett Jr
1649 Forest Glenn Cir
Chester VA 23836

Call Sign: WD4AFD
Keith E Snavely
619 Fulcher Ln
Chester VA 23831

Call Sign: KD4GAU
James D Clark
3901 Glen Oaks Ct
Chester VA 23831

Call Sign: N4GAU
James D Clark
3901 Glen Oaks Ct
Chester VA 23831

Call Sign: KR4UL
Daniel E Ashworth
10325 Glen Oaks Dr
Chester VA 23831

Call Sign: N2HEU
Dennis H Bailey
4818 Glenmorgan Ct
Chester VA 238316596

Call Sign: WA4QDM
John R Youell
12801 Gloria Ct
Chester VA 23831

Call Sign: KJ4FEI
Jeffrey S Gaskins
13800 Golf Course Rd
Chester VA 23836

Call Sign: KJ4QZD
Carmen C Johnson
11214 Great Branch Dr
Chester VA 23831

Call Sign: KD6OZF
Michael H Lackey Jr
12800 Greenside Dr
Chester VA 23836

Call Sign: AK4NT
Michael H Lackey Jr
12800 Greenside Dr
Chester VA 23836

Call Sign: KI4JLN
Norris O Brickhouse
3901 Hamlin Ter
Chester VA 23831

Call Sign: KF4ONW
Annette Thomas
4106 Hamlin Ter
Chester VA 23831

Call Sign: KG4ZTC
Ronald Moorman
12801 Harrowgate Rd
Chester VA 23831

Call Sign: KI4AE
Samuel R Killen
15000 Harrowgate Rd
Chester VA 23831

Call Sign: N2WHD
Terence L Brooks
13130 B Harrowgate Rd
Chester VA 23831

Call Sign: KG4LUL
Eric T Gensheimer
3901 Hilltop Field Dr
Chester VA 23831

Call Sign: KB4YYM
Eugene B Call
13330 Inge Rd
Chester VA 23831

Call Sign: WA3J
Allan F Johnson
12750 Jefferson Davis Hwy 159
Chester VA 238315308

Call Sign: KF4SVH
Jacob E Bridgman
143 Lakeview Dr
Chester VA 23831

Call Sign: KF4IGA
Kenneth G Davis
146 Lakeview Dr
Chester VA 23831

Call Sign: KE4RAI
Gary W Frame
12310 Laprade St
Chester VA 23831

Call Sign: WA4SCO
Gary W Frame
12310 Laprade St
Chester VA 23831

Call Sign: KE4NHB
Stefan Hofmaenner
4616 Laurel Spring Ct
Chester VA 23831

Call Sign: KE4NHC
Eric A Hofmaenner
4616 Laurel Spring Ct
Chester VA 23831

Call Sign: KD4MUG
Jed M Birch
10801 Lunswood Rd

Chester VA 23831

Call Sign: KG4HIU
Varina High School ARC
600 Martineau Dr
Chester VA 23836

Call Sign: KD4MJN
Michael L Adkins
2418 Mistwood Forest Dr
Chester VA 23831

Call Sign: W4QWX
Albert C Miles
3811 Mooring Way
Chester VA 23831

Call Sign: KW8O
Don Runyon Jr
10510 Morehead Dr
Chester VA 23831

Call Sign: WA4DR
Don Runyon Jr
10510 Morehead Dr
Chester VA 23831

Call Sign: KW8O
Don Runyon Jr
10510 Morehead Dr
Chester VA 23831

Call Sign: WA4DR
Don Runyon Jr
10510 Morehead Dr
Chester VA 23831

Call Sign: N4CCA
Don Runyon Jr
10510 Morehead Dr
Chester VA 23831

Call Sign: KA4YDW
Lewis R Mabry
12521 Mt Blanco Ct
Chester VA 23836

Call Sign: KB4BPY
Ann C Mabry

12521 Mt Blanco Ct
Chester VA 23836

Call Sign: KG4ENZ
Charles M Mc Cauley
117 N Elm Ave
Chester VA 23075

Call Sign: WA4CMI
Albert C Miles
3828 N Light Dr
Chester VA 23831

Call Sign: W4CMS
Christopher M Service
12802 Norlanya Dr
Chester VA 23836

Call Sign: KD4LTY
Wanda C Ward
523 Old Bermuda Hundred Rd
Chester VA 23836

Call Sign: KF4QAN
John E Styles
4201 Old Hundred Rd
Chester VA 23831

Call Sign: KC4ULH
James B Connelly
3335 Osborne Rd
Chester VA 23831

Call Sign: K3KAM
Kim L Jensen
12531 Parker Ln
Chester VA 23831

Call Sign: KG4YYO
James E Harris Jr
2700 Perdue Ct
Chester VA 23831

Call Sign: W4UPW
James L Summers
3196 Poplar View Pl
Chester VA 23831

Call Sign: KF4TOD

Richard L Young
12869 Richmond St
Chester VA 238314749

Call Sign: WA8NNX
Michael A Likavec
4715 Rieves Pond Dr
Chester VA 23831

Call Sign: KD4GIV
Janet R Lynch
4715 Rieves Pond Dr
Chester VA 23831

Call Sign: WC4VAA
VA Ares Races Inc Area A
2318 Rio Vista St
Chester VA 238312242

Call Sign: N4NI
Jeremy N Marlowe
1318 River Tree Dr Apt 201
Chester VA 23836

Call Sign: K4KZI
Philip H Hope Jr
14414 Rivermont Rd
Chester VA 23831

Call Sign: KE4KLD
William B Sowers III
14422 Rivermont Rd
Chester VA 23831

Call Sign: KE4WXS
David L Lastovica
14529 Rivermont Rd
Chester VA 23831

Call Sign: WF4D
David L Lastovica
14529 Rivermont Rd
Chester VA 23836

Call Sign: N1AXS
Julian P Bell Jr
11510 Rochelle Rd
Chester VA 23831

Call Sign: KJ4HGN
Carl M Kersey Jr
4107 S Cresthill Ct
Chester VA 23831

Call Sign: KE4FGH
Herman A Edwards
14304 Shale Pl
Chester VA 23831

Call Sign: N4RVR
John C Mc Colman
10436 Shumark Dr
Chester VA 238311167

Call Sign: KI4AES
Warren T Nuckols Jr
10448 Shumark Dr
Chester VA 238311167

Call Sign: W4TNJ
Warren T Nuckols Jr
10448 Shumark Dr
Chester VA 238311167

Call Sign: KG4BEM
Ronald J Mingos
10836 Stilton Dr
Chester VA 23831

Call Sign: KD4VMX
Harold A Hodges
13330 Stoneway Dr
Chester VA 23831

Call Sign: KG4RFL
Keith J Andrews
4620 Stoney Creek Pkwy
Chester VA 23831

Call Sign: KJ4EEI
Matthew Z Bryant
2205 Sula Dr
Chester VA 23831

Call Sign: KG4EOB
Kevin D Mc Donald
10525 Surry Rd
Chester VA 23831

Call Sign: WB4VWR
George A Starke Jr
14610 Tranor Ave
Chester VA 23836

Call Sign: N4TKK
Jeannie L Kirby
14403 Traywick Dr
Chester VA 238366085

Call Sign: N4RMB
Mark E Kirby
14403 Traywick Dr
Chester VA 238366085

Call Sign: KD4YCS
David C Payne
Vicki Ct
Chester VA 23831

Call Sign: KD4ODU
Robert A Lee
12336 Villas Dr
Chester VA 238362759

Call Sign: KJ4OUV
Donald E Manlove Jr
4019 W Dogwood Ave
Chester VA 23831

Call Sign: W4JJB
James J Bishop
508 W Hundred Rd
Chester VA 23831

Call Sign: KK4CSI
Raymond J Kunkle III
3315 Walnut Cove Ct
Chester VA 23831

Call Sign: KC8NNC
William Frey
1500 Walnut Dr
Chester VA 238366144

Call Sign: KG4DPY
Robert L Wilson Sr
1508 Walnut Dr

Chester VA 23836

Call Sign: WW4RL
Robert L Wilson Sr
1508 Walnut Dr
Chester VA 238366144

Call Sign: WB8HYL
William A Brown
500 Wellshire Pl
Chester VA 23836

Call Sign: N5WZB
Barry M Sushinsky
509 Wellshire Pl
Chester VA 23836

Call Sign: AC4LL
Joseph A Gagliano
2801 Wilton Ct
Chester VA 23831

Call Sign: K4RIC
Richard W Mcgrath
15807 Windseeker Ct
Chester VA 23831

Call Sign: KG4YQU
Richard W Mcgrath
15807 Windseeker Ct
Chester VA 23861

Call Sign: N8WEA
Patricia L Johnson
12836 Winfree St
Chester VA 238315036

Call Sign: KF4ONY
Richard W Walkup
12148 Winfree St Apt N2
Chester VA 23831

Call Sign: KD4KWP
Michael Melnyk Jr
4701 Wraywood Ave
Chester VA 23831

Call Sign: WD4DLH
Walter M Hall Jr

3712 Yantis Ct
Chester VA 23831

Call Sign: KI4GTY
VA Races Inc For Chippenham
Medical Center
Chester VA 23831

Call Sign: KI4GTZ
VA Races Inc For Community
Memorial Hospital
Chester VA 23831

Call Sign: KI4GUA
VA Races Inc For Henrico
DoctorS Hospital - Forest
Chester VA 23831

Call Sign: KI4GUB
VA Races Inc For Henrico
DoctorS Hospital - Parham
Chester VA 23831

Call Sign: KI4GUC
VA Races Inc For Halifax
Regional Hospital
Chester VA 23831

Call Sign: KI4GUD
VA Races Inc For John
Randolph Medical Center
Chester VA 23831

Call Sign: KI4GUE
VA Races Inc For Johnston -
Willis Hospital
Chester VA 23831

Call Sign: KI4GUF
VA Races Inc For Memorial
Regional Medical Center
Chester VA 23831

Call Sign: KI4GUG
VA Races Inc For Richmond
Community Hospital
Chester VA 23831

Call Sign: KI4GUH

VA Races Inc For Retreat
Hospital
Chester VA 23831

Call Sign: KI4GUI
VA Races Inc For Southside
Community Hospital
Chester VA 23831

Call Sign: KI4GUJ
VA Races Inc For Saint MaryS
Hospital
Chester VA 23831

Call Sign: KI4GUK
VA Races Inc For Southside
Regional Medical Center
Chester VA 23831

Call Sign: KI4GUL
VA Races Inc For Southern VA
Regional Medical Center
Chester VA 23831

Call Sign: KI4GUM
VA Races Inc For VA
Commonwealth University
Medical Center
Chester VA 23831

Call Sign: KI4GUN
VA Races Inc For Mc Guire
Veterans Hospital
Chester VA 23831

Call Sign: KI4GWF
VA Races Inc For Martha
Jefferson Hospital
Chester VA 23831

Call Sign: KI4GWG
VA Races Inc For University Of
VA Hospital
Chester VA 23831

Call Sign: W4SVR
VA Races Inc For Southern VA
Regional Medical Center
Chester VA 23831

Call Sign: N4DHF
VA Races Inc For Henrico
DoctorS Hospital - Forest
Chester VA 23831

Call Sign: K4MVH
VA Races Inc For Mc Guire
Veterans Hospital
Chester VA 23831

Call Sign: WC4RH
VA Races Inc For Retreat
Hospital
Chester VA 23831

Call Sign: KC4CMC
VA Races Inc For Chippenham
Medical Center
Chester VA 23831

Call Sign: W4VCU
VA Races Inc For VA
Commonwealth University
Medical Center
Chester VA 23831

Call Sign: KC4JRM
VA Races Inc For John
Randolph Medical Center
Chester VA 23831

Call Sign: K4SRM
VA Races Inc For Southside
Regional Medical Center
Chester VA 23831

Call Sign: W4CMH
VA Races Inc For Community
Memorial Hospital
Chester VA 23831

Call Sign: N4HRH
VA Races Inc For Halifax
Regional Hospital
Chester VA 23831

Call Sign: K4MRM

VA Races Inc For Memorial
Regional Medical Center
Chester VA 23831

Call Sign: W4SMH
VA Races Inc For Saint MaryS
Hospital
Chester VA 23831

Call Sign: N4SCH
VA Races Inc For Southside
Community Hospital
Chester VA 23831

Call Sign: N4JWH
VA Races Inc For Johnston -
Willis Hospital
Chester VA 23831

Call Sign: W4DHP
VA Races Inc For Henrico
DoctorS Hospital - Parham
Chester VA 23831

Call Sign: WC4RC
VA Races Inc For Richmond
Community Hospital
Chester VA 23831

Call Sign: K4UVH
VA Races Inc For University Of
VA Hospital
Chester VA 23831

Call Sign: N4MJH
VA Races Inc For Martha
Jefferson Hospital
Chester VA 23831

Call Sign: WA4FC
Fieldcomm Association
Chester VA 23831

Call Sign: KB4FQB
Diane P Howard
Chester VA 23831

Call Sign: KD4BPZ
James H Lovelady Jr

Chester VA 23831

Call Sign: KE4AUD
Rocky L Shaffer
Chester VA 23831

Call Sign: WC4VAC
VA Ares Races Inc Area C
Chester VA 23831

Call Sign: K4JSG
Jeffrey S Gaskins
Chester VA 23831

Call Sign: KR4UQ
Anthony M Amato
Chester VA 238318444

FCC Amateur Radio Licenses in Chester Gap

Call Sign: KG4FLT
Catherine P Switzer
8 Avery Dr
Chester Gap VA 22623

Call Sign: KG4FLU
Wayne J Switzer
8 Avery Dr
Chester Gap VA 22623

FCC Amateur Radio Licenses in Chesterfield

Call Sign: KA4NCB
Thelma E Davis
9800 3rd Branch Dr
Chesterfield VA 23832

Call Sign: KA4NCC
Winston C Davis
9800 3rd Branch Dr
Chesterfield VA 23832

Call Sign: KB1JOO
Kayle B Miller
9206 Alcove Grove Rd
Chesterfield VA 23832

Call Sign: K4KSR
William B Cunningham
15031 Badestowe Dr
Chesterfield VA 23832

Call Sign: KD4KVE
Lawrence T Brown
6216 Barrister Rd
Chesterfield VA 23832

Call Sign: AK4PQ
Lawrence T Brown
6216 Barrister Rd
Chesterfield VA 23832

Call Sign: KO4PI
Ronald E Searle
6333 Barrister Rd
Chesterfield VA 23832

Call Sign: KE4RTU
Mark D Sylvester
11514 Beach Rd
Chesterfield VA 23838

Call Sign: KB4WWK
Wendy D Moseley
13021 Beach Rd
Chesterfield VA 23838

Call Sign: KI4HHY
Joseph M Walker
11911 Beechwod Forest Dr
Chesterfield VA 23838

Call Sign: WB4H
Frederick E Bennett Jr
11920 Beechwood Forest Dr
Chesterfield VA 23838

Call Sign: WA4FEH
Richard O Arnold
6920 Belmont Rd
Chesterfield VA 238328222

Call Sign: WA4DFI
Robert W Almond Jr
8300 Belmont Rd
Chesterfield VA 23832

Call Sign: N6WAG
David M Billikopf
4507 Boones Trl Ter
Chesterfield VA 23832

Call Sign: KG4QIW
Glen R Le Blanc
13700 Bradley Bridge Rd
Chesterfield VA 23838

Call Sign: N1XII
Dana F Love
11413 Braidstone Ln
Chesterfield VA 23838

Call Sign: WA4WPG
Mark L Garris
13700 Brandy Oaks Dr
Chesterfield VA 23832

Call Sign: KC4AYE
Richard C Bozarth
13713 Brandycrest Dr
Chesterfield VA 23832

Call Sign: KC4YVF
Michael G Sacco
4016 Bronholly Rd
Chesterfield VA 23832

Call Sign: KD4NGR
Michael W Jezierski
4706 Brookridge Rd
Chesterfield VA 23832

Call Sign: KK4MR
Steven B Reynolds
12020 Buckhorn Rd
Chesterfield VA 23832

Call Sign: WB2HOF
Wallis M Mc Cormick
9006 Canvasback Cir
Chesterfield VA 238385275

Call Sign: N4GO
George P Oberto
4324 Carafe Dr

Chesterfield VA 23234

Call Sign: N4KDE
Douglas M Edwards
11712 Carters Creek Dr
Chesterfield VA 23838

Call Sign: AA2ER
Carl A Mc Kissack Sr
13410 Carters Creek Pl
Chesterfield VA 23838

Call Sign: KG4BIZ
Harry Thomas Ebbert
9509 Cattail Rd
Chesterfield VA 238385421

Call Sign: KC4EUW
Chad W Glass
10321 Cattail Rd
Chesterfield VA 23832

Call Sign: N5FRA
Dorothy T Goerner
15530 Chesdin Landing Ct
Chesterfield VA 23838

Call Sign: KI4GK
Malcolm R Petitt
10101 Clearwood Rd
Chesterfield VA 23832

Call Sign: KF4VIY
Lenville F Hall Jr
6612 Corcoran Dr
Chesterfield VA 23832

Call Sign: KJ4WLI
Herman W Clarke Jr
4633 Cordova Ln
Chesterfield VA 23832

Call Sign: KA4NTT
John R Kirk
7121 Courthouse Rd
Chesterfield VA 23832

Call Sign: KE4CPY
Charles A Rhoton

11330 Danforth Rd
Chesterfield VA 23838

Call Sign: KJ4WHY
Mark A Merritt
12520 Donegal Dr
Chesterfield VA 23832

Call Sign: KE4MAR
John C Morris
12601 Donegal Dr
Chesterfield VA 23832

Call Sign: KC4ZRG
Gerald F Fuss Sr
12760 Donegal Dr
Chesterfield VA 23832

Call Sign: NP3CZ
Jose E Berrios Rodriguez
10025 E Alberta Ct
Chesterfield VA 23832

Call Sign: KG4VZZ
George E Ackinclose Jr
10901 Eades Ct
Chesterfield VA 23838

Call Sign: W4GNE
George E Ackinclose Jr
10901 Eades Ct
Chesterfield VA 23838

Call Sign: W4YEN
August L Johnston Jr
10849 Egret Ct
Chesterfield VA 23838

Call Sign: KD4MAA
Thomas H Watson Jr
6621 Elvas Ln
Chesterfield VA 23832

Call Sign: KF4UQA
Margaret E Myers
6654 Elvas Ln
Chesterfield VA 238388705

Call Sign: KJ4JZI

Gilbert W Bishop
15312 Exter Mill Rd
Chesterfield VA 23838

Call Sign: KD7EWN
Benjamin J Dolle
3712 Farmhill Ln
Chesterfield VA 23832

Call Sign: N7ATF
Christopher W Ogle
8607 Finstown Ln
Chesterfield VA 23838

Call Sign: KB4CBB
Paul D Maxwell Jr
6008 Gatesgreen Dr
Chesterfield VA 23832

Call Sign: KA4PER
William R Justice
6229 Gatesgreen Dr
Chesterfield VA 23832

Call Sign: W4JGS
John G Skora
6300 Glebe Point Rd
Chesterfield VA 23838

Call Sign: KC2JT
John G Skora
6300 Glebe Point Rd
Chesterfield VA 23838

Call Sign: KC2JT
John G Skora
6300 Glebe Point Rd
Chesterfield VA 23838

Call Sign: N2NQ
John G Skora
6300 Glebe Point Rd
Chesterfield VA 23838

Call Sign: KJ4TRE
Carl F Robinson
7739 Hampton Green Dr
Chesterfield VA 23832

Call Sign: KE4TNR
Anthony L Gilreath
5660 Hereld Green Dr
Chesterfield VA 23832

Call Sign: KJ4KVL
Ricky A West
4216 Litchfield Dr
Chesterfield VA 23832

Call Sign: W4KQB
Ricky A West
4216 Litchfield Dr
Chesterfield VA 23832

Call Sign: KJ4KVH
Brian K Davis
8231 Macandrew Pl
Chesterfield VA 23838

Call Sign: KF4HEV
Benjamin Vecchio
14415 Mission Hills Cir
Chesterfield VA 238322671

Call Sign: KF4JVP
Jennifer Vecchio
14415 Mission Hills Cir
Chesterfield VA 238322671

Call Sign: KG4FWJ
Troy L Zornes
11801 N Brook Cir
Chesterfield VA 23838

Call Sign: WA4CBV
Garland E Heath
9921 Newbys Bridge Rd
Chesterfield VA 23832

Call Sign: K4UVA
Randolph L Bradshaw
4919 Newbys Mill Ct
Chesterfield VA 23832

Call Sign: KI4MCX
Tyler R Schultz
8203 Outpost Cir
Chesterfield VA 23832

Call Sign: KE4WXT
John F Chasse
9301 Owl Trace Ct
Chesterfield VA 23832

Call Sign: KC4MQF
Donald K Waybright II
9601 Pampas Dr
Chesterfield VA 23832

Call Sign: KE4CWQ
Leroy C Lin
10921 Pintail Pl
Chesterfield VA 23832

Call Sign: N1KEA
Drexel N Harris
13536 Poplardell Ct
Chesterfield VA 23832

Call Sign: W3CPU
Michael B Mitchum
13712 Prince James Dr
Chesterfield VA 23832

Call Sign: W4RBA
Robert B Allin Jr
12200 Princess Mary Ter
Chesterfield VA 23838

Call Sign: AD4NB
Freddie Mercado
9916 Qualla Rd
Chesterfield VA 23832

Call Sign: KC4PVO
Marc A Avinger
9933 Qualla Rd
Chesterfield VA 23832

Call Sign: WA4GUV
Calvin J Willard Sr
12700 Raven Wing Ct
Chesterfield VA 23832

Call Sign: KI4UWU
Charles J Kunowsky
9411 Raven Wing Dr

Chesterfield VA 23832

Call Sign: WA3JTQ
Peter G Fundinger
9510 Raven Wing Dr
Chesterfield VA 23832

Call Sign: AA4PF
Peter G Fundinger
9510 Raven Wing Dr
Chesterfield VA 23832

Call Sign: KJ4BYC
Charles R Jennings
10201 Reedy Branch Rd
Chesterfield VA 23838

Call Sign: KC4CYZ
Vicki P Welch
6109 Richland Rd
Chesterfield VA 23832

Call Sign: WD4BBD
Robert J Welch
6109 Richland Rd
Chesterfield VA 23832

Call Sign: KE4KFI
Roland T Scott III
10400 Ridgerun Rd
Chesterfield VA 23832

Call Sign: KE4HRM
Adam Blath III
4141 Round Hill Dr
Chesterfield VA 23832

Call Sign: K4LJF
A Frederick Berger Jr
6000 Round Rock Rd
Chesterfield VA 238386052

Call Sign: KA4ESO
Joseph R Vest
16101 Rowlett Rd
Chesterfield VA 23838

Call Sign: N4NIL
Harrison E Poole

15413 Saddlebrook Rd
Chesterfield VA 23838

Call Sign: KI4UWR
Gordon F Terry Sr
9313 Salix Grove Ln
Chesterfield VA 23832

Call Sign: KC8OPV
James D Wiersma
7552 Sambar Rd
Chesterfield VA 23832

Call Sign: KG4SEE
William T Ellinger
16810 Sandy Ford Rd
Chesterfield VA 23838

Call Sign: KO4WI
Rex D Curtiss
14540 Skybird Rd
Chesterfield VA 23838

Call Sign: KJ4TRH
Thomas E Fenner Sr
14237 Spyglass Hill Cir
Chesterfield VA 23832

Call Sign: KJ4GBV
John L Ratcliff
14648 Spyglass Hill Cir
Chesterfield VA 23832

Call Sign: KG4UFG
Thomas G Surface Jr
9300 Squirrel Tree Ct
Chesterfield VA 23838

Call Sign: N4HFB
John P Kirby
9330 Squirrel Tree Ct
Chesterfield VA 23838

Call Sign: KB6HCT
Joanalee G Horn
9400 Squirrel Tree Ct
Chesterfield VA 238388922

Call Sign: KC6KDP

Marilee K Horn
9400 Squirrel Tree Ct
Chesterfield VA 238388922

Call Sign: KB6HCU
Wayne F Stack
9400 Squirrel Tree Ct
Chesterfield VA 238388922

Call Sign: K5HTZ
John G De Majo
6001 Statute St
Chesterfield VA 23832

Call Sign: WA3SRO
Richard R Williams
9602 Summercliff Ct
Chesterfield VA 23832

Call Sign: WD4FAZ
Daniel W Salisbury
10524 Sunne Ct
Chesterfield VA 23832

Call Sign: KT4RE
Raymond W Earley Jr
13713 Swiftrock Ridge Dr
Chesterfield VA 23838

Call Sign: K4BGE
Brenda G Earley
13713 Swiftrock Ridge Dr
Chesterfield VA 23838

Call Sign: WB9DZS
Thomas K Williams
8700 Taylor Landing Pl
Chesterfield VA 23838

Call Sign: KF4SVI
Ralph W Sites
10700 Timberun Rd
Chesterfield VA 23832

Call Sign: KG4FRC
Francis M Jarrelle
4330 Tracker Dr
Chesterfield VA 23832

Call Sign: W4FMJ
Francis M Jarrelle
4330 Tracker Dr
Chesterfield VA 23832

Call Sign: KG4LJL
David P Hope
10710 Trailwood Dr
Chesterfield VA 23832

Call Sign: KJ4MTD
Paul W Childress
6632 W Denny Ct
Chesterfield VA 23832

Call Sign: KJ4KTT
Howard F Lang
6634 W Denny Ct
Chesterfield VA 23832

Call Sign: W4BDW
Frank N Strickler
6710 Welch Dr
Chesterfield VA 23832

Call Sign: KD4FKI
Jerimiah J Cox
6611 West Rd
Chesterfield VA 23832

Call Sign: WA1UQO
Armand R Hamel
9070 Whistling Swan Rd
Chesterfield VA 238388900

Call Sign: KJ4WYT
Thomas J Delgado
15106 Winding Ash Dr
Chesterfield VA 23832

Call Sign: KC4WCQ
William A Hixson
9600 Winterpock Rd
Chesterfield VA 23832

Call Sign: WB4SDP
Jimmy R Mullins
11141 Winterpock Rd
Chesterfield VA 23832

Call Sign: KI4NFY
John D Beeler
7800 Woodpecker Rd
Chesterfield VA 23838

Call Sign: K4VAG
John D Beeler
7800 Woodpecker Rd
Chesterfield VA 23838

Call Sign: KI4NFZ
Judith C Henry
7800 Woodpecker Rd
Chesterfield VA 23838

Call Sign: N5JCH
Judith C Henry
7800 Woodpecker Rd
Chesterfield VA 23838

Call Sign: KC4VUN
Michelle R Grate
Chesterfield VA 23832

Call Sign: KF4VVG
Mark A Swearengen
Chesterfield VA 23832

Call Sign: KI4NCG
Chesterfield County Emergency
Management
Chesterfield VA 238320040

Call Sign: KO4FN
Earl G Johnson
Chesterfield VA 238329112

FCC Amateur Radio Licenses
in Chilhowie

Call Sign: KC4VLB
Gilda W Dingler
211 4 Apple Dr
Chilhowie VA 24319

Call Sign: NU4R
Robert N Porterfield
494 Cole Crest Dr

Chilhowie VA 24319

Call Sign: KC4TTF
Gary L Heath
1203 Horseshoe Bend Rd
Chilhowie VA 24319

Call Sign: WG4LH
Gary L Heath
1203 Horseshoe Bend Rd
Chilhowie VA 24319

Call Sign: KJ4QYJ
Angela M Dixon
3310 Little Grannys Ln
Chilhowie VA 24319

Call Sign: KJ4QYK
Rebecca L Saltz
3310 Little Grannys Ln
Chilhowie VA 24319

Call Sign: KD4HIQ
John W Martin
37363 Loves Mill Rd
Chilhowie VA 24319

Call Sign: KJ4WAL
William J Garrison Jr
17001 Mill Creek Rd
Chilhowie VA 24319

Call Sign: KJ4WAM
Charles S Schmidtka
38581 Twin Forks Dr
Chilhowie VA 24319

Call Sign: KD4JDH
Wayne E Carter
Chilhowie VA 24319

Call Sign: KE4EJV
Herbert D Barbrow
Chilhowie VA 24319

Call Sign: KF4YBA
Tracy T Peery
Chilhowie VA 24319

Call Sign: KG4FBI
Candice E Barbrow
Chilhowie VA 24319

Call Sign: W4VAW
VA Appalachian Wireless
Association
Chilhowie VA 24319

Call Sign: KI4AEC
Michael W Lagerholm
Chilhowie VA 24319

Call Sign: AB4X
Michael W Lagerholm
Chilhowie VA 24319

FCC Amateur Radio Licenses
in Chincoteague

Call Sign: N3MK
Donald G Snider Jr
7465 Beebe Rd
Chincoteague VA 23336

Call Sign: N4UZC
Rickie L Gegenheimer
Rr 1 E Side Dr Box 553D
Chincoteague VA 23336

Call Sign: W4NGW
Thomas E Brown Jr
4221 Fillmore St
Chincoteague VA 23336

Call Sign: KJ4WKG
Nicholas J Debrita
4210 Main St
Chincoteague VA 23336

Call Sign: WA2GRI
Sandra S Birmingham
6140 Martin Ln
Chincoteague VA 23336

Call Sign: WB2IFC
Kenneth G Birmingham
6140 Martin Ln
Chincoteague VA 23336

Call Sign: KE7PHG
Clifford F Murphy
6465 Phipps Ln
Chincoteague VA 23336

Call Sign: KG4KYG
Jenny W Somers
6140 Quillen Dr
Chincoteague VA 23336

Call Sign: KE4NQT
Vaughn W Davis Jr
4271 Ridge Rd
Chincoteague VA 23336

Call Sign: KB3BD
William S Ward
4034 Ridge Rd
Chincoteague VA 23336

Call Sign: KE4NQR
Jesse W Speidel
8245 Seaweed Dr
Chincoteague VA 23336

Call Sign: KD4LLM
Charles R Cook
Chincoteague VA 23336

Call Sign: KG4VEP
Henry W Herndon Jr
Chincoteague VA 233361011

FCC Amateur Radio Licenses in Chincoteague Island

Call Sign: WA0WHT
Thomas A Larson
5563 Hibiscus Dr
Chincoteague Island VA
233360211

Call Sign: K3GFK
John C Lang
2569 Main St
Chincoteague Island VA 23336

Call Sign: KG4UKP

Charles R Davis
4175 Main St
Chincoteague Island VA 23336

Call Sign: KK4CEJ
Henry Barnaby III
5320 Main St
Chincoteague Island VA 23336

Call Sign: AF4CP
Jane C Peake
7156 Piney Island Rd
Chincoteague Island VA 23336

Call Sign: KC2AP
Warren C Peake Jr
7156 Piney Island Rd
Chincoteague Island VA 23336

Call Sign: K3LAN
John D Subasic
7533 Pony Cove Ln
Chincoteague Island VA 23336

Call Sign: WB2CQO
Clarence E Staeb
Chincoteague Island VA 23336

FCC Amateur Radio Licenses in Christiansburg

Call Sign: KD4CIW
Mason Wallace
185 Ash Dr
Christiansburg VA 24073

Call Sign: W4CIW
Mason Wallace
185 Ash Dr
Christiansburg VA 24073

Call Sign: KF4BGM
Paul J Newman
80 Belmont Dr
Christiansburg VA 24073

Call Sign: KB8ETX
Lee E Barker
190 Belmont Dr

Christiansburg VA 24073

Call Sign: KJ4NEB
Anna J Hysell
255 Berkshire Dr
Christiansburg VA 24073

Call Sign: KI4CKP
Phil J Hysell
255 Berkshire Dr
Christiansburg VA 24073

Call Sign: K4AST
John A Wikstrom
2652 Beulah Ln
Christiansburg VA 24073

Call Sign: KB4JIO
John E Wonderley
Rt 4 Box 142
Christiansburg VA 24073

Call Sign: WB4DQZ
Le Roy J Kniskern
225 Briarwood Dr
Christiansburg VA 24073

Call Sign: KC4MM
Le Roy J Kniskern
225 Briarwood Dr
Christiansburg VA 24073

Call Sign: N1AOV
Gregg H Shadel
1050 Cambria NW
Christiansburg VA 24073

Call Sign: KG4OQI
New River Valley ARC
600 Cambria St
Christiansburg VA 24073

Call Sign: WA4CKQ
Willard E Denton
1840 Cambria St
Christiansburg VA 24073

Call Sign: KB7DAR
Christopher L Mc Nabb

600 Cambria St NW
Christiansburg VA 24073

Call Sign: K3GX
Stanley D Kingma
450 Canterbury St
Christiansburg VA 24073

Call Sign: KJ4NDQ
Scott A Cook
600 Capitol Way
Christiansburg VA 24073

Call Sign: KF4VNW
Irvin R Saul Jr
680 Carson Dr
Christiansburg VA 24073

Call Sign: WA4NOB
Thomas R Stricker
1110 Cassatt Ln
Christiansburg VA 24073

Call Sign: AA4HC
Harlan B Caldwell
635 Charles St
Christiansburg VA 24073

Call Sign: KG4OVH
Joshua L Regnaud
420 Cherokee Dr
Christiansburg VA 24073

Call Sign: KC4YWG
Arlene H Cecil
2208 Childress Rd
Christiansburg VA 24073

Call Sign: WB3S
Robert B Cecil
2208 Childress Rd
Christiansburg VA 24073

Call Sign: KG4ECL
Richard L Bailey II
3420 Childress Rd
Christiansburg VA 240735956

Call Sign: KK4BWL

Daniel B Goff
70 Chrisman St
Christiansburg VA 24073

Call Sign: KG4JAW
Kathryn J Ward
295 Church St
Christiansburg VA 24073

Call Sign: KK4KAT
Kathryn J Ward
295 Church St
Christiansburg VA 24073

Call Sign: KG4JSN
Dylan J Ward
295 Church St
Christiansburg VA 24073

Call Sign: NS4NS
Randolph W Ward
295 Church St
Christiansburg VA 24073

Call Sign: KG4BYT
Randolph W Ward
295 Church St
Christiansburg VA 240731539

Call Sign: KG4DPL
Colin R Ward
295 Church St
Christiansburg VA 240731539

Call Sign: K4AUG
Mack W Edwards
325 Coal Hollow Rd
Christiansburg VA 24073

Call Sign: N4QBB
Pauline A Edwards
325 Coal Hollow Rd
Christiansburg VA 24073

Call Sign: KJ4BTG
Robert V Speiden
657 Coal Hollow Rd
Christiansburg VA 24073

Call Sign: K4RVS
Robert V Speiden
657 Coal Hollow Rd
Christiansburg VA 24073

Call Sign: N4ANK
Wayne A Spence
910 Collins St
Christiansburg VA 24073

Call Sign: KS4MQ
Sandra J Curd
175 Colonial Dr
Christiansburg VA 24073

Call Sign: KS4MR
Jennifer M Curd
175 Colonial Dr
Christiansburg VA 24073

Call Sign: KG4GRE
Garland L Linkous
190 Colonial Dr
Christiansburg VA 24073

Call Sign: K9RES
Garland L Linkous
190 Colonial Dr
Christiansburg VA 24073

Call Sign: KR4FD
Dennis L Curd
175 Colonial Dr
Christiansburg VA 24073

Call Sign: KE4OMX
Hubert T Stephenson
25 Cullen Ct
Christiansburg VA 24073

Call Sign: KJ4NDU
Pamela L Hodge
265 Depot St NE
Christiansburg VA 24073

Call Sign: KF4AMC
Herbert E Garlick
835 E Main St
Christiansburg VA 24073

Call Sign: KB4Q
Herbert E Garlick
835 E Main St
Christiansburg VA 24073

Call Sign: KC4MQE
Nancy C Baker
228 Easy St
Christiansburg VA 24073

Call Sign: KF4PCU
Benny C Mullens Jr
260 Easy St
Christiansburg VA 24073

Call Sign: KF4CPK
Benny C Mullens
260 Easy St
Christiansburg VA 24073

Call Sign: AJ4SZ
Benny C Mullens
260 Easy St
Christiansburg VA 24073

Call Sign: KE4JDD
Kemp E Cunningham
485 Emerald Blvd
Christiansburg VA 24073

Call Sign: KG4QJY
Jason E Krisch
802 Falls Ridge Rd
Christiansburg VA 24073

Call Sign: WD4DQR
Cyrus O Hall Jr
1095 Flint Dr
Christiansburg VA 24073

Call Sign: AB4FA
Fredric N Jones
1680 Gallimore St
Christiansburg VA 24073

Call Sign: KU8Z
Roger M Galloway
905 George Edward Via

Christiansburg VA 24073

Call Sign: KE4JHH
Scot E Shippee
1010 George Edward Via
Christiansburg VA 24073

Call Sign: KI4ED
Robert C Bratton
205 Gold Leaf Dr
Christiansburg VA 24073

Call Sign: KJ4NEX
Anne F Taylor
630 Gold Leaf Dr
Christiansburg VA 24073

Call Sign: N4YCL
Carl B Dietrich Jr
295 Gold Leaf Dr
Christiansburg VA 24073

Call Sign: KE4CIB
Allen W Bishop
120 Gum Dr
Christiansburg VA 24073

Call Sign: KE4FBT
Dale F Ashworth
113 Hagan St
Christiansburg VA 24073

Call Sign: KE4JKH
Katherine M Ashworth
113 Hagan St
Christiansburg VA 24073

Call Sign: N4WMM
Charles S Correll
1120 Hans Meadow Rd
Christiansburg VA 240732301

Call Sign: KB4MRH
Christopher C Peters
240 Harkrader St
Christiansburg VA 240734259

Call Sign: K4HZ
Christopher C Peters

240 Harkrader St
Christiansburg VA 240734259

Call Sign: WQ3C
Joseph M Davis
425 Harmon Cir
Christiansburg VA 24073

Call Sign: KB4AUL
Frank M Robinson Jr
300 Hickok St SW
Christiansburg VA 24073

Call Sign: WA4HBC
Howard C Newman
203B Hill St
Christiansburg VA 24073

Call Sign: KC9LC
Clyde R Shake
735 Holly Dr
Christiansburg VA 24073

Call Sign: KF4TRT
Stephen R Shake
735 Holly Dr
Christiansburg VA 24073

Call Sign: KF4DOW
Michael L Ashwell
490 Independence Blvd
Christiansburg VA 24073

Call Sign: KG4ECD
Rodney L Sheppard
1525 Jackson St
Christiansburg VA 24073

Call Sign: KE4EOT
James E Hudgins Jr
30 Johns Ct
Christiansburg VA 24073

Call Sign: KI4HFQ
Jeff G Legge
1185 Juniper Dr
Christiansburg VA 24073

Call Sign: N8HCR

Lonnie L Goodman Jr
50 Kays Dr
Christiansburg VA 24073

Call Sign: KB8BOE
Linda J Goodman
50 Kays Dr
Christiansburg VA 24073

Call Sign: KB4JHO
James H Billingsley Jr
70 Kimball Ln
Christiansburg VA 24073

Call Sign: KE4FPB
James A Murphy Jr
2299 Leather Rd
Christiansburg VA 24073

Call Sign: KI4UAZ
Kevin B Salyers
117 Lester St
Christiansburg VA 24073

Call Sign: KD4IOM
James C Robinette
725 Liberty Via
Christiansburg VA 24073

Call Sign: KF4ZJD
Monta Elkins
1974 Lynnwood Ln
Christiansburg VA 24073

Call Sign: KE4UMK
Rene Fonseca Jr
940 Magnolia Ln
Christiansburg VA 24073

Call Sign: KI4EYJ
Danny L Wylam
710 McDaniel Dr
Christiansburg VA 24073

Call Sign: AI4RC
Danny L Wylam
710 McDaniel Dr
Christiansburg VA 24073

Call Sign: KE4AJV
Daniel S Corkey Sr
106 Miller St
Christiansburg VA 24073

Call Sign: W4OUC
William R Hawkins
109 Miller St
Christiansburg VA 24073

Call Sign: KG4OMK
Jennifer A Cease
440 Montgomery St
Christiansburg VA 24073

Call Sign: N4QMB
Jerry W Akers
475 Montgomery St
Christiansburg VA 24073

Call Sign: WD4BSB
Douglas B Minnick
740 Montgomery St
Christiansburg VA 24068

Call Sign: KI4FYG
Marcus W Thompson
40 Mulberry Dr
Christiansburg VA 24073

Call Sign: KA4VXH
Clifford S Costigan
45 Mulberry Dr
Christiansburg VA 24073

Call Sign: KI4IME
Malcolm S Mcpherson
430 Mulberry Dr
Christiansburg VA 24073

Call Sign: KE4FBN
Gregory W Branscome
30 Newcomb St
Christiansburg VA 24073

Call Sign: KD1MF
Robert T Gallagher
1280 Orange Leaf Ct
Christiansburg VA 24073

Call Sign: W4RJP
Robert J Pearsall
335 Overland Dr
Christiansburg VA 240734715

Call Sign: KC4SII
Arron W Tuggle
380 Overland Dr
Christiansburg VA 24073

Call Sign: KC4SIJ
Allen W Tuggle
380 Overland Dr
Christiansburg VA 24073

Call Sign: KI4JMF
Peter G Sanders
422 Peppers Ferry Rd NW 109
Christiansburg VA 24073

Call Sign: KK4BWV
James B Perkins
461 Pike Ln
Christiansburg VA 24073

Call Sign: KK4BWQ
Linda C Perkins
461 Pike Ln
Christiansburg VA 24073

Call Sign: KJ4NDS
Donald R Yearout
2301 Plateau Dr
Christiansburg VA 24073

Call Sign: W3WEQ
Winfield E Burkey
1375 Providence Blvd
Christiansburg VA 24073

Call Sign: KC4TAB
Terrence T Shrader
1040 Radford St Apt 5
Christiansburg VA 24073

Call Sign: KG4CNH
Donald E Dudding
655 Reading Rd

Christiansburg VA 24073

Call Sign: N7SDL
Robert A Lewit
1335 Red Hawk Run
Christiansburg VA 24073

Call Sign: KE4JDG
John E Reeder
595 Republic St Apt L 113
Christiansburg VA 24073

Call Sign: N4LCL
Linda D Lucas
1224 Rock Rd 12
Christiansburg VA 24073

Call Sign: KA4HMJ
Paul A Haynes
160 Rose Hill Dr
Christiansburg VA 24073

Call Sign: K4BFO
Harold W Irwin
10 Rosehill Dr SW
Christiansburg VA 240734430

Call Sign: KB4INA
Homer D Sawyer
609 S Franklin St
Christiansburg VA 24073

Call Sign: KB5ZYZ
Charles F Bass
125 Sapphire Ave
Christiansburg VA 240735895

Call Sign: KE4HER
Jan C Jackson
1250 Scott St
Christiansburg VA 24073

Call Sign: KF4BCT
Christopher S Lacy
1635 Sherwood Dr
Christiansburg VA 24073

Call Sign: KF7NFH
Michael W Rutherford Jr

480 Silverleaf Dr
Christiansburg VA 24073

Call Sign: KG4MFO
Michael Brown
1590 Sleepy Hollow Rd
Christiansburg VA 24073

Call Sign: WA4FUZ
Grayson E Wright
870 Smith Creek Rd
Christiansburg VA 24073

Call Sign: KJ4NDX
Leonard B Akers
1200 Stafford Dr
Christiansburg VA 240734040

Call Sign: KF4PHV
Joshua J Rancourt
60 Summit Ridge Rd
Christiansburg VA 24073

Call Sign: KC4CZN
Edwin C Sheffield Jr
1041 Switchback Rd
Christiansburg VA 24073

Call Sign: KD4LQM
Marvin B Smith Jr
265 Tanglewood Dr
Christiansburg VA 24073

Call Sign: KB4GCF
Gary F Kendall
420 Tanglewood Dr
Christiansburg VA 24073

Call Sign: KE4HXA
Earnest H Alderman
1609 Testerman Dr
Christiansburg VA 24073

Call Sign: KE4TIV
Karen G Vahl
2596 Townhouse St
Christiansburg VA 24073

Call Sign: KJ4TRT

Patrick M Johnson
3478 Tyler Rd
Christiansburg VA 24073

Call Sign: KF4MCZ
Jennifer L Vaden
810 Unicorn Ln
Christiansburg VA 24073

Call Sign: N8QEG
William D Tilson
360 Wakeman Ct
Christiansburg VA 240731390

Call Sign: KJ4TRV
Andrew T Mcelvery
1335 Wall St
Christiansburg VA 24073

Call Sign: KJ4TRU
Heather N Mcelvery
1335 Wall Strret
Christiansburg VA 24073

Call Sign: K9EZO
Dale W Schutt
380 Walters Dr NW
Christiansburg VA 24073

Call Sign: AJ4WB
Peter H Johnson
1430 Westview Dr
Christiansburg VA 24073

Call Sign: WA4EPX
Carlos G Wright
2183 Whispering Pine Cir
Christiansburg VA 24073

Call Sign: N4ATV
Thomas C Lawrence Sr
1824 White Oak Ln
Christiansburg VA 24073

Call Sign: KA3WVD
Jenny K Riffe
1542 Whitman Ln
Christiansburg VA 24073

Call Sign: W4AAR
Charles J Albright
220 Windsong Ln
Christiansburg VA 24073

Call Sign: KK4EWT
James B Williams
755 Wing St
Christiansburg VA 24073

Call Sign: KB3KDD
David J Jasinski
1014 Woodrow Rd
Christiansburg VA 24073

Call Sign: KC4WIM
Herbert E Zimmerman
3026 Zimmerman Ln
Christiansburg VA 24073

Call Sign: K3IW
Robert A Barrow
Christiansburg VA 24068

Call Sign: K3IWH
Deborah L Barrow
Christiansburg VA 24068

Call Sign: WD4APV
Lettie P Minnick
Christiansburg VA 24068

Call Sign: W4LPQ
Ellis W Carner
Christiansburg VA 24073

Call Sign: K3WPI
Barrow Lodge Qrp Group
Christiansburg VA 24068

Call Sign: KB4GEF
Susan K Fritz
Christiansburg VA 24068

Call Sign: KE4JDF
James E Cash Jr
Christiansburg VA 24068

Call Sign: KF4GJG

Elizabeth C Lancaster
Christiansburg VA 24068

Call Sign: KI4CY
David C Fritz
Christiansburg VA 24068

Call Sign: KJ4JRC
Scott D Pritchard
Christiansburg VA 240680301

Call Sign: K4ALC
Harold G Shelton
Christiansburg VA 240730512

Call Sign: KI4BJP
VA Highlands Amateur Group
Chrsitiansburg VA 24073

FCC Amateur Radio Licenses in Church Road

Call Sign: KB4VAC
John T Belvin
12211 Browns Rd
Church Road VA 23833

Call Sign: WB4EZ
John T Belvin
12211 Browns Rd
Church Road VA 23833

Call Sign: KA9AWF
Dennis W Stinnett
13024 Cox Rd
Church Road VA 23833

Call Sign: KI4DW
Dennis W Stinnett
13024 Cox Rd
Church Road VA 23833

FCC Amateur Radio Licenses in Church View

Call Sign: KJ4ZLJ
Ian S Abbott
Church View VA 23032

FCC Amateur Radio Licenses in Churchville

Call Sign: KE4CKE
Patrick J Conroy
Rt 1 Box 553
Churchville VA 24421

Call Sign: KB4DJK
Boyd W Hevener
266 Hankey Mtn Hwy
Churchville VA 24421

Call Sign: W4XD
Valley ARA
1344 Hankey Mtn Hwy
Churchville VA 24421

Call Sign: W4MUS
Valley ARA
1344 Hankey Mtn Hwy
Churchville VA 24421

Call Sign: W4PJW
Jeffrey M Rinehart
1344 Hankey Mtn Hwy
Churchville VA 24421

Call Sign: K4PJJ
Patsy S Rinehart
1344 Hankey Mtn Hwy
Churchville VA 24421

Call Sign: KI4FZX
Ronald F Mecum
1019 Moffett Branch Rd
Churchville VA 24421

Call Sign: KG4CHZ
Jade A Ashley
1773 Moffett Branch Rd
Churchville VA 24421

Call Sign: KJ4VVP
Glenn J Mingo
44 Sillings Rd
Churchville VA 244212030

Call Sign: KC4AWW

Arthur W Woolfrey Sr
439 Union Church Rd
Churchville VA 24421

Call Sign: KB2IK
Donald M O Connor
1157 Union Church Rd
Churchville VA 24421

Call Sign: WA4RPH
Kenneth J Indart
311 Varner Rd
Churchville VA 244212216

Call Sign: KG4GZH
Danny S Clatterbaugh
670 Whiskey Creek Rd
Churchville VA 24421

FCC Amateur Radio Licenses in Clarksville

Call Sign: KC4IZH
Jonathan G Pharr
Rt 2 Box 107
Clarksville VA 23927

Call Sign: KC4RXP
Jessie J Redd
Rt 2 Box 111C
Clarksville VA 23927

Call Sign: KC4ITN
Christopher W Hamlett
Rt 1 Box 203
Clarksville VA 23927

Call Sign: KC4RXK
David W Pulliam
Rt 1 Box 42
Clarksville VA 23927

Call Sign: KC4RXJ
Micheal A Newton
Rt 2 Box 552G
Clarksville VA 23927

Call Sign: N4ZSX
George G Clack

Rt 1 Box 82D
Clarksville VA 23927

Call Sign: KC4EAZ
Marie Garratt
153 Cheverly Rd
Clarksville VA 239273536

Call Sign: KE4HBO
Carol Ann Garratt
153 Cheverly Rd
Clarksville VA 239273536

Call Sign: N4YMI
Richard Garratt
153 Cheverly Rd
Clarksville VA 239273536

Call Sign: WA4UQV
Charles J Farmer
315 E 5th St
Clarksville VA 23927

Call Sign: KK4DPM
Aaron B Cornett
142 Eagle Porch Ct
Clarksville VA 23927

Call Sign: KC4ITG
Les L Elliott
115 Forest Hill St
Clarksville VA 23927

Call Sign: KM4JX
Wayne D Brenckman Jr
600 Highpoint Bvld
Clarksville VA 23927

Call Sign: KI4TXC
Edward T Hite Jr
718 Jones Rd
Clarksville VA 23927

Call Sign: K9EOG
Kenneth L Haskett Jr
114 Marshall Dr
Clarksville VA 23927

Call Sign: KI4ITC

David P House
3784 Shiney Rock Rd
Clarksville VA 23927

Call Sign: KJ4BMO
Jennifer L Jacker-House
3784 Shiney Rock Rd
Clarksville VA 23927

Call Sign: KJ4BMM
Joshua M Hibbert
3784 Shiney Rock Rd
Clarksville VA 23927

Call Sign: KJ4BMN
Jonathan F Hudson
3784 Shiney Rock Rd
Clarksville VA 23927

Call Sign: N4UOL
Legare Hairston
801 VA Ave
Clarksville VA 23927

Call Sign: KA4KBP
Kenneth R Cope
103 Willow Oak Dr
Clarksville VA 23927

Call Sign: KC4ITE
Gary L Kent
Clarksville VA 23927

Call Sign: KC4ITO
Daphane M Terry
Clarksville VA 23927

Call Sign: KC4QXC
Ellis E Maxon
Clarksville VA 23927

Call Sign: KC4RXS
Patrick L Callahan
Clarksville VA 23927

Call Sign: KD4KDC
Thomas W Riggan
Clarksville VA 23927

Call Sign: KG4CBQ
James F Lessing
Clarksville VA 23927

Call Sign: KS4HS
James Norris
Clarksville VA 23927

Call Sign: N4NNK
Arthur H Edwardson
Clarksville VA 23927

FCC Amateur Radio Licenses in Claudville

Call Sign: KC4DCD
James E Slate Sr
Rt 1 Box 47
Claudville VA 24076

Call Sign: KK4BJW
Robert S Martin
1248 Unity Church Rd
Claudville VA 240763540

Call Sign: W5RJE
William W Patterson
Claudville VA 24076

FCC Amateur Radio Licenses in Clear Brook

Call Sign: KI4TTK
Kenneth M Guida
150 Orchard Dale Dr
Clear Brook VA 22624

Call Sign: KI4WPF
Kenneth M Guida
150 Orchard Dale Dr
Clear Brook VA 22624

Call Sign: KG4LVU
John R Andrick III
344 Orchard Dale Dr
Clear Brook VA 22624

Call Sign: KD8FHJ
Denise R Andrick

344 Orchard Dale Dr
Clear Brook VA 22624

Call Sign: KF4TNW
Timothy L Putprush
445 Orchard Dale Dr
Clear Brook VA 22624

Call Sign: KJ4EK
John A Anastas
142 Peach Grove Ln
Clear Brook VA 22624

Call Sign: KE4OBG
Derek J Hewett
189 Peach Grove Ln
Clear Brook VA 22624

Call Sign: KG6IPN
Michael H Wysong
292 Ruebuck Rd
Clear Brook VA 22624

Call Sign: KI4SEU
Timothy W Hartley
214 Walnut Dr
Clear Brook VA 22624

Call Sign: WA8BIW
Gary D Yonally
217 Walnut Dr
Clear Brook VA 22624

Call Sign: KE4JJR
James M Hodson Jr
Clear Brook VA 22624

FCC Amateur Radio Licenses in Cleveland

Call Sign: KJ4OOO
Brett W Edmonds
74 Angel Way Ave
Cleveland VA 24225

Call Sign: KJ4YNT
Brett W Edmonds
74 Angel Way Ave
Cleveland VA 24225

Call Sign: KC4RBI
David A Musick
Rt 2 Box 187
Cleveland VA 24225

Call Sign: KE4ACP
Betty L Lane
Rt 1 Box 347
Cleveland VA 24225

Call Sign: KA4ZOJ
Clarence R Rasnake
Rt 1 Box 442
Cleveland VA 24225

Call Sign: KC4MTC
Thermon H Powers
Rt 1 Box 71
Cleveland VA 24225

Call Sign: KC4RER
Linda M Powers
3972 Jessees Mill Rd
Cleveland VA 24225

Call Sign: KB0YFJ
Brian S Osborne
3080 Spring City Rd
Cleveland VA 242253307

Call Sign: KA4JND
Nancy S Elswick
Cleveland VA 24225

FCC Amateur Radio Licenses in Clifton

Call Sign: W4OGS
William V Tranavitch Jr
7503 Amkin Ct
Clifton VA 22024

Call Sign: N4GSH
Carolyn H Rash
11711 Amkin Dr
Clifton VA 20124

Call Sign: N4HCR

Wayne Rash Jr
11711 Amkin Dr
Clifton VA 20124

Call Sign: KG4HAN
Brittany L Rash
11711 Amkin Dr
Clifton VA 20124

Call Sign: KA4DMN
Donald E Ralston
11716 Amkin Dr
Clifton VA 22024

Call Sign: W4TFW
Thomas O Ruppert Jr
12100 Beaver Creek Rd
Clifton VA 22024

Call Sign: KF4PTA
Randy L Garrett I
7817 Blackacre Rd
Clifton VA 20124

Call Sign: KI4POQ
John S Mcclure
6801 Bluff Ridge Ln
Clifton VA 20124

Call Sign: KI4OWK
Charles T Rau
6801 Bluff Ridge Ln
Clifton VA 201241643

Call Sign: WD4KGC
Christopher B Kubelick
6714 Bunkers Ct
Clifton VA 20124

Call Sign: NO5P
George O Nossaman
6715 Bunkers Ct
Clifton VA 201242533

Call Sign: KC4YWL
Randal K Allison
13500 Canada Goose Ct
Clifton VA 20124

Call Sign: KD4HAF
Thomas J Boggess
13400 Cavalier Wds Dr
Clifton VA 22024

Call Sign: KC4FJO
Stanley G Cawelti
11621 Chapel Rd
Clifton VA 22024

Call Sign: W3YY
Robert T Peterson
12601 Chapel Rd
Clifton VA 201241926

Call Sign: KJ4EPD
Houston G Dewey
12216 Cliffwood Ct
Clifton VA 20124

Call Sign: W6BV
Houston G Dewey
12216 Cliffwood Ct
Clifton VA 20124

Call Sign: W2RX
Mark S Weiss
12402 Clifton Hunt Dr
Clifton VA 20124

Call Sign: KJ4FQO
Jeffrey J Weiss
12402 Clifton Hunt Dr
Clifton VA 20124

Call Sign: W4JWX
Jeffrey J Weiss
12402 Clifton Hunt Dr
Clifton VA 20124

Call Sign: KJ4YHD
Laurence H Gary
6289 Clifton Rd
Clifton VA 20124

Call Sign: KG4YQQ
Bruce C Hunter
6409 Clifton Rd
Clifton VA 20124

Call Sign: KG4RRM
Aaron C Hunter
6409 Clifton Rd
Clifton VA 201241404

Call Sign: K8ZOA
Jack R Smith
7236 Clifton Rd
Clifton VA 20124

Call Sign: KI4WFY
Stephen R Holmes
7241 Clifton Rd
Clifton VA 201240246

Call Sign: N3BRF
Stephen R Holmes
7241 Clifton Rd
Clifton VA 201240246

Call Sign: KE4PCU
Mark Mc Cormack
7372 Clifton Rd
Clifton VA 22024

Call Sign: K3KRK
Kenneth R Kranz
13504 Covey Ln
Clifton VA 20124

Call Sign: KK4HDM
Tosha M Kranz
13504 Covey Ln
Clifton VA 20124

Call Sign: N4ANW
Leroy H Black
13800 Foggy Hills Ct
Clifton VA 22024

Call Sign: KK4AQR
Raymond E Helms III
13815 Foggy Hills Ct
Clifton VA 20124

Call Sign: KF4LGU
Tracy A Keeter
13309 Green Mallard Ct

Clifton VA 20124

Call Sign: WB3GBL
Richard C Pomaibo
13309 Green Mallard Ct
Clifton VA 20124

Call Sign: N7THZ
Brian D Eubanks
11501 Henderson Rd
Clifton VA 20124

Call Sign: KJ4NXJ
Nathaniel K Eubanks
11501 Henderson Rd
Clifton VA 20124

Call Sign: KU4YK
Gary L Page
12218 Henderson Rd
Clifton VA 20124

Call Sign: AF4RO
Gary L Page
12218 Henderson Rd
Clifton VA 20124

Call Sign: KJ4EPG
Vicky S Page
12218 Henderson Rd
Clifton VA 20124

Call Sign: KI4FVW
Jacqueline Gulick
12219 Henderson Rd
Clifton VA 20124

Call Sign: W1TEW
Jacqueline Gulick
12219 Henderson Rd
Clifton VA 20124

Call Sign: KJ4OTQ
Kevin P Latchford
13311 Jaybird Ct
Clifton VA 201241096

Call Sign: KG4TAL
Ronald A Gustafson

13212 Johnny Moore Ln
Clifton VA 201241420

Call Sign: KA4WRV
Jackson D Harper
8301 Knights Forest Dr
Clifton VA 22024

Call Sign: KE0EK
John C Nolan
6608 Ladyslipper Ln
Clifton VA 22024

Call Sign: KG4OWP
Mitch L Guess
13787 Laurel Rock Dr
Clifton VA 20124

Call Sign: WB2GVQ
Michael S Kolansky
6419 Melstone Ct
Clifton VA 20124

Call Sign: KF4BCS
Shick C Hom
6420 Melstone Ct
Clifton VA 20124

Call Sign: KF4CKD
Charles L Lynch
13338 Moore Rd
Clifton VA 22024

Call Sign: KC4RFO
Cynthia M Stone
6401 Noble Rock Ct
Clifton VA 20124

Call Sign: WA1JQC
George M Stone Jr
6401 Noble Rock Ct
Clifton VA 201242515

Call Sign: KF4JHB
Noah R Hillstrom
7615 Partridge Berry Ln
Clifton VA 20124

Call Sign: KF4CFZ

Harry T Rensel Jr
13016 Quartz Ln
Clifton VA 22032

Call Sign: KF4ZTO
Phillip W Sperry
13026 Quartz Ln
Clifton VA 201241002

Call Sign: KD6BYT
David N Garten
6508 Rock Crystal Dr
Clifton VA 20124

Call Sign: KJ4VTA
David P Mehfoud
6449 Rock Hollow Ln
Clifton VA 20124

Call Sign: KG4EXY
John L Scarfone
13632 S Springs Dr
Clifton VA 201242442

Call Sign: N2SJZ
Christina K Nelson
13641 S Springs Dr
Clifton VA 20124

Call Sign: KB1BD
Robert G Nelson
13641 S Springs Dr
Clifton VA 20124

Call Sign: KE4GDU
Kie Bum Eom
13823 S Springs Dr
Clifton VA 22024

Call Sign: N2UMK
Patrick M Dunlap
6115 Sandstone Ct
Clifton VA 201242324

Call Sign: KJ4JWH
James L Kindig
6235 Sandstone Way
Clifton VA 20124

Call Sign: N4PXI
Wilson L Abbott
13969 Shalestone Dr
Clifton VA 22024

Call Sign: W8HLN
Edward C Rozelle
6302 Stonehunt Way
Clifton VA 22024

Call Sign: N3GJO
Sara K Meinders
13415 Trey Ln
Clifton VA 20121

Call Sign: KA3VOE
Sara E Meinders
13415 Trey Ln
Clifton VA 20124

Call Sign: N0GTV
Marvin D Meinders
13415 Trey Ln
Clifton VA 20124

Call Sign: W4BFD
Robert W Payton Jr
6405 Union Mill Rd
Clifton VA 201241110

Call Sign: KA4FFK
Michael J Kirchner
13604 Union Village Cir
Clifton VA 201242355

Call Sign: WB2VYM
Robert A Hollander
13628 Union Village Cir
Clifton VA 22024

Call Sign: WA8MXX
Peter A Williams
12631 Water St
Clifton VA 20124

Call Sign: AB4UM
Terry S Berman
5409 Willow Valley Rd
Clifton VA 201241091

Call Sign: KI3C
Terry S Berman
5409 Willow Valley Rd
Clifton VA 201241091

Call Sign: W4UF
Howard C Gay
Clifton VA 20124

FCC Amateur Radio Licenses in Clifton Forge

Call Sign: WB4ZET
Stewart E Shannon Sr
Rt 1 Box 478A
Clifton Forge VA 24422

Call Sign: KC4WSA
Jarrell B Peery
Rt 1 Box 523 Wilson Creek Ln
Clifton Forge VA 24422

Call Sign: KK4DRA
Emily K Timbrook
735 Callie Mines Rd
Clifton Forge VA 24422

Call Sign: K4QEL
Edward L Crance
516 Douglas St
Clifton Forge VA 24422

Call Sign: KI4QEO
John P Zeek
801 Douglas St
Clifton Forge VA 24422

Call Sign: KB3PPA
Wayne A Starkey
511 E Ridgeway St Apt 13
Clifton Forge VA 24422

Call Sign: KF4VTN
Denyse A Rothe
97 Ferrol Ave
Clifton Forge VA 24422

Call Sign: K4HWP

Norman C Scott
812 Gardner St
Clifton Forge VA 24422

Call Sign: KJ4LNH
Glenn E Clements
1400 Grace Ave
Clifton Forge VA 24422

Call Sign: WD4OXR
Vernon C Hudson
1414 Grace Ave
Clifton Forge VA 24422

Call Sign: K4UMO
Ernest B Young
1600 Jefferson Ave
Clifton Forge VA 24422

Call Sign: KJ4PGD
John T Fury
3812 Longdale Furnace Rd
Clifton Forge VA 24422

Call Sign: WD4NRV
Bernard M Campbell
1120 Madison Ave
Clifton Forge VA 24422

Call Sign: K4GJC
John G Sanders
808 McCormick St
Clifton Forge VA 24422

Call Sign: N4IFW
Miriam S Boyd
4915 McKinney Hollow Rd
Clifton Forge VA 24422

Call Sign: N4DLN
William E Boyd Jr
4915 McKinney Hollow Rd
Clifton Forge VA 24422

Call Sign: KI4UBD
Wayne A Crawford
1812 N Oakwood Dr
Clifton Forge VA 24422

Call Sign: KJ4KFW
Ron Gashgai
100 Nicholas Dr Box 4945
Clifton Forge VA 24422

Call Sign: KG4DQD
Reba P Cartwright
1606 Oak Hill Ave Apt 1
Clifton Forge VA 24422

Call Sign: KF4UYJ
John W Riley Jr
302 Reverse St
Clifton Forge VA 24422

Call Sign: KF4VJF
Winfred B Unroe
612 W Ridgeway St
Clifton Forge VA 24422

Call Sign: K4TKP
Lawrence Salvemini
800 W Ridgeway St Apt Rv408
Clifton Forge VA 24422

Call Sign: KF4PSH
Anthony B Smith
100 Wintergreen Ave
Clifton Forge VA 24422

Call Sign: KG4DYV
Elizabeth A Bartley
Clifton Forge VA 244220175

FCC Amateur Radio Licenses in Clinchburg

Call Sign: KC4AUO
John W Heath Jr
Rt 2 Box 402
Clinchburg VA 24361

FCC Amateur Radio Licenses in Clinchco

Call Sign: AE4HZ
Dana K Witt
Rt 1 Box 630
Clinchco VA 24226

Call Sign: KF4MML
Myra A Witt
4568 Nealy Ridge
Clinchco VA 24226

FCC Amateur Radio Licenses in Clinchport

Call Sign: WA4IFW
Glenn J Edwards
Rt 2 Box 180
Clinchport VA 24244

Call Sign: KE4TXU
Mickey L Gilliam
Rt 4 Box 210
Clinchport VA 24244

Call Sign: KE4VQS
Christopher D Gilliam
Rt 4 Box 210
Clinchport VA 24244

Call Sign: KD4NPG
Tony R Dockery
Rt 4 Box 44
Clinchport VA 24244

Call Sign: KI4DPI
Donnie D Sloan
Rt 3 Box 58A
Clinchport VA 24244

FCC Amateur Radio Licenses in Clintwood

Call Sign: KF4ABG
Cyrus N Vanover
Rt 2 Box 106H
Clintwood VA 24228

Call Sign: KI4DIH
Patricia N Mullins
Rt 2 Box 142
Clintwood VA 24228

Call Sign: WD4DRI
Joseph M Sykes

Rt 3 Box 197
Clintwood VA 24228

Call Sign: KE4ONM
Harold P Akens
Rt 1 Box 209A
Clintwood VA 24228

Call Sign: KE4URM
Christopher N Smith
Rt 3 Box 309 K
Clintwood VA 24228

Call Sign: KC4TQC
Gobel Johnson
Rt 2 Box 323H
Clintwood VA 24228

Call Sign: KF4DMW
Miranda D Mc Coy
Rt 1 Box 372
Clintwood VA 24228

Call Sign: KF4ICE
Cindy L Newberry
Rt 1 Box 372 H
Clintwood VA 24228

Call Sign: KE4ZAO
Brian S Newberry
Rt 1 Box 372H
Clintwood VA 24228

Call Sign: KE4ZAP
Randy L Newberry
Rt 1 Box 372H
Clintwood VA 24228

Call Sign: KF4MNV
Stella A Newberry
Rt 1 Box 373
Clintwood VA 24228

Call Sign: KF4FLP
Roger W Newberry
Rt 1 Box 373 B
Clintwood VA 24228

Call Sign: KF4FFE

Connie L Newberry
Rt 1 Box 373B
Clintwood VA 24228

Call Sign: KF4ABD
Roger W Newberry
Rt 1 Box 374
Clintwood VA 24228

Call Sign: KF4ABE
Shana L Newberry
Rt 1 Box 374
Clintwood VA 24228

Call Sign: KF4ABF
Christopher D Kincaid
Rt 1 Box 385C
Clintwood VA 24228

Call Sign: KF4FEK
Dennis J Rose
Rt 1 Box 408 A
Clintwood VA 24228

Call Sign: KF4FFB
Linda N Rose
Rt 1 Box 408A
Clintwood VA 24228

Call Sign: KF4IKG
Jason J Rose
Rt 1 Box 408A
Clintwood VA 24228

Call Sign: KE4QZR
Ronnie L Robbins
Rt 1 Box 427
Clintwood VA 24228

Call Sign: WB4ZIP
Oval W Hillman
Rfd 1 Box 440
Clintwood VA 24228

Call Sign: W9NQH
L C Sykes
R 3 Box 543
Clintwood VA 24228

Call Sign: KC4EYN
Corbett L Mc Cowan
Rt 1 Box 543
Clintwood VA 24228

Call Sign: K4AKI
Vilous T Mullins
Rt 2 Box 69K
Clintwood VA 24228

Call Sign: KC4WBH
Dwayne L Ramey
202 Chickadee Dr
Clintwood VA 24228

Call Sign: KD4HIO
Roger L Ramey
202 Chickadee Dr
Clintwood VA 24228

Call Sign: AB4TI
Danny W Mullins
590 Hill Rdg
Clintwood VA 24228

Call Sign: N4YEY
Rita J Mullins
590 Hill Rdg
Clintwood VA 24228

Call Sign: KB4KTH
Donnie P Dotson
775 Honeycamp Rd
Clintwood VA 24228

Call Sign: KF4MMJ
Janice D Mc Cowan
141 Hummingbird Ln
Clintwood VA 24228

Call Sign: NR4I
Dennis C Vandyke
187 J P Ln
Clintwood VA 24228

Call Sign: KI4UAQ
Danny C Wampler
110 Jp Ln
Clintwood VA 24228

Call Sign: K4TDW
Danny C Wampler
110 Jp Ln
Clintwood VA 24228

Call Sign: KJ4LOA
Kathy M Wampler
110 Jp Ln
Clintwood VA 24228

Call Sign: KG4IKJ
Rustina L Mullins
358 Lower Georges Fork
Hollow
Clintwood VA 242285964

Call Sign: KG4NAL
Randy Mullins
388 Lower Georges Fork
Hollow
Clintwood VA 24228

Call Sign: KF4TDB
Adam D Vanover
309 Phipps Cir
Clintwood VA 24228

Call Sign: KE4CSD
Freel J Vanover
Clintwood VA 24228

Call Sign: N4NUX
Ben W Johnston
Clintwood VA 24228

Call Sign: WD4JPZ
Bobby G Garrett
Clintwood VA 24228

Call Sign: KB4AKS
Mark W Mullins
Clintwood VA 24228

Call Sign: KF4KTH
Joshua A Moore
Clintwood VA 24228

Call Sign: KF4QKM

Timothy R Redden
Clintwood VA 24228

Call Sign: WA4EUK
Robert L Lyall
Clintwood VA 24228

Call Sign: WD4PLO
Garry W Kendrick
Clintwood VA 24228

Call Sign: KI4PYN
Michael V Miller
Clintwood VA 24228

Call Sign: W9MVM
Michael V Miller
Clintwood VA 24228

Call Sign: KC8ERJ
Mark D Womack
Clintwood VA 242280365

FCC Amateur Radio Licenses in Clover

Call Sign: KC4UHQ
Kevin M Lindsey
Rt 1 Box 108
Clover VA 24534

Call Sign: KE4LHK
Sean E Collins
Rt 1 Box 126
Clover VA 24534

Call Sign: KD4IQI
Paul J Whitlow Jr
Rt 1 Box 133 B5
Clover VA 24534

Call Sign: KE4EDK
Calvin L Dixon
Rt 1 Box 67
Clover VA 24534

Call Sign: KC4OQD
Steven L Long
4A Church St

Clover VA 24534

Call Sign: KJ4MNY
William R Nicklin
3081 Neals Corner Rd
Clover VA 24534

Call Sign: KB4YSV
Jerry O Russell Sr
Clover VA 24534

FCC Amateur Radio Licenses in Cobbs Breek

Call Sign: KE4RDU
Bobby D Brooks
359 Cobbs Creek Ln
Cobbs Creek VA 23035

Call Sign: N2GFC
Francis G Gaul
1570 Ebenezer Church Rd
Cobbs Creek VA 23035

Call Sign: N2GFD
Patricia Gaul
1570 Ebenezer Church Rd
Cobbs Creek VA 23035

Call Sign: KB1HP
James L O Brien
106 Hudgin Point Ln
Cobbs Creek VA 230350701

Call Sign: KH6JAU
Lionel Mew
190 King Fisher Ln
Cobbs Creek VA 230350337

Call Sign: W3EDR
Richard A Graziano Sr
237 Proctor Ln
Cobbs Creek VA 23035

Call Sign: N6DEN
C William Lapworth
Providence
Cobbs Creek VA 23035

Call Sign: KK4FXL
Josiah Waldron
195 Roane Point Dr
Cobbs Creek VA 23035

Call Sign: KK4GXL
Nathanael Waldron
195 Roane Point Dr
Cobbs Creek VA 23035

Call Sign: KK4GXJ
Cassia S Waldron
195 Roane Point Dr
Cobbs Creek VA 23035

Call Sign: K3LEN
Carl T Bochau
629 Skipjack Ln
Cobbs Creek VA 23035

Call Sign: K4SXF
Luther C Farmer
Box 161 Vauxhall Rd
Cobbs Creek VA 23035

Call Sign: K1NLF
Jennifer L Graziano
Cobbs Creek VA 23035

Call Sign: KF4CDQ
Robert A May Jr
Cobbs Creek VA 23035

Call Sign: N4GHI
Geraldine G Sweeney
Cobbs Creek VA 23035

Call Sign: N6ANQ
John L Sweeney
Cobbs Creek VA 23035

FCC Amateur Radio Licenses in Coeburn

Call Sign: KF4MNR
Elmer M Kiser
Rt 2 Box 123
Coeburn VA 24230

Call Sign: KF4ABH
Alfred M Mullins
Rt 2 Box 222
Coeburn VA 24230

Call Sign: KI4AMC
Dwayne E Mullins
Rt 2 Box 244B
Coeburn VA 24230

Call Sign: KE4VBV
Delphina J Peters
Rt Hc 05 Box 604A
Coeburn VA 24230

Call Sign: KE4ACO
Betty J Barnette
Rt 1 Box 65A
Coeburn VA 24230

Call Sign: KC4UBV
Melissa A Perry
Rt 3 Box 972
Coeburn VA 24230

Call Sign: KF4LDM
Michael L Ring
7430 Caney Rd
Coeburn VA 24230

Call Sign: KE4ACL
Bradley L Barnette
6493 Caney Ridge Rd
Coeburn VA 24230

Call Sign: KK4MW
Lloyd D Elswick
6496 Caney Ridge Rd
Coeburn VA 24230

Call Sign: KF4MNS
Chris M Ring
7428 Caney Ridge Rd
Coeburn VA 24230

Call Sign: KF4MNT
Carla Y Ring
7428 Caney Ridge Rd
Coeburn VA 24230

Call Sign: KF4HXK
Phyllis A Ring
7430 Caney Ridge Rd
Coeburn VA 24230

Call Sign: W4DJP
David L Peters
5387 Dr Ralph Stanley Hwy
Coeburn VA 24230

Call Sign: WD4RJV
Leonard C Ferguson
2520 Dungannon Rd
Coeburn VA 24230

Call Sign: KG6OJQ
Sara E Young
2589 Dungannon Rd
Coeburn VA 24230

Call Sign: KG6MUS
Virgel J Young
2589 Dungannon Rd
Coeburn VA 24230

Call Sign: NR4VT
Virgel J Young
2589 Dungannon Rd
Coeburn VA 24230

Call Sign: WD4RJU
Luther W Nichols
830 E Front St
Coeburn VA 24230

Call Sign: KE4FFF
Brian N Rose
3992 Happy Hollow Rd
Coeburn VA 24230

Call Sign: KC4MTD
Mark R Hughes
E Rt 58 House 1004
Coeburn VA 24230

Call Sign: W4MJH
Eugene L Hillman
11947 Jaybird Branch Rd

Coeburn VA 242306041

Call Sign: KG4ZCN
Angela R Perry
4225 Kiser Rd
Coeburn VA 24230

Call Sign: KG4ZCO
Jonathan A Perry
4225 Kiser Rd
Coeburn VA 24230

Call Sign: KC4UBU
Geoffrey W Perry
4225 Kiser Rd
Coeburn VA 24230

Call Sign: KI4ENM
Ronnie B Yates
273 Little Brushy Rd
Coeburn VA 24230

Call Sign: KF4MNU
Bert W Ring
11407 C Lyons Fork Rd
Coeburn VA 24230

Call Sign: KB4LDF
Frank D Collins
301 May Ave
Coeburn VA 24230

Call Sign: KF4DOX
Mark R Mefford
11018A Pine Camp Rd
Coeburn VA 24230

Call Sign: KE4DQV
William L Davidson
304 Poplar Ave
Coeburn VA 24230

Call Sign: KD4JDL
Daniel F Anderson
4613 Pyramid Rd
Coeburn VA 24230

Call Sign: KE4CSE
Raymond G Roop

5805 Starnes Rd
Coeburn VA 24230

Call Sign: KE4FFE
Jason G Roop
5805 Starnes Rd
Coeburn VA 24230

Call Sign: KE4HYH
Pamela S Roop
5805 Starnes Rd
Coeburn VA 24230

Call Sign: KE4QZS
Shallon L Roop
5805 Starnes Rd
Coeburn VA 24230

Call Sign: KE4VQU
Richard E Jones
12225 Toms Creek Rd
Coeburn VA 24230

Call Sign: KE4BVX
Christena N L Cook
Coeburn VA 24030

Call Sign: AD4NZ
Dennis C Boggs Sr
Coeburn VA 24230

Call Sign: AD4OV
Clinton W Hawkins Jr
Coeburn VA 24230

Call Sign: KC4PXN
Herbert T Jones
Coeburn VA 24230

Call Sign: KD4VEX
Nolan L Kilgore
Coeburn VA 24230

Call Sign: KE4BRL
Bobby A Addington Jr
Coeburn VA 24230

Call Sign: KE4BRM
Lisa N Addington

Coeburn VA 24230

Call Sign: KE4BRN
Ella M Franks
Coeburn VA 24230

Call Sign: KE4BVW
Lester G Cook
Coeburn VA 24230

Call Sign: KE4FFC
Thomas L Jackson Jr
Coeburn VA 24230

Call Sign: KE4FUA
Warren T Jackson
Coeburn VA 24230

Call Sign: N4YDZ
Radene H Cook
Coeburn VA 24230

Call Sign: AB4YJ
James S Cook
Coeburn VA 24230

Call Sign: KB4VGQ
Patricia K Culbertson
Coeburn VA 24230

Call Sign: KB4VPG
John J Hamm
Coeburn VA 24230

Call Sign: KC4MAH
Janice M King
Coeburn VA 24230

Call Sign: KC4MAJ
Jerry W King
Coeburn VA 24230

Call Sign: KC4MEX
Robert F Stout
Coeburn VA 24230

Call Sign: KC4QAV
Mary J Collins
Coeburn VA 24230

Call Sign: KC4RGI
Frankie W Barlow Sr
Coeburn VA 24230

Call Sign: KC4VLO
Bob A Addington Sr
Coeburn VA 24230

Call Sign: KE4BRO
Threva L Boggs
Coeburn VA 24230

Call Sign: KE4ONO
Allen A Hamm
Coeburn VA 24230

Call Sign: KE4PJF
Tishia R Boggs
Coeburn VA 24230

Call Sign: KE4UUP
Kevin W Donelson
Coeburn VA 24230

Call Sign: KF4FFC
Dennis C Boggs Jr
Coeburn VA 24230

Call Sign: KF4WUS
Robert E Estep
Coeburn VA 24230

Call Sign: N4KXU
Kerry A Culbertson
Coeburn VA 24230

Call Sign: N4XGF
Robert T Barnette
Coeburn VA 24230

Call Sign: KG4ISA
Terry D Ramey
Coeburn VA 24230

Call Sign: KJ4OOS
Brian A Maiden
Coeburn VA 24230

Call Sign: KG4WZH
Karaneena B Brickey
Coeburn VA 24230

Call Sign: KI4MWD
Melvin L Wardrup
Coeburn VA 24230

Call Sign: KE4SCL
Eulane B Hamm
Coeburn VA 242301026

FCC Amateur Radio Licenses in Coleman Falls

Call Sign: KF4FYF
Lavelon C Sydnor 3Rd
Rt 1 Box 1217
Coleman Falls VA 24536

FCC Amateur Radio Licenses in Coles Point

Call Sign: KA3YLH
Samuel H Smith
Coles Point VA 22442

FCC Amateur Radio Licenses in Collinsville

Call Sign: WB4JLW
Alfred H Merrill
61 Autumn Dr
Collinsville VA 240782649

Call Sign: W4MAD
Alfred H Merrill
61 Autumn Dr
Collinsville VA 240782649

Call Sign: WA1NRQ
Thomas L Emerson
100 Burroughs White St
Collinsville VA 24078

Call Sign: WA4ACO
Thomas R Gibbs
148 Clyde Cir
Collinsville VA 24078

Call Sign: KA4SYJ
James E Headen
3236 Daniels Creek Rd
Collinsville VA 24078

Call Sign: KD4MHB
Calvin E Rains Sr
44 Fall Dr
Collinsville VA 24078

Call Sign: K4WVU
Harold O Nofsinger
774 Ferndale Dr
Collinsville VA 24078

Call Sign: N4UIV
Dwayne M Martin
1094 Hilltop Dr
Collinsville VA 24078

Call Sign: WA4RAH
James I Marshall
176 Lackey Rd
Collinsville VA 24078

Call Sign: KC4CVQ
Carole L Webb
202 Laurel Ln
Collinsville VA 24078

Call Sign: W4AAH
Frank L Webb
1192 Laurel Ln
Collinsville VA 24078

Call Sign: KJ4BPL
Randall F Glover
124 Lee St Apt 2
Collinsville VA 24078

Call Sign: KA5WMU
Randall F Glover
120 Lee St Apt B2
Collinsville VA 24078

Call Sign: W4YTY
Tarcisius A Chaput
3278 Longview Dr

Collinsville VA 24078

Call Sign: KC4GMX
James A Vaught
502 Oak Rd
Collinsville VA 24078

Call Sign: KC4SFO
John T Vaught
502 Oak Rd
Collinsville VA 24078

Call Sign: KG4YEI
James R Newman
360 Paul St
Collinsville VA 240782016

Call Sign: KE4MBB
Harold D Hawks
3134 Sunset Rd
Collinsville VA 24078

Call Sign: KC4OKS
Stephen P Kerr
712 Woodlyn Dr
Collinsville VA 24078

Call Sign: KA4NZO
Ann S Hopkins
Collinsville VA 24078

Call Sign: KC4LXA
Walter M Bondurant Jr
Collinsville VA 24078

Call Sign: KG4IXQ
John W Mayhorn
Collinsville VA 24078

Call Sign: KG4JJL
John D Hopkins
Collinsville VA 24078

Call Sign: AB4L
Cornelius D Hopkins Jr
Collinsville VA 240780337

FCC Amateur Radio Licenses in Colonial Beach

Call Sign: KD4LTE
Eugene W Reid Jr
210 2nd St
Colonial Beach VA 22443

Call Sign: KD4UUH
Ronald W Peter
149 8th St
Colonial Beach VA 22443

Call Sign: KE4JXH
Emily A Peter
149 8th St
Colonial Beach VA 22443

Call Sign: KE4CLK
Brian D Jones
Rt 1 Box 288
Colonial Beach VA 22443

Call Sign: WA4UBC
Alvin V Mountford
Rt 1 Box 443
Colonial Beach VA 22443

Call Sign: WB4LPK
William G Lee
Rt 1 Box 480
Colonial Beach VA 22443

Call Sign: KA4FCX
Edward W Kern
Rt 2 Box 842
Colonial Beach VA 22443

Call Sign: KG4BSW
Russell C Mc Cauley
212 Fairfax Dr
Colonial Beach VA 22443

Call Sign: WD4PPY
James E Travis
480 Holly Way
Colonial Beach VA 22443

Call Sign: WA2VTO
Ernest P Du Bois
1519 Irving Ave

Colonial Beach VA 22443

Call Sign: KF4TIS
Nick T Mc Daniel Sr
197 Mattox Ave
Colonial Beach VA 22443

Call Sign: N3JFP
Albert M Wurm Jr
1518 Monroe Bay Cir
Colonial Beach VA 22443

Call Sign: KD4ZPK
John H Jenkins
20735 Ridge Rd
Colonial Beach VA 22443

Call Sign: W3KI
Paul C Christie
165 Sebastian Ave
Colonial Beach VA 22443

Call Sign: KE4EV
Jacob B Waltermire Jr
462 Thompson Cir
Colonial Beach VA 22443

Call Sign: N4LKA
Kathlyn H Waltermire
462 Thompson Cir
Colonial Beach VA 22443

Call Sign: W4ACN
Jacob B Waltermire Jr
462 Thompson Cir
Colonial Beach VA 22443

Call Sign: KC4VVB
Wayne A Lloyd
Colonial Beach VA 22443

Call Sign: N3KWA
Joseph M Hammel Jr
Colonial Beach VA 224430601

**FCC Amateur Radio Licenses
in Colonial Heights**

Call Sign: KG4YJB

Rob C Turner
19306 Braebrook Dr
Colonial Heights VA 23834

Call Sign: WD4NYN
Kirby G Rakes Sr
17020 Branders Bridge Rd
Colonial Heights VA 23834

Call Sign: KG4KXU
Claire D Ellery
2 Brandywine Ct
Colonial Heights VA 23834

Call Sign: KU4AZ
Allen R Ellery
2 Brandywine Ct
Colonial Heights VA
238342161

Call Sign: KG4JDV
Richard A Ellery
2 Brandywine Ct
Colonial Heights VA
238342161

Call Sign: AG4ET
Allen R Ellery
2 Brandywine Ct
Colonial Heights VA
238342161

Call Sign: KG4VRI
Doris H Bailey
231 Breezy Hill Dr
Colonial Heights VA 23834

Call Sign: KJ4EEF
Roger L Nida Jr
98 Carroll Ave
Colonial Heights VA 23834

Call Sign: KE4CVL
Michael J Landers
2007 Circlestone Ct
Colonial Heights VA 23834

Call Sign: KE4EUE
Michael J Landers

2007 Circlestone Ct
Colonial Heights VA 23834

Call Sign: K4RUE
Barry P Mapp II
113 Clearfield Cir Apt D
Colonial Heights VA 23834

Call Sign: WB4ZEB
Horace S Whitmore
1203 Clifton Dr
Colonial Heights VA 23834

Call Sign: N4ON
Curtis E Anderson Jr
4814 Conduit Rd
Colonial Heights VA 23834

Call Sign: AA4JN
James T Navary
914 Conjurers Dr
Colonial Heights VA 23834

Call Sign: W4LKW
Stephen J Travis
1513 Creek Knoll Ct
Colonial Heights VA 23834

Call Sign: KG4OVL
Darrell L Gregg
113 Deerwood Dr
Colonial Heights VA 23834

Call Sign: W4DLG
Darrell L Gregg
113 Deerwood Dr
Colonial Heights VA
238342209

Call Sign: KB2HH
James N Heasley
419 Dick Ewell Ave
Colonial Heights VA 23834

Call Sign: KC4QOF
Floyd M Humphries
301 Fairfax Ave
Colonial Heights VA 23834

Call Sign: KC4QOG
Barbara S Humphries
301 Fairfax Ave
Colonial Heights VA 23834

Call Sign: KB4NNT
Garry K Jones
2012 Franklin Ave
Colonial Heights VA 23834

Call Sign: KD4OSV
Lewis T Monroe
3211 Glenview Ave
Colonial Heights VA 23834

Call Sign: KB4VWY
Henry R Geiger
810 Hamilton Ave
Colonial Heights VA 23834

Call Sign: KI4BKK
Matthew W Hendricks
1202 Hermitage Rd
Colonial Heights VA 23834

Call Sign: K4IEG
Ennis W Ramey
3220 Holly Ave
Colonial Heights VA 23834

Call Sign: WD4HYY
Genevieve Ramey
3220 Holly Ave
Colonial Heights VA 23834

Call Sign: N4BBX
Garred A Pelfrey
213 Honeycreek Ct
Colonial Heights VA
238341757

Call Sign: KF4IWP
Chris Coppler
14101 Howlett Line Dr
Colonial Heights VA 23834

Call Sign: KF4JUB
Christopher D Coppler
14101 Howlett Line Dr

Colonial Heights VA 23834

Call Sign: KD4YVV
Jeffrey C Seymour
203 Lafayette Ave
Colonial Heights VA 23834

Call Sign: KG4AXO
James H Maddox
806 Lafayette Ave
Colonial Heights VA 23834

Call Sign: KC4ZCI
David W Gregory
16902 Lansmill Dr
Colonial Heights VA 23834

Call Sign: KJ4WRL
Thomas R Lester
1536 Mt Pleasant Dr
Colonial Heights VA 23834

Call Sign: W3EC
William A Mason
304 Newcastle Dr
Colonial Heights VA
238342415

Call Sign: AC4IY
Mitchell E Winkle
421 Nottingham Dr
Colonial Heights VA 23834

Call Sign: KB4FFA
Donna E Wawner
1320 Oakwood Dr
Colonial Heights VA 23834

Call Sign: KD4YEL
Mitchell F Leininger
612 Old Town Dr
Colonial Heights VA 23834

Call Sign: KG4ZIN
Nell M Fisher
2510 Pine Forest Dr
Colonial Heights VA 23834

Call Sign: KF4DTV

Robert W Allen
1250 Riveroaks Dr
Colonial Heights VA 23834

Call Sign: KI4BWJ
Bradley Price
563 Riverview Rd
Colonial Heights VA 23834

Call Sign: KF4RXL
Sean P Higgins
426 Roslyn Ave
Colonial Heights VA 23834

Call Sign: AC4AF
Charles H Hibbitts
1500 Ruffin Mill Rd
Colonial Heights VA 23834

Call Sign: KG4EOC
Michael T Robbins
126A Suffolk Ave
Colonial Heights VA
238343453

Call Sign: N2GNS
Michael T Robbins
126A Suffolk Ave
Colonial Heights VA
238343453

Call Sign: KG4USJ
Robert M Tench
1209 W Roslyn Rd
Colonial Heights VA 23834

Call Sign: KF4JUC
Steve W Haskett
2211 Wakefield Av
Colonial Heights VA 23834

Call Sign: KJ4TRD
Catherine C Sebastian
1801 Walthall Creek Dr
Colonial Heights VA 23834

Call Sign: KI4NGB
Michele L Melnyk
314 Washington Ave

Colonial Heights VA 23834

Call Sign: KG4YYN
Thomas F Sweeney
305 Washington NE
Colonial Heights VA 23834

Call Sign: KC4UYV
Charles N Thompson Jr
Colonial Heights VA
238340929

FCC Amateur Radio Licenses in Columbia

Call Sign: N4MOJ
David R Young
1367 Columbia Rd
Columbia VA 23038

Call Sign: K4RCK
Travis D Cox
2620 Elk Island Rd
Columbia VA 23038

Call Sign: WD4KUK
John C Williams Sr
3001 Lowry Rd
Columbia VA 23038

Call Sign: N4EHJ
Ralph R Fetty Sr
4228 Shannon Hill Rd
Columbia VA 23038

Call Sign: W4FEG
Ralph R Fetty Sr
4228 Shannon Hill Rd
Columbia VA 23038

Call Sign: K4KKN
Homer C Waits Jr
Columbia VA 23038

FCC Amateur Radio Licenses in Concord

Call Sign: KF4WBH
Paul Mc Rae

1415 Archer Mill Rd
Concord VA 245387590

Call Sign: N4CCF
Frank J Poynter
Rr 2 Box 108P
Concord VA 24538

Call Sign: WB4YWV
Robert D Greep
Rr 2 Box 65A
Concord VA 24538

Call Sign: WA4ZNF
Stephen C Pool Sr
Rt 2 Box 7t
Concord VA 24538

Call Sign: WA4ZNG
Rosalie G Pool
Rt 2 Box 7t
Concord VA 24538

Call Sign: K4DER
William L Wheaton
101 Carriage Ln
Concord VA 24538

Call Sign: KF4RWZ
Cecil W Kidd
1950 Chestnut Mtn Rd
Concord VA 24538

Call Sign: KG4AXB
Lawrence E Randall
243 Jackson Ln
Concord VA 24538

Call Sign: KJ4EIU
Gerald B Martin
132 Kimball Rd
Concord VA 24538

Call Sign: K2YJE
William E O Donnell Sr
3999 Nowlins Mill Rd
Concord VA 24538

Call Sign: KK4BIV

Jeffrey A Lewis
394 Phoebe Pond Rd
Concord VA 24538

Call Sign: KC4MDI
Harvey G Morgan Jr
8458 Spring Mill Rd
Concord VA 24538

Call Sign: KG4POW
Michael A Rivera
10378 Spring Mill Rd
Concord VA 24538

Call Sign: KG4POQ
Miguel Rivera
10378 Springhill Rd
Concord VA 24538

Call Sign: KG4PTZ
Kenneth W Lewis Jr
377 Truline Dr
Concord VA 24538

Call Sign: K4NNW
Kenneth W Lewis Jr
377 Truline Dr
Concord VA 24538

Call Sign: WA4JJE
William E Lawrie
8274 Village Hwy
Concord VA 24538

Call Sign: WA4BJH
Marvin O Ledbetter
9634 Village Hwy
Concord VA 24538

Call Sign: KE4SVQ
Roger A Hunter Jr
117 Village Ter
Concord VA 24538

Call Sign: WA4DBK
Harvey G Morgan Sr
1293 Vineyard Rd
Concord VA 24538

Call Sign: KE4JRW
Matthew G Guthrie
Concord VA 24538

Call Sign: K6YWQ
William D Cox
Concord VA 24538

FCC Amateur Radio Licenses in Copper Hill

Call Sign: KB4TAM
Miriam P Gregory
Rt 1 Box 107E
Copper Hill VA 24079

Call Sign: KJ4WRQ
Marcus A Wanner
11308 Countyline Rd NE
Copper Hill VA 24079

Call Sign: WD4GDO
James G Gray
613 Graysville Rd
Copper Hill VA 24079

Call Sign: N3XBH
Walter L Epperly
1602 Graysville Rd
Copper Hill VA 24079

Call Sign: KE4WDO
Marvin K Beckner
9427 Sweet Annie Dr
Copper Hill VA 24079

Call Sign: KF4RFY
Sylvia L Beckner
9427 Sweet Annie Dr
Copper Hill VA 24079

Call Sign: KJ4ZKA
Bryan C Dowd
Copper Hill VA 24079

Call Sign: KJ4ZKB
Jeffrey A Dowd
Copper Hill VA 24079

FCC Amateur Radio Licenses in Corbin

Call Sign: KJ4NYG
Corbin ARC
Corbin VA 22446

Call Sign: NI4VA
Corbin ARC
Corbin VA 22446

FCC Amateur Radio Licenses in Courtland

Call Sign: WB4NTV
Kenneth J Gelhaus
30127 Country Club Rd
Courtland VA 23837

Call Sign: WB4ZNB
Ralph B Atkinson
30137 Country Club Rd
Courtland VA 23837

Call Sign: K4LAB
Linwood A Bailey
25350 Hyders Dr
Courtland VA 23837

Call Sign: KF6QXT
Kent W Daniel
25111 Oak Trl D
Courtland VA 23837

FCC Amateur Radio Licenses in Covesville

Call Sign: KF4UTB
Willie J Nichols III
Covesville VA 229310156

FCC Amateur Radio Licenses in Covington

Call Sign: N3BA
Robert C Anderson Jr
2416 Almost Heaven Rd
Covington VA 24426

Call Sign: KD4NFS
Michael L Vandevender
1001 Apache Ct
Covington VA 24426

Call Sign: KE4APW
William A Potter
2525 Bethany St
Covington VA 24426

Call Sign: KC4ZTD
Richard L Lacks
208 Big Run Rd
Covington VA 24428

Call Sign: KE4LIJ
Steve D Dawson
4409 Blue Spring Run Rd
Covington VA 24426

Call Sign: KN4AD
James R Mc Allister
Rt 1 Box 80B
Covington VA 24426

Call Sign: K4BY
Robert F Grady
209 Broken Arrow Ln
Covington VA 24426

Call Sign: KD4BAX
Stanley E Wright Jr
1101 Brookhaven Dr
Covington VA 24426

Call Sign: KE4SWO
Laura L Giles
4512 Cartwright Ln
Covington VA 24426

Call Sign: KE4TRN
Frederick J Giles
4512 Cartwright Ln
Covington VA 24426

Call Sign: N4IF
Charles F Merica
4306 Castile Rd

Covington VA 24426

Call Sign: WD4RYP
Donald A Lugar
210 Chapel Dr
Covington VA 24426

Call Sign: KB3DAY
Marcy L Brown
1301 Cherokee Pl
Covington VA 24426

Call Sign: KG4SIR
Darrell L Tucker
909 Cherokee Trl
Covington VA 24426

Call Sign: KB4UCA
Jason A Hill
1201 Cherokee Trl
Covington VA 24426

Call Sign: KC4EJE
Tamara B Hill
1201 Cherokee Trl
Covington VA 24426

Call Sign: KB4URU
Eric B Hill
1316 David Ave
Covington VA 24426

Call Sign: KE4OHW
David W Palmer
4218 Dunlap Cr Rd
Covington VA 24426

Call Sign: KG4IUF
Lewis R Mcallister
7310 Dunlap Creek Rd
Covington VA 24426

Call Sign: KE4NYF
Michael W Kelley
7717 Dunlap Crk Rd
Covington VA 24426

Call Sign: KC4ZTE
Ryland E Craft

217 E Chestnut St
Covington VA 24426

Call Sign: W4REC
Ryland E Craft
217 E Chestnut St
Covington VA 24426

Call Sign: KD4BAW
Michael W Landis
1023 E Dolly Ann Dr
Covington VA 24426

Call Sign: K4NWO
Michael W Landis
1023 E Dolly Ann Dr
Covington VA 24426

Call Sign: KN4FT
James V Whitehead Sr
203 E Gray St
Covington VA 24426

Call Sign: KE4DZY
Dwight M Rohr
347 E Gray St
Covington VA 24426

Call Sign: KE4IDL
Joseph M Rohr
347 E Gray St
Covington VA 24426

Call Sign: KE4UUI
Betty E Rohr
347 E Gray St
Covington VA 24426

Call Sign: W4SPJ
Dwight M Rohr
347 E Gray St
Covington VA 24426

Call Sign: KG4BEU
Tom J Smith III
318 E Main St
Covington VA 24426

Call Sign: KE4DDM

Joseph E Cash Jr
76 Grande Rd
Covington VA 244261374

Call Sign: KG4IHP
Joseph E Cash Jr
241 Grande Rd
Covington VA 24426

Call Sign: KE4YKF
Roy D Cary Jr
1019 Hattie St
Covington VA 24426

Call Sign: N4MLM
Arnold M Pullin
702 Highland Ave
Covington VA 24426

Call Sign: N4DCJ
Gregory C Mc Mullen
315 Horse Mtn View
Covington VA 24426

Call Sign: KG4SIQ
Clyde H Landis Jr
401 Jackson Dr
Covington VA 24426

Call Sign: KJ4FJW
Lindsay E Cartwright
4710 Johnson Creek Rd
Covington VA 24426

Call Sign: K4NJV
Zandy G De Priest
5120 Kanawha Trl
Covington VA 24426

Call Sign: K4MX
Jeri D O Rourke
1208 N Pocahontas Ave
Covington VA 24426

Call Sign: WD4RGS
Elizabeth S Johnson
807 Oneida Trl
Covington VA 24426

Call Sign: WB4CAV
Maurice L Johnson
807 Oneida Trl
Covington VA 24426

Call Sign: KD4OOQ
John D Seay
822 Oneida Trl
Covington VA 24426

Call Sign: WV4L
Wayne A Crawford
642 Overlook Dr
Covington VA 24426

Call Sign: K4DP
James S Woodson
3154 Pitzers Ridge Rd
Covington VA 24426

Call Sign: KD4OOP
Fontaine C Forbes
1115 Pocahontas Ave
Covington VA 24426

Call Sign: KC4DVI
Donna K Biggs
803 Potts Creek Rd
Covington VA 24426

Call Sign: WB4LCO
William C Biggs Jr
803 Potts Creek Rd
Covington VA 24426

Call Sign: KD4BAY
Lynda S Hill
1923 S Arden Ave
Covington VA 24426

Call Sign: KD4HJJ
Bobby L Miller
1923 S Arden Ave
Covington VA 24426

Call Sign: KB4TZS
Robert E Wood
1349 S David St
Covington VA 24426

Call Sign: W4COV
VA Mountain ARC
1349 S David St
Covington VA 24426

Call Sign: WA4PGI
Howard E Wood Jr
1349 S David St
Covington VA 244262238

Call Sign: WD4IPJ
Edith S Wood
1349 S David St
Covington VA 244262238

Call Sign: WA4HTI
Danny B Hill
1339 S Dee Ave
Covington VA 244262206

Call Sign: WD4JBC
Rhoda R Hill
1339 S Dee Ave
Covington VA 244262206

Call Sign: KE4DDN
Donald E Ross
1413 S Franklin Ave
Covington VA 24426

Call Sign: WB4BSS
Robert L Smith
1527 S Franklin Ave
Covington VA 24426

Call Sign: KC4EJD
Robin B Jennings
2910 S Greenway Dr
Covington VA 24426

Call Sign: KC4WNB
Harley R Bender
1904 S Jefferson Ave
Covington VA 24426

Call Sign: AB4WW
Roger L Pullin
1239 S Mound Ave

Covington VA 24426

Call Sign: KI4SIM
Timothy T Barbour
215 Sherry May St
Covington VA 24426

Call Sign: WD4JHW
James B Linkenhoker
2602 Valley Ridge Rd
Covington VA 24426

Call Sign: N4MOL
Gene G Pullin
2614 Valley Ridge Rd
Covington VA 24426

Call Sign: KG4IJW
Elizabeth F Ruggiero
104 W Country Club Ln
Covington VA 24426

Call Sign: KG4DYX
Joshua M Ruggiero
104 W Country Club Ln
Covington VA 244266318

Call Sign: KD4BAV
Grayson H Broce Jr
205 W Morris Hill Rd
Covington VA 24426

Call Sign: N1NP
Benjamin I Gayle
217 W Parrish St
Covington VA 24426

Call Sign: K4GKW
John C Snyder Sr
123 W Phillip St
Covington VA 24426

Call Sign: KC4JWF
David R Gwinn
448 W Riverside
Covington VA 24426

Call Sign: KB4DCW
Caroline F De Priest

102 Waller Ave
Covington VA 24426

Call Sign: KE4RTH
Roger J Kirk
109 White Rock Gap Rd
Covington VA 24426

Call Sign: KC4EJH
Francis F Clinedinst
433 Winding Way
Covington VA 244266407

Call Sign: KD4UFU
Janet W Brown
461 Winding Way
Covington VA 24426

Call Sign: K4HAJ
Janet W Brown
461 Winding Way
Covington VA 24426

Call Sign: AE4AD
Harry G Brown
461 Winding Way
Covington VA 244269026

Call Sign: KC4LSZ
Daniel F Kidd Jr
403 Woodland Rd
Covington VA 24426

Call Sign: WD4JHX
Ernest W Williams Sr
712 Wrightstown Ave
Covington VA 24426

Call Sign: KC4PTL
Gary C Hodges
Covington VA 24426

Call Sign: KE4UUH
Erskine M Cottrell Jr
Covington VA 24426

Call Sign: KJ4TOZ
Terrance D Roberts
Covington VA 24426

Call Sign: KE4ARJ
William W Faddis
Rt 1 Box 1105
Crewe VA 23930

Call Sign: KC4ALL
Terry L Reeves
Rt 2 Box 122
Crewe VA 23930

Call Sign: KC4KUK
Paul W Ashman
Rt 2 Box 510
Crewe VA 23930

Call Sign: N4VXN
William C Redman
615 E Carolina Ave
Crewe VA 23930

Call Sign: WA4NEL
Lewis H Greene Jr
505 E Pennsylvania Ave
Crewe VA 23930

Call Sign: KF4MBM
William K Warriner
107 Gatewood Ave
Crewe VA 23930

Call Sign: KF4SPW
Mary L Morris
1308 Melody Ln
Crewe VA 23930

Call Sign: W4UWL
Julius C Morris
1308 Melody Ln
Crewe VA 23930

Call Sign: KG4JII
Derrick P Fellows
507 Moncure Ave
Crewe VA 239301513

Call Sign: KG4SNO
Franklin L Reid
7324 Namozine Rd
Crewe VA 239302516

Call Sign: KB4YYT
Robert J Schnell
3553 Old Nottoway Rd
Crewe VA 239309577

Call Sign: N4VFY
Charles H Branch Jr
204 Oliver Ave
Crewe VA 23930

Call Sign: KG4QZI
Josh D Knight
307 Rock Castle Ave
Crewe VA 23930

Call Sign: KC4BTH
Edward C Mc Nett
3887 Snead Spring Rd
Crewe VA 23930

Call Sign: KI4NQT
Paul W Ashman
260 Twisted Spur Ln
Crewe VA 23930

Call Sign: N2LV
William R Huff
107 W Tennessee
Crewe VA 23930

Call Sign: KJ4YSW
Sparc ARC
110 W Tennessee Ave
Crewe VA 23930

Call Sign: KJ4YVG
Nottaway County Skywarn
110 W Tennessee Ave
Crewe VA 23930

Call Sign: KJ4YVH
Nottaway County Aries
110 W Tennessee Ave
Crewe VA 23930

Call Sign: WB3HPE
John R Aloi Sr
506 W VA Ave
Crewe VA 23930

Call Sign: WB3HTY
Celia L Aloi
506 W VA Ave
Crewe VA 23930

Call Sign: KG4PMH
John R Aloi Jr
506 W VA Ave
Crewe VA 239301742

Call Sign: KE4VOM
Russell E Wade II
1417 Woodmans Rd
Crewe VA 239304219

FCC Amateur Radio Licenses in Criders

Call Sign: K3JRR
Lawrence T Harrison Jr
23733 German River Rd
Criders VA 22820

FCC Amateur Radio Licenses in Crimora

Call Sign: KF4CZM
Thomas C Kieffer
87 Belvidere Rd
Crimora VA 24431

Call Sign: KF4BFM
James E Shoemaker
Rt 1 Box 3174
Crimora VA 24431

Call Sign: KA4EKK
Patricia R Almquist
57 Chriss Cir
Crimora VA 24431

Call Sign: W4PNT
Dee C Almquist
57 Chriss Cir
Crimora VA 24431

Call Sign: KA4NMG
Betty L Martin
145 Crimora Mine Rd
Crimora VA 24431

Call Sign: WD4HJK
Everett H Martin Jr
145 Crimora Mine Rd
Crimora VA 24431

Call Sign: KE4HVE
Kenneth W Tullis
80 Jenni Lynn Cir
Crimora VA 24431

Call Sign: KF4PFS
James T Bess
271 Lake Dr Lake Hideaway
Crimora VA 24431

Call Sign: KC4GQZ
Jerome D Almquist
Crimora VA 24431

Call Sign: KE4CKL
Walter F Johnson
Crimora VA 24431

Call Sign: N4SIH
Richard A Thompson Sr
Crimora VA 24431

FCC Amateur Radio Licenses in Critz

Call Sign: W4COX
Mitchell W Cox
641 Cedar Ln
Critz VA 24082

Call Sign: KC4HBL
Bobbi B Cox
641 Cedar Ln
Critz VA 24082

Call Sign: WB4COX

Bobbi B Cox
641 Cedar Ln
Critz VA 24082

Call Sign: KF4SGG
High Mountain RC
Critz VA 24082

Call Sign: KI4DSY
Jason S Walters
996 Crockett Rd
Crockett VA 24323

Call Sign: AI3B
Jason S Walters
996 Crockett Rd
Crockett VA 24323

Call Sign: KI4RRJ
Angel Fairbanks
159 Greek Miller Rd
Crockett VA 24323

Call Sign: KI4JPR
Douglas Fairbanks
159 Greek Miller Rd
Crockett VA 24323

Call Sign: N3EQL
Joey B Eversole
841 St Paul Church Rd
Crockett VA 24323

Call Sign: K3DJD
Donald J Duclos
1306 Bloomery Pike
Cross Junction VA 22625

Call Sign: KI4YNB
Mackenzie A Duclos
1306 Bloomery Pike
Cross Junction VA 22625

Call Sign: KD4DIG
Dale L Lund
Hc2 Box 125
Cross Junction VA 22625

Call Sign: N4RAB
Lynda M Ames
Hc3 Box 171
Cross Junction VA 22625

Call Sign: N4PBC
David G Rosen
149 Cacapon Ln
Cross Junction VA 22625

Call Sign: WB4YSQ
Ellen J Sylvester
1909 Collinsville Rd
Cross Junction VA 22621

Call Sign: WA4FJJ
Paul D Sylvester
1909 Collinsville Rd
Cross Junction VA 22625

Call Sign: KK4BQA
Stephen E Bancroft
192 Cumberland Trl Rd
Cross Junction VA 22625

Call Sign: KJ4TCA
William M Bergen III
130 Damaris Ln
Cross Junction VA 22625

Call Sign: KA4NAS
Michael J Sweeney
124 Down Hill Cir
Cross Junction VA 22625

Call Sign: KB2HLC
Robin A Streyle
150 Lake Holiday Rd
Cross Junction VA 22625

Call Sign: N2IKY
Dale G Streyle
150 Lake Holiday Rd
Cross Junction VA 22625

Call Sign: KJ4CRF
John B Platt
1084 Lakeview Dr
Cross Junction VA 22625

Call Sign: KA0TFM
Carisa A Dueweke
1096 Lakeview Dr
Cross Junction VA 22625

Call Sign: KJ4BNZ
Samuel E Morris
319 Laurel Dr
Cross Junction VA 22625

Call Sign: N4HRK
Lynda H Du Bose
8397 N Frederick Pike
Cross Junction VA 22625

Call Sign: WD4LNH
Joseph S Du Bose Jr
8397 N Frederick Pike
Cross Junction VA 22625

Call Sign: KE4YAD
Ronald E Medley
245 Wesley Chaple Ln
Cross Junction VA 22625

Call Sign: AF4GN
Victor M Franco
Cross Junction VA 22625

Call Sign: KF4NDM
Romuald N Nickles
Cross Junction VA 22625

Call Sign: KD4BZI
Nathan L Williamson
Rt 2 Box 340B
Crozet VA 22932

Call Sign: KA4IRR
Marshall A Armentrout

5511 Brookwood Rd
Crozet VA 22932

Call Sign: KI4CGJ
Patsy Crosby
5571 Brookwood Rd
Crozet VA 22932

Call Sign: K4PMC
Patsy Crosby
5571 Brookwood Rd
Crozet VA 22932

Call Sign: WD4HMW
James E Crosby
5571 Brookwood Rd
Crozet VA 229329370

Call Sign: K4JEC
James E Crosby
5571 Brookwood Rd
Crozet VA 229329370

Call Sign: KC4RRY
John M Apperson
1609 Buck Rd
Crozet VA 229322720

Call Sign: KE8DH
James R Fisher
419 Burchs Creek Rd
Crozet VA 22932

Call Sign: KI4RIW
Linda L Beard
6424 Burnt Acres Ct
Crozet VA 22932

Call Sign: KI5LLB
Linda L Beard
6424 Burnt Acres Ct
Crozet VA 22932

Call Sign: KK4EDU
Roland K Beard III
6424 Burnt Acres Ct
Crozet VA 22932

Call Sign: KK4FJY

Michael C Elliott
5020 Clearfields Ct
Crozet VA 22932

Call Sign: K4WDV
Michael C Elliott
5020 Clearfields Ct
Crozet VA 22932

Call Sign: KJ4RPV
David W Booth
1142 Greenwood Rd
Crozet VA 22932

Call Sign: KE5BTL
Thomas G Hartsell
6696 Highlander Way
Crozet VA 22932

Call Sign: W4BLL
William T Woodson Jr
4924 Jones Mill Rd
Crozet VA 229322609

Call Sign: WA4YUS
Roderick H Beitzel
5754 Myrtle St
Crozet VA 229323123

Call Sign: W1MPR
Matthew P Robertson
5459 Park Rd
Crozet VA 22932

Call Sign: KF7DOR
Kenneth O Johnson
5604 Park Rd
Crozet VA 22932

Call Sign: KC4BMR
Wendy L Morris
Pink Hill Rr 2
Crozet VA 22932

Call Sign: N3YBY
James D Stearns III
2687 Shiffletts Mill Rd
Crozet VA 22932

Call Sign: W4OUD
James R Copeland
5763 St George Ave
Crozet VA 22932

Call Sign: N4YMR
Dorsey L Thacker
5080 Still Pond Ct
Crozet VA 22932

Call Sign: AG4JM
Dorsey L Thacker
5080 Still Pond Ct
Crozet VA 22932

Call Sign: WD4LT
Dorsey L Thacker
5080 Still Pond Ct
Crozet VA 22932

Call Sign: KI4EPD
Kevin K Ward
6438 Sugar Hollow Rd
Crozet VA 22932

Call Sign: KD4EAP
Dale B Castle
2012 Vista View Ln
Crozet VA 22932

Call Sign: K5KIP
Kip R Chatterson
5950 Weston Ln
Crozet VA 22932

Call Sign: KC4OVE
Heinz J Strasser
Crozet VA 22932

Call Sign: KG4OXX
Dan Shumard
Crozet VA 22932

Call Sign: N6DJS
Dan Shumard
Crozet VA 22932

Call Sign: KI4HWH
Pamela J Burke

Crozet VA 22932

FCC Amateur Radio Licenses in Crozier

Call Sign: N4MI
Madison M Long
1975 Covington Rd
Crozier VA 230390235

Call Sign: KC4TAT
Carter C Lucas
2156 Sheppard Town Rd
Crozier VA 23039

FCC Amateur Radio Licenses in Culpeper

Call Sign: K6GSW
Daniel D Tharp
514 2nd St
Culpeper VA 22701

Call Sign: KG4JAN
Kermit H Wagner Jr
525 Azalea St
Culpeper VA 22701

Call Sign: NR3D
Kent L Slocum
20106 Batna Rd
Culpeper VA 22701

Call Sign: AF4CY
John T Berry
1278 Beahm Town Rd
Culpeper VA 22701

Call Sign: KC2ACW
Anthony T Nazzaro
1880 Blue Bell Ln
Culpeper VA 22701

Call Sign: KI4QZB
Anthony T Nazzaro
1880 Blue Bell Ln
Culpeper VA 22701

Call Sign: AI4ZH

Anthony T Nazzaro
1880 Blue Bell Ln
Culpeper VA 22701

Call Sign: WD4LHP
Henry C Lewis Jr
Rt 3 Box 126C
Culpeper VA 22701

Call Sign: N4RVW
Daniel Harrer
Rt 3 Box 137A
Culpeper VA 22701

Call Sign: KC4QFD
Luke F Harding
Rt 3 Box 195A
Culpeper VA 22701

Call Sign: KC4QFE
Justin A Harding
Rt 3 Box 195A
Culpeper VA 22701

Call Sign: KB4CUJ
Kaye B Lenn
Rfd 2 Box 243
Culpeper VA 22701

Call Sign: KC4SWH
Katie E Jenkins
Rt 2 Box 36
Culpeper VA 22701

Call Sign: KF4AFH
Lucian W Hoffman
19065 Brandy Frizz Ct
Culpeper VA 22701

Call Sign: N4YKD
Daniel L Burns III
1822 Broad St
Culpeper VA 22701

Call Sign: K4YLF
Ella M Nelles
14190 Chesterfield Ln
Culpeper VA 22701

Call Sign: KE4WKX
Jeffery L Davis
15137 Chestnut Fork Rd
Culpeper VA 22701

Call Sign: KG4GZI
Robert F Beard III III
513 Clubhouse Way
Culpeper VA 22701

Call Sign: AF4YE
Robert F Beard III
513 Clubhouse Way
Culpeper VA 22701

Call Sign: KD4FKU
Thomas J Gerhart
520 Clubhouse Way
Culpeper VA 22701

Call Sign: KC4IDL
Charles E Goslin
525 Clubhouse Way
Culpeper VA 22701

Call Sign: N9FIZ
Steven P Koeller
620 Clubhouse Way
Culpeper VA 22701

Call Sign: KB4INQ
Joseph D Martin
516 Cromwell Ct
Culpeper VA 22701

Call Sign: KF4REA
Kevin J Hales
15324 Dragonfly Ln
Culpeper VA 22701

Call Sign: KF4AFI
Morris P Hoffman
320 Duke St Apt A
Culpeper VA 22701

Call Sign: NC4JD
Robert F Beard III
823 E Piedmont St
Culpeper VA 227012835

Call Sign: KA2HRT
Michael E Babbitt
301 Elmwood Dr
Culpeper VA 22701

Call Sign: KI4DOO
Aneesa M Jones
702 Fairfax St 3
Culpeper VA 22701

Call Sign: KE4CAW
Warren D Blatz Jr
1812 Fairway Ct
Culpeper VA 22701

Call Sign: K4CAW
Warren D Blatz Jr
1812 Fairway Ct
Culpeper VA 22701

Call Sign: K4RCH
Raymond C Hansohn
15498 Fox Chase Ln
Culpeper VA 22701

Call Sign: KF4QKE
Hemant M Garg
800 Friendship Way 302
Culpeper VA 22701

Call Sign: KB2LJX
Darla L Berthold
11410 Gen Jeb Stuart Ln
Culpeper VA 22701

Call Sign: KB2LJZ
Timothy D Dilks
11410 Gen Jeb Stuart Ln
Culpeper VA 22701

Call Sign: KI4YFY
James M Wilkerson
16556 Gibson Mill Rd
Culpeper VA 22701

Call Sign: K4SFO
James M Wilkerson
16556 Gibson Mill Rd

Culpeper VA 22701

Call Sign: KB4FOU
Stephen H Osborn
14445 Glen Verdant Dr
Culpeper VA 22701

Call Sign: W4LTU
Walter F Bain
16201 Glenhollow Ct
Culpeper VA 22701

Call Sign: N3OCQ
Andrew C Ohnstad
540 Greenbriar Dr
Culpeper VA 22701

Call Sign: KG4RXN
Lee A Ohnstad
540 Greenbriar Dr
Culpeper VA 22701

Call Sign: WD5IRR
Bill W Dunn
19479 Hickory Dr
Culpeper VA 227018313

Call Sign: W5BWD
Bill W Dunn
19479 Hickory Dr
Culpeper VA 227018313

Call Sign: W4TLG
Theodore L Gausmann
507 Hitt Ct
Culpeper VA 22701

Call Sign: KF4MBC
Robert P Childress
638 Holly Crest Dr
Culpeper VA 22701

Call Sign: KK4HUT
Daniel P Conlan
715 Holly Crest Dr
Culpeper VA 22701

Call Sign: K3VB
Vincent C Braxton

9104 James Monroe Hwy
Culpeper VA 227016933

Call Sign: KJ4ZPR
Mark A Attanasio
9398 Jamesons Mill Rd
Culpeper VA 22701

Call Sign: KC4VVJ
Christine M Mroczek
430 Jenkins Ave
Culpeper VA 22701

Call Sign: KC7WAO
Matthew G Woolston
641 Keswick Dr
Culpeper VA 22701

Call Sign: WD4EHF
George R Ferrell
2402 Kirtley Trl
Culpeper VA 22701

Call Sign: KD4MVI
Walter J Barlow
210 Lakemont Dr
Culpeper VA 22701

Call Sign: KC4HLL
Joanne L Pyle
17268 Lakemont Dr
Culpeper VA 22701

Call Sign: KI4KLV
Walter J Barlow
17286 Lakemont Dr
Culpeper VA 22701

Call Sign: WA2NGV
Frank J Iacono
15461 Laurel Springs Rd
Culpeper VA 22701

Call Sign: KC4KLN
Walter M Mocarski
1101 Lee St
Culpeper VA 22701

Call Sign: KC4KLO

Edith E Mocarski
1101 Lee St
Culpeper VA 22701

Call Sign: K4EU
Stephen G Hawley
12006 Lord Willing Dr
Culpeper VA 22701

Call Sign: W4ECK
Jane M Hawley
12006 Lord Willing Dr
Culpeper VA 22701

Call Sign: WA4UAZ
Hawley Amateur Mentoring
Society
12006 Lord Willing Dr
Culpeper VA 22701

Call Sign: KD4OL
Mulford H Smith III
13457 Loyds Ln
Culpeper VA 22701

Call Sign: W4CYS
Mulford H Smith III
13457 Loyds Ln
Culpeper VA 22701

Call Sign: KA3STW
Deborah L Ray
2312 Maplewood Dr
Culpeper VA 22701

Call Sign: N1NZL
William A Scherr IV
15121 Montanus Pkwy
Culpeper VA 22701

Call Sign: KI4DJT
John A Turchi
734 Moonlight Dr
Culpeper VA 22701

Call Sign: WA3TSJ
Eric J Berty
121 Morningside Dr
Culpeper VA 22701

Call Sign: AF4ZC
Eric J Berty
121 Morningside Dr
Culpeper VA 22701

Call Sign: W3EU
Eric J Berty
121 Morningside Dr
Culpeper VA 22701

Call Sign: KC4BHW
Gary L Norman
1303 Mtn Run Lake Rd
Culpeper VA 22701

Call Sign: KC4ZBM
Charles R Cowherd
16503 Mtn Run Ln
Culpeper VA 22701

Call Sign: KC4BJD
Colby A Cowherd
16503 Mtn Run Ln
Culpeper VA 227017959

Call Sign: KC4KLQ
Laura V Cowherd
16503 Mtn Run Ln
Culpeper VA 227017959

Call Sign: KC4QFH
Mary A Cowherd
16503 Mtn Run Ln
Culpeper VA 227017959

Call Sign: KC4ZBN
Leonard M Cowherd III
16503 Mtn Run Ln
Culpeper VA 227017959

Call Sign: N4AQC
Leonard M Cowherd
16503 Mtn Run Ln
Culpeper VA 227017959

Call Sign: KD4LIN
Paul M Baker
920 N Aspen St

Culpeper VA 22701

Call Sign: KI4MNK
Christopher L Addison
510 N East St Apt 2
Culpeper VA 22701

Call Sign: KK4GWX
Adam J Gausmann
507 N Hitt Ct
Culpeper VA 22701

Call Sign: N4CY
Theodore L Gausmann
507 N Hitt Ct
Culpeper VA 22701

Call Sign: KK4VU
William E Anderson
15012 N Ridge Blvd
Culpeper VA 22701

Call Sign: N3ERZ
Scott D Smith
11413 Nether Ct
Culpeper VA 22701

Call Sign: KO4VQ
Hubert Turley
19137 Old Orange Rd
Culpeper VA 227018332

Call Sign: KI4SXP
Larry E Doyle
9383 Old Tpke Rd
Culpeper VA 22701

Call Sign: KG4JAS
Ronald J Young
11420 Pauline Ct
Culpeper VA 22701

Call Sign: KD7IWT
Michael E Duby
9288 Piedmont Springs Rd
Culpeper VA 22701

Call Sign: KG4JMZ
Tobin M Duby

9288 Piedmont Springs Rd
Culpeper VA 22701

Call Sign: KC4FWB
Rita A Simpson
1530 Queen St
Culpeper VA 22701

Call Sign: KG4YLZ
James J Vital
12217 Randle Ln
Culpeper VA 22701

Call Sign: W4WHY
Quinten C Laster
13824 Ridgelea Ave
Culpeper VA 22701

Call Sign: KE4GDX
Timothy A Dreas
14028 Ridglea Ave
Culpeper VA 22701

Call Sign: KE6TBA
Robert D Burget
966 Riverdale Cir
Culpeper VA 22701

Call Sign: KC4KLY
Richard C Hall
1742 Rolling Hills Dr
Culpeper VA 22701

Call Sign: KE4MGJ
Raymond H Hansohn
12310 Rose Cottage Ln
Culpeper VA 22701

Call Sign: KB3EZS
James C Deaver Jr
13447 Scantlin Mtn Rd
Culpeper VA 22701

Call Sign: WA4FPT
John R Benenson
13389 Scotts Mill Rd
Culpeper VA 22701

Call Sign: KJ4DGC

Thomas C Verdino
17100 Shady Ct
Culpeper VA 22701

Call Sign: KD4OGS
Fransiscus R Yulianto
670A Southview Ct
Culpeper VA 22701

Call Sign: KB4RVM
Ellis H Jenkins
1321 Sperryville Pike
Culpeper VA 22701

Call Sign: N1LSP
Karl H Knapp
11411 Sperryville Pk
Culpeper VA 22701

Call Sign: KJ4IYB
Jason L Deal
1345 Spring Meadow Ln 301
Culpeper VA 22701

Call Sign: N3UHI
Douglas R Lingenfelter
13144 Stonehouse Mtn Rd
Culpeper VA 22701

Call Sign: KE4BWD
Donald E Crow
1601 Stoneybrook Ln
Culpeper VA 22701

Call Sign: AB4N
Samuel S Yates
14394 Temple Ln
Culpeper VA 22701

Call Sign: N4SIG
Brenda J Yates
14394 Temple Ln
Culpeper VA 22701

Call Sign: W3YB
Samuel S Yates
14394 Temple Ln
Culpeper VA 22701

Call Sign: W4WQ
Samuel S Yates
14394 Temple Ln
Culpeper VA 22701

Call Sign: KX4AA
Samuel S Yates
14394 Temple Ln
Culpeper VA 22701

Call Sign: W4WQ
Samuel S Yates
14394 Temple Ln
Culpeper VA 22701

Call Sign: W4BJY
Brenda J Yates
14394 Temple Ln
Culpeper VA 22701

Call Sign: KW4SS
Samuel S Yates
14394 Temple Ln
Culpeper VA 22701

Call Sign: W4WQ
Samuel S Yates
14394 Temple Ln
Culpeper VA 22701

Call Sign: W5KD
Samuel S Yates
14394 Temple Ln
Culpeper VA 22701

Call Sign: K4KAI
Samuel S Yates
14394 Temple Ln
Culpeper VA 22701

Call Sign: KJ4NAP
Jason R Stanley
917 Terrace St
Culpeper VA 22701

Call Sign: KD4LIB
Ralph L Whalen Jr
19424 Throughfare Ln
Culpeper VA 22701

Call Sign: WD4BAB
Larry W Specht
9436 Timbertrail Ct
Culpeper VA 22701

Call Sign: NP2IL
Stephen A Cruse
305 W Asher St
Culpeper VA 22701

Call Sign: WB5QVN
Robert A Stohlman
223 W Park Ave
Culpeper VA 22701

Call Sign: K4RCG
Robert A Stohlman
223 W Park Ave
Culpeper VA 22701

Call Sign: KF4YYU
William W Platts
215 W Piedmont St
Culpeper VA 22701

Call Sign: WB4IVF
Enos H Campbell
9228 Watersedge Ln
Culpeper VA 22701

Call Sign: W3MZO
Lawrence A Neureither
12290 Waverly Pl
Culpeper VA 227014355

Call Sign: K4HE
James F Lanier
9133 White Dove Way
Culpeper VA 22701

Call Sign: KC4IZO
VA L Lanier
9133 White Dove Way
Culpeper VA 22701

Call Sign: KC8PYO
Timothy L Waltz
664 Windermere Dr

Culpeper VA 22701

Call Sign: K4CLW
Berkeley D Evans
29067 Windsor Rd
Culpeper VA 22701

Call Sign: K4CLX
Alice J Evans
29067 Windsor Rd
Culpeper VA 22701

Call Sign: KC4BCI
George H Moltz Jr
18015 Winterwood Ct
Culpeper VA 227017983

Call Sign: KU4ND
George H Moltz III
18015 Winterwood Ct
Culpeper VA 227017983

Call Sign: N4RMF
Kevin L Walton
Culpeper VA 22701

Call Sign: AB3FX
Johnathan D Mayo
Culpeper VA 22701

Call Sign: KB3NVH
Robert C Mayo
Culpeper VA 22701

FCC Amateur Radio Licenses in Cumberland

Call Sign: KE4HBK
Raymond R Williams
Rt 1 Box 43A
Cumberland VA 23040

Call Sign: WB7UWN
Michael E Tillett
45 Ruby Ln
Cumberland VA 23040

Call Sign: KI4SHB
Aaron B Hickman

55 Sports Lake Rd
Cumberland VA 23040

Call Sign: KF4MHT
Robert K Mulleins
557 Stoney Point Rd
Cumberland VA 23040

Call Sign: AA3BM
Robert K Mulleins
557 Stoney Point Rd
Cumberland VA 23040

Call Sign: KF4NZR
Brian S Kronmeister
81 Wilsion Russell Dr
Cumberland VA 230402704

Call Sign: KA4DOM
Ralph W Seal
Cumberland VA 23040

Call Sign: KG4LUK
James H Carrigan Jr
Cumberland VA 23040

FCC Amateur Radio Licenses in Dahlgren

Call Sign: KA3UOI
James H Jensen
Dahlgren VA 22448

Call Sign: KA4TDH
John H Smith
Dahlgren VA 22448

Call Sign: KB4TRV
Michael J Kramer
Dahlgren VA 22448

Call Sign: KB4TRW
Ruth E Kramer
Dahlgren VA 22448

Call Sign: KD4ATE
Brian H Cloud
Dahlgren VA 22448

Call Sign: WB1FNM
Michael E Mc Ginn
Dahlgren VA 22448

Call Sign: WJ4B
Joseph D Harrop
Dahlgren VA 22448

Call Sign: AA2FD
Robert Kenny
Dahlgren VA 22448

Call Sign: KB4FWM
William M Horton
Dahlgren VA 22448

Call Sign: KD4KLS
James A Culpepper
Dahlgren VA 22448

Call Sign: KJ4CQH
Charles E Spooner
Dahlgren VA 22448

Call Sign: WA4GGL
Charles J Hershfield Jr
Dahlgren VA 22448

Call Sign: KB6RZO
Bruce R Hewston
Dahlgren VA 224480700

FCC Amateur Radio Licenses in Dale City

Call Sign: KE4QWJ
Brian J Ford
3105 Adams St
Dale City VA 22193

Call Sign: KA2SAE
Richard O Best
3491 Beale Ct
Dale City VA 22193

Call Sign: KA4TTI
William E Hartman
3490 Bonita Ct
Dale City VA 221931419

Call Sign: AF4SK
William E Hartman
3490 Bonita Ct
Dale City VA 221931419

Call Sign: KD4WGA
Sean C Smith
15020 Cordell Ave
Dale City VA 22193

Call Sign: KA4UST
Joseph S Williams
14422 Cotton Ln
Dale City VA 22193

Call Sign: KB4CIF
Daniel De Stephanis
15229 Crescent St
Dale City VA 22193

Call Sign: KD4VZP
Harvey J Hindin
14739 Darbydale Ave
Dale City VA 22193

Call Sign: N4DXS
Stephen R Veader
14754 Darbydale Ave
Dale City VA 221931938

Call Sign: KE4QWH
Jeremy M Schwartz
3905 Del Mar Dr
Dale City VA 22193

Call Sign: N4MX
John Martinez
14804 Dillon Ave
Dale City VA 22193

Call Sign: N3XJN
Daniel J Mouer
4501 Eaton Ct
Dale City VA 22193

Call Sign: AE4DB
John E Gray
14711 Edgewater Dr

Dale City VA 22193

Call Sign: N4VCL
William B Fugitt
14730 Endsley Turn
Dale City VA 22193

Call Sign: KA3DHV
James E Hale Jr
4390 Evansdale Rd
Dale City VA 22193

Call Sign: KI4KXF
Corby T Ivey
4531 Evansdale Rd
Dale City VA 22193

Call Sign: WH6AUF
Charles M Hooke
4534 Evansdale Rd
Dale City VA 22193

Call Sign: WB5OOD
Joseph H Aldridge
14310 Fallbrook Ln
Dale City VA 22193

Call Sign: KI4VUR
Theo S Abramovich
3553 Forestdale Ave
Dale City VA 221932053

Call Sign: W3RPM
Theo S Abramovich
3553 Forestdale Ave
Dale City VA 221932053

Call Sign: KG4CGQ
James E Richardson
14219 Fullerton Rd
Dale City VA 22193

Call Sign: K4WDM
James E Richardson
14219 Fullerton Rd
Dale City VA 22193

Call Sign: KG4SGY
Lorenzo Lo Piccolo

13706 Gilbert Rd
Dale City VA 22193

Call Sign: KD4JQU
Stan R Turner Jr
4127 Glendale Rd
Dale City VA 22193

Call Sign: K9FBI
David R Morgan
4207 Glendale Rd
Dale City VA 22193

Call Sign: KC4RFM
Theresa M Moyers
4510 Glendale Rd
Dale City VA 22193

Call Sign: N4ZAF
Linda M Melia
4204 Hemingway Dr
Dale City VA 22193

Call Sign: KC4LPE
Andrea M Tidd
13702 Kaywood Dr
Dale City VA 22193

Call Sign: KI4KLX
Rita M Russell
4801 Kelly Rd
Dale City VA 22193

Call Sign: KI4EVF
Tod J Titus
4501 Kenwood Dr
Dale City VA 22193

Call Sign: N3OF
Tod J Titus
4501 Kenwood Dr
Dale City VA 22193

Call Sign: KZ5BZN
Bobby J Cook
4612 Kenwood Dr
Dale City VA 22193

Call Sign: KS4BY

Robert D Muller
4608 Kerrydale Pl
Dale City VA 22193

Call Sign: KE4DFI
Jared C Mc Elwee
13237 Kurtz Rd
Dale City VA 22193

Call Sign: KD4RFC
Kyle C Straker
13900 Lynhurst Dr
Dale City VA 221934335

Call Sign: KD4ZPE
John G Dome
5303 Macwood Dr
Dale City VA 22193

Call Sign: N0ESG
James M Murph
5281 Miles Ct
Dale City VA 22193

Call Sign: KJ4BIJ
Christine Spargur
13887 Montoclair Ln
Dale City VA 22193

Call Sign: KG4TJX
Angela D Tyson
5635 Naylor Ct
Dale City VA 22192

Call Sign: KG4DFI
Michael A Bates
5594 Neddleton Ave
Dale City VA 221934166

Call Sign: KC4FXH
Jeffrey M Smithberger
13316 Nickleson Dr
Dale City VA 22193

Call Sign: KH6JKW
Ellery D De Santo Jr
13227 Nickleson Rd
Dale City VA 22193

Call Sign: KC4NDU
Martin D Morris
6127 Plainville Ln
Dale City VA 22193

Call Sign: KI4FNB
Richard C Sudberry
6058 Ponhill Dr
Dale City VA 22193

Call Sign: KK4FMT
Joseph Johnston Jr
13401 Princedale Dr
Dale City VA 22193

Call Sign: K3EER
Clifford L Parody
13445 Princedale Dr
Dale City VA 22193

Call Sign: KG4HTM
Ashfaq Ahmad
14339 Rehfield Ct
Dale City VA 22193

Call Sign: KG4IEO
Habib Ahmad
14339 Renfield Ct
Dale City VA 22193

Call Sign: KE4VIG
Dennis J Diaz
13920 Ruler Ct
Dale City VA 22193

Call Sign: N0EUV
Milan Seifert
14360 Salsbury Ct
Dale City VA 22193

Call Sign: N3KXI
Peter V Porrello
14445 Simmons Ln
Dale City VA 221933546

Call Sign: KC4KZM
Teri D Schaeffer
4853 Tobacco Way
Dale City VA 22193

Call Sign: WD4FSB
Larry E Walker
4875 Tobacco Way
Dale City VA 22193

Call Sign: KK4CWO
James T Stocks
15492 Travailer Ct
Dale City VA 22193

Call Sign: KG4DQF
Brian D Martin
6096 Trident Ln
Dale City VA 22193

FCC Amateur Radio Licenses in Daleville

Call Sign: KI4CJA
John S Dickerson
75 Alpine Dr
Daleville VA 24083

Call Sign: KI4CJB
Shaun M Petersen
471 Azalea Dr
Daleville VA 24083

Call Sign: KE4CMY
Robby L Hogan
1823 Azalea Dr
Daleville VA 24083

Call Sign: KG4HEE
Betsy C Robison
471 Azalea Rd
Daleville VA 24083

Call Sign: KG4FPA
Kirk E Robison
471 Azalea Rd
Daleville VA 24083

Call Sign: AI4EX
Kirk E Robison
471 Azalea Rd
Daleville VA 24083

Call Sign: N4HNR
Vernon Schultz
Rt 1 Box 487
Daleville VA 24083

Call Sign: N4OII
Charles S Mc Neill III
Rt 2 Box 92
Daleville VA 24083

Call Sign: KI4ZNE
Scott A Johnston
130 Butler Ct
Daleville VA 24083

Call Sign: K4AON
Wilbur L Newcomb
225 Camellia Dr
Daleville VA 240833503

Call Sign: WD4DUY
Steve E Nation
28 Daleview Dr
Daleville VA 240832684

Call Sign: KS3H
Larry G Dennis
460 Glebe Rd
Daleville VA 24083

Call Sign: KK4KX
Robert R Warner
246 Harvest Ln
Daleville VA 24083

Call Sign: K4CGP
Stephen N Gillespie
109 Ivy Ln
Daleville VA 24083

Call Sign: KD7UWJ
Jeffery A Anzaldi
44 Kingston Dr 132
Daleville VA 240832574

Call Sign: KJ4QOE
Austin B Warren
39 Pinehurst Dr
Daleville VA 24083

Call Sign: WA4RJJ
Robert C Patten
1930 Roanoke Rd
Daleville VA 24083

Call Sign: WB4RKO
Jerry L Wilkinson
2444 Roanoke Rd
Daleville VA 24083

Call Sign: KO4SD
Harold N Klaser Jr
21 Stonewall Dr
Daleville VA 240833185

Call Sign: N4FTN
John S Garman Jr
110 Summit Ridge Rd
Daleville VA 24083

Call Sign: KJ4WYI
Kevin P Hines
28 Winthrop Pl
Daleville VA 24083

FCC Amateur Radio Licenses in Damascus

Call Sign: KD4NGK
Fred R Badger
22381 Alvarado Rd
Damascus VA 24236

Call Sign: WA4KBE
Ralph L Garrett
Rt 1 Box 176
Damascus VA 24236

Call Sign: N4RJJ
David C Patrick
Rt 1 Box 59
Damascus VA 24236

Call Sign: KI4AAZ
Walter L Baldree
826 S Beaver Dam Ave
Damascus VA 242361102

Call Sign: KF4UMO
James B Thrasher
115 W Laurel Ave Apt A
Damascus VA 24236

FCC Amateur Radio Licenses in Dann Loring

Call Sign: KG4TSZ
Thomas P Lennertz
7927 Tire Swing Rd
Dann Loring VA 22027

FCC Amateur Radio Licenses in Dante

Call Sign: KE4ACM
Amanda D Diets
Hc 67 Box 179A
Dante VA 24237

Call Sign: KA4AGU
William E Litton
Hc 67 Box 222
Dante VA 24237

Call Sign: KE4ZAN
Carmella L Counts
Hc 67 Box 321
Dante VA 24237

Call Sign: KS4WP
Danny M Counts
Hc 67 Box 321
Dante VA 24237

Call Sign: KF4DWD
Carlos E Perkins
355 Cigarette Hollow
Dante VA 24237

Call Sign: KF4OLS
Janet A Perkins
355 Cigarette Hollow
Dante VA 24237

Call Sign: KC4PWC
Robert A Diets
Rt 657 Hazel Mtn Rd

Dante VA 24237

Call Sign: KC4RFJ
Bessie L Powers
Rt 657 Hazel Mtn Rd
Dante VA 24237

Call Sign: KC4DX
Donald R Powers Jr
Hazel Mtn Rd
Dante VA 24237

Call Sign: W4AMR
Ardel E Shreve
Box 634 Roanoke Hill
Dante VA 24237

Call Sign: KC4RDG
Glen H Diets
Dante VA 24237

Call Sign: KG4RXJ
Adam L Powers
Dante VA 24237

Call Sign: KG4SGL
Aaron C Powers
Dante VA 24237

Call Sign: N4ZBR
James T Cline Sr
Dante VA 24237

FCC Amateur Radio Licenses in Danville

Call Sign: N4QCI
Todd A Turner
566 Arlington Rd
Danville VA 24541

Call Sign: WD4BXR
Bruce L Hutcheson Jr
738 Arlington Rd
Danville VA 24541

Call Sign: WD4HXV
Betty T Hutcheson
738 Arlington Rd

Danville VA 245414906

Call Sign: KC4YRF
Steven S Hendrickson
314 Arnett Blvd
Danville VA 24540

Call Sign: KC4KJR
Jackie D Hill
901 Arnett Blvd
Danville VA 24540

Call Sign: KM4GG
Errol D Morton III
411 Avondale Dr
Danville VA 24541

Call Sign: K4FNA
Walter E Singleton Jr
208 Bailey Pl
Danville VA 24540

Call Sign: K4OAK
Charles E Jones
74 Baltimore Ave
Danville VA 24541

Call Sign: K4FNF
Horton L Pribble
684 Berry Hill Rd
Danville VA 245419759

Call Sign: N2JTM
Jean G Fee
Rte 5 Box 1060 Ridgecrest Dr
Danville VA 24540

Call Sign: KA4UDM
Garland D Eaton
Rt 6 Box 1495
Danville VA 24541

Call Sign: KE4NDY
Michael S Pritchett
Rt 6 Box 1557
Danville VA 24541

Call Sign: KD4RUY
Michael T Barker

Rt 8 Box 322
Danville VA 24540

Call Sign: KI4LEW
Craig K Wilkes
138 Broad St
Danville VA 24541

Call Sign: KI4KEN
Ronald L Martin
112 Brook Cir
Danville VA 24541

Call Sign: KF4JPV
Fred R Turner Jr
184 Camberth Dr 10
Danville VA 24541

Call Sign: KM4XF
Eric S Harvey
130 Cambridge Cir
Danville VA 24541

Call Sign: KJ4BPJ
Jettie S Towler
1112 Campview Rd
Danville VA 24540

Call Sign: K4UO
William E Carson
165 Canterbury Rd
Danville VA 24541

Call Sign: W4EGA
Charles S Bumgarner Jr
206 Cathy Dr
Danville VA 24540

Call Sign: W4MAV
J Mike Harris
615 Clairborne St
Danville VA 245403265

Call Sign: KG4MYC
Alan T Pinekenstein
153 Clarendon Cir
Danville VA 24541

Call Sign: KB4NCN

Clarence A Edmonds
313 Clover Ln
Danville VA 24540

Call Sign: KJ4TAX
Jeffrey B Lance
124 Coleman St
Danville VA 24540

Call Sign: KG4MEQ
Clay R Mullins II
3325 Conrad Ct
Danville VA 24540

Call Sign: WB4ZGP
William J Erwin Jr
2 Creekside Dr
Danville VA 24541

Call Sign: KI4KAU
David E Hyler
332 Deercrest Ln
Danville VA 24541

Call Sign: KE4DH
Lemuel M Nash
781 Deercrest Ln
Danville VA 245419326

Call Sign: KD4OMD
John R Shanks
336 Dogwood Dr
Danville VA 24541

Call Sign: K2CAS
Harold Evans
168 Dogwood Ln
Danville VA 24540

Call Sign: N8NDA
Henry H Dempsey
616 Dover Pl
Danville VA 24541

Call Sign: K4GL
Central Va Dx And Contest
Club
140 Dovie Ct
Danville VA 24541

Call Sign: KU4VY
Carl A Mc Intire III
140 Dovie Ct
Danville VA 24541

Call Sign: KA4KEG
Luke E Lassiter
563 Downing Dr
Danville VA 24541

Call Sign: NI4E
Max E Lassiter
563 Downing Dr
Danville VA 24541

Call Sign: N4QCH
Eugene W Barker Sr
582 Elizabeth St Ext
Danville VA 245417211

Call Sign: KE4VSB
Mitchell R Childrey
2953 Finch Dr
Danville VA 24540

Call Sign: KF4HUC
Emily V Ware
2953 Finch Dr
Danville VA 24540

Call Sign: KA4KGL
James W Shelton
104 Forestroad Dr
Danville VA 24540

Call Sign: KC3PJ
William R Gardner
145 Foxberry Ln
Danville VA 24541

Call Sign: KI4KAO
Madlyn M Gauldin
473 Gemstone Ln
Danville VA 24541

Call Sign: K4QIZ
James T De Boe
130 Gilliland Dr

Danville VA 24541

Call Sign: WB4RAF
Dale F Watson
14 Glen Oak Dr
Danville VA 24541

Call Sign: N4WTG
Barry L Parker
98 Glen Oak Dr
Danville VA 24541

Call Sign: KD4FJW
Betty M Wells
831 Glendale Ave
Danville VA 24540

Call Sign: K4NKW
Norma K Williams
123 Grandin Ct
Danville VA 24541

Call Sign: KC4AO
Michael K Williams
123 Grandin Ct
Danville VA 24541

Call Sign: KC4CIG
Barbara M George
127 Greencroft Pl
Danville VA 24541

Call Sign: AB4FZ
James L Bond
1204 Greenwood Ave
Danville VA 24541

Call Sign: N4RNQ
Etta J Bond
1204 Greenwood Ave
Danville VA 24541

Call Sign: N4WST
Michael H Bond
1204 Greenwood Ave
Danville VA 24541

Call Sign: KE4YUE
Edward W Fisher Jr

235 Grove Park Cir
Danville VA 24541

Call Sign: KE4NDZ
Harold W Evans
240 Hamlin Ave
Danville VA 24540

Call Sign: WD4BWL
David G Emerson
425 Haynesworth Dr
Danville VA 24541

Call Sign: KE4NEA
Mario J Doggett
219 Hermitage Dr
Danville VA 24541

Call Sign: N4YHR
Charles A Wells
319 Hillcrest Ave
Danville VA 24540

Call Sign: KD4AEN
Carroll D Hensley
813 Holland Rd
Danville VA 24541

Call Sign: KI4KAK
Eddie R Walker
4352 Horseshoe Rd
Danville VA 24541

Call Sign: KI4KAF
Geraldine S Walker
4352 Horseshoe Rd
Danville VA 24541

Call Sign: KI4KAG
Elizabeth Shorter
4400 Hoseshoe Rd
Danville VA 24541

Call Sign: WA4CNE
Alton L Corpening Jr
15 Howeland Cir
Danville VA 24541

Call Sign: WD4BLE

William O Watts
135 Howeland Cir
Danville VA 24541

Call Sign: KE4WQI
Laura Y Snead
1640 Hunting Hills Rd
Danville VA 24540

Call Sign: NZ4H
William R Snead III
1640 Hunting Hills Rd
Danville VA 24540

Call Sign: KD4MWM
Alma J Hurst
448 Iris Ln
Danville VA 24540

Call Sign: WA4UFU
Mildred E Davidson
500 Iris Ln
Danville VA 24540

Call Sign: N4DBX
James R Davidson Jr
520 Iris Ln
Danville VA 24540

Call Sign: N4XFP
William R Meigs
615 Jackson Hts
Danville VA 245401051

Call Sign: K4HRJ
Bill B Motley
406 Kemper Rd
Danville VA 24541

Call Sign: AE4WG
George W Astin
3516 Laniers Mill Rd
Danville VA 24540

Call Sign: K4WWI
Thomas S Taylor
346 Laurelwoods Dr
Danville VA 24540

Call Sign: WA4HBH
Robert C Hunt Jr
1640 Leemont Ct
Danville VA 24541

Call Sign: KT4HS
Brett Parrish
1063 Linden Ln
Danville VA 24541

Call Sign: K4EWH
Dalton R Taylor
152 Longview Dr
Danville VA 24541

Call Sign: N4AE
Paschal L Anderson Jr
428 Maple Ln
Danville VA 24541

Call Sign: N4KYC
Samuel P Cobb
149 Marshall Ter
Danville VA 245412806

Call Sign: KG4KTX
Matthew B Biggs
146 Martindale Dr
Danville VA 24541

Call Sign: KD4SSF
Charles W Keen
122 McLaughlin Dr
Danville VA 24540

Call Sign: KB4NLT
Edward De Miller
130 Meadowbrook Dr
Danville VA 24540

Call Sign: KD4FJX
Alice L De Miller
130 Meadowbrook Dr
Danville VA 24540

Call Sign: KI4KAP
Linda R Mills
101 Medical Center Rd
Danville VA 24540

Call Sign: KE4SIH
Butch Mann
775 Melrose Ave
Danville VA 24540

Call Sign: KB4NTK
Charles G Roach Jr
823 Melrose Ave
Danville VA 24540

Call Sign: KG4ZEZ
Royce B Agee
806 Melville Ave
Danville VA 245402208

Call Sign: KC4LIM
Deborah S Barker
3104 Moorefield Bridge Rd
Danville VA 245418340

Call Sign: KI4KAV
Pearl D Harris
1119 N Main St
Danville VA 24540

Call Sign: KB4KPR
Joseph L Dickerson
2912 N Main St
Danville VA 24540

Call Sign: N4LMG
Roger H Lea
111 Naples St
Danville VA 24541

Call Sign: K4QNL
Glen A Williamson
372 Norwood
Danville VA 24540

Call Sign: KI4KOO
James E Davis
380 Oakwood Dr
Danville VA 24541

Call Sign: WB4HVZ
Robert S Shumate
2481 Old Mayfield Rd

Danville VA 24541

Call Sign: KI4KAH
James S Mauldin
403 Old Spring Rd
Danville VA 24540

Call Sign: KB4PX
Carl E Manasco
1614 Olde Hunting Trl
Danville VA 24540

Call Sign: WA4HBI
William C Drumwright
139 Orchard Dr
Danville VA 24541

Call Sign: KF4FBE
Thomas O Ruhland
552 Parker Rd
Danville VA 24540

Call Sign: KE4BRW
Kenneth A Latchum
563 Parker Rd
Danville VA 24540

Call Sign: K6GLJ
Eugene F Boaz
526 Parkland Dr
Danville VA 24540

Call Sign: KD4PGM
La Juana L Manasco
1105 Piney Forest Rd
Danville VA 24540

Call Sign: KJ4VEU
Sammy L Quarles
479 Princeton Rd
Danville VA 24541

Call Sign: KU4I
David A Hart
146 Reese Dr
Danville VA 24540

Call Sign: KI4YCK
Philip M Dorsey

104 Reid Ct
Danville VA 24540

Call Sign: W4AKL
Clayton B Reed
113 Riceland St
Danville VA 24540

Call Sign: N4WSM
Wesley S Mc Bride
6171 Riverside Dr Apt D4
Danville VA 24541

Call Sign: KG4EOZ
Wesley S Mc Bride
154 Robinwood Pl
Danville VA 24540

Call Sign: WA4EHB
William U Schwarz
803 Rosemary Ln
Danville VA 24541

Call Sign: N4QCJ
Sharon S Marshall
520 S Woodberry Ave
Danville VA 24540

Call Sign: W4XQ
William R Woodle
102 Schoolfield Dr
Danville VA 24541

Call Sign: KC4YKG
Peter A George III
212 Sedgefield Ln
Danville VA 24541

Call Sign: WB4QZN
Dorothy T Reynolds
416 Skyline Ave
Danville VA 24540

Call Sign: K4YZR
Glenwood D Reynolds
416 Skyline Ave
Danville VA 245401926

Call Sign: KI4KAR

Al R Hill Jr
911 I Springfield Rd
Danville VA 24540

Call Sign: KA4DWH
David W Hartman
116 Still Spring Dr
Danville VA 24541

Call Sign: KI4QJF
David W Hartman
116 Still Spring Rd
Danville VA 24541

Call Sign: KI4RNT
Keith A Moore
1053 Stoney Mill Rd
Danville VA 24540

Call Sign: KB2FVV
James H Van Ornum
1009 Stony Mill Rd
Danville VA 24540

Call Sign: KA2LEF
Leonard A Bernstein
308 Sutherlin Pl
Danville VA 24541

Call Sign: KC4FYQ
David C Parrott
315 Swain Dr
Danville VA 24540

Call Sign: N4QBC
Curtis E Fain
143 Tamworth Dr
Danville VA 24540

Call Sign: W4AYB
Kermit F White
644 Timber Lake Dr
Danville VA 24540

Call Sign: KU4TJ
Ronald W Williams Jr
332 Updike Pl
Danville VA 24541

Call Sign: KF4CIM
John L Losee
237 VA Ave
Danville VA 24541

Call Sign: KF4ENY
Kimberly A Losee
237 VA Ave
Danville VA 24541

Call Sign: K4WWA
Earl T Conner Jr
1095 Walnut Creek Rd
Danville VA 24540

Call Sign: N4XNI
Larry Scott
1425 Walnut Creek Rd
Danville VA 24540

Call Sign: KF4JDT
Samuel F Myers
209 Washburn Dr
Danville VA 24541

Call Sign: KF4JDV
Dan P Myers
209 Washburn Dr
Danville VA 24541

Call Sign: WA4API
Hugh J Soyars
4515 Westover Dr
Danville VA 24541

Call Sign: KB3CLJ
Raymond E Bell
4530 Westover Dr
Danville VA 24541

Call Sign: KJ4RL
Harold W Mustain Sr
700 Westridge Dr
Danville VA 24541

Call Sign: KB4JPE
John D Hudson Sr
114 Wheatley Rd
Danville VA 24540

Call Sign: WA4TRG
Gene T Morris
424 Williamson Rd
Danville VA 24541

Call Sign: N4QCK
A Earle Garrett III
119 Winston Ct
Danville VA 24541

Call Sign: KD4CRN
Joseph D Wooten
2035 Woodlake Dr
Danville VA 24540

Call Sign: WA6RZI
Mark W Welch
432 Woodlawn Dr
Danville VA 24541

Call Sign: N4BLG
Leonard M Tiller
200 Woodside Rd
Danville VA 24541

Call Sign: W4NSX
Pete M Wilson
311 Woodside Rd
Danville VA 24540

Call Sign: KB4BRA
Job J G Reynolds
502 Worsham St
Danville VA 24540

Call Sign: KE4EDO
Maynard W Sandridge Jr
Danville VA 24541

Call Sign: KN4UN
Charles C Swain
Danville VA 24543

Call Sign: W4RKM
Douglas L Motley
Danville VA 24541

Call Sign: KG4QLT

George A Crowell
Danville VA 24543

Call Sign: AD4AX
Marvin E Wilborne III
Danville VA 245430479

Call Sign: KC4CPU
Mark Kevin Wolf Mcsherry
Danville VA 245435001

Call Sign: W0LFM
M K Wolf Mcsherry
Danville VA 245435001

FCC Amateur Radio Licenses in Davenport

Call Sign: KC4VXQ
Randy C Breeding
Davenport VA 24239

FCC Amateur Radio Licenses in Dayton

Call Sign: KG4YLE
Bradley C Anderson
7181 Autumn View Dr
Dayton VA 22821

Call Sign: KA4EEH
Marvin E Ulrich
Rt 3 Box 100
Dayton VA 22821

Call Sign: W4BRH
James T Landram Jr
Rt 1 Box 221
Dayton VA 22821

Call Sign: KE4EXG
Clint E Showalter
Rt 3 Box 40
Dayton VA 22821

Call Sign: KA4EEG
Lowell E Ulrich
Rt 3 Box 99
Dayton VA 22821

Call Sign: KD4AGL
Robert G Plaugher
7511 Briery Branch Rd
Dayton VA 22821

Call Sign: KK4BPF
Jonathan B Cromer
1219 Clover Hill Rd
Dayton VA 22821

Call Sign: KI4HIQ
Chad D Stover
3124 Clover Hill Rd
Dayton VA 22821

Call Sign: KI4HIP
Clay P Shiplet
3128 Clover Hill Rd
Dayton VA 22821

Call Sign: KD4AGM
La Dawn F Knicely
3667 Dry Hollow Rd
Dayton VA 22821

Call Sign: KJ4BXP
George W Arey
9866 Jess Arey Ln
Dayton VA 22821

Call Sign: KA4NVE
Rose E Flory
3269 Limestone Ln
Dayton VA 22821

Call Sign: K4FSU
Seymour Paul
8147 Ottobine Rd
Dayton VA 22821

Call Sign: WD4HVM
Robert M Weaver
2047 W Dry River Rd
Dayton VA 22821

Call Sign: KE4LLL
Peter L Hartzler
4475 Woodcock Ln

Dayton VA 22821

Call Sign: KD4OCN
Jonathan E Hartzler
4475 Woodcock Ln
Dayton VA 22821

Call Sign: N4MQR
Ralph J Alger
Dayton VA 22821

FCC Amateur Radio Licenses in Deerfield

Call Sign: KI4CQQ
Carson R Ralston
3441 Deerfield Valley Rd
Deerfield VA 24432

Call Sign: KE4BVP
Tama M Bird
Deerfield VA 24432

FCC Amateur Radio Licenses in Delaplane

Call Sign: KG4VEM
Michael A Potter
10205 Cobbler Ln
Delaplane VA 20144

Call Sign: WA1DYR
Charles H Mitchell
3806 Cobbler Mt Rd
Delaplane VA 201442105

Call Sign: KD4UQJ
William F Owens Jr
3574 Cobbler Mtn Rd
Delaplane VA 20144

Call Sign: KI4JSD
Kevin W Rose
11173 Oak View Rd
Delaplane VA 20144

Call Sign: KI4BTR
Tree Bangers Field Day Society
10230 Stillhouse Rd

Delaplane VA 20144

Call Sign: KA1TB
John L D Ausilio
10230 Stillhouse Rd
Delaplane VA 20144

FCC Amateur Radio Licenses in Deltaville

Call Sign: K4GZE
Robert P Mason
Hcr 01 Box 444
Deltaville VA 23043

Call Sign: WD4NIL
Thomas L Thompson
32 Cardinal Trl
Deltaville VA 23043

Call Sign: KI4CVT
Cornelia Grothe
144 Dogfish Ln Cove
Deltaville VA 23043

Call Sign: WB4IMX
William J Ulrich
353 Farmers Dell Ln
Deltaville VA 23043

Call Sign: N1IOR
Louis L Abernethy
29 Harbor Dr
Deltaville VA 230430012

Call Sign: K1HDR
Christopher J Woodbury
52 Netties Ln
Deltaville VA 230430633

Call Sign: KC4QHP
Anthony G Evans
Rt 1105
Deltaville VA 23043

Call Sign: KD4KWS
Cheryl A Evans
Rt 1105
Deltaville VA 23043

Call Sign: KG4WPN
Pierre M Trehard
1224 Timberneck Rd
Deltaville VA 23043

Call Sign: KC4EGV
Susan H Golembicki
Deltaville VA 23043

Call Sign: KC4EWY
Ethel M Musbach
Deltaville VA 23043

Call Sign: KC4ZCB
Donald L Arendt
Deltaville VA 23043

Call Sign: KC4ZCC
Robert J Golembicki
Deltaville VA 23043

Call Sign: KD4LLE
William D Mc Kee
Deltaville VA 23043

Call Sign: KD4QMD
Robert C Livingstone
Deltaville VA 23043

Call Sign: KE4LRB
Maude M Walker
Deltaville VA 23043

Call Sign: WA1MDY
Milton W Musbach
Deltaville VA 23043

Call Sign: AD4VI
Peter W D Wright
Deltaville VA 23043

Call Sign: KB4JGN
Thomas F Kelsey Jr
Deltaville VA 23043

Call Sign: KF4LCU
Pamela D Wright
Deltaville VA 23043

Call Sign: KI4HNH
Stuart F Wallace
Deltaville VA 23043

Call Sign: KK4HJW
Elizabeth M Elliott
Deltaville VA 23043

Call Sign: KB2FQF
John J Neill
Deltaville VA 23043

Call Sign: KF4ZBT
William A Pinekenstien
Deltaville VA 23043

FCC Amateur Radio Licenses in Dendron

Call Sign: N4IAR
Lyle A Hedden
471 Azalea Ln
Dendron VA 238392405

Call Sign: WD4EIQ
Louis E Conary
2194 Colonial Trl W
Dendron VA 23839

Call Sign: KK4HLO
Douglas A Leidy
Dendron VA 23839

FCC Amateur Radio Licenses in Dewitt

Call Sign: N2AQY
Robert G Hardy
11407 Patillo Rd
Dewitt VA 23840

Call Sign: KE4CIO
William A Edwards Sr
12817 White Oak Rd
Dewitt VA 23840

Call Sign: KF4TMY
Gladys P Edwards

12817 White Oak Rd
Dewitt VA 23840

Call Sign: KJ4RQJ
Chris A Herb
14355 Wilkinson Rd
Dewitt VA 23840

Call Sign: KJ4VFH
George A Herb
14355 Wilkinson Rd
Dewitt VA 23840

FCC Amateur Radio Licenses in Dillwyn

Call Sign: KG4MPO
James C Legrand
850 Back Mtn Rd
Dillwyn VA 23936

Call Sign: KF4EGI
Frank A Cowan Jr
Rt 3 Box 109
Dillwyn VA 23936

Call Sign: KE4OSE
Ronald W Senger
Rt 3 Box 152A
Dillwyn VA 23936

Call Sign: KD4EJE
Karen A Dulaney
Rr 2 Box 7190
Dillwyn VA 23936

Call Sign: K4HIP
Harold T Scott
Rt 2 Box 9160
Dillwyn VA 23936

Call Sign: KI4BBO
Josh D Powell
838 Main St
Dillwyn VA 23936

FCC Amateur Radio Licenses in Dinwiddie

Call Sign: KB3UEZ
React International Inc
12114 Botdton Plank Rd
Dinwiddie VA 23841

Call Sign: KD4EET
Steve Pories
18804 Carson Rd
Dinwiddie VA 23841

Call Sign: KD4KAQ
Darryl M Wrenn
23411 Carson Rd
Dinwiddie VA 23841

Call Sign: KF4IKE
William M Bullock
Dinwiddie VA 23841

FCC Amateur Radio Licenses in Disputanta

Call Sign: KA4TZE
Robert B Dyer Sr
Rt 2 Box 236X
Disputanta VA 23842

Call Sign: KF4ONT
Richard J Wagner
9600 Golf Course Dr
Disputanta VA 23842

Call Sign: KE4OFO
Charles R Arnold
9714 Golfcourse Dr
Disputanta VA 23842

Call Sign: KF4LOV
Richard B ARCher
5730 Hair Rd
Disputanta VA 23842

Call Sign: KC4GHR
Ray F Leptic
13600 Hines Rd
Disputanta VA 23842

Call Sign: W4WJJ
Everett E Worrell Jr

8004 Holdsworth Rd
Disputanta VA 238427127

Call Sign: KJ4JPS
Mark W Warthan
15220 James River Dr
Disputanta VA 23842

Call Sign: AA4XD
James D Kanak
9801 Kanak Dr
Disputanta VA 23842

Call Sign: KD4KWV
Linda C Collins
18461 Loving Union Rd
Disputanta VA 23842

Call Sign: KI4AER
John J Seckora Sr
18461 Loving Union Rd
Disputanta VA 23842

Call Sign: KF4HGT
Hilal S Syouf
4501 Pamela Dr
Disputanta VA 23842

Call Sign: WA4QFP
William F Gandel
14216 Pole Run Rd
Disputanta VA 238428417

Call Sign: KG4WUR
Forest N Motto
12822 Prince George Dr
Disputanta VA 23842

Call Sign: KE4YSO
Michael S Pond
9410 Springfield Ln
Disputanta VA 23842

FCC Amateur Radio Licenses in Doe Hill

Call Sign: KG4APB
Leonidas M Schwartz
Rt 1 Box 138

Doe Hill VA 24433

FCC Amateur Radio Licenses in Dolphin

Call Sign: KJ4QKH
William C Poulton
46 Peaceable Kingdom Dr
Dolphin VA 23843

FCC Amateur Radio Licenses in Doran

Call Sign: KE4MHM
Lewis L Campbell
Doran VA 24612

FCC Amateur Radio Licenses in Doswell

Call Sign: KD4CPX
Kristin A Swain
15092 King Rd
Doswell VA 23047

Call Sign: KD4KYS
Michael D Mc Makin
15046 Melody Hills Dr
Doswell VA 230472075

Call Sign: KC4YVJ
Patrick O Brady Jr
12436 Noel Rd
Doswell VA 23047

Call Sign: KF4IUC
Clarice T Oldham
12276 Welling Hall Rd
Doswell VA 23047

Call Sign: KS4LB
Robert W Oldham
12276 Welling Hall Rd
Doswell VA 23047

Call Sign: W2MG
Martin N Gary
16261 Winding Trl
Doswell VA 23047

FCC Amateur Radio Licenses in Drakes Branch

Call Sign: WB4BDC
William M Firestone Jr
300 Cake Ln
Drakes Branch VA 23937

Call Sign: KI4FQN
S Marlene Gilliam
6761 Westpoint Stevens Rd
Drakes Branch VA 23937

Call Sign: WB1HAC
Roland W Poitras
Drakes Branch VA 23937

Call Sign: KI4GIG
Charlotte County ARC
Drakes Branch VA 23937

FCC Amateur Radio Licenses in Draper

Call Sign: KB4KGK
Effie Hasson
Rt 1 Box 299
Draper VA 24324

Call Sign: KB4TXG
Dorothy S Hasson
Rt 1 Box 299
Draper VA 24324

Call Sign: WB4IVE
Albert Pugh
Rt 1 Box 397F
Draper VA 24324

Call Sign: K4ISB
Milton N Aust
3830 Draper Valley Rd
Draper VA 24324

Call Sign: KB4TVC
Brenda B Aust
3830 Draper Valley Rd
Draper VA 243243701

Call Sign: KI4GXM
Bruce A Martin
2531 Forest Hill Dr
Draper VA 24324

Call Sign: WB4NSF
David F Pohlig
3560 Sayers Rd
Draper VA 24324

Call Sign: WD5HLO
Franklin M Caldwell
1737 Wysor Hwy
Draper VA 243243009

Call Sign: K4HZS
William E Mc Neely
3028 Wysor Hwy
Draper VA 24324

Call Sign: KB4FHW
Carmine A Di Nitto
2758 Wysor Rd
Draper VA 24324

Call Sign: KG4AMC
Larry J Martin Sr
Draper VA 24324

Call Sign: KG4CAL
Teena P Martin
Draper VA 24324

FCC Amateur Radio Licenses in Dry Fork

Call Sign: KC4YRG
Maurice A Twilley
Rt 2 Box 185C
Dry Fork VA 24549

Call Sign: WB4YIG
Glenn A Kirks
Rt 2 Box 55A
Dry Fork VA 24549

Call Sign: KI4EJP
Natalie P Welker

640 F C Beverly Rd
Dry Fork VA 24549

Call Sign: KJ4SNU
Edward Schnell Jr
14118 Franklin Tnpk
Dry Fork VA 24549

Call Sign: KJ4NSL
Andrea E Robbins
14688 Franklin Tpke
Dry Fork VA 24549

Call Sign: KJ4NSK
VA R Hylton
217 Hylton Ln
Dry Fork VA 24549

Call Sign: K4USV
Michael H Pruitt
540 Junior Oaks Rd
Dry Fork VA 24549

Call Sign: KG4IXR
David J Morgan
241 Olde Shoppe Rd
Dry Fork VA 24549

Call Sign: K4MZ
David J Morgan
241 Olde Shoppe Rd
Dry Fork VA 24549

Call Sign: KI4JWD
Susan M Morgan
241 Olde Shoppe Rd
Dry Fork VA 24549

Call Sign: KB4OGG
Ruby S Stoots
1025 W I Powell Rd
Dry Fork VA 245499628

Call Sign: WD4AWL
Willard H Stoots
1025 W I Powell Rd
Dry Fork VA 245499628

Call Sign: N4OMC

Victoria J Cundiff
1413 W I Powell Rd
Dry Fork VA 245499628

Call Sign: N4PHF
Garry J Cundiff
1413 W I Powell Rd
Dry Fork VA 245499628

Call Sign: KG4MEP
Frederick A Mckague Jr
4141 Whitmell School Rd
Dry Fork VA 24549

Call Sign: K4FAM
Frederick A Mckague Jr
4141 Whitmell School Rd
Dry Fork VA 24549

FCC Amateur Radio Licenses in Dryden

Call Sign: AF4FB
Charlie J Poe
Rt 1 Box 1540
Dryden VA 24243

Call Sign: KJ4DBI
Larry G Crabtree
Rt 1 Box 164
Dryden VA 24243

Call Sign: AJ4GJ
Larry G Crabtree
Rt 1 Box 164
Dryden VA 24243

Call Sign: KF4NYD
Marsha L Sturgill
Rr 1 Box 1687
Dryden VA 24243

Call Sign: KU4GN
David M Sturgill
Rr 1 Box 1687
Dryden VA 24243

Call Sign: KF4HOX
William H Gilliam

Rt 1 Box 995
Dryden VA 24243

Call Sign: W4WHG
William H Gilliam Jr
Rt 1 Box 995
Dryden VA 24243

Call Sign: KG4YCQ
Ruth E Gilliam
Rt 1 Box 995
Dryden VA 24243

Call Sign: WB4VUH
Charlie J Poe
148 Cave Springs Rd
Dryden VA 24243

Call Sign: KI4VNN
Clarence E Collins Jr
Dryden VA 24243

FCC Amateur Radio Licenses in Dublin

Call Sign: W4SE
Samuel F Krunsberg
5422 Aldrin St
Dublin VA 24084

Call Sign: N4NRV
New River Valley ARC
5190 Bowling St
Dublin VA 24084

Call Sign: KF4ABN
Michael G Slate
5231 Bowling St
Dublin VA 24084

Call Sign: KC5EJR
Lenford A Sutphin
5190 Bowling St
Dublin VA 24084

Call Sign: KI4EWG
Andrew D Dye
Hc 8 Box 109B
Dublin VA 24084

Call Sign: K4DYE
Andrew D Dye
Hc 8 Box 109B
Dublin VA 24084

Call Sign: KI4EWF
Randall L Meadows
Hc 8 Box 110
Dublin VA 24084

Call Sign: N4LSM
Michael L Trail
Rt 4 Box 120
Dublin VA 24084

Call Sign: KD4EMO
James H Payne Sr
Hc 8 Box 67 B
Dublin VA 24084

Call Sign: K9HPO
James E Lucas
Hrc 8 Box 87
Dublin VA 24084

Call Sign: W4DFD
Roy R Wall Jr
5607 Cloydsview Dr Lot 6
Dublin VA 24084

Call Sign: KJ4NGC
John C Lawson
6049 Dolphus Ave
Dublin VA 24084

Call Sign: W8HJ
Benjamin M Reed
508 Hanks Ave
Dublin VA 24084

Call Sign: W8BMR
Benjamin M Reed
5832 Hanks Ave
Dublin VA 24084

Call Sign: AB4I
Donnie S Coleman
6235 Highland Rd

Dublin VA 24084

Call Sign: KF4PCX
Diane H Coleman
6235 Highland Rd
Dublin VA 24084

Call Sign: KD4NWP
Christopher W Clark
4736 Highview Dr
Dublin VA 24084

Call Sign: WD4JIX
Steve R Allen
5691 Howell Dr
Dublin VA 24084

Call Sign: KE4FX
Gerald D Wood
5866 Jewell Ave
Dublin VA 24084

Call Sign: N8KLS
Roger W Hermann
5791 Jones Dr
Dublin VA 240842113

Call Sign: KD4LQL
Mark S Tuell
5394 Katie Cir
Dublin VA 24084

Call Sign: KA4LOK
Walter G Barker
7415 Lillydell Cir
Dublin VA 24084

Call Sign: KE4YKD
Raymond R Peck
12094 Little Creek Hwy
Dublin VA 24084

Call Sign: KI4IJM
Nicholas J Capobianco
5991 Lyons Rd
Dublin VA 24084

Call Sign: W4FLE
Colbern E Linkous

436 Maple St
Dublin VA 24084

Call Sign: WB4LMD
Eugene C Smith
4851 Mecca W Dr
Dublin VA 24084

Call Sign: KE4NGW
Danny B Mann
5616 Rolling Hills Dr
Dublin VA 24084

Call Sign: KD4SAH
Cindy C Tuell
6252 Skyview Cr
Dublin VA 240842627

Call Sign: KI4HSW
Carolyn L Meadows
1786 Spur Branch Rd
Dublin VA 24084

Call Sign: W4SUV
Carolyn L Meadows
1786 Spur Branch Rd
Dublin VA 24084

Call Sign: K4YLJ
Randall L Meadows
1786 Spur Branch Rd
Dublin VA 24084

Call Sign: KF4GWK
Mark E Lucas
Star Rt Box 87
Dublin VA 24084

Call Sign: KI4SSG
Christopher T Akers
5761 Stephen Dr
Dublin VA 24084

Call Sign: K4DFD
Christopher T Akers
5761 Stephen Dr
Dublin VA 24084

Call Sign: WA4MPJ

Donnie R Linkous
5092 Vally View Dr
Dublin VA 24084

Call Sign: KQ4XI
Randall F Potts
429 Vermillion St
Dublin VA 24084

Call Sign: N4RAN
Randall F Potts
429 Vermillion St
Dublin VA 24084

Call Sign: KE4CMW
Larry R Lytton
444 Vermillion St
Dublin VA 24084

Call Sign: KE4WSV
Roy L Bond
17 Wesley Ln
Dublin VA 24084

Call Sign: KE4CWU
Daniel R Williams
5877 Wesley St
Dublin VA 24084

Call Sign: KI4JTE
Allen D Shields
5290 Wilderness Rd
Dublin VA 24084

Call Sign: KE4TJA
Barry R Ashburn
135 Wright Ave
Dublin VA 24084

Call Sign: KA4ZHK
Patrick A Bryant
Dublin VA 24084

Call Sign: KE4CIF
Rubin O Lineberry Jr
Dublin VA 24084

Call Sign: KE4TIW
Roy S Martin

Dublin VA 24084

Call Sign: KF4BGN
Edith S Lineberry
Dublin VA 24084

Call Sign: KF4BGO
Bobby R Coleman Sr
Dublin VA 24084

Call Sign: KF4JFF
Pamela S Miller
Dublin VA 24084

Call Sign: W4CBM
Richard D Shupe
Dublin VA 24084

Call Sign: WB4MIG
Jeff D Arnold
Dublin VA 24084

Call Sign: KG4EZV
Fred E Phillips
Dublin VA 24084

Call Sign: KG4IRL
Larry W Dixon
Dublin VA 24084

Call Sign: N4MJP
Fred E Phillips
Dublin VA 24084

Call Sign: W1PAB
Patrick A Bryant
Dublin VA 24084

Call Sign: KI4AQI
Patrick J Murray Jr
Dublin VA 24084

Call Sign: K4JXL
Patrick J Murray Jr
Dublin VA 24084

Call Sign: KX4JL
Patrick J Murray Jr
Dublin VA 24084

Call Sign: KI4SSI
Roy R Wall Jr
Dublin VA 24084

Call Sign: WS4J
Rubin O Lineberry Jr
Dublin VA 24084

Call Sign: KJ4JBS
Sarah L Prescott
Dublin VA 24084

Call Sign: WX4NRV
Sarah L Prescott
Dublin VA 24084

Call Sign: KF4ZUU
Steve A Smith
Dublin VA 240841665

FCC Amateur Radio Licenses in Duffield

Call Sign: KT4PJ
James L Tomlinson
Rt 1 Box 121
Duffield VA 24244

Call Sign: KI4USC
Randall L Ward Sr
Rt 1 Box 134B
Duffield VA 24244

Call Sign: KD4MBR
Garnie B Dorton Jr
Rt3 Box 16A
Duffield VA 24244

Call Sign: KG4UIQ
Charles H Sloan Jr
Rt 3 Box 62Aa
Duffield VA 24244

Call Sign: KI4LWY
Ronnie D Dow
123 Cecil D Quillen Dr
Duffield VA 24244

Call Sign: KI4VYN
Judy J Kilgore
274 Cecil D Quillen Dr
Duffield VA 24244

Call Sign: WA4GEZ
Stermell G Bledsoe
258 Cecil D Quillen Dr
Duffield VA 24244

Call Sign: KG4MBB
Bryan D Osborne
116 Kane Ct
Duffield VA 24244

Call Sign: KG4MXP
Ernie Osborne
116 Kane Ct
Duffield VA 24244

Call Sign: KI4UDA
Samuel B Salling
5155 Rye Cove Memorial Rd
Duffield VA 24244

Call Sign: AB4TX
Rodney S Penley
191 Union Dr
Duffield VA 24244

Call Sign: KD4DZA
Anthony G Ewing
Duffield VA 24244

Call Sign: KG4DFZ
Roger C Taylor
Duffield VA 24244

Call Sign: N4KBQ
Michael K Pease
Duffield VA 24244

Call Sign: KI4RYN
William F Litton
Duffield VA 24244

FCC Amateur Radio Licenses in Dugspur

Call Sign: KF4NBK
Wendell R Carpenter
Rt 1 Box 177E
Dugspur VA 24325

Call Sign: WB4JSO
Douglas A Cahill
1960 Burkes Ford Rd
Dugspur VA 24325

Call Sign: WB2JMP
Clarence R Lounsberry
997 Duncan Mill Rd
Dugspur VA 243253844

Call Sign: KM4XE
Jimmy D Osborne
13 Kanawha Ridge Rd
Dugspur VA 24325

Call Sign: KI4ONE
Harry T Macmullan
3225 Panther Creek Rd
Dugspur VA 24325

Call Sign: KI4WWO
Joanna B Macmullan
3225 Panther Creek Rd
Dugspur VA 24325

Call Sign: KJ4CIP
James E Macmullan
3225 Panther Creek Rd
Dugspur VA 24325

Call Sign: KI4JTV
Beverly A Tipton
396 Rd Creek Ford
Dugspur VA 24325

Call Sign: KI4TSS
Andrew M Goad
2792 River Rd
Dugspur VA 24325

Call Sign: KI4OMX
Joseph D Goad
2792 River Rd
Dugspur VA 24325

Call Sign: KA4GUZ
Thomas E Largen II
306 Silverleaf Rd
Dugspur VA 24325

Call Sign: KG4RMK
Amy M Watson
2444 Silverleaf Rd
Dugspur VA 24325

Call Sign: KG4RML
Kermit M Watson
2444 Silverleaf Rd
Dugspur VA 24325

Call Sign: KA4JPS
Kenneth E Reece
1187 Sutphin Town Rd
Dugspur VA 24325

Call Sign: KI4JTO
Stuart G Dalton
1230 Sutphintown Rd
Dugspur VA 24325

FCC Amateur Radio Licenses in Dulles

Call Sign: KE5ZRX
Lester E Whitt
2030 Addis Ababa Pl
Dulles VA 20189

Call Sign: KE6SYZ
John Roger Lackups
4170 Ait Taipei Pl
Dulles VA 201894170

Call Sign: KB9GTD
Fred R Nelson
6030 Algiers Pl
Dulles VA 20189

Call Sign: KJ4RDA
Thomas E Dinkins
7200 Bangkok Pl
Dulles VA 201897200

Call Sign: KO4PH
Douglas H Wise
2045 Beacon Pl
Dulles VA 201892019

Call Sign: KA2WAN
Samuel S Kwok
7300 Beijing Pl Unit 0450
Dulles VA 201897300

Call Sign: KI4QAY
Richard G Romero
5110 Bern Pl
Dulles VA 20189

Call Sign: KF6FFN
Paul M Fermoile
6250 Calcutta Pl
Dulles VA 201896250

Call Sign: WA1LBP
David F Cowhig Jr
4080 Chengdu Pl
Dulles VA 201894080

Call Sign: KI4AWT
David J Ifversen
2120 Cotonou Pl
Dulles VA 201892120

Call Sign: KC9BVZ
Joshua I Reitz
2170 Gaborone Pl
Dulles VA 20189

Call Sign: KI4CON
Richard J Hill Jr
2180 Harare Pl
Dulles VA 201892180

Call Sign: KG4YDH
Gwen Sell
2220 Kinshasa Pl
Dulles VA 201892220

Call Sign: KG4YIN
Mark A Shepler
2300 Lome Pl
Dulles VA 201892300

Call Sign: KI4OTI
Crayon C Efird Jr
2550 Luanda Pl
Dulles VA 201892550

Call Sign: N9MDH
John B Everman Jr
2330 Maputo Pl
Dulles VA 20189

Call Sign: KA3MHB
Guadalupe Pinon
2330 Maputo Pl
Dulles VA 201892330

Call Sign: KF4UNB
Charles M Vansickle Jr
6240 Mumbai Pl
Dulles VA 201896240

Call Sign: KG4OJV
Frank W Landymore III
9000 New Delhi Pl
Dulles VA 20189

Call Sign: W4MSL
Michael S Lundy
9000 New Delhi Pl
Dulles VA 201899000

Call Sign: N4HX
James R Bullington
2420 Niamey Pl
Dulles VA 20189

Call Sign: KC2EVM
Karen L Norton
9300 Pretoria Pl
Dulles VA 201899300

Call Sign: KG2QB
James C Norton
9300 Pretoria Pl
Dulles VA 201899300

Call Sign: N3URB
Loretta H Hall
9300 Pretoria Pl

Dulles VA 201899300

Call Sign: N3VLT
David J Hall
9300 Pretoria Pl
Dulles VA 201899300

Call Sign: KW1O
Mark W Lukinovich
9300 Pretoria Pl
Dulles VA 201899300

Call Sign: WA9UZM
Heinz G Stroebel
5640 Reykjavik Pl
Dulles VA 201895640

Call Sign: KE6GRC
Nael Sabha
6300 Riyadh Pl
Dulles VA 201896300

Call Sign: KI4CNT
Michael J Fotheringham
5740 Sofia Pl
Dulles VA 201895740

Call Sign: KG4URX
Itay Eshet
21025 Stanford Sq No 202
Dulles VA 20166

Call Sign: KC2BOB
Warren K Kumari
43479 Stukely Dr
Dulles VA 20166

Call Sign: AC4WK
Warren K Kumari
43479 Stukely Dr
Dulles VA 20166

Call Sign: KF5IJ
David M Reinert
7110 Tashkent Pl
Dulles VA 20189

Call Sign: KI4CNS
Stuart F Moss

9510 Tirana Pl
Dulles VA 20189

**FCC Amateur Radio Licenses
in Dumfries**

Call Sign: WA4KSO
Curt A Cochran
17070 4 Seasons Dr
Dumfries VA 220251889

Call Sign: KG4YQO
Pamela M Cochran
17070 4 Seasons Dr
Dumfries VA 220251889

Call Sign: K4JK
John Kendra
17456 4 Seasons Dr
Dumfries VA 22025

Call Sign: N4LJS
John Kendra
17456 4 Seasons Dr
Dumfries VA 22025

Call Sign: KG4OWW
Nestor V Torres
4272 Ashmere Cir
Dumfries VA 22026

Call Sign: KJ4GWK
Donald G Goff Jr
17745 Avenel Ln
Dumfries VA 22026

Call Sign: N4MDX
Donald G Goff Jr
17745 Avenel Ln
Dumfries VA 22026

Call Sign: KA3EHL
Charles E Helverson
3090 Azalea Sands Ln
Dumfries VA 22026

Call Sign: KC4BIR
Rodger A Barney
15708 Buck Ln

Dumfries VA 22026

Call Sign: KG4GSS
Brian M De Muth
15223 Cedar Knoll Ct
Dumfries VA 220251068

Call Sign: AA3TX
William R Askew III
2015 Cherry Hill Rd
Dumfries VA 22026

Call Sign: KD4QQZ
Fred Tillman Jr
3109 Chesapeke Dr 302
Dumfries VA 22026

Call Sign: KA0WZV
Timothy E Halpin
15723 Cranberry Ct
Dumfries VA 22025

Call Sign: KA0WZW
Sharon J Halpin
15723 Cranberry Ct
Dumfries VA 22026

Call Sign: K4KEE
Robert C Hamlin
15729 Cranberry Ct
Dumfries VA 220251751

Call Sign: N3AF
Romuald A Stone
3815 Dalebrook Dr
Dumfries VA 220261801

Call Sign: KG4PVF
John D Pivk
3717 Dalebrook Dr
Dumfries VA 22025

Call Sign: KT4AD
John T Grout
15798 Fawn Pl
Dumfries VA 220251427

Call Sign: KI4GSK
Paul A Young

1913 Fort Monroe Ct
Dumfries VA 22026

Call Sign: KU4RJ
Ronald A Doby
17637 Hampstead Ridge Ct
Dumfries VA 22026

Call Sign: AI4FB
Ronald A Doby
17637 Hampstead Ridge Ct
Dumfries VA 22026

Call Sign: AE4RD
Ronald A Doby
17637 Hampstead Ridge Ct
Dumfries VA 22026

Call Sign: KF4YFU
Darala A Doby
17637 Hampstead Ridge Ct
Dumfries VA 220264549

Call Sign: KI4FHI
Darala A Doby
17637 Hampstead Ridge Ct
Dumfries VA 220264549

Call Sign: WB4USA
Darala A Doby
17637 Hampstead Ridge Ct
Dumfries VA 220264549

Call Sign: KI4MIL
Gerald T Gillis
15121 Holley Side Dr
Dumfries VA 22025

Call Sign: AI4SG
Gerald T Gillis
15121 Holley Side Dr
Dumfries VA 22025

Call Sign: K4RG
Robert J Graham Jr
15095 Holleyside Dr
Dumfries VA 22025

Call Sign: N4LRA

Wilbert H Hull
3218 John Rolfe Ct
Dumfries VA 22026

Call Sign: KJ4OXM
Jay R Young
4319 Jonathan Ct
Dumfries VA 22025

Call Sign: WB4HG
William H Gibbs
17439 Kagera Dr
Dumfries VA 22025

Call Sign: WB4TG
William H Gibbs
17439 Kagera Dr
Dumfries VA 22025

Call Sign: KK5HU
James L Federwisch
16601 Kensington Pl
Dumfries VA 22026

Call Sign: KI4IAJ
Clifton J Mccullough
17354 Kildare Ln
Dumfries VA 220263303

Call Sign: KJ4EPB
Daniel J Krause
17364 Kildare Ln
Dumfries VA 22026

Call Sign: KJ4WEA
Maria C Hershfield
16209 Kings Valley Dr
Dumfries VA 22025

Call Sign: W2YPT
Vincent L Napoli
4918 Live Oaks Ct
Dumfries VA 22026

Call Sign: KA5JJV
John C Peacock
17878 Lounsbury Dr
Dumfries VA 22026

Call Sign: KI4KFC
Brian A Shaw
17886 Main St 2
Dumfries VA 22026

Call Sign: KC4QYQ
Eric T Kelley
3637 McDowell Ct
Dumfries VA 22026

Call Sign: K5ESO
Dale D Barr Jr
15786 Moncure Ct
Dumfries VA 22026

Call Sign: WA5YIM
Marjorie A Barr
15786 Moncure Ct
Dumfries VA 22026

Call Sign: KJ4SOH
Kevin P Logan
2905 Myrtlewood Dr
Dumfries VA 22026

Call Sign: KF4ZDQ
Chirstopher A Long
2970 Myrtlewood Dr
Dumfries VA 22026

Call Sign: KJ4WEC
Pierre R Benjamin
3358 Mystic Ct
Dumfries VA 22026

Call Sign: W4IY
James D Hale
17569 Old Stagecoach Rd
Dumfries VA 22026

Call Sign: N5UIR
Frank F Mc Cann
15561 Outlook Pl
Dumfries VA 22026

Call Sign: WB4DAM
Derek W Kelly
18069 Possum Point Rd
Dumfries VA 22026

Call Sign: KC4ARX
Louis L Simpleman
16006 Prestwick Ct
Dumfries VA 22026

Call Sign: KC4ASB
Christopher L Simpleman
16006 Prestwick Ct
Dumfries VA 22026

Call Sign: KF4YPV
Francis R Kotulak
16011 Prestwick Ct
Dumfries VA 22026

Call Sign: W4QBA
Edward J Driscoll Jr
15526 Ridgecrest Dr
Dumfries VA 22026

Call Sign: KC4SZT
James E Catalano
17336 Rocky Mt Ln
Dumfries VA 22026

Call Sign: WB4PYZ
Charles V Hoffmann
5122 Spring Branch Blvd
Dumfries VA 22026

Call Sign: K4QJZ
George W Hill III
4639 Timber Ridge Dr
Dumfries VA 220251059

Call Sign: KK4FMQ
Dorothea D Barr
18055 Tompkins Ct
Dumfries VA 22026

Call Sign: WA7QQL
Randy L Woolf
17563 Wayside Dr
Dumfries VA 22026

Call Sign: KI4AFJ
Donald M Hamilton Jr
15774 Widewater Dr

Dumfries VA 22026

Call Sign: K4MPT
Fred G Kern III
15800 Widewater Dr
Dumfries VA 22026

Call Sign: KD4ACC
Fred G Kern III
15800 Widewater Dr
Dumfries VA 22026

Call Sign: K4XXZ
Fred G Kern III
15800 Widewater Dr
Dumfries VA 22026

Call Sign: KI4VUQ
Michael A Barton
3301 William Johnston Ln Apt
14
Dumfries VA 22026

Call Sign: KG4TOQ
Daniel J Coburn
15516 Yorktown Dr
Dumfries VA 22026

Call Sign: KD4UFI
Bradley J Ketchum
Dumfries VA 22026

Call Sign: KE4OIJ
Ian B Littlejohn
Dumfries VA 22026

Call Sign: KF6JLP
Bruce M Mac Kay
Dumfries VA 22026

Call Sign: KI4ZGY
Andrew J Suski
Dumfries VA 22026

**FCC Amateur Radio Licenses
in Dungannon**

Call Sign: KC4RDY
Lois A Powers

3104 7th Ave
Dungannon VA 24245

Call Sign: KC4MVJ
Donald R Powers Sr
3104L 7th Ave
Dungannon VA 24245

Call Sign: KF4GOH
Charles D Dorton
Rt 1 Box 189
Dungannon VA 24245

Call Sign: KF4BGV
James M Sergent
Rt 1 Box 211
Dungannon VA 24245

Call Sign: KF4BGY
Perry C Quillen
Rt 1 Box 233
Dungannon VA 24245

Call Sign: KE4WFF
Angela F Brickey
Dungannon VA 24245

Call Sign: KF4GOF
Samantha D Brickey
Dungannon VA 24245

Call Sign: KF4GOG
Candace N Brickey
Dungannon VA 24245

Call Sign: KS4DD
Daniel S Brickey Jr
Dungannon VA 24245

Call Sign: KG4SZP
Jeffrey N Bellamy
Dungannon VA 24245

**FCC Amateur Radio Licenses
in Dunn Loring**

Call Sign: KF4PJE
Gary A Dixon
2300 Arden St

Dunn Loring VA 22027

Call Sign: KJ4NXK
Caroline A Bauer
7980 Foxmoor Dr
Dunn Loring VA 22027

Call Sign: KJ4FBO
Dstc
2216 Gallows Rd
Dunn Loring VA 22027

Call Sign: KE4TCQ
Paul A Haag
2212 Harithy Dr
Dunn Loring VA 22027

Call Sign: K3RV
Carl G Kratzer
Dunn Loring VA 22027

Call Sign: WA3WQZ
Charles D Suit
Dunn Loring VA 22027

FCC Amateur Radio Licenses in Dunnsville

Call Sign: KF4ZSE
Harry C Byron Jr
Hc 1 Box 1913
Dunnsville VA 22454

Call Sign: KB4HMS
Jennifer S May
Rt 1 Box 582
Dunnsville VA 22454

Call Sign: WD4GOY
Edgar C Robinson Jr
161 Cedar Dr
Dunnsville VA 224542121

Call Sign: N3EMT
William L Hankison Jr
689 Eastern View Rd
Dunnsville VA 22454

Call Sign: KG4RPP

George R Winder
2326 Johnville Rd
Dunnsville VA 22454

Call Sign: KD4GRW
George R Winder
2326 Johnville Rd
Dunnsville VA 22454

Call Sign: N2BPH
Joseph E Farrington III
1530 Muddy Gut Rd
Dunnsville VA 22454

Call Sign: KB4GAZ
Hollis W Wolcott Jr
Dunnsville VA 22454

Call Sign: AJ4DO
Nathaniel E Wolcott
Dunnsville VA 22454

FCC Amateur Radio Licenses in Dutton

Call Sign: N4TVB
John F Satterly
826 Irishmen Ln
Dutton VA 23050

Call Sign: WA2OFU
George Zhoroff
Dutton VA 23050

Call Sign: KG4KQL
Frank V Rose
Dutton VA 23050

FCC Amateur Radio Licenses in Dyke

Call Sign: N4NVK
Richard E Bunch Jr
25 Brills Ln
Dyke VA 22935

Call Sign: KD4SCV
Ean H Schiller
2387 Brokenback Mtn Rd

Dyke VA 22935

Call Sign: KI4HCB
Eugene Aragona
2393 Brokenback Mtn Rd
Dyke VA 22935

Call Sign: AC6FE
Jonathan E Sjordal
1042 Morning Glory Pl
Dyke VA 22935

Call Sign: KE6TLL
Kristie L Sjordal
1042 Morning Glory Pl
Dyke VA 22935

FCC Amateur Radio Licenses in Eagle Rock

Call Sign: KC4EJG
Joseph M Ledford
Rt 2 Box 100C
Eagle Rock VA 24085

Call Sign: N4DUB
Joe L Coggin
Rt 1 Box 1580
Eagle Rock VA 24085

Call Sign: WB4UUE
Gerard J King
Rt 2 Box 71
Eagle Rock VA 24085

Call Sign: KG4DBP
Robert K Crowder
7387 Craig Creek Rd
Eagle Rock VA 24085

Call Sign: KD4AID
Ronald W Wright
49 Lakeview Ct
Eagle Rock VA 24085

Call Sign: KG4BEV
Leslie C Dunbar
2670 Mt Moriah Rd
Eagle Rock VA 24085

Call Sign: KG4BEW
Lee F Dunbar Jr
2670 Mt Moriah Rd
Eagle Rock VA 24085

Call Sign: KK4EVN
Harold L Bradley
19 Salt Petre Cave Rd
Eagle Rock VA 24085

Call Sign: AE4HB
Harold L Bradley
19 Salt Petre Cave Rd
Eagle Rock VA 24085

Call Sign: KG4DYW
Stephen D Pendleton
639 Solders Retreat Rd
Eagle Rock VA 24085

Call Sign: KC4EJF
Beverly D Mayo
623 Soldiers Retreat Rd
Eagle Rock VA 24085

Call Sign: N4PWX
David L Mayo
623 Soldiers Retreat Rd
Eagle Rock VA 24085

Call Sign: KC4IIB
Bonnie G Kestner
1374 Sunset Dr
Eagle Rock VA 24085

FCC Amateur Radio Licenses in Earlysville

Call Sign: W4HIR
Michael Brown
5082 Advance Mills Rd
Earlysville VA 229361828

Call Sign: KJ4VJR
Shannon R Tevendale
551 Allen Rd
Earlysville VA 22936

Call Sign: N4IQH
Warren K Crady
620 Allen Rd
Earlysville VA 22936

Call Sign: KJ4TRJ
Warren K Crady
620 Allen Rd
Earlysville VA 22936

Call Sign: N4IQH
Warren K Crady
620 Allen Rd
Earlysville VA 22936

Call Sign: K8EV
Richard H Dale Sr
3720 Bleak House Rd
Earlysville VA 229362201

Call Sign: KC4VYK
Jesse B Mercer
Hc 01 Box 31B
Earlysville VA 22936

Call Sign: KF4NUO
Tareq S Tahboub
282 Buck Mtian Rd
Earlysville VA 22936

Call Sign: KK4EDT
James G Lawrence
700 Caro Ct
Earlysville VA 22936

Call Sign: W4DGN
Philip D Lawrence Jr
700 Caro Ct
Earlysville VA 229369694

Call Sign: WB4CWP
Jim P Wade
4425 Carriage Hill Dr
Earlysville VA 229369584

Call Sign: KB2B
Margaret C Flavin
9 Cedar Creek Rd
Earlysville VA 22936

Call Sign: KB2C
John E Flavin
9 Cedar Creek Rd
Earlysville VA 22936

Call Sign: N4DGR
James R Scuffham Jr
176 Claymont Dr
Earlysville VA 22936

Call Sign: KJ4MWS
Carrie J Brownhill
1232 Durrett Ridge Rd
Earlysville VA 22936

Call Sign: KJ4MWV
Mark D Brownhill
1232 Durrett Ridge Rd
Earlysville VA 22936

Call Sign: N4TAV
Eloise S Heeschen
2590 Earlysville Rd
Earlysville VA 22936

Call Sign: K8HC
Harold J Crosthwaite
3000 Earlysville Rd
Earlysville VA 229369663

Call Sign: KJ4WOI
Michael R Jones
565 Eyre Rd
Earlysville VA 22936

Call Sign: KE4KJB
John W Holman
515 Fishing Creek Ln
Earlysville VA 22936

Call Sign: KB4WBV
John A King
1410 Forest Spring Ln
Earlysville VA 22936

Call Sign: KF4RKQ
Roy A Emert Jr
1135 Fox Ridge Dr

Earlysville VA 22936

Call Sign: K4RKQ
Roy A Emert Jr
1135 Fox Ridge Dr
Earlysville VA 22936

Call Sign: KE4SSE
Karen C Taylor
1195 Fox Ridge Dr
Earlysville VA 22936

Call Sign: KB4ZUM
Gerhard Spindler
1200 Fox Ridge Dr
Earlysville VA 22936

Call Sign: WA1A
Mark J Gorlinsky
576 Frays Ridge Rd
Earlysville VA 22936

Call Sign: KE4OIB
Brian E Scott
435 Hickory Dr
Earlysville VA 22936

Call Sign: WD4LOU
Charles M Adkins III
700 Lochridge Ln
Earlysville VA 22936

Call Sign: KS4NW
Charles J Gross
3867 Loftlands Dr
Earlysville VA 22936

Call Sign: KK4GEN
Duncan Townsend
3200 Monroe St
Earlysville VA 22936

Call Sign: KI4UQV
Donald H Eason Jr
725 Montei Dr
Earlysville VA 22936

Call Sign: N4UVA
Donald H Eason Jr

725 Montei Dr
Earlysville VA 22936

Call Sign: KI4HWF
Britt M Grimm
915 Quail Ridge Cir
Earlysville VA 22936

Call Sign: N4WJQ
Howard S Gentry
623 Reas Ford Rd
Earlysville VA 22936

Call Sign: N4YER
Alice G Gentry
623 Reas Ford Rd
Earlysville VA 22936

Call Sign: KJ4UEA
Woodrow P Gimbel Jr
799 Reas Ford Rd
Earlysville VA 22936

Call Sign: WD4ALY
Donald J Wigent
820 Reas Ford Rd
Earlysville VA 22936

Call Sign: N1FBQ
Frank S Cruickshank
4200 Rowan Ct
Earlysville VA 22936

Call Sign: KA4RBW
Clinton H Estes
635 Windrift Dr
Earlysville VA 22936

Call Sign: KC4ZZP
John A Roder
4255 Windy Cove
Earlysville VA 22936

Call Sign: W4TJ
William J Lakatosh
735 Yorkshire Rd
Earlysville VA 22936

Call Sign: KE4DDP

Kenas L Shiflett Jr
Earlysville VA 22936

Call Sign: KJ4OP
Jonathan T Katz
Earlysville VA 22936

Call Sign: KC4UCK
Guy W Taylor Jr
Earlysville VA 22936

Call Sign: WB4AIO
Kevin A Strom
Earlysville VA 22936

Call Sign: K4WOA
Guy W Taylor Jr
Earlysville VA 22936

Call Sign: KA2CIJ
Lorie F Schultz
Earlysville VA 229360132

FCC Amateur Radio Licenses in East Stone Gap

Call Sign: KG4IEH
Lonnie W Brooks
3913 Logan Ave
East Stone Gap VA 24246

Call Sign: KG4ONF
Danna M Fuson
East Stone Gap VA 24246

Call Sign: KI4USR
James A Swan
East Stone Gap VA 24246

Call Sign: KK4DXK
Steve J Bobrosky Jr
East Stone Gap VA 24246

FCC Amateur Radio Licenses in Eastville

Call Sign: KK4CEK
Talib-Din M Akbar
Eastville VA 23347

FCC Amateur Radio Licenses in Ebony

Call Sign: N3LDS
D Freeman Carroll
377 Hideaway Pl
Ebony VA 23845

Call Sign: N3NXN
Annette W Carroll
377 Hideaway Pl
Ebony VA 23845

FCC Amateur Radio Licenses in Edinburg

Call Sign: KE4NBS
James C Patrick
4676 Alum Springs Rd
Edinburg VA 22824

Call Sign: KC4CQC
Vaughn L Blankenship
Rt 1 Box 581A
Edinburg VA 22824

Call Sign: KC4KOP
Clifford Guetter
139 Cliffside Dr
Edinburg VA 228243564

Call Sign: W2FIB
Donald L Howell
542 Coffman Rd
Edinburg VA 22824

Call Sign: KJ4JMN
Bryan L Estep
1387 Edinburg Gap Rd
Edinburg VA 22824

Call Sign: KI4ZKY
Gary T Barb
115 Harmony Ln
Edinburg VA 22824

Call Sign: KJ4PUN
Gary T Barb
115 Harmony Ln
Edinburg VA 22824

Call Sign: WD4KNX
John L Whitmer
356 Hillcrest Rd
Edinburg VA 22824

Call Sign: KJ4KGC
John L Whitmer
356 Hillcrest Rd
Edinburg VA 22824

Call Sign: WD4KNX
John L Whitmer
356 Hillcrest Rd
Edinburg VA 22824

Call Sign: KF4OAA
John S Jones
75 Jewell Ln
Edinburg VA 22824

Call Sign: KI4HLU
Tonya S Frazier
178 Millertown Rd
Edinburg VA 22824

Call Sign: KG6AEZ
Michael S Kessinger
897 Palmyra Church Rd
Edinburg VA 22824

Call Sign: KC8IVN
Jeremy M Keckley
761 Race Track Rd
Edinburg VA 22824

Call Sign: N8BJT
Matthew J Keckley II
761 Race Track Rd
Edinburg VA 228242738

Call Sign: KI4HLT
Norm C Barb
2324 Ridge Hollow Rd
Edinburg VA 22824

Call Sign: KD4WIE
Wayne A Frye
545 S Ox Rd
Edinburg VA 22824

Call Sign: WB5YAK
Jessie J Granier Jr
1597 S Ox Rd
Edinburg VA 22824

Call Sign: KF4QLB
David E Markham
20422 Senedo Rd
Edinburg VA 22824

Call Sign: KD4TAB
Jerry L Pryor
534 Windsor Knit Rd
Edinburg VA 22824

Call Sign: KJ4UFF
Andrew E Smith
Edinburg VA 22824

FCC Amateur Radio Licenses in Eggleston

Call Sign: W4PAJ
Brian D Squibb
221 Sleepy Hollow Ln
Eggleston VA 24086

Call Sign: KG4PBW
Carine L Squibb
221 Sleepy Hollow Ln
Eggleston VA 24086

Call Sign: AC4XO
Ben E Cline
Eggleston VA 24086

Call Sign: KD4LQO
Sue Ellen J Cline
Eggleston VA 24086

Call Sign: K4ZDF
Samuel B Thomason
Eggleston VA 24086

FCC Amateur Radio Licenses in Elberon

Call Sign: KK4CYZ
William C Cole
883 Bellevue Rd
Elberon VA 23846

Call Sign: KK4RE
James D Acree
534 Golden Hill Rd
Elberon VA 23846

FCC Amateur Radio Licenses in Elk Creek

Call Sign: W4FMP
Bill M Bland
Rt 1 Box 139
Elk Creek VA 24326

Call Sign: KI4DP
Bayne G Fielder
Rfd 1 Box 44
Elk Creek VA 24326

Call Sign: KD4LHS
Nancy M Hale
1700 Comers Rock Rd
Elk Creek VA 24326

Call Sign: N4MGH
Bronson D Hale
1700 Comers Rock Rd
Elk Creek VA 24326

Call Sign: KB4KNX
Edward W Hines
8153 Elk Creek Pkwy
Elk Creek VA 24326

Call Sign: WA4IGT
Rodney C Rhudy
1826 Mt Zion Rd
Elk Creek VA 24326

Call Sign: KI4PZV
Darren L Shepherd
985 Powder Mill Rd
Elk Creek VA 24326

Call Sign: K4ROC
Darren L Shepherd
985 Powder Mill Rd
Elk Creek VA 24326

Call Sign: KI4TYI
Eddie L Shepherd
985 Powder Mill Rd
Elk Creek VA 24326

FCC Amateur Radio Licenses in Elkton

Call Sign: K4TMH
Todd M Harrison
501 4th St
Elkton VA 22827

Call Sign: KG4LRH
Patricia A Hensley
92 Ashby Ave
Elkton VA 22827

Call Sign: K4PAH
Patricia A Hensley
92 Ashby Ave
Elkton VA 22827

Call Sign: KJ4VVO
Kenneth E Copeland Jr
3675 Bloomer Springs Rd
Elkton VA 22827

Call Sign: KD4ZSD
Jonathan W Lee
Rt 4 Box 113
Elkton VA 22827

Call Sign: KF4CJS
Rebecca L Gooden
Rt 3 Box 285
Elkton VA 22827

Call Sign: N4YRZ
Claude E Wheelbarger III
Rt 3 Box 5 End Rockingham St
Ext

Elkton VA 22827

Call Sign: KC4VLE
Tracey L Fisher
Rt 3 Box 8
Elkton VA 22827

Call Sign: KE4UFL
Duffy J Essman
3474 Branch Ln
Elkton VA 22827

Call Sign: KE4ZLE
Rebecca A Essman
3474 Branch Ln
Elkton VA 22827

Call Sign: WA4NUF
Eugene A Sullivan
4200 Brown Mtn Ln
Elkton VA 22827

Call Sign: N4DRN
Donald R Nichols
6701 Dovel Rd
Elkton VA 228272417

Call Sign: KG4RDH
Donnie L Williams
21651 Dry Run Falls Trl
Elkton VA 22827

Call Sign: N4YSA
Mark D Hensley
3109 Homestead Rd
Elkton VA 22827

Call Sign: KG4ZDP
Matthew W Dean
2816 Rodney Ln
Elkton VA 22827

Call Sign: KJ4HFO
Gene P Frazier
17610 Spotswood Trl
Elkton VA 22827

Call Sign: KK4HUO
William R Beaulieu

6946 Thoroughrare Rd
Elkton VA 22827

Call Sign: W3MVZ
Earl H Dilley
129 Washington Ave
Elkton VA 22827

Call Sign: WB7FEY
Richard C Mc Gregor
264 Windsong Hills Dr
Elkton VA 22827

FCC Amateur Radio Licenses in Elkwood

Call Sign: W4IMA
Belmont L Worman
19775 Edwards Shop Rd
Elkwood VA 22718

Call Sign: W3TIM
Timothy R Malony
17319 Red Fox Run
Elkwood VA 22718

Call Sign: K1AEP
Jerry Smith
Elkwood VA 22701

FCC Amateur Radio Licenses in Elliston

Call Sign: N4QMK
ARChibald G Smith III
3406 Bardshaw Rd
Elliston VA 24087

Call Sign: KF4TUH
Michael A Russell
4748 Calloway St
Elliston VA 24087

Call Sign: WD6FLL
John G Garrett
2467 Cannery Rd Lot 10
Elliston VA 24087

Call Sign: KC4WMO

Hunter T Walden
131 Dark Run Rd
Elliston VA 24087

Call Sign: KD4SAF
Robert A Repass
131 Dark Run Rd 160
Elliston VA 24087

Call Sign: KJ4CGQ
Dennis C Hartman
5467 Lafayette Rd
Elliston VA 24087

Call Sign: WD4NRN
Heston Cooksey Jr
1600 Moomaw Cir
Elliston VA 24087

Call Sign: K1GG
Gordon G Garrett
4528 N Fork Rd
Elliston VA 24087

Call Sign: K4KAT
Melissa A Garrett
4528 N Fork Rd
Elliston VA 24087

Call Sign: K4ROA
Southwestern VA Wireless
Assn Inc
4528 N Fork Rd
Elliston VA 24087

Call Sign: N4SBK
Deborah H Garrett
4528 N Fork Rd
Elliston VA 24087

Call Sign: KF4UOP
Dimitri I Vlasenko
4528 N Fork Rd
Elliston VA 24087

Call Sign: WC4VAB
VA Ares Races Inc Area B
4528 N Fork Rd
Elliston VA 24087

Call Sign: WD8IHE
Donna A Conner
5520 N Fork Rd
Elliston VA 24087

Call Sign: KI4MGB
John G Conner
5520 N Fork Rd
Elliston VA 24087

Call Sign: KI4HDH
James F Small
3771 Northfork Rd
Elliston VA 24087

Call Sign: KB4NIU
Carson A Mills
2962 Reesedale Rd
Elliston VA 24087

Call Sign: KO4AM
Joe M Francis
2849 Sarver Rd
Elliston VA 24087

FCC Amateur Radio Licenses in Emory

Call Sign: WA4PME
James W Hill
Linden St
Emory VA 24327

Call Sign: WA4PMK
John R Hill
Linden St
Emory VA 24327

Call Sign: N4OGD
John A Neal III
Emory VA 24327

Call Sign: KI4FTB
Dallas G Breedlove
Emory VA 24327

FCC Amateur Radio Licenses in Emporia

Call Sign: KA8IGC
Larry E Lambert
136 Courtland Rd
Emporia VA 28033

Call Sign: KI4GFG
Gerald L Delbridge
1452 James River Junction
Emporia VA 23847

Call Sign: KD4ELA
Derrick Carpenter Sr
404 Lee St
Emporia VA 23847

Call Sign: KI4FXG
Steve M Maitland Jr
3331 Low Ground Rd
Emporia VA 238476723

Call Sign: K4FOY
David E Roberts
1623 Walnut Dr
Emporia VA 23847

Call Sign: KG4UQP
Jerry S Whitehead
415 Watkins St
Emporia VA 23847

Call Sign: K4TEK
Jerry S Whitehead
415 Watkins St
Emporia VA 23847

FCC Amateur Radio Licenses in Esmont

Call Sign: KE4JYS
Thomas Donnelly
Esmont VA 22937

FCC Amateur Radio Licenses in Etlan

Call Sign: KA4DFJ
Robert A Falls
Hc 6 Box 132A

Etlan VA 22719

Call Sign: W4RAF
Robert A Falls
672 Church Hill Rd
Etlan VA 22719

FCC Amateur Radio Licenses in Ettrick

Call Sign: KC4IUN
Lloyd D Bell
3112 E River Rd
Ettrick VA 23803

Call Sign: KI4HNJ
Charles D Fasano
20305 Hickory Branch Dr
Ettrick VA 23803

Call Sign: KD4PDB
Horace Dickerson
20201 Sheffield Pl
Ettrick VA 23803

FCC Amateur Radio Licenses in Evington

Call Sign: KE4PID
Sean L Braswell
150 Baywood Ct
Evington VA 24550

Call Sign: KF4JKF
Daniel B Mc Millan
1255 Blackberry Ln
Evington VA 245503953

Call Sign: N4QPA
Rodney P Dotson
Rt 1 Box 745
Evington VA 24550

Call Sign: KD4RBV
Richard D Sanders
Rt 1 Box 965
Evington VA 24550

Call Sign: KJ4BZ

David L Higgins
397 Bridge Tree Ct
Evington VA 24550

Call Sign: KD4ZTP
Charles H Benedict
200 Chestnut Creek Dr
Evington VA 24550

Call Sign: KE4SWP
Tracy A Tweedy
Box 38 Clayton Estates
Evington VA 24550

Call Sign: KE4JGV
James T Jewell
5879 Colonial Hwy
Evington VA 245501887

Call Sign: NG4Q
Robert W Weber
193 Davids Way
Evington VA 24550

Call Sign: KD4OOM
Jeffrey D Demers
3201 Evington Rd
Evington VA 245504126

Call Sign: N4LFJ
Jeffrey D Seay
76 Holly Ridge Ct 3
Evington VA 24550

Call Sign: KI4IXL
Paul C Prose Sr
3105 Johnson Mtn Rd
Evington VA 24550

Call Sign: KR4AK
James M Brower Sr
20 Luenburg Dr
Evington VA 24550

Call Sign: K9JMB
James M Brower Sr
20 Luenburg Dr
Evington VA 24550

Call Sign: KI4SIT
Judy L Brower
20 Luenburg Dr
Evington VA 24550

Call Sign: W4JLB
Judy L Brower
20 Luenburg Dr
Evington VA 24550

Call Sign: KI4SAO
Janice Mata
33 Luenburg Dr
Evington VA 24550

Call Sign: KA4JEM
Janice E Mata
33 Luenburg Dr
Evington VA 24550

Call Sign: KJ4MYV
Juan R Mata
33 Luenburg Dr
Evington VA 24550

Call Sign: W4ABT
Jean A Rogers
115 Luenburg Dr
Evington VA 24550

Call Sign: K4ABT
Glynn E Rogers Sr
115 Luenburg Dr
Evington VA 245501705

Call Sign: WB4EDZ
Jean A Rogers
115 Luenburg Dr
Evington VA 245501705

Call Sign: AD4A
Ronald L Miles
232 Mortimer Dr
Evington VA 245502247

Call Sign: KU4MP
Mark B Viers
830 One Mile Rd
Evington VA 245509762

Call Sign: KI4AWN
Maynard E Sawyer Jr
865 Orrix Creek Rd
Evington VA 24550

Call Sign: KF4NKK
Diana M Kislo
124 Ritz St
Evington VA 24550

Call Sign: KI4AWO
Robert L Andrews
2550 Town Fork Rd
Evington VA 24550

Call Sign: KI4PMN
Janice P Mclaughlin
276 Wahoo Ct
Evington VA 24550

Call Sign: KD4YFE
Barry N Yost Jr
Evington VA 24550

Call Sign: KD4BH
Alva B Lloyd Jr
Evington VA 24550

Call Sign: KG4MPQ
Howard E Floyd
Evington VA 24550

Call Sign: N4EUQ
Daniel P Baker
Evington VA 24550

Call Sign: KD4BH
Howard E Floyd
Evington VA 24550

Call Sign: KI4LYV
Jeffrey W Miles
Evington VA 24550

FCC Amateur Radio Licenses in Ewing

Call Sign: KJ4RLR

Debbie L Brooks
109 Bamboo Dr
Ewing VA 24248

Call Sign: KE4LVI
Eugene L Chadwell
Rt 2 Box 204
Ewing VA 24248

Call Sign: KF4CMH
Clarence A Hampton
Rt 2 Box 29
Ewing VA 24248

Call Sign: KE4FHK
Bruce O Ferguson
Rt 2 Box 299Aa
Ewing VA 24240

Call Sign: KD4YNX
Ricky D Baker
Rt 2 Box 407
Ewing VA 24248

Call Sign: KD4KVY
Terry E Lewis
Rt 2 Box 419 A
Ewing VA 24248

Call Sign: KD4YHJ
Pamela B Lewis
Rt 2 Box 419 A
Ewing VA 24248

Call Sign: KD4WMV
Willis Hounshel
Rt 2 Box 510
Ewing VA 24248

Call Sign: KC4JUB
Arthur T Payne
Rt 1 Box 73A
Ewing VA 24248

Call Sign: KD4GFP
Tilman V Grubb
297 Neighborhood Ln
Ewing VA 242488611

Call Sign: KD4GFQ
Tyson J Grubb
297 Neighborhood Ln
Ewing VA 242488611

Call Sign: KD4GFR
Deborah C Grubb
297 Neighborhood Ln
Ewing VA 242488611

**FCC Amateur Radio Licenses
in Exmore**

Call Sign: K2DFZ
Dudley B Field
2196 Clear View Rd
Exmore VA 23350

Call Sign: AA3W
Terry W Sawyer
3170 Eden Meadows Dr
Exmore VA 23350

Call Sign: N4JNG
Jerry D Ellerbe
4530 Seaside Rd
Exmore VA 233500645

Call Sign: KD4PPF
Arnold G Coston
Exmore VA 23350

Call Sign: KG4PEX
Jeffrey A Flournoy
Exmore VA 23350

Call Sign: KK4HKT
Andrew C Muender
Exmore VA 23350

Call Sign: KD4NVY
Leonard R Sturgis
Exmore VA 23350

**FCC Amateur Radio Licenses
in Faber**

Call Sign: KE4SCT
Richard J Lawrence

Rt 1 Box 175 L
Faber VA 22938

Call Sign: N4UWL
Thomas Sanacuore
6599 Faber Rd
Faber VA 229382780

Call Sign: KM4OZ
Colin E Ramirez
514 Rainbow Ridge Rd
Faber VA 22938

Call Sign: KG4FOK
Lars P Larsen
33 Tiffany Ln
Faber VA 22938

Call Sign: WB6HFI
Jack G Evans Jr
171 Turkey Run
Faber VA 22938

Call Sign: W4KOV
Jack G Evans Jr
171 Turkey Run
Faber VA 22938

**FCC Amateur Radio Licenses
in Fairfax**

Call Sign: KA4NAU
William J Porter Jr
10841 1st St
Fairfax VA 22030

Call Sign: KB4GND
David M Radtke
9821 5 Oaks Rd
Fairfax VA 22031

Call Sign: N4JNH
Susan C Goodall
9821 5 Oaks Rd
Fairfax VA 22031

Call Sign: KJ4YHC
John M Righi
10935 Adare Dr

Fairfax VA 22032

Call Sign: KG4PBV
Matthew Moulton
5518 Akridge Ct
Fairfax VA 22032

Call Sign: W4POQ
William E Elder
3322 Albion Ct
Fairfax VA 22031

Call Sign: KD4CUM
Wanda J Wyborski
4211 Allison Cir
Fairfax VA 22030

Call Sign: KE4MO
Tice F De Young
4312 Alta Vista Dr
Fairfax VA 22030

Call Sign: WD4EEA
Joe T Reeves
4401 Alta Vista Dr
Fairfax VA 22030

Call Sign: W4JJS
John J Schumacher
4337 Andes Dr
Fairfax VA 22030

Call Sign: N4XBH
Raymond J Bayerl
5502 Andrews Chapel Ct
Fairfax VA 220323109

Call Sign: KB4IKT
Marilyn C Cunningham
5557 Ann Peake Dr
Fairfax VA 22032

Call Sign: WD5DBC
Howard F Cunningham Jr
5557 Ann Peake Dr
Fairfax VA 220323001

Call Sign: WA6YOU
Ronald C Payne

10203 Antietam Ave
Fairfax VA 22030

Call Sign: KD4MTW
Michael T Sheleheda
10207 Antietam Ave
Fairfax VA 220302101

Call Sign: KI4EKH
John D Mairs
4126 Appleby Way
Fairfax VA 22030

Call Sign: WA4CPZ
Michael O Warren
11911 Appling Valley Rd
Fairfax VA 22030

Call Sign: N5IPK
Harold A Chadsey
11931 Appling Valley Rd
Fairfax VA 220305701

Call Sign: KF4SMV
Carol C Chadsey
11931 Appling Valley Rd
Fairfax VA 220305901

Call Sign: KI4ZHB
Thomas A Dalton
11317 Aristotle Dr 413
Fairfax VA 22030

Call Sign: KE4JEK
Luis A Llamosas
9130 Arlington Blvd
Fairfax VA 22031

Call Sign: KF4HNM
Kelvin D Hodge
9481 Arlington Blvd 103
Fairfax VA 22031

Call Sign: AB5TY
Macalee L Hime
9229 Arlington Blvd Apt 353
Fairfax VA 22031

Call Sign: KG4KZY

Charles H Nelson
855 Arlington Blvd Ste 101
Fairfax VA 22042

Call Sign: KF4ZXX
William K Cassidy
10436 Armstrong St
Fairfax VA 220303616

Call Sign: KC4SQK
Gerald L Brunson
10511 Arrowood St
Fairfax VA 22032

Call Sign: KJ4NJI
Sheila B Adams
10513 Arrowood St
Fairfax VA 22032

Call Sign: KK4ADS
Dane J Larsen
10624 Ashby Pl
Fairfax VA 22030

Call Sign: K4AS
Robert L Fischer
9802 Ashby Rd
Fairfax VA 220313516

Call Sign: KB3GHH
Stephen J Svoboda
9819 Ashby Rd
Fairfax VA 22031

Call Sign: N4DGS
John D Gallivan III
9124 Ashmeade Dr
Fairfax VA 22032

Call Sign: N4UCC
John D Gallivan IV
9124 Ashmeade Dr
Fairfax VA 22032

Call Sign: KG4WAF
Tony Cristofano
13189 Ashvale Dr
Fairfax VA 22033

Call Sign: KG4EWG
Adam D Burgh
13104 Autumn Woods Way Apt
C
Fairfax VA 22033

Call Sign: KD4VZN
Jeffrey W Holmes
13117 Autumn Woods Way Apt
F
Fairfax VA 22033

Call Sign: KJ4DFO
Satoshi Tabata
13101 Autumn Woods Way Apt
G
Fairfax VA 22033

Call Sign: WA4SQX
John E E Dehnel
3115 Barbara Ln
Fairfax VA 220312741

Call Sign: AA4JJ
John R Karickhoff
3235 Barbara Ln
Fairfax VA 22031

Call Sign: N4MWP
Michael J Dinolfo
4027 Barbour Dr
Fairfax VA 22030

Call Sign: K4TFK
Howard C Junkermann
3501 Barkley Dr
Fairfax VA 22031

Call Sign: W3AWU
Alfred J Cammarata
9542 Barkwood Ct
Fairfax VA 22032

Call Sign: KD4DGT
Pablo A Estrada
9924 Barnsbury Ct
Fairfax VA 22031

Call Sign: WD9COZ

Barry L Barton
9200 Barrick St Apt 202
Fairfax VA 22031

Call Sign: NJ9L
Jameson Burt
9156 Barrick St Apt 3
Fairfax VA 22031

Call Sign: WB5PAQ
Hans K Crosthwait
3480 Barristers Keepe Cir
Fairfax VA 22031

Call Sign: KC4PQW
Joshua A Powers
4610 Battenburg Ln
Fairfax VA 22030

Call Sign: WA2DLL
Robert L Freeman
3139 Bayswater Ct
Fairfax VA 22031

Call Sign: WB4FDS
Zardis R Hoffman
10314 Beaumont St
Fairfax VA 22030

Call Sign: KG4KUT
William P Chamberlin
9544 Belglade St
Fairfax VA 22031

Call Sign: KI4AFN
John L Trevey Jr
6036 Berwynd Rd
Fairfax VA 220304532

Call Sign: WB4OPZ
Edward J Cyran
4310 Birch Pond Ln
Fairfax VA 22033

Call Sign: KI4GRY
Thinnappan Subramanian
9547 Blair Ln 201
Fairfax VA 22031

Call Sign: KI4EEH
Sae R Kim
12312 Blair Ridge Rd
Fairfax VA 220331800

Call Sign: N4CVZ
Fred A Scheihing
8910 Blue Gate Dr
Fairfax VA 220311404

Call Sign: N3NQB
Dennis E Renken
10445 Breckinridge Ln
Fairfax VA 22030

Call Sign: KF4HGI
George L Price
5104 Brentwood Farm Dr
Fairfax VA 22030

Call Sign: N4YDP
Richard W Cramer II
4610 Briar Patch Ct
Fairfax VA 22032

Call Sign: KJ4CNN
Jorg R Anderson
4618 Briar Patch Ct
Fairfax VA 220322120

Call Sign: KD4LJC
Bruce E Copping
3714 Brices Ford Ct
Fairfax VA 22033

Call Sign: N4CZO
Michael W Jenkins
5526 Bridgewood Dr
Fairfax VA 22032

Call Sign: N2OXQ
Paul R Coleman
4901 Briggs Rd
Fairfax VA 22030

Call Sign: K3IOB
Christopher F Mayol
4901 Briggs Rd 312
Fairfax VA 220305708

Call Sign: KC4CZA
Daniel M Cash
10823 Broadwater Dr
Fairfax VA 22032

Call Sign: KF4OSR
Brian J Goldsmith
3227 Brookings Ct
Fairfax VA 220313004

Call Sign: KG4UNO
Andrew T Coleman
3708 Broomsedge Ct
Fairfax VA 22033

Call Sign: KD4NFG
Mark C Baban
3307 Buckeye Ln
Fairfax VA 22033

Call Sign: N4XLC
George J Flood
11328 Bulova Ln
Fairfax VA 22030

Call Sign: W4TQS
Richard O St Clair
4223 Burke Station Rd
Fairfax VA 22032

Call Sign: KK4BMA
Stanton C Fox
3513 Burrows Ave
Fairfax VA 22030

Call Sign: WB4EVT
Oliver J De Zoute
11020 Byrd Dr
Fairfax VA 22030

Call Sign: K3KST
Gary M Citrenbaum
4330 Cannon Ridge Ct Unit K
Fairfax VA 22033

Call Sign: KF4MQD
Rene Winnik
12312 Cannonball Rd

Fairfax VA 22030

Call Sign: KI4LGL
Joseph H Kim
11501 Cardoness Ln 102
Fairfax VA 22030

Call Sign: KA4COW
Robert B Doherty
10813 Carol St
Fairfax VA 22030

Call Sign: K5FY
Bruce P Hellmann
4720 Carterwood Dr
Fairfax VA 22032

Call Sign: KC0ZIR
Daniel E Wesely
11104 Cavalier Ct Apt 3E
Fairfax VA 22030

Call Sign: WD8QAX
Linda M Johnston
10811 Cedar Ave Apt 2
Fairfax VA 220304720

Call Sign: KF4PIY
Regis A Gottus
3106 Cedar Grove Dr
Fairfax VA 22031

Call Sign: KJ4ETF
Eric N Tapp
3152 Cedar Grove Dr
Fairfax VA 22031

Call Sign: KJ4NIZ
Leonardo Leonato
12408 Cedar Lakes Dr
Fairfax VA 22033

Call Sign: WA4ACH
Kenneth A Chayt
9712 Ceralene Dr
Fairfax VA 220321704

Call Sign: WD4PTR
Carl W Kain

9723 Ceralene Dr
Fairfax VA 22032

Call Sign: KD4RET
Laszlo Taba
3748 Chain Bridge Rd
Fairfax VA 22030

Call Sign: KJ4PVL
Yaw Ampofo Kwarteng
3545 Chain Bridge Rd 209
Fairfax VA 22030

Call Sign: KJ4YPQ
Chalew D Anteneh
3545 Chain Bridge Rd 209
Fairfax VA 22030

Call Sign: KJ4YPR
Mary Coleen F Cas
3545 Chain Bridge Rd 209
Fairfax VA 22030

Call Sign: WA6HRB
Steven E Brown
5335 Chalkstone Way
Fairfax VA 22030

Call Sign: KJ4CNJ
Claude W Kirkland
4900 Chantery Ct
Fairfax VA 220322309

Call Sign: KK4CWK
Claude W Kirkland
4900 Chantery Ct
Fairfax VA 220322309

Call Sign: KF4NMO
Richard J W Tryon
4902 Chantery Ct
Fairfax VA 22032

Call Sign: WB7CSL
Walter E Ireland
4310 Chariot Crt
Fairfax VA 22030

Call Sign: KG4LTW

ARC Of Itu Delegates
4310 Chariot Crt
Fairfax VA 22030

Call Sign: K4ITU
ARC Of Itu Delegates
4310 Chariot Ct
Fairfax VA 22030

Call Sign: AG4QV
Robert T Campbell
5505 Chestermill Ct
Fairfax VA 22030

Call Sign: KA4REI
Glenn Moore
4100 Chestnut St
Fairfax VA 22030

Call Sign: AB4CY
Paul E Wilkins
3208 Chichester Ln
Fairfax VA 22031

Call Sign: WK4M
Lewis S Norman Jr
3211 Chichester Ln
Fairfax VA 22031

Call Sign: KJ4CNV
James R Spiller
4822 Christie Jane Ln
Fairfax VA 22030

Call Sign: AJ4IV
James R Spiller
4822 Christie Jane Ln
Fairfax VA 22030

Call Sign: AJ4RS
James R Spiller
4822 Christie Jane Ln
Fairfax VA 22030

Call Sign: KA6DOF
Martin H Mc Gay
11138 Church St
Fairfax VA 22030

Call Sign: KK4DON
Joshua E Mann
10908 Clara Barton Ct
Fairfax VA 22032

Call Sign: N4TWI
David J Shrewsbury
3901 Clares Ct
Fairfax VA 220334640

Call Sign: KJ4HSU
Victor Youk
6113 Colchester Rd
Fairfax VA 22030

Call Sign: KI4BPC
A Glenn Richardson
6301 Colchester Rd
Fairfax VA 22030

Call Sign: KG4UIY
Blane J Jackson
8915 Colebury Pl
Fairfax VA 22301

Call Sign: N4GRW
James B Bean
5062 Coleridge Dr
Fairfax VA 22032

Call Sign: KF4VWC
John M Williamson
5082 Coleridge Dr
Fairfax VA 220322416

Call Sign: WB4JJJ
Alan A Wheeler
4206 Collier Rd
Fairfax VA 22030

Call Sign: KD6YOX
Edward H You
10320 Collingham Dr
Fairfax VA 22032

Call Sign: K3PRE
Edward R Kowalski
10430 Collingham Dr
Fairfax VA 220322608

Call Sign: KG4TLR
William R Kincaid
10432 Collingham Dr
Fairfax VA 22032

Call Sign: N3QQE
Xiangjun Liu
3952 Collis Oak Ct
Fairfax VA 22033

Call Sign: KI4PI
Ralph M Pool
9912 Colony Rd
Fairfax VA 22030

Call Sign: KJ4KTS
Edwin C Gardner
9932 Colony Rd
Fairfax VA 22030

Call Sign: K4JUB
Frank H Nelson
10812 Colton St
Fairfax VA 22032

Call Sign: KI4FYM
Brent E Marshall
9818 Commonwealth Blvd
Fairfax VA 22032

Call Sign: K4EMC
Brent E Marshall
9818 Commonwealth Blvd
Fairfax VA 22032

Call Sign: KI4JQB
John D Marshall
9818 Commonwealth Blvd
Fairfax VA 220322406

Call Sign: AA4PX
Adam Albrett
9905 Commonwealth Blvd
Fairfax VA 220322408

Call Sign: KC4LX
Ryoji Ikeda
10221 Confederate Ln

Fairfax VA 22030

Call Sign: N4EFK
Malcolm C Mercer Jr
10301 Confederate Ln
Fairfax VA 22030

Call Sign: K2HRM
Malcolm C Mercer Jr
10301 Confederate Ln
Fairfax VA 22030

Call Sign: W1CHQ
Arthur W Pattee
10319 Confederate Ln
Fairfax VA 220302131

Call Sign: WA4BXO
Ron S Stultz
3516 Cornell Rd
Fairfax VA 22030

Call Sign: K0ADY
Richard H Williams
10430 Courtney Dr
Fairfax VA 22030

Call Sign: KG4LYE
Daniel A Colcher
3083 Covington St
Fairfax VA 22031

Call Sign: KJ4HSQ
Michael A Cummings
3086 Covington St
Fairfax VA 22031

Call Sign: KM4AO
Charles E Mc Cullough III
3098 Covington St
Fairfax VA 22031

Call Sign: KE4YXP
Darrin J Benson
5348 Cristfield Ct
Fairfax VA 22032

Call Sign: KF4VZY
Bryan W Stange

5440 Crows Nest Ct
Fairfax VA 22032

Call Sign: KM4ML
Richard A Rucker
10426 Darby St
Fairfax VA 22030

Call Sign: N1FPF
Daniel E Hunt
9350 Deer Glen Ct
Fairfax VA 22031

Call Sign: KA3YIJ
Norman R Solis
2911 Deer Hollow Way 119
Fairfax VA 22031

Call Sign: KD4KYR
Michael D Mc Makin Jr
2921 Deer Hollow Way 214
Fairfax VA 22031

Call Sign: KC4APU
Geoffrey R Battersby
4603 Demby Dr
Fairfax VA 22032

Call Sign: KD4KBP
Lee G Cassetty
10703 Deneale Pl
Fairfax VA 22032

Call Sign: KI4SMK
Joshua S Hunter
5024 Dequincey Dr
Fairfax VA 22032

Call Sign: KB4IWD
Jeffrey A Barr
5038 Dequincey Dr
Fairfax VA 22032

Call Sign: KC2EWT
Aaron T S Fenner
4403 Dixie Hill Rd Apt 201
Fairfax VA 22030

Call Sign: N2JDY

Aaron T S Fenner
4403 Dixie Hill Rd Apt 201
Fairfax VA 22030

Call Sign: WA4KUH
David H Mooney
4028 Dogberry Ln
Fairfax VA 22033

Call Sign: KI4NOG
Donald R Hensley Jr
12722 Dogwood Hills Ln
Fairfax VA 22033

Call Sign: KI4OBP
Kylie B Hensley
12722 Dogwood Hills Ln
Fairfax VA 22033

Call Sign: KC4ZPR
Edward A Swoboda
3612 Dorado Ct
Fairfax VA 220313836

Call Sign: KG4JBM
Andrew J Perash
10002 Duncan St
Fairfax VA 22031

Call Sign: K4AJP
Andrew J Perash
10002 Duncan St
Fairfax VA 22031

Call Sign: WD4PWK
David D Hawkins
12613 Dusty Wheel Ln
Fairfax VA 22033

Call Sign: KD4ORW
John C Aulabaugh
3164 Eakin Park Ct
Fairfax VA 22031

Call Sign: KJ4OOJ
Alex J Aulabaugh
3164 Eakin Park Ct
Fairfax VA 22031

Call Sign: KJ4OOI
John M Aulabaugh
3164 Eakin Pk Ct
Fairfax VA 22031

Call Sign: KC4IDG
Bruce C Ball
9932 Eastlake Dr
Fairfax VA 22032

Call Sign: W4EXS
Arthur R Ashley
3636 Elderberry Pl
Fairfax VA 22033

Call Sign: KG4LUN
Robert M Weiss
3136 Ellenwood Dr
Fairfax VA 220312039

Call Sign: KG4VEV
Kimberly M Coffield
5403 Ellzey Dr
Fairfax VA 22032

Call Sign: N2LEQ
John W Downey
3622 Embassy Ln
Fairfax VA 22030

Call Sign: N8AKK
Debra L Tolson
5304 Esabella Ct
Fairfax VA 22032

Call Sign: KI4IHC
Daniel T Olewine
2929 Eskridge Rd Ste S
Fairfax VA 22031

Call Sign: K9BAE
George A Hanover
4139 Evergreen Dr
Fairfax VA 22032

Call Sign: KJ4BQZ
Gary M Jackson
2906 Everleigh Way
Fairfax VA 22031

Call Sign: KG4NBK
Gregory A Bogle
12627 Fair Crest Ct
Fairfax VA 22033

Call Sign: KK4HDP
Kevin M Fennell
12587 Fair Lakes Cir 191
Fairfax VA 22033

Call Sign: K4KMF
Kevin M Fennell
12587 Fair Lakes Cir 191
Fairfax VA 22033

Call Sign: N4CHM
William L Mega
3911 Fairfax Farms Rd
Fairfax VA 220332721

Call Sign: W1FHU
William L Mega
3911 Fairfax Farms Rd
Fairfax VA 220332721

Call Sign: WN8VEF
Vince E Foley
11616 Fairfax Meadows Cir
19003
Fairfax VA 22030

Call Sign: N2WCA
Jerry B Hernandez
3880 Fairfax Sq
Fairfax VA 22031

Call Sign: N0CHX
Richard H Garrett
9852 Fairfax Sq 225
Fairfax VA 22031

Call Sign: KJ4EAA
John L Foster II
4125 Fairfax St
Fairfax VA 22030

Call Sign: KC9RHA
Joseph F Trefilek V

11735 Fairfax Woods Way Apt
6203
Fairfax VA 22030

Call Sign: KD4QVW
Stanley E Jones
2928 Fairlee Dr
Fairfax VA 22031

Call Sign: KG4JCN
Amanda Marie Bohrer
3906 Fairview Dr
Fairfax VA 22031

Call Sign: WA3RGH
Craig B Kendall
12399 Falkirk Dr
Fairfax VA 22033

Call Sign: KK4EKZ
Marilyn L Hilbers
12461 Falkirk Dr
Fairfax VA 22033

Call Sign: W4LBL
Joseph E Herrmann
10116 Farmington Dr
Fairfax VA 22030

Call Sign: WB4NPQ
Leslie J Brown
12303 Field Lark Ct
Fairfax VA 22033

Call Sign: KJ4HDC
Bruce O Burnside
3134 Flintlock Rd
Fairfax VA 22030

Call Sign: KE4LF
Joe R Dickhudt
11111 Flora Lee Dr
Fairfax VA 22039

Call Sign: K4ELF
Joe R Dickhudt
11111 Flora Lee Dr
Fairfax VA 22039

Call Sign: KI4FNC
Bruce O Ferratt
10309 Forest Ave
Fairfax VA 220303529

Call Sign: K4BOF
Bruce O Ferratt
10309 Forest Ave
Fairfax VA 220303529

Call Sign: KD4QVV
Carolyn D Williams
4202 Forest Ct
Fairfax VA 22032

Call Sign: KE4JPD
James T Fortune
5109 Forsgate Pl
Fairfax VA 22030

Call Sign: KG4HMT
Anna C Fortune
5109 Forsgate Pl
Fairfax VA 22030

Call Sign: KE4FZI
Francisca V Alonso
12263 Fort Buffalo Cir
Fairfax VA 22033

Call Sign: KE4TXP
Jesse B Tucker
10287 Friendship Ct
Fairfax VA 22030

Call Sign: N3TWP
Andrew R Leister
11106 Gainsborough Ct Apt 3
Fairfax VA 22030

Call Sign: K3PZM
Frank J Silver
5119 Gainsborough Dr
Fairfax VA 220322712

Call Sign: KI4JJM
Keith A Bare II
5219 Gainsborough Dr
Fairfax VA 22032

Call Sign: KE4CYB
Gary L Haddox
5377 Gainsborough Dr
Fairfax VA 22032

Call Sign: KD4OXL
Joseph C Liberti Jr
12103 Gary Hill Dr
Fairfax VA 22030

Call Sign: KD4RNF
Michael A Barrett
11960 Glen Alden Rd
Fairfax VA 22030

Call Sign: W4YWF
John A Massie
3903 Glenbrook Rd
Fairfax VA 22031

Call Sign: N2RPJ
Eugene D Mc Gee
8921 Glenbrook Rd
Fairfax VA 22031

Call Sign: KA4YZG
Keith P Newman
9110 Glenbrook Rd
Fairfax VA 22031

Call Sign: KB4BJI
Robert J Hickey Jr
10114 Glenmere Rd
Fairfax VA 22032

Call Sign: WA4EQY
Grover G Heiman Jr
2881 Glenvale Dr
Fairfax VA 220311436

Call Sign: KC4OIG
Rebecca J Fleischer
4052 Glostonbury Way
Fairfax VA 22030

Call Sign: WB4PBI
John P Korb
10612 Goldeneye Ln

Fairfax VA 220323151

Call Sign: W4GHJ
Roy A Benson
5427 Governor Yeardley Dr
Fairfax VA 22032

Call Sign: KI4RDA
Daniel C Benson
5427 Governor Yeardley Dr
Fairfax VA 22032

Call Sign: WA1YIG
John M Feeney
4606 Gramlee Cir
Fairfax VA 22032

Call Sign: KJ4WRJ
Joseph A Hoover
12933C Grays Pointe Rd
Fairfax VA 220332134

Call Sign: N3TG
William T Free Jr
3627 Great Laurel Ln
Fairfax VA 22033

Call Sign: KJ4EGY
Mary A Free
3627 Great Laurel Ln
Fairfax VA 220331212

Call Sign: K3MAF
Mary A Free
3627 Great Laurel Ln
Fairfax VA 220331212

Call Sign: WA4OAP
Jane M Wenger
6112 Green Cap Pl
Fairfax VA 22030

Call Sign: WA4DXC
Neil D Fox
5502 Greenshank Ct
Fairfax VA 220323144

Call Sign: KG4PSZ
Thomas W Creedon

4115 Grover Glen Ct
Fairfax VA 22030

Call Sign: AG4QP
Thomas W Creedon
4115 Grover Glen Ct
Fairfax VA 22030

Call Sign: N4BIA
Richard E Runyon
9116 Hamilton Dr
Fairfax VA 22031

Call Sign: N4WFX
Mark F Moynihan
5609 Hampton Forest Way
Fairfax VA 22030

Call Sign: KB3ASP
Robert M Silber
5611 Hampton Forest Way
Fairfax VA 22203

Call Sign: KJ4SZH
Raja Waseem
5020 Head Ct
Fairfax VA 22032

Call Sign: KB7VR
Jesse M Richards III
5403 Heatherford Ct
Fairfax VA 22030

Call Sign: KJ4LPS
Alexander L Garmew
4505 Herend Pl
Fairfax VA 22032

Call Sign: AF3T
Peter S Jaworski
3621 Heritage Ln
Fairfax VA 22030

Call Sign: KA4SMT
Palmer G Tunstall
3619 Highland Pl
Fairfax VA 22033

Call Sign: AA0TH

Jill C Kamienski
3017 Hightower Pl 308
Fairfax VA 22031

Call Sign: KI4DRL
Gregory S Matson
4406 Hillyer St
Fairfax VA 22032

Call Sign: W4TAX
Gregory S Matson
4406 Hillyer St
Fairfax VA 22032

Call Sign: K4JDM
James D Hawkins
5202 Holden St
Fairfax VA 22032

Call Sign: KG6UJX
Thomas P Gresham
4307 Hollowview Ct
Fairfax VA 22032

Call Sign: KI4BTB
Amy A Zwirko
4426 Holly Ave
Fairfax VA 22030

Call Sign: KB4EYL
Cecil E Barker Jr
4445 Holly Ave
Fairfax VA 22030

Call Sign: KI4ZYJ
Shawn D Morrow
4754 Holly Ave
Fairfax VA 22030

Call Sign: W4SDM
Shawn D Morrow
4754 Holly Ave
Fairfax VA 22030

Call Sign: KI4KLY
Joshua N Wilkes
5409 Honey Brook Ct
Fairfax VA 22030

Call Sign: KD4OFV
Timothy J Kilby
10607 Howerton Ave
Fairfax VA 22030

Call Sign: KH2FX
Anita R Hofferth
10707 Howerton Ave
Fairfax VA 22030

Call Sign: NH2A
Kerry B Hofferth
10707 Howerton Ave
Fairfax VA 22030

Call Sign: AK4LR
Andrew P Mikulski
4232 Hunt Club Cir Apt 1134
Fairfax VA 22033

Call Sign: KK4DPU
Dane A Smith
4240 Hunt Club Cir Apt 1231
Fairfax VA 22033

Call Sign: KB4MYU
Charles N Haggard
4212 Hunt Club Cir Apt 722
Fairfax VA 22033

Call Sign: W4HFZ
Charles A Richard
3605 Irish Moss Ct
Fairfax VA 22033

Call Sign: KD7SCV
Charles A Richard Jr
3605 Irish Moss Ct
Fairfax VA 22033

Call Sign: KD7SCW
Lisa M Richard
3605 Irish Moss Ct
Fairfax VA 22033

Call Sign: KI4QYJ
Allison B Richard
3605 Irish Moss Ct
Fairfax VA 22033

Call Sign: KB1RFK
Emily N Richard
3605 Irish Moss Ct
Fairfax VA 22033

Call Sign: KE4POI
Walter C Herbert Jr
8310 Ivy Green Rd
Fairfax VA 22039

Call Sign: AI4VL
Walter C Herbert Jr
8310 Ivy Green Rd
Fairfax VA 22039

Call Sign: KE4CW
Albert G Hutchins
10819 James Halley Dr
Fairfax VA 22032

Call Sign: W4MFM
Sean P O Mara
4260 Jefferson Oaks Cir Apt H
Fairfax VA 22033

Call Sign: KD4FRJ
Joan M Newman
3623 Jermantown Rd
Fairfax VA 22030

Call Sign: KD4LJD
John P Bisset
10599 John Ayres Dr
Fairfax VA 22032

Call Sign: KE4FNC
Jay C Conner
10708 John Ayres Dr
Fairfax VA 22032

Call Sign: N7UTF
Joshua B Hunley
10710 John Turley Pl
Fairfax VA 22032

Call Sign: K8LOS
Richard A Golden
10627 Jones St 101B

Fairfax VA 22030

Call Sign: KD6NRI
Robert A Book
9117 Kahle St
Fairfax VA 22032

Call Sign: K9DZI
James E Girard
6328 Karmich St
Fairfax VA 22039

Call Sign: N5PYJ
Gerald W Whatley
3917 Kathryn Jean Ct
Fairfax VA 22033

Call Sign: KD4YEP
Stanley R Sulak
5248 Kaywood Ct
Fairfax VA 22032

Call Sign: KF4WZC
Aaron M Sulak
5248 Kaywood Ct
Fairfax VA 220322618

Call Sign: KB6KBA
Robert H Shaw
5251 Kaywood Ct
Fairfax VA 220322614

Call Sign: K4UNF
Frank N Winn
3908 Keith Ave
Fairfax VA 22030

Call Sign: KF4YMZ
Leilani G De Witt
7700 Kelly Ann Ct
Fairfax VA 22039

Call Sign: KJ4IMU
Matthew M Hauler
4137 Kentmere Sq
Fairfax VA 22030

Call Sign: KJ4NJE
James R Alford

3914 Kernstown Ct
Fairfax VA 22033

Call Sign: KF4YXV
Richard W Cummings
4306 Kilbourne Dr
Fairfax VA 22032

Call Sign: WY4Z
Harry W Johnson
9209 Kilmarnock Dr
Fairfax VA 22031

Call Sign: WD4PYF
Robert R Hadley
6119 Kings Color Dr
Fairfax VA 22030

Call Sign: WA3LHV
Regis P Eannarino
9706 Kingsbridge Dr 1
Fairfax VA 22031

Call Sign: K2ZQW
Kenneth M Bohling
9720 Kingsbridge Dr 101
Fairfax VA 22031

Call Sign: KJ4UYF
Katherine Habermas
9712 Kingsbridge Dr Unit 101
Fairfax VA 22031

Call Sign: AK4BJ
Katherine Habermas
9712 Kingsbridge Dr Unit 101
Fairfax VA 22031

Call Sign: KC0QZS
Adam M Hiatt
9912 Kinsgbridge Dr
Fairfax VA 22031

Call Sign: KG4UIR
Keith A Robertory
9117 Kristin Ln
Fairfax VA 22032

Call Sign: N4VJS

David P Timpe
9219 Kristin Ln
Fairfax VA 22032

Call Sign: KC5RPD
Mark T Devlin
5508 La Cross Ct
Fairfax VA 22032

Call Sign: KJ4SES
Mark W Hartong
4039 Lake Glen Dr
Fairfax VA 22033

Call Sign: AJ4YI
Mark W Hartong
4039 Lake Glen Dr
Fairfax VA 22033

Call Sign: KD4SO
Kenneth J Hintz
11727 Lakewood Ln
Fairfax VA 22039

Call Sign: KG4NXQ
Ray J Mahoney
5510 Landmark Pl
Fairfax VA 22032

Call Sign: KG4QXR
Ray J Mahoney
5510 Landmark Pl
Fairfax VA 22032

Call Sign: AG4TR
Ray J Mahoney
5510 Landmark Pl
Fairfax VA 22032

Call Sign: KE4NKR
Dennis H Carlough
5512 Landmark Pl
Fairfax VA 22032

Call Sign: N4VJT
Donna A Feller
3605 Landon Ct
Fairfax VA 22031

Call Sign: KC4FPC
Roy E Grisham
10302 Latney Rd
Fairfax VA 22032

Call Sign: KE4BUK
William S Powell
5384 Laura Belle Ln
Fairfax VA 22032

Call Sign: KE4BUL
Tina M Powell
5384 Laura Belle Ln
Fairfax VA 22032

Call Sign: N4SUR
Edward A Parsons
5387 Laura Belle Ln
Fairfax VA 22032

Call Sign: KB4LK
Keith W Reiss
3522 Laurel Leaf Ln
Fairfax VA 220313213

Call Sign: KI4YMB
Lora J Mclain
3605 Laurel Leaf Ln
Fairfax VA 220313214

Call Sign: KK4DBD
Matthew Roney
4203 Lauries Way
Fairfax VA 22033

Call Sign: KA3WRL
Charles M Capps
3331 Lauriston
Fairfax VA 22031

Call Sign: N4FSW
Earl B Hohbein
4602 Lawn Ct
Fairfax VA 22032

Call Sign: N4JMJ
Arthur Van Wagenen
4602 Lawn Ct
Fairfax VA 220322015

Call Sign: AG4PO
John M Gray
4613 Lawn Ct
Fairfax VA 220322016

Call Sign: KE4QMR
Michael L Hastings
10336 Layton Hall Dr 508
Fairfax VA 220302327

Call Sign: KJ4BQW
Luis A Aguilar
13296 Leafcrest Ln 202C
Fairfax VA 22033

Call Sign: KJ4EPC
Sameer Chandra
9335 Lee Hwy 204
Fairfax VA 22031

Call Sign: KI4KPP
John P Selph
9335 Lee Hwy 506
Fairfax VA 22031

Call Sign: KJ4MFB
Jason Sandiford
9335 Lee Hwy Apt 410
Fairfax VA 22031

Call Sign: WD4OXP
Daniel P May
4438 Legato Rd
Fairfax VA 22030

Call Sign: KA4OTN
Naoma L May
4501 Legato Rd
Fairfax VA 22030

Call Sign: W4LUE
Clifford D May Jr
4501 Legato Rd
Fairfax VA 22030

Call Sign: WB4VCQ
David R Wolf
4143 Lenox Dr

Fairfax VA 22032

Call Sign: KK4AQS
Kenneth N Moreau
4145 Lenox Dr
Fairfax VA 22032

Call Sign: KA3RQR
Shawn P Stokes
12550 Levau Ct 103
Fairfax VA 22033

Call Sign: KA1UTB
John J Marino
5224 Lewisham Rd
Fairfax VA 22030

Call Sign: KD4ICD
Justin G Marino
5224 Lewisham Rd
Fairfax VA 22030

Call Sign: KD4LTA
Carol A Marino
5224 Lewisham Rd
Fairfax VA 22030

Call Sign: KR1O
John G Marino
5224 Lewisham Rd
Fairfax VA 22030

Call Sign: WB4YHB
Ernest P Fakoury
9717 Limoges Dr
Fairfax VA 22032

Call Sign: KB5JNF
Andrew R West
12154 Lincoln Lake Way 4309
Fairfax VA 22030

Call Sign: KD5ETH
Joseph C Moran Jr
12175 Lincoln Lake Way 7302
Fairfax VA 22030

Call Sign: KC4BQI
John C Bailey Jr

4219 Linden St
Fairfax VA 22030

Call Sign: KD4DEN
Laila S Bailey
4219 Linden St
Fairfax VA 22030

Call Sign: KA2CAI
Christopher G Treston
9583 Lindenbrook St
Fairfax VA 220311154

Call Sign: KJ4PRX
Paul D Graves
3167 Lindenwood Ln
Fairfax VA 22031

Call Sign: KE5WQ
Victoria L Phillips
12012 Lisa Marie Ct
Fairfax VA 22033

Call Sign: KD4LRP
Robert E Duggar
4129 Locust Ln
Fairfax VA 220303551

Call Sign: KI4RSD
Daniel J Dubray
11456 Log Ridge Dr
Fairfax VA 220308571

Call Sign: KI4MNL
Edgar Guerra-Erazo
3329 Lothian Rd
Fairfax VA 22031

Call Sign: N6XDG
Tine J Brajnik
3216 Lothian Rd Apt 202
Fairfax VA 22031

Call Sign: K3SLO
Tine J Brajnik
3216 Lothian Rd Apt 202
Fairfax VA 22031

Call Sign: KI4CNP

John C Galido
3890 Lyndhurst Dr 203
Fairfax VA 22031

Call Sign: N4KRD
Theresa T Cann
10060 Maclura Ct
Fairfax VA 22032

Call Sign: WA4YCC
William A Cann
10060 Maclura Ct
Fairfax VA 22032

Call Sign: KJ4FDJ
Steven Topolovec
9866 Main St
Fairfax VA 22031

Call Sign: KD4QVX
Dee D Sharp
10310 Main St 260
Fairfax VA 22030

Call Sign: AJ4YB
Nicholas A Bloom
10570 Main St Apt 221
Fairfax VA 22030

Call Sign: N5XEG
David D Carter
9820 Main St Apt 401
Fairfax VA 220314215

Call Sign: W8BBR
Graham W Casserly
4409 Majestic Ln
Fairfax VA 220333536

Call Sign: KC0GFA
Abby M Carey
4003 Majestic Ln B
Fairfax VA 22033

Call Sign: KG4NME
Tedd P Knarr
4421 Manor Hall Ln
Fairfax VA 22033

Call Sign: WD4OMI
Davis S Johnson
4114 Maple St
Fairfax VA 22030

Call Sign: KJ4PUQ
Justin L Scott
10607 Maple St
Fairfax VA 22030

Call Sign: KE4ISB
Byrna O West
13010 Maple View Ln
Fairfax VA 22033

Call Sign: W4OOV
John E Frank
4322 Mariner Ln
Fairfax VA 22033

Call Sign: WD4ASI
Thomas H Parker
4330 Mariner Ln
Fairfax VA 22030

Call Sign: KC4FYA
George E Karch
4817 Marymead Dr
Fairfax VA 22030

Call Sign: KK4WQ
Laquetta A Karch
4817 Marymead Dr
Fairfax VA 22030

Call Sign: KI4AWR
Mohammad A Chaudhry
4224 Mayport Ln
Fairfax VA 22033

Call Sign: W2SNH
Donn Mc Giehan
8318 McNeil
Fairfax VA 22180

Call Sign: KK4HMV
John E Conrick
11431 Meath Dr
Fairfax VA 22030

Call Sign: AD4WA
Andrew W Huttner
13234 Memory Ln
Fairfax VA 22033

Call Sign: N4USK
Claude W Johnson
4104 Middle Ridge Dr
Fairfax VA 22033

Call Sign: KI4VYH
Michael A Hughes
4303 Middle Ridge Dr
Fairfax VA 22033

Call Sign: KE4RRC
Matthew G Mc Ilwain
3302 Midland Rd
Fairfax VA 22031

Call Sign: KC8EGY
Brian G Willis
3314 Midland Rd
Fairfax VA 22031

Call Sign: K4JHU
Samuel C Coroniti
3305 Mill Springs Dr
Fairfax VA 220323016

Call Sign: WD4BFB
Harlan N Olson
4427 Miniature Ln
Fairfax VA 22033

Call Sign: W4JLF
John L Foster II
4439 Miniature Ln
Fairfax VA 22033

Call Sign: W4NIJ
Herbert Greenberg
4114 Minstrell Ln
Fairfax VA 22033

Call Sign: KK4HMY
Rocco R Soraci
12799 Misty Creek Ln

Fairfax VA 22033

Call Sign: KJ4SZK
Jose R Ramos
13118 Misty Glen Ln
Fairfax VA 22033

Call Sign: KI4YGU
Steven M Sears
4164 Monument Hillway 13306
Fairfax VA 22030

Call Sign: NT4AT
Darwin B Bingham
4231 Monument Wall Way Apt
339
Fairfax VA 22030

Call Sign: KB3XC
Van E Evans
9160 Moonstone Dr
Fairfax VA 22031

Call Sign: W4ICN
Walter J Tolson
10010 Morningside Ct
Fairfax VA 22030

Call Sign: WD4GQP
John E Shepherd
3716 Morningside Dr
Fairfax VA 22031

Call Sign: W4NUA
Francis J Haynes
10113 Mosby Woods Dr
Fairfax VA 220301719

Call Sign: KC4IGS
William J Mc Clain
10133 Mosby Woods Dr
Fairfax VA 220301719

Call Sign: KC4FQO
Glenn E Cavert
5115 Myrtle Leaf Dr
Fairfax VA 22032

Call Sign: KI4EKG

Oliver H Richter
11320 Nancyann Way
Fairfax VA 22030

Call Sign: KJ4MTL
Wolfgang O Richter
11320 Nancyann Way
Fairfax VA 22030

Call Sign: KE4GHT
Clifford R R Krieger
5416 New London Park Dr
Fairfax VA 22032

Call Sign: WZ4V
Robert E Bledsoe
10616 Norman Ave
Fairfax VA 22030

Call Sign: KI4QER
Glenda G Jenkins
10802 Norman Ave
Fairfax VA 22030

Call Sign: K4GGJ
Glenda G Jenkins
10802 Norman Ave
Fairfax VA 22030

Call Sign: KG4RRR
Mark E Caputa
4405 Oak Creek Ct 408
Fairfax VA 22033

Call Sign: KJ4OCE
Deapesh Misra
12321 Oak Creek Ln 1719
Fairfax VA 22033

Call Sign: KC2QCY
Nicholas B Leghorn
12313 Oak Creek Ln Apt 1518
Fairfax VA 22033

Call Sign: KC6TUE
Bradley D Strausbaugh
12316 Oak Creek Ln Apt 724
Fairfax VA 22033

Call Sign: KC5HQS
Brandon T Royster
4865 Oakcrest Dr
Fairfax VA 22030

Call Sign: KK4EPQ
Jonathan Posey
4486 Oakdale Crescent Ct 4312
Fairfax VA 22030

Call Sign: KG4JJV
Daniel J Ternes
4458 Oakdale Crescent Ct Apt
1235
Fairfax VA 22030

Call Sign: KA4ORH
Lori J Draheim
3513 Old Post Rd
Fairfax VA 22030

Call Sign: WA2HWR
Stephen C Moss
5911 Old Sawmill Rd
Fairfax VA 22030

Call Sign: W4RJA
Samuel C Wagner
4100 Olley Ln
Fairfax VA 22032

Call Sign: KG4KUM
Michael R Neill
10813 Orchard St
Fairfax VA 22030

Call Sign: N3NRP
Andrew J Guenther
5311 Orchardson Ct
Fairfax VA 22032

Call Sign: KT4XC
Ernest A Harris Jr
12317 Ox Hill Rd
Fairfax VA 22033

Call Sign: N4TVG
Michael R Kelley
3623 Parklane Rd

Fairfax VA 22030

Call Sign: WA4LYH
Robert F Gordon
3314 Parkside Ter
Fairfax VA 22031

Call Sign: KB7MXI
Curtis A Lamb
13101 Parson Ln
Fairfax VA 22033

Call Sign: KA5BME
Fred L Thornhill
13102 Pavilion Ln
Fairfax VA 22033

Call Sign: N4DVS
Michael S Friedman
13130 Pavilion Ln
Fairfax VA 22033

Call Sign: KD4EKU
Joseph S Minus
10907 Paynes Church Dr
Fairfax VA 22032

Call Sign: KI4ARR
Sylvia Perez-Fasano
10911 Paynes Church Dr
Fairfax VA 22032

Call Sign: KA3VZR
Michael S Twedt
13106 Peach Leaf Pl
Fairfax VA 22030

Call Sign: K6HPR
J Bradley Flippin
13127 Peachleaf Pl
Fairfax VA 220308128

Call Sign: NP4NL
Lourdes C Centeno
10418 Pearl St
Fairfax VA 22032

Call Sign: N7FEH
Terence L Johnson

13306 Pearsall Ln
Fairfax VA 22033

Call Sign: KC5UYA
Glen T Smith
13103 Pelfrey Ln
Fairfax VA 220333029

Call Sign: AI4ZA
Glen T Smith
13103 Pelfrey Ln
Fairfax VA 220333029

Call Sign: KG4MZG
Michael D Henderson
13108 Pelfrey Ln
Fairfax VA 22033

Call Sign: KC2HTK
Matthew Carver
3904 Penderview Dr 728
Fairfax VA 22033

Call Sign: KD4NEM
Charles D Attaway
12155 Penderview Ter Apt 802
Fairfax VA 22033

Call Sign: WA4PNS
William F Amon III
13312 Pennypacker Ln
Fairfax VA 220333451

Call Sign: WB3ERA
Jonathan V Siverling
3508 Perry St
Fairfax VA 22030

Call Sign: N4FIB
Deborah C Mc Lain
3510 Perry St
Fairfax VA 22030

Call Sign: KI4LJD
Haoqi Li
3842 Persimmon Cir
Fairfax VA 22031

Call Sign: AA4QA

Robert L Burton Jr
3943 Persimmon Dr Apt E F F
Fairfax VA 22031

Call Sign: N4NST
Richard H Garrett
3943 Persimmon Dr Eff
Fairfax VA 22031

Call Sign: W1AWA
Richard H Garrett
3943 Persimmon Dr Eff
Fairfax VA 22031

Call Sign: W4PUH
William A Cann
4718 Pickett Rd
Fairfax VA 22032

Call Sign: KG4TVN
Claude M Hennessey
2927 Piney Grove Ct
Fairfax VA 220312021

Call Sign: W4AT
Claude M Hennessey
2927 Piney Grove Ct
Fairfax VA 220312021

Call Sign: KI4BEF
Marcia F Ferreira-Hennessey
2927 Piney Grove Ct
Fairfax VA 220312021

Call Sign: KD4RE
Donald L Garlock Jr
3163 Plantation Pky
Fairfax VA 22030

Call Sign: KI4EXI
Amateur Radio Emergency
Communications Support
3867 Plaza Dr
Fairfax VA 22030

Call Sign: KJ4NXI
Christopher S Moore
13229 Pleasantview Ln
Fairfax VA 22033

Call Sign: W4CGK
Sydney S Wagoner Jr
4144 Point Hollow Ln
Fairfax VA 22033

Call Sign: KF4KWC
Robert P Cannon
12107 Polo Dr Apt 114
Fairfax VA 22033

Call Sign: WB3BTI
Sharon L Hodgkins
5221 Pommeroy Dr
Fairfax VA 22032

Call Sign: KI4YVQ
Glenna L Meade
11611 Popes Head Rd
Fairfax VA 22030

Call Sign: W4IYH
Glenna L Meade
11611 Popes Head Rd
Fairfax VA 22030

Call Sign: WA4RHC
Carl E Parsons
11008 Popeshead Rd
Fairfax VA 220304608

Call Sign: KI4FBB
David B Davies
9521 Poplar Leaf Ct
Fairfax VA 22031

Call Sign: KB4LZS
Oscar Salesky
5004 Porstmouth Rd
Fairfax VA 22032

Call Sign: WA8AHZ
Michael A Aimone
4835 Powell Rd
Fairfax VA 22032

Call Sign: KF4NTS
Patricia A Mitchell
4824 Prestwick Dr

Fairfax VA 22030

Call Sign: KE8TW
Brett S Mason
3712 Prince William Dr
Fairfax VA 22031

Call Sign: N8VPP
Cheryl L Mason
3712 Prince William Dr
Fairfax VA 22031

Call Sign: W4BRA
Eugene L Cave
3750 Prosperity Ave
Fairfax VA 22031

Call Sign: AE4JG
Michael E O Brien
3752 Prosperity Ave
Fairfax VA 22031

Call Sign: KE4YXS
Joan C Obrien
3752 Prosperity Ave
Fairfax VA 22031

Call Sign: KB7GII
Ryan D Taylor
2665 Prosperity Ave 132
Fairfax VA 22031

Call Sign: KE4LOK
Gemal J Brangman
12183 Queens Brigade Dr
Fairfax VA 22030

Call Sign: WA4CLK
Timothy G Donovan
4502 Rachael Manor Dr
Fairfax VA 22032

Call Sign: W4CLK
Timothy G Donovan
4502 Rachael Manor Dr
Fairfax VA 22032

Call Sign: KA4JFO
Allen D Dayton

10221 Raider Ln
Fairfax VA 22030

Call Sign: AC6NN
Craig M Young
3723 Randolph St
Fairfax VA 22030

Call Sign: KE6SYC
Milagros Cobos
3723 Randolph St
Fairfax VA 22030

Call Sign: K4IJ
Clinton C Halstead
10108 Ranger Rd
Fairfax VA 22030

Call Sign: KE4GDY
Glenn K Thompson
10151 Red Spruce Rd
Fairfax VA 22032

Call Sign: KD4UPD
Paul H Brown
10180 Red Spruce Rd
Fairfax VA 22032

Call Sign: KE4QES
Kathryn W Brown
10180 Red Spruce Rd
Fairfax VA 22032

Call Sign: KC7DNR
Blaine W Brown
10180 Red Spruce Rd
Fairfax VA 22032

Call Sign: KC7DWF
Karen T Brown
10180 Red Spruce Rd
Fairfax VA 22032

Call Sign: KC7VAU
David W Brown
10180 Red Spruce Rd
Fairfax VA 22032

Call Sign: KF4TOG

Christopher M Moretz
3022 Regent Tower St 245
Fairfax VA 22031

Call Sign: N4UU
Robert C Sommer
3806 Richard Ave
Fairfax VA 22031

Call Sign: KE4KAO
Christina M Glover
5223 Richardson Dr
Fairfax VA 22032

Call Sign: KB4WEV
John M Grieg
5231 Richardson Dr
Fairfax VA 22032

Call Sign: N4DCN
John B Coleman Jr
5233 Richardson Dr
Fairfax VA 22032

Call Sign: N4RER
Peter S Jensen
4211 Ridge Top Rd Apt 2415
Fairfax VA 22030

Call Sign: WA2ODN
Thomas F Calarco
10803 Rippon Lodge Dr
Fairfax VA 22032

Call Sign: N4LZG
Christopher A Suleske
4450 Rivanna Ln F114
Fairfax VA 22030

Call Sign: WN2SGI
Joseph N Graif
3303 Rocky Mt Rd
Fairfax VA 22031

Call Sign: KG4KAI
Patrick V Rumley
11002 Roma St
Fairfax VA 220305316

Call Sign: W4PVR
Patrick V Rumley
11002 Roma St
Fairfax VA 220305316

Call Sign: W7TBG
Tom B Garcia
10524 Rosehaven St Apt 111
Fairfax VA 22030

Call Sign: KD4ICU
Peter D Bergstrom Jr
4017 Rosemeade Dr
Fairfax VA 22033

Call Sign: KC4HF
David T Armstrong
8917 Royal Hannah Ln
Fairfax VA 22031

Call Sign: WA2KHO
Frederick L Sandel
8620 Running Fox Ct
Fairfax VA 220392723

Call Sign: WB2KHQ
Ronald H Feary
7513 S Reach Dr
Fairfax VA 22039

Call Sign: N2TAD
Ahmed N Amin
3215 Saber Cir
Fairfax VA 220301905

Call Sign: KG4KCX
Thomas F Clark
5451 Safe Harbor Ct
Fairfax VA 22032

Call Sign: N2AW
Robert B Collidge
10328 Sager Ave Unit 224
Fairfax VA 22030

Call Sign: K3US
John F Shell
2903 Saintsbury Plaza 205
Fairfax VA 220311166

Call Sign: WA4MKL
Gerrald J Gantt
4409 San Carlos Dr
Fairfax VA 22030

Call Sign: KI4NXH
Michael D Andersen
3807 Sandalwood Ct
Fairfax VA 22031

Call Sign: KF4WDD
Benjamin J Hofstatter
3906 Sandalwood Ct
Fairfax VA 22031

Call Sign: WA4RBX
Carroll N Guin Jr
10864 Santa Clara Dr
Fairfax VA 220304463

Call Sign: KC4DIA
Edward Burr II
9201 Santayana Dr
Fairfax VA 22031

Call Sign: KB5YDL
Brandt L Welker
10812 Scott Dr
Fairfax VA 22030

Call Sign: N4TOV
Lama Kanawati
10111 Scout Dr
Fairfax VA 22030

Call Sign: N4TPY
Majd Kanawati
10111 Scout Dr
Fairfax VA 22030

Call Sign: WA5UNA
Claude D Stephenson Jr
10203 Scout Dr
Fairfax VA 22030

Call Sign: KG4GYH
James W Robinson Secondary
School ARC

5035 Sideburn Rd
Fairfax VA 22032

Call Sign: KA5GER
Charles E Tompkins III
3804 Skyview Ln
Fairfax VA 220313102

Call Sign: N4UTZ
Isadore J Schoen
3830 Skyview Ln
Fairfax VA 22031

Call Sign: KA5DWZ
Darrel L Adams
12321 Sleepy Lake Ct
Fairfax VA 22033

Call Sign: N8XBP
David A Houde
3080 Southern Elm Ct
Fairfax VA 220311129

Call Sign: WA3IMT
Richard G Marshall
5405 Southport Ln
Fairfax VA 22032

Call Sign: K4HAM
Arthur I Mahler
8911 Southwick St
Fairfax VA 220313236

Call Sign: WD4RMS
Paul S Dell Aria
11209 Split Rail Ln
Fairfax VA 22039

Call Sign: KJ4WCO
Eduardo C Esguerra Jr
3509 Springlake Ter
Fairfax VA 22030

Call Sign: KI4STU
Detrick T Merz
4742 Spruce Ave
Fairfax VA 220306222

Call Sign: K4YT

Karl J Renz
10725 Spruce St
Fairfax VA 22030

Call Sign: KB2BLB
Marisa S Renz
10725 Spruce St
Fairfax VA 22030

Call Sign: KH7CD
Winfried Kriegl
10725 Spruce St
Fairfax VA 22030

Call Sign: N4RDI
Andrew G Fuller
10907 Spurlock Ct
Fairfax VA 22032

Call Sign: KK4GOV
Benjamin J Hosek
10908 Spurlock Ct
Fairfax VA 22032

Call Sign: KK4GOO
Timothy J Hosek
10908 Spurlock Ct
Fairfax VA 22032

Call Sign: W4JT
John P Kingman
9207 St Marks Pl
Fairfax VA 22031

Call Sign: KK4AQP
Philip H Spector
9210 St Marks Pl
Fairfax VA 22031

Call Sign: KD4RGU
Evan P Jayson
9513 Stevebrook Rd
Fairfax VA 22032

Call Sign: N4ZYP
Thomas H Forrest
3009 Steven Martin Dr
Fairfax VA 22031

Call Sign: N4JRL
Arthur D Hurtado
9011 Stoneleigh Ct
Fairfax VA 22031

Call Sign: KF6LWR
Gabriel T Lau
9904 Stoughton Rd
Fairfax VA 22032

Call Sign: KA5SJN
Jerome M Myers
2842 Subtle Ln
Fairfax VA 220311435

Call Sign: KB3GWD
James A Rusinko
3758 Sudley Ford Ct
Fairfax VA 22033

Call Sign: K6MDA
M Dewayne Adams
4241 Summit Corner Dr 258
Fairfax VA 220308444

Call Sign: KJ4JDF
Michael C Shaffer
5223 Summit Dr
Fairfax VA 22030

Call Sign: WB8AGY
James R Cline
11406 Sunflower Ln
Fairfax VA 220306031

Call Sign: KI4STC
James W Kiker
12495 Sweet Leaf Ter
Fairfax VA 22033

Call Sign: KE4KBA
Marvin B Cardon
3258 Sydenham St
Fairfax VA 22031

Call Sign: KI4PHG
Lara C Coutinho
3308 Sydenham St 204
Fairfax VA 22031

Call Sign: K4JYK
Charles F Pollock Jr
3027 Talking Rock Dr
Fairfax VA 22031

Call Sign: KD4UPC
Todd H Mc Namara
10158 Tapestry Ct
Fairfax VA 22032

Call Sign: KD4DET
Marilyn J Jackson
4783 Tapestry Dr
Fairfax VA 22032

Call Sign: W4VG
Barnett C Jackson Jr
4783 Tapestry Dr
Fairfax VA 22032

Call Sign: WA3YYG
Duncan E Mc Bride
4608 Tara Dr
Fairfax VA 22032

Call Sign: WB4RVL
Francis P Cahill
9353 Tartan View Dr
Fairfax VA 22032

Call Sign: WA4MM
Nova Qrp
9353 Tartan View Dr
Fairfax VA 22032

Call Sign: KE4YMM
Gretchen H Anderson
13368 Teaberry Ct
Fairfax VA 220331109

Call Sign: KR4YO
Robert S Anderson
13368 Teaberry Ct
Fairfax VA 220331109

Call Sign: WD4ONJ
Panos P Siatis
7529 Thistledown Trl

Fairfax VA 22039

Call Sign: N1CJV
Christopher S Livingston
3273D Tilton Valley Dr
Fairfax VA 22033

Call Sign: KK4GPA
Shawn L Mccarty
5227 Tooley Ct
Fairfax VA 22032

Call Sign: KK4GOS
Stephen G Mccarty
5227 Tooley Ct
Fairfax VA 22032

Call Sign: KI4FBH
William E Beasley II
13026 Tortoise Pl
Fairfax VA 22033

Call Sign: KJ4FDI
Samantha L Debee
9291 Tower Side Dr 417
Fairfax VA 22031

Call Sign: KE7CNO
John S Anevski
9290 Tower Side Dr Apt 109
Fairfax VA 22031

Call Sign: KI4CNQ
Joerg Zeppenfeld
8232 Townsend St
Fairfax VA 22031

Call Sign: KK4ARQ
Jonathan E Nuckolls
10002 Tumbleweed Ct
Fairfax VA 22032

Call Sign: W4PGA
William C Fuchs
3885 Tusico Pl
Fairfax VA 22030

Call Sign: W4VC
Hal S Christensen

4605 Twinbrook Rd
Fairfax VA 220322041

Call Sign: W4RIM
Hal S Christensen
4605 Twinbrook Rd
Fairfax VA 220322041

Call Sign: KD4VOF
Kevin J Smith
4701 Twinbrook Rd
Fairfax VA 22032

Call Sign: KA4PIL
Albert W Adams
4814 Twinbrook Rd
Fairfax VA 220322049

Call Sign: WB0ZPP
John F Wallin
3582 University Dr
Fairfax VA 22030

Call Sign: W4FMD
Steven R Glickstein
3850 University Dr
Fairfax VA 22030

Call Sign: KG4DFJ
S Adam Nissley
4203 University Dr
Fairfax VA 22030

Call Sign: WD4RPX
Robert W Wedan Jr
4214 Upper Park Dr
Fairfax VA 22030

Call Sign: KC8PLB
David K Stipp
3954 Valley Ridge Dr
Fairfax VA 22033

Call Sign: KI6AWA
Donald S Pitchford
4100 Vandervilt Ct 302
Fairfax VA 22030

Call Sign: N3GES

Robert A Kuhn
12600 Varny Pl
Fairfax VA 22033

Call Sign: KD4QCK
Kenneth D Kalunian
10807 Verde Vista Dr
Fairfax VA 22030

Call Sign: KB4NRU
Richard P Van Doren
10814 Verde Vista Dr
Fairfax VA 22030

Call Sign: KD4STB
Henry L Hansen
3626 W Ox Rd
Fairfax VA 22033

Call Sign: KA2GXU
Dianne M Hansen
3626 W Ox Rd
Fairfax VA 22033

Call Sign: KB4FGG
Anthony F Chaikowski
4207 Waller Rd
Fairfax VA 22032

Call Sign: KD6FOL
Matthew D Sambora
4080 Walnut Cove Cir
Fairfax VA 22033

Call Sign: KE4VIM
David P Boger
10816 Warwick Ave
Fairfax VA 22030

Call Sign: KC4UWS
James E Terrell
10901 Warwick Ave
Fairfax VA 22030

Call Sign: N4POT
Kenneth W Shoopman
9723 Water Oak Dr
Fairfax VA 22031

Call Sign: KA5TMI
William R Pinney
10497 West Dr
Fairfax VA 220308124

Call Sign: KI4QNM
Amanda R West
10727 West Dr Apt 103
Fairfax VA 22030

Call Sign: KJ4JQC
James E Ingram
11302 Westbrook Mill Ln 304
Fairfax VA 22030

Call Sign: K4JEI
James E Ingram
11302 Westbrook Mill Ln 304
Fairfax VA 22030

Call Sign: KA3KYA
Harry Nagel Jr
5007 Wheatstone Dr
Fairfax VA 22032

Call Sign: KF4RHE
Anthony T Owens
4234 Wheeled Caisson Sq
Fairfax VA 22033

Call Sign: KF4RHF
Mary B Bolton Owens
4234 Wheeled Caisson Sq
Fairfax VA 22033

Call Sign: KC4ZYQ
John D Warburton
5211 Whisper Willow Dr
Fairfax VA 22030

Call Sign: KD4CRI
Andrew J Warburton
5211 Whisper Willow Dr
Fairfax VA 22030

Call Sign: KJ4RBB
Scott K Persky
4209 Whitacre Rd
Fairfax VA 22032

Call Sign: KF4TRH
James K Wilson
3913 Wilcoxson Dr
Fairfax VA 22031

Call Sign: AI4SV
John J Welch Jr
3925 Wilcoxson Dr
Fairfax VA 22031

Call Sign: KI4SNF
Thomas R Morrissey Jr
5539 Winford Ct
Fairfax VA 22032

Call Sign: N4GZ
Thomas R Morrissey Jr
5539 Winford Ct
Fairfax VA 22032

Call Sign: KE4AJL
Richard M Morani
3096 Winter Pine Ct
Fairfax VA 22031

Call Sign: KJ4VTM
Nicholas J Beauregard
3070 Winter Pine Ct
Fairfax VA 22031

Call Sign: KE4MKD
Donald C Tison
9107 Wood Pointe Wy
Fairfax VA 22039

Call Sign: KE4AVI
John M Orr
10135 Wood Rd
Fairfax VA 22030

Call Sign: K4QIE
David B Frohman
10308 Wood Rd
Fairfax VA 22030

Call Sign: W4NND
Charles B Orr Jr
10315 Wood Rd

Fairfax VA 22030

Call Sign: KI4AFT
Jose A Barros
10412 Woodbury Woods Ct
Fairfax VA 22032

Call Sign: K4MM
Joseph W Miller
10919 Woodfair Rd
Fairfax VA 22039

Call Sign: WB4CCM
Dale E Pace
4021 Woodland Dr
Fairfax VA 22030

Call Sign: KG4MCM
Anthony G Dibenedetto
13131 Wren Hollow Ln
Fairfax VA 22033

Call Sign: KT4UG
Kie B Nahm
10201 Wrens Ct
Fairfax VA 22032

Call Sign: AG4WF
Kie B Nahm
10201 Wrens Ct
Fairfax VA 22032

Call Sign: KB9N
Kie B Nahm
10201 Wrens Ct
Fairfax VA 22032

Call Sign: KA4FSC
George V Clark
4901 Wycliff Ln
Fairfax VA 22032

Call Sign: KU4MZ
Steve M Antosh
3237 Wynford Dr 37
Fairfax VA 220312828

Call Sign: KJ4MFK
Rainer A Sommer

10335 Zion Dr
Fairfax VA 22032

Call Sign: W2AUS
Rainer A Sommer
10335 Zion Dr
Fairfax VA 22032

Call Sign: KK4FFP
Clark V Wallace
10503 Zion Dr
Fairfax VA 22032

Call Sign: W4NDR
Clark V Wallace
10503 Zion Dr
Fairfax VA 22032

Call Sign: N4DRT
Richard G Pinto
Fairfax VA 22038

Call Sign: KB2EJU
Daniel P Parker
Fairfax VA 22031

Call Sign: KC4ICR
Allen T Santora
Fairfax VA 22038

Call Sign: KB2LEB
Timothy J Bultman
Fairfax VA 220380011

FCC Amateur Radio Licenses in Fairfax Station

Call Sign: KG4UVK
Noel F Wolber
7121 12 Oaks Dr
Fairfax Station VA 220391527

Call Sign: NW5N
Noel F Wolber
7121 12 Oaks Dr
Fairfax Station VA 220391527

Call Sign: N5FJC
Mark A Oliva

11505 4 Penny Ln
Fairfax Station VA 220391111

Call Sign: KK4EXV
Michael J Carey
8314 Armetale Ln
Fairfax Station VA 22039

Call Sign: KC7FR
Douglas W Webster
9103 Autumn Oak Ct
Fairfax Station VA 22039

Call Sign: KK4FQU
Michael S Walker
7855 Bressingham Dr
Fairfax Station VA 22039

Call Sign: KI4KFB
Peter Lunt
7856 Bressingham Dr
Fairfax Station VA 22039

Call Sign: W4PEL
Peter Lunt
7856 Bressingham Dr
Fairfax Station VA 22039

Call Sign: KK4AII
Jacob L Wallace
8300 Cathedral Forest Dr
Fairfax Station VA 22039

Call Sign: W4VGH
Jacob L Wallace Jr
8300 Cathedral Forest Dr
Fairfax Station VA 22039

Call Sign: KQ4MJ
Gozef L Hennigan
8501 Century Oak Ct
Fairfax Station VA 22039

Call Sign: AG4NL
Jozef L Hennigan
8501 Century Oak Ct
Fairfax Station VA 22039

Call Sign: W3CZ

Jozef L Hennigan
8501 Century Oak Ct
Fairfax Station VA 220393343

Call Sign: KJ4EAH
John E Whalan
8650 Chase Glen Cir
Fairfax Station VA 22039

Call Sign: K4RBP
Marvin W Lawley
10911 Chimney Ln
Fairfax Station VA 22039

Call Sign: KC4MH
Jacqueline S Lawley
10911 Chimney Ln
Fairfax Station VA 22039

Call Sign: W4OKO
Robert C Hoyler
11503 Clara Barton Dr
Fairfax Station VA 220391336

Call Sign: KF4GF
Joseph R Lowry
11539 Clara Barton Dr
Fairfax Station VA 22039

Call Sign: AA3ZU
Junichi Nishiyama
11801 Clara Way
Fairfax Station VA 22039

Call Sign: KJ4HCX
James B Clayton
8212 Copperglow Trl
Fairfax Station VA 22039

Call Sign: K3DSI
James B Clayton
8212 Copperglow Trl
Fairfax Station VA 22039

Call Sign: W3JH
James B Clayton
8212 Copperglow Trl
Fairfax Station VA 22039

Call Sign: W3AH
James B Clayton
8212 Copperglow Trl
Fairfax Station VA 22039

Call Sign: K4WY
John D Kelley
10617 Donovans Hill Dr
Fairfax Station VA 22039

Call Sign: KI4HD
Robert P Arnold
8001 Eddy Bend Trl
Fairfax Station VA 22039

Call Sign: KA3DZV
Timothy D Maclay
11524 Fairfax Station Rd
Fairfax Station VA 220391121

Call Sign: WB7EYY
Fraser Yeung
5811 Fairview Woods Dr
Fairfax Station VA 22039

Call Sign: W4YHD
Stephen M Floyd
11118 Flora Lee Dr
Fairfax Station VA 22039

Call Sign: KC4NEI
Andras Kereki
9910 Hampton Rd
Fairfax Station VA 22039

Call Sign: KJ4BRI
Edward R Grosvenor II
10422 Hampton Rd
Fairfax Station VA 22039

Call Sign: WD4EKO
Roger L Eisinger
8930 Harrivan Ln
Fairfax Station VA 22039

Call Sign: KD4FKH
Robert B Le Blanc
11651 Havenner Rd
Fairfax Station VA 22039

Call Sign: KI4BEA
Thomas L Peterson
8010 Hollington Pl
Fairfax Station VA 22039

Call Sign: KD4NSH
Robert E Emard
6102 Housatonic Ct
Fairfax Station VA 22039

Call Sign: W4GDP
Gene A Del Polito
8300 Ivy Green Rd
Fairfax Station VA 22039

Call Sign: KO4UA
John Bradbury
10870 Jennifer Marie Pl
Fairfax Station VA 22039

Call Sign: KG4KWX
Thomas D Schrader
6412 Jumet Ct
Fairfax Station VA 22039

Call Sign: KK4FFO
Matthew C Cummings
9606 Larkview Ct
Fairfax Station VA 22039

Call Sign: KI4YMC
Clifford E Mclain
7816 Manor House Dr
Fairfax Station VA 220392215

Call Sign: KA2HAN
Gary G Swenson
8603 Oak Chase Cir
Fairfax Station VA 22039

Call Sign: N0CLN
Matthew P Donovan
9105 Oak Chase Ct
Fairfax Station VA 220393333

Call Sign: N0ZMB
Philip R Devoe
7911 Oak Hollow Ln

Fairfax Station VA 22039

Call Sign: N6FYG
Carl E Rodgers
7925 Oak Hollow Ln
Fairfax Station VA 22039

Call Sign: KE4LYN
Scott C Willis
5913 One Penny Dr
Fairfax Station VA 220391118

Call Sign: KF4KKO
Aida P Willis
5913 One Penny Dr
Fairfax Station VA 220391118

Call Sign: KG4NXR
Michael C Willis
5913 One Penny Dr
Fairfax Station VA 220391118

Call Sign: KJ4LBY
Scott M Rix
8304 Pinyon Pine Ct
Fairfax Station VA 22039

Call Sign: WA2VRF
Mark S Weiss
9414 Ravina Ct
Fairfax Station VA 22039

Call Sign: N2PJ
Paul F James Jr
8304 Richlawn Ter
Fairfax Station VA 220393221

Call Sign: KG4GUC
Robert E Breazeale
9731 Rolling Ridge Dr
Fairfax Station VA 22039

Call Sign: KI4MUN
John H Wherry
7414 S Reach Dr
Fairfax Station VA 22039

Call Sign: KD4KUN
Sheryl L Dickinson

9691 S Run Oaks Dr
Fairfax Station VA 22039

Call Sign: KI4HRC
Victor Kernus
9701 S Run Oaks Dr
Fairfax Station VA 22039

Call Sign: KB4WKJ
James A Hagerty Jr
7315 Scarlet Oak Ct
Fairfax Station VA 220391928

Call Sign: KG4VXP
James A Hagerty Jr
7315 Scarlet Oak Ct
Fairfax Station VA 220391928

Call Sign: W4JHU
James A Hagerty Jr
7315 Scarlet Oak Ct
Fairfax Station VA 220391928

Call Sign: NS2O
Gregory Yadzinski
10901 Shadow Ln
Fairfax Station VA 22039

Call Sign: WO6Z
Kenneth W Holtkamp
9751 Thorn Bush Dr
Fairfax Station VA 22039

Call Sign: KF4VVX
Marsha F White
9012 Triple Ridge Rd
Fairfax Station VA 22039

Call Sign: KD4MFA
Clarence R Brown
9016 Triple Ridge Rd
Fairfax Station VA 22039

Call Sign: KD4MFB
Richelle C Brown
9016 Triple Ridge Rd
Fairfax Station VA 22039

Call Sign: KJ4YSH

David B Moxley
6117 Union Camp Dr
Fairfax Station VA 22039

Call Sign: K9MOX
David B Moxley
6117 Union Camp Dr
Fairfax Station VA 22039

Call Sign: KF4BPE
Matthew J Hanlon
8404 Westpointe Dr
Fairfax Station VA 22039

Call Sign: WA1FFG
Daniel Katcher
7523 Wilderness Way
Fairfax Station VA 22039

Call Sign: KE4LYM
Rosita K Villanueva
7904 Willfield Ct
Fairfax Station VA 20039

Call Sign: KE4LYL
Dean A Villanueva
7904 Willfield Ct
Fairfax Station VA 22039

Call Sign: KB6ESF
Deborah A W Cooper
6916 Winners Cir
Fairfax Station VA 22039

Call Sign: WB7AXT
John D Schoedel Jr
7507 Wolf Run Shoals Rd
Fairfax Station VA 22039

Call Sign: KK4EGE
Umberto Fornario
11042 Wolfs Landing
Fairfax Station VA 22039

Call Sign: KE4MGF
Jennifer L Tison
9107 Wood Pointe Way
Fairfax Station VA 22035

Call Sign: KE4L
Michael H Williams
Fairfax Station VA 220390372

FCC Amateur Radio Licenses
in Fairfield

Call Sign: KC4IQH
Jeffrey W Grey
Rt 2 Box 165 A3
Fairfield VA 24435

Call Sign: KB4FP
Jeremiah N Partrick
190 Henry Hill Dr
Fairfield VA 24435

Call Sign: KC4AS
George L Howe Jr
91 Huffman Ln
Fairfield VA 24435

Call Sign: KF4EKU
Betty J Ralston
304 Jonestown Rd
Fairfield VA 24435

Call Sign: KA4NAX
Donald E Franklin
4508 N Lee Hwy
Fairfield VA 24435

Call Sign: KF4FYL
Albert Tkacik
7174 N Lee Hwy
Fairfield VA 244350402

Call Sign: NJ1ED
Edward F Culp
3974 N Lee Hwy
Fairfield VA 24435

Call Sign: N4YEX
Robert W Day
Fairfield VA 24435

Call Sign: K2TKN
Willis L Ashby
Fairfield VA 24435

Call Sign: KE4NRH
Deborah T Day
Fairfield VA 24435

FCC Amateur Radio Licenses
in Fairlawn

Call Sign: AD4LD
Lon J Berman
7467 Bluff View Dr
Fairlawn VA 24141

Call Sign: N4IEF
Robert E Hancock
Rt 2 Box 421A
Fairlawn VA 24141

Call Sign: KI4AWM
David W Sherrer II
7586 Old Peppers Ferry Loop
Fairlawn VA 24141

Call Sign: KE4RGY
Michael J Herring
6218 Schooler Hill Dr Apt 36
Fairlawn VA 24141

FCC Amateur Radio Licenses
in Falls Church

Call Sign: KC6TUD
Heather D Barden
1811 Anderson Rd
Falls Church VA 22043

Call Sign: AA4XU
Benjamin A Shaver Jr
3162 Annandale Rd
Falls Church VA 22042

Call Sign: KF4JMZ
Robert W Dewekas
506 Anne St
Falls Church VA 22046

Call Sign: WB4RPJ
Stephen J Mc Carthy
6077 Arlington Blvd

Falls Church VA 22044

Call Sign: WA3ONL
Roy A Rathbun
6001 Arlington Blvd 910
Falls Church VA 22044

Call Sign: KF4LWJ
Raytheon Falls Church ARC
7700 Arlington Blvd MS N 210
Falls Church VA 22046

Call Sign: K4OCI
Benjamin R Mc Elroy
6651 Avignon Blvd
Falls Church VA 22043

Call Sign: KK4FRA
Richard P Herrell
2532 Avon Ln
Falls Church VA 22043

Call Sign: AJ4PD
Erik B Svedberg
2405 Barbour Rd
Falls Church VA 22043

Call Sign: KE4SSQ
Manuel A Galdo
2414 Barbour Rd
Falls Church VA 22043

Call Sign: K4ML
James W Tucker
6112 Beachway Dr
Falls Church VA 22041

Call Sign: W5AOC
Kenneth W Miller
3716 Bent Branch Rd
Falls Church VA 22041

Call Sign: W4POI
William A Sincek
130 Birch St
Falls Church VA 22046

Call Sign: WB4NIW
Alvin M Pesachowitz

306 Bishops Ct
Falls Church VA 22046

Call Sign: WA4WSZ
Harold C Cutright
2824 Bolling Rd
Falls Church VA 22042

Call Sign: KC4YME
Arthur J Kyle
7428 Brad St
Falls Church VA 220423605

Call Sign: KC3C
Arthur J Kyle
7428 Brad St
Falls Church VA 220423605

Call Sign: KD4DGR
David A Buckingham
1004 Broadmont Ter
Falls Church VA 22046

Call Sign: KD4DZF
Rachel B Cochran
1004 Broadmont Ter
Falls Church VA 22046

Call Sign: N0DQN
Susan A Buckingham
1004 Broadmont Ter
Falls Church VA 22046

Call Sign: W0SQ
William A Buckingham Jr
1004 Broadmont Ter
Falls Church VA 22046

Call Sign: WA6SWA
Ivan D Hafstrom
6053 Brook Dr
Falls Church VA 22044

Call Sign: KG6GX
Sam Levine
2230 G C Marshall Dr Apt 515
Falls Church VA 22043

Call Sign: K4JDU

Edward B Mc Devitt
7501 Camp Alger Ave
Falls Church VA 22042

Call Sign: KG4FSP
Andy W Arnold
7521 Camp Alger Ave
Falls Church VA 22042

Call Sign: KA4VNE
Sterling E Springston
7005 Carlton Ave
Falls Church VA 22042

Call Sign: KC4VDM
Roger S Girdwood
7221 Carol Ln
Falls Church VA 22042

Call Sign: KA2VUI
Joseph J Seifried
6423 Cavalier Corridor
Falls Church VA 22044

Call Sign: KJ4YSG
Jimmy R Hickey Sr
3121 Celadon Ln
Falls Church VA 22044

Call Sign: K4JRH
Jimmy R Hickey Sr
3121 Celadon Ln
Falls Church VA 22044

Call Sign: KI4VUS
Tara B Olson
2041 Cherri Dr
Falls Church VA 22043

Call Sign: WD4EYK
David E Sauer
6704 Chestnut Ave
Falls Church VA 22042

Call Sign: KI4YPH
Andrew M Messner
3144 Cofer Rd
Falls Church VA 22042

Call Sign: WB4AYW
Robert E Winter
6205 Colmac Dr
Falls Church VA 22044

Call Sign: N3JEE
Christopher L Buehler
6308 Colubia Pike
Falls Church VA 22041

Call Sign: WA3GLA
Philip W Savitz
3139 Creswell Dr
Falls Church VA 22044

Call Sign: KC4UIA
Roger L Hoskin
6359 Crosswoods Dr
Falls Church VA 22044

Call Sign: KA4YMA
John R Birch
3108 Dashiell Rd
Falls Church VA 22042

Call Sign: KJ4GYJ
Philip M Kania
7231 Deborah Dr
Falls Church VA 22046

Call Sign: KB4TKB
Thomas W Wolfe
6379 Dockser Ter
Falls Church VA 22041

Call Sign: KB4SGE
William C Burry III
6381 Dockser Ter
Falls Church VA 22041

Call Sign: KB4SNN
Christine M Burry
6381 Dockser Ter
Falls Church VA 22041

Call Sign: KJ4BVF
Martin W Elthon
404 E Broad St
Falls Church VA 22046

Call Sign: KA4HTZ
Charles W H Barnett
800 E Broad St
Falls Church VA 22046

Call Sign: KD4LSR
John E Fredenburg
606 E Columbia St
Falls Church VA 22046

Call Sign: KD4LSS
Marion G Fredenburg
606 E Columbia St
Falls Church VA 22046

Call Sign: KE4GFR
Brian L Mc Laughlin
208 E Jefferson St
Falls Church VA 22046

Call Sign: KG4SUB
Jeffrey H Leach
3579 Ellery Cir
Falls Church VA 22041

Call Sign: KC4SKM
Arthur E Jeffers III
3327 Elm Ter
Falls Church VA 22042

Call Sign: N4DCC
William H Kreher
6522 Elmhirst Dr
Falls Church VA 220431916

Call Sign: KC4NEJ
Michael Picone
3318 Executive Ave
Falls Church VA 220423332

Call Sign: K3HOT
Gregory W Guise
3113 Faber Dr
Falls Church VA 22044

Call Sign: K4KXK
John C Bartone II
2901 Fairmont St

Falls Church VA 22042

Call Sign: KA4LCI
John P Morrison
3009 Fairmont St
Falls Church VA 22042

Call Sign: N4HCP
Charles A Rexroad Jr
7511 Fairwood Ln
Falls Church VA 22046

Call Sign: N4CFI
Robert L Lisbeth
7525 Fairwood Ln
Falls Church VA 22046

Call Sign: K4RWI
Marion R Hales
7011 Falls Reach Dr Apt 307
Falls Church VA 22043

Call Sign: WA4VDR
Jose L Ardai Jr
303 Forest Dr
Falls Church VA 22046

Call Sign: W4HVG
H John Heffernan
316 Forest Dr
Falls Church VA 220463627

Call Sign: WB4OXA
Chadwick S Johnson
2230 George C Marshall Dr
Falls Church VA 220432584

Call Sign: WQ2M
Michael B Jeffrey
2230 George C Marshall Dr Apt
528
Falls Church VA 22043

Call Sign: N8GNQ
James H Monaghan
2230 George C Marshall Dr
Unit 1119
Falls Church VA 220432584

Call Sign: N4CSJ
Chadwick S Johnson
2230 George C Marshall Dr
Unit 1119
Falls Church VA 220432584

Call Sign: K4HZW
Lester M Heller
3506 Georges Ln
Falls Church VA 22044

Call Sign: KQ4DX
William B Allen
3440 Glavis Rd
Falls Church VA 22044

Call Sign: KB4PGC
Michael C Trahos
6613 Goldsboro Rd
Falls Church VA 22042

Call Sign: WB4ZTT
Thomas C Rozzell
6728 Gouthier Rd
Falls Church VA 220422734

Call Sign: K4AHS
John E Nagley
2234 Great Falls St
Falls Church VA 22046

Call Sign: KM4WS
Roger H Denker
6190 Greenwood Dr 2
Falls Church VA 22044

Call Sign: KG4OTP
Alexander Jack
1831 Griffith Rd
Falls Church VA 22043

Call Sign: KI4THM
Aric G Letzring
1853 Griffith Rd
Falls Church VA 22043

Call Sign: K4PJO
Michael W Craven
3111 Hall Ct

Falls Church VA 22042

Call Sign: KG4FHW
Linda S Craven
3111 Hall Ct
Falls Church VA 22042

Call Sign: N9FV
Adam T Carpenter
6935 Haycock Rd
Falls Church VA 220432304

Call Sign: KG4TIF
August H Vandermer
7023 I Haycock Rd
Falls Church VA 22043

Call Sign: K4ERS
Michael J Rivers
3039 Hazelton St
Falls Church VA 22044

Call Sign: KM6HI
Holcombe H Thomas Jr
7292 Highland Estates Pl
Falls Church VA 22043

Call Sign: N2EPK
Linda G Hill
3515 Highview Pl
Falls Church VA 220441125

Call Sign: W4WXL
Edwin A Bondurant
411 Hillwood Ave
Falls Church VA 220463541

Call Sign: KC4TDG
Thomas A Kaye
905 Hillwood Ave
Falls Church VA 22042

Call Sign: KF4DJI
Catherine A Kaye
905 Hillwood Ave
Falls Church VA 22042

Call Sign: KF4YWQ
Robert M Petillo

1011 Hillwood Ave
Falls Church VA 22042

Call Sign: N3FRU
Alice E Petillo
1011 Hillwood Ave
Falls Church VA 22042

Call Sign: KB5JEN
Darrell L Young
2555 Holly Manor Dr
Falls Church VA 22043

Call Sign: KF4AJS
R Randolph Ritter
7714 Holmes Run Dr
Falls Church VA 22042

Call Sign: KF4BTH
Elizabeth B Ritter
7714 Holmes Run Dr
Falls Church VA 22042

Call Sign: N4YQ
George L Axford
3140 Holmes Run Rd
Falls Church VA 22042

Call Sign: W4NYJ
Lionel J Wollner
3306 Horseman Ln
Falls Church VA 22042

Call Sign: WU3G
Toshiro Ogino
7306 Idylbrook Ct
Falls Church VA 220431513

Call Sign: KJ4JHC
Joe Anshien
7212 Idylwood Ct
Falls Church VA 22043

Call Sign: KJ4JHJ
Sol C Anshien
7212 Idylwood Ct
Falls Church VA 22043

Call Sign: WA4GVE

Donald L Cockrell
7607 Idylwood Rd
Falls Church VA 22043

Call Sign: KE5IOQ
Nathaniel Gist
2290 Idylwood Station Ln
Falls Church VA 22043

Call Sign: KD5TZH
Scott F Winter
2188 Iroquois Ln
Falls Church VA 22043

Call Sign: KG4GTY
Joseph H Speredelozzi
2146 Iroquois Ln 103
Falls Church VA 22043

Call Sign: KJ4IDB
David A Wilkey
6906 Jackson Ave
Falls Church VA 22042

Call Sign: NA4RX
David A Wilkey
6906 Jackson Ave
Falls Church VA 22042

Call Sign: KJ4EMI
David W Shaw
405 Jackson St
Falls Church VA 22046

Call Sign: KD4DGP
Bruce M Bates
605 Jackson St
Falls Church VA 22046

Call Sign: WA4SMI
Kurt F Wehle Jr
608 Jackson St
Falls Church VA 22046

Call Sign: KJ4CJM
Rafael Villasmil
355 James St
Falls Church VA 22046

Call Sign: KF4PGK
Chaim A Smith
6913 Jefferson Ave
Falls Church VA 22042

Call Sign: KD4SIA
Darla J Lee
6923 Jefferson Ave
Falls Church VA 22042

Call Sign: KK4COW
Julius Suyat
7000 Jenkins Ln
Falls Church VA 22043

Call Sign: KJ4SZN
Qusai Shabsigh
3232 Juniper Ln
Falls Church VA 22044

Call Sign: KE4JHL
Joseph L Van Meter
1000 Kennedy St
Falls Church VA 22046

Call Sign: KE4WYF
Anh T Ma
2910 Kingchapel Rd 7
Falls Church VA 22042

Call Sign: KG4VKN
William J Kelleher
6643 Kirby Ct
Falls Church VA 22043

Call Sign: KD4HEF
Donald W Combs
7600F Lakeside Village Dr
Falls Church VA 22042

Call Sign: KB3GON
Walter R Cate
6329 Lakeview Dr
Falls Church VA 220411324

Call Sign: AI4MA
Richard E Hardy
6440 Lakeview Dr
Falls Church VA 22041

Call Sign: K4DHP
Richard E Hardy
6440 Lakeview Dr
Falls Church VA 22041

Call Sign: WA4QXN
Carleton R Woodard
3904 Larchwood Rd
Falls Church VA 22041

Call Sign: KE4PDS
Clifford L Mauck
2845 Lawrence Dr
Falls Church VA 22042

Call Sign: W3VDL
John W Brogden
6020 Lebanon Dr
Falls Church VA 22041

Call Sign: K4VD
Kevin Der Kinderen
2807 Lee Landing Ct
Falls Church VA 22043

Call Sign: N1MKC
Timothy M Bielawa
7642 Lee Landing Dr
Falls Church VA 22043

Call Sign: KE4SLA
James R Revell Jr
2808 Lee Oaks Pl 201
Falls Church VA 22046

Call Sign: W1ROY
Royal M Proulx
2212 Leeland Dr
Falls Church VA 220431950

Call Sign: KE4DSD
Charles W Frey
7201 Leesburg Pike
Falls Church VA 22043

Call Sign: KI4TO
Robert G Lepelletier Jr
5119A Leesburg Pike

Falls Church VA 220413207

Call Sign: KC4REV
George T Hertzog
1917 Leonard Rd
Falls Church VA 22043

Call Sign: KK4GSH
Dwight D Muse
1929 Leonard Rd
Falls Church VA 22043

Call Sign: KK4ADN
Richard P Perri
3103 Lewis Pl
Falls Church VA 22042

Call Sign: KI4QNJ
Peter H Dittmar
702 Lincoln Ave
Falls Church VA 220462507

Call Sign: KF2F
Peter H Dittmar
702 Lincoln Ave
Falls Church VA 220462507

Call Sign: KG4FRM
Mark L Martin
7630 Lisle Ave
Falls Church VA 220431208

Call Sign: AG4BR
Mark L Martin
7630 Lisle Ave
Falls Church VA 220431208

Call Sign: KE4ILZ
Tommy O Johnson
7708 Lisle Ave
Falls Church VA 22043

Call Sign: KJ4PZP
Gary L Mannering
7716 Lisle Ave
Falls Church VA 22043

Call Sign: K2TGE
Anthony J Tether

6400 Lyric Ln
Falls Church VA 22044

Call Sign: KI4DRJ
Michael H Doherty
6132 Madison Crest Ct
Falls Church VA 22041

Call Sign: KC4IJD
Joseph C White
3716 Madison Ln
Falls Church VA 22041

Call Sign: KE8US
Kristine L Svinicki
3676 Madison Watch Way
Falls Church VA 22041

Call Sign: KI4OQJ
Titus T Edeke
7423 Magarity Rd
Falls Church VA 22043

Call Sign: KD4VON
Nathan F Shaifer
3621 Malibu Cir 206
Falls Church VA 22041

Call Sign: KE3ZS
Tamas Gal
3659 Malibu Cir Apt 204
Falls Church VA 22041

Call Sign: KG4SEM
John J Garcia
3621 Malibu Cir Apt T7
Falls Church VA 22041

Call Sign: K9OAD
Jack S Rugh
3037 Manor Rd
Falls Church VA 22042

Call Sign: KI4TZD
Abdriel Garcia- Velez
3133 Manor Rd
Falls Church VA 22042

Call Sign: W4OBO

Jack J Keith
3435 Mansfield Rd
Falls Church VA 22041

Call Sign: K4HZF
David J Kennedy
6545 Mapledale Ct
Falls Church VA 22041

Call Sign: KJ4DFZ
Chris K Gibilisco
6412 Maplewood Dr
Falls Church VA 22041

Call Sign: W4UWY
Mary H Budlong
6421 Maplewood Dr
Falls Church VA 22041

Call Sign: KJ4GOI
John R Bumgarner Jr
7101 Marbury Ct
Falls Church VA 22046

Call Sign: AA1RB
John R Bumgarner Jr
7101 Marbury Ct
Falls Church VA 22046

Call Sign: K4SQP
Joseph W Paljug
7405 Marc Dr
Falls Church VA 22042

Call Sign: KG4TLK
Heather M Sinclair
7735 Marshall Heights Ct
Falls Church VA 22043

Call Sign: KB1FHG
Rajesh A Dhanaraj
7612 Matera St Apt 1
Falls Church VA 22043

Call Sign: WB4BSR
Robert W Beausoliel
2028 Maynard Dr
Falls Church VA 22043

Call Sign: KA4FID
Kathleen S Rutter
2110 McKay St
Falls Church VA 22043

Call Sign: KI4GNM
Shawn W Firth
2110 McKay St
Falls Church VA 22043

Call Sign: KJ4DFT
Robert M Brown
2127 McKay St
Falls Church VA 22043

Call Sign: N3IPT
Jeffrey A Sherer
6806 McLean Province Cir
Falls Church VA 22043

Call Sign: AA9AT
Takashi Mori
6852 McLean Province Cir
Falls Church VA 220431668

Call Sign: KB4PXK
William A Linne II
2830 Meadow Ln
Falls Church VA 22042

Call Sign: KJ4SEY
David E Howell Sr
7251 Mendota Ave
Falls Church VA 22042

Call Sign: N4SNK
Gerald W Gangl
2237 Meridian St
Falls Church VA 22046

Call Sign: KC4CAY
Joseph C Kelly III
2811 Middleboro Dr
Falls Church VA 22042

Call Sign: KI4EAV
Christopher A Strong
2861 Middleboro Dr
Falls Church VA 22042

Call Sign: KM4VJ
William M Russell
6636 Midhill Pl
Falls Church VA 220431833

Call Sign: K4WGB
William G Beyer
2603 Midway St
Falls Church VA 22046

Call Sign: WD4IZM
Warren H Frayne
2608 Midway St
Falls Church VA 220461927

Call Sign: KF4PPF
Michael D Davis
3329 Military Dr
Falls Church VA 22044

Call Sign: K4MDD
Michael D Davis
3329 Military Dr
Falls Church VA 22044

Call Sign: KE4MFF
John F Felter
1915 Miracle Ln
Falls Church VA 22043

Call Sign: WB4HAV
Samuel J Lebowich
2009 Miracle Ln
Falls Church VA 22043

Call Sign: KE4LXY
Jennifer A Clausen
2244 Mohegan Dr Apt 203
Falls Church VA 22043

Call Sign: KJ4LYA
James M Adriansen
2852 Monroe St
Falls Church VA 22042

Call Sign: KJ4QAH
James M Adriansen
2852 Monroe St

Falls Church VA 22042

Call Sign: W8JQS
David J South
6800 Montour Dr
Falls Church VA 22043

Call Sign: KI4EVG
Charles I Arms
5915 Munson Ct
Falls Church VA 22041

Call Sign: KG3C
Charles I Arms
5915 Munson Ct
Falls Church VA 22041

Call Sign: KJ4RFJ
John F Langford
218 N Cherry St
Falls Church VA 22046

Call Sign: KI4RM
Joseph J De Poorter
209 N Oak St
Falls Church VA 220463237

Call Sign: AJ4AK
Hideaki Suyama
505 N Roosevelt Blvd
Falls Church VA 22044

Call Sign: WA7GTX
William H Philo
507 N Roosevelt Blvd C201
Falls Church VA 22044

Call Sign: WB2EXT
Hillel Weinberg
311 N Underwood St
Falls Church VA 22046

Call Sign: KF4RQL
Paul V Jaffe
105 N Virginia Ave
Falls Church VA 22046

Call Sign: KG4YZB
Christopher S Norloff

508 N West St
Falls Church VA 220462517

Call Sign: K4CXP
Richard H Garrett
508 N West St
Falls Church VA 22046

Call Sign: N4CZF
Colleen E Shelley
2112 Natahoa Ct
Falls Church VA 22043

Call Sign: WD4SMA
Jeffrey B Miller
2112 Natahoa Ct
Falls Church VA 22043

Call Sign: W4LCD
James F Mc Arthur
3236 Nealon Dr
Falls Church VA 220423635

Call Sign: KJ4NJG
Brady N Itkin
3313 Nevins St
Falls Church VA 22041

Call Sign: W4HE
Charles A Stay
3321 Nevius St
Falls Church VA 22041

Call Sign: KD4YFN
Timothy A Nibbe
7742 New Providence Dr 104
Falls Church VA 22042

Call Sign: KD4YXU
Thomas W Massie
7761 New Providence Dr 46
Falls Church VA 22042

Call Sign: KC8IVF
Edwin W Cox
6344 Nicholson St
Falls Church VA 220441912

Call Sign: KA0SER

John R Bowers
3015 Nicosh Cir 2304
Falls Church VA 22042

Call Sign: AJ3O
Richard A Folger
3003 Nicosh Cir Unit 3409
Falls Church VA 22042

Call Sign: KA4HOV
David D Beattie Jr
3234 Norfolk Ln
Falls Church VA 22042

Call Sign: KK4CBU
David Kolet-Tassara
2407 Nottingham Dr
Falls Church VA 22043

Call Sign: KE4ICT
Perry E Browning
7728 Oak St
Falls Church VA 22043

Call Sign: KF4HVF
Carl A Risheim
517 Oak St N
Falls Church VA 22046

Call Sign: KJ4ZMT
Kenneth L Rosenbaum
6540 Oakwood Dr
Falls Church VA 22041

Call Sign: K4MEL
Deane E Parker
6605 Oakwood Dr
Falls Church VA 22041

Call Sign: KC1AD
Keith A Christianson
1110 Offutt Dr
Falls Church VA 22046

Call Sign: KG4EXZ
Carol Chaney
1110 Offutt Dr
Falls Church VA 22046

Call Sign: KG4NII
Christina A Christianson
1110 Offutt Dr
Falls Church VA 22046

Call Sign: KG4LAA
John E Leonard
1811 Olney Rd
Falls Church VA 22043

Call Sign: KK4CJL
Jean-Marie Leonard
1811 Olney Rd
Falls Church VA 22043

Call Sign: KB4CMC
Nicolaus G Makris
6548 Orland St
Falls Church VA 22043

Call Sign: AF4PD
John R Transue
303 Parker Ave
Falls Church VA 220463913

Call Sign: WB4PZL
Edward D Andrus III
2497 Patricia Ct
Falls Church VA 22043

Call Sign: KJ4HPP
Anna T Hallahan
1827 Peabody Dr
Falls Church VA 22043

Call Sign: KG4ZRZ
Francis B Hallahan
1827 Peabody Dr
Falls Church VA 22043

Call Sign: KI4YNG
Joseph P Hallahan
1827 Peabody Dr
Falls Church VA 22043

Call Sign: N3SNI
Michael S Calhoon
2016 Peach Orchard Dr Apt 12
Falls Church VA 22043

Call Sign: W3DEQ
Michael S Calhoon
2016 Peach Orchard Dr Apt 12
Falls Church VA 22043

Call Sign: KI4JPX
Jason P Miele
2018 Peach Orchard Dr Apt 24
Falls Church VA 22043

Call Sign: K4CEM
Charles E Mc Cullough III
2022 Peach Orchard Dr Apt 34
Falls Church VA 22043

Call Sign: KG4WXJ
James R White
200 Pennsylvania Ave
Falls Church VA 22046

Call Sign: WA4TQI
Walter F Seaberg Jr
1801 Pimmit Dr
Falls Church VA 220431114

Call Sign: N4YJ
Marshall S Epstein
2300 Pimmit Dr Unit 919
Falls Church VA 220432825

Call Sign: KJ4RBG
Hiroshi Hongo
2282 Pimmit Run Ln 4
Falls Church VA 22043

Call Sign: W4NSL
Michael C Horowitz
1015 Poplar Dr
Falls Church VA 22046

Call Sign: W3HXF
William E Scholtz Jr
1032 Poplar Dr
Falls Church VA 220462002

Call Sign: KJ4PV
Gary Bleasdale
3800 Powell Ln 1115

Falls Church VA 22041

Call Sign: KJ4BRT
Amy J Mills
3800 Powell Ln 1125
Falls Church VA 22041

Call Sign: W3BSA
Scout Venture Crew 80 Natl
Cap Area Cnl Bsa
3800 Powell Ln Ph 5
Falls Church VA 22041

Call Sign: K4BSA
Demetrios G Pulas Jr
3800 Powell Ln Ph 5
Falls Church VA 220413660

Call Sign: KJ4BSG
Kyle G Mills
3800 Powell Ln Unit 1125
Falls Church VA 22041

Call Sign: KJ4NXL
Elizabeth G Lovegrove
1925 Powhatan St
Falls Church VA 22043

Call Sign: KA5PRD
Diane K Lum
3430 Putnam St
Falls Church VA 22042

Call Sign: NH6E
Dickson Y Lum
3430 Putnam St
Falls Church VA 220423727

Call Sign: W4LQD
Walter A Pappas
6443 Queen Anne Ter
Falls Church VA 22044

Call Sign: KO4DE
Earl J Diehl
805 Randolph St
Falls Church VA 22046

Call Sign: KG4WSS

Sean P Smith
7711 Random Run Ln Apt 204
Falls Church VA 22042

Call Sign: N4KSN
Volkert Werbeck
3154 Ravenwood Dr
Falls Church VA 22044

Call Sign: W4YKH
William N Parker
3154 Ravenwood Dr
Falls Church VA 22044

Call Sign: KI4QNI
Steven G Herbst
803 Ridge Pl
Falls Church VA 22046

Call Sign: WB4IUN
James R Buscher
323 Riley St
Falls Church VA 22046

Call Sign: K8JRB
James R Buscher
323 Riley St
Falls Church VA 22046

Call Sign: WB4IUN
James R Buscher
323 Riley St
Falls Church VA 22046

Call Sign: W4CNO
James R Buscher
323 Riley St
Falls Church VA 22046

Call Sign: KJ4KWT
Josiah C Boning
333 Riley St
Falls Church VA 22046

Call Sign: N2LPQ
Lisa T Kosoff
7310 Rockford Dr
Falls Church VA 22043

Call Sign: W1BKA
Tom L Parker
2857 Rogers Dr
Falls Church VA 22042

Call Sign: WB4AZA
James D Elliott
7328 Ronald St
Falls Church VA 22046

Call Sign: KC4MLC
Phillip J Smith
7310 Roosevelt Ave
Falls Church VA 22042

Call Sign: KI4AOG
Keith R Fulton
505 Roosevelt Blvd B715
Falls Church VA 22044

Call Sign: KD4ETX
Garey C Engle
6512 Roosevelt St
Falls Church VA 22043

Call Sign: KK4CBR
Donald L Goff
6613 Rosecroft Pl
Falls Church VA 22043

Call Sign: W4ILL
Donald L Goff
6613 Rosecroft Pl
Falls Church VA 22043

Call Sign: N3BYE
Maurice E Skinner IV
3356 Roundtree Estates Ct
Falls Church VA 22042

Call Sign: KA8ZJM
Ray O Johnson
2160 Royal Lodge Dr
Falls Church VA 22043

Call Sign: KB4DKD
Jeffrey H Latker
3418 Rusticway Ln
Falls Church VA 220441243

Call Sign: KC4WFM
Hugh E Mills Jr
101 S Cherry St
Falls Church VA 22046

Call Sign: W4RWJ
Arnold A Shostak
Apt 1706W 3713 S Geo Mason
Dr
Falls Church VA 22041

Call Sign: WB4HIZ
Wilson D Haigler Sr
3701 S Geo Mason Dr 715N
Falls Church VA 22041

Call Sign: WB4TXH
John E Hohl
3705 S George Mason Dr 1205
Falls Church VA 22041

Call Sign: KD4CGU
Mahmoud A Omari
3701 S George Mason Dr
1618N
Falls Church VA 22041

Call Sign: W8UFW
James R Durbin
3701 S George Mason Dr 508N
Falls Church VA 22041

Call Sign: KJ4QKK
Ray D Howell
3705 S George Mason Dr 715 S
Falls Church VA 22041

Call Sign: KJ4RDK
Judith M Howell
3705 S George Mason Dr 715S
Falls Church VA 22041

Call Sign: KF4EWJ
Nameer S Azalddin
3713 S George Mason Dr Apt
1316W
Falls Church VA 22041

Call Sign: W4JSG
Gordon M Larson
3440 S Jefferson St
Falls Church VA 22041

Call Sign: WB4OAT
John A Bartelt
3440 S Jefferson St Apt 1024
Falls Church VA 22041

Call Sign: KB4EBG
Edgar H Parsons
3440 S Jefferson St Apt 1136
Falls Church VA 22041

Call Sign: WA4BNV
Phillip N Bennett Jr
3440 S Jefferson St Apt 1236
Falls Church VA 22041

Call Sign: W4NDK
Duncan D Peters
3440 S Jefferson St Apt 818
Falls Church VA 220413127

Call Sign: KE4AJO
Bernie V Sevilla
7000 S Kenfig Dr
Falls Church VA 22042

Call Sign: WD8SBA
Darryl O Wilkinson
3101 S Manchester St Apt 403
Falls Church VA 22044

Call Sign: N3CRG
David M Matonick
410 S Maple Ave Apt 618
Falls Church VA 22046

Call Sign: N4BUY
Leo Ferrari
608 S Oak St
Falls Church VA 22046

Call Sign: KF4ESZ
Victoria T Behrens
512 S Spring St
Falls Church VA 22046

Call Sign: W4GP
Mark A Behrens
512 S Spring St
Falls Church VA 22046

Call Sign: KE4WYE
Richard B Mullen
213 S West St
Falls Church VA 22046

Call Sign: KJ4OCB
Robert R Magnuson
7516 Salem Rd
Falls Church VA 22043

Call Sign: KB3GJI
Rick J Christensen
5563 Seminary Rd
Falls Church VA 22041

Call Sign: KB7YHD
Peter W Hubber
5505 Seminary Rd 1303 N
Falls Church VA 22041

Call Sign: N2YQF
Steven D Hane
5505 Seminary Rd 1318N
Falls Church VA 22041

Call Sign: KJ4QKL
Veronica A Abraham
5505 Seminary Rd 1609 N
Falls Church VA 22041

Call Sign: W4ER
Ralph H Albers
5597 Seminary Rd 2013S
Falls Church VA 22041

Call Sign: WA4ZGX
Charles L Bristor
5505 Seminary Rd 315N
Falls Church VA 22041

Call Sign: KA0MGE
Kenneth R Jaskowiak
5505 Seminary Rd 414

Falls Church VA 22041

Call Sign: KK4XB
Albert N Zodun
5601 Seminary Rd 505N
Falls Church VA 220413507

Call Sign: KC4ZPK
Barry R Fine
5501 Seminary Rd 603 S
Falls Church VA 22041

Call Sign: KG4RAY
Joshua J Abraham
5505 Seminary Rd Apt 1609 N
Falls Church VA 22041

Call Sign: KF4BPU
William H Wallace
5597 Seminary Rd Apt 2007 S
Falls Church VA 22041

Call Sign: KI4CYJ
Harry Johnson
5597 Seminary Rd Apt 2014S
Falls Church VA 22041

Call Sign: KW4U
John A Mc Cann
5501 Seminary Rd Apt 214
Falls Church VA 220413902

Call Sign: N4CHP
Robert R Dasenbrock
5501 Seminary Rd Apt 2606
Falls Church VA 220413913

Call Sign: KQ4HD
Michael F Wenz Jr
5505 Seminary Rd Unit 819
Falls Church VA 22041

Call Sign: N2MOS
Larry J Clark
6312 Seven Corners Center
Falls Church VA 22044

Call Sign: AA2NC
Daniel C Mota

6312 Seven Corners Ctr Pmb
174
Falls Church VA 220442409

Call Sign: AD4UO
Anne Lundin
6312 Seven Corners Ctr Pmb
174
Falls Church VA 220442409

Call Sign: NO4I
Carl Janow
3053 Shadeland Dr
Falls Church VA 22044

Call Sign: KD4ITJ
Gary E Moss
7713 Shreve Rd
Falls Church VA 220433315

Call Sign: KE4BVQ
Barbara L Moss
7713 Shreve Rd
Falls Church VA 220433315

Call Sign: KA8CES
Steven T Koenig
7801 Shreve Rd
Falls Church VA 22043

Call Sign: WA9GVK
Bruce J Brown
3422 Silver Maple Pl
Falls Church VA 22042

Call Sign: KB9EZV
Mathew S Schuck
3340 Skyview Ter
Falls Church VA 22042

Call Sign: KG4TSY
Mathew S Schuck
3340 Skyview Ter
Falls Church VA 22042

Call Sign: KJ4VTG
Matthew B Jensen
7802 Snead Ln
Falls Church VA 220433510

Call Sign: KC4VCD
Roger R Oliva
7842 Snead Ln
Falls Church VA 22043

Call Sign: KF4TZT
Jason A Smingler
3330 Spring Ln D12
Falls Church VA 22041

Call Sign: N4CDF
Richard B Demaret
6451 Spring Ter
Falls Church VA 22042

Call Sign: K7MU
Charles Ives ARC
2957 Strathmeade St
Falls Church VA 22042

Call Sign: W3IO
Burt Thompson
2957 Strathmeade St
Falls Church VA 22042

Call Sign: KF4PJU
Carol J Mack
2839 Summerfield Rd
Falls Church VA 22042

Call Sign: KG5IB
Michael D Sawyer
2839 Summerfield Rd
Falls Church VA 22042

Call Sign: W4RVJ
William Hansel
2925 Summerfield Rd
Falls Church VA 22042

Call Sign: K3HB
Judith A Booker
3442 Surrey Ln
Falls Church VA 22042

Call Sign: KG4AKG
Qrv Society
3442 Surrey Ln

Falls Church VA 220423536

Call Sign: W3WV
James M Wilcox
3442 Surrey Ln
Falls Church VA 220423536

Call Sign: N3RLM
Laurie S Brown
3018 Sylvan Dr
Falls Church VA 220424314

Call Sign: KG4YQM
Dennis J Shannon
3029 Sylvan Dr
Falls Church VA 22042

Call Sign: WD4MXW
Robert E Duggar
7430 Tillman Dr
Falls Church VA 22043

Call Sign: KK4FQZ
Thomas L Croxton
303 Timber Ln
Falls Church VA 22046

Call Sign: KG4WAM
Peter M Kiesel
7615 Trail Run Rd
Falls Church VA 22042

Call Sign: KB4QYL
Paul D Yoder
6512 Truman Ln
Falls Church VA 22043

Call Sign: N4RXQ
Laurie G Caldwell
7219 Tyler Ave
Falls Church VA 22042

Call Sign: W4FFV
John H Mc Mahon
2233 Underwood St
Falls Church VA 22043

Call Sign: WA4PBG
Montie F Cone

317 Van Buren St
Falls Church VA 22046

Call Sign: KD7SSM
James L Quinn Jr
2086 Van Tuyl Pl
Falls Church VA 22043

Call Sign: KE4DMP
Sidney H Shaw
802 Villa Ridge Rd
Falls Church VA 22046

Call Sign: KG4OAQ
Benjamin H Shaw
802 Villa Ridge Rd
Falls Church VA 22046

Call Sign: W4ZPQ
Walter W Wurfel
502 W Broad St 512
Falls Church VA 22046

Call Sign: AA1TE
Daniel J Sullivan
207 W Cameron Rd
Falls Church VA 22046

Call Sign: KI4HTE
John D Porter
213 W Cameron Rd
Falls Church VA 22046

Call Sign: NT8B
Leon H Bruner
305 W Columbia St
Falls Church VA 22046

Call Sign: KB1TFF
Jacob H Bruner
305 W Columbia St
Falls Church VA 22046

Call Sign: KG4SEL
James R Becerra
2803 W George Mason Rd
Falls Church VA 22042

Call Sign: KE4WGN

Herbert W Hicks
2823 W George Mason Rd
Falls Church VA 22042

Call Sign: KC2ENC
Ricarda L Koc
7506 Walnut Hill Ln
Falls Church VA 22042

Call Sign: KC2END
Peter B Best
7506 Walnut Hill Ln
Falls Church VA 22042

Call Sign: W0PDU
Jerry L Dowell
6204 Waterway Dr
Falls Church VA 22044

Call Sign: KI4FNE
Penelope A Talleur
6365 Waterway Dr
Falls Church VA 22044

Call Sign: KI4BXQ
Thomas J Talleur
6365 Waterway Dr
Falls Church VA 22044

Call Sign: KE4WKY
Edward E Greer
6804 Westcott Rd
Falls Church VA 22042

Call Sign: WA3USW
William C Walsh
6916 Westlawn Dr
Falls Church VA 22042

Call Sign: KE4ALT
Jose Bernabe III
6845 Westmoreland Rd
Falls Church VA 22042

Call Sign: W4IBJ
John A Vignali
2030 Westmoreland St Apt 221
Falls Church VA 22043

Call Sign: K4NOV
Anthony P Kancler
2769 Winchester Way
Falls Church VA 22042

Call Sign: KI4AZU
Charles F Savich
2801 Woodlawn Ave
Falls Church VA 22042

Call Sign: WA4IHQ
Robert C Martin
2847 Woodlawn Ave
Falls Church VA 22042

Call Sign: WA2BSL
David J Allen
6110 Wooten Dr
Falls Church VA 22044

Call Sign: KI4ZGU
Howard L Miller Jr
312 Wrens Way
Falls Church VA 220463517

Call Sign: WD6CPV
Alexander L Popof
Falls Church VA 22040

Call Sign: KI4IPO
Macel A Sharland
Falls Church VA 22040

Call Sign: KK4BBI
Joseph E Friedel
Falls Church VA 22041

Call Sign: WL7AF
Carl F Langford
Falls Church VA 22042

Call Sign: KI4RGC
Peter R Shanklin
Falls Church VA 220400321

Call Sign: WB5OYP
George E Lemaster
Falls Church VA 220407424

Call Sign: KD4CXM
Katherine M Hubble
Rt 3 Box 177A
Falls Mills VA 24613

Call Sign: KD4MSP
De Wayne K Hubble
Rt 3 Box 177A
Falls Mills VA 24613

Call Sign: KC4QQO
Thomas Kelly
Rt 3 Box 503B4
Falls Mills VA 24613

Call Sign: KC4RVR
Wanda F Kelly
130 Capri St
Falls Mills VA 24613

Call Sign: KE4FAQ
James W Brewster
Falls Mills VA 24613

Call Sign: KI4TYG
Jean E Jarrett
Falls Mills VA 24613

Call Sign: KI4TYH
William T Jarrett
Falls Mills VA 24613

Call Sign: K4RFP
Mark A Seymour
252 Anderson Dr
Falmouth VA 224051626

Call Sign: KG4KUO
Mark A Seymour
914 Anderson Dr
Falmouth VA 22405

Call Sign: KI4JHG

Michael P Carr
222 Betty Lewis Dr
Falmouth VA 22405

Call Sign: KF4QH
Lloyd E Perkins Sr
520 Brooke Rd
Falmouth VA 22405

Call Sign: WB4JKT
Bernard E Fallin
198 Caisson Rd
Falmouth VA 22405

Call Sign: WB4EDB
William L White
534 Caisson Rd
Falmouth VA 22405

Call Sign: KC4LGK
Paul W Thompson
807 Cresthill Rd
Falmouth VA 22405

Call Sign: WA1YVO
Douglas Anderson
915 Ficklen Rd
Falmouth VA 224052103

Call Sign: KG4VTS
Gary V Markum
89 Hickory Hill Ln
Falmouth VA 22405

Call Sign: AI4MC
Gary V Markum
89 Hickory Hill Ln
Falmouth VA 22405

Call Sign: KE4BSX
Herbert W Embrey
841 Kellogg Mill Rd
Falmouth VA 22406

Call Sign: N4NNN
Juan C Chaves III
44 Little Falls Rd
Falmouth VA 22405

Call Sign: W4ULM
Hilbert A Newton
67 McCarty Rd
Falmouth VA 22405

Call Sign: NL7SE
William H Morrison
9 N Pointe Dr
Falmouth VA 22405

Call Sign: WL7BVV
Sheila S Morrison
9 N Pointe Dr
Falmouth VA 22405

Call Sign: AC4SK
Carolyn E Cavanagh
223 N Randolph Rd
Falmouth VA 22405

Call Sign: KB4XF
John F Cavanagh
223 N Randolph Rd
Falmouth VA 22405

Call Sign: KC4YJZ
Robert T Garrow
89 New Hope Church Rd
Falmouth VA 22405

Call Sign: KD4JTI
George M Payne Jr
175 Newton Rd
Falmouth VA 22405

Call Sign: KD4PPD
Patricia M Jones
21 Plumosa Dr
Falmouth VA 22405

Call Sign: KE4ATH
Gerald W Lucas
1012 Ramoth Church Rd
Falmouth VA 22406

Call Sign: WD6FIX
Frank C Valentine
230 Richards Ferry Rd
Falmouth VA 22406

Call Sign: WB4JYM
Alan D Albert
302 Ridgemore St
Falmouth VA 22401

Call Sign: KF4EPO
Dennis R Dudley
181 Rocky Run Rd
Falmouth VA 22406

Call Sign: KD4FMD
Hugh G Newton Jr
17 Salvington Rd
Falmouth VA 22405

Call Sign: N9IVZ
Trevor M Boyd
265 Salvington Rd
Falmouth VA 22405

Call Sign: K9MX
David G Boyd
265 Salvington Rd
Falmouth VA 224053459

Call Sign: KB9CYU
Jennifer H Campbell
265 Salvington Rd
Falmouth VA 224053459

Call Sign: KD4JTH
James R Clore Jr
940 White Oak Rd
Falmouth VA 22405

Call Sign: KJ4ENU
Grayson Willis
608 Winterberry Dr
Falmouth VA 22405

Call Sign: K9PLY
Grayson Willis
608 Winterberry Dr
Falmouth VA 22405

Call Sign: KC7CYD
James V Correia
710 Winterbury Dr

Falmouth VA 224052054

Call Sign: KD4OBY
Richard W Carpenter Jr
Falmouth VA 22403

Call Sign: KI4SWM
Stafford ARA
Falmouth VA 22403

Call Sign: WS4VA
Stafford ARA
Falmouth VA 22403

Call Sign: WW4VA
Stafford ARA
Falmouth VA 22403

FCC Amateur Radio Licenses in Fancy Gap

Call Sign: W4DSU
Qcwa Chapter 126
196898 Blue Ridge Pkwy
Fancy Gap VA 24328

Call Sign: W4TJE
Thomas J Emerson Jr
196898 Blue Ridge Pkwy
Fancy Gap VA 24328

Call Sign: K4JOH
Jackson C Steele
Rt 2 Box 28 Elk Spur Rd
Fancy Gap VA 24328

Call Sign: KF4GUR
Joel A Dantzler
Rt 2 Box 614
Fancy Gap VA 24328

Call Sign: N4VMB
David Nicholson
Dogwood Mtn
Fancy Gap VA 24328

Call Sign: WA4TLC
Mikel C Strickland
894 Elk Spur Rd

Fancy Gap VA 24328

Call Sign: K4GI
Mikel C Strickland
894 Elk Spur Rd
Fancy Gap VA 24328

Call Sign: KI4YTX
Jared J Strickland
1511 Elk Spur Rd
Fancy Gap VA 24328

Call Sign: KI4OMW
Brenda D Marrah
7018 Joy Ranch Rd
Fancy Gap VA 24328

Call Sign: KI4EYP
Michael E Rossi
1767 Misty Trl
Fancy Gap VA 24328

Call Sign: K4MOD
Michael E Rossi
1767 Misty Trl
Fancy Gap VA 24328

Call Sign: K4EYP
Michael E Rossi
1767 Misty Trl
Fancy Gap VA 24328

Call Sign: KJ4AUX
Stephen J A Hayward
102 Overland Trl
Fancy Gap VA 24328

Call Sign: K2VRT
Stephen J A Hayward
102 Overland Trl
Fancy Gap VA 24328

Call Sign: KJ4FDX
John A Mount
1546 Turner Spur Rd
Fancy Gap VA 24328

Call Sign: KI4JTM
William A Brownlee Jr

1546 Turner Spur Rd
Fancy Gap VA 243284208

Call Sign: KF4GWJ
Carlos W Rigney
Fancy Gap VA 24328

FCC Amateur Radio Licenses in Farmville

Call Sign: KB4TAN
Matthew A Merkle
711 1st Ave
Farmville VA 23901

Call Sign: KD4NZF
Fred H Hanbury
312 3rd Ave
Farmville VA 23901

Call Sign: KN4LF
Fred H Hanbury
312 3rd Ave
Farmville VA 23901

Call Sign: KI4WOC
Roger D Rogerson
1103 4th Ave
Farmville VA 23901

Call Sign: N4CFA
John M Austin
1001 7th Ave
Farmville VA 23901

Call Sign: KE4GEF
Vern W Clark Jr
205 Agee St Apt A
Farmville VA 23901

Call Sign: KF4JKC
Bradley L Slayton
79 Allen Farm Rd
Farmville VA 23901

Call Sign: N4YHF
Carolyn H Statzer
Hc 6 Box 1726
Farmville VA 23901

Call Sign: KC4CVW
Billy L Dempsey Jr
Rt 3 Box 250
Farmville VA 23901

Call Sign: KF4GFR
Linwood S Vaughan
220 Calloway Ln
Farmville VA 23901

Call Sign: KE4UQI
David E Clark
2705 Charles Wood Ln
Farmville VA 23901

Call Sign: KZ5RO
Ronald M Guilliams
890 Douglas Church Rd
Farmville VA 239019356

Call Sign: KE4ZBH
Southside ARA
311 E 2nd St
Farmville VA 23901

Call Sign: N3JJQ
Billie S Dixon
311 E 2nd St
Farmville VA 23901

Call Sign: N4TVM
Brian T Butler
401 E 2nd St
Farmville VA 23901

Call Sign: KB4TBX
David L Brown
817 Early St
Farmville VA 23901

Call Sign: KJ4UFP
Jason E Brooks
292 Fairgrounds Rd
Farmville VA 23901

Call Sign: W4AGP
Alvin G Profitt
344 Fork Rd

Farmville VA 23901

Call Sign: KG4KXX
Constance J Kershner
117 Garnett Rd
Farmville VA 23901

Call Sign: KG4KXT
Sherie L Gwin
117 Garnett Rd
Farmville VA 23901

Call Sign: KA4WBW
Irvin M Robertson
2005 Germantown Rd
Farmville VA 23901

Call Sign: N4RKM
David W Statzer
208 Germantown Rd
Farmville VA 23901

Call Sign: WB3K
David W Statzer
208 Germantown Rd
Farmville VA 23901

Call Sign: K4WL
David W Statzer
208 Germantown Rd
Farmville VA 23901

Call Sign: KE7AUH
Steven R Huff
348 Holly Farms Rd
Farmville VA 23966

Call Sign: KE4MTM
Michael E Woolard
701 Meadowview Ln
Farmville VA 23901

Call Sign: KE4WQJ
Lois M Woolard
701 Meadowview Ln
Farmville VA 23901

Call Sign: WM4DX
Michael E Woolard

701 Meadowview Ln
Farmville VA 23901

Call Sign: KD4YVJ
Leslie D Phaup Jr
1100 Milnwood Rd
Farmville VA 23901

Call Sign: KE4RPL
Nancy C Phaup
1100 Milnwood Rd
Farmville VA 23901

Call Sign: KE4VOC
Amanda S Phaup
1100 Milnwood Rd
Farmville VA 23901

Call Sign: KT4QB
Garret C Jensma
707 Northview Dr
Farmville VA 239013050

Call Sign: KE4QXY
Jeremy S Woolard
1131 Old Ridge Rd
Farmville VA 23901

Call Sign: KG4AHJ
Dan G Wickizer
707 Orchard St
Farmville VA 23901

Call Sign: WA4PGM
Kyle P Chavis
826 Plank Rd
Farmville VA 239010127

Call Sign: W5BR
Robert L Risacher
1735 Price Dr
Farmville VA 23901

Call Sign: KA3SAG
Billie F Risacher
1735 Price Dr
Farmville VA 239012812

Call Sign: KE4RPN

Katherine M Austin
1001 Seventh Ave
Farmville VA 239012317

Call Sign: K4KJU
William F Kelly
205 Smith Dr
Farmville VA 23901

Call Sign: KE4JYO
Shannon D Rodgers
420C Winston St
Farmville VA 23901

Call Sign: KE4GXQ
Robert C Blosser III
Farmville VA 23901

Call Sign: K4VWK
Scott M Harwood Sr
Farmville VA 23901

Call Sign: KE4SFU
Harold M Garrett
Farmville VA 23901

Call Sign: KF4EAS
Jason R Garrett
Farmville VA 23901

Call Sign: WB4NWP
Michael A Silveira Jr
Farmville VA 23901

FCC Amateur Radio Licenses in Farnham

Call Sign: N4KBP
Vernon W Cooke
Rt 1 Box 179
Farnham VA 22460

Call Sign: KF4EVK
William R Nash
1116 Bryants Town Rd
Farnham VA 22460

FCC Amateur Radio Licenses in Ferrum

Call Sign: N4MHF
Albert J Anderson
Rt 2 Box 35A
Ferrum VA 24088

Call Sign: KA3NZR
Harry W Weiss Jr
2873 Haw Patch Rd
Ferrum VA 24088

Call Sign: KE4JFV
Clarence R Wilcox IV
Ferrum VA 24088

Call Sign: KE4MBC
Lisa H Wilcox
Ferrum VA 240880555

FCC Amateur Radio Licenses in Fieldale

Call Sign: KG4KUA
Gale W Walker
3979 Dillon Forks Rd
Fieldale VA 24089

Call Sign: W4GWW
Gale W Walker
3979 Dillon Forks Rd
Fieldale VA 24089

Call Sign: KE4APX
Joe R Bryant
80 Patrick Ave
Fieldale VA 24089

Call Sign: KD4POE
Joseph D Handy
1191 Valley Dr
Fieldale VA 24089

Call Sign: KC4DIQ
William R Turner
Fieldale VA 24089

Call Sign: KF4YUU
Wilma S Harrison
Fieldale VA 24089

Call Sign: KI4MTJ
William L Huffling
Fieldale VA 24089

FCC Amateur Radio Licenses in Fincastle

Call Sign: WA4WXP
Eugene F Strickler
Rfd 1 Box 32
Fincastle VA 24090

Call Sign: KC4LDR
Thomas E Eide
Rt 1 Box 329
Fincastle VA 24090

Call Sign: KE4APO
James H Eads
102 Catawba St Box 161
Fincastle VA 24090

Call Sign: WA2DTA
Luther P Quick
1766 Lees Gap Rd
Fincastle VA 24090

Call Sign: WD4NZP
David W Oxley
1538 Lugar Ln
Fincastle VA 24090

Call Sign: KC4QN
Michael R Brumfield
1078 Mildred St
Fincastle VA 24090

Call Sign: WD4DUX
James B Booze
27 Murray St
Fincastle VA 24090

Call Sign: WA4DQC
William H Belcher
3155 Nace Rd
Fincastle VA 24090

Call Sign: KI4QXV

Anna M Wallace
562 Oak Hill Rd
Fincastle VA 24090

Call Sign: N4RPY
Henry B Wallace
562 Oak Hill Rd
Fincastle VA 24090

Call Sign: KB8MXZ
Jonathan L Lester
7691 Old Fincastle Rd
Fincastle VA 24090

Call Sign: KK4BXM
Todd L Flood
101 Regent St
Fincastle VA 24090

Call Sign: N4PXG
Timothy M Brady
128 Ridge Trl
Fincastle VA 24090

Call Sign: WD4OXS
George E Tehan
Fincastle VA 24090

Call Sign: W4WIC
Thomas E Chamblin Jr
Fincastle VA 24090

FCC Amateur Radio Licenses in Fishersville

Call Sign: KJ4BBM
Octavio De Los Reyes
34 Bedford Ln
Fishersville VA 22939

Call Sign: AJ4YE
Octavio De Los Reyes
34 Bedford Ln
Fishersville VA 22939

Call Sign: WB4KIT
John S Harvey
Rt 2 Box 127
Fishersville VA 22939

Call Sign: W1AL
Arthur J Lore
Rr 1 Box 321A
Fishersville VA 22939

Call Sign: KD4OXO
Preston Barker
R 1 Box 394C
Fishersville VA 22939

Call Sign: W4ZEE
Ronald K Burch
23 Goose Meadow Ct
Fishersville VA 22939

Call Sign: KJ4VTT
Jason P Bibeau
46 Hamshire Way
Fishersville VA 22939

Call Sign: KB4GUA
Oscar L Price
37 Hereford Dr
Fishersville VA 229392101

Call Sign: KI4QNN
Amc ARC
78 Medical Center Dr
Fishersville VA 22939

Call Sign: KE4AMC
Amc ARC
78 Medical Center Dr
Fishersville VA 22939

Call Sign: KE4JSX
Neil D Beidler
71 Princeton Ln
Fishersville VA 22939

Call Sign: KG4IUH
Scott H Hevener
445 Ramsey Rd
Fishersville VA 22939

Call Sign: KA4VMP
Edward P Taylor
537 Ramsey Rd

Fishersville VA 229392314

Call Sign: K5DXR
Mark E Sutherland
18 S Cobblestone Ct
Fishersville VA 22939

Call Sign: W4MES
Mark E Sutherland
18 S Cobblestone Ct
Fishersville VA 22939

Call Sign: K5DXR
Mark E Sutherland
18 S Cobblestone Ct
Fishersville VA 22939

Call Sign: AG4XN
Andrew J Barbour
516 St James Rd
Fishersville VA 22939

Call Sign: KF4DQ
Fred M Castello
70 Twin Hills Ln
Fishersville VA 22939

Call Sign: KB2CBV
Walter M Sigmund
310 Westminister Dr
Fishersville VA 22939

Call Sign: KE4NNY
Stephen M Shepherd
Box W 58 Woodrow Wilson Rehab Ctr
Fishersville VA 22939

Call Sign: KG4VOQ
Morris I Peltz
85 Wyndham Hill Dr
Fishersville VA 22939

Call Sign: N4WVK
Barbara J Barr
Fishersville VA 22939

Call Sign: KI4FZW
John M Schroeder

Fishersville VA 22939

Call Sign: KJ4ZOT
Robert L Thomas III
Fishersville VA 22939

FCC Amateur Radio Licenses in Flint Hill

Call Sign: KG4VXJ
Randall G Bartlett
125 Bear Wallow Rd
Flint Hill VA 226270392

Call Sign: KA4AFA
Edwin G Streapy
Flint Hill VA 22627

Call Sign: KC4NSQ
John A Proper
Flint Hill VA 22627

FCC Amateur Radio Licenses in Floyd

Call Sign: KF4OOQ
Joseph A Stone
Blue Ridge Mtn Common 4
Floyd VA 24091

Call Sign: KG4VMI
Dierdre M Dannewitz
100 Blue Ridge Mtn Rd 11
Floyd VA 24091

Call Sign: KC4SVC
Carl E Harmon
Rr 1 Box 675
Floyd VA 24091

Call Sign: KJ4MHZ
Luis A Garcia
401 Cannadays Gap Rd SE
Floyd VA 24091

Call Sign: WA3BAR
Alisha L Rupprecht
110 Clinger Xing
Floyd VA 24091

Call Sign: W7JAR
James M Rupprecht
110 Clinger Xing
Floyd VA 24091

Call Sign: KK4CXB
Floyd ARS
201 E Main St Ste 9
Floyd VA 24091

Call Sign: W4FCV
Floyd ARS
201 E Main St Ste 9
Floyd VA 24091

Call Sign: N4WRT
John B Hughlett
432 E Oxford
Floyd VA 24091

Call Sign: KI4TSJ
Faith M King
2787 Floyd Hwy S
Floyd VA 24091

Call Sign: W4FIC
Faith M King
2787 Floyd Hwy S
Floyd VA 24091

Call Sign: WB4HQW
Kathleen A Becker
2787 Floyd Hwy S
Floyd VA 240913055

Call Sign: WK4AB
Kathleen A Becker
2787 Floyd Hwy S
Floyd VA 240913055

Call Sign: KI4RRK
Rhonda D Graham
503 Harvestwood Rd
Floyd VA 24091

Call Sign: KC4VAJ
Jabe D Graham
503 Harvestwood Rd SE

Floyd VA 240912476

Call Sign: KK4ESM
Jason T Gallimore
885 Music Rd NW
Floyd VA 24091

Call Sign: KI4OSJ
Carmen R Hamlin
563 New Haven Rd
Floyd VA 24091

Call Sign: KF4PHA
Robert N Shelor Sr
525 Oakhill Ln
Floyd VA 24091

Call Sign: KF4HDX
Donna R Johnson
429 Penn Rd NW
Floyd VA 240912431

Call Sign: KF4HDW
Benny D Johnson
429 Penn Rd NW
Floyd VA 240912431

Call Sign: KK4ESL
Robert E Clark Jr
1138 Penn Rd NW
Floyd VA 24091

Call Sign: WB4WQY
Joseph S Williamson II
Pine St
Floyd VA 24091

Call Sign: KC4VJA
Steven K Graham
1612 Sandy Flats Rd SE
Floyd VA 24091

Call Sign: W4VZH
Thomas J King Jr
285 Silverleaf Ln
Floyd VA 24091

Call Sign: K2XX
Bartolo J Giacobello

187 Slusher Store Rd
Floyd VA 24091

Call Sign: K2XXX
Anne C Wilmot
187 Slusher Store Rd
Floyd VA 24091

Call Sign: N4TJE
Michael Lengwiler
233 Turtle Rock Dr
Floyd VA 24091

Call Sign: KE4UGF
Donald F Clemens
405 Walnut Ridge Dr
Floyd VA 24091

Call Sign: KF4EKH
Martha K Clemens
405 Walnut Ridge Dr
Floyd VA 24091

Call Sign: KJ4SNT
Michael L Finch
2610 Webbs Mill Rd
Floyd VA 24091

Call Sign: KI4SMG
Kelly R Thompson
1031 White Rock Rd NW
Floyd VA 24091

Call Sign: KG4KRA
Alan E Thompson
1031 White Rock Rd NW
Floyd VA 24091

Call Sign: KF4GUU
Robert N Shelor Jr
209 Woods Gap Rd
Floyd VA 24091

Call Sign: KF4HRK
Beth K Shelor
209 Woods Gap Rd
Floyd VA 24091

Call Sign: K1WE

Victor V Goncharsky
Floyd VA 24091

Call Sign: KD4PNV
Oles Yaremenko
Floyd VA 24091

Call Sign: KD4QAV
Peter P Choporov
Floyd VA 24091

Call Sign: KD4QAW
Igor M Shevtchuk
Floyd VA 24091

Call Sign: KE4AEZ
Md Mahmudul Gani
Floyd VA 24091

Call Sign: KE4BJC
Taimur Rahman
Floyd VA 24091

Call Sign: KE4EKL
George G Alferyev
Floyd VA 24091

Call Sign: KE4EKM
Victor N Golutvin
Floyd VA 24091

Call Sign: KE4EKN
Eugene A Smirnov
Floyd VA 24091

Call Sign: KE4EKO
Alex G Malikov
Floyd VA 24091

Call Sign: KE4EKP
Vyacheslav P Baranov
Floyd VA 24091

Call Sign: KE4EKR
Dmytry D Coondel
Floyd VA 24091

Call Sign: KE4EKS
Victor V Pivovarov

Floyd VA 24091

Call Sign: KE4EKT
Gennady V Treus
Floyd VA 24091

Call Sign: KE4EKU
Yuri P Gritsenko
Floyd VA 24091

Call Sign: KE4EKV
Victor L Bobrow
Floyd VA 24091

Call Sign: KK4WWW
Gaynell M Larsen
Floyd VA 24091

Call Sign: KR4AL
Igor W Shekhovtsev
Floyd VA 24091

Call Sign: N4USA
Foundation For Amateur
International Rad Serv
Floyd VA 24091

Call Sign: KB0KNA
Valentin I Kudryavtsev
Floyd VA 24091

Call Sign: KD4QAU
Serge N Tarasov
Floyd VA 24091

Call Sign: KD4STR
Yuri V Katyutin
Floyd VA 24091

Call Sign: KE4AEU
Sohel M Awrangzeb
Floyd VA 24091

Call Sign: KE4AEV
Manjurul Haque
Floyd VA 24091

Call Sign: KE4AEW
Saiful A Bhuiyan

Floyd VA 24091

Call Sign: KE4AEX
Md Abul Bashar
Floyd VA 24091

Call Sign: KE4AEY
Syed Shabiu Ahsan
Floyd VA 24091

Call Sign: KE4AFA
M Saiful Islam
Floyd VA 24091

Call Sign: KE4AFB
Muhammad O Gani
Floyd VA 24091

Call Sign: KE4AFC
Mohammed Arif
Floyd VA 24091

Call Sign: KE4AFD
Gazi Golam Mobin
Floyd VA 24091

Call Sign: KE4AFE
S M Abdul Majed
Floyd VA 24091

Call Sign: KE4AFG
Ahm Shamsul Islam Dipu
Floyd VA 24091

Call Sign: KE4AFH
A E Talukde Pavel
Floyd VA 24091

Call Sign: KE4BRE
A B M Ferdous
Floyd VA 24091

Call Sign: KE4HJB
Vlad N July
Floyd VA 24091

Call Sign: KK4WW
David G Larsen
Floyd VA 24091

Call Sign: KT4RP
Helen V Goncharsky
Floyd VA 24091

Call Sign: KT4RQ
Vladimir N Goncharsky
Floyd VA 24091

Call Sign: K3RSP
Richard S Pence Jr
Floyd VA 24091

FCC Amateur Radio Licenses in Ford

Call Sign: WA3RP
Richard J Pruhs
4931 Old Plantation Dr
Ford VA 23850

Call Sign: WB4LSQ
Richard E Isabelle
1543 Wills Rd
Ford VA 238502833

FCC Amateur Radio Licenses in Forest

Call Sign: AC4RG
Judy S Friel
1128 2 Church Ln
Forest VA 245514134

Call Sign: KC4AHV
Glen P Friel
1128 2 Church Ln
Forest VA 245514134

Call Sign: KI4AUA
Sara J Friel
1265 2 Church Ln
Forest VA 24551

Call Sign: KD4HVT
Cynthia D Wilson
113 Abbey Pl
Forest VA 24551

Call Sign: AD4YY
William J Glahn
752 Alum Springs Rd
Forest VA 24551

Call Sign: KA4CZU
Donald R Griffis
1246 Ashburn Dr
Forest VA 24551

Call Sign: KG4IHM
Ashley R Overstreet
350 Barbour Dr
Forest VA 245514007

Call Sign: K4RSQ
Ashley R Overstreet
350 Barbour Dr
Forest VA 245514007

Call Sign: W4AFL
Charles B Morrison
102 Berkley Pl
Forest VA 245511312

Call Sign: W4SKD
William D Wright
1302 Bethel Church Rd
Forest VA 24551

Call Sign: KJ4IFX
Martin B Akers
1380 Bethel Church Rd
Forest VA 24551

Call Sign: KJ4IFY
Sherry H Akers
1380 Bethel Church Rd
Forest VA 24551

Call Sign: KJ4QBX
Blaine K Akers
1380 Bethel Church Rd
Forest VA 24551

Call Sign: KD4GMU
James M Lugar
1486 Bethel Church Rd
Forest VA 245513401

Call Sign: K4LUL
Edwin G Orgera
349 Bob Cir
Forest VA 245514026

Call Sign: N4WYI
Douglas S Russell
Rt 2 Box 198
Forest VA 24551

Call Sign: N5ORC
David R Grunert
Rt 6 Box 200
Forest VA 24551

Call Sign: KB4MK
Boyce A Clodfelter
Rt 4 Box 55
Forest VA 24551

Call Sign: N4ZEH
Anson W Mays
Rt 2 Box 558
Forest VA 24551

Call Sign: KC4RBA
Bernard W Henegan
78 Briery Creek Rd
Forest VA 24551

Call Sign: KF5JR
Wayne N Lewis
1206 Brigade Pl
Forest VA 24551

Call Sign: KC4ZXA
Roger A Harris
25 Carters Crossing Ln
Forest VA 24551

Call Sign: KD4AEM
Lisa J Harris
25 Carters Crossing Ln
Forest VA 24551

Call Sign: KC6JLT
John S Mustol
204 Casaloma Dr

Forest VA 24551

Call Sign: KD6CFV
David M Mustol
204 Casaloma Dr
Forest VA 24551

Call Sign: N4TER
Colton S Johnson
1C Cedar Haven Ct
Forest VA 24551

Call Sign: KC2IMD
Robert J Winberry
1116 Cedar Rock Dr
Forest VA 24551

Call Sign: AK4LP
Robert J Winberry
1116 Cedar Rock Dr
Forest VA 24551

Call Sign: N3OG
Justin L Ogden
1365 Cedar Rock Dr
Forest VA 24551

Call Sign: KE4VUZ
Kristine L C Lee
104 Chelsea Dr
Forest VA 24551

Call Sign: N4USS
Jeffrey T Lee
104 Chelsea Dr
Forest VA 24551

Call Sign: WB4JBI
Victor C Bosiger
230 Chelsea Dr
Forest VA 24551

Call Sign: K4YB
Mountain Top Associates Of
VA
1704 Cottontown Rd
Forest VA 24551

Call Sign: KJ4ILH

Karrie R Seeberger
1141 Cuddington Ln
Forest VA 24551

Call Sign: KJ4ILI
Robert B Seeberger
1141 Cuddington Ln
Forest VA 24551

Call Sign: K4CUE
Richard T Boswell II
107 Cygnet Cir
Forest VA 24551

Call Sign: KC4CTS
Richard L Ramsey
112 Declaration Ter
Forest VA 24551

Call Sign: KG4POZ
Michael E Vogt
313 Eastwind Dr
Forest VA 24551

Call Sign: KD4CAT
Brenda F Harvey
1221 Equestrian Ridge Cir
Forest VA 24551

Call Sign: WD4KQI
Robert E Harvey
1221 Equestrian Ridge Cir
Forest VA 24551

Call Sign: N3MS
Matthew D Snyder
4165 Everett Rd
Forest VA 245513864

Call Sign: WA6CRL
Joel D Kramar
103 Field Brook Pl
Forest VA 24551

Call Sign: W0ID
Richard W Ehrhorn
11261 Forest Rd
Forest VA 245510645

Call Sign: KS4Q
Richard W Ehrhorn
11261 Forest Rd
Forest VA 245510645

Call Sign: K4TDI
Thomas G Wolcott Sr
107 Fox Hall Rd
Forest VA 24551

Call Sign: KI4FGT
Jeremy E Potts
1661 Fox Ridge Rd
Forest VA 24551

Call Sign: W4MKO
Robert K Johnson
1053 Governors Ln
Forest VA 24551

Call Sign: N6NI
Thomas M Hoyne
1073 Governors Ln
Forest VA 24551

Call Sign: KJ4IGF
John P Davison
102 Graves Dr
Forest VA 24551

Call Sign: KB4MPK
Doris F Turner
2308 Graves Mill Rd
Forest VA 245511947

Call Sign: W4ITP
Myron A Turner Jr
2308 Graves Mill Rd
Forest VA 245511947

Call Sign: KI4FGW
Carl J Weber
1683 Great Oak Rd
Forest VA 24551

Call Sign: KC0MCV
Joseph J Milhorn II
1076 Green Way Trl
Forest VA 24551

Call Sign: KK4GDG
Brenda D Glass
2095 Gumtree Rd
Forest VA 24551

Call Sign: WB5JJK
Don W Baker
114 Haines Point Ter
Forest VA 24551

Call Sign: KQ4NP
Raymond L Hawkins
115 Haines Point Ter
Forest VA 24551

Call Sign: KG4DDP
Jeffery W Williams Jr
105 Hickory Winds Ct
Forest VA 24551

Call Sign: KG4HQI
Timothy B Yeatts
108 Hickory Winds Ct
Forest VA 24551

Call Sign: KI4TSZ
Jerry S Cornelius
214 Hitching Post Ln
Forest VA 24551

Call Sign: W4TJV
Tammy J Veres
1168 Homestead Garden Ct 5
Forest VA 24551

Call Sign: KI4SFQ
Tammy V Rogers
1168 Homestead Garden Ct 5
Forest VA 24551

Call Sign: KG4PTY
Cary P Cofer
1307 Homestead Gardens Ct
Forest VA 24551

Call Sign: WA4SNY
David L Suchodolski
3484 Hooper Rd

Forest VA 24551

Call Sign: KD4KWD
J Greg Snow
199 Hydaway Dr
Forest VA 245514147

Call Sign: KB4AT
Larry D Hatch Sr
1143 Irvine Ct
Forest VA 24551

Call Sign: W4JAM
John A Mann Sr
107 Ivy Lea Dr
Forest VA 24551

Call Sign: AD4ZF
Jay B Tomlinson
1131 Ivy Woods Dr
Forest VA 24551

Call Sign: W0MAN
Susanne L Mann-Moore
107 Ivylea Dr
Forest VA 245513201

Call Sign: WB4JBJ
Larry Y Lewis
187 Jane Randolph St
Forest VA 24551

Call Sign: WA4IWT
Barry W Blankenship
504 Jane Randolph St
Forest VA 24551

Call Sign: KC4GDF
Dennis R Layne
1335 Jeb Stuart Pl
Forest VA 24551

Call Sign: KK4BJA
Thomas L White Sr
1156 Jefferson Way
Forest VA 24511

Call Sign: KG4KCG
Kelly D Taylor

109 Jefferson Woods Dr
Forest VA 24551

Call Sign: W4WWQ
Peter L Lascell
261 Kirkley Cir
Forest VA 245511613

Call Sign: WD4GCD
Shirley T Garbee
384 Kirkley Cir
Forest VA 24551

Call Sign: W3PKL
Henry B Stamps
203 Lake Ridge Dr
Forest VA 24551

Call Sign: KD4PKA
Hugh E Owen II
412 Lake Vista Dr
Forest VA 24551

Call Sign: KG4POT
Dwight L Patton
506 Lake Vista Dr
Forest VA 24551

Call Sign: WA3GKI
Stephen R Downs
725 Lake Vista Dr
Forest VA 24551

Call Sign: KD6IA
Walter J Majewski
734 Lake Vista Dr
Forest VA 24551

Call Sign: W7KUK
George E Hayner
121 Londonberry Rd
Forest VA 245511609

Call Sign: WA4PRI
Samuel F Serio
101 Lyon Dr
Forest VA 24551

Call Sign: N4JLQ

Deirdre E Serio
101 Lyon Dr
Forest VA 245512317

Call Sign: K0CYF
John D Benson
202 Manor Dr
Forest VA 24551

Call Sign: KI4QYI
Thomas A Taylor
106 Maplewood Dr
Forest VA 24551

Call Sign: KE4JHT
Gregory L Durham
2161 Matthew Talbot Rd
Forest VA 24551

Call Sign: N1RKZ
Robert W Weber
1610 Meadow Down Dr
Forest VA 24551

Call Sign: AA4RW
Robert W Weber
1610 Meadow Down Dr
Forest VA 24551

Call Sign: KD4TNQ
Dallas T Scott
1900 Meadow Down Dr
Forest VA 24551

Call Sign: KE4HBR
Frances A Scott
1900 Meadow Down Dr
Forest VA 24551

Call Sign: N2ICW
Edward E Schwabe
103 Meadowgate Dr
Forest VA 24551

Call Sign: N8AID
Daryl G Popowitch
217 Millspring Dr
Forest VA 24551

Call Sign: WB4CEF
David L Roberson
111 Millstone Ter
Forest VA 24551

Call Sign: N4KRV
Richard L Harper
1131 Mont View Ln
Forest VA 24551

Call Sign: KF4JKE
Ronald S Merkal
202 Mt Haven Dr
Forest VA 24551

Call Sign: AG4VI
Joseph G Kislo
11 Orion Ct Apt 103
Forest VA 245513119

Call Sign: KI4RJS
Alfred L Pisarek
203 Persimmon Way
Forest VA 24551

Call Sign: WB4URF
Jeffrey R Johnson
202 Pocahontas Dr
Forest VA 24551

Call Sign: KJ4PYF
Mike Mullins
1060 Pond View Cir
Forest VA 24551

Call Sign: K4LNB
Mike Mullins
1060 Pond View Cir
Forest VA 24551

Call Sign: WD4OLV
Richard L Brown
3 Poplar Forest Dr
Forest VA 24551

Call Sign: NN4RB
Richard L Brown
3 Poplar Forest Dr
Forest VA 24551

Call Sign: KA4JWR
Keaner C Brown
3 Poplar Forest Dr
Forest VA 245511623

Call Sign: N4KCB
Keaner C Brown
3 Poplar Forest Dr
Forest VA 245511623

Call Sign: KG4KNP
Michael R Lee
266 Poplar Forest Dr
Forest VA 24551

Call Sign: K4YCR
Henry L Wyatt II
306 Quail Ridge Dr
Forest VA 245511018

Call Sign: KF4OBF
Joanne J Wyatt
306 Quail Ridge Dr
Forest VA 245511018

Call Sign: K1SE
William B De Lage
203 Quail Ridge Dr
Forest VA 245511019

Call Sign: N4CNH
Joseph F Nuccio
504 Ramblewood Rd
Forest VA 24551

Call Sign: K4NYY
Joseph F Nuccio
504 Ramblewood Rd
Forest VA 24551

Call Sign: KI4MPY
Colby I York Jr
801 Ramblewood Rd
Forest VA 24551

Call Sign: KE4UDN
Todd Owen
1732 Rocky Branch Dr

Forest VA 24551

Call Sign: KG4VEL
Donald R Harris Jr
3493 Rocky Mtn Rd
Forest VA 245513624

Call Sign: KF4ZTG
Wade J Baumgartner
1033 S Oak Lawn Dr
Forest VA 24551

Call Sign: WB4DAI
Lawrence L Lineberry Jr
116 Sailview Dr
Forest VA 24551

Call Sign: KD4LJS
Kenneth S Howard
1142 Shadow Peak Rd
Forest VA 24551

Call Sign: N4RLW
Robert L Woodlief
112 Simsbury Ln
Forest VA 24551

Call Sign: KF4ZBU
David W Rainey
211 Simsbury Ln
Forest VA 24551

Call Sign: KB6NRA
Patricia P Barber
1372 Smartview Ln
Forest VA 24551

Call Sign: AJ4AZ
David F Barber
1372 Smartview Ln
Forest VA 24551

Call Sign: KD4ARK
Timothy G Haynie
1107 Smoketree Dr
Forest VA 24551

Call Sign: W4DTX
Wayne D Dalton

311 Spring Lake Rd
Forest VA 245511971

Call Sign: N2DA
Craig F Szczutkowski
403 Spring Lake Rd
Forest VA 245511978

Call Sign: KF4ZTF
James L Tyree
105 Summerwood Ln
Forest VA 24551

Call Sign: WA4VQC
Carl F Sensabaugh
2368 Terrace View Rd
Forest VA 245519742

Call Sign: N4CCR
Anthony L Iovinetti
3143 Thomas Jefferson Rd
Forest VA 24551

Call Sign: KG4PJW
Jacob E Thomas
2909 Thomas Jefferson Rd
Forest VA 24551

Call Sign: KC4GHS
Robert E De Long
20 Timber Ridge Dr
Forest VA 24551

Call Sign: WB4RQQ
Larry L Roberts
110 Twin Creek Ter
Forest VA 24551

Call Sign: WJ4R
Larry L Roberts
110 Twin Creek Ter
Forest VA 24551

Call Sign: N2QT
Mark M Sihlanick
121 Twin Creek Ter
Forest VA 24551

Call Sign: KF4SXM

Forest Dx Assn
121 Twin Creek Ter
Forest VA 24551

Call Sign: N4KEV
Kevin A Sihlanick
121 Twin Creek Ter
Forest VA 24551

Call Sign: WE4M
Forest Contest Club
121 Twin Creek Ter
Forest VA 24551

Call Sign: KG4GYI
Forest Contest Club
121 Twin Creek Ter
Forest VA 24551

Call Sign: KG4ANH
Charles W Lee III
1324 Twin Springs Ct
Forest VA 24551

Call Sign: AK4CK
Kevin Markey
18 Valleywood Dr
Forest VA 24551

Call Sign: KF4RJQ
Dan I Bachman
1606 H Waterlick Rd
Forest VA 24551

Call Sign: KI4TDS
Raul C Wilson
5485 Waterlick Rd Apt 5
Forest VA 24551

Call Sign: AI4WX
Raul C Wilson
5485 Waterlick Rd Apt 5
Forest VA 24551

Call Sign: K4KDT
Kelly D Taylor
846 Wellington Dr
Forest VA 24551

Call Sign: KF4WBE
Timothy R Minney
1005 Whispering Pines Cir
Forest VA 24551

Call Sign: KI4JZR
Bill Hoy
1256 Whistling Swan Dr
Forest VA 24551

Call Sign: KN0R
Duane W Erby
317 Willow Oak Ter
Forest VA 24551

Call Sign: KG4POV
Jake W Bell
670 Willow Oak Ter
Forest VA 24551

Call Sign: KG4BAC
David L Mc Kinney
1319 Winewood Rd
Forest VA 24551

Call Sign: N4JHT
Judith C Reel
206 Woodville Dr
Forest VA 24551

Call Sign: WN4H
Michael R Reel
206 Woodville Dr
Forest VA 24551

Call Sign: N4NCC
Michael G Baber
111 Yukon Dr
Forest VA 24551

Call Sign: KJ4GMM
Blue Ridge Alpha Club
Forest VA 24551

Call Sign: W4ETO
Blue Ridge Alpha Club
Forest VA 24551

Call Sign: KK4AM

Duane W Erby
Forest VA 24551

FCC Amateur Radio Licenses in Fork Union

Call Sign: KG4JLL
Peter R Thorsen Jr
Rt 1 Box 57 Lll
Fork Union VA 23055

Call Sign: KV4R
Michael E Smith
Fork Union VA 23055

Call Sign: KI4UQT
Aldwin B Williams
Fork Union VA 23055

Call Sign: W4BCE
Aldwin B Williams
Fork Union VA 23055

FCC Amateur Radio Licenses in Fort A P Hill

Call Sign: KJ4WRN
John W Haefner
1 Hopemont 1
Fort A P Hill VA 22427

Call Sign: AI4JH
John W Haefner
1 Hopemont 1
Fort A P Hill VA 22427

Call Sign: NG2E
John W Haefner
1 Hopemont 1
Fort A P Hill VA 22427

Call Sign: KK4HMM
Lucas E Haefner
1 Hopemont 1
Fort A P Hill VA 22427

Call Sign: KK4HMN
Tonya S Haefner
1 Hopemont 1

Fort A P Hill VA 22427

Call Sign: KK4ECV
Cora G Haefner
1 Hopemont Apt 1
Fort A P Hill VA 22427

FCC Amateur Radio Licenses in Fort Belvoir

Call Sign: KI4LFG
Nicholas J Curcuru
9601 Barlow Rd
Fort Belvoir VA 22060

Call Sign: KI4QCR
Greg Robison
9665 Barlow Rd
Fort Belvoir VA 22060

Call Sign: WA3AOB
Ralph F Ives Jr
9120 Belvoir Woods Pkwy
Fort Belvoir VA 22060

Call Sign: N4LEO
Leo A Brooks
9002 Belvoir Woods Pky 206
Fort Belvoir VA 22060

Call Sign: WA4KTW
John B Laugerman
9100 Belvoir Woods Pky 308
Fort Belvoir VA 22060

Call Sign: K4RQ
Charles F Concannon
9002 Belvoir Woods Pky Apt 405
Fort Belvoir VA 22060

Call Sign: K6CLM
Cameron L Mackenzie
5503 Boxwood Ct N
Fort Belvoir VA 22060

Call Sign: N4PZA
Carl P Mc Kinney
5911 Chalkely Rd

Fort Belvoir VA 22060

Call Sign: KG4HOE
Audra L Zeibel
6930 Cove Inlet Ct
Fort Belvoir VA 22060

Call Sign: N1JZ
Jason G Zeibel
6930 Cove Inlet Ct
Fort Belvoir VA 22060

Call Sign: KI4DKU
James L Brinkley
6954 Farrcove Ct
Fort Belvoir VA 22060

Call Sign: NP4LM
Excell Jones
10417 Forney Loop Fairfax Village
Fort Belvoir VA 22060

Call Sign: KJ4EAE
James T Jackson
5518 Gristmill Ct N
Fort Belvoir VA 22060

Call Sign: KC4MJR
Jason M Inman
108 Gunston Rd
Fort Belvoir VA 22060

Call Sign: KJ4EYB
Robert K OMara
5977 Hallebeck Blvd
Fort Belvoir VA 22060

Call Sign: KB5UOY
Paul K Routhier
8221 Ice House Ct
Fort Belvoir VA 22060

Call Sign: N8EQA
Charles E Varsogea
5607 Marshall Rd
Fort Belvoir VA 22060

Call Sign: KC0OWD

Henry W Tye
9555 Mero Way
Fort Belvoir VA 22060

Call Sign: N0TXL
Robert J Au Buchon
5970 Sitgreaves Rd
Fort Belvoir VA 22060

Call Sign: KG4LGG
Jeffrey L Amos
5216 Stable Ct 1
Fort Belvoir VA 22060

Call Sign: KC5OCS
Yew Yuan
7020 Stone Inlet Dr
Fort Belvoir VA 22060

Call Sign: KJ4NSC
John G Vigil
5402 York Rd
Fort Belvoir VA 22060

FCC Amateur Radio Licenses in Fort Blackmore

Call Sign: KF4CAN
Charlie B Peters
Rt 1 Box 1500
Fort Blackmore VA 24250

Call Sign: KE4DQU
Fred R Gillenwater
Rr 1 Box 1506
Fort Blackmore VA 24250

Call Sign: KD4AVX
James L Grizzle
Rt 1 Box 32A
Fort Blackmore VA 24250

Call Sign: KF4BGU
Buford V Salling
Rt 1 Box 405
Fort Blackmore VA 24250

Call Sign: KB9GHI
Timothy J Carico

12859 Clinch River Hwy
Fort Blackmore VA 24250

Call Sign: KI4SFX
James S Currier
167 Fort Blackmore Ln
Fort Blackmore VA 24250

Call Sign: KJ4ADV
James S Currier
167 Fort Blackmore Ln
Fort Blackmore VA 24250

Call Sign: W7BWC
James S Currier
167 Fort Blackmore Ln
Fort Blackmore VA 24250

Call Sign: KD4EDG
Sherman P Cox
4817 Hill Station Alley Rd
Fort Blackmore VA 24250

Call Sign: KE4QCD
Rhonda A Cox
4817 Hill Station Alley Rd
Fort Blackmore VA 24250

Call Sign: KE4ICQ
James W Summers Jr
Rt Box 160
Fort Blackmore VA 24250

Call Sign: KC4JPR
J T Greear
Fort Blackmore VA 24250

FCC Amateur Radio Licenses in Fort Defiance

Call Sign: KE4RMA
Kevin E Mongold
828 Battlefield Rd
Fort Defiance VA 24437

Call Sign: NE4F
Preston H Hadley III
790 Battlefield Rd
Fort Defiance VA 24437

Call Sign: AE4I
Preston H Hadley III
790 Battlefield Rd
Fort Defiance VA 24437

Call Sign: KF4FPX
Eddie S Hooke
Rt 1 Box 131
Fort Defiance VA 24437

Call Sign: KC4HYU
Timothy D Queensberry
Rt 1 Box 56
Fort Defiance VA 24437

Call Sign: W4CAF
Charles A Frederickson
664 New Hope Crimora Rd
Fort Defiance VA 24437

FCC Amateur Radio Licenses in Fort Eustis

Call Sign: KI4BMC
Robert K Whiteley
1164 Butner St Unit B
Fort Eustis VA 23604

Call Sign: KD4MAL
Jamie S Dement
124H Richardson St
Fort Eustis VA 23604

Call Sign: KD4MAM
Anthony N Dement
124 Richardson St H
Fort Eustis VA 23604

Call Sign: WP4KDL
Marcos I Rosa III
2372 D Smith Cir
Fort Eustis VA 23604

Call Sign: KF4API
Wesley W Michael III
2335B Somervell St
Fort Eustis VA 23604

Call Sign: KM4QB
Alfred M Durtschi
103G Stillwell
Fort Eustis VA 23604

Call Sign: KJ4UNN
Sandra L Grover
1988 Van Voorhis St Apt A
Fort Eustis VA 23604

Call Sign: KI4SHV
Charles R Alexander
Fort Eustis VA 23604

FCC Amateur Radio Licenses in Fort Lee

Call Sign: K1STY
Kirsty J Waller
327A Bataan Rd
Fort Lee VA 23801

Call Sign: N3OY
Michael L Waller
327A Bataan Rd
Fort Lee VA 23801

Call Sign: WN4HRN
Garvin M Ficklin
387 A Buna Rd
Fort Lee VA 23801

Call Sign: KE4J
Garvin M Ficklin
387 A Buna Rd
Fort Lee VA 23801

Call Sign: KA4JOB
Jennifer T Haste
372A Coral Sea Dr
Fort Lee VA 23801

Call Sign: K0TAK
Thomas A Kirchhoefer
1853 Harrison Ct
Fort Lee VA 238011311

Call Sign: KF4NGW
Frederick L Johnson

426A Ledo Rd
Fort Lee VA 23801

Call Sign: AA7ZU
Barbara K Sherer
72 St Lo Rd
Fort Lee VA 23801

Call Sign: KK4FLL
Edgardo D Academia
Fort Lee VA 23801

FCC Amateur Radio Licenses in Fort Monroe

Call Sign: KE4PWP
Gene C Kamena
65 Ingalls Rd
Fort Monroe VA 23651

Call Sign: AC0CR
Andrew D Murray
33 Tidball Rd
Fort Monroe VA 236511030

FCC Amateur Radio Licenses in Fort Valley

Call Sign: KM4UH
Kenneth L Moan
99 Bethany Ln
Fort Valley VA 226520299

Call Sign: KG4VPE
Karma M Hengst
2965 Boliver Rd
Fort Valley VA 22652

Call Sign: KG4UPM
Claude H Hengst III
2965 Boliver Rd
Fort Valley VA 226522406

Call Sign: KC4VCF
Fred R Cortese
3753 Boliver Rd
Fort Valley VA 22652

Call Sign: KI4ITE

John T Rush
308 Bowman Ln
Fort Valley VA 22652

Call Sign: KC4IDJ
Gail E Garner
Hc 60 Box 1604
Fort Valley VA 22652

Call Sign: KJ4GYG
Brian J West
1083 Camp Roosevelt Rd
Fort Valley VA 22652

Call Sign: KG4QVR
Carroll E Koller
1672 Camp Roosevelt Rd
Fort Valley VA 22652

Call Sign: KG4QXL
John M Harrell
116 Coverstone Rd
Fort Valley VA 22652

Call Sign: N8OVM
James G Stonemetz Jr
7487 Fort Valley Rd
Fort Valley VA 22652

Call Sign: W4QFY
Dan W Cronin
11590 Fort Valley Rd
Fort Valley VA 22652

Call Sign: KG4QFH
William G Melson
14056 Fort Valley Rd
Fort Valley VA 22652

Call Sign: W4WRS
George R Borsari Jr
7355 Moreland Gap Rd
Fort Valley VA 22652

Call Sign: KK4DQV
James F Stephenson
1557 S Fort Valley Rd
Fort Valley VA 22652

Call Sign: KJ4MTR
Anthony C Durso
2764 St Davids Church Rd
Fort Valley VA 22652

Call Sign: KA3IKJ
John A Proudman
Fort Valley VA 22652

Call Sign: AG4BQ
William D Gentry
Fort Valley VA 22652

Call Sign: KJ4MTQ
Marie E Moan
Fort Valley VA 22652

FCC Amateur Radio Licenses in Franconia

Call Sign: KB4NTW
Timothy G Fleming
6203 Marilyn Dr
Franconia VA 22310

FCC Amateur Radio Licenses in Franklin

Call Sign: KG4QAQ
R Bruce Edwards
705 Canterbury Ct
Franklin VA 23851

Call Sign: KG4QAP
Michael I Futrell
31154 Cardinal Ave
Franklin VA 23851

Call Sign: KJ4VPX
Alexandra J Kokich
113 Carrie Dr
Franklin VA 23851

Call Sign: KJ4WEG
Lori L Kokich
113 Carrie Dr
Franklin VA 23851

Call Sign: KJ4WEH

Rudy E Kokich
113 Carrie Dr
Franklin VA 23851

Call Sign: WA5LNI
John W Rankin
1034 Clay St
Franklin VA 23851

Call Sign: WB4MNJ
Robert L Putze
1320 Clay St
Franklin VA 23851

Call Sign: KG4QAR
Brent O Gayle
824 Hunterdale Rd
Franklin VA 23851

Call Sign: KE4HVK
Linda S Alvis
106 Irving St
Franklin VA 23851

Call Sign: KJ4VPY
Zeljka J Mitrovic
112 Kings Ln
Franklin VA 23851

Call Sign: KG4YEY
Linwood A Bailey
32001 Monroe Rd
Franklin VA 23851

Call Sign: K4MLD
Clifford A Hedgepeth Jr
109 Pocahontas St
Franklin VA 238512330

Call Sign: KJ4ZFH
John P Oliver Sr
512 Pretlow St
Franklin VA 23851

Call Sign: KJ4ZFI
Karen E Oliver
512 Pretlow St
Franklin VA 23851

Call Sign: KI4VPO
Roscoe L Fleming Jr
121 Regency Ln
Franklin VA 23581

Call Sign: W4RLF
Roscoe L Fleming Jr
121 Regency Ln
Franklin VA 23581

Call Sign: KJ4J
James B Menendez
35388 S Quay Rd
Franklin VA 238514142

Call Sign: KD4QOA
Dewey L Corbin Jr
36010 S Quay Rd
Franklin VA 23851

Call Sign: W4DCJ
Dewey L Corbin Jr
36010 S Quay Rd
Franklin VA 23851

Call Sign: KJ4IBV
Lori R Livesay
34743 Sandy Ridge Rd
Franklin VA 23851

Call Sign: WA2UBY
Steven M Hager
22376 Scojo Dr
Franklin VA 23851

Call Sign: W4RTI
Steven M Hager
22376 Scojo Dr
Franklin VA 23851

Call Sign: K4SPS
Joseph E Gillette Sr
23165 Scottswood Dr
Franklin VA 23851

Call Sign: WA4CHJ
John E Beale III
503 South St
Franklin VA 23851

Call Sign: N4DWM
Bernice H Lance
510 Vaughans Ln
Franklin VA 23851

Call Sign: NC4N
Garland F Lance
510 Vaughans Ln
Franklin VA 23851

Call Sign: AE4LG
Justin Gray
31223 Walters Hwy
Franklin VA 23851

Call Sign: K4FOR
William C Billings
128 Woodland Cir
Franklin VA 23851

FCC Amateur Radio Licenses in Franktown

Call Sign: KD4NVP
Jacob D Jolly
9213 Bay Side Rd
Franktown VA 23354

Call Sign: KF4OQJ
Ellen R Grimes
Franktown VA 23354

FCC Amateur Radio Licenses in Fredericksburg

Call Sign: KI4VXW
Susan E Harrelson
100 Air Park Blvd
Fredericksburg VA 22405

Call Sign: KI4VXX
William C Harrelson
100 Air Park Blvd
Fredericksburg VA 22405

Call Sign: N3KCG
Michael C Rock
3809 Alberta Dr N

Fredericksburg VA 22408

Call Sign: KA1NCI
Jeffrey S Mootrey Sr
1074 Allie Dr
Fredericksburg VA 22408

Call Sign: N4QLV
Claude D Phillippy
1114 Amherst Ave
Fredericksburg VA 22405

Call Sign: KF4NUG
Stanley W Roberts
1202 Amherst Ave
Fredericksburg VA 22405

Call Sign: KJ4UYD
Edward L Foxwell
249 Anderson Dr
Fredericksburg VA 22405

Call Sign: W8ELF
Edward L Foxwell
249 Anderson Dr
Fredericksburg VA 22405

Call Sign: W4VQX
Jack M Williams
264 Anderson Dr
Fredericksburg VA 22405

Call Sign: KJ4IWK
Mark D Pressley
2813 Angela Ct
Fredericksburg VA 22408

Call Sign: WB4RIY
Robert T Goss
9305 Antler Ct
Fredericksburg VA 22407

Call Sign: K4ZIP
Daniel R Altman
11580 Arend Ct
Fredericksburg VA 22408

Call Sign: KE4VTG
Charles M Blackmon

1808 Artillery Rdg Rd
Fredericksburg VA 22408

Call Sign: W4UMC
Frank E Brooks
1209 Augustine Ave
Fredericksburg VA 22402

Call Sign: K4AAV
William M Mcray Jr
13740 Avalon River Dr
Fredericksburg VA 22407

Call Sign: N0HRB
Matthew W Hartwig
302 Azalia Dr
Fredericksburg VA 22408

Call Sign: KJ4BFL
Thomas L Lombard
5405 Balls Bluff Rd
Fredericksburg VA 22407

Call Sign: WD8ONZ
Russell E Etheridge Jr
14 Banbury Ct
Fredericksburg VA 22406

Call Sign: KD4WXX
Mary G Johnson
715 Barkley Dr
Fredericksburg VA 22407

Call Sign: WA4CRL
George H Johnson
715 Barkley Dr
Fredericksburg VA 22407

Call Sign: KJ4CKF
Matthew J Oravec
408 Barrows Ct
Fredericksburg VA 22406

Call Sign: WD4JDB
Robert B Freeman
52 Basalt Dr
Fredericksburg VA 22406

Call Sign: KI4MPG

Joseph V Saitta
164 Basalt Dr
Fredericksburg VA 22406

Call Sign: W3GHU
Lewis T Ankerbrand
6004 Battlefield Green Dr
Fredericksburg VA 22407

Call Sign: K6AGC
Barbara W Ankerbrand
6004 Battlefield Green Dr
Fredericksburg VA 22407

Call Sign: KB4CFP
Gregory S Mickle
6011 Battlefield Green Dr
Fredericksburg VA 22407

Call Sign: KG4SOL
David C Hansinger
6012 Battlefield Green Dr
Fredericksburg VA 22407

Call Sign: KD4CGR
Allen P Hansen
13104 Beckman Ct
Fredericksburg VA 22408

Call Sign: KJ4NQU
Gary D Dunn
10 Bedford Ct
Fredericksburg VA 22406

Call Sign: KV4U
Carl T Froehlich
40 Beechcraft Ct
Fredericksburg VA 22405

Call Sign: KI4SXK
Scott S Harlow
7314 Beechplum Rd
Fredericksburg VA 22407

Call Sign: KI4KSF
Herbert M Knerr Jr
6008 Benevolent St
Fredericksburg VA 22407

Call Sign: KI4EEL
Scott E Gaber
9207 Bishops Ln
Fredericksburg VA 22407

Call Sign: W3SEG
Scott E Gaber
9207 Bishops Ln
Fredericksburg VA 22407

Call Sign: KJ4PBN
Dean A Gayle
15 Blair Rd
Fredericksburg VA 22405

Call Sign: KA4UMQ
J Michael P Wood
210 Braehead Dr
Fredericksburg VA 224012210

Call Sign: KB2NP
Philip W Fitzhugh
304 Braehead Dr
Fredericksburg VA 224012212

Call Sign: KG4HWK
Paul E Mann
200 Braemar Pl
Fredericksburg VA 22405

Call Sign: WA4ONR
Dorsey W Akers
1203 Bragg Rd
Fredericksburg VA 22407

Call Sign: KC4ZPN
James A Hereford
1703 Bragg Rd
Fredericksburg VA 22407

Call Sign: W4JAH
James A Hereford
1703 Bragg Rd
Fredericksburg VA 22407

Call Sign: KA1VFF
Michael A Paquette
11901 Branchwater St
Fredericksburg VA 22407

Call Sign: KK4DWM
William J Armstrong
11907 Branchwater St
Fredericksburg VA 22407

Call Sign: KD4TTQ
Albert J Corda
3910 Braxton St
Fredericksburg VA 22408

Call Sign: AC3D
Richard L Gulatsi Jr
421 Breezewood Dr
Fredericksburg VA 22407

Call Sign: AD4AB
Jon P Beckett
1401 Brent St
Fredericksburg VA 22401

Call Sign: KJ4YNN
Wayne L Whitley
433 Bridgewater St
Fredericksburg VA 22401

Call Sign: KJ4LGK
Christopher W Schmidt
900 Brompton St
Fredericksburg VA 22401

Call Sign: K4KSQ
Christopher W Schmidt
900 Brompton St
Fredericksburg VA 22401

Call Sign: K4GMH
Michael L Sims
410 Brooke Rd
Fredericksburg VA 22405

Call Sign: K4TS
Rappahannock Valley ARC
410 Brooke Rd
Fredericksburg VA 22405

Call Sign: KJ4ZUZ
Clyde E Mccall Jr
471 Brooke Rd

Fredericksburg VA 224051884

Call Sign: KB8RTZ
Patrick S Schwarz
1330 Brooke Rd
Fredericksburg VA 22405

Call Sign: KA4RNJ
Douglas A Cherry
418 Bunker Hill St
Fredericksburg VA 22401

Call Sign: KC4DD
Wayne R Johnson
5206 Calvert Ct
Fredericksburg VA 22407

Call Sign: K1NOC
Wayne R Johnson
5206 Calvert Ct
Fredericksburg VA 22407

Call Sign: KG4SQM
Carl L Darron
3 Camelot Ct
Fredericksburg VA 22405

Call Sign: KG4SOI
Thomas M Darron
3 Camelot Ct
Fredericksburg VA 22405

Call Sign: KJ4JUT
Kevin W Johnson
3514 Carlyle Ct
Fredericksburg VA 22408

Call Sign: KI4ZPH
George F Omohundro
2 Carmine Cir
Fredericksburg VA 22407

Call Sign: W4ZPH
George F Omohundro
2 Carmine Cir
Fredericksburg VA 22407

Call Sign: KK4BGI
Nicholas J Mccormick

3632 Carolina Ct
Fredericksburg VA 22408

Call Sign: KJ4CML
Carol D Steele
3634 Carolina Ct
Fredericksburg VA 22408

Call Sign: N4AND
James R Steele
3634 Carolina Ct
Fredericksburg VA 22408

Call Sign: N9JH
James R Steele
3634 Carolina Ct
Fredericksburg VA 22408

Call Sign: NX4Q
James R Steele
3634 Carolina Ct
Fredericksburg VA 22408

Call Sign: KF4ATH
Christine E Stone
103 Caroline St
Fredericksburg VA 22401

Call Sign: KJ4WVX
Fpf ARC
130 Caroline St
Fredericksburg VA 22401

Call Sign: W4FPF
Fpf ARC
130 Caroline St
Fredericksburg VA 22401

Call Sign: K4IA
Craig E Buck
130 Caroline St
Fredericksburg VA 22401

Call Sign: W5TUY
Joseph R Wilson
309 Caroline St
Fredericksburg VA 22401

Call Sign: KJ4YNJ

Allen J Wineland
130 Caroline St Apt A
Fredericksburg VA 22401

Call Sign: KG4JCT
Joseph D Black
5908 Cascade Dr
Fredericksburg VA 28540

Call Sign: AD4GA
Edward J Schiess
5800 Castle Ct
Fredericksburg VA 224077614

Call Sign: KC0UEJ
James A Butikofer
6010 Cathederal Rd
Fredericksburg VA 22407

Call Sign: KC0UEI
Jeanette M Butikofer
6010 Cathedral Rd
Fredericksburg VA 224075032

Call Sign: KI4QFW
Lawrence J Cerritelli
7208 Cattail Ct
Fredericksburg VA 224072503

Call Sign: KK4BCQ
William P Berens
3225 Cavalry Ridge Ct
Fredericksburg VA 22408

Call Sign: KK4DBA
Christopher Bey
4 Cavalry Ridge Rd
Fredericksburg VA 22405

Call Sign: KF4YCC
William J Murray
5504 Cedar Ridge Dr
Fredericksburg VA 22407

Call Sign: N4WJM
William J Murray
5504 Cedar Ridge Dr
Fredericksburg VA 22407

Call Sign: W4KMS
Wheeler T Thompson
12100 Chancellors Village Apt 3201
Fredericksburg VA 22407

Call Sign: W4ACM
Carleton H Gray
12100 Chancellors Village Ln 4011
Fredericksburg VA 22407

Call Sign: WB4TYS
John R Cross
96 Chapel Heights Dr
Fredericksburg VA 22405

Call Sign: N4FFT
Stephen C Schreppler
12909 Chapel Heights Ln
Fredericksburg VA 22407

Call Sign: KA3AZJ
Charles T Bosch III
22 Cherry Laurel Dr
Fredericksburg VA 22405

Call Sign: N5HIK
Beverly L Barge
16 Christian Ct
Fredericksburg VA 224052304

Call Sign: KJ4WTH
Derek T Sprinz
12 Clarion Dr
Fredericksburg VA 22405

Call Sign: KI4CQD
Daniel F Lawlor
33 Clarion Dr
Fredericksburg VA 22405

Call Sign: W4ONV
William H Bass Sr
1007 Clear View Ave
Fredericksburg VA 22405

Call Sign: KG4WXG
Emmanuel Karras

1019 Clearview Ave
Fredericksburg VA 22405

Call Sign: KJ4VXU
Norb Raddatz
107 Cleremont Dr
Fredericksburg VA 22405

Call Sign: KA4IBG
Edward F Hlywa
118 Cleremont Dr
Fredericksburg VA 22405

Call Sign: AD4SY
John W Stone Sr
1445 Clover Dr
Fredericksburg VA 22407

Call Sign: KK4EJE
Kenneth A Buszta
8 Cloverleaf Ct
Fredericksburg VA 22406

Call Sign: KE4MMQ
Richard A Ploshay
4407 Club Cart Cir
Fredericksburg VA 22408

Call Sign: KA1KXZ
Lewis P Darley
71 Coakley Ln
Fredericksburg VA 22406

Call Sign: KI4IIU
Brian L Howell
10402 Colechester St
Fredericksburg VA 22408

Call Sign: KC4QH
Brian L Howell
10402 Colechester St
Fredericksburg VA 22408

Call Sign: KD4OOH
Kevin W Karpin
1901 Coleman Ln
Fredericksburg VA 22407

Call Sign: KJ4RTO

Brittany N Adams
1701 College Av
Fredericksburg VA 22401

Call Sign: N4ZXB
Herbert F Smith Jr
1714 College Ave
Fredericksburg VA 22401

Call Sign: K4RTO
Brittany N Adams
1701 College Ave Box 1857
Univ Mary Washington
Fredericksburg VA 22401

Call Sign: KE4MMS
John Ferro
6010 Collier Dr
Fredericksburg VA 22407

Call Sign: W4BGX
Daniel S Boutchyard
11710 Collinwood Ct
Fredericksburg VA 22407

Call Sign: KG4RSK
Edgar D Morris Jr
907 Conway Rd
Fredericksburg VA 22405

Call Sign: WB6BHL
Larry E Gray
60 Cornwallis Dr
Fredericksburg VA 22405

Call Sign: KK4GWS
Lloyd D Lyle
23 Country Manor Dr
Fredericksburg VA 22406

Call Sign: KI4RCZ
Arlen D Raasch
3 Countryside Dr
Fredericksburg VA 22406

Call Sign: N0NCM
Arlen D Raasch
3 Countryside Dr
Fredericksburg VA 22406

Call Sign: KE4IWT
William S Keyer
2219 Cowan Blvd 49A
Fredericksburg VA 22401

Call Sign: K5IWT
William S Keyer
2219 Cowan Blvd 49A
Fredericksburg VA 22401

Call Sign: W3AJL
Jan Rychlik
2221 Cowan Blvd 55B
Fredericksburg VA 224014443

Call Sign: KD4TTO
Larry E Barker
2342 Cowan Blvd Apt 102
Fredericksburg VA 22401

Call Sign: W2MPD
Stephen A Mccarthy
2600 Cowan Blvd Apt 222
Fredericksburg VA 22401

Call Sign: KG4RZM
Jeffrey L Adams
2219 Cowan Blvd Apt 51B
Fredericksburg VA 22401

Call Sign: KI4STB
Matthew W Genack
2318 Cowan Blvd Apt B
Fredericksburg VA 22401

Call Sign: WT9V
David G Gower
40 Craft Ct
Fredericksburg VA 22405

Call Sign: KJ4EYD
Theodore J Elsenman
153 Cranes Corner Rd
Fredericksburg VA 22405

Call Sign: KC5YNN
Brian S Crumpler
6901 Craven Ln

Fredericksburg VA 22407

Call Sign: K4ME
Carl J Schlegel
901 Crest Hill Rd
Fredericksburg VA 22405

Call Sign: KK4CWP
Michael R Doornbos
11310 Crown Ct
Fredericksburg VA 22407

Call Sign: KI4TPS
Daniel R Kuzel
7105 Crown Jewels Ct
Fredericksburg VA 22407

Call Sign: KB4KUZ
Daniel R Kuzel
7105 Crown Jewels Ct
Fredericksburg VA 22407

Call Sign: KI4WZV
Joshua A Kuzel
7105 Crown Jewels Ct
Fredericksburg VA 22407

Call Sign: KB4JAK
Joshua A Kuzel
7105 Crown Jewels Ct
Fredericksburg VA 22407

Call Sign: KI4WZU
Aaron R Kuzel
7105 Crown Jewels Ct
Fredericksburg VA 22407

Call Sign: KB4ARK
Aaron R Kuzel
7105 Crown Jewels Ct
Fredericksburg VA 22407

Call Sign: KJ4NMV
Katerina M Kuzel
7105 Crown Jewels Ct
Fredericksburg VA 22407

Call Sign: KB4KMK
Katerina M Kuzel

7105 Crown Jewels Ct
Fredericksburg VA 22407

Call Sign: N4YVY
Noel M Freeman
803 Culpeper St
Fredericksburg VA 22405

Call Sign: KJ4MKF
Mufrad Zaman
41 Cynthias Pl Apt 202
Fredericksburg VA 22406

Call Sign: KJ4MHD
Daniel B Lien
56 Cynthias Pl Apt 301
Fredericksburg VA 22406

Call Sign: KJ4ZNJ
Gregory D Bonzo
9513 Dabney Ct
Fredericksburg VA 22408

Call Sign: KG4SUM
David L Seals
7400 Danalu Ct
Fredericksburg VA 224077366

Call Sign: W6AAV
William M Mc Ray Jr
7404 Danalu Ct
Fredericksburg VA 22407

Call Sign: KA9KIT
Elizabeth M Womble
9825 Danford St
Fredericksburg VA 224078369

Call Sign: KE4BWE
Kelly D Gilbert
5909 Danielle Dr
Fredericksburg VA 22407

Call Sign: N4IPF
Victor R Wiss
21 Dawson Dr
Fredericksburg VA 22405

Call Sign: KG4OXH

Brandon E Meade
6 Deep Run Rd
Fredericksburg VA 22406

Call Sign: KE4LYG
Jeffrey L Meade
6 Deep Run Rd
Fredericksburg VA 22406

Call Sign: KG4CVT
Joshua P Meade
6 Deep Run Rd
Fredericksburg VA 22406

Call Sign: K3NC
Neal P Campbell
120 Delmar Ct
Fredericksburg VA 22407

Call Sign: KF4BAN
Robert P Cannon Jr
17 Devonshire Dr
Fredericksburg VA 22401

Call Sign: KB4GQM
Felton M Trusel Jr
5153 Dominion Dr
Fredericksburg VA 22401

Call Sign: KJ4YCQ
Gabriel P Leonhard
5164 Dominion Dr
Fredericksburg VA 22407

Call Sign: N1RRQ
Steven T Hiller
9614 Dominion Forest Cir
Fredericksburg VA 22408

Call Sign: KD6VMA
Kenneth R Bosley
11805 Doryl Dr
Fredericksburg VA 22407

Call Sign: KI4OQB
Fred R Ott
11809 Doryl Dr
Fredericksburg VA 22407

Call Sign: KF4UYL
Ted J Schubel
320 Durham Dr
Fredericksburg VA 22407

Call Sign: KD4EES
Linda K Becker
92 E River Bend Rd
Fredericksburg VA 22407

Call Sign: KD4MVE
Gary M Manes
7 Edgewood Cir
Fredericksburg VA 22405

Call Sign: N4CKZ
William B Simpson
1906 Elmhurst Ave
Fredericksburg VA 22401

Call Sign: KQ4KH
Maurice R Blankenbaker
10014 Elys Ford Rd
Fredericksburg VA 22407

Call Sign: WD4BLI
Robert E Cann
20 Evanshire Dr
Fredericksburg VA 22406

Call Sign: KG4RZE
Walter E Lyons III
500 Excaliber Cir Apt 103
Fredericksburg VA 22406

Call Sign: K4IPM
Ian P Mc Daniel
602 Excaliber Cir Apt 203
Fredericksburg VA 22406

Call Sign: KK4FJA
Cynthia L Cross
1913 Fall Hill Ave
Fredericksburg VA 22401

Call Sign: KC4JM
Barry J Kefauver
3315 Fall Hill Ave
Fredericksburg VA 224013040

Call Sign: KD4WYC
Cyrus E Phillips V
608 Falmouth Dr
Fredericksburg VA 22405

Call Sign: N2RLJ
Richard J Haas Jr
1228 Farrish Dr
Fredericksburg VA 22401

Call Sign: NL7P
William A Hatch
311 Fauquier St
Fredericksburg VA 22401

Call Sign: KB5YNG
Marlene B Ray
9826 Fendale Ln
Fredericksburg VA 22408

Call Sign: W4NEZ
Edward A Ray
9826 Fendale Ln
Fredericksburg VA 22408

Call Sign: KE3XE
Mark R Weiss
11704 Fillmore Ln
Fredericksburg VA 22407

Call Sign: KC5QPX
Pierre N Bahizi
7107 Finch Ln
Fredericksburg VA 22407

Call Sign: KB4MOX
Michael V Morrelli
9513 Flint Hill Ct
Fredericksburg VA 22407

Call Sign: KG4DFK
Betty J Naghdi
9721 Flint Hill Ct
Fredericksburg VA 22407

Call Sign: KF4WDE
David J Miller
9721 Flint Hill Ct

Fredericksburg VA 22407

Call Sign: AF4SL
David J Miller
9721 Flint Hill Ct
Fredericksburg VA 22407

Call Sign: KJ4RXI
Dmitriy Zavyalov
7504 Flippo Dr
Fredericksburg VA 22408

Call Sign: WD4HCN
Gail H Alderson
6226 Forest Grove Dr
Fredericksburg VA 22407

Call Sign: KG4HSK
Mid Atlantic Island Crew
27 Fox Run Ln
Fredericksburg VA 22405

Call Sign: K3USI
Mid Atlantic Island Crew
27 Fox Run Ln
Fredericksburg VA 22405

Call Sign: AE4MK
Jay F Chamberlain
27 Fox Run Ln
Fredericksburg VA 22405

Call Sign: NS4J
Jay F Chamberlain
27 Fox Run Ln
Fredericksburg VA 22405

Call Sign: KJ4MKG
Guillermo R Gonzalez III
7 Gable Ct
Fredericksburg VA 22406

Call Sign: KB0DOA
Cindy L Thrush
5620 Glen Eagles Ct
Fredericksburg VA 22407

Call Sign: W0PK
Leo J Thrush

5620 Glen Eagles Ct
Fredericksburg VA 22407

Call Sign: KI4QFU
Patricia C Perrault
5828 Glen Eagles Dr
Fredericksburg VA 22407

Call Sign: KI4ZFS
Steven W Stone
40 Glen Oak Rd
Fredericksburg VA 22405

Call Sign: N4LZJ
James R Mc Cloud Jr
8205 Gold Mine Ct
Fredericksburg VA 22407

Call Sign: KU4C
James R Mc Cloud Jr
8205 Gold Mine Ct
Fredericksburg VA 22407

Call Sign: KD4CVH
Sue G Mc Cloud
8205 Gold Mine Ct
Fredericksburg VA 22407

Call Sign: KE4GHR
Lauren A Mccloud
8205 Gold Mine Ct
Fredericksburg VA 22407

Call Sign: KI4BEB
Samuel A Mccloud
8205 Gold Mine Ct
Fredericksburg VA 22407

Call Sign: KK4GSC
Christopher S Mattes
13300 Golden Oaks Dr
Fredericksburg VA 22407

Call Sign: KK4GOK
Samuel S Mattes
13300 Golden Oaks Dr
Fredericksburg VA 22407

Call Sign: KC4PMK

Theresa A Mechem
13350 Golden Oaks Dr
Fredericksburg VA 22401

Call Sign: WA4YVM
Bradley D Mechem
13350 Golden Oaks Dr
Fredericksburg VA 22407

Call Sign: W4CHT
Frederick E Chapman
205 Goldvein Dr
Fredericksburg VA 22407

Call Sign: KC4HVX
Timothy D Stapp
310 Green Arbor Dr
Fredericksburg VA 22401

Call Sign: N1IJR
Roger A Lee
6608 Green Arbor Dr
Fredericksburg VA 22407

Call Sign: KJ4BQG
Michael P Petrone
1400 Green Tree Rd Apt 103
Fredericksburg VA 22406

Call Sign: N3WQO
Michael T Rush
2300 Green Tree Rd Apt 103
Fredericksburg VA 22406

Call Sign: KE4RZF
Tommy L Cowger
608 Greenbriar Ct Apt L
Fredericksburg VA 22401

Call Sign: KK4FXO
John M Corrigan
4031 Guinea Station Rd
Fredericksburg VA 22408

Call Sign: N4TPQ
Jason R Jarnagin
9714 Gunston Hall Rd
Fredericksburg VA 22408

Call Sign: W4YCW
James T Chinn Jr
5703 Halifax Ct
Fredericksburg VA 224077120

Call Sign: KF4YDL
Carl M Nasal Jr
405 Hamilton St
Fredericksburg VA 22408

Call Sign: WA1RWY
James R Bouchard
6800 Hanover Ct
Fredericksburg VA 22407

Call Sign: K4HWK
Paul E Mann
921 Hanover St
Fredericksburg VA 22401

Call Sign: KA4ELP
Jack R Thompson
305 Hanson Ave
Fredericksburg VA 22401

Call Sign: KG4PZZ
Fred W Payne Jr
6101 Harrison Rd
Fredericksburg VA 22407

Call Sign: KG4RZG
Fred W Payne Sr
6101 Harrison Rd
Fredericksburg VA 22407

Call Sign: WD4MJT
Edward C Rowe
300 1 Harrison Rd
Fredericksburg VA 22401

Call Sign: KJ4IES
Ernest W Legg Jr
210 Hartlake Dr
Fredericksburg VA 22406

Call Sign: KJ4ATM
Scott M Jennings
88 Hartwood Meadows Dr
Fredericksburg VA 22406

Call Sign: KD4YCO
Thomas J D Epiro
11517 Harvestdale Dr
Fredericksburg VA 22407

Call Sign: WB2LUU
William C Cronk
11517 Harvestdale Dr
Fredericksburg VA 22407

Call Sign: KD4NEJ
Charles J Pitts Jr
11609 Harvestdale Dr
Fredericksburg VA 22407

Call Sign: KJ4DXT
Nicholas Weresnick
7208 Hearthside Tr
Fredericksburg VA 22407

Call Sign: KG4VYI
Carroll W Moore
1420 Heatherstone Dr
Fredericksburg VA 22407

Call Sign: W4JUR
Paul J Nutter
1625 Heatherstone Dr
Fredericksburg VA 22407

Call Sign: KI4CGA
George R Kennedy
7403 Heathrow Dr
Fredericksburg VA 22407

Call Sign: KE4NAT
Waldo W Keister
17 Heritage Rd
Fredericksburg VA 22405

Call Sign: KB3DSS
John S Reitwiesner
44 Heritage Rd
Fredericksburg VA 22405

Call Sign: KF4QQR
George R Gentile
13103 Hickory Ct

Fredericksburg VA 22407

Call Sign: WB4CDU
John M Tokar
1020 Hillcrest Ter
Fredericksburg VA 22405

Call Sign: K8RKF
John M Tokar
1020 Hillcrest Ter
Fredericksburg VA 22405

Call Sign: KC4REP
Robert A Devereaux
10402 Hillside Ln
Fredericksburg VA 22408

Call Sign: KF4PKX
Stephan D Masson
4404 Hilltop Ct
Fredericksburg VA 22408

Call Sign: KD4ZPF
Stephen L Sellers
52 Holly Berry Rd
Fredericksburg VA 22406

Call Sign: KJ4BRG
Daniel E Carroll
407 Holly Corner Rd
Fredericksburg VA 22406

Call Sign: WA4CWM
Gilbert F Du Val Jr
648 Holly Corner Rd
Fredericksburg VA 22406

Call Sign: KJ4CPD
Francis W Bacon
360 Hollywood Farm Rd
Fredericksburg VA 22405

Call Sign: AJ4ZC
Richard H Anderson
53 Hunton Dr
Fredericksburg VA 22405

Call Sign: KG4RCN
Michael P Apicella

63 Hunton Dr
Fredericksburg VA 22405

Call Sign: WB3JFR
Kenneth M Chiocchio
11905 Hyacinth Ct
Fredericksburg VA 22407

Call Sign: N3WMZ
William D Dubensky
1005 Jefferson Davis Hwy 234
Fredericksburg VA 22401

Call Sign: KA4ERP
James P Brodhead
901 Jefferson Davis Hwy Apt
105
Fredericksburg VA 22401

Call Sign: KA4WIT
David F Eliezer
1003 Jefferson Davis Hwy Apt
244
Fredericksburg VA 22401

Call Sign: N1USH
Dana F Greenwood Sr
8701 Jenny Ln
Fredericksburg VA 22407

Call Sign: KG4RBF
Nathan J White
604 Jett St
Fredericksburg VA 22405

Call Sign: NL7JT
Joseph M Cassel
7 Jolie Ct
Fredericksburg VA 224067237

Call Sign: N1VA
Frank S Baechtel
10711 Joshua Ln
Fredericksburg VA 22408

Call Sign: KB1EMZ
Krikor Kolandjian
55 Journeys Way
Fredericksburg VA 22406

Call Sign: KG4CKG
John R Dunnivan
2225 Karen Ter
Fredericksburg VA 22405

Call Sign: KG4CVM
Lisa M Dunnivan
2225 Karen Ter
Fredericksburg VA 22405

Call Sign: KE2MI
Kenneth J Burns
137 Kelley Rd
Fredericksburg VA 22405

Call Sign: K0RWB
Robert W Broeking
114 Kellogg Mill Rd
Fredericksburg VA 22406

Call Sign: KU3C
Robert W Broeking
114 Kellogg Mill Rd
Fredericksburg VA 22406

Call Sign: KG4SQJ
Taylor L Drew
625 Kellogg Mill Rd
Fredericksburg VA 22406

Call Sign: AC4P
Carl E Espeland Jr
870 Kellogg Mill Rd
Fredericksburg VA 22406

Call Sign: N4OJB
Charles H Clark
5 Kendale Ln
Fredericksburg VA 22401

Call Sign: KI4KUP
Basil M Fedun
34 King Georges Grant
Fredericksburg VA 22405

Call Sign: N4XEN
Eric J Horne
211 Kings Mill Ct Apt 6

Fredericksburg VA 22401

Call Sign: N4KEA
John E Peterson
42 Kinsley Ln
Fredericksburg VA 22406

Call Sign: AJ4JE
James P Marvin
3902 Lafayette Blvd
Fredericksburg VA 22408

Call Sign: N4XOP
Gary W Folden
4301 Lafayette Blvd
Fredericksburg VA 22401

Call Sign: KJ4ETX
Carla J Marvin
3902 Lafayette Blvd
Fredericksburg VA 22408

Call Sign: NI4F
Gerald D Mullinix
116 Lake Shore Dr
Fredericksburg VA 22405

Call Sign: W4VAD
James W Poole
121 Lake Shore Dr
Fredericksburg VA 22405

Call Sign: KC4QKV
John H Chichester
135 Lake Shore Dr
Fredericksburg VA 22405

Call Sign: WB4IUB
Carlton W Earl
309 Laurel Ave
Fredericksburg VA 22408

Call Sign: WB4LRO
Russell W Stallings
416 Laurel Ave
Fredericksburg VA 224081536

Call Sign: KD4IQD
Robert N Sargeant

458 Laurel Ave
Fredericksburg VA 22408

Call Sign: KI4GRZ
Jeffrey S Lawson
9319 Laurel Oak Dr
Fredericksburg VA 22407

Call Sign: WB3INK
Christopher Dunlap
5407 Leavells Crossing Dr
Fredericksburg VA 22407

Call Sign: KE4YWC
William N Hart
10615 Limburg Ct
Fredericksburg VA 22408

Call Sign: KJ4MHC
Barbara S Doyal
34 Little Creek Ln
Fredericksburg VA 22405

Call Sign: WE4BSD
Barbara S Doyal
34 Little Creek Ln
Fredericksburg VA 22405

Call Sign: KJ4BPM
Charles T Doyal
34 Little Creek Ln
Fredericksburg VA 224053621

Call Sign: W4CTD
Charles T Doyal
34 Little Creek Ln
Fredericksburg VA 224053621

Call Sign: KF4EWM
Thomas K Staples
20 Little St
Fredericksburg VA 22405

Call Sign: KD4DEP
Charlotte W Hartman
11316 Loch Ness Dr
Fredericksburg VA 22407

Call Sign: KC4WQC

William C Hartman
11316 Loch Ness Dr
Fredericksburg VA 22407

Call Sign: KG4LFE
Dennis A Kieper
107 Lombardy Dr
Fredericksburg VA 22408

Call Sign: K4GZS
Dennis A Kieper
107 Lombardy Dr
Fredericksburg VA 22408

Call Sign: W3ZUM
James E Swanekamp
31 Lord Fairfax Dr
Fredericksburg VA 22405

Call Sign: AD4SX
Ken J Converse
113 Lorenzo Dr
Fredericksburg VA 22405

Call Sign: KE4BSV
Terri L Gray
113 Lorenzo Dr
Fredericksburg VA 22405

Call Sign: N4GW
Ken J Converse
113 Lorenzo Dr
Fredericksburg VA 22405

Call Sign: AD4SX
Ken J Converse
113 Lorenzo Dr
Fredericksburg VA 22405

Call Sign: KF4YYD
Thomas E Butchers
6112 Loriella Park Dr
Fredericksburg VA 224075068

Call Sign: KE4WJK
Heidi M Knouff
10716 Lotus Ct
Fredericksburg VA 22407

Call Sign: WA3CVB
Gerald W Knouff
10716 Lotus Ct
Fredericksburg VA 22407

Call Sign: KC5ZOU
James E Mc Ginley
11303 Lynchburg Dr
Fredericksburg VA 22407

Call Sign: KD4DGS
Mary A Moul
11307 Lynchburg Dr
Fredericksburg VA 22407

Call Sign: W4DE
Robert G Moul
11307 Lynchburg Dr
Fredericksburg VA 22407

Call Sign: KJ4AVZ
John M Palmer
22 Lynchester Dr
Fredericksburg VA 224066270

Call Sign: KC0SHU
Carl W Braun
12910 Macneil Ct
Fredericksburg VA 22407

Call Sign: NY4L
Carl W Braun
12910 Macneil Ct
Fredericksburg VA 22407

Call Sign: KF6JEF
Richard M Corrigan
12 Maggie Ct
Fredericksburg VA 22406

Call Sign: KF6NUS
Eric P Corrigan
12 Maggie Ct
Fredericksburg VA 22406

Call Sign: N0RMC
Richard M Corrigan
12 Maggie Ct
Fredericksburg VA 22406

Call Sign: KI4EEF
Mary C Jenkins
433 Malvern Lakes Cir 202
Fredericksburg VA 22406

Call Sign: KE4RLX
Thomas A Jenkins
433 Malvern Lakes Cir 202
Fredericksburg VA 22406

Call Sign: KI4CGC
Thomas A Jenkins
433 Malvern Lakes Cir 202
Fredericksburg VA 22406

Call Sign: KI4GIA
Sherry A Jenkins
433 Malverne Lake Cir Apt 202
Fredericksburg VA 22406

Call Sign: KD4USJ
Roy E Mc Afee
202 Mansfield St
Fredericksburg VA 22408

Call Sign: KD4ZPI
Linda W Mc Afee
202 Mansfield St
Fredericksburg VA 22408

Call Sign: KG4VBW
John T Magerowski
12903 Maple Springs Dr
Fredericksburg VA 224080248

Call Sign: W5UOW
Dwight G Garretson
12910 Maple Springs Dr
Fredericksburg VA 224080248

Call Sign: KI4MKW
Gordon R Olson
6503 Marsh Ct
Fredericksburg VA 22407

Call Sign: KG4SGV
Jason A Snellings
805 Marye St

Fredericksburg VA 22401

Call Sign: W4BEO
Bruce E Owen
6034 Massaponax Dr
Fredericksburg VA 22407

Call Sign: W4DXU
Bruce E Owen
6034 Massaponax Dr
Fredericksburg VA 22407

Call Sign: KI4MUP
Bruce E Owen
6034 Massaponax Dr
Fredericksburg VA 22407

Call Sign: WD4NIP
William R Hardenburgh Jr
112 McCarty Rd
Fredericksburg VA 22405

Call Sign: KJ4CKE
John B Morton Jr
362 McCarty Rd
Fredericksburg VA 22405

Call Sign: KG4FCM
David F Rolls
11 McLanie Hollow Ln
Fredericksburg VA 22405

Call Sign: KD4JTO
Marvin E Yoder
5206 McManus Dr
Fredericksburg VA 22407

Call Sign: KH2SF
Judith B Moshenek
1403 Meadow Dr
Fredericksburg VA 22405

Call Sign: WH2S
Mark P Stacy
1403 Meadow Dr
Fredericksburg VA 224058706

Call Sign: WA4GSV
Wilbur M Anderson

3500 Meekins Dr Apt 319
Fredericksburg VA 224070128

Call Sign: KK4BC
Joseph M Thompson
10 Mercer Ln
Fredericksburg VA 22405

Call Sign: KD4ZTR
Quinton L Duffy
101 Merlin Way Apt 102
Fredericksburg VA 22406

Call Sign: KG4GRH
Cynthia A Brandel
13003 Mill Rd
Fredericksburg VA 22407

Call Sign: KI4SLR
Christiana J Brandel
13003 Mill Rd
Fredericksburg VA 22407

Call Sign: KI4JVC
Robert L Brandel III
13003 Mill Rd
Fredericksburg VA 22407

Call Sign: KG4CGP
Robert L Brandel Jr
13003 Mill Rd
Fredericksburg VA 224072225

Call Sign: WN2G
Robert L Brandel Jr
13003 Mill Rd
Fredericksburg VA 224072225

Call Sign: KG4OWV
Dennis M Boyce
13103 Mill Rd
Fredericksburg VA 22407

Call Sign: AG4PH
Dennis M Boyce
13103 Mill Rd
Fredericksburg VA 22407

Call Sign: W4IDC

John S Guzewicz
3948 Mine Rd
Fredericksburg VA 22408

Call Sign: KB5LNC
Ronald F Startzel Jr
6 Morningmist Dr
Fredericksburg VA 22406

Call Sign: K6SO
David M Ridderhof
913 Mortimer Ave
Fredericksburg VA 22401

Call Sign: KG2CY
Vincent C Rizzotto
243 Morton Rd
Fredericksburg VA 22405

Call Sign: WA2VR
Vincent C Rizzotto
243 Morton Rd
Fredericksburg VA 22405

Call Sign: KG4TFU
David C Finley
4202 Mt Vernon Pl
Fredericksburg VA 224089530

Call Sign: N3FBB
Thomas J Morris
10102 Mulligan Ct
Fredericksburg VA 224089214

Call Sign: KJ4VOV
Bernhard W Behling
22 Myers Dr
Fredericksburg VA 22405

Call Sign: KJ4WEB
Thomas B Hoover
4008 N Andover Ln
Fredericksburg VA 22408

Call Sign: KJ4RXJ
Jason Judd
10417 N Mcclellan Dr
Fredericksburg VA 22408

Call Sign: KV1JVJ
Jason Judd
10417 N Mcclellan Dr
Fredericksburg VA 22408

Call Sign: KJ4QNN
Timothy R Kirk
33 Neabsco Dr
Fredericksburg VA 22405

Call Sign: WW4ACE
Timothy R Kirk
33 Neabsco Dr
Fredericksburg VA 22405

Call Sign: KI4YVR
Jeffrey Nelson
24 Norfolk St
Fredericksburg VA 22406

Call Sign: KI4OGC
Sara C Speer
29 Norfolk St
Fredericksburg VA 22406

Call Sign: KK4HIG
Jorge A Bermudez
3203 Normandy Ave
Fredericksburg VA 22401

Call Sign: KE4MAP
Mark Y Johnson
4007 Norris Dr
Fredericksburg VA 22407

Call Sign: KG4SOJ
Harold M Bell III
801 Northside Dr
Fredericksburg VA 22405

Call Sign: KJ4PBM
Lamont A Brown
9609 Norwick
Fredericksburg VA 22408

Call Sign: KA8SFP
Stanley D Musick
4204 Oakhill Rd
Fredericksburg VA 22408

Call Sign: K8PDQ
Stanley D Musick
4204 Oakhill Rd
Fredericksburg VA 22408

Call Sign: KG4YXO
John K Hord
6529 Old Plank Rd
Fredericksburg VA 22407

Call Sign: KA4UJK
William A Masi Jr
8501 Old Plank Rd
Fredericksburg VA 22407

Call Sign: KJ4MKP
Amy N Bartenfelder
5 Oliver Ct
Fredericksburg VA 22406

Call Sign: KJ4JST
Edward J Cain
6 Oliver Ct
Fredericksburg VA 22406

Call Sign: KG4RZD
Frank W Ransom
6819 Orchid Ln
Fredericksburg VA 22407

Call Sign: W3VHY
Frank W Ransom
6819 Orchid Ln
Fredericksburg VA 224078503

Call Sign: KD5KQD
Jeremy W Matlock
12645 Osborne Dr
Fredericksburg VA 22407

Call Sign: KD4WUO
Robert D Cherry
3505 Overview Dr
Fredericksburg VA 22408

Call Sign: KG4OBT
April L Frantz-Severin
3601 Overview Dr

Fredericksburg VA 22408

Call Sign: KE4RBP
Bryan E Browe
3604 Overview Dr
Fredericksburg VA 22408

Call Sign: KI4CWJ
Glen L Clark
3818 Overview Dr
Fredericksburg VA 22408

Call Sign: AK4BQ
Glen L Clark
3818 Overview Dr
Fredericksburg VA 22408

Call Sign: KG4RBE
Bryan L Travers
4518 Papillion Ct
Fredericksburg VA 22408

Call Sign: KJ4JSS
Alexei Frolov
4535 Papillion Ct
Fredericksburg VA 22408

Call Sign: KJ4KDC
Alexei Frolov
4535 Papillion Ct
Fredericksburg VA 22408

Call Sign: N4AFT
Alexei Frolov
4535 Papillion Ct
Fredericksburg VA 22408

Call Sign: KJ4KDB
Konstantin Frolov
4535 Papillion Ct
Fredericksburg VA 22408

Call Sign: KK4FFN
Bryan A Steckler
1224 Parcell St
Fredericksburg VA 22401

Call Sign: KK4CBA
Darin D Ramey

10819 Peach Tree Dr
Fredericksburg VA 22407

Call Sign: K4DDR
Darin D Ramey
10819 Peach Tree Dr
Fredericksburg VA 22407

Call Sign: KC4STH
Marilyn Z Thompson
100 Pecan Ln
Fredericksburg VA 22405

Call Sign: KD4USY
Kurt D Sokolowski
49 Pendleton Rd
Fredericksburg VA 224053037

Call Sign: AJ4KV
Aaron J Needham
10 Pennsbury Ct
Fredericksburg VA 22406

Call Sign: N6VCR
James D Christian
13500 Perimeter Dr
Fredericksburg VA 22407

Call Sign: KG4JMX
Richard L Oasen
1108 Perry St
Fredericksburg VA 224051937

Call Sign: N4YMJ
Carroll E Blake
509 Persimmon Ln
Fredericksburg VA 22408

Call Sign: KB4QPV
Millard E Carr
65 Pierce Ct
Fredericksburg VA 22406

Call Sign: KG4UFV
Joshua J Darkow
175 Pine View Dr
Fredericksburg VA 22406

Call Sign: KK4ER

Michael D Goretsas
60 Piper Pl
Fredericksburg VA 22405

Call Sign: WD4EFA
William E Jones
4035 Plank Rd
Fredericksburg VA 22401

Call Sign: KD4PRP
William L Jones
5933 Plank Rd
Fredericksburg VA 22407

Call Sign: KJ4RJB
Geraldine E Crisp
527 Pleasants Dr
Fredericksburg VA 22407

Call Sign: KJ4MTM
Rudolf W Crisp
527 Pleasants Dr
Fredericksburg VA 22407

Call Sign: W3RWC
Rudolf W Crisp
527 Pleasants Dr
Fredericksburg VA 22407

Call Sign: WB0HCO
Thomas M Westhoff
84 Plume Ct
Fredericksburg VA 22406

Call Sign: KE4WFE
William L Frostick Jr
40 Plumosa Dr
Fredericksburg VA 22405

Call Sign: N4OLM
Arseny J Melnick
335 Poplar Rd
Fredericksburg VA 22406

Call Sign: KD4YWM
Harry L Wood
107 Powell St
Fredericksburg VA 22408

Call Sign: KJ4FAI
Robert G Pedersen
407 Pratt St
Fredericksburg VA 22405

Call Sign: KB5OTP
Russell C Rochte Jr
10 Prestonwood Ct
Fredericksburg VA 22406

Call Sign: KD5YKE
Rachel C Rochte
10 Prestonwood Ct
Fredericksburg VA 22406

Call Sign: KD5YKD
Rebekah C Rochte
10 Prestonwood Ct
Fredericksburg VA 22406

Call Sign: KA7NWC
Jennifer T Rochte
10 Prestonwood Ct
Fredericksburg VA 22406

Call Sign: KF6ILN
Steven M Draper Sr
10712 Priest Ct
Fredericksburg VA 22407

Call Sign: WA1ZFB
Michael O Christie
11206 Prince Ct
Fredericksburg VA 22407

Call Sign: W1ZFB
Michael O Christie
11206 Prince Ct
Fredericksburg VA 22407

Call Sign: KE4NAU
Betty J Smith
11206 Prince Ct
Fredericksburg VA 224077616

Call Sign: WA4TUF
Craig E Buck
1203 Prince Edward St
Fredericksburg VA 22401

Call Sign: N8POB
Alan J Currence
1013 Princess Anne St
Fredericksburg VA 22401

Call Sign: KJ4CJB
Sarah F Southworth
205 Princess Elizabeth St
Fredericksburg VA 22401

Call Sign: KN3F
Evan T Pert
309 Princess Elizabeth St
Fredericksburg VA 22401

Call Sign: WB4KCL
Frederick J Smith
27 Princess Gillian Ct
Fredericksburg VA 22406

Call Sign: KG4ETM
Dennis N Currence
32 Princess Gillian Ct
Fredericksburg VA 22406

Call Sign: KG4SPY
Carl-Eric M Currence
32 Princess Gillian Ct
Fredericksburg VA 22406

Call Sign: KI4HRN
Allan R Bacon Jr
6107 Prospect St
Fredericksburg VA 224078344

Call Sign: AI4TK
Allan R Bacon Jr
6107 Prospect St
Fredericksburg VA 224078344

Call Sign: KI4LUT
Edward L Shelkey
9 Quartz Cir
Fredericksburg VA 224052791

Call Sign: WA4ZKF
John L Bean
68 Rainwater Ln

Fredericksburg VA 224064740

Call Sign: KA5EGQ
Stephen J Webb
5507 Rainwood Dr
Fredericksburg VA 22401

Call Sign: KG4PLM
Dee E Mc Daniel
431 Rann Ct
Fredericksburg VA 22401

Call Sign: KB0EWM
James N Javinsky
11712 Ravensclaw Ln Apt 203
Fredericksburg VA 22407

Call Sign: KD4MVJ
Everette M Royster
6823 Red Rose Village Dr
Fredericksburg VA 22407

Call Sign: KK4BCT
Hal R Taylor
41 Richards Ferry Rd
Fredericksburg VA 22406

Call Sign: WH6TB
Marko H Davis Jr
337 Richards Ferry Rd
Fredericksburg VA 22406

Call Sign: KJ4PBO
John A Kennedy
7 Ridge Pointe Ln
Fredericksburg VA 22405

Call Sign: KC4EAT
Michael C Albrycht
7 Ridgemore Cir
Fredericksburg VA 22405

Call Sign: KG4SQK
Rachel E Ingram
2 Ridgeview Cir
Fredericksburg VA 22406

Call Sign: KG4SQN
Dennis J Ingram

2 Ridgeview Cir
Fredericksburg VA 22406

Call Sign: KI4PPP
Camden L Bullock
120 Ridgeway St
Fredericksburg VA 224012256

Call Sign: KJ4YDE
Charles W Pritchett Jr
7714 Riparian Ct
Fredericksburg VA 22408

Call Sign: WD5ACJ
David J Adams
7720 Riparian Ct
Fredericksburg VA 224088804

Call Sign: K5DJA
David J Adams
7720 Riparian Ct
Fredericksburg VA 224088804

Call Sign: KD4DIQ
Susan R Eshbaugh
10501 Rising Ridge Rd 303
Fredericksburg VA 22407

Call Sign: KD4DIS
Eric W Eshbaugh
10501 Rising Ridge Rd 303
Fredericksburg VA 22407

Call Sign: NH6IQ
Richard D Minton
6313 River Rd
Fredericksburg VA 22407

Call Sign: NH6JX
Marie A Minton
6313 River Rd
Fredericksburg VA 22407

Call Sign: N3EFO
Karl J Alsheimer
207 Riverside Manor Blvd
Fredericksburg VA 224014937

Call Sign: WB5LXX

Kathryn D Sturdivant
3 Roanoke Ct
Fredericksburg VA 224076385

Call Sign: KG4UVJ
Michael C Mancini
552 Rocky Run Rd
Fredericksburg VA 224065415

Call Sign: AA4HA
Marianne Houser
504 Rogers St
Fredericksburg VA 22405

Call Sign: AA4HB
John F Houser Jr
504 Rogers St
Fredericksburg VA 22405

Call Sign: WA4YEZ
John D Daly
4 Rosecroft Dr
Fredericksburg VA 224072345

Call Sign: KK4EYB
Michael J Carrancho
51 Rubins Walk
Fredericksburg VA 22405

Call Sign: KK4GSD
Carl S Lynn IV
203 Rumford Rd
Fredericksburg VA 22405

Call Sign: K7NAT
Thomas F Wells
6943 Runnymede Trl
Fredericksburg VA 22407

Call Sign: KI4RUO
James D Reynolds
11716 Rutherford Dr
Fredericksburg VA 22407

Call Sign: KJ4RJC
John A Piedel Jr
11815 Rutherford Dr
Fredericksburg VA 22407

Call Sign: KJ4DFN
Jeffrey S Burnett
5907 S Cedar Ridge Ln
Fredericksburg VA 22407

Call Sign: KC4HWI
Shannon C Williams
260 Salvington Rd
Fredericksburg VA 22405

Call Sign: KD4MAG
Mary J Simpson
10827 Samantha Pl
Fredericksburg VA 22408

Call Sign: KT4HX
David A Simpson
10827 Samantha Pl
Fredericksburg VA 22408

Call Sign: N4IAG
Stephen L English
245 Sandy Ridge Rd
Fredericksburg VA 22405

Call Sign: KI4UDE
William S Hare
6 Sanford Cir
Fredericksburg VA 22407

Call Sign: KJ4YDA
Jose M Toves
344 Sanford Dr
Fredericksburg VA 22406

Call Sign: W0ZGR
Richard B Heil
11016 Scottwood Ln
Fredericksburg VA 22407

Call Sign: KD4DNF
Cecil K Vandegrift Jr
5407 Sean Dr
Fredericksburg VA 22407

Call Sign: KK4GBC
David B Perrussel
2130 Sebastian Rd
Fredericksburg VA 22405

Call Sign: KE4NGS
David M Broach
1220 Semple Ct
Fredericksburg VA 22401

Call Sign: N0JOK
Barry R Miller
6 Seneca Ter
Fredericksburg VA 224011115

Call Sign: KJ4GYR
Jonathan M Branker
11 Shadowbrook Ln
Fredericksburg VA 22406

Call Sign: KI4IGQ
David C Kleinberg Md
131 Shady Creek Ln
Fredericksburg VA 22406

Call Sign: WQ8Z
Andrew C Thompson
10120 Sharon Spring Dr
Fredericksburg VA 224080259

Call Sign: N9VT
Andrew C Thompson
10120 Sharon Springs Dr
Fredericksburg VA 224080259

Call Sign: KI4QIY
Luis A Ortega-Rodriguez
2015 Sierra Dr
Fredericksburg VA 22405

Call Sign: KK4FVH
Kyle M Hotchkiss
5118 Signal Corps Dr
Fredericksburg VA 22408

Call Sign: N4SJX
Tommy J Pittman
7005 Soulier Ln
Fredericksburg VA 224076409

Call Sign: KJ4ZSA
Michael J Kramer
15400 Spotswood Furnace Rd

Fredericksburg VA 22407

Call Sign: AK4FS
Michael J Kramer
15400 Spotswood Furnace Rd
Fredericksburg VA 22407

Call Sign: KG4YYC
Michael L Delapp
419 Spotted Tavern Rd
Fredericksburg VA 22406

Call Sign: WA4NDT
William S Lenzi
221 Spring Knoll Cir
Fredericksburg VA 22405

Call Sign: WB0AOD
Stephen L Moore
11009 Spring Meadow Blvd
Fredericksburg VA 22407

Call Sign: KI4HRL
Timothy J King
712 Spring Valley Dr
Fredericksburg VA 22405

Call Sign: N2CLB
Camden L Bullock
134 Spring Wood Dr
Fredericksburg VA 22401

Call Sign: KJ4MYX
David A Algert
208 Springknoll Cir
Fredericksburg VA 22405

Call Sign: KF4LCZ
Darren K Hobbs
43 Spruce Ln
Fredericksburg VA 22406

Call Sign: KG4SGU
Lynne E Cunningham
10 Stable Way
Fredericksburg VA 22407

Call Sign: KG4SOK
Ben W Cunningham

10 Stable Way
Fredericksburg VA 22407

Call Sign: KG4SQL
James P Cunningham
10 Stable Way
Fredericksburg VA 22407

Call Sign: KA5MMF
Brenda F Crusenberry
11004 Stacy Run
Fredericksburg VA 22408

Call Sign: KB5VEA
Dennis W Crusenberry
11004 Stacy Run
Fredericksburg VA 22408

Call Sign: KD5BF
Wendell W Crusenberry Sr
11004 Stacy Run
Fredericksburg VA 22408

Call Sign: KD4VNP
Jack M Tiger
7706 Stockwell Dr
Fredericksburg VA 22407

Call Sign: N4PVL
William F Potter
509 Sullivan Dr
Fredericksburg VA 22405

Call Sign: KJ4YCY
Jennifer A Styles
6404 Summer Breeze Ct
Fredericksburg VA 22407

Call Sign: KJ4YCZ
Jeremy D Styles
6404 Summer Breeze Ct
Fredericksburg VA 22407

Call Sign: KJ4YDF
Philip S Bradshaw
6404 Summer Breeze Ct
Fredericksburg VA 22407

Call Sign: KG4RXM

Durwood L Young
11140 Sunburst Ln
Fredericksburg VA 22407

Call Sign: KR4JK
James J Bradley
11146 G Sunburst Ln
Fredericksburg VA 22407

Call Sign: KC4SUW
Michael Y Chang
110 Sycamore Ridge Rd
Fredericksburg VA 22405

Call Sign: AF4UV
Michael Y Chang
110 Sycamore Ridge Rd
Fredericksburg VA 22405

Call Sign: KI4DJS
Christina J Chang
110 Sycamore Ridge Rd
Fredericksburg VA 22405

Call Sign: KI4GCV
Christopher Y Chang
110 Sycamore Ridge Rd
Fredericksburg VA 22405

Call Sign: KE6PBM
David C Algert
4 Tally Ho Dr
Fredericksburg VA 22405

Call Sign: KA4VYU
Joseph M Overman Sr
202 Taylor St
Fredericksburg VA 22405

Call Sign: N1RYX
Michael A Kosior
209 Taylor St
Fredericksburg VA 224052909

Call Sign: KB1JTU
Susan C Kosior
209 Taylor St
Fredericksburg VA 224052909

Call Sign: KA4UMP
Jimmie D Wing
221 Taylor St
Fredericksburg VA 22405

Call Sign: KI4LTR
Jimmie D Wing
221 Taylor St
Fredericksburg VA 22405

Call Sign: KG4KTJ
Lee Peters III
5 Teak Ct
Fredericksburg VA 22405

Call Sign: N4FOA
Raymond W Gill Jr
10938 Tidewater Tr
Fredericksburg VA 224082023

Call Sign: K4CQU
Raymond W Gill Jr
10938 Tidewater Tr
Fredericksburg VA 224082023

Call Sign: KG4JZG
Patrick A Mcdonald
11321 Tidewater Trl
Fredericksburg VA 22408

Call Sign: K4CWR
Christopher W Reed
85 Tracey Ln
Fredericksburg VA 22406

Call Sign: N3MHF
Mark J Episcopo
12913 Trench Ct
Fredericksburg VA 22407

Call Sign: KB2RJW
Craig J Steckowski
9 Trey Ct
Fredericksburg VA 22405

Call Sign: K4ZRL
Emmett L Snellings
315 Truslow Rd
Fredericksburg VA 22405

Call Sign: KG4IQW
Connie L Cornett
1379 Truslow Rd
Fredericksburg VA 22406

Call Sign: KK4COU
Warren T Lee
1566 Truslow Rd
Fredericksburg VA 22406

Call Sign: W4SHS
Warren T Lee
1566 Truslow Rd
Fredericksburg VA 22406

Call Sign: N6DEU
James A Bass
16 Twin Lake Ct
Fredericksburg VA 22405

Call Sign: KF3N
Raymond E Babineau Jr
210 Twinlakes Dr
Fredericksburg VA 22401

Call Sign: AE4GM
Brockman H Winfrey
11328 Tyrell Ct
Fredericksburg VA 22407

Call Sign: KV4GK
David N Rosenblum
5520 W Rich Mtn Way
Fredericksburg VA 22407

Call Sign: WB8PFT
Preston E Simms
103 W Wildwood Ln
Fredericksburg VA 224056125

Call Sign: KG4FCL
Jerry R Redding
112 W Wildwood Ln
Fredericksburg VA 22405

Call Sign: KA8Q
Jerry R Redding
112 W Wildwood Ln

Fredericksburg VA 22405

Call Sign: KJ4RXH
Adam W Schreiber
10714 Wakeman Dr
Fredericksburg VA 22407

Call Sign: KI4BCK
John F Rowley
7 Wallace Farm Ln
Fredericksburg VA 22406

Call Sign: KG4ZIZ
Kelli E Martin
8 Wallace Farms Ln
Fredericksburg VA 22406

Call Sign: W3DGG
Donald Kling
204 Walnut Dr
Fredericksburg VA 22405

Call Sign: W4XA
Ronald R Akers
11500 Warner Dr
Fredericksburg VA 22407

Call Sign: N4UZU
Richard B Pennington
1908 Washington Ave
Fredericksburg VA 22401

Call Sign: N3DSB
Randall C Jenkins
85 Wateredge Ln
Fredericksburg VA 22406

Call Sign: KK4BCR
Charles S Campbell
10407 Watford Ln
Fredericksburg VA 22408

Call Sign: W4JIO
Carl S Wilson
3212 Waverly Dr
Fredericksburg VA 224076919

Call Sign: WD4SAW
Roger M Vines

3320 Waverly Dr
Fredericksburg VA 22401

Call Sign: KI4VLR
Matt I Mcdaniel
36 Welford Ln
Fredericksburg VA 22405

Call Sign: KI4SLQ
Ian B Mcdaniel
36 Welford Ln
Fredericksburg VA 224053642

Call Sign: KC4YHI
Kathryn J Hitt
8 Westmoreland Pl
Fredericksburg VA 22405

Call Sign: K4THY
Kathryn J Hitt
8 Westmoreland Pl
Fredericksburg VA 22405

Call Sign: W4LLK
E Thomas Hitt III
8 Westmoreland Pl
Fredericksburg VA 224053056

Call Sign: KC2LJN
Russell C Erickson
1211 Westview Dr
Fredericksburg VA 22405

Call Sign: KG4DBC
Rance P Rupp
485 White Oak Rd
Fredericksburg VA 22405

Call Sign: WA4MLN
Linwood Jones
6 Wickham Ct
Fredericksburg VA 22405

Call Sign: WB0PCZ
Rick L Blank
3804 Wilburn Dr
Fredericksburg VA 22407

Call Sign: KD4ZPG

Laurie J Cavanagh
1805 William St Apt 210C
Fredericksburg VA 22401

Call Sign: N3CCK
Michael H Hubbard
14 Williams Dr
Fredericksburg VA 22405

Call Sign: N8WZH
Donald S Corbin
6509 Willow Pond Dr
Fredericksburg VA 22407

Call Sign: K3DSC
D Scott Corbin
6509 Willow Pond Dr
Fredericksburg VA 22407

Call Sign: KI4HMJ
Mark Lepire
6515 Willow Pond Dr
Fredericksburg VA 22407

Call Sign: KQ6NT
Ted A Ruane
6610 Willow Pond Dr
Fredericksburg VA 22407

Call Sign: AF4LE
William J Oxford
6704 Willow Pond Dr
Fredericksburg VA 224078409

Call Sign: KE4JPG
Jose B De Leon Jr
13014 Willow Pt Dr
Fredericksburg VA 22408

Call Sign: KG4FCS
Linnea E Wissting
1200 Winchester St
Fredericksburg VA 22401

Call Sign: AG4AK
Charles J Albright
10032 Windridge Dr
Fredericksburg VA 22407

Call Sign: AC4IU
David L Wilson
6116 Windsor Dr
Fredericksburg VA 22407

Call Sign: KG4LFD
Shomir J Wilson
6116 Windsor Dr
Fredericksburg VA 22407

Call Sign: KG4VXO
Alpana Wilson
6116 Windsor Dr
Fredericksburg VA 22407

Call Sign: KE4NNE
William G Cornell Sr
802 Wolfe St
Fredericksburg VA 22401

Call Sign: KD4OOV
Ruby J Thomas
11 Wood Landing Rd
Fredericksburg VA 22405

Call Sign: W0STY
Charles E Crown
3 Woodland Ter
Fredericksburg VA 224052264

Call Sign: WB4LNT
Gordon F Thomas
11 Woodlanding Rd
Fredericksburg VA 22405

Call Sign: NW3Z
Nathan A Miller
12501 Wye Oaks Ln
Fredericksburg VA 22407

Call Sign: KU4IY
Timothy L Gajewski
11303 Wytheville Ln
Fredericksburg VA 22407

Call Sign: KD4ESY
Ward M Le Hardy
Fredericksburg VA 22402

Call Sign: KD4ESX
Judy N Le Hardy
Fredericksburg VA 22032

Call Sign: KJ4YCX
Rachel E White
Fredericksburg VA 22402

Call Sign: KJ4RBF
Samuel D Jones
Fredericksburg VA 22403

Call Sign: K2DCA
John F Feet
Fredericksburg VA 22403

Call Sign: KA7LGG
Michael J Lovingier
Fredericksburg VA 22404

Call Sign: N4LDS
Larry D Sumner
Fredericksburg VA 22404

Call Sign: KK4GXK
Jim R Andrus
Fredericksburg VA 22404

Call Sign: WA4PAG
Franklin M Haas
Fredericksburg VA 224048222

FCC Amateur Radio Licenses in Free Union

Call Sign: KF4TMD
Joel Z Slezak
3567 Ballards Mill Rd
Free Union VA 22940

Call Sign: KD4CUB
Suzanne Z Slezak
3567 Ballards Mill Rd
Free Union VA 22940

Call Sign: KD4CUA
Mark Z Slezak
3567 Ballards Mill Rd
Free Union VA 229402027

Call Sign: KD4BZH
Noah Y Mcmurray
4337 Ballards Mill Rd
Free Union VA 22940

Call Sign: KD4CTZ
David Slezak
Rt 1 Box 185
Free Union VA 22940

Call Sign: KD4KWJ
Denise R Zito
Rt 1 Box 185
Free Union VA 22940

Call Sign: KA1ZTB
Daniel J Seideman
2470 Cascades Dr
Free Union VA 22940

Call Sign: KI4ICP
Julian D Heislup Jr
1808 Old Orchard Rd
Free Union VA 22940

Call Sign: KI4GCU
Charles M Davis Jr
Free Union VA 22940

Call Sign: W4CMD
Charles M Davis Jr
Free Union VA 22940

FCC Amateur Radio Licenses in Freeman

Call Sign: KJ4BML
David M Fuller Jr
2275 5 Forks Rd
Freeman VA 23856

Call Sign: WB4OHC
Chester P Royster
674 Big Horn Rd
Freeman VA 23856

Call Sign: K4DAL
Walter M Hall Sr

363 Harris Ln
Freeman VA 23856

Call Sign: KJ4BMP
Timothy W Jones
1949 Reedy Creek Rd
Freeman VA 23856

Call Sign: KJ4BMJ
Katherin G Anglin
Freeman VA 23856

FCC Amateur Radio Licenses in Fries

Call Sign: KK4CWI
Bob M Hines
469 Blue Spruce Ln
Fries VA 24330

Call Sign: KB4OTX
Marie S Combs
Rt 2 Box 113
Fries VA 24330

Call Sign: AA4OW
Larry L Jones
122 Half Mile Ln
Fries VA 24330

Call Sign: WD4LHB
Joe J Vaughan
94 Iron Mtn Ln
Fries VA 243303840

Call Sign: KF4WEZ
Michael D Hackler
160 Lee Dr
Fries VA 24330

Call Sign: KG4NBV
Elaine A Hackler
160 Lee Dr
Fries VA 24330

Call Sign: WA4DFH
Oscar B Underwood
426 Sheep Grove Rd
Fries VA 243303771

Call Sign: WA3ZGN
Donald E Sexton
Fries VA 24330

Call Sign: KI4TSU
Bobbie R Jones
Fries VA 24330

FCC Amateur Radio Licenses in Front Royal

Call Sign: KG4TBX
Ian C Hitchcock
200 Academy Dr
Front Royal VA 22630

Call Sign: KG4VXF
Randolph-Macon Academy
Ham RC
200 Academy Dr Box C6
Front Royal VA 22630

Call Sign: WA4RMA
Randolph-Macon Academy
Ham RC
200 Academy Dr Box C6
Front Royal VA 22630

Call Sign: WA4BIV
Robert A Barbour
458 Acton St
Front Royal VA 22630

Call Sign: N4SOR
David E Kidd
343 Amherst Dr
Front Royal VA 22630

Call Sign: WB4VKY
Anthony Del Grosso
1019 Applewood Dr
Front Royal VA 22630

Call Sign: KI4JSC
Michael B Davidsen
149 Bens Ct
Front Royal VA 22630

Call Sign: W1AMR
Michael B Davidsen
149 Bens Ct
Front Royal VA 22630

Call Sign: KB5UAB
Christopher M Timmons
81 Bens Ct
Front Royal VA 22630

Call Sign: AB4PD
Eugene B Lunsford
182 Blair Rd
Front Royal VA 22630

Call Sign: N4NTH
Thelma R Lunsford
182 Blair Rd
Front Royal VA 22630

Call Sign: N3LGF
R Thomas Chase
647 Blue Mtn Rd
Front Royal VA 226303847

Call Sign: KJ4YLK
Mark D Ferguson
2775 Blue Mtn Rd
Front Royal VA 22630

Call Sign: WB4TTN
Robert E Bishop
3968 Blue Mtn Rd
Front Royal VA 22630

Call Sign: KD4CBG
Steve D Dillon
Rt 3 Box 439
Front Royal VA 22630

Call Sign: K4CTR
Kenneth R Doege
Rt 1 Box 4556
Front Royal VA 22630

Call Sign: KC4VCP
John W Paulson
Rt 5 Box 572
Front Royal VA 22630

Call Sign: AD4RM
Walter D Smith
1058 Braxton Rd
Front Royal VA 22630

Call Sign: KF4AIL
John S Bell
2468 Browntown Rd
Front Royal VA 22630

Call Sign: KF4LRS
Susan R Bell
2468 Browntown Rd
Front Royal VA 22630

Call Sign: W3DOS
Department Of State ARC
3446 Browntown Rd
Front Royal VA 22630

Call Sign: WB6SBW
George O Glavis
3446 Browntown Rd
Front Royal VA 22630

Call Sign: KB4KRO
Marc A Dominguez
3069 Cardinal Dr
Front Royal VA 22630

Call Sign: N4MKH
William R Thomas Jr
3071 Cardinal Dr
Front Royal VA 22630

Call Sign: KG4EHK
Joshua J Long
134 Christundom Dr
Front Royal VA 22630

Call Sign: KI4RWR
John F Ohlinger
237 Church St
Front Royal VA 22630

Call Sign: KJ4YKR
Thomas S Madden
268 Creekside Way

Front Royal VA 22630

Call Sign: K4BLB
Barry L Barton
272 Creekside Way
Front Royal VA 22630

Call Sign: KJ4YES
Michael W Kosko
180 Crest Ln
Front Royal VA 226306369

Call Sign: KG4FUE
Andrew J Mandela
421 Criser Rd 302
Front Royal VA 22630

Call Sign: W4JK
Charles E Marshall
455 Dowing Farm Rd
Front Royal VA 22636

Call Sign: KD4WIF
Kerwin A Ralls
603 Duck St
Front Royal VA 22630

Call Sign: KJ4EOZ
James D Swann
302 Duncan Ave
Front Royal VA 22630

Call Sign: W3CN
Carroll E Nickens
124 E 19th St
Front Royal VA 226304135

Call Sign: WA2MGC
Charles K Guy
1078 E Goodview Dr
Front Royal VA 22630

Call Sign: KC4ALF
Ralph J Di Muccio
65 Ehlers Dr
Front Royal VA 226305455

Call Sign: KD4TNT
Pamela F Thompson

492 Ellen Dr
Front Royal VA 22630

Call Sign: W7YAL
Clyde O Price
400 Grand Ave
Front Royal VA 22630

Call Sign: KK4FSP
Michael E Reed
115 Grebe Dr
Front Royal VA 22630

Call Sign: W4MER
Michael E Reed
115 Grebe Dr
Front Royal VA 22630

Call Sign: AB4YY
Michael J Kelly
64 Greenhill Ridge Ct
Front Royal VA 22630

Call Sign: KE4DDS
Darlene J Kelly
64 Greenhill Ridge Ct
Front Royal VA 22630

Call Sign: WB4WRH
Robert C Rae
512 Happy Creek Rd
Front Royal VA 22630

Call Sign: W4RKN
Robert C Rae
512 Happy Creek Rd
Front Royal VA 22630

Call Sign: KE4CAU
Thomas E Zinn II
901 Happy Creek Rd
Front Royal VA 22630

Call Sign: KG4VPG
Alan J Baldwin
2382 Harmony Hollow Rd
Front Royal VA 22630

Call Sign: KD4CAS

Roger C Roberts Sr
158 Heavens Tree Trl
Front Royal VA 22630

Call Sign: W4ROG
Roger C Roberts Sr
158 Heavens Tree Trl
Front Royal VA 22630

Call Sign: WA4TMG
Robert A Gould
92 High Knob Rd
Front Royal VA 22630

Call Sign: KG4IJD
Ervin M Beekman
635 High Knob Rd
Front Royal VA 22630

Call Sign: KI4UVA
Ervin M Beekman
635 High Knob Rd
Front Royal VA 22630

Call Sign: N9QLM
Thomas I Breed
1017 Horseshoe Dr
Front Royal VA 22630

Call Sign: KC3FF
Donald N Haw
4353 Howellsville Rd
Front Royal VA 22630

Call Sign: W3HTJ
Dominic J Repici
6289 Howellsville Rd
Front Royal VA 22630

Call Sign: KJ4NXF
Carla L Repici
6289 Howellsville Rd
Front Royal VA 22630

Call Sign: AA4GM
John T Seely
93 Joanwood Ln
Front Royal VA 22630

Call Sign: KB4ZDR
Phylis H Seely
93 Joanwood Ln
Front Royal VA 22630

Call Sign: WB4JFC
David F Jones
1520 John Marshall Hwy
Front Royal VA 226304505

Call Sign: WA4PMD
Thomas M Cross
1256 Kesler Rd
Front Royal VA 22630

Call Sign: N4TBL
Larry W Kirby Sr
27 Lake Ave
Front Royal VA 22630

Call Sign: K4LWK
Larry W Kirby Sr
27 Lake Ave
Front Royal VA 22630

Call Sign: W4LWK
Larry W Kirby Sr
27 Lake Ave
Front Royal VA 22630

Call Sign: W4DOG
Larry W Kirby Sr
27 Lake Ave
Front Royal VA 22630

Call Sign: KF4ZJG
Theda L Dawson
231 Leach St
Front Royal VA 22630

Call Sign: KD4DEF
William R Grandy
303 Leach St
Front Royal VA 22630

Call Sign: KI4HFH
Van A Knight II
524 Lena Ct
Front Royal VA 22630

Call Sign: KG4TAE
William J Harrison
1481 Linden St
Front Royal VA 22630

Call Sign: KG4VPH
Lucille E Harrison
1481 Linden St
Front Royal VA 22630

Call Sign: KG4WQE
William J Harrison
1481 Linden St
Front Royal VA 22630

Call Sign: AG4YF
William J Harrison
1481 Linden St
Front Royal VA 22630

Call Sign: WB4KTC
Robert J Traister Sr
513 Manassas Ave
Front Royal VA 22630

Call Sign: K4AC
Roy A Cartier
600 Mt View St Apt 101
Front Royal VA 226302357

Call Sign: KJ4IXX
Ray Q Miller Jr
119 Mtn Heights Rd
Front Royal VA 22630

Call Sign: W3HEY
Raymond A Hart
799 Mtn Heights Rd
Front Royal VA 22630

Call Sign: KG4FUG
James P O Conner
746 Mtn Rd
Front Royal VA 22630

Call Sign: KG4DGH
Robert E Clayton
1271 Mtn Rd

Front Royal VA 22630

Call Sign: N4NRO
Gerald R Soucy
235 Mtn Top Rd
Front Royal VA 22630

Call Sign: NO4N
Gerald R Soucy
235 Mtn Top Rd
Front Royal VA 22630

Call Sign: N4ZSF
John B Gentry
28 N Marshall St
Front Royal VA 22630

Call Sign: K4JNA
Thomas S Strickler
1043 Northview Ave
Front Royal VA 22630

Call Sign: KF4BPL
Daniel R Hart
705 Oak Ln
Front Royal VA 22630

Call Sign: KI4NAR
John D Zeits Sr
476 Old Oak Ln
Front Royal VA 22630

Call Sign: WB4DQF
William R Whitlock
981 Osprey Ln
Front Royal VA 226305514

Call Sign: KG4CPT
Patrick G Desbois
2467 Panhandle Rd
Front Royal VA 22630

Call Sign: KG4DGI
Charity H Martin
5172 Panhandle Rd
Front Royal VA 22630

Call Sign: KG4DGJ
Carol A Martin

5172 Panhandle Rd
Front Royal VA 22630

Call Sign: N3QOF
Donald R Martin
5172 Panhandle Rd
Front Royal VA 226306636

Call Sign: N2ECO
Hugh C Martin Sr
78 Park Ridge Ct
Front Royal VA 22630

Call Sign: KG4FLZ
Thomas H Krebs
328 Paw Paw Dr
Front Royal VA 22630

Call Sign: KG4FMA
Michele R Krebs
328 Paw Paw Dr
Front Royal VA 22630

Call Sign: KJ4YOY
Joseph Roberts
292 Pine Ridge Dr
Front Royal VA 22630

Call Sign: KG4FUB
Judith P Schiminsky
255 Pine Shores Dr
Front Royal VA 22630

Call Sign: KB4LMJ
Natashya A Wilson
449 Poca Bella Dr
Front Royal VA 22630

Call Sign: KD3T
James L Wilson Sr
449 Poca Bella Dr
Front Royal VA 22630

Call Sign: KG4QVS
Steven L Wilson
449 Poca Bella Dr
Front Royal VA 22630

Call Sign: N4EG

David O Armstrong
542 Pow Morr Dr
Front Royal VA 226032308

Call Sign: W3IPL
James W Ramsey
116 Richmond Rd
Front Royal VA 22630

Call Sign: KJ4LBK
Thomas E Harrison
3944 River Mt Dr
Front Royal VA 22630

Call Sign: W4FBF
William R Miller
97 River Overlook Rd
Front Royal VA 22630

Call Sign: KG4TAD
David A Harrison
3944 Rivermont Dr
Front Royal VA 22630

Call Sign: KI4AVU
Benjamin W Harrison
3944 Rivermont Dr
Front Royal VA 22630

Call Sign: KI4AVV
Halimah R Harrison
3944 Rivermont Dr
Front Royal VA 22630

Call Sign: KG4VXI
Jenny L Harrison
3944 Rivermont Dr
Front Royal VA 22630

Call Sign: KG4VPI
Rachel A Harrison
3944 Rivermont Dr
Front Royal VA 22630

Call Sign: KG4SPS
Rick I Droege
97 Riverside Ln
Front Royal VA 226305100

Call Sign: AB4D
James W Jones
151 Robinson Rd
Front Royal VA 22630

Call Sign: K2EZY
Fred L Holt
220 Rolling View Dr
Front Royal VA 22630

Call Sign: KC4YMO
Gregory L Williams
1182 S Fork Dr
Front Royal VA 22630

Call Sign: KD4DEQ
Sharon A Kirby
27 S Lake Ave
Front Royal VA 22630

Call Sign: KF4VLZ
Richard R Jacobus
424 S Shenandoah Ave
Front Royal VA 22630

Call Sign: WA4PVM
Steven W Sagar
565 Sagar Dr
Front Royal VA 22630

Call Sign: WA4RAX
VA L Sagar
565 Sagar Dr
Front Royal VA 22630

Call Sign: KJ4YKT
Luke W Bieryla
108 Salem Ave
Front Royal VA 22630

Call Sign: KA4RGW
Cheryl D Lavezza
Apt 304 Shenandoah Commons
Way
Front Royal VA 22630

Call Sign: KG4AUX
Richard E Shane

5 Shenandoah Commons Way
Apt 103
Front Royal VA 22630

Call Sign: KG4FLY
Harold D Brock
115 Simons Way
Front Royal VA 22630

Call Sign: KC4MTA
Paul E Griffis
715 Stockton Rd
Front Royal VA 22630

Call Sign: KG4FLV
Darryl J Adams
135 Stonegate Ct
Front Royal VA 22630

Call Sign: KG4DOD
Annemarie V Wouters
900 Thunder Rd
Front Royal VA 22630

Call Sign: KG4DUX
Jacqueline M Catterton
900 Thunder Rd
Front Royal VA 22630

Call Sign: KC4LCR
Philip R Compton
108 VA Ave
Front Royal VA 22630

Call Sign: KD4ANU
Nicholas A Johnson
427 Vesey Dr
Front Royal VA 22630

Call Sign: KG4FKB
Carl M Schmitt
41 View Dr
Front Royal VA 22630

Call Sign: KC4MEL
Gerard A Martin
840 Village Ct
Front Royal VA 22630

Call Sign: AD4HS
Lewis E Wharton
413 Viscose Ave
Front Royal VA 22630

Call Sign: AG4MT
Matthew B Biggs
424 W 15th St
Front Royal VA 22630

Call Sign: KI4AVW
Bryon T Biggs
424 W 15th St
Front Royal VA 22630

Call Sign: KI4AVX
Liesle M Biggs
424 W 15th St
Front Royal VA 22630

Call Sign: KI4BAP
Michael J Biggs
424 W 15th St
Front Royal VA 22630

Call Sign: KF4EJY
Ricky L Shepherd
136 W 17th St
Front Royal VA 22630

Call Sign: KC4HTU
William L Woods
22 W 1st Apt 12
Front Royal VA 22630

Call Sign: KG4VPD
Thomas B Hindley
227 W 8th St
Front Royal VA 22630

Call Sign: KG4WJD
Jolea Hindley
227 W 8th St
Front Royal VA 22630

Call Sign: K4DAS
Donald A Sabella
152 W Duck St
Front Royal VA 22630

Call Sign: W3EVI
Henry F Mc Cauley Jr
146 W Strasburg Rd
Front Royal VA 22630

Call Sign: KF4LAA
Jim A Burton Jr
299 Walnut Dr
Front Royal VA 22630

Call Sign: KG4EBY
Clyde M Cornwell
1311 Warren Ave
Front Royal VA 22630

Call Sign: KG4EHH
Kevin D Cornwell
1311 Warren Ave
Front Royal VA 22630

Call Sign: KM4KR
David W Johnson
92 Windy Ridge Rd
Front Royal VA 226307201

Call Sign: N4UIM
Joseph W Johnson
92 Windy Ridge Rd
Front Royal VA 226307201

Call Sign: WA4DJ
David W Johnson
92 Windy Ridge Rd
Front Royal VA 226307201

Call Sign: K4OD
Carl D Bethel Jr
Front Royal VA 22630

Call Sign: KC4CQE
Audrey E Glass
Front Royal VA 22630

Call Sign: KC4NTE
Richard D Ellinger
Front Royal VA 22630

Call Sign: KD4BBD

Ralph L Mallonee
Front Royal VA 22630

Call Sign: WA4AKO
Nathan T Brooks
Front Royal VA 22630

Call Sign: KC4LVQ
David M Ellinger
Front Royal VA 22630

Call Sign: W4FRR
Charles E Glass
Front Royal VA 22630

Call Sign: KG4FKC
Joe D Bergida
Front Royal VA 22630

Call Sign: KG4FKD
Mary E Bergida
Front Royal VA 22630

Call Sign: KG4FLW
James E Bergida
Front Royal VA 22630

Call Sign: KG4FLX
Marvin M Bergida
Front Royal VA 22630

Call Sign: KG4FMB
Edward J Leptich
Front Royal VA 22630

Call Sign: KG4FMC
Draper J Warren
Front Royal VA 22630

Call Sign: KG4FUF
John R Bergida
Front Royal VA 22630

Call Sign: KE4FFG
Roger L Skidmore
Front Royal VA 226300956

**FCC Amateur Radio Licenses
in Fulks Run**

Call Sign: KD4HDL
Russell M Turner
11920 Brocks Gap Rd
Fulks Run VA 22830

Call Sign: KJ4LDL
Kevin N Mcdonaldson
12423 Dusty Ln
Fulks Run VA 22830

**FCC Amateur Radio Licenses
in Gainesville**

Call Sign: N4DS
Richard C Spencer
14955 Alpine Bay Loop
Gainesville VA 201552808

Call Sign: KE4IDQ
Clifford J Webb
13560 Amal Ln
Gainesville VA 20155

Call Sign: WA1STU
John W Zorger
5711 Artemus Rd
Gainesville VA 201551542

Call Sign: KK4BBJ
Steven M Curry
6503 Atkins Way
Gainesville VA 20155

Call Sign: N4TKJ
Thomas A Beckett
8632 Belgrove Gardens Ln
Gainesville VA 20155

Call Sign: N3VT
Thomas A Beckett
8632 Belgrove Gardens Ln
Gainesville VA 20155

Call Sign: KB2BZK
L S Newman Jr
7490 Bosedge Dr
Gainesville VA 20155

Call Sign: KG4IVT
Peter C Boswell
14064 Breeders Cup Dr
Gainesville VA 20155

Call Sign: K4WRG
William M Hinely
14371 Breezewood Ct
Gainesville VA 201551238

Call Sign: K9ZD
William M Hinely
14371 Breezewood Ct
Gainesville VA 201551238

Call Sign: W2SBI
Donald C Eaton
6551 Bullen Bluff Ter
Gainesville VA 20155

Call Sign: N9RPC
James A Williams
14133 Catbird Dr
Gainesville VA 20155

Call Sign: N4MQ
George K Woodworth
4800 Catharpin Rd
Gainesville VA 20155

Call Sign: K3SS
Hugh C Maddocks
13891 Chelmsford Dr A 303
Gainesville VA 201553132

Call Sign: KA4WJJ
Jane F Maddocks
13891 Chelmsford Dr A 303
Gainesville VA 201553132

Call Sign: K6SLK
Timothy C Tatum
6281 Culverhouse Ct
Gainesville VA 20155

Call Sign: KI4ISW
John J Bisaga
6825 Derby Run Way
Gainesville VA 20155

Call Sign: K4BLZ
Leon Medler
6828 Derby Run Way
Gainesville VA 20155

Call Sign: KJ4UNL
Charles B Harding
6721 Edgartown Way
Gainesville VA 20155

Call Sign: W4WKB
Walter E Alward
7501 Falkland Dr
Gainesville VA 20155

Call Sign: KB4BZN
Gary M Alward
7501 Falkland Dr
Gainesville VA 22065

Call Sign: KK4ADQ
Andrew W Higgins
13293 Fieldstone Way
Gainesville VA 20155

Call Sign: WD4DBV
Thomas C Roth
13314 Fieldstone Way
Gainesville VA 20155

Call Sign: KB4LOS
Marilyn W Lamm
13322 Fieldstone Way
Gainesville VA 20155

Call Sign: W4LAM
Franklin C Lamm
13322 Fieldstone Way
Gainesville VA 20155

Call Sign: WA2LSN
Christopher E Mankiewich
13333 Fieldstone Way
Gainesville VA 201556615

Call Sign: WA2PAT
Frederick S Deitz
14112 Flicker Ct

Gainesville VA 201555868

Call Sign: K4ET
George H Moltz III
6854 General Lafayette Way
Gainesville VA 20155

Call Sign: N4MSU
Eugene R Arbogast
14532 Jansbury St
Gainesville VA 20155

Call Sign: KJ4MTB
Finnian G Cornelison
14584 Kylewood Way
Gainesville VA 20155

Call Sign: W4WSW
Luis A Vellon
14258 Ladderbacked Dr
Gainesville VA 20155

Call Sign: N3CCR
Ronald A King
4220 Lawnvale Dr
Gainesville VA 201551100

Call Sign: KK4HKD
William L Payne II
14222 Lee Hwy B 11
Gainesville VA 20155

Call Sign: KB4IFT
Matthew T Ramsey
4529 Lynn Forest Dr
Gainesville VA 20155

Call Sign: KJ4JMZ
Byron L Brigham
4559 Lynn Forest Dr
Gainesville VA 20155

Call Sign: K1IZ
Volodymyr Andryeyev
4808 Maurine Ct
Gainesville VA 20155

Call Sign: WF3J
Boris A Platonov

4808 Maurine Ct
Gainesville VA 20155

Call Sign: KG4JZR
Volodymyr Andryeyev
4808 Maurine Ct
Gainesville VA 20155

Call Sign: KG4KCY
Vasiliy M Voliy
4808 Maurine Ct
Gainesville VA 20155

Call Sign: KT4ER
Scott C Bellefeuille
13614 Morris Ct
Gainesville VA 20155

Call Sign: KJ4LAS
Justin W Anderle
14333 Newbern Loop
Gainesville VA 20155

Call Sign: KI4YNO
Stephen A Crouch
13500 Norwick Pl
Gainesville VA 20155

Call Sign: KI4SA
Stephen A Crouch
13500 Norwick Pl
Gainesville VA 20155

Call Sign: W4DOJ
Homero Ruiz Jr
7811 Ontario Rd
Gainesville VA 20155

Call Sign: KD7QLQ
Susan K Morgan
5975 Pageland Ln
Gainesville VA 20155

Call Sign: KD7QLR
Malachi J Morgan
5975 Pageland Ln
Gainesville VA 20155

Call Sign: K2RFC

Robert F Corriel
10629 Rembert Ct
Gainesville VA 20155

Call Sign: K3WV
Robert F Corriel
10629 Rembert Ct
Gainesville VA 20155

Call Sign: K3PXR
Alfred E Resnick
6347 Retriever Ln
Gainesville VA 201556604

Call Sign: N1PLK
Carol B Resnick
6347 Retriever Ln
Gainesville VA 201556604

Call Sign: KB4OAJ
Andrew S Wells
8031 Rocky Run Rd
Gainesville VA 20155

Call Sign: KM4AE
William J Crandall
7693 Royal Sydney Dr
Gainesville VA 20155

Call Sign: N4WJC
William J Crandall
7693 Royal Sydney Dr
Gainesville VA 20155

Call Sign: W4DGA
Walter E Szuminski
13574 Ryton Ridge Ln
Gainesville VA 201553007

Call Sign: K4FTO
Augustus Arthur Hackett Jr
6837 Saddle Run Way
Gainesville VA 201553027

Call Sign: KC4TL
Michael A Machtinger Dpm
6234 Settlers Trl Pl
Gainesville VA 20155

Call Sign: KC4ATU
William H Rowlett
6260 Settlers Trl Pl
Gainesville VA 201551375

Call Sign: KK4ARB
Christopher Andersen
14468 Sharpshinned Dr
Gainesville VA 20155

Call Sign: KE4ZDV
Elaine G Miller
4360 Snow Hill Dr
Gainesville VA 20155

Call Sign: KI4SPX
Jacob F Guepe
4239 Stepney Rd
Gainesville VA 20155

Call Sign: KD7UHR
William N Radicic
13514 Tackhouse Ct
Gainesville VA 20155

Call Sign: N6ZLB
Douglas J Boone
8197 Tillinghast Ln
Gainesville VA 20155

Call Sign: WA0MET
Jay M Lough
4501 Tullamore Estates Rd
Gainesville VA 20155

Call Sign: KK4ARP
Nathaniel L Hatfield
15520 Vint Hill Rd
Gainesville VA 20155

Call Sign: KK4ARO
Seth T Hatfield
15520 Vint Hill Rd
Gainesville VA 20155

Call Sign: W4TNQ
John F Delean
6947 Walnut Hill Dr
Gainesville VA 20155

Call Sign: N4UQI
Jonathan F Schupp
7844 Waverley Mill Ct
Gainesville VA 22065

Call Sign: KC4ZA
Alan L Skerker
6700 Whirlaway Ct
Gainesville VA 20155

Call Sign: N0HNN
Lawrence J Hogya Jr
14008 Willet Way
Gainesville VA 201555915

Call Sign: KF4UQF
Dustin M White
Gainesville VA 20156

FCC Amateur Radio Licenses in Galax

Call Sign: KI4ONG
Rodney A Roberts
308 Alderman St
Galax VA 24333

Call Sign: KF4NZE
John H Mullins
308 Armory Rd Apt B
Galax VA 24333

Call Sign: KE4QAA
Richard G Hudson
105 Barger St
Galax VA 24333

Call Sign: KE4JUG
James F Billings
152 Bee Line Dr
Galax VA 24333

Call Sign: N4GGU
Paul S Hill
170 Bee Line Dr
Galax VA 24333

Call Sign: KJ4ASH

William M Perkins
1087 Beech Grove Ln
Galax VA 243332187

Call Sign: K4TLT
Tony L Truitt
1288 Beech Grove Ln
Galax VA 24333

Call Sign: WD4LJD
Leroy Mc Kenzie
1903 Beech Grove Ln
Galax VA 24333

Call Sign: KF4ESX
Todd G Hash
Rt 8 Box 121
Galax VA 24333

Call Sign: KE4ATF
Lois G Williams
Rt 4 Box 205
Galax VA 24333

Call Sign: KE4ATG
Johnny M Williams
Rt 4 Box 205
Galax VA 24333

Call Sign: KE4TEB
Dennis P Winesett
Rt 2 Box 27
Galax VA 24333

Call Sign: KF4JRU
Daniel D Adams
Rt 4 Box 353A1
Galax VA 24333

Call Sign: WD4BXW
Barry C Hill
Rfd 4 Box 381
Galax VA 24333

Call Sign: WD4BXX
Larry C Hill
Rt 4 Box 381
Galax VA 24333

Call Sign: KF4USL
Stacy C Dalton
Rt 3 Box 55
Galax VA 24333

Call Sign: WA4IGC
Carmel L Brown
Rt 1 Box 95 Memory Ln
Galax VA 24333

Call Sign: WB4BRQ
William C Davis
133 Camp Zion Rd
Galax VA 24333

Call Sign: KI4NXA
Gail W Davis
133 Camp Zion Rd
Galax VA 24333

Call Sign: N4VL
Glenn J Diamond Jr
8233 Carrollton Pike
Galax VA 24333

Call Sign: N4DQZ
Sue C Diamond
8233 Carrollton Pk
Galax VA 24333

Call Sign: KI4SYS
Edward L Reavis
307 Chestnut Dr
Galax VA 24333

Call Sign: KF4GCU
Harold D Nelson
111 Circle Dr
Galax VA 24333

Call Sign: N4XWL
James L Swiney
139 Clover St
Galax VA 24333

Call Sign: KC4VKX
James R Poe
145 Clover St
Galax VA 24333

Call Sign: KA4GVA
Robert N Andrews
1879 Cold Springs Ln
Galax VA 24333

Call Sign: N4FRP
Ruth S Andrews
1879 Cold Springs Ln
Galax VA 24333

Call Sign: KF4PWW
Michael W Spence
179 Commonwealth Rd
Galax VA 24333

Call Sign: KI4TSR
Harvey B Forrest
556 Coon Ridge Ln
Galax VA 24333

Call Sign: KI4GCZ
Edward J Pasley
402 Country Club Ln
Galax VA 24333

Call Sign: W4AEG
Edward J Pasley
402 Country Club Ln
Galax VA 24333

Call Sign: N9ZBW
Edward J Pasley
Country Club Ln
Galax VA 24333

Call Sign: KA4VTK
Gene P Stoneman
Country Club Ln S
Galax VA 24333

Call Sign: KB5OMZ
Ronald B Higgins
1065 Cranberry Rd
Galax VA 24333

Call Sign: AJ4VU
Ronald B Higgins
1065 Cranberry Rd

Galax VA 24333

Call Sign: KI4NEU
Linda D Galyean
1681 Cross Rds Dr
Galax VA 24333

Call Sign: WA4ZIV
Ronald D Leagan
3849 Delhart Rd
Galax VA 24333

Call Sign: WA4ZCR
Jerry L Felty
5522 Delhart Rd
Galax VA 24333

Call Sign: KG4GZN
Samuel C Brumfield Jr
1090 Dickey Dr
Galax VA 24333

Call Sign: KI4JTP
Janet G Hill
325 Fox Run
Galax VA 243333343

Call Sign: WD4IVZ
Robert K Kirby
309 Fox Run Dr
Galax VA 24333

Call Sign: KI4OMS
Roger J Billings
406 Fries Rd
Galax VA 24333

Call Sign: WD4CQB
Linda L Leonard
819 Fries Rd
Galax VA 24333

Call Sign: AE4DX
Jamie D Ayers
2825 Fries Rd
Galax VA 24333

Call Sign: KE4EVX
Christi G Ayers

2825 Fries Rd
Galax VA 24333

Call Sign: KI4OMY
Kenneth W Carico
1101 Gambetta Rd
Galax VA 24333

Call Sign: NW4N
Thomas M Lineberry
102 Highland St
Galax VA 24333

Call Sign: AE4HK
Patricia A Hill
1189 Iron Ridge Rd
Galax VA 24333

Call Sign: KI4KTR
Carl G Hill
1189 Iron Ridge Rd
Galax VA 24333

Call Sign: KB4EXG
Ida M Shaw
370 Kenbrook Dr
Galax VA 24333

Call Sign: KE4LI
William F Shaw
370 Kenbrook Dr
Galax VA 24333

Call Sign: KE4UML
Bobby R Choate
108 King Arthur Ct
Galax VA 24333

Call Sign: N4DOE
Ann T Austin
285 Knoll Ridge Ln
Galax VA 24333

Call Sign: WW4B
William R Austin
285 Knoll Ridge Ln
Galax VA 24333

Call Sign: KF4BWR

Jamie L Blythe
202 Locust St
Galax VA 24333

Call Sign: KG4GJN
Judith C Blythe
202 Locust St
Galax VA 24333

Call Sign: KC4VPP
Linwood B Lawrence
971 Longview Ln
Galax VA 24333

Call Sign: K4UTJ
Thomas S Whittle Jr
425 Meadow Creek Rd
Galax VA 24333

Call Sign: AD4QY
Leonard C Wright
6480 Meadow Creek Rd
Galax VA 24333

Call Sign: N1TW
Thomas H West
59 Melrose Ln
Galax VA 24333

Call Sign: KI4BMV
Sarah V Sizemore
500 Mischief Valley Rd
Galax VA 24333

Call Sign: K4TOG
Richard T Mayer
187 Northwoods Ln
Galax VA 243333195

Call Sign: KI4NFP
James C Christman
452 Nuckolls Curve Rd
Galax VA 24333

Call Sign: KG4NBU
Philip M Hash
650 Nuckolls Curve Rd
Galax VA 24333

Call Sign: KI4NET
Katie H Walls
3416 Old Baywood Rd
Galax VA 24333

Call Sign: KF4GUQ
Wayne A Dalton
111 Painter St Apt 3
Galax VA 24333

Call Sign: KI4JTS
David W Fowler
82 Paradise Ln
Galax VA 24333

Call Sign: KI4JTU
Joshua D Fowler
82 Paradise Ln
Galax VA 24333

Call Sign: W2RCJ
Robert C Johnson
206A Partridge St
Galax VA 24333

Call Sign: K4LLC
Larry L Cornett
117 Pine Knoll Dr
Galax VA 24333

Call Sign: KF4ZIH
Lois L Cornett
117 Pine Knoll Dr
Galax VA 24333

Call Sign: K4TLL
Thomas L Lineberry
3379 Pipers Gap Rd
Galax VA 24333

Call Sign: KE4QAB
Rodney W Hall
3937 Pipers Gap Rd
Galax VA 24333

Call Sign: KJ4NFP
Robert J Campbell Jr
5616 Pipers Gap Rd
Galax VA 24333

Call Sign: KI4KTS
Brian K Paschall
8075 Pipers Gap Rd
Galax VA 24333

Call Sign: KF4YNT
Steven E Semones
2019 Poplar Knob Rd
Galax VA 24333

Call Sign: KG4FLA
Craig W Patton
250 Rippey Hollow Rd
Galax VA 24333

Call Sign: KA4JIL
Wanda G Spurlin
664 Riverhill Rd
Galax VA 24333

Call Sign: KB4ZC
Ronald D Spurlin
664 Riverhill Rd
Galax VA 24333

Call Sign: N4XLJ
William O Bray
114 Robinhood Rd
Galax VA 24333

Call Sign: KI4TST
Leshanna C Patton
538 Rolling Wood Ln
Galax VA 24333

Call Sign: KG4VNI
Herbert L Hash
34 Running Horse Rd
Galax VA 24333

Call Sign: KE4PEV
Steven F Galyean
1241 S Main St
Galax VA 24333

Call Sign: KI4NES
Beth G Robinson
675 Savannah Rd

Galax VA 24333

Call Sign: KI4ONA
James W Larue
1411 Skyline Hwy
Galax VA 24333

Call Sign: KE4QHM
Charles W Meadows Jr
112 Spring St
Galax VA 24333

Call Sign: KE4LGP
Charles W Meadows
118 Spring St
Galax VA 24333

Call Sign: KG4DJT
Ronald P Harmon
127 Stonebrook Dr
Galax VA 24333

Call Sign: WW4EE
Claude E Evans
209 Swanson St
Galax VA 24333

Call Sign: N8PNC
Roger L Combs
207 Terrace Ln
Galax VA 24333

Call Sign: N4TC
Stephen M Collins
296 Timberline Dr
Galax VA 24333

Call Sign: KI4JTT
David R Jones
383 Timberline Dr
Galax VA 24333

Call Sign: KI4JTK
Karina D Jones
383 Timberline Dr
Galax VA 24333

Call Sign: KI4BAX
Zachary J Phipps

41 Trudy Ln
Galax VA 24333

Call Sign: WA4ZIN
Nathan E Smith
509 W Center St
Galax VA 24333

Call Sign: KI4ONF
Charles L Reeves
807 W Stuart Dr
Galax VA 24333

Call Sign: KA4GUY
Dan H Rector
1010 W Stuart Dr
Galax VA 24333

Call Sign: KE4HKS
Anthony P Davis
300 W Washington St
Galax VA 24333

Call Sign: KF4TBH
Matt C Wood
115 Wild Flower Ln
Galax VA 24333

Call Sign: W8CYT
James C Wood
115 Wild Flower Ln
Galax VA 24333

Call Sign: KG4VLJ
James A Haga Jr
284 Winterberry Rd
Galax VA 24333

Call Sign: AJ4HD
James A Haga Jr
284 Winterberry Rd
Galax VA 24333

Call Sign: AJ4JH
James A Haga Jr
284 Winterberry Rd
Galax VA 24333

Call Sign: KA4HAN

Gay D Wright
Galax VA 24333

Call Sign: KF4LKI
Cathy A Rogers
Galax VA 24333

Call Sign: WD4P
James A Litz
Galax VA 24333

Call Sign: KI4JTL
Vernon S Bedwell
Galax VA 24333

Call Sign: K3SPC
Joseph J Snyder
Galax VA 243331371

FCC Amateur Radio Licenses in Gamaca

Call Sign: KK4AIN
Aaron W Abbott
23032 Union Show Ln
Gamaca VA 23032

FCC Amateur Radio Licenses in Garrisonville

Call Sign: KE4MDK
Larry Brunson
Garrisonville VA 22463

Call Sign: KG4GYY
Kenneth T Franks
Garrisonville VA 22463

Call Sign: AA4PB
Robert W Lewis
Garrisonville VA 224630522

FCC Amateur Radio Licenses in Gate City

Call Sign: KG4PIC
Aaron M Hammond
121 Adams Cemetery Ln
Gate City VA 24251

Call Sign: KG4SUZ
Roy L Hammond
121 Adams Cemetery Ln
Gate City VA 24251

Call Sign: KJ4UHB
Andrew T Shearin
677 Apple Orchard Rd
Gate City VA 24251

Call Sign: K4UOE
Danny I Ward
900 Apple Orchard Rd
Gate City VA 24251

Call Sign: K4LKP
John T Gillenwater
184 Bluebird Ln
Gate City VA 24251

Call Sign: N4RPT
Anthony R Smith
137 Bobwhite Dr
Gate City VA 242512644

Call Sign: KE4QCE
Charlotte K Cleek
Rt 2 Box 148
Gate City VA 24251

Call Sign: KE4QCF
Gary W Cleek
Rt 2 Box 148
Gate City VA 24251

Call Sign: KA4KLL
Jack R Johnson
Rr 7 Box 1590
Gate City VA 24251

Call Sign: KF4KLN
Linda S Johnson
Rt 7 Box 1590
Gate City VA 24251

Call Sign: KF4WLG
William T Lawson
Rt 3 Box 196A

Gate City VA 24251

Call Sign: KI4AAO
Glen C Poore
Rt 1 Box 264A
Gate City VA 24251

Call Sign: KI4LWW
Gerald D Griffin
Rt 3 Box 287 X
Gate City VA 24251

Call Sign: KI4LWV
Sherry N Griffin
Rt 3 Box 287 X
Gate City VA 24251

Call Sign: KI4LIR
James A Fansler
Rt 3 Box 288A
Gate City VA 24251

Call Sign: KI4DWB
James D Fansler
Rt 3 Box 288A
Gate City VA 24251

Call Sign: KC4YQY
Jerry L Burke
Rt 3 Box 316
Gate City VA 24251

Call Sign: KG4MXO
Andrew T Tate
Rt 3 Box 318H
Gate City VA 24251

Call Sign: KG4MXN
Harold G Tate
Rt3 Box 318H
Gate City VA 24251

Call Sign: KE4PQR
Terry L Wolfe
Rt 6 Box 322
Gate City VA 24251

Call Sign: KG4MXQ
Randy D Bise

Rt 1 Box 341
Gate City VA 24251

Call Sign: KD4YVZ
Anthony H Robinson
Rt 4 Box 358A
Gate City VA 24251

Call Sign: KF4YJG
Vanessa L Wininger
Rt 3 Box 408 E
Gate City VA 24251

Call Sign: KG4WCK
Kenneth W Wininger Jr
Rt 3 Box 408E
Gate City VA 24251

Call Sign: KI4LQV
John T Gillenwater
Rr 7 Box 4175
Gate City VA 24251

Call Sign: KF4EIN
Kimberly R Henderson
Rt 3 Box 468
Gate City VA 24251

Call Sign: KF4TKE
Matthew C Mc Clellan
Rt 3 Box 470
Gate City VA 24251

Call Sign: KF4EIM
Kenneth W Wininger Sr
Rr 3 Box 480
Gate City VA 24251

Call Sign: KD4NPH
Ronnie G Dingus Jr
Rt 1 Box 492
Gate City VA 24251

Call Sign: KI4AAP
Ivan K Moore
Rt 3 Box 522
Gate City VA 24251

Call Sign: KI4AAQ

Nancy J Moore
Rt 3 Box 522
Gate City VA 24251

Call Sign: KF4HAF
Joe E Quillian
Rr 2 Box 60 F
Gate City VA 24251

Call Sign: KF4JVL
Christy D Quillian
Rr 2 Box 60 F
Gate City VA 24251

Call Sign: KD4NGJ
Otis P Pierson
Rt 6 Box 675
Gate City VA 24251

Call Sign: KN4PA
Vernon Cook
4706 Bristol Hwy
Gate City VA 24251

Call Sign: W4CSN
Christopher S Newton
1764 Bristol Hwy
Gate City VA 24251

Call Sign: KF4VTM
Scott County ARS
196 Compton Hollow Lake
Gate City VA 24251

Call Sign: K4GV
Jimmy L Flanary
196 Compton Hollow Ln
Gate City VA 24251

Call Sign: KD4IES
Billie J Flanary
196 Compton Hollow Ln
Gate City VA 24251

Call Sign: K4CNK
Arthur L Verthein
605 Cypress St
Gate City VA 24251

Call Sign: KG4IKI
Christopher T Starnes
1640 Daniel Boone Rd
Gate City VA 24251

Call Sign: KE4WGU
James E Stallard
410 Ernie Dr
Gate City VA 24251

Call Sign: KG4EIS
Christopher S Gillenwater
1130 Hales Spring Rd
Gate City VA 24251

Call Sign: KG4KMP
Vickie D Gillenwater
1130 Hales Spring Rd
Gate City VA 24251

Call Sign: N4FYS
Dannie L Elliott
186 Henderson Ln
Gate City VA 24251

Call Sign: KI4RVM
Bryan W Shelton
3078 Little Valley Rd
Gate City VA 24251

Call Sign: KD4HIM
William K Pierson II
326 Marble Point Cir
Gate City VA 24251

Call Sign: KD4HIZ
Katheryn S Pierson
326 Marble Point Cir
Gate City VA 24251

Call Sign: KG4LWL
Donnie L Tate
185 Memory Ln Dr
Gate City VA 24251

Call Sign: KG4LWN
Terry A Bise
176 Military Ln
Gate City VA 24251

Call Sign: KJ4HKI
Stephen G Stanley
213 Military Ln
Gate City VA 24251

Call Sign: W4TRC
Kingsport ARC
213 Military Ln
Gate City VA 242512875

Call Sign: WA4KIP
David L Turner
345 Misty Morning Cir
Gate City VA 242514322

Call Sign: W4AAI
Claude R Keith
369 Mtn View School Ln
Gate City VA 24251

Call Sign: KC4MAW
Dana M Mann Ms
2756 Nickelsville Hwy
Gate City VA 24251

Call Sign: KF4BGW
Stephen J Stewart
220 Parker Estates Rd
Gate City VA 24251

Call Sign: WB4REK
Robert L Riner
365 Slabtown Cir
Gate City VA 24251

Call Sign: KF4UJA
Jerry Hensley
2027 Snowflake Rd
Gate City VA 24251

Call Sign: K4VDH
Jerry Hensley
2027 Snowflake Rd
Gate City VA 24251

Call Sign: KG4IRY
Frederick M Miller III
424 Solon St N

Gate City VA 24251

Call Sign: KI4BBN
James P Henderson
117 Spring Dr
Gate City VA 24251

Call Sign: KC4YRA
Michael B Reed
130 Starnes St
Gate City VA 24251

Call Sign: KD4BND
Franklin E Glover
230 Tennessee Dr
Gate City VA 24251

Call Sign: KG4FBE
Keith E Depew Jr
188 Tucker
Gate City VA 24251

Call Sign: KO4PZ
David D Minnich
115 Tucker St
Gate City VA 24251

Call Sign: KG4EZJ
Ronnie L Jones
4735 Upper Possum Creek Rd
Gate City VA 24251

Call Sign: KG4BRS
Nannie M Wininger
4935 Upper Possum Creek Rd
Gate City VA 24251

Call Sign: KD4NZR
Jeffrey D Henderson
6521 Upper Possum Creek Rd
Gate City VA 24251

Call Sign: KJ4ZYX
Thomas D Fields II
7042 Upper Possum Creek Rd
Gate City VA 24251

Call Sign: KI4KGU
James R Peters

422 Westhighland St
Gate City VA 24251

Call Sign: KG4LWM
Daniel L Tate
5182 Yuma Rd
Gate City VA 24251

Call Sign: KD4QKS
James B Blevins
Gate City VA 24251

Call Sign: W4UIR
William E Wing
Gate City VA 24251

Call Sign: WB4CDS
Hargis Flanary
Gate City VA 24251

Call Sign: AF4GU
Walt M Sickmen
Gate City VA 24251

Call Sign: KE4DNU
Kenneth R Hickam
Gate City VA 24251

Call Sign: KG4CYU
James M Cole
Gate City VA 24251

Call Sign: N4ROA
William D Wolfe
Gate City VA 24251

Call Sign: N4WWB
Robert G Parsons
Gate City VA 24251

Call Sign: WD4GTA
James V Craft
Gate City VA 24251

Call Sign: KJ4SLE
Morris W Person
Gate City VA 24251

Call Sign: KD4UCV

Kermit M Swan III
Gate City VA 24251

Call Sign: KA4TUR
Micheal L Brickey Jr
Gate City VA 24251

FCC Amateur Radio Licenses in Glade Hill

Call Sign: KF4OKG
Shilynn A Brooks
212 Ocala Rd
Glade Hill VA 24092

Call Sign: WM3T
Glen A Brooks
212 Ocala Rd
Glade Hill VA 24092

Call Sign: KF4ZBW
Philip R Smith
930 Old Carriage Rd
Glade Hill VA 24092

Call Sign: KD4RRL
James T Riddle
1733 Webster Rd
Glade Hill VA 24092

Call Sign: KE4FAP
Mary P Riddle
1733 Webster Rd
Glade Hill VA 24092

FCC Amateur Radio Licenses in Glade Spring

Call Sign: KM4TJ
Charles T Maiden
Rt 2 Box 524
Glade Spring VA 24340

Call Sign: KO4ZV
Arthur D Strange
7364 Buchanan Rd
Glade Spring VA 24340

Call Sign: KI4ZDU

Carolyn L Strange
7364 Buchanan Rd
Glade Spring VA 24340

Call Sign: N4KSO
Edward L Dingler III
403 Cherry St
Glade Spring VA 24340

Call Sign: KG4SZO
Michael A Doane
31283 Lee Hwy
Glade Spring VA 24340

Call Sign: KC4HEH
Chris M Nickels
36012 Loves Mill Rd
Glade Spring VA 24340

Call Sign: KI4SZB
David R Fields
12246 Minor Ln
Glade Spring VA 24340

Call Sign: KI4OSK
Debbie K Fields
31208 Old Stage Rd
Glade Spring VA 24340

Call Sign: K4DKF
Debbie K Fields
31208 Old Stage Rd
Glade Spring VA 24340

Call Sign: KI4MTF
Rowland B Fields Jr
31208 Old Stage Rd
Glade Spring VA 24340

Call Sign: K4RBF
Rowland B Fields Jr
31208 Old Stage Rd
Glade Spring VA 24340

Call Sign: N5SMB
James L Johnson
335 Peachtree St
Glade Spring VA 24340

Call Sign: KG4EPL
Jo A Debusk
15537 Prices Bridge Rd
Glade Spring VA 24340

Call Sign: KI4AMD
Michael R Debusk
15537 Prices Bridge Rd
Glade Spring VA 24340

Call Sign: KC4WSS
Josephine S Ridgway
Ridgvue Farm
Glade Spring VA 24340

Call Sign: N4LSK
Walter W Ridgway
Ridgvue Farms
Glade Spring VA 24340

Call Sign: N4NCE
James A Snapp
36513 Snapp Siding Ln
Glade Spring VA 243404749

Call Sign: N4ODB
Karen J Snapp
36513 Snapp Siding Ln
Glade Spring VA 243404749

Call Sign: WB6JZZ
Timothy G Sexton
34150 Stagecoach Rd
Glade Spring VA 243405160

Call Sign: KF4WTG
John S Casey
116 Walnut St
Glade Spring VA 24340

Call Sign: N4QJK
James W Walton
Glade Spring VA 24340

FCC Amateur Radio Licenses in Gladstone

Call Sign: KE4JYT
Jerel Matthews

Rt 2 Box 105E
Gladstone VA 24553

Call Sign: KD4YFH
Robert L Mulder
Rt 2 Box 149
Gladstone VA 24553

Call Sign: KI4UTI
William S Grimes
9943 Oakville Rd
Gladstone VA 24553

Call Sign: KG4HQJ
Christopher A Phelps
10118 Oakville Rd
Gladstone VA 24553

Call Sign: KE4DVT
Robert M Wilkes
Rt 2
Gladstone VA 24553

Call Sign: W4RKR
Robert K Reed Jr
631 Union School Dr
Gladstone VA 24553

FCC Amateur Radio Licenses in Gladys

Call Sign: KE4SWR
Darrell L St John
Rt 1 Box 160
Gladys VA 24554

Call Sign: KD4YFJ
Scott C Gunn
Rt 2 Box 223H
Gladys VA 24554

Call Sign: KC4DFW
Sheila M Tuck
Rt 1 Box 237D
Gladys VA 24554

Call Sign: N4SJM
Jerry D Irby
Rt 1 Box 237D

Gladys VA 24554

Call Sign: KF4FYM
Darryl Foreman
Rt 2 Box 366 A
Gladys VA 24554

Call Sign: N4SCI
Richard M Disher
Rt 2 Box 5
Gladys VA 24554

Call Sign: KG4POX
Anthony A Dunkley
2878 Long Island Rd
Gladys VA 24554

Call Sign: KJ4IGC
Jonathan W Crawford
5193 Marrysville Rd
Gladys VA 24554

Call Sign: KJ4IGB
James L Crawford Jr
5193 Marysville Rd
Gladys VA 24554

Call Sign: W3WJS
William J Stiffler Jr
1230 Mitchell Mill Rd
Gladys VA 24554

Call Sign: WA4UML
Norvell E Godsie
1131 Tabor Rd
Gladys VA 24554

Call Sign: KC4SWT
Vernon B Wallace Jr
168 William Campbell Dr
Gladys VA 24554

Call Sign: N4TIU
Charles P Carter Jr
458 Winfall Rd
Gladys VA 24554

Call Sign: KE4RPM
Steve R Irby

Gladys VA 24554

Call Sign: N4MJZ
Kurt W Riegel
Rt 1 Box 225A
Glasgow VA 24555

Call Sign: KK4IEL
Robert Cash
1843 Pineview Dr
Glasgow VA 24555

Call Sign: KG4KCO
Austin A Hemmings
345 Serenity Dr
Glasgow VA 24555

Call Sign: N4WVE
Gregory C Hemmings
500 Serenity Dr
Glasgow VA 24555

Call Sign: KI4ZBP
Michelle F Johnson
11489 Abbots Cross Ln
Glen Allen VA 23059

Call Sign: W4VDF
Michelle F Johnson
11489 Abbots Cross Ln
Glen Allen VA 23059

Call Sign: KI4YTU
Julie C Wine
9912 Alf Ct
Glen Allen VA 23060

Call Sign: KK4GDA
Robert L Fox Jr
10429 Attems Way
Glen Allen VA 23060

Call Sign: N4OLK

Donald L Sykes
5340 Axe Handle Ln
Glen Allen VA 23060

Call Sign: KI4FDF
Sejo Sudic
9322 Becton Rd
Glen Allen VA 23060

Call Sign: KJ4ZLG
Santhosh S R
5009 Belair Pl
Glen Allen VA 23059

Call Sign: KG4BEN
Sean T Blosser
1405 Berrymeade Hills Ct
Glen Allen VA 23060

Call Sign: KJ4CJK
F E Jens II
3500 Bohannon Dr
Glen Allen VA 23060

Call Sign: W4AAO
F E Jens II
3500 Bohannon Dr
Glen Allen VA 23060

Call Sign: WA3ZDN
Howard A Bohm
9207 Broad Meadows Rd
Glen Allen VA 23060

Call Sign: KG4FPN
Stephen S Meredith
3112 Brookemoor Ct
Glen Allen VA 23060

Call Sign: W4PPY
Arthur M Atchison
9812 Brookemoor Pl
Glen Allen VA 23060

Call Sign: KK4BHO
Clifford Middlebrook Jr
4715 Candlelight Pl
Glen Allen VA 23060

Call Sign: KA2DOV
Richard A Morrisey
5905 Carrington Green Ct
Glen Allen VA 23060

Call Sign: N3BVB
Bob Pectelidis
11417 Caruthers Way
Glen Allen VA 23059

Call Sign: KJ4SDC
Michael C Waters
5016 Castle Point Ct
Glen Allen VA 23060

Call Sign: W8UDB
Robert F Koch
9112 Castle Point Dr
Glen Allen VA 23060

Call Sign: KI4KIJ
Michael D Presley
11177 Cauthorne Rd
Glen Allen VA 23059

Call Sign: KB4JJP
Steven M Atkins
11200 Cedar Post Pl
Glen Allen VA 23060

Call Sign: N4SOU
Charles W Miller Jr
2700 Cemetery Rd
Glen Allen VA 23060

Call Sign: KA2RSX
Patricia L Schmitz
6005 Chestnut Hill Dr
Glen Allen VA 23059

Call Sign: KD4IAY
Ryan M Mitchell
10100 Christiano Dr
Glen Allen VA 23060

Call Sign: KO4XB
James W Mitchell Jr
10100 Christiano Dr
Glen Allen VA 23060

Call Sign: KF4ZSG
Timothy R Swingle Sr
11268 Cobbs Rd
Glen Allen VA 23059

Call Sign: N4DGB
Douglas L Harvey
9312 Coleson Rd
Glen Allen VA 23060

Call Sign: KI4NAK
David W Hawkins
11415 Colfax Rd
Glen Allen VA 23059

Call Sign: WB4DKE
Owen W Hawkins Jr
11415 Colfax Rd
Glen Allen VA 230591008

Call Sign: KI4ITV
Charles A Pollard III
9717 Country Way Rd
Glen Allen VA 23060

Call Sign: KI4VGG
VA Southbears
Sbc Of Virginia 4101 Cox Rd
Ste 100
Glen Allen VA 23060

Call Sign: N4IGU
Thomas M Witt
9354 Crystal Brook Ter
Glen Allen VA 230606349

Call Sign: N4OQI
Terry D Crabb
10213 Delray Rd
Glen Allen VA 23060

Call Sign: AK4PE
Terry D Crabb
10213 Delray Rd
Glen Allen VA 23060

Call Sign: KB2MLF
Jason Caravaglia

5853 Dorton Ln
Glen Allen VA 23060

Call Sign: KE4JXG
Lucy M Moses
5003 Eddings Dr
Glen Allen VA 23060

Call Sign: KJ4NPQ
David P Hines
2853 Fairway Homes Way
Glen Allen VA 23059

Call Sign: K4HIN
David P Hines
2853 Fairway Homes Way
Glen Allen VA 23059

Call Sign: K2WYP
Ronald G Long
2865 Fairway Homes Way
Glen Allen VA 23059

Call Sign: N4MYK
Ronald W Thomas
4620 Fort Mc Henry Pky
Glen Allen VA 23060

Call Sign: KI4GCW
Philip N Theurer
4713 Ft Mchenry Pkwy
Glen Allen VA 23060

Call Sign: KF7RMM
Andrew M Winsor
4810 Garden Spring Ln 303
Glen Allen VA 23059

Call Sign: KE4UDP
Stuart B Longest
14152 Gordons Ln
Glen Allen VA 23059

Call Sign: KF6TDA
William J Tumulty
12212 Greenwich Dr
Glen Allen VA 23060

Call Sign: KG4W

Edwin J Hughes
3175 Greenwood Ct
Glen Allen VA 23060

Call Sign: W4FEG
VA ARA Inc
3175 Greenwood Ct
Glen Allen VA 23060

Call Sign: WD4HLA
Fred A Ochs
10710 Greenwood Rd
Glen Allen VA 23060

Call Sign: KD4HFH
William A Baughan Jr
711 Harmony Rd
Glen Allen VA 23060

Call Sign: KD4QCD
Alan S Winfield
4211 Harwin Pl 306
Glen Allen VA 23060

Call Sign: K1YOR
William H Roy
3809 Haylors Beach Way
Glen Allen VA 23060

Call Sign: KE4ZNP
Darrell W Basinger
10103 Heritage Ln
Glen Allen VA 23060

Call Sign: WW4F
Darrell W Basinger
10103 Heritage Ln
Glen Allen VA 23060

Call Sign: KN4XJ
Frank J Humphreys II
10110 Heritage Ln
Glen Allen VA 23060

Call Sign: KI4JQV
Thomas J Banholzer
10232 Heritage Ln
Glen Allen VA 23060

Call Sign: N4RZO
Warren B Bell Sr
2208 High Bush Cir
Glen Allen VA 23060

Call Sign: KI4ZZH
Daniel P Vorster
5521 Holman Dr
Glen Allen VA 23059

Call Sign: NI4T
Daniel P Vorster
5521 Holman Dr
Glen Allen VA 23059

Call Sign: WB4UET
William A Haase
9311 Howze Rd
Glen Allen VA 23060

Call Sign: KC9MAM
Meng Yu
12044 Ivy Hollow Ct
Glen Allen VA 23059

Call Sign: KC9MHH
Wanyu Zang
12044 Ivy Hollow Ct
Glen Allen VA 23059

Call Sign: KJ4JPX
Cheryl A Hackett
5312 Jacobs Creek Dr
Glen Allen VA 23060

Call Sign: N4LFU
David E White
2724 Jon Page Ct
Glen Allen VA 230604474

Call Sign: W4AHC
Melvin L Ford Jr
3001 Kellipe Rd
Glen Allen VA 230594752

Call Sign: KO3Q
James S Carroll
9006 Kellywood Ct
Glen Allen VA 23060

Call Sign: W3QY
James S Carroll
9006 Kellywood Ct
Glen Allen VA 23060

Call Sign: N4ZLM
Christine K F Gyurik
1936 Kings Rd
Glen Allen VA 23059

Call Sign: N4EZQ
Willard M Perkins Jr
10550 Lambeth Rd
Glen Allen VA 23060

Call Sign: K4QLL
William W Martin
10809 Leabrook Dr
Glen Allen VA 23060

Call Sign: KC4WOW
William D Smith
1418 Lee Ave
Glen Allen VA 23060

Call Sign: KF4EFX
David W Hartley
11432 Long Meadow Dr
Glen Allen VA 230595101

Call Sign: KO4JY
Kevin S Mahler
9904 Mistyview Ct
Glen Allen VA 23060

Call Sign: W4RWE
Roy W Efford
2925 Mtn Rd
Glen Allen VA 23060

Call Sign: KK4AIK
Patrick G Foster
13080 Mtn Rd
Glen Allen VA 23059

Call Sign: WA4EZA
Arthur D Blake
4710 N Lakefront Dr

Glen Allen VA 23060

Call Sign: KB4JEB
Donna L Duke
11451 New Farrington Ct
Glen Allen VA 230591629

Call Sign: WG4O
James H Duke Jr
11451 New Farrington Ct
Glen Allen VA 230591629

Call Sign: K2RMM
Jens Christian Mueller
12300 Nuthatch Ct
Glen Allen VA 230597123

Call Sign: WB4UJS
Walter H Conoly III
5129 Old Forester Ln
Glen Allen VA 23060

Call Sign: KD4ZDQ
Joshua C Cease
2809 Olde Belo Ct
Glen Allen VA 23060

Call Sign: N4DDL
Thomas C Foster
13135 Overhill Dr
Glen Allen VA 23059

Call Sign: K8YFM
Drew W Koontz
1316 Pennsylvania Ave
Glen Allen VA 23060

Call Sign: KF4UJU
Joseph J Alexis
1415 Pennsylvania Ave
Glen Allen VA 23060

Call Sign: KD4HBT
Richard A Repp
3504 Poquoson Ct
Glen Allen VA 230607245

Call Sign: KC4PKK
Evelyn C Osterloh

10920 Rickey Ct
Glen Allen VA 23060

Call Sign: N4ICT
Robert E Osterloh
10920 Rickey Ct
Glen Allen VA 23060

Call Sign: KC4AUG
James A Holbrook
11217 Rocky Ridge Rd
Glen Allen VA 23059

Call Sign: K4DET
David E Tiller
11236 Rocky Ridge Rd
Glen Allen VA 23059

Call Sign: KJ4SDB
Robert S Amos
4733 Rollingwood Ln
Glen Allen VA 23060

Call Sign: KB3PH
Harry Deutsch
4928 Sadler Glen Ct
Glen Allen VA 23060

Call Sign: KC4YVL
Ronald L Miller
9512 Sara Beth Cir
Glen Allen VA 23060

Call Sign: KJ4QZC
John T Matsumoto
11012 Scattered Flock Ct
Glen Allen VA 23059

Call Sign: KA4PTP
Kimberly A Chase
5243 Shady Grove Rd
Glen Allen VA 23059

Call Sign: KB4INE
Gail L Sublett
5243 Shady Grove Rd
Glen Allen VA 23059

Call Sign: KD4IT

Margaret E Chase
5243 Shady Grove Rd
Glen Allen VA 23059

Call Sign: KC4ZUJ
William P Partenheimer IV
11912 Shady Willow Ter
Glen Allen VA 23059

Call Sign: KD4EEB
Keith A Nichols
4654 Snow Goose Ln
Glen Allen VA 23060

Call Sign: W4EEB
Keith A Nichols
4654 Snow Goose Ln
Glen Allen VA 23060

Call Sign: KI4IZU
George W Chabalewski
4532 Spring Moss Cir
Glen Allen VA 23060

Call Sign: K4KIU
Matthew Harper
12028 Stonewick Pl
Glen Allen VA 23059

Call Sign: KE4OFN
Charles C Fishburne III
14178 Stuart Oaks Dr
Glen Allen VA 23059

Call Sign: KG4ZTF
Jeffrey S Conklin
12425 Summer Creek Ct
Glen Allen VA 23059

Call Sign: W2FFQ
Jeffrey S Conklin
12425 Summer Creek Ct
Glen Allen VA 23059

Call Sign: KI4NTK
Tracy R Barlow
10931 Tiller Rd
Glen Allen VA 23060

Call Sign: N4PCU
Jerry E Geil
3217 Trillium Pl
Glen Allen VA 23060

Call Sign: K4OAH
Garey K Barrell
10912 VA Forest Ct
Glen Allen VA 230606503

Call Sign: WA4HUJ
Joseph H Kuhns IV
4511 Village Run Dr
Glen Allen VA 23060

Call Sign: WD4HDN
Charles C Smith
10510 Warren Rd
Glen Allen VA 23060

Call Sign: KI4UIL
Wolfgang P Gebhardt
10033 Washington Blvd
Glen Allen VA 23059

Call Sign: K4WMA
William R Heltzel
5231 Willane Rd
Glen Allen VA 23059

Call Sign: KC4LGN
Ronald W Sprouse
11270 Winfrey Rd
Glen Allen VA 23059

Call Sign: KI4VYM
Lee A Horton
5420 Wintergreen Rd
Glen Allen VA 23060

Call Sign: WB4IXS
David L Cadora Sr
10215 Wolfe Manor Ct Unit
507
Glen Allen VA 23060

Call Sign: W4TWS
Mack T Ruffin III
11422 Wood Brook Rd

Glen Allen VA 23060

Call Sign: KD4RJQ
Monique R Enders
Glen Allen VA 23060

Call Sign: KE4GEH
Lois A Sax Barbour
Glen Allen VA 23060

Call Sign: N4VT
Roger P Dull
Glen Allen VA 23058

Call Sign: KV4FS
John G Skora
Glen Allen VA 23058

Call Sign: KV4GG
John G Skora
Glen Allen VA 23058

Call Sign: N4IXJ
Michael D Geipel
Glen Allen VA 23058

Call Sign: N9WMU
Joseph J Silvio
Glen Allen VA 23060

Call Sign: KG4LBH
Thomas A Pace
Glen Allen VA 23060

Call Sign: W4RMA
Richard M Anthony
Glen Allen VA 230582662

Call Sign: KF4RNF
Marm
Glen Allen VA 230586673

Call Sign: N0PSB
Walter G Green III
Glen Allen VA 230600799

**FCC Amateur Radio Licenses
in Glen Lyn**

Call Sign: KA4OCP
Jerry W Surber
Glen Lyn VA 24093

Call Sign: KG4FWH
Jerry W Surber
Glen Lyn VA 24093

**FCC Amateur Radio Licenses
in Gloucester**

Call Sign: KJ4VSH
Micah S Reffo
6864 Ark Rd
Gloucester VA 23061

Call Sign: KJ4VSI
Josiah C Reffo
6864 Ark Rd
Gloucester VA 23061

Call Sign: KB4OPR
Thomas C Mosca III
6977 Ark Rd
Gloucester VA 23061

Call Sign: N4MYO
Denise M Mosca
6977 Ark Rd
Gloucester VA 23061

Call Sign: W4ACD
Alfred C Drnec
5300 Beechwood Knoll Tr
Gloucester VA 230613712

Call Sign: N4BLQ
Edwen K Gause
6289 Belroi Rd
Gloucester VA 23061

Call Sign: KG4WCZ
Kara N Wertman
6543 Belroi Rd
Gloucester VA 23061

Call Sign: KC4BNN
Brenda L Almeida
Rt 1 Box 108

Gloucester VA 23061

Call Sign: KC4DYZ
Melanie M Head
Rt 1 Box 108
Gloucester VA 23061

Call Sign: KC4EQZ
Rebecca L Head
Rt 1 Box 108
Gloucester VA 23061

Call Sign: KF4GFS
Andrew R Stiltner
Rt 5 Box 1126
Gloucester VA 23061

Call Sign: KC4PXC
Rosser B West
Rt 2 Box 174 X2
Gloucester VA 23061

Call Sign: N4IUR
Donald L Austin
Rt 2 Box 267H
Gloucester VA 23061

Call Sign: KC4QIS
Kevin L Smith
Rt 1 Box 338
Gloucester VA 23061

Call Sign: WA4KSP
Jack E Pennington
Rt 5 Box 514
Gloucester VA 23061

Call Sign: N9XLM
Jason L Rentz
10132 Bumpy Rd
Gloucester VA 23061

Call Sign: KA9YOQ
John R Capin
3138 Cappahosic Rd
Gloucester VA 23061

Call Sign: N4QEX
John T Myles

7342 Cary Ave
Gloucester VA 23061

Call Sign: KD4EVA
Dale W Shankle
4642 Cedar Point Rd
Gloucester VA 23061

Call Sign: AJ4XX
Dale W Shankle
4642 Cedar Point Rd
Gloucester VA 23061

Call Sign: KM4VR
Eric I Forman
4513 Chestnut Fork Rd
Gloucester VA 230613940

Call Sign: KI4QAU
Roger A West
5323 Dogwood Forest Dr
Gloucester VA 23061

Call Sign: KI4JYR
Elisabeth M Drechsel
5676 Dogwood Forest Dr
Gloucester VA 23061

Call Sign: N7KZN
David C Roddy
12325 Dogwood Trl
Gloucester VA 23061

Call Sign: KA1FBC
Eileen D Razinha
9954 Figg Shop
Gloucester VA 23061

Call Sign: WA1TJR
Frank A Razinha
9954 Figg Shop Rd
Gloucester VA 23061

Call Sign: KJ4BTQ
Dreux A Elliott II
1697 Fletcher Rd
Gloucester VA 23061

Call Sign: K4ASI

William H Eacho Jr
4721 Fletcher Rd
Gloucester VA 23061

Call Sign: KK4GXM
Rachael R Zabel
5049 Fletcher Rd
Gloucester VA 23061

Call Sign: KJ4BTO
Larry R Mccready
6219 Fletcher Rd
Gloucester VA 23061

Call Sign: KE4PGT
Merlin D Martin
10004 Forest Grove Dr
Gloucester VA 23061

Call Sign: KF4KAC
Levi J Martin
10004 Forest Grove Dr
Gloucester VA 23061

Call Sign: KA7HWW
Richard E Miner
8263 Founders Mill Way
Gloucester VA 23061

Call Sign: KI4EIJ
Wesley D Jones
6850 Fox Mill Ct
Gloucester VA 23061

Call Sign: AI4FH
Wesley D Jones
6850 Fox Mill Ct
Gloucester VA 23061

Call Sign: KC0FHX
Jonathan D White
8246 Hamilton Dr
Gloucester VA 23061

Call Sign: KE4LUF
Elmerson G Deloso
4638 Hermitage Ln
Gloucester VA 23061

Call Sign: KF4AMG
Katherine S Deloso
4638 Hermitage Ln
Gloucester VA 23061

Call Sign: KF4HDK
Carolyn W Stiltner
2830 Hickory Fork Rd
Gloucester VA 23061

Call Sign: KF4IGX
Donald E Stiltner
2830 Hickory Fork Rd
Gloucester VA 23061

Call Sign: KJ4OQQ
Steven A White
3489 Hickory Fork Rd
Gloucester VA 230613935

Call Sign: KJ4CYD
Elizabeth R Safranek
4894 Hickory Fork Rd
Gloucester VA 23061

Call Sign: KK4AUS
Tyler J Safranek
4894 Hickory Fork Rd
Gloucester VA 23061

Call Sign: KF4WSN
James O Santore
5261 Hickory Fork Rd
Gloucester VA 23061

Call Sign: KG4BUC
Kimberly A Santore
5261 Hickory Fork Rd
Gloucester VA 23061

Call Sign: KG4SMU
James A Santore
5261 Hickory Fork Rd
Gloucester VA 23061

Call Sign: KG4ZCS
Joshua D Santore
5261 Hickory Fork Rd
Gloucester VA 23061

Call Sign: KJ4TYV
James W Conner
4618 Hill Trl
Gloucester VA 23061

Call Sign: KE4CXP
Richard B Stillman
6782 Hilltop Dr
Gloucester VA 23061

Call Sign: WB4OLE
John L Goldstone
6821 Honeycutt Ln
Gloucester VA 23061

Call Sign: KF4DTT
Charles W Riedell II
7302 Jefferson Ct
Gloucester VA 23061

Call Sign: W4CWR
Charles W Riedell II
7302 Jefferson Ct
Gloucester VA 23061

Call Sign: KF4ZET
Keri M Riedell
7302 Jefferson Ct
Gloucester VA 230615276

Call Sign: N1LO
Mark D Lowell
7322 Jefferson Ct
Gloucester VA 23061

Call Sign: KE4RIS
Richard C Vermillion
6745 Kimberly Dr
Gloucester VA 23061

Call Sign: KG4GYT
Phillip C Fenstermacher
5876 Ladysmeade Ln
Gloucester VA 23061

Call Sign: KG4HVZ
Douglas S Fenstermacher
5876 Ladysmeade Ln

Gloucester VA 23061

Call Sign: AG4GO
Douglas S Fenstermacher
5876 Ladysmeade Ln
Gloucester VA 23061

Call Sign: WD4GES
Solange M Gause
7797 Lonesome Dove Ln
Gloucester VA 23061

Call Sign: N1UYS
Daniel D Hitsman
7059 Lord Carrington
Gloucester VA 23061

Call Sign: KG4LZU
Joseph J Safranek
8778 Marlfield Rd
Gloucester VA 23061

Call Sign: KG4NSH
Joy M Safranek
8778 Marlfield Rd
Gloucester VA 23061

Call Sign: K4JJS
Joseph J Safranek
8778 Marlfield Rd
Gloucester VA 23061

Call Sign: W2JMS
Joy M Safranek
8778 Marlfield Rd
Gloucester VA 23061

Call Sign: WB4JPM
James E Sterling Jr
7657 Meredith Dr
Gloucester VA 23061

Call Sign: KK4AUU
Greta J Alto
9216 Moran Cir
Gloucester VA 23061

Call Sign: KK4AUT
Shelby L Alto

9216 Moran Cir
Gloucester VA 23061

Call Sign: KJ4TJU
Lee R Alto
9216 Moran Cir
Gloucester VA 230612814

Call Sign: AJ4ZU
Lee R Alto
9216 Moran Cir
Gloucester VA 230612814

Call Sign: KG4YEH
William W Fenstermacher
6710 Muggins Creek Rd
Gloucester VA 23061

Call Sign: KF4APK
Joe S Downes
6722 Muggins Creek Rd
Gloucester VA 23061

Call Sign: K2VIJ
James J Mc Neil
8880 Nelson Wood Ln
Gloucester VA 23061

Call Sign: KC5UDV
Martha E V Huie
5179 Pampa Rd
Gloucester VA 23061

Call Sign: KC5UDW
Mark A Huie
5179 Pampa Rd
Gloucester VA 23061

Call Sign: KG4GMY
Paul C Springe
8168 Pinetta Rd
Gloucester VA 23061

Call Sign: WA4YTL
Charles R Collier
8006 Pinetta Rd
Gloucester VA 23061

Call Sign: W4OUK

William B Brown
4337 Point Breeze Ln
Gloucester VA 230610327

Call Sign: KD4VPB
Mary S Walters
4823 Primrose Path
Gloucester VA 230613518

Call Sign: WA4QEY
Samuel C Snader
11999 Roane Ave
Gloucester VA 23061

Call Sign: W4ONE
Theodore J Zuk
12067 Roane Ave
Gloucester VA 23061

Call Sign: K4TED
Theodore P Liaros
7581 Roaring Springs Rd
Gloucester VA 23061

Call Sign: N4XND
James T Rogers
4810 Rosewell Dr
Gloucester VA 23061

Call Sign: KE4NBX
Earl E Evans Jr
4931 Rosewell Dr
Gloucester VA 23061

Call Sign: KE4QNX
Patricia S Evans
4931 Rosewell Dr
Gloucester VA 23061

Call Sign: KC4NUB
Melvin H Sawyer
9477 Running Horse Ln
Gloucester VA 23061

Call Sign: KJ4OQO
John V Ertel
8240 Sheffield Dr
Gloucester VA 23061

Call Sign: N3VDI
Edward C Engle
7601 Springfield Ct
Gloucester VA 23061

Call Sign: NB4P
Paul D Steiner
4326 Taliaferro Ln
Gloucester VA 23061

Call Sign: KD4GJC
William L Hankison Jr
6807 Village S Dr Apt 2
Gloucester VA 23061

Call Sign: KG4GDI
Tanya W Conley
7294 Wellford Ln
Gloucester VA 23061

Call Sign: KF4LCW
Melissa A Knuteson
7312 Wellford Ln
Gloucester VA 23061

Call Sign: KF4MID
Luanne C Knuteson
7312 Wellford Ln
Gloucester VA 23061

Call Sign: KU4BB
Dennis M Knuteson
7312 Wellford Ln
Gloucester VA 23061

Call Sign: AJ4CJ
Harold E Weissler II
7557 Windy Hill Rd
Gloucester VA 23061

Call Sign: KK4CET
Sandra N Unverferth
8261 Woodhaven Dr
Gloucester VA 23061

Call Sign: KJ4SCW
Jerome D Unverferth
8261 Woodhaven Dr
Gloucester VA 23061

Call Sign: K4SKD
Jerome D Unverferth
8261 Woodhaven Dr
Gloucester VA 23061

Call Sign: KE4BHM
William H Altemus Jr
Gloucester VA 23061

Call Sign: KC4DZA
Bradford B Allen
Gloucester VA 23061

Call Sign: KF4GFV
Felton S Graham
Gloucester VA 23061

Call Sign: N4MYY
George D Wells
Gloucester VA 230610599

FCC Amateur Radio Licenses in Gloucester Point

Call Sign: KC4DZC
Stephen S Heaney
Hc 1 Box 87Aa
Gloucester Point VA 23062

Call Sign: KC4GYQ
Elizabeth F Heaney
Hc1 Box 87Aa Rt 1202
Gloucester Point VA 23062

Call Sign: KC4PSQ
John B Falkinburg
1525 Lafayette Rd
Gloucester Point VA 23062

Call Sign: KA3TIX
W Michael Greaney Jr
1682 Laurel Dr
Gloucester Point VA 23062

Call Sign: KB4DWX
Edmund A Brummer III III
Rte 1235
Gloucester Point VA 23062

Call Sign: AC4BH
William F Mc Millan
7856 Terapin Cove Rd
Gloucester Point VA 23062

Call Sign: NT3G
Charles E Teclaw
7801 Terrapin Cove Rd
Gloucester Point VA 23062

Call Sign: KF4TNV
Carolyn G Teclaw
7801 Terrapin Cove Rd
Gloucester Point VA
230622117

Call Sign: KC4RYB
Carol S Mc Millan
7856 Terrapin Cove Rd
Gloucester Point VA 23062

Call Sign: KJ4BTS
Robert B Howe Jr
7662 Terrepin Cove Rd
Gloucester Point VA 23062

Call Sign: KF4DTU
Louis P Stark
7785 Tillage Estate Ln
Gloucester Point VA
230620628

Call Sign: N4JFY
Steven J Clukey
1562 Trouville Ct
Gloucester Point VA
230621318

Call Sign: KE4BHL
Ronald D Cagle
Gloucester Point VA 23062

Call Sign: KE4ENF
Kathleen A Cagle
Gloucester Point VA 23062

Call Sign: KI4GG
Robert A Reid

Gloucester Point VA 23062

Call Sign: N8VQ
Roger C Simmons
Gloucester Point VA 23062

Call Sign: WB8FIU
Milton W Wegener
Gloucester Point VA 23062

Call Sign: KB4BIB
James S Cumbee
Gloucester Point VA 23062

Call Sign: KB4BIC
Rosalie M Cumbee
Gloucester Point VA 23062

Call Sign: KB4MKE
Marlene S Brummer
Gloucester Point VA 23062

Call Sign: KF4APH
David L Wilson
Gloucester Point VA 23062

Call Sign: W4HZL
Middle Peninsula ARC
Gloucester Point VA 23062

Call Sign: WD4NYW
Milford S Holben Jr
Gloucester Point VA 23062

Call Sign: KK4CNF
David R Craft
Gloucester Point VA 23062

Call Sign: KI4JNV
Douglas W Lindsay
Gloucester Point VA 23062

Call Sign: N1SFR
Robert B Clemons
Gloucester Point VA
230621305

Call Sign: N1XBH
Sandra V Clemons

Gloucester Point VA
230621305

FCC Amateur Radio Licenses in Goade

Call Sign: KG4RJC
Glen A Styles
8672 Charlemont Rd
Goade VA 245562587

FCC Amateur Radio Licenses in Goldbond

Call Sign: KK4GSU
Shawn M Jack
129 Iron Spring Dr
Goldbond VA 24150

FCC Amateur Radio Licenses in Goldvein

Call Sign: KB4LUH
Melanie L Billingsley
13231 Blackwells Mill Rd
Goldvein VA 22720

Call Sign: KJ4GSW
Larry R Shannon
12615 Camden Dr
Goldvein VA 22720

Call Sign: KK4FXP
Michael I Randall
3315 Deepview Ct
Goldvein VA 22720

Call Sign: KI4FBC
James R Stevens
4062 Goldmine Rd
Goldvein VA 22720

FCC Amateur Radio Licenses in Goochland

Call Sign: KT4PH
John C Holtz
5254 Island Ct

Goochland VA 23063

Call Sign: KA2UGF
Charles T Huffman
2211 Jackson Shop Rd
Goochland VA 230633023

Call Sign: KK4BO
Clarence L Bryant
2167 Sandy Hook Rd
Goochland VA 23063

Call Sign: KG4NWO
Central VA Contest Club
5303 St Paul S Church Rd
Goochland VA 23063

Call Sign: W4ML
Central VA Contest Club
5303 St Paul S Church Rd
Goochland VA 23063

Call Sign: W4MYA
Robert S Morris
5303 St Pauls Church Rd
Goochland VA 23063

Call Sign: KF4QQY
Barry D Twigg
5311 St Pauls Church Rd
Goochland VA 23063

Call Sign: KI4TOQ
Bradley D Twigg
5311 St Pauls Church Rd
Goochland VA 23063

Call Sign: KF7NN
Laszlo G Vagner
5012 Tori Ln
Goochland VA 23063

Call Sign: KK4BHJ
Douglas R Shackelford
2605 Turner Rd
Goochland VA 23063

Call Sign: KC4PVQ
Shawn M Powers

Goochland VA 23063

Call Sign: KG4CSW
Cynthia L Duke
Goochland VA 23063

Call Sign: KG4FPM
Aaron M Duke
Goochland VA 23063

Call Sign: KG4MRT
Aaron M Duke
Goochland VA 23063

Call Sign: W4JST
Aaron M Duke
Goochland VA 23063

FCC Amateur Radio Licenses in Goode

Call Sign: KE4KEH
George C Kelly
1104 Ashton Ct
Goode VA 24556

Call Sign: KG4TDE
Ryszard Dedor
1243 Ashton Ct
Goode VA 24556

Call Sign: N2KDA
Anne Riely Popper
Rr 2 Box 45
Goode VA 24556

Call Sign: KD4AZY
Edwin D Bosiger Sr
6830 Charlemont Rd
Goode VA 24556

Call Sign: KC5LVF
Mack A Turner
1356 Colony Heights Rd
Goode VA 24556

Call Sign: KB2HBN
Arlette M Stanecker
106 E Otter Ridge Dr

Goode VA 24556

Call Sign: WA2OLP
Lawrence G Stanecker
106 E Otter Ridge Dr
Goode VA 24556

Call Sign: WB4QXE
Norvell W White Jr
133 E Otter Ridge Dr
Goode VA 24556

Call Sign: KZ4AK
Norvell W White Jr
133 E Otter Ridge Dr
Goode VA 24556

Call Sign: N4CH
Herman Cone III
305 Foxwood Dr
Goode VA 24556

Call Sign: N4RXL
Donna M Cone
305 Foxwood Dr
Goode VA 24556

Call Sign: KG4ACQ
Glenn C Shaeff
3010 Goode Rd
Goode VA 24556

Call Sign: K4ISY
James V Mitchell
3905 Goode Rd
Goode VA 24556

Call Sign: N1UGW
Jerald D Stratton
1300 Goode Station Rd
Goode VA 24556

Call Sign: N2DEJ
Serge Popper
1691 Happy Ours Ln P O Box 67
Goode VA 245560067

Call Sign: KA4YNO

Harold J De Vuyst
135 Hunting Ln
Goode VA 24556

Call Sign: KG4BAF
Christine De Vuyst
135 Hunting Ln
Goode VA 245561016

Call Sign: KA4TJK
Michael S Fulk
202 Hunting Ln
Goode VA 24556

Call Sign: W4PK
Samuel A Leslie
1038 Lone Pine Ter
Goode VA 245562545

Call Sign: KC4YF
John D Benson
205 Meadowhill Cir
Goode VA 24556

Call Sign: KK4LD
Dennis P Mc Faden
3400 Oslin Creek Rd
Goode VA 245569714

Call Sign: KJ4MHI
Kent B Munson
6195 Otterville Rd
Goode VA 24556

Call Sign: KK4GGP
Randall S Houck
1932 Prophet Rd
Goode VA 24556

Call Sign: KG4TCN
Jeff Bills
3403 Roaring Run Rd
Goode VA 24556

Call Sign: KG4TCP
Zachary W Bills
3403 Roaring Run Rd
Goode VA 24556

Call Sign: N4TEP
John E Harvey
2345 Roaring Run Rd
Goode VA 24556

Call Sign: N4UA
George S Dubovsky
1225 Telegraph Ln
Goode VA 24556

Call Sign: WA4FRH
Lawrence N Mc Kinney
1254 Telegraph Ln
Goode VA 24556

Call Sign: W4YV
Melvin G Brafford
125 Whitcomb Ln
Goode VA 24556

Call Sign: W4TEL
Hy Tower Dxers And Twisted
Pairs
125 Whitcomb Ln
Goode VA 245561024

Call Sign: AC4PD
Peaks Of Otter Dxers
125 Whitcomb Ln
Goode VA 245561024

Call Sign: NK4DX
Hy Tower Dxers And
Contesters
125 Whitcomb Ln
Goode VA 245561024

Call Sign: WK4CQ
New Bedford Contesters
125 Whitcomb Ln
Goode VA 245561024

Call Sign: KJ4IPU
Richard Jones
Goode VA 24556

Call Sign: K4WTX
Richard Jones
Goode VA 24556

Call Sign: KA4GFZ
Steven W Elmore
102 Bowles St
Goodview VA 240952204

Call Sign: KB4JKW
Michael B Ferguson
Rt 2 Box 249A
Goodview VA 24095

Call Sign: KD4QDR
Larry W Dodd
Rt 1 Box 359
Goodview VA 24095

Call Sign: KC4KMK
Thomas L Dillon Jr
1141 Dillons Draw Rd
Goodview VA 24095

Call Sign: KK4GBE
Ve David Brown
101 Dove Valley Dr
Goodview VA 24095

Call Sign: K4YD
James L Powell III
6878 Goodview Rd
Goodview VA 24095

Call Sign: KE4HES
Allen L Reed Jr
2831 Goodview Town Rd
Goodview VA 24095

Call Sign: KG4NIQ
Brian E Brindle Jr
304 Hemlock Shores Dr
Goodview VA 24095

Call Sign: N4VPO
Michael B Hall
401 Hemlock Shores Dr
Goodview VA 24095

Call Sign: KS4HK
James S Jones
106 Hensley Ct
Goodview VA 24095

Call Sign: N4NZ
Eugene B Barfield Sr
1276 Marigold Dr
Goodview VA 24095

Call Sign: KF4WBC
James S Pait Jr
1365 Mill Iron Rd
Goodview VA 24095

Call Sign: KJ4ZJY
Linda Steed
3071 Morgans Mill Rd
Goodview VA 24095

Call Sign: KE4DOI
Julie M Jones
1173 Navigation Point
Goodview VA 24095

Call Sign: NX1G
James S Jones
1173 Navigation Point
Goodview VA 24095

Call Sign: KI9M
Jimmie L O Neil
1269 Quail Dr
Goodview VA 240952849

Call Sign: KI4DMV
Benjamin V Ports
409 Ridgelake Rd
Goodview VA 24095

Call Sign: KI4EAQ
Patrick W Ports
409 Ridgelake Rd
Goodview VA 24095

Call Sign: W1ZQG
Merle C Dutton
1123 Roanoke Dr
Goodview VA 24095

Call Sign: AE4CJ
John H Carroll III
2534 Sandy Level Rd
Goodview VA 24095

Call Sign: KG4KDI
Leo D Cullen
1658 Trails End Rd
Goodview VA 24095

FCC Amateur Radio Licenses in Gordonsville

Call Sign: KA4GIY
Mark S Eubank Jr
Rt 2 Box 374
Gordonsville VA 22942

Call Sign: NH7FG
Donald R Danielson
42 Branch Ln
Gordonsville VA 22942

Call Sign: W4BAF
John W Winn
18276 Cameron Rd
Gordonsville VA 229428000

Call Sign: KJ4LM
Bryan P Lovetere
6079 Chestnut Ln
Gordonsville VA 22942

Call Sign: K4LTX
Bryan P Lovetere
6079 Chestnut Ln
Gordonsville VA 22942

Call Sign: KE4ULA
Ruth A Clowater
339 Columbia Rd
Gordonsville VA 22942

Call Sign: KB8KXT
Ballard L Jewell
12391 Cox Mill Rd
Gordonsville VA 22942

Call Sign: KC4TOS
Erno M Hanz
14325 Cox Mill Rd
Gordonsville VA 229428805

Call Sign: WB1FKV
James B Thurber
600 Gordon Ave
Gordonsville VA 22942

Call Sign: KC4ZZJ
Shane L Henning
1684 Hanback Rd
Gordonsville VA 22942

Call Sign: KO4LT
Patricia E Henning
1684 Hanback Rd
Gordonsville VA 22942

Call Sign: N8HUJ
Richard H Johnson
58 Meghans Ln
Gordonsville VA 22942

Call Sign: K4LCO
Richard H Johnson
58 Meghans Ln
Gordonsville VA 22942

Call Sign: AB4AK
Emmet C Hughes
6291 Old Barboursville Rd
Gordonsville VA 22942

Call Sign: KJ4TKG
Stefan D Tinsley
100 Orange Ave
Gordonsville VA 22942

Call Sign: K0STP
Stefan D Tinsley
100 Orange Ave
Gordonsville VA 22942

Call Sign: KK4CEQ
Douglas D Goode
642 Red Hill Rd
Gordonsville VA 22942

Call Sign: K2WK
Walter Kornienko
2930 Red Hill Rd
Gordonsville VA 229426110

Call Sign: KD4RYS
Kenneth E Turpin
Gordonsville VA 22942

Call Sign: KK4FJX
John A Klei
Gordonsville VA 22942

Call Sign: KI4CGH
Jack F Thompson Jr
Gordonsville VA 229420445

FCC Amateur Radio Licenses in Gore

Call Sign: KG4FGO
Willis A F Mcdowell
980 Cove Rd
Gore VA 22637

Call Sign: KD4CRE
Boy Scouts Of America-Camp
Rock Enon
292 Rock Enon Springs Rd
Gore VA 22637

FCC Amateur Radio Licenses in Goshen

Call Sign: KJ4KWE
Robert E Walker Jr
1888 Big River Rd
Goshen VA 24439

FCC Amateur Radio Licenses in Gouchland

Call Sign: KI4UDF
Erick C Coffman
5303 St Pauls Church Rd
Gouchland VA 23063

FCC Amateur Radio Licenses in Grafton

Call Sign: KJ4DWS
Dena M Proctor
133 Bailey Dr
Grafton VA 23692

Call Sign: KE4HTU
Herman R Wiant
206 Brook Ln
Grafton VA 23692

Call Sign: WD4FTK
John C Murray
101 Buckingham Dr
Grafton VA 23695

Call Sign: KF4YQN
Keith U Bruffey
103 Castellow Ct
Grafton VA 23692

Call Sign: KA4VYD
James R Tyeryar Jr
205 Choisy Cres
Grafton VA 23692

Call Sign: KD4WHL
Benjamin E Collier Sr
418 Dare Rd
Grafton VA 23692

Call Sign: N4TPI
Michael C Forbes
209 Fielding Lewis Dr
Grafton VA 23692

Call Sign: KI4EIK
Mark S Lawrence
107 Holden Ln
Grafton VA 236922859

Call Sign: AI4FI
Mark S Lawrence
107 Holden Ln
Grafton VA 236922859

Call Sign: N4WRV

Erik S Willke
205 Hollywood Blvd
Grafton VA 23692

Call Sign: K4UMI
David C E Holmes
200 Holmes Blvd
Grafton VA 23692

Call Sign: WA4ZNY
Hubert M Squires
300 Old Lakeside Dr
Grafton VA 23692

Call Sign: KC4CKY
Michael C Necaise
101 Pinehurst Dr
Grafton VA 23692

Call Sign: KB4OQD
F Ambert Dail
508 Piney Point Rd
Grafton VA 23692

Call Sign: WB4AOA
Mark Flockhart
107 Quartermarsh Dr
Grafton VA 23692

Call Sign: KC4HEA
Russell W Brierly
102 School Ln
Grafton VA 23692

Call Sign: KD4EIL
Charles A Burnside Jr
106 School Ln
Grafton VA 23692

Call Sign: KF4UDP
Rebecca L Gavrila
100 Shanna Ct
Grafton VA 23692

Call Sign: N2CDK
Ernest F Doherty
103 Waterside Pl
Grafton VA 23692

Call Sign: WB4KNU
Peninsula Emergency Amateur
Repeater Soc
Grafton VA 23692

Call Sign: KF4DJY
Andrew C Laroy
Grafton VA 236920707

FCC Amateur Radio Licenses in Great Falls

Call Sign: KJ4JGZ
Douglas K Gustaveson
11305 Antrim Ct
Great Falls VA 22066

Call Sign: W4YXL
Douglas K Gustaveson
11305 Antrim Ct
Great Falls VA 22066

Call Sign: K1ZX
Douglas K Gustaveson
11305 Antrim Ct
Great Falls VA 22066

Call Sign: KB4RAZ
Michael J O Connell
9306 Arnon Chapel Rd
Great Falls VA 22066

Call Sign: K4CQQ
Albert G Reitan Jr
10900 Beckman Way
Great Falls VA 220663318

Call Sign: K4KQT
Brice Eldridge
208 Bliss Ln
Great Falls VA 22066

Call Sign: KC4RWA
Carol C Crawford
11641 Blue Ridge Ln
Great Falls VA 22066

Call Sign: KD4CAL
Garrett N Funkhouser

11107 Bowen Ave
Great Falls VA 22066

Call Sign: KF4ZSH
Jason J Smart
11127 Bowen Ave
Great Falls VA 22066

Call Sign: N1RQW
James W Smart III
11127 Bowen Ave
Great Falls VA 22066

Call Sign: N1RQY
Patricia M Smart
11127 Bowen Ave
Great Falls VA 22066

Call Sign: KK4COS
Anna M Dulik
10507 Cambridge Ct
Great Falls VA 22066

Call Sign: KK4COT
Erik S Dulik
10507 Cambridge Ct
Great Falls VA 22066

Call Sign: AK4JC
Richard P Dulik
10507 Cambridge Ct
Great Falls VA 22066

Call Sign: KB4IKG
Nancy R Raybold
10206 Carol St
Great Falls VA 22066

Call Sign: KI4SCG
Charles J Givans
250 Carrwood Rd
Great Falls VA 22066

Call Sign: N4BA
Frederick H Essig
520 Clear Spring Rd
Great Falls VA 22066

Call Sign: K4JYG

Walter R Key
321 Club View Dr
Great Falls VA 22066

Call Sign: KF4TTE
Lauren M Burt
916 Constellation
Great Falls VA 22066

Call Sign: KD4ENP
Tim L Reid
908 Constellation Dr
Great Falls VA 22066

Call Sign: KF4TSI
Leslie Burt
916 Constellation Dr
Great Falls VA 22066

Call Sign: KJ4JWP
Carlos Berrios
10102 Cottesmore Ct
Great Falls VA 22066

Call Sign: KE4VH
Patrick S Korten
927 Cup Leaf Holly Ct
Great Falls VA 22066

Call Sign: KC4JCW
John M Turner
1032 Cupleaf Holly Ct
Great Falls VA 22066

Call Sign: KI4CTY
Michael P Siddall
9700 Darelene Ln
Great Falls VA 22066

Call Sign: KI4OCZ
Lost Mountain Operators Club
9700 Darlene Ln
Great Falls VA 22066

Call Sign: N8ZJ
Lost Mountain Operators Club
9700 Darlene Ln
Great Falls VA 22066

Call Sign: K3ZJ
David R Siddall
9700 Darlene Ln
Great Falls VA 22066

Call Sign: KJ4LYF
Eric A Ams
9703 Darlene Ln
Great Falls VA 22066

Call Sign: KU4LF
Stephen P Gerke
131 Eaglesmere Rd
Great Falls VA 220664116

Call Sign: KI4EUF
Purvis W Bane
205 Eaton Ct
Great Falls VA 22066

Call Sign: KC4SZU
Michael A Attebury
11923 Fallen Holly Ct
Great Falls VA 22066

Call Sign: KE4LBM
Matthew B Russ
719 Forest Park Rd
Great Falls VA 22066

Call Sign: W4ECS
John S Ward
724 Forest Ridge Dr
Great Falls VA 22066

Call Sign: KB4QPW
Keith C Johnson
918 Golden Arrow St
Great Falls VA 22066

Call Sign: KC4UQ
Charles K Johnson
918 Golden Arrow St
Great Falls VA 22066

Call Sign: KC4YJX
Ralph J Arrington
751 Gouldman Ln
Great Falls VA 22066

Call Sign: AB6W
Thomas R Talbott
20019 Great Falls Forest Dr
Great Falls VA 22066

Call Sign: KI4IAI
John A Owens
1006 Harriman St
Great Falls VA 22066

Call Sign: KI4LSC
Jeffrey M Owens
1006 Harriman St
Great Falls VA 22066

Call Sign: KI4LGI
Jeffrey D Cooper
904 Holly Blossom Ct
Great Falls VA 22066

Call Sign: KI4QKS
Michael A Cooper
904 Holly Blossom Ct
Great Falls VA 22066

Call Sign: KM4MAC
Michael A Cooper
904 Holly Blossom Ct
Great Falls VA 22066

Call Sign: N3ZYU
Paul Konigsburg
920 Holly Run Ct
Great Falls VA 22066

Call Sign: K3MZ
Paul Konigsburg
920 Holly Run Ct
Great Falls VA 22066

Call Sign: W4AOL
Aol ARC
920 Holly Run Ct
Great Falls VA 22066

Call Sign: KI4YPJ
Frederick P Weidinger
558 Innsbruck Ave

Great Falls VA 22066

Call Sign: KJ4QKI
Andrew H Watson
96 Interpromontory Rd
Great Falls VA 22066

Call Sign: KR4QW
John J Knab
903 Jaysmith St
Great Falls VA 22066

Call Sign: KI4YNE
Justin L Green
911 Jaysmith St
Great Falls VA 22066

Call Sign: KB4SWL
Robert M Olshan
1110 Kelso Rd
Great Falls VA 22066

Call Sign: KB3ENK
George M Smith
1267 Kenmore Dr
Great Falls VA 22066

Call Sign: KC4YMG
Dino A Lorenzini
10892 Lake Windermere Dr
Great Falls VA 22066

Call Sign: KI4GLQ
Rory Kronmiller
961 Leigh Mill Rd
Great Falls VA 22066

Call Sign: KJ4SEW
Theodore G Kronmiller
961 Leigh Mill Rd
Great Falls VA 22066

Call Sign: KJ4EGO
Dana M Mastropole
965 Leigh Mill Rd
Great Falls VA 22066

Call Sign: AI4TF
James W Mastropole

965 Leigh Mill Rd
Great Falls VA 22066

Call Sign: KG4JBP
Surendra Safaya
10813 Lockmeade Ct
Great Falls VA 22066

Call Sign: K7MPP
Terry L Thompson
9507 Locust Hill Dr
Great Falls VA 22066

Call Sign: N4ZZD
Gloria D Thompson
9507 Locust Hill Dr
Great Falls VA 22066

Call Sign: AC4I
Raphael W H Wong
9522 Locust Hill Dr
Great Falls VA 22066

Call Sign: KI4ZGT
Carlos H Montes
10807 Monticello Dr
Great Falls VA 22066

Call Sign: KB3CDF
John L Murphy III
10809 Monticello Dr
Great Falls VA 220064225

Call Sign: N3QT
John L Murphy III
10809 Monticello Dr
Great Falls VA 220664225

Call Sign: K3JGB
Edward C Miller
10844 Monticello Dr
Great Falls VA 22066

Call Sign: KE4PDQ
Jeffrey K Meunier
1109 Morningwood Ln
Great Falls VA 220661609

Call Sign: WA4LRN

Tony K Meunier
1109 Morningwood Ln
Great Falls VA 220661609

Call Sign: KK4FPI
Amanda C Steffy
10105 Nedra Dr
Great Falls VA 20066

Call Sign: KJ4BRQ
Jeffrey A Rainey
1086 Pensive Ln
Great Falls VA 22066

Call Sign: KG4YQT
Michael J Murphy
9410 Piscataway Ln
Great Falls VA 22066

Call Sign: WA3IDS
Barry D Bergman
476 River Bend Rd
Great Falls VA 22066

Call Sign: K4AA
Joseph Squarzini Jr
688 Rossmore Ct
Great Falls VA 220662641

Call Sign: KG4WNF
William R Claybaugh II
10616 Runaway Ln
Great Falls VA 22066

Call Sign: WA3HDX
Richard L Elkins
10114 Sanders Ct
Great Falls VA 22066

Call Sign: WA2BCK
Thomas H Nail
9720 Schreiner Ln
Great Falls VA 22066

Call Sign: KN4LI
John W Small
10418 Shesue St
Great Falls VA 22066

Call Sign: AG1X
James W Zirkle
302 Springvale Rd
Great Falls VA 22066

Call Sign: KJ4BVG
Carlton Q Brown
507 Springvale Rd
Great Falls VA 220663424

Call Sign: K4CQB
Carlton Q Brown
507 Springvale Rd
Great Falls VA 220663424

Call Sign: KG4WTM
Gaige B Paulsen
513 Springvale Rd
Great Falls VA 22066

Call Sign: WB3BUL
Stuart J Statland
1100 Springvale Rd
Great Falls VA 22066

Call Sign: WA4STU
Stuart J Statland
1100 Springvale Rd
Great Falls VA 22066

Call Sign: KD4SHW
Alfred G Woldin
498 St Ives Rd
Great Falls VA 22066

Call Sign: K4EVH
Kenneth C Bass III
9800 Thunderhill Ct
Great Falls VA 22066

Call Sign: KF6JAJ
Kathy W Manifold
J Mueller 1143 Towiston Rd
Great Falls VA 22066

Call Sign: KA0YJG
Kannon K Shanmugam
1286 Towlston Rd
Great Falls VA 22066

Call Sign: KK4HVW
Stephen D Moxley
1290 Towlston Rd
Great Falls VA 220662213

Call Sign: KG4RJX
Norman R Eaglestone
11525 Tralee Dr
Great Falls VA 220661364

Call Sign: W4YT
Arthur F Reinhardt
414 Walker Rd
Great Falls VA 22066

Call Sign: K3MT
Michael J Toia
723 Walker Rd
Great Falls VA 22066

Call Sign: KF4LGR
Lynda M Toia
723 Walker Rd
Great Falls VA 220662801

Call Sign: KG4ABD
Joyce L Toia
723 Walker Rd
Great Falls VA 220662801

Call Sign: K3XA
William P Rohde
916 Walker Rd
Great Falls VA 22066

Call Sign: KR4YS
Jeffrey P Hahn
11009 Warwickshire Dr
Great Falls VA 22066

Call Sign: KT4LN
Frank S Smith III
10865 Wolfe Hill Ln
Great Falls VA 22066

Call Sign: K0BRA
Frank H Gentges
9251 Wood Glade Dr

Great Falls VA 22066

Call Sign: N4OGE
Margaret H Gentges
9251 Wood Glade Dr
Great Falls VA 22066

Call Sign: AI4UX
Margaret H Gentges
9251 Wood Glade Dr
Great Falls VA 22066

Call Sign: KJ4VHS
Aaron R Aragon
10985 Woodland Falls
Great Falls VA 22066

Call Sign: W0YVA
Robert A Sullivan
Great Falls VA 22066

Call Sign: W2ZL
John H Hardman
Great Falls VA 22066

FCC Amateur Radio Licenses in Green Bay

Call Sign: K3RRZ
George W White
Rt 1 Box 128
Green Bay VA 239429718

Call Sign: AA4OG
Walter Patterson
Rt 1 Box 83
Green Bay VA 23942

Call Sign: KF4YAK
John D Ward
338 Hatters Creek Dr
Green Bay VA 23942

FCC Amateur Radio Licenses in Greenbackville

Call Sign: KD4NFH
Cathy T Fleming
39022 Church St

Greenbackville VA 23356

Call Sign: KE4NYV
Jason R Rausch
37400 Davey Jones Blvd
Greenbackville VA 23356

Call Sign: KV4AN
Steven M Krumm
2395 Jolly Rodger Dr
Greenbackville VA 23356

Call Sign: KG4OTL
Andrew M Krumm
2395 Jolly Rodger Dr
Greenbackville VA 23356

Call Sign: KG4TVP
Yvonne S Krumm
2395 Jolly Rodger Dr
Greenbackville VA 23356

Call Sign: KE3ND
Charles R Jacob
3070 Navigator Dr
Greenbackville VA 23356

Call Sign: KG4SCY
Thomas Moskios
3326 Scimitar Way
Greenbackville VA 23356

Call Sign: KD4NVR
William L Mariner
Greenbackville VA 23356

Call Sign: AC4NV
Orville N Fleming Jr
Greenbackville VA 23356

FCC Amateur Radio Licenses in Greenbush

Call Sign: KJ4QZF
Walter Gray
22414 Drummonds Mill Rd
Greenbush VA 23357

FCC Amateur Radio Licenses in Greenville

Call Sign: KF4RK
Kenneth P Bassett
Rt 1 Box 534
Greenville VA 24440

Call Sign: KD4RBU
Arethelia C Kinsey
3372 Coldspring Rd
Greenville VA 244401820

Call Sign: KI4LLA
Darrell L Little
360 Deer Trl
Greenville VA 24440

Call Sign: KE4CKJ
Scott L Fielding
393 Greenville School Rd
Greenville VA 24440

Call Sign: KJ4AAG
Sylvia C Fielding
393 Greenville School Rd
Greenville VA 24440

Call Sign: KK4CGI
Chase A Harris
95 Main St
Greenville VA 24440

Call Sign: KG4VOR
Charles R Young
61 Park Dr
Greenville VA 24440

Call Sign: KD4CNJ
Carlton E Wiseman
49 Peyton Hill Rd
Greenville VA 24440

Call Sign: K4KPB
Kenneth P Bassett
1397 Stover School Rd
Greenville VA 24440

Call Sign: KG4MZZ

Helen L Bassett
1397 Stover School Rd
Greenville VA 24440

Call Sign: W4HLB
Helen L Bassett
1397 Stover School Rd
Greenville VA 244402005

Call Sign: KJ4CSC
Evan B Wilder
71 Turkey Ridge Rd
Greenville VA 24440

Call Sign: W1LDR
Evan B Wilder
71 Turkey Ridge Rd
Greenville VA 24440

Call Sign: KJ4INE
Rebecca A Wilder
71 Turkey Ridge Rd
Greenville VA 24440

Call Sign: KB4WLI
William L Blackburn Jr
Greenville VA 24440

Call Sign: KI4RKD
Charles E Mccracken
Greenville VA 24440

FCC Amateur Radio Licenses in Greenwood

Call Sign: K4MBL
Thomas M Knasel
825 Greenwood Hollow Rd
Greenwood VA 22943

Call Sign: K4LDO
Adam C Dudley
850 Greenwood Rd
Greenwood VA 22943

Call Sign: WA0RWL
Thomas C Jorgensen
8675 Little York Heights
Greenwood VA 22943

Call Sign: KB2BLI
Gerald H Siegel
Greenwood VA 22943

Call Sign: KC4CFY
William G Merrill
Greenwood VA 22943

Call Sign: KI4UQS
Adam C Dudley
Greenwood VA 22943

Call Sign: KI4UQR
Larry T Frazier
Greenwood VA 22943

Call Sign: KK4COV
Peter G Farrell
Greenwood VA 22943

FCC Amateur Radio Licenses in Gretna

Call Sign: WB3EPF
Clyde A Tuck
4393 Blue Ridge Dr
Gretna VA 24557

Call Sign: KE4ARL
Jody A Adkins
2744 Boxwood Rd
Gretna VA 24557

Call Sign: KI4EDK
Adam M Custer
820 Cedar Rd
Gretna VA 24557

Call Sign: KA4GND
Rickey L Boyd
386 Cocke Ln
Gretna VA 24557

Call Sign: KI4KAQ
Eleanor M Osborne
105 Coffey St
Gretna VA 24557

Call Sign: KG4YBE
Arthur C Wilton
471 Long Branch Ln
Gretna VA 24557

Call Sign: KG4VXL
David S Wilton
180 Long Branch Ln
Gretna VA 24557

Call Sign: KC9ELT
Dale E Vinton
120 Magnolia Rd
Gretna VA 24557

Call Sign: K4CQM
Paul Murry
1985 Midway Rd
Gretna VA 24557

Call Sign: KE4RG
Kenneth R Talbott
1512 Millstream Dr
Gretna VA 24557

Call Sign: KF4CQZ
Joseph H Talbott
1512 Millstream Dr
Gretna VA 24557

Call Sign: K1VSP
Joseph H Talbott
1512 Millstream Dr
Gretna VA 24557

Call Sign: KI4KAN
Mary E Cote
4501 Old Mine Rd
Gretna VA 24557

Call Sign: KD4FJY
Christopher L Dalton
175 Owens Mill Rd
Gretna VA 24557

Call Sign: KI4PMR
Lyle D Shelton
789 Ray Mill Rd
Gretna VA 24557

Call Sign: WD4CXQ
Gerald M Cooper
2396 Renan Rd
Gretna VA 24557

Call Sign: KF4WKE
Michael G Mayhew
8253 Rockford School Rd
Gretna VA 24557

Call Sign: KF4WKF
Eugenia P Mayhew
8253 Rockford School Rd
Gretna VA 24557

Call Sign: KD4HKK
Elwood L Dalton
8808 Rockford School Rd
Gretna VA 24557

Call Sign: N6VLS
Raul J Salas
719 S Main St
Gretna VA 24557

Call Sign: WA4PEP
Frank T Montgomery
1841 Tucker Rd
Gretna VA 245579293

Call Sign: KE4AGG
Larry D Roach
Gretna VA 24557

**FCC Amateur Radio Licenses
in Grimstead**

Call Sign: N4RXJ
John W Mahaffey II
Rt 633
Grimstead VA 23064

Call Sign: W1GYN
Kenneth G Smith
Grimstead VA 23064

**FCC Amateur Radio Licenses
in Grottoes**

Call Sign: KF4WDG
Vickie L Pitsenbarger
200 12th St
Grottoes VA 24441

Call Sign: KB4LCI
David B Gordon
407 17th St
Grottoes VA 24441

Call Sign: KC8LXE
Tamara R Gordon
407 17th St
Grottoes VA 24441

Call Sign: KG4JOF
William A Hooke
204 19th St
Grottoes VA 24441

Call Sign: KF4GNY
Ronald Garton
206 2nd St
Grottoes VA 24441

Call Sign: KE4WPF
Timothy L Henderson
204 8th St
Grottoes VA 24441

Call Sign: KJ4SIP
Charles M Baber III
600 8th St
Grottoes VA 24441

Call Sign: KJ4SIR
Toma-Cine P Baber
600 8th St
Grottoes VA 24441

Call Sign: KJ4BXR
Daniel L Chapman
223 Aspen Ave
Grottoes VA 24441

Call Sign: KJ4CSD
Tammarie D Sutherland
223 Aspen Ave

Grottoes VA 24441

Call Sign: KE4LKR
John W Phillips
Rt 1 Box 229B
Grottoes VA 24441

Call Sign: KE4HVM
Cheryl A Risley
Rt 1 Box 623
Grottoes VA 24441

Call Sign: WB4SHJ
Paul E Ipock
Rt 2 Box 668
Grottoes VA 24441

Call Sign: N4TMY
Glen R Saufley
10412 Browns Gap Rd
Grottoes VA 24441

Call Sign: KI4NQA
Dion D Bailey
3440 Eastside Hwy
Grottoes VA 24441

Call Sign: KF4CZH
Garry L Thompson Jr
3322 Eastside Hwy
Grottoes VA 24441

Call Sign: K4AXF
James N Stoneback
9738 Greenleaf St
Grottoes VA 24441

Call Sign: KA4EWG
Pamela L Stoneback
9738 Greenleaf St
Grottoes VA 24441

Call Sign: KI4GSS
Todd A Jenkins
95 Jenkins Ln
Grottoes VA 24441

Call Sign: KC4JXC
Kevin W Johnson

126 Mercer Cir
Grottoes VA 24441

Call Sign: N4ZFQ
Colin B Hester
521 Point Lookout Rd
Grottoes VA 24441

Call Sign: KF4BMN
Rickie L Bradshaw
4273 Rockfish Rd
Grottoes VA 24441

Call Sign: KI4QVA
Rickie L Bradshaw
4273 Rockfish Rd
Grottoes VA 24441

Call Sign: K4WMM
William M Mundy Jr
222 Trayfoot Rd
Grottoes VA 24441

Call Sign: KD4VPE
Kenneth M Anderson
Grottoes VA 24441

Call Sign: KC4VMG
Michael A Smith
Grottoes VA 24441

Call Sign: KE4JYL
Stephen M Fitzgerald
Grottoes VA 24441

FCC Amateur Radio Licenses in Grundy

Call Sign: KF4UYR
Jerrett C Thomas
Rr 2 Box 216
Grundy VA 24614

Call Sign: KK4EH
Arthur Stiltner
Rt 4 Box 89
Grundy VA 24614

Call Sign: WB4RBE

James S Looney
1135 Harman Junction Rd
Grundy VA 24614

Call Sign: KE4CXB
Eugene D Rife
Hcr Box 9
Grundy VA 24614

Call Sign: N1KAL
Christopher E King
1063 Lower Mill Branch Rd
Grundy VA 246146916

Call Sign: KC4AWG
Leslie K Stiltner
1044 Musky Rd
Grundy VA 24614

Call Sign: K4HWQ
Charles Osborne Jr
1013 Safe Way Dr
Grundy VA 24614

Call Sign: KE5UQY
Justin L Ekis
1888 Woosley Branch Rd
Grundy VA 24614

Call Sign: KK4SY
Matthew Stiltner
Grundy VA 24614

Call Sign: N4OBG
Jackie L Mc Clanahan
Grundy VA 24614

Call Sign: NO4G
Johnny L Ratliff
Grundy VA 24614

Call Sign: N4SWD
Roger Mayhorn
Grundy VA 24614

Call Sign: K4NRR
Gary D Street
Grundy VA 24614

Call Sign: KE4ZTR
Stephanie L Slone
Grundy VA 24614

Call Sign: KE4ZTS
Roger L Potter
Grundy VA 24614

Call Sign: KE4ZTT
Carol S Potter
Grundy VA 24614

Call Sign: KG4UAE
Charles D Church
Grundy VA 24614

Call Sign: N4JVG
James E Slone
Grundy VA 24614

FCC Amateur Radio Licenses in Gum Spring

Call Sign: KD4OCK
Wanda B Clemons
3691 Broad St Rd
Gum Spring VA 23065

Call Sign: WB4IKL
Ray G Clemons
3691 Broad St Rd
Gum Spring VA 23065

Call Sign: KC4IRJ
Richard W Shanks
4562 Broad St Rd
Gum Spring VA 23065

Call Sign: N4UPT
Andrea A Newlin
3243 Countryside W Dr
Gum Spring VA 23065

Call Sign: KE4ANP
Charles C Hardie
5595 New Line Rd
Gum Spring VA 23065

Call Sign: KF4RAM

Cynthia P Pendergraft
4819 Newline Rd
Gum Spring VA 23065

Call Sign: WD4JCI
Joseph R Gouldman Jr
Rt 634
Gum Spring VA 23065

Call Sign: W4AWN
Arthur W Nixon
4401 Spring Rock Ln
Gum Spring VA 23065

Call Sign: KE4KLE
Erin C Statzer
Gum Spring VA 23065

FCC Amateur Radio Licenses in Gwynns Island

Call Sign: W4RZB
Anthony R Tanner
835 Buckschase Rd
Gwynns Island VA 23066

FCC Amateur Radio Licenses in Hadensville

Call Sign: NP4RII
Lawrence Kelsey
Crow Hill Farm
Hadensville VA 23067

FCC Amateur Radio Licenses in Hague

Call Sign: KD5FCY
Brian J Byers
8268 Cople Hwy
Hague VA 22469

Call Sign: KA3TZM
Stafford L Gooch
45 Drum Bay Ln
Hague VA 22469

Call Sign: KE4YXR
Reginald R Follin

428 Fithians Ln
Hague VA 22469

Call Sign: W3HRZ
David J Brack
670 Quiet Harbor Dr
Hague VA 22469

Call Sign: KG4DTM
Carole A Alexander
636 Travelers Rest Rd
Hague VA 22469

Call Sign: KB4LPP
Jack A Klinefelter
266 Wilton Woods Dr
Hague VA 22469

Call Sign: KI4OPZ
William B Mason
Hague VA 22469

FCC Amateur Radio Licenses in Halifax

Call Sign: KD4ISK
Kelly R Bear
Rt 1 Box 413
Halifax VA 24558

Call Sign: KE4EDG
James V Medley
Rt 1 Box 584
Halifax VA 24558

Call Sign: KF4GTK
Walter D Gilmore Jr
Rt 1 Box 653 E
Halifax VA 24558

Call Sign: KE4EDL
Joseph W Watson
Rt 1 Box 68
Halifax VA 24558

Call Sign: WD4LBM
Harvey E Heath
R 2 Box 710A
Halifax VA 24558

Call Sign: KE4EDI
Charles T Salley
Rt 2 Box 887
Halifax VA 24558

Call Sign: W4JPN
John L Cole Jr
509 Buena Vista Dr
Halifax VA 24558

Call Sign: KJ4QEW
Richard C Shaw
751 Canterbury Dr
Halifax VA 24558

Call Sign: KI4YLL
Joseph H Boutwell III
1076 Cowford Rd
Halifax VA 24558

Call Sign: N4VVM
James M Wright
114 Evergreen Tr Rt 2
Halifax VA 24558

Call Sign: KF4FBO
Edward T Reagan
1214 Golf Course Rd
Halifax VA 24558

Call Sign: KF4PWN
Kevin S Lovelace
2075 Grubby Rd
Halifax VA 24558

Call Sign: K4REC
Kevin S Lovelace
2075 Grubby Rd
Halifax VA 24558

Call Sign: KC4LYD
Howard T Glascock
Hwy 729 Highland Hill
Halifax VA 24558

Call Sign: KD4MWL
Henry A Terry
1041 Highland Hills Dr

Halifax VA 24558

Call Sign: KI4YAH
Charles E Dyer
5153 Lp Bailey Mem Hwy
Halifax VA 24558

Call Sign: KJ4QEX
Matthew A Dyer
5153 Lp Bailey Mem Hwy
Halifax VA 24558

Call Sign: KJ4APT
David C Lawson Jr
1050 Occaoneechee Trl
Halifax VA 24558

Call Sign: WA4BKZ
Andrew A Hupp
2063 Swain Rd
Halifax VA 24558

Call Sign: KF4JDU
Jimmy W Ford Jr
2230 Swain Rd
Halifax VA 24558

Call Sign: WA7YHT
Dennis E Robinson
2001 Younger Rd
Halifax VA 245582987

Call Sign: AC4IF
Anthony S Jackson
Halifax VA 24558

Call Sign: KD4ZVK
James W Rutherford Jr
Halifax VA 24558

Call Sign: N4ZAO
Calvin J Willis
Halifax VA 24558

Call Sign: KF4ISE
Richard W Fallen Jr
Halifax VA 245580802

FCC Amateur Radio Licenses in Hallieford

Call Sign: KB4QZ
Kemp L Parrish
Rt 666
Hallieford VA 23068

FCC Amateur Radio Licenses in Hallwood

Call Sign: KG4VEQ
Barry J Budenos
28263 Main St
Hallwood VA 23359

Call Sign: KC4UHH
Charles F Russell
Hallwood VA 23359

Call Sign: KJ4UYN
Michael A Maciejewski
Hallwood VA 23359

Call Sign: KE4AKU
Frankie C Hall
Hallwood VA 23359

FCC Amateur Radio Licenses in Hamilton

Call Sign: KF4RCC
Michael T Clark
114 Applewood Ct
Hamilton VA 20158

Call Sign: KI4LUI
George A Bongiovano
124 Applewood Ct
Hamilton VA 201589736

Call Sign: WA0STX
John W Beasley
17526 Bates Dr
Hamilton VA 20158

Call Sign: KI4HVI
Michael N Ceo
17545 Bates Dr

Hamilton VA 20158

Call Sign: KE4KGQ
Joe O Pallanez
39801 E Colonial Hwy
Hamilton VA 20158

Call Sign: K1SPY
John J Wilber
17351 Hamilton Station Rd
Hamilton VA 20158

Call Sign: KJ4BRO
James H Moore III
10 Hamilton Ter Dr
Hamilton VA 20158

Call Sign: K3TZY
James D Baker
15901 Hampton Rd
Hamilton VA 20158

Call Sign: K4REL
James A Slagle
16459 Hampton Rd
Hamilton VA 20158

Call Sign: KC5BSM
Elizabeth A S Slagle
16459 Hampton Rd
Hamilton VA 201589418

Call Sign: K4RLZ
George K Wilmoth
17778 Harmony Church Rd
Hamilton VA 201583528

Call Sign: K0RAJ
Frederick H Davidson
16868 Heather Knolls Pl
Hamilton VA 20158

Call Sign: KB0PAL
Polly A Davidson
16868 Heather Knolls Pl
Hamilton VA 20158

Call Sign: KC4HTH
William E Knickerbocker

210 Madison Ave
Hamilton VA 22068

Call Sign: W3TNC
Charles A Gobs Jr
17637 Madison Ave
Hamilton VA 20158

Call Sign: KK4FFL
Peter E Burt
70 N Ivandale
Hamilton VA 20158

Call Sign: K4LJH
Charles T Preston
48 N Ivandale St
Hamilton VA 20158

Call Sign: KF4AFG
Joseph J Marker
67 N Laycock Ct Box 162
Hamilton VA 22068

Call Sign: WA4FEY
Ruth M Heitfield
308 Orchard Cir
Hamilton VA 20158

Call Sign: K4MSG
Paul H Bock Jr
38661 Pheasant Hill Ln
Hamilton VA 20158

Call Sign: KD4LSL
Dale A Cabaniss
363 W VA Ave
Hamilton VA 201589037

Call Sign: N2KVV
Robert J Myers
17585 Wadell Ct
Hamilton VA 20158

Call Sign: KB3COY
Nathaniel D George
38515 Wooded Hollow Dr
Hamilton VA 20158

Call Sign: W4AU

John D Unger
Hamilton VA 201590095

FCC Amateur Radio Licenses in Hampden Sydney

Call Sign: KB4VAO
Kenneth N Townsend
Cherry Hill
Hampden Sydney VA 23943

Call Sign: KB7QVY
Earl W Fleck
265 College Rd
Hampden Sydney VA
239430006

Call Sign: KB4YGN
Carl W Anderson
Box 4 Hsc
Hampden Sydney VA 23943

Call Sign: W4JAS
Jorge A Silveira
Hampden Sydney VA 23943

FCC Amateur Radio Licenses in Hampton

Call Sign: KJ4TJV
Paul Wolf
1302 Addison Rd
Hampton VA 23663

Call Sign: WO4LFP
Paul Wolf
1302 Addison Rd
Hampton VA 23663

Call Sign: KD4JVJ
David W Kelly
7 Admiral Ct
Hampton VA 236691001

Call Sign: K0IPA
Edward G Lembcke
4 Alamo Ct
Hampton VA 236691103

Call Sign: KJ4LVA
Saundra D Harvey
138 Alaric Dr
Hampton VA 23664

Call Sign: KJ4ACW
Charles M Heath III
47 Alleghany Rd
Hampton VA 23661

Call Sign: N4POX
Donald L Richards
474 Alma Ct
Hampton VA 23669

Call Sign: KI4LIB
Patrick L S Crandol
48 Apple Ave
Hampton VA 23661

Call Sign: W4POB
Walter A Leyland
116 Apple Ave
Hampton VA 23661

Call Sign: KJ4LVB
Maria C Larios De Ullman
133 Apple Ave
Hampton VA 23661

Call Sign: KE4WLS
Harold E Brown Jr
33 Aspenwood Dr
Hampton VA 23666

Call Sign: KE4NXZ
Edward M Manning
108 Aspenwood Dr
Hampton VA 23666

Call Sign: KI4VKH
Thomas G Cline
30 Banister Dr
Hampton VA 23666

Call Sign: W4TGC
Thomas G Cline
30 Banister Dr
Hampton VA 23666

Call Sign: KD4MAN
Jeffery L Barbour
20 Barnes Ct
Hampton VA 23664

Call Sign: KG4DAC
Paul R Bauer
36 Bay Front Pl
Hampton VA 236641791

Call Sign: KG4DAA
Thomas A Pantelides
51 Bay Front Pl
Hampton VA 23664

Call Sign: KI4HIA
Karen L Rowe
61 Beach Rd
Hampton VA 23664

Call Sign: KD4GLA
Me Lisa D Aycock
162 Beach Rd
Hampton VA 23664

Call Sign: WA4OHX
Jerry C Aycock
162 Beach Rd
Hampton VA 236642043

Call Sign: KE4SBM
Fred R Everett
308 Beach Rd
Hampton VA 236642006

Call Sign: KG4ZYY
Richard A Mars
1008 Beach Rd
Hampton VA 236642109

Call Sign: KD7PJQ
Scott B Hedberg
244 Beauregard Heights
Hampton VA 23669

Call Sign: KK4HLI
Nancy E Gruttman-Tyler
307 Beauregard Heights

Hampton VA 23669

Call Sign: N4EGT
Nancy E Gruttman-Tyler
307 Beauregard Heights
Hampton VA 23669

Call Sign: WA4OCU
Elmer F Smith
304 Beauregard Hgts
Hampton VA 23669

Call Sign: KJ4OZE
Thomas W Weidner
2812 Bending Oak Dr
Hampton VA 23666

Call Sign: K4LI
Thomas W Weidner
2812 Bending Oak Dr
Hampton VA 23666

Call Sign: KJ4CEQ
Frances M Doyle
2817 Bending Oak Dr
Hampton VA 236663001

Call Sign: KD4KJM
Richard G Thompson
101 Benson Dr
Hampton VA 23664

Call Sign: KI4ZWR
David H Verlander
423 Berkshire Ter
Hampton VA 23666

Call Sign: W3BHB
Robert M Mills
24 Bickfield Dr
Hampton VA 236662308

Call Sign: KD4NCL
William D Mace
108 Bickfield Dr
Hampton VA 23666

Call Sign: KJ4EBU

Liberty Baptist Church Disaster
Relief
1921 Big Bethel Rd
Hampton VA 23666

Call Sign: KB4DJD
Mark W Byerly
12 Big Bethel Rd Apt B
Hampton VA 23666

Call Sign: KJ4UIG
David P Rush
12 Bimini Crossing Apt H
Hampton VA 23666

Call Sign: W4DPR
David P Rush
12 Bimini Crossing Apt H
Hampton VA 23666

Call Sign: KD4FNS
Naomi V Reynolds
8 Blackberry Ln
Hampton VA 23669

Call Sign: K4AAO
Madell B Reynolds
8 Blackberry Ln
Hampton VA 236696003

Call Sign: KJ4HTX
Vivian E Taylor
303 Bond St
Hampton VA 23666

Call Sign: KC0GQQ
Deborah K Atkinson
82 Breakwater St
Hampton VA 23669

Call Sign: KB4DXO
Charles R Le Compte
1631 Briarfield Rd
Hampton VA 23661

Call Sign: KA8SGK
Mary L Rodehorst
449 Bridge St
Hampton VA 236694169

Call Sign: KA4INA
Patricia A Pittman
107 Bristol Ct
Hampton VA 23666

Call Sign: W4TEC
Harold R Pittman
107 Bristol Ct
Hampton VA 23666

Call Sign: KI4HPF
Richard J Hartung
1812 Broadstreet Rd
Hampton VA 236664325

Call Sign: KE4NBP
Eddie L Jones
307 Bromsgrove Dr
Hampton VA 23666

Call Sign: KD6JBP
Bryan L Burks
312 Bromsgrove Dr
Hampton VA 23666

Call Sign: KG4MYI
David F Warren Jr
13 Brough Ln
Hampton VA 23669

Call Sign: KI4JNH
Teresa E Vess
605 Buckroe Ave
Hampton VA 23664

Call Sign: K8SI
James E Gaskins Jr
32 Buffalo Dr
Hampton VA 23664

Call Sign: KI4RUN
Geoffrey M Tennille
309 Burgh Westra Dr
Hampton VA 23669

Call Sign: KI4MJY
John S Crane
615 Burton St

Hampton VA 23666

Call Sign: KI4VPI
John S Crane
615 Burton St
Hampton VA 23666

Call Sign: KY4VT
John S Crane
615 Burton St
Hampton VA 23666

Call Sign: KI4WKS
Gregory Greene
717 Burton St
Hampton VA 23666

Call Sign: W4QR
Southern Peninsula Amateur
Radio Klub
811 Burton St
Hampton VA 23666

Call Sign: WD4IAV
Addison T Inge
811 Burton St
Hampton VA 236661912

Call Sign: AA4AV
Addison T Inge
811 Burton St
Hampton VA 236661912

Call Sign: K4GAW
Andrew B Lucas Jr
16 C C Spaulding Dr
Hampton VA 23666

Call Sign: AC4GZ
George E Hunt III
1305 Caldwell Dr
Hampton VA 23666

Call Sign: KJ4LVF
Elyse L Hunt
1305 Caldwell Dr
Hampton VA 23666

Call Sign: KI4JZS

Cynthia K Verser
406 Calvert St
Hampton VA 23669

Call Sign: AI4OO
Cynthia K Verser
406 Calvert St
Hampton VA 23669

Call Sign: KI4TPB
Nathan C Verser
406 Calvert St
Hampton VA 23669

Call Sign: KF4OLU
Wayne T Berry
3407 Candlewood Dr
Hampton VA 23666

Call Sign: W3AF
Robert H Uiterwyk
16 Capps Quarters
Hampton VA 23669

Call Sign: KF4NPD
Daniel A Oneill
4018 Catesby Jones Dr
Hampton VA 23669

Call Sign: KE4ZHZ
Russell D Luttig
4029 Catesby Jones Dr
Hampton VA 23699

Call Sign: KE4ZII
Philip C Acol
64 Cavalier Rd
Hampton VA 23669

Call Sign: W4PTF
Clarence D Ray
417 Cedar Dr
Hampton VA 23669

Call Sign: AE4HV
Charles A Bogert
16A Chamberlin Ave E
Hampton VA 236631554

Call Sign: KE4KYM
William M Miller
629 Chapel St
Hampton VA 23669

Call Sign: KF4NOY
V Lee Miller
629 Chapel St
Hampton VA 23669

Call Sign: KF4NPC
Nancy L K Miller
629 Chapel St
Hampton VA 23669

Call Sign: KF4NQD
Garth L Miller
629 Chapel St
Hampton VA 23669

Call Sign: KK4HLN
Garth L Miller
629 Chapel St
Hampton VA 23669

Call Sign: KJ4CES
Mary F Mathes
34 Charlene Loop
Hampton VA 23666

Call Sign: KI4UPX
Garry S Mc Lemore
108 Charlton Dr
Hampton VA 23666

Call Sign: WA4VVY
Edwin E Davenport
106 Cherokee Rd
Hampton VA 236613504

Call Sign: KE4UWV
Paul E Van Norman Jr
18 Cherry Acre Dr
Hampton VA 23669

Call Sign: KF4KLI
Karla D Van Norman
18 Cherry Acre Dr
Hampton VA 23669

Call Sign: K4AEN
Thomas F Morehouse III
2222 Chesapeake Ave
Hampton VA 236613205

Call Sign: K4EGW
Willard E Granger
3011 Chesapeake Ave
Hampton VA 236613438

Call Sign: KE4LUD
Martin W Steffens
4000 Chesapeake Ave
Hampton VA 23669

Call Sign: KB4VJZ
Warren B Wood
4 Chipanbeth Ct
Hampton VA 23669

Call Sign: KJ4DWQ
Michael W Levy
22 Claremont Ave
Hampton VA 23661

Call Sign: KJ4DWP
Oliver J Hayes
11 Claymore Dr
Hampton VA 23669

Call Sign: KI4TPC
David A Thompson
129 Clifton St
Hampton VA 23661

Call Sign: KK4HNV
Dominic J Thompson
129 Clifton St
Hampton VA 23661

Call Sign: KI4PTU
John D Thompson
129 Clifton St
Hampton VA 23661

Call Sign: KB4DSB
David S Saunders
3 Colonies Landing

Hampton VA 23669

Call Sign: K4DKC
James M Cubbage Jr
10 Commander Dr
Hampton VA 23666

Call Sign: KT4UB
George P Spencer Jr
222 Commodore Dr
Hampton VA 23669

Call Sign: KB4OPZ
Michael F Harris
229 Commodore Dr
Hampton VA 23669

Call Sign: KA8DIY
Roxie A Mertz
6 Compass Cir
Hampton VA 236691026

Call Sign: WA8KLH
Bruce W Mertz
6 Compass Cir
Hampton VA 236691026

Call Sign: KC4YTF
Terry L Pridgen
1 Cooks Cir
Hampton VA 23669

Call Sign: WA4DLH
James A Brown
15 Cornelius Dr
Hampton VA 23666

Call Sign: W4JNT
Robert W Vernon Sr
25 Cornwall Ter
Hampton VA 23666

Call Sign: WA4VFW
Armand E Girard
3305 Custer Ct
Hampton VA 23666

Call Sign: WB4PDC
Zack W Washington

3306 Custer Ct
Hampton VA 23666

Call Sign: N4GGG
Luther L Briggins
3319 Custer Ct
Hampton VA 23666

Call Sign: KF4QJL
Robert L Tyson
305 Cynthia Dr
Hampton VA 23666

Call Sign: KD4MBE
Eugene R Thibeault
1903 Demetro Dr
Hampton VA 23663

Call Sign: K4OHO
Eugene R Thibeault
1903 Demetro Dr
Hampton VA 23663

Call Sign: K4GMK
William M Tweed
1909 Demetro Dr
Hampton VA 23663

Call Sign: KJ4GBW
Eugene A Urick Jr
1524 Denton Dr
Hampton VA 23664

Call Sign: KB4MHD
William L Hinspeter
1 Denver Cir
Hampton VA 23666

Call Sign: KE4WMC
VA L Soule
261 Derosa Dr
Hampton VA 23666

Call Sign: WD4LPA
Gordon F Bullock
38 Diamond Hill Rd
Hampton VA 23666

Call Sign: W6WQD

Robert J Allen
48 Diamond Hill Rd
Hampton VA 236666011

Call Sign: KC4YWX
Joseph David
34 Diggs Dr
Hampton VA 23666

Call Sign: KJ4CEV
Nathaniel T Smith
120 Downes St
Hampton VA 236631811

Call Sign: KJ4TIM
Nathaniel T Smith
120 Downes St
Hampton VA 236631811

Call Sign: W8KMJ
Robert A Bollenbacher
220 Drummonds Way
Hampton VA 23669

Call Sign: W4MRX
Robert A Bollenbacher
220 Drummonds Way
Hampton VA 23669

Call Sign: KF4NOX
Huyen V Nguyen
404 Dunham Massie Dr
Hampton VA 23669

Call Sign: KE4UP
John F Howe
205 Dunn Cir
Hampton VA 236665678

Call Sign: KI4JZW
Valerie A Howe
205 Dunn Cir
Hampton VA 236665687

Call Sign: WN0N
Tsuneo Masui
516 Dunn Cir
Hampton VA 23666

Call Sign: KE4FBL
Emery B Shoemaker
2061 E Bronco Dr
Hampton VA 23665

Call Sign: KI4LVD
Charles A Bogert
16 A E Chamberlain Ave
Hampton VA 23663

Call Sign: KE4NBL
James E Benbow Sr
12 E Chamberlin Ave
Hampton VA 23663

Call Sign: KD4YMR
Robert E Leavell
1043 E Little Backriver Rd
Hampton VA 23669

Call Sign: AG4JE
Robert E Leavell
1043 E Little Backriver Rd
Hampton VA 23669

Call Sign: KI4RXA
Donna M Leavell
1043 E Little Backriver Rd
Hampton VA 236691037

Call Sign: KF4JBT
Deborah M Wetmore
110 E Sewell Ave
Hampton VA 23663

Call Sign: N4XSW
Mark W Mc Laughlin
30 Eagles Landing
Hampton VA 23669

Call Sign: KJ4TJN
Harold V Horten Jr
3231 B Easy St
Hampton VA 23666

Call Sign: KD4SVN
Mark R King
5 Eberly Ter
Hampton VA 23669

Call Sign: KD4UFH
Theresa B King
5 Eberly Ter
Hampton VA 23669

Call Sign: N4DDK
Sarah M King
5 Eberly Ter
Hampton VA 23669

Call Sign: KE4MCA
Kathleen M Harbin
3 Edgewood Dr
Hampton VA 23666

Call Sign: KC4YTD
Alexander W Walker Jr
606 Essex Park Dr
Hampton VA 23669

Call Sign: W4ALX
Alexander W Walker Jr
606 Essex Park Dr
Hampton VA 23669

Call Sign: KB4VIU
Charles R Belcher Sr
813 Fairfield Blvd
Hampton VA 23669

Call Sign: KC4IUE
James R Youngblood
102 Fairmont Dr
Hampton VA 23666

Call Sign: KE6LUK
Andrew T Nevins
205 Forrest St
Hampton VA 23669

Call Sign: KE6UCR
Muriel M Nevins
205 Forrest St
Hampton VA 23669

Call Sign: KK4DIA
Raymond E Gose
202 Fort Worth St

Hampton VA 23669

Call Sign: KE4SCP
David S Triplett
457 Fort Worth St
Hampton VA 23669

Call Sign: WD4MOO
James K Ballard
155 Frissell St
Hampton VA 23663

Call Sign: W4NRM
John P Morgan
7 Garland St
Hampton VA 23669

Call Sign: WD4PRU
James A Venable
1 Garrett Dr
Hampton VA 23669

Call Sign: WA4AIQ
Willie O Mitchell
17 Garrett Dr
Hampton VA 23669

Call Sign: KE4ZXW
Vasc Amateur Radio Group Inc
115 Garrett Dr
Hampton VA 23669

Call Sign: KI4JZX
Stuart G Flechner
115 Garrett Dr
Hampton VA 236693624

Call Sign: N4STU
Stuart G Flechner
115 Garrett Dr
Hampton VA 236693624

Call Sign: K4LUD
Otis L Price Jr
28 Genhaven Dr
Hampton VA 23664

Call Sign: KD4SVL
Christopher A Sanford

20 Glen Forest Dr
Hampton VA 23669

Call Sign: N6EH
Frank H Gleason
109 Greenbriar Ave
Hampton VA 23661

Call Sign: KI4DJP
Edward R Potts
705 Greenville Ct
Hampton VA 23669

Call Sign: KD4IEK
Richard K Pendergraft
1223 Hale Dr
Hampton VA 23663

Call Sign: KE4PGU
John T Ellington
34 Hall Rd
Hampton VA 23664

Call Sign: KE4VCR
Mark D Craig
70 Hall Rd
Hampton VA 23664

Call Sign: W4KZC
Sheldon T Peterson
301 Hamrick Dr
Hampton VA 23666

Call Sign: W4CUI
William J Briglia Sr
215 Hankins Dr
Hampton VA 23369

Call Sign: KI4IMU
Brian S Roy
343 Harris Ave
Hampton VA 23665

Call Sign: KJ4ACT
Michael A Mitchell
495 Harwin Dr
Hampton VA 23666

Call Sign: KD4EIT

Edward C Snyder
1503 Hastings Dr
Hampton VA 23663

Call Sign: KF4HPD
James R Bense
1517 Hastings Dr
Hampton VA 23663

Call Sign: KA3MYK
Larry W Story
2 Hatteras Landing
Hampton VA 23669

Call Sign: KI4MNE
Milissa L Story
2 Hatteras Landing
Hampton VA 23669

Call Sign: KF4CDN
Vance L Reynolds
5 Hatteras Landing
Hampton VA 23669

Call Sign: KF4ZFW
David L Simons
3 Hawknest Ct
Hampton VA 23666

Call Sign: KG4NUD
Linda S Simons
3 Hawknest Ct
Hampton VA 23666

Call Sign: K4LKG
David L Simons
3 Hawknest Ct
Hampton VA 23666

Call Sign: K4LSS
Linda S Simons
3 Hawknest Ct
Hampton VA 23666

Call Sign: KG4TZU
Woodrow W Howell II
57 Henry St
Hampton VA 23669

Call Sign: KD4GSE
Suzanne E Miller
408 Hollomon Dr
Hampton VA 23666

Call Sign: AJ4MK
Mark A Elgert
4 Holloway Dr
Hampton VA 23666

Call Sign: KG4OIJ
David W Bridges
3613 Hollyberry St
Hampton VA 23661

Call Sign: KI4JNC
John B Hobler
100 Hollywood Ave
Hampton VA 23661

Call Sign: KJ4LVE
Douglas A Rogers
118 Hollywood Ave
Hampton VA 23661

Call Sign: KJ4ACU
Raymond R Holt
40 Huffman Dr
Hampton VA 23669

Call Sign: KI4HNK
Winfield S Arnott
17 Hunter Trace
Hampton VA 23669

Call Sign: W4AFA
Winfield S Arnott
17 Hunter Trace
Hampton VA 23669

Call Sign: KI4MQS
Christine K Arnott
17 Hunter Trace
Hampton VA 236691053

Call Sign: KD4ZTJ
Barry A Pierce
70 Ireland St
Hampton VA 23663

Call Sign: KB4OPU
Phillips A Hurlock
32 Ivy Home Rd
Hampton VA 236694547

Call Sign: WD4EKP
Benjamin L Daughtry
327 Ivy Home Rd
Hampton VA 23669

Call Sign: KI4DNV
Andrew T Shumate
2915 Kecoughtan Rd
Hampton VA 23661

Call Sign: W4CEU
Blair Blanton
3509 Kenmore Dr
Hampton VA 23661

Call Sign: N4IIC
Albert S Evans
1842 Kensington Dr
Hampton VA 23663

Call Sign: KA4IZE
Robert O Schade
19 Kenwood Dr
Hampton VA 23666

Call Sign: KI4MMI
Darren Spencer
34 Kincaid Ln
Hampton VA 23666

Call Sign: WD0FYV
Edward Shuman
2 Kings Landing Ln
Hampton VA 236692335

Call Sign: WR4H
Robert Holt
214 Kove Dr
Hampton VA 236692154

Call Sign: KA4ODF
David M Lambert
1741 Lafayette Dr

Hampton VA 236641753

Call Sign: WA7OCS
Daniel J Patch
19 Lake Ferguson Ct
Hampton VA 23669

Call Sign: W4LIJ
Maxwell F Mc Near
113 Lancaster Ter
Hampton VA 23666

Call Sign: KI4IYW
Hampton Public-Service Team
119 Lancaster Ter
Hampton VA 23666

Call Sign: W4HPT
Hampton Public-Service Team
119 Lancaster Ter
Hampton VA 23666

Call Sign: KI4TPA
Heather R Stevens
119 Lancaster Ter
Hampton VA 23666

Call Sign: KG4YEX
Christopher L Hosman
119 Lancaster Ter
Hampton VA 23666

Call Sign: KC4F
Christopher L Hosman
119 Lancaster Ter
Hampton VA 23666

Call Sign: N4RBS
Diana C Commander
7 Laurel Dr
Hampton VA 23669

Call Sign: KI4JZU
Robert W Limpus
25 Lawrence Ave
Hampton VA 236631345

Call Sign: KJ4TJS
Elizabeth A Hughes

3 Lillian Ct
Hampton VA 23669

Call Sign: KK4FOO
Frank Simmons Jr
305 Little Round Top Ct
Hampton VA 236691519

Call Sign: KJ4ACZ
Thomas P Yuhas Sr
6 Locksley Dr
Hampton VA 23666

Call Sign: KI4CQP
Jesse Walton
39 Locksley Dr
Hampton VA 23666

Call Sign: K4WLF
Jesse Walton
39 Locksley Dr
Hampton VA 23666

Call Sign: KI4RXF
Justin M Walton
39 Locksley Dr
Hampton VA 23666

Call Sign: N4RKO
John M Whytsell
802 Loura Ct
Hampton VA 23666

Call Sign: N3DUI
John H Brackbill
210 Lowden Hunt Dr
Hampton VA 23666

Call Sign: KF4WPE
Randall T Michalos
228 Lynnhaven Dr
Hampton VA 23666

Call Sign: KC1HW
John M Nuttall Sr
324 Lynnhaven Dr
Hampton VA 23666

Call Sign: KD5NVO

Vincent D Elia Jr
29 Madrid Dr
Hampton VA 23669

Call Sign: NQ4H
William A Smith
49 Manilla Ln
Hampton VA 23669

Call Sign: W4PQB
Gary A Herman
6 Manor Hill Ct
Hampton VA 23666

Call Sign: KB0HIH
Alain L M Jones
260 Marcella Dr 703
Hampton VA 23666

Call Sign: WB4GUY
Max Milien Sr
260 Marcella Rd Apt 821
Hampton VA 23666

Call Sign: KA6AJA
Neil M Blum
15 Marina Rd
Hampton VA 23669

Call Sign: K4FVI
Charles A Morgan
100 Martha Lee Dr Apt 184
Hampton VA 23666

Call Sign: KE4NBW
R Wayne Kelley
16 Mary Ann Dr
Hampton VA 23666

Call Sign: KJ4YRH
Justin R Lynch
1029 Mary Peake Blvd
Hampton VA 23666

Call Sign: KI4BTN
Ronald L Foreman
203 Maryfield Ct
Hampton VA 23666

Call Sign: KJ4MQX
Kathleen A Faron
3001 Matoaka Rd
Hampton VA 23661

Call Sign: KG4IDK
Mark L Faron
3001 Matoaka Rd
Hampton VA 236613014

Call Sign: K4MLF
Mark L Faron
3001 Matoaka Rd
Hampton VA 236613014

Call Sign: KI4PTV
Jayson R Stiffler
3004 Matoaka Rd
Hampton VA 23661

Call Sign: W6EYZ
Thomas A Polsley
103 Michaels Woods Dr
Hampton VA 23666

Call Sign: KE9AH
Gregory W Johnson
12 Mill Creek Ter
Hampton VA 23663

Call Sign: KE4MJE
Allan Tobin
164 Mill Point Dr
Hampton VA 23669

Call Sign: KF4WPF
John D Jordan Jr
36 Mizzen Cir
Hampton VA 236641778

Call Sign: KJ4CVR
Donald C Mertz Jr
4010 Monitor Dr
Hampton VA 23669

Call Sign: KJ4IRG
Donald C Mertz Jr
4010 Monitor Dr
Hampton VA 23669

Call Sign: KJ4MZ
Donald C Mertz Jr
4010 Monitor Dr
Hampton VA 23669

Call Sign: KI4TOX
Joseph G Caruso
10 Monte Volpe Ln
Hampton VA 23664

Call Sign: KG4EAL
Randy L Vaughan
23 Myra Dr
Hampton VA 23661

Call Sign: KB4LPI
Marian E Davis
348 N 1st St
Hampton VA 23664

Call Sign: KD7FGG
Bryce L Bills
711 N 5th St
Hampton VA 23664

Call Sign: W4WRM
Wallace R Morgan Jr
1796 N Armistead Ave
Hampton VA 23666

Call Sign: KA3KOE
Craig D Mc Clure
1711 N King St 17
Hampton VA 23669

Call Sign: W5NOA
Charles E Parnell
2016 N Mallory St
Hampton VA 23664

Call Sign: KD4CGZ
Tony C Woodard
331 Nassau Pl
Hampton VA 23666

Call Sign: W4ANY
William A Reece Jr
8 Natalie Dr

Hampton VA 236665564

Call Sign: KD4NBQ
Ronald L Dezern
10 Nathan St
Hampton VA 236691328

Call Sign: KG4IBR
Ralph D Eanes Jr
2 Neff Dr
Hampton VA 23669

Call Sign: KI4MKC
Jennifer L Parker
11 Neff Dr
Hampton VA 23669

Call Sign: KI4MKD
Kenneth A Parker
11 Neff Dr
Hampton VA 23669

Call Sign: N4KXJ
William F Adkins
19 Neff Dr
Hampton VA 236691123

Call Sign: KI4VFJ
Gina M Rhoden
314 Nelson Pkwy
Hampton VA 23669

Call Sign: KI4ROA
Steven L Dobbs
703 New Bern Ave
Hampton VA 23669

Call Sign: W4GMT
Steven L Dobbs
703 New Bern Ave
Hampton VA 23669

Call Sign: WA4RJG
Charles W Moore Sr
33 Newby Dr
Hampton VA 23666

Call Sign: WD4MUD
John D Darden

59 Newby Dr
Hampton VA 23666

Call Sign: K4PSD
Robert Maclachlan
427 Newport News Ave
Hampton VA 236693926

Call Sign: KF4NPA
Daryl A Maclachlan
427 Newport News Ave
Hampton VA 236693926

Call Sign: WA4EVD
George A Woodcock
812 Nottingham Dr
Hampton VA 23669

Call Sign: KD4FNT
James E Wallace Sr
718 Oakland Ave
Hampton VA 23663

Call Sign: WB4GXC
Jack G Barbour
1659 Old Buckroe Rd
Hampton VA 23664

Call Sign: KE4BDZ
Frances E Williams
1860 Olde Buckingham Rd
Hampton VA 23669

Call Sign: KE4BEA
Gloria B Rowell
1860 Olde Buckingham Rd
Hampton VA 23669

Call Sign: WB4SNG
Robert L Webb
11 Orchard Ave
Hampton VA 23361

Call Sign: KK4APU
David L Hedrick
39 Pacific Dr
Hampton VA 23666

Call Sign: N6DLH

David L Hedrick
39 Pacific Dr
Hampton VA 23666

Call Sign: KK4EMR
Roxanne Brickhouse
39 Pacific Dr
Hampton VA 23666

Call Sign: KC4YRO
Phillip M Smith
152 Pacific Dr
Hampton VA 23666

Call Sign: AF4SJ
Phillip M Smith
152 Pacific Dr
Hampton VA 23666

Call Sign: KE4WLU
Eric C Jones
611 Page Dr
Hampton VA 23669

Call Sign: KF4HPE
Howard C Jones
611 Page Dr
Hampton VA 23669

Call Sign: KA4RRT
William L Terrill
816 Park Pl
Hampton VA 23669

Call Sign: KD4EAQ
John S Osborn
316 Pasture Ln
Hampton VA 23669

Call Sign: KO4HO
Thomas M Portanova
316 Pasture Ln
Hampton VA 23669

Call Sign: WA4AJH
George C Hilton Jr
310 Patrician Dr
Hampton VA 23666

Call Sign: KF4PAS
Megan M Timm
102 Pear Ave
Hampton VA 23661

Call Sign: KK4HLJ
William C Simmons III
3319 Pershing Ct
Hampton VA 23666

Call Sign: KD4OQD
Jesse G Barbour
15 Phelps Cir
Hampton VA 23663

Call Sign: KG6JEV
Steven D Peterson
1714 Piazza Pl
Hampton VA 236662981

Call Sign: KA4VKZ
Kenneth P Rivas
19 Pine Lake Ct
Hampton VA 23669

Call Sign: KG4UNA
Sharon K Freeman-Raines
2 Poulas Ct
Hampton VA 23669

Call Sign: KE4JLR
Ronald T Carson
9 Poulas Ct
Hampton VA 23669

Call Sign: KJ4ZFG
Moore L Benjamin
134 Powhatan Pkwy
Hampton VA 23661

Call Sign: WD4HZB
Francis D Stone
26 Prince James Dr
Hampton VA 23669

Call Sign: KV4HE
Francis D Stone
26 Prince James Dr
Hampton VA 23669

Call Sign: WD4CEJ
Robert E Fago
150 Ransone St
Hampton VA 23669

Call Sign: KE4YLK
Derrick A Ward
1933 Rawood Dr
Hampton VA 23663

Call Sign: KJ4DEV
Ronald P Foster
2202 Rawood Dr
Hampton VA 23663

Call Sign: KD4ECR
Davis H Crawford
9 Raymond Dr
Hampton VA 23666

Call Sign: KG4DAB
William J Cournoyer Sr
500 Regina Ct
Hampton VA 23669

Call Sign: KJ4OLX
Nancy R Cournoyer
500 Regina Ct
Hampton VA 23669

Call Sign: KF4GFM
Juan R Cruz
47 Ridge Wood Dr
Hampton VA 236665646

Call Sign: KA4SVN
Richard W Ruehe
311 Riverside Dr
Hampton VA 23669

Call Sign: N4YCB
Francisco X Berna
109G Roane Dr
Hampton VA 23669

Call Sign: N4OEM
Artie D Jessup
77 Rockwell Rd

Hampton VA 23669

Call Sign: N4XYX
Michael B Jenkins Sr
526 Rogers Ave
Hampton VA 23664

Call Sign: KF4AMI
Gordon F Langille
533 Rogers Ave
Hampton VA 23664

Call Sign: KE4QDR
Henry C Vann
632 Rolfe St
Hampton VA 23661

Call Sign: WB4GSF
Donald A Johnson
17 Routten Rd
Hampton VA 23664

Call Sign: KE4SGH
Robert R Beuerlein
14 Royston Dr
Hampton VA 23669

Call Sign: KB4CAU
Michael G Hawk
38 S Boxwood St
Hampton VA 236693269

Call Sign: N4VIK
Scott B Zack
21 Sacramento Dr 12C
Hampton VA 23666

Call Sign: KG4VGF
Michael E Theriot Jr
27 Sacramento Dr Apt 61
Hampton VA 23666

Call Sign: W4ZMF
Robert A Magoun
20 Salem St
Hampton VA 23669

Call Sign: KI4JZV
Michelle L Justiniano

7 Samantha Ct
Hampton VA 23663

Call Sign: KC4JST
Michelle L Justiniano
7 Samantha Ct
Hampton VA 23663

Call Sign: KK4GXE
Colleen M Dudley
48 Sanlun Lakes Dr
Hampton VA 23666

Call Sign: WI4B
Stewart T Bowden
31 Santa Barbara Dr
Hampton VA 23666

Call Sign: N1VTT
Randall L Braddock Jr
63 Santa Barbara Dr
Hampton VA 23666

Call Sign: KH7WU
Robert P Devega Jr
42 Santa Barbara Dr
Hampton VA 23666

Call Sign: KC4YJP
Irma S White
310 Sea Breeze Ct
Hampton VA 23669

Call Sign: KJ4DWR
Lawrence R Peters
20 Seaview Dr
Hampton VA 23664

Call Sign: KF4IGY
David O Bruckheimer Jr
520 Settlers Landing Rd
Hampton VA 23669

Call Sign: KC4DVR
Tod Caldwell
2018 Seward Dr
Hampton VA 23663

Call Sign: AF4SI

David J Priddy
336 Shawen Dr
Hampton VA 23669

Call Sign: WD4LOZ
Rebecca J Priddy
336 Shawen Dr
Hampton VA 236692254

Call Sign: KG4DKA
Paul W Ferris
504 Shelton Rd
Hampton VA 23663

Call Sign: KJ4YKD
Angela J Russell
36 Sherry Dell Dr
Hampton VA 23666

Call Sign: WZ4DX
Henry P Russell Jr
36 Sherry Dell Dr
Hampton VA 236661822

Call Sign: WK4W
Ernest M Baumeister
51 Sherry Dell Dr
Hampton VA 23666

Call Sign: W6VQ
Ernest M Baumeister
51 Sherry Dell Dr
Hampton VA 23666

Call Sign: W6VQ
Ernest M Baumeister
51 Sherry Dell Dr
Hampton VA 236661869

Call Sign: KE4WLX
Harry R Simpson
417 Shoreline Dr
Hampton VA 23669

Call Sign: N8AHT
George B Beeler
422 Shoreline Dr
Hampton VA 23669

Call Sign: KG4AWN
Matthew J Spurlock
109 Signature Way 615
Hampton VA 23666

Call Sign: AF4CS
Gregory A Lesko
100 Signature Way 827
Hampton VA 23666

Call Sign: N3CKW
Lynn M Lesko
100 Signature Way 827
Hampton VA 23666

Call Sign: KC8EXR
Shannon B Moser
117 Signature Way Apt 436
Hampton VA 23666

Call Sign: WA2OYK
Anthony V Cassini
315A Silver Isles Blvd
Hampton VA 23664

Call Sign: AE4RB
William G Sale
104 Southerland Dr
Hampton VA 236692422

Call Sign: KA4REN
Marjorie B Sale
104 Southerland Dr
Hampton VA 236692422

Call Sign: WB4ZHQ
Joe H Andis
92D Spanish Trl
Hampton VA 23669

Call Sign: KD4JJO
Charles A Bogert
26 Steeplechase Lp
Hampton VA 23666

Call Sign: KO4MR
Richard S Eckman
9 Still Harbor Ct
Hampton VA 23669

Call Sign: W3IT
Richard S Eckman
9 Still Harbor Ct
Hampton VA 23669

Call Sign: KB5FWC
Dana C Kuecker
8 Stirrup Ct
Hampton VA 23664

Call Sign: KB7UCC
Sarah L Razee
409 Stockton St
Hampton VA 23669

Call Sign: KB4WDD
William E Lipford III
409 Summit Ct
Hampton VA 23666

Call Sign: KJ4KDH
Gerald G Blankenberg
304 Talley Farm Retreat
Hampton VA 23669

Call Sign: KJ4KDG
Richard O Mccarty Sr
401 Tappan Ave
Hampton VA 23664

Call Sign: KJ4ACR
Lonnie R Shaw
422 Tappan Ave
Hampton VA 23664

Call Sign: W4PS
Walter T Pickrell
14 Teresa Dr
Hampton VA 23666

Call Sign: K4OGT
John W Carter Jr
35 Teresa Dr
Hampton VA 23666

Call Sign: WB4LLO
Russell W Frum
1 Terrace Rd

Hampton VA 23661

Call Sign: KI4JNG
Donna R Nourse
848 Thames Dr
Hampton VA 23666

Call Sign: KC4HUK
Harry E Bryant
905 Thornhill Dr
Hampton VA 23661

Call Sign: WA4RQU
Jerry R Oxenburg
117 65C Tide Mill Ln
Hampton VA 23666

Call Sign: KE4WHN
Arthur W Lott
99 Tidemill Ln 100
Hampton VA 23666

Call Sign: KE4VCZ
Richard Shaw Jr
1610 Todds Ln
Hampton VA 23666

Call Sign: WB4ODZ
Edward F Von Bergen
26 Trail St
Hampton VA 23669

Call Sign: W4AVN
Richard D Hofler
16 Turner Ter
Hampton VA 23666

Call Sign: KE4WLT
John P Palen
19 Turner Ter
Hampton VA 23666

Call Sign: KD4YWR
Charles L Bell
218 Valirey Dr
Hampton VA 23669

Call Sign: KB6QWP
Jeffrey T Newmaster

8 Veneris Ct
Hampton VA 23669

Call Sign: KE4QDT
Ann M Newmaster
8 Veneris Ct
Hampton VA 23669

Call Sign: AG4CV
Jeffrey T Newmaster
8 Veneris Ct
Hampton VA 23669

Call Sign: KS4GC
David L Hamm
4603 Victoria Blvd
Hampton VA 236694139

Call Sign: WA4WX
David L Hamm
4603 Victoria Blvd
Hampton VA 236694139

Call Sign: KJ4AUG
Jeffrey M Leckemby
36 W Big Sky Dr
Hampton VA 23666

Call Sign: AJ0ML
Jeffrey M Leckemby
36 W Big Sky Dr
Hampton VA 23666

Call Sign: KE4WLW
Alvah M Blake
1 W Creek Ct
Hampton VA 23666

Call Sign: WA4YOB
Bonner L Johnson
25 W Lamington Rd
Hampton VA 23669

Call Sign: KA4IMZ
Charles R Hall Sr
101 W Lewis Rd
Hampton VA 23666

Call Sign: WB4DYS

William T Brock
509 W Lewis Rd
Hampton VA 23666

Call Sign: K4WKK
Kenneth H Smith
2519 W Pembroke Ave
Hampton VA 23661

Call Sign: KG4PME
Dave Russell
47 W Queens Way
Hampton VA 23669

Call Sign: AG4MU
Dave Russell
47 W Queens Way
Hampton VA 23669

Call Sign: KB3IVF
Robert G Brown
18 W Riverpoint Dr
Hampton VA 23669

Call Sign: WD4EOP
Robert Holt
305 Ward Dr
Hampton VA 23669

Call Sign: W4OKK
Alfred L Jones
24 Westbrook Dr
Hampton VA 23666

Call Sign: W4TRB
Thomas R Breeden
16 Westminister Dr
Hampton VA 23666

Call Sign: KC4JGR
Robert E Deming
14 Westmont Dr
Hampton VA 23666

Call Sign: KC4TJH
Francis X La Chance Jr
14 Westmont Dr
Hampton VA 23666

Call Sign: N4NIE
Clyde E Johnson Jr
10 Westmoreland Dr
Hampton VA 23669

Call Sign: WA4SRM
Leemon R Reed Jr
807 Westwood Ave
Hampton VA 23661

Call Sign: KA4VXR
Kim A Raines
31 Wexford Hill Rd
Hampton VA 23666

Call Sign: KI4WA
Manly L Hare
339 Whealton Rd
Hampton VA 23666

Call Sign: KD4LEL
Saunders B Moon IV
40 Whetstone Dr
Hampton VA 23666

Call Sign: KG4ZCT
Roy M Vaughn
128 Wilderness Rd
Hampton VA 23669

Call Sign: KK4HLT
Joshua A Belt
143 Wilderness Rd
Hampton VA 23669

Call Sign: KB8MOA
Jaris E Tankersley Jr
320 Wilderness Rd
Hampton VA 23669

Call Sign: KB4ZEC
Winston N Beverly
304 Willow Oaks Blvd
Hampton VA 23669

Call Sign: KI4TOY
Roger L Mowery
128 Winchester Dr
Hampton VA 23666

Call Sign: W4VYZ
Clyde E Murphy
147 Winchester Dr
Hampton VA 236662215

Call Sign: KC5SE
Evelyn A Thompson
103 Winchester Dr
Hampton VA 23666

Call Sign: K4OR
Stuart L Seaton
460 Windmill Point
Hampton VA 23664

Call Sign: W4OYA
Lamar E Williams
454 Windmill Point Rd
Hampton VA 23664

Call Sign: N4MYX
Roland G Kitts
2028 Winfree Rd
Hampton VA 23663

Call Sign: WA6DPF
Layne D Hurst
348 Wrexham Ct
Hampton VA 23669

Call Sign: AG4DW
Layne D Hurst
348 Wrexham Ct
Hampton VA 23669

Call Sign: WA4GIS
Charles A Downing
411 Yale Dr
Hampton VA 23666

Call Sign: KE4AZI
Patrick D W Power
Hampton VA 23664

Call Sign: N4CZV
Robert W Smith
Hampton VA 23666

Call Sign: N4RVT
Ivy J Lay
Hampton VA 23666

Call Sign: KE5FSI
Mark L Ghigliotti
Hampton VA 23661

Call Sign: KJ4TJO
William D Arnold
Hampton VA 23663

Call Sign: KI4YGS
Gregory A Snyder
Hampton VA 23664

Call Sign: N1HF
Huey M Fourquet
Hampton VA 23665

Call Sign: WA2DYF
James R Branstetter
Hampton VA 23666

Call Sign: KG4LZR
Peninsula Electronic Ars
Hampton VA 23666

Call Sign: KD7LYT
Charles A Hall
Hampton VA 23669

Call Sign: KD7LYU
Kathryn B Hall
Hampton VA 23669

Call Sign: KI4GEN
Jesse W White
Hampton VA 23669

Call Sign: KI4ELR
Michael A Sanborn
Hampton VA 23669

Call Sign: KA4WAN
Vermont D Moore
Hampton VA 23670

Call Sign: KI4JZT

Brian C Simon
Hampton VA 236640025

Call Sign: KQ6IN
Miguel A Doncell
Hampton VA 236655801

FCC Amateur Radio Licenses in Hanover

Call Sign: W4RTH
Robert T Harris
8173 Long Ln
Hanover VA 23069

Call Sign: KG4AOK
James R Connor
12 Oak Grove Ln
Hanover VA 230699607

Call Sign: KE4RAJ
Jack A Butts
32450 Richmond Tpke
Hanover VA 23069

Call Sign: KE6DMZ
Robert S Heer Jr
8061 St Pauls Church Rd
Hanover VA 23069

Call Sign: W4JHK
Marm
Hanover VA 23069

Call Sign: KF4ADF
Donna L Gattuso
Hanover VA 23069

FCC Amateur Radio Licenses in Harborton

Call Sign: WB2KUW
Charles R Belensky
14262 Shore Dr
Harborton VA 23389

Call Sign: KA4TPR
Karl F Steinbach
Harborton VA 23389

FCC Amateur Radio Licenses in Hardy

Call Sign: KE4FBO
Edmund F Kline
128 Bailey Blvd
Hardy VA 24101

Call Sign: N4UZY
Robert N Capper
22 Boulder Point Dr
Hardy VA 24101

Call Sign: KB9HTQ
Richard J Bixby
1089 Commonwealth Dr
Hardy VA 24101

Call Sign: KK4DGG
James E Martin IV
411 Daytona Dr
Hardy VA 24101

Call Sign: AK4LB
James E Martin III
411 Daytona Dr
Hardy VA 24101

Call Sign: N4MIF
Wilfred G Davis
8715 Edwardsville Rd
Hardy VA 24101

Call Sign: KJ4SNS
Raymond J Matthews Jr
52 Farm Park Dr
Hardy VA 24101

Call Sign: KD4HZF
Ricky A Williams
12253 Hardy Rd
Hardy VA 24101

Call Sign: KA4NQP
Cecil O Jamison
80 Jamison Ln
Hardy VA 24101

Call Sign: AE4AK
David E Sidener
370 Lakeshore Ter Rd
Hardy VA 24101

Call Sign: K4PK
Donald M Aldridge
170 Lenoir Ln
Hardy VA 24101

Call Sign: KJ4FTQ
Shaun M Bennett
200 Meadow Dr
Hardy VA 24101

Call Sign: WB2LCR
Paul M Cooper
65 Middle Valley Rd
Hardy VA 24101

Call Sign: KF4RGB
Benjamin T Perdue
1446 Morewood Rd
Hardy VA 24101

Call Sign: KG4NIN
Johnson H Mills Jr
32 Mtn Breeze Dr
Hardy VA 24101

Call Sign: KD4OSS
Ronald C Addis
1343 Northridge Rd
Hardy VA 241014245

Call Sign: KD4MLT
Gary L Cochran
2645 Northridge Rd
Hardy VA 24101

Call Sign: N8XZX
Henry M Stephens
19 Overlook Rd
Hardy VA 24101

Call Sign: N8IAH
Dennis J Guza
290 Par 5 Ln
Hardy VA 24101

Call Sign: AJ4MO
Luke J Huybrechts
260 Saddleback Trl
Hardy VA 24101

Call Sign: WB2CJU
Neil P Flynn
1300 Walnut Run Dr
Hardy VA 24101

Call Sign: NF9J
Neil P Flynn
1300 Walnut Run Dr
Hardy VA 24101

FCC Amateur Radio Licenses in Hardyville

Call Sign: W3JW
Jefferson H Walker Jr
271 Chick Cove Dr
Hardyville VA 230709705

Call Sign: AD4RG
James G O Sullivan
410 Mallard Dr
Hardyville VA 23070

Call Sign: KE3GM
Kenneth C Hill
115 Point Cove Ln
Hardyville VA 23070

Call Sign: KB4NGO
Fay E Smith
Hardyville VA 23070

FCC Amateur Radio Licenses in Harrisonburg

Call Sign: K4EJG
Elroy W Kauffman
1466 2 Penny Dr
Harrisonburg VA 228022339

Call Sign: KJ4DNZ
Jerry E Wright
319 7th St

Harrisonburg VA 22802

Call Sign: WB6SPD
Michael E Smilowitz
474 Andergren Dr
Harrisonburg VA 228014302

Call Sign: KB4YSP
John J Bobbio
3510 Apple Tree Dr
Harrisonburg VA 22802

Call Sign: KC4YTC
David M Hammer
3226 Arrowhead Rd
Harrisonburg VA 22801

Call Sign: KC4HYS
Roger P Gingerich
1021 Ashwood St
Harrisonburg VA 22801

Call Sign: KK4IFB
Dustin T Gladwell
2363 Avalon Woods Dr
Harrisonburg VA 22801

Call Sign: KB2QIF
Brian M Latuga
2363 Avolon Woods Dr
Harrisonburg VA 22801

Call Sign: KI4EDB
Charles L Kahler III
185 Bel Ayr View
Harrisonburg VA 22801

Call Sign: KF4YGO
Douglas E Alder
278 Bellview Rd
Harrisonburg VA 22802

Call Sign: N4DUG
Douglas E Alder
278 Bellview Rd
Harrisonburg VA 22802

Call Sign: KG4RMX
Ruel J Burkholder

145 Belmont Dr
Harrisonburg VA 22801

Call Sign: KI4NTP
Michael D Stouwie
1027 Blue Ridge Dr
Harrisonburg VA 22802

Call Sign: KY4FOX
Michael D Stouwie
1027 Blue Ridge Dr
Harrisonburg VA 22802

Call Sign: K4RMY
Bryan E Daniels
2327 Blue Stone Hill Dr
Harrisonburg VA 22801

Call Sign: KI4ILU
Phillip A Long
1027 Blueridge Dr
Harrisonburg VA 22802

Call Sign: KF4BFJ
Daryl A Alligood
1248 Bluewater Rd
Harrisonburg VA 22801

Call Sign: KK4IFC
Richard C French
1475 Bluewater Rd
Harrisonburg VA 22801

Call Sign: WD4OQI
Ronald W Allen
Rr 11 Box 310
Harrisonburg VA 22801

Call Sign: KF4EKW
Jason E Zirk
Rt 2 Box 407
Harrisonburg VA 22801

Call Sign: KC4HYQ
Steven R Brunk
Rt 8 Box 48
Harrisonburg VA 22801

Call Sign: KC4IDK

Benjamin G Brunk
Rt 8 Box 48
Harrisonburg VA 22801

Call Sign: KG4HMU
Charles M Andes
2402 Breckenridge Ct
Harrisonburg VA 22801

Call Sign: K4CMA
Charles M Andes
2402 Breckenridge Ct
Harrisonburg VA 22801

Call Sign: KI4TOF
Ernest Frank III
741 Broadview Dr
Harrisonburg VA 22802

Call Sign: KJ4DNY
Daryl E Tonini
3130 Brookshire Dr
Harrisonburg VA 22801

Call Sign: KJ4DOC
Sheryl M Tonini
3130 Brookshire Dr
Harrisonburg VA 22801

Call Sign: KG4LRC
Steven M Sites
101 Brookside Pl
Harrisonburg VA 22802

Call Sign: KK4BPD
Thomas H Pike
2948 Brookstone Dr
Harrisonburg VA 22801

Call Sign: KI4TAJ
Michael D Showalter
300 Cedar Hill Dr
Harrisonburg VA 22802

Call Sign: KD4SZR
Michael D Showalter
3000 Cedar Hill Dr
Harrisonburg VA 22801

Call Sign: N1QEQ
Robert J Steere
1652 Central Ave
Harrisonburg VA 22801

Call Sign: KJ4AAH
David B Walton
1726 Central Ave
Harrisonburg VA 22801

Call Sign: AJ4FF
David B Walton
1726 Central Ave
Harrisonburg VA 22801

Call Sign: KF4BFG
David A Crider
1060 Cherrybrook Dr
Harrisonburg VA 22801

Call Sign: KF4WDH
Mark D Hartman
1057 Chicago Ave
Harrisonburg VA 22802

Call Sign: KK4IEZ
Andrew R Kniss
621 Circle Dr
Harrisonburg VA 22801

Call Sign: KG4BLF
Winston E Rhodes
3694 Clayborn Rd
Harrisonburg VA 22802

Call Sign: K3RFP
William R Nash
878 College Ave
Harrisonburg VA 22802

Call Sign: KB4NXR
Margaret M Wyse
1481 College Ave
Harrisonburg VA 22802

Call Sign: W4PFM
Paul M Wyse
1481 College Ave
Harrisonburg VA 22802

Call Sign: KE4CKF
Simon D Riggleman
919 Collicello
Harrisonburg VA 22802

Call Sign: KD4ATS
John M Miller
1265 Crescent Rd
Harrisonburg VA 22801

Call Sign: KK4IFA
William H Groce
121 Crestridge Ct
Harrisonburg VA 22802

Call Sign: W4JVC
Jeffrey W Holsinger
1285 Cumberland Dr
Harrisonburg VA 22801

Call Sign: N4ORR
Lucinda M Umberger
93D Dutchmill Jct
Harrisonburg VA 22801

Call Sign: N4KKI
Mary E Mc Caskill
250 E Elizabeth St 203
Harrisonburg VA 22801

Call Sign: KB4YSP
John J Bobbio
518 E Market St
Harrisonburg VA 22801

Call Sign: KG4EBQ
Spencer T Gibson
238 E Water St Apt 118
Harrisonburg VA 22801

Call Sign: KD4OYE
Bruce P Matthias
54 E Weaver Ave
Harrisonburg VA 22801

Call Sign: AC4AR
Donald W Miller
1208 Edgewood Dr

Harrisonburg VA 22801

Call Sign: W4BAR
Robert G Veith
718 Elmwood Dr
Harrisonburg VA 22801

Call Sign: WA4LVE
R William Shifflet
825 Elmwood Dr
Harrisonburg VA 22801

Call Sign: KC4SFD
Marian U Taylor
48 Emery St
Harrisonburg VA 22801

Call Sign: KI4WTN
Amateur Radio Missionary
Service
2457 Eversole Rd
Harrisonburg VA 22802

Call Sign: KA2RMS
Amateur Radio Missionary
Service
2457 Eversole Rd
Harrisonburg VA 22802

Call Sign: K4RBZ
Gerald R Brunk
2457 Eversole Rd
Harrisonburg VA 22802

Call Sign: KD4DCX
Robert A Jones
61 Garbers Church Rd
Harrisonburg VA 22801

Call Sign: KE4CKN
Allen L Dean
3330 General Jackson Ln
Harrisonburg VA 22801

Call Sign: KG4KKU
Dawn M Dean
3330 General Jackson Ln
Harrisonburg VA 22801

Call Sign: N4NXS
Allen L Dean
3330 General Jackson Ln
Harrisonburg VA 22801

Call Sign: KJ4IK
Roy K Patteson Jr
4525 Grattan Price Dr 1
Harrisonburg VA 22801

Call Sign: KE4RMD
Douglas S Zirk
538 Gravels Rd
Harrisonburg VA 22802

Call Sign: KE4WIE
Karen S Zirk
538 Gravels Rd
Harrisonburg VA 22802

Call Sign: WA4RXY
David R Cave
555 Gravels Rd
Harrisonburg VA 22802

Call Sign: WA4NIC
Lewis A Hensley
2152 Gravels Rd
Harrisonburg VA 22802

Call Sign: KC4VLD
Michael F Quimby
3150 Harness Ln
Harrisonburg VA 22801

Call Sign: W8HGH
Robert E Dixon
1560 Hawthorne Cir
Harrisonburg VA 22802

Call Sign: W3IFE
Grant C Riggle
429 Highlands Pl
Harrisonburg VA 22801

Call Sign: AD4IZ
Alexander H Forman
1604 Hillcrest Dr
Harrisonburg VA 228025517

Call Sign: KK4IET
Joseph W Yarber
1340 Hunters Rd
Harrisonburg VA 22801

Call Sign: N4JKX
Carol P Landes
8644 Indian Trl Rd
Harrisonburg VA 228021869

Call Sign: WX4CPL
Carol P Landes
8644 Indian Trl Rd
Harrisonburg VA 228021869

Call Sign: WX4C
Donald N Landes
8644 Indian Trl Rd
Harrisonburg VA 228021869

Call Sign: N4WVY
Stephen E Winegard
2314 Irish Path
Harrisonburg VA 22802

Call Sign: KK4IEY
Brandon E Peavy
2439 Isaac Ln
Harrisonburg VA 22801

Call Sign: KG4IJC
Randy L Weber
3693 Izaak Walton Dr
Harrisonburg VA 22801

Call Sign: KB3EDO
Paul R Boisen
1091 James Pl
Harrisonburg VA 22801

Call Sign: KB3O
Paul R Boisen
1091 James Pl
Harrisonburg VA 22801

Call Sign: KJ4UEB
John J Bobbio
304 Kelley St

Harrisonburg VA 22802

Call Sign: WB4PWP
William D Fawcett
8645 Koontz Corner Rd
Harrisonburg VA 22802

Call Sign: KG4APC
Gene B Hoover
5214 Kratzer Rd
Harrisonburg VA 22802

Call Sign: W4HOV
Gene B Hoover
5214 Kratzer Rd
Harrisonburg VA 22802

Call Sign: KD4TBO
Tom M Callahan
1078 Lacey Ln
Harrisonburg VA 22802

Call Sign: KC4LTP
Phillip N Helmuth
2250 Lake Terrace Dr
Harrisonburg VA 22802

Call Sign: W4QDC
Jay M Suter
2252 Lake Terrace Dr
Harrisonburg VA 228026193

Call Sign: KC9OXE
Nathan W Cooper
2316 Lancelot Ln
Harrisonburg VA 22801

Call Sign: WL7WC
Russell G Lockey
79 Laurel St
Harrisonburg VA 22801

Call Sign: KB4MZE
Floyd J See
526 Lee Ave
Harrisonburg VA 22801

Call Sign: WB3FZK
Ronald S Kraybill

1371 Lincolnshire Dr
Harrisonburg VA 228028355

Call Sign: KI4DMC
Charles L Kline
613 Locust Hill Dr
Harrisonburg VA 22801

Call Sign: KF4ZXO
Robert S Edmunds
361 Maryland Ave
Harrisonburg VA 22801

Call Sign: W5VEY
Walter C Berryman Jr
681 Maryland Ave
Harrisonburg VA 228011749

Call Sign: WB4DQX
Maynard D Johnson
1742 Massanetta Sprgs Rd
Harrisonburg VA 22801

Call Sign: N4FXH
Robert N Landes
2808 Mattie Dr
Harrisonburg VA 22801

Call Sign: KJ4INF
Fred R Mcdavid Jr
128 Media Ln
Harrisonburg VA 22801

Call Sign: KD4LRY
James E Hiter Jr
1950 Melrose Rd
Harrisonburg VA 22802

Call Sign: N4TXB
Arthur E Albrecht
3340 Mesinetto Creek Dr
Harrisonburg VA 228018533

Call Sign: KC4UZI
Raymond J Schneider
77 Middlebrook St
Harrisonburg VA 22801

Call Sign: KB4IZY

Anita G Baker
908 Mockingbird Dr
Harrisonburg VA 22801

Call Sign: KB4IZZ
Meade H Baker
908 Mockingbird Dr
Harrisonburg VA 22801

Call Sign: KF4BFE
Lois B Bowman
1390 Mt Clinton Pike
Harrisonburg VA 228022338

Call Sign: AJ4JI
Lois B Bowman
1390 Mt Clinton Pike
Harrisonburg VA 228022338

Call Sign: WF4O
Foster D Farone
5919 Mt Clinton Pike
Harrisonburg VA 22802

Call Sign: KG4RMW
Christopher A Burkholder
1398A Mt Clinton Pike
Harrisonburg VA 22802

Call Sign: KJ4MWQ
Ray N Hensley Jr
12 N Dogwood Dr A
Harrisonburg VA 22802

Call Sign: KE4WIF
Joyce K Sutherly
698 N Liberty St
Harrisonburg VA 22801

Call Sign: KF4BFH
Donald L Sutherly
698 N Liberty St
Harrisonburg VA 22801

Call Sign: KI4DMF
Nevin J Blankenship
7648 N Valley Pike
Harrisonburg VA 22802

Call Sign: N8VRP
Vickie S Blankenship
7648 N Valley Pike
Harrisonburg VA 22802

Call Sign: KG4LRE
Erich W Lantz
9989 N Valley Pike
Harrisonburg VA 22802

Call Sign: KD4ZRY
Alan W Mann
1196 Nelson Dr
Harrisonburg VA 22801

Call Sign: W4AZR
Michael W Mc Kay
675 New York Ave
Harrisonburg VA 22801

Call Sign: WA4FEI
Edgar W Denton
278 Newman Ave
Harrisonburg VA 22801

Call Sign: KJ4DOE
Mark E Reed
895 Northfield Ct
Harrisonburg VA 22802

Call Sign: KG4VOP
James M Conis
705 Oak Hill Dr
Harrisonburg VA 22801

Call Sign: KF4UKZ
Christopher F Mullins
1041 Oak View Ct
Harrisonburg VA 22801

Call Sign: KC3AN
Richard I Haxton
5676 Oak Villa Ln
Harrisonburg VA 22801

Call Sign: N4VZC
Phyllis M Haxton
5676 Oak Villa Ln
Harrisonburg VA 22801

Call Sign: W4KTT
William M Pollard Sr
5701 Oak Villa Ln
Harrisonburg VA 22801

Call Sign: KF4ZEB
Daniel Kvitko
1098 Oakdale Ct
Harrisonburg VA 22801

Call Sign: KV1TKO
Daniel Kvitko
1098 Oakdale Ct
Harrisonburg VA 22801

Call Sign: WB1CKP
Ken Purdy
1184A Old Furnace Rd
Harrisonburg VA 22801

Call Sign: KG4RMY
Bryan E Daniels
116A Old S High St
Harrisonburg VA 228013642

Call Sign: KE4OIE
Kenneth D Brunk
3095 Old Thirty Three
Harrisonburg VA 22801

Call Sign: KC4UZF
Trent W Bowman
1246 Old Windmill Cir
Harrisonburg VA 22802

Call Sign: N4VVJ
Paul D Helmuth
1286 Old Windmill Cir
Harrisonburg VA 22802

Call Sign: KF4BFB
Herbert W Lam
1209D Old Windmill Cir
Harrisonburg VA 228026178

Call Sign: KG4OPO
Kyle Klosinski
1054 Oriole Ln

Harrisonburg VA 22802

Call Sign: KG4IJA
Antonio Martinez
481 Ott St
Harrisonburg VA 22801

Call Sign: KD4UWY
Daniel L Johnson Jr
922 C Parkwood Dr
Harrisonburg VA 22801

Call Sign: N3WGM
William J Hampton
2441 Peake Mtn Rd
Harrisonburg VA 22802

Call Sign: W4IPD
Roger D Sack
126 A Pleasant Hill Rd
Harrisonburg VA 22801

Call Sign: KG4TZI
Young Choe
126A Pleasant Hill Rd
Harrisonburg VA 22801

Call Sign: NS4K
Dennis W Phillips
25 Port Republic Rd
Harrisonburg VA 22801

Call Sign: KE4HVQ
Richard E Sedwick
3235 Port Republic Rd
Harrisonburg VA 22801

Call Sign: KG4JAY
Dorman H Hensley
3587 Port Republic Rd
Harrisonburg VA 228018008

Call Sign: W3HXH
Richard S Weaver
3842 Rawley Pike
Harrisonburg VA 22801

Call Sign: K4AXL
Owen B Showalter

4577 Rawley Pike
Harrisonburg VA 22801

Call Sign: KF4BFF
Enos P Nauman
1127 Rockingham Dr
Harrisonburg VA 22802

Call Sign: KN4FM
Gerald E Nauman
1127 Rockingham Dr
Harrisonburg VA 22802

Call Sign: KG4MWI
Terry J Kielbasa Jr
181 Rockingham Dr Apt N
Harrisonburg VA 22802

Call Sign: KI4TOJ
Alfred E Passarelli
554 Roosevelt St
Harrisonburg VA 22801

Call Sign: KI4HYK
Matthew S Dovel
2050 Rosedale Ct
Harrisonburg VA 22801

Call Sign: W4MSD
Matthew S Dovel
2050 Rosedale Ct
Harrisonburg VA 22801

Call Sign: KD4GZV
James R Veazey
750 S Dogwood Dr
Harrisonburg VA 22801

Call Sign: WB4YEX
James D Cline
1032 S Dogwood Dr
Harrisonburg VA 22801

Call Sign: KE4KKZ
Thomas A Flick
1613 S Main St
Harrisonburg VA 22801

Call Sign: WA4KQX

John N Nelson
4035 S Main St
Harrisonburg VA 22801

Call Sign: N3JN
John N Nelson
4035 S Main St
Harrisonburg VA 22801

Call Sign: KF4YJB
William B Hodges
1347 S Main St Apt D
Harrisonburg VA 22801

Call Sign: AK4OG
C Austin Wright
2420 S Main St Ste 4
Harrisonburg VA 22801

Call Sign: N4NOL
Albert W Mc Nett Sr
485 5 S Mason St
Harrisonburg VA 22801

Call Sign: W4JQT
Kenneth B Anderson
2105 Secrist Ln
Harrisonburg VA 22801

Call Sign: W2GCW
Harry Taubin
2151 Secrist Ln
Harrisonburg VA 22801

Call Sign: N4ALS
Glendon L Heatwole
3530 Seneca Rd
Harrisonburg VA 22801

Call Sign: N4TRF
Michael D Weaver
1545 Shank Dr
Harrisonburg VA 22801

Call Sign: KI4DLM
Chad O Allen
3285 Shen Lake Dr
Harrisonburg VA 22801

Call Sign: KE4ZLD
David W Napier
3361 Shen Lake Dr
Harrisonburg VA 22801

Call Sign: KF4QPD
Brian J Moshier
1131 Shenandoah St
Harrisonburg VA 22801

Call Sign: KF4QPC
Joseph L Moshier
1131 Shenandoah St
Harrisonburg VA 22802

Call Sign: KF4QPE
Eric J Moshier
1161 Shenandoah St
Harrisonburg VA 22801

Call Sign: W4POL
James D Lehman
1180 Shenandoah St
Harrisonburg VA 22801

Call Sign: KI4LLC
Brian S Cowger
5385 Sky Rd
Harrisonburg VA 22802

Call Sign: KB4IDP
Edwina H Willis
1945 Smithland Rd
Harrisonburg VA 22802

Call Sign: KE4EHN
Buffi L Jones
116 South Ave
Harrisonburg VA 22801

Call Sign: KJ4HFP
Jon J Guinn
1320 Star Crest Dr
Harrisonburg VA 22802

Call Sign: N4FGY
Joseph W Puffenbarger Sr
270 Stoneleigh Dr
Harrisonburg VA 228019062

Call Sign: KG4VOS
Riley A Knowles Jr
831 Stuart St
Harrisonburg VA 22802

Call Sign: WB4IXG
George R Brunk
983 Summit Ave
Harrisonburg VA 22802

Call Sign: W4RY
Paul W Brunk Sr
987 Summit Ave
Harrisonburg VA 22801

Call Sign: KC4EQW
Jeffrey C Crider
330 Sunrise Ave
Harrisonburg VA 22801

Call Sign: KD4UFP
Regena M Crider
330 Sunrise Ave
Harrisonburg VA 22801

Call Sign: K8SJP
James R Alpine
536 Tabb Ct
Harrisonburg VA 22801

Call Sign: N4OIS
George C Johnson
32 Tamela Ct
Harrisonburg VA 22801

Call Sign: K4AVW
Ira T Lowe Jr
1027 Toppin Blvd
Harrisonburg VA 22801

Call Sign: KJ4UDX
James E Derrer Jr
595 Trinity Church Rd
Harrisonburg VA 22802

Call Sign: KC4IZP
Jeanne L Fahrney
760 VA Ave

Harrisonburg VA 22801

Call Sign: KC4HYR
Dowl F Sherman Jr
1654 VA Ave
Harrisonburg VA 22801

Call Sign: KB4ELE
Myron G Good
Oak Lea Nrsing Hm 1475 VA
Ave
Harrisonburg VA 22802

Call Sign: W4YJ
Oscar L Short
1491 VA Ave 321
Harrisonburg VA 22802

Call Sign: K3AXA
Floyd G Kulp
1501 VA Ave Apt 143
Harrisonburg VA 22802

Call Sign: KD4ZOP
Charles P Knowles III
1200 VA Ave Lot 9
Harrisonburg VA 22801

Call Sign: KE4CKC
George C Bowers Jr
1456 Valley St
Harrisonburg VA 22801

Call Sign: N4NRA
George C Bowers Jr
1456 Valley St
Harrisonburg VA 22801

Call Sign: WA4CSG
Lee E Eshleman
13 Village Sq
Harrisonburg VA 22802

Call Sign: KJ4EYR
Valerie M Rodney
521 D Vine St
Harrisonburg VA 22802

Call Sign: KR4PO

Maurice W Parsley
930 Vine St Apt G
Harrisonburg VA 228024952

Call Sign: KA4CHX
Bruce W Ritchie
339 W Bruce St
Harrisonburg VA 22801

Call Sign: K1DB
David M Burgess
1254 W Dogwood Dr
Harrisonburg VA 228025537

Call Sign: KB3ODP
Scott A Baker
1424 W Market St
Harrisonburg VA 22801

Call Sign: AA4TC
Lawrence K Heatwole
212 Wakefield Pl
Harrisonburg VA 22801

Call Sign: N4YET
Zane R Bowman Jr
1220 Walnut Creek Dr
Harrisonburg VA 22801

Call Sign: W4IMS
William H Edmonson Jr
1170 Westmoreland Dr
Harrisonburg VA 22801

Call Sign: N1PG
Harry A Brooks Jr
1199 Westmoreland Dr
Harrisonburg VA 22801

Call Sign: KC4HYT
Pamela B Wilkins
2916 Windy Heights Ln
Harrisonburg VA 22802

Call Sign: KR4V
Richard L Wilkins
2916 Windy Heights Ln
Harrisonburg VA 22802

Call Sign: N4XN
Donald W Miller
976 Woodland Hills Dr
Harrisonburg VA 22802

Call Sign: KB5UTU
Rachel Friesen
1145 Woodleigh Ct
Harrisonburg VA 22802

Call Sign: KA4KUS
Clarence C Brand
4058 Woodside Dr Apt 16
Harrisonburg VA 22801

Call Sign: KD4ZOR
Jeffrey A Farnsworth
Harrisonburg VA 22801

Call Sign: N4UZA
Earl C Litten
Harrisonburg VA 22801

Call Sign: KJ4PTU
Amanda R Haddock
Harrisonburg VA 22801

Call Sign: KJ4MWW
Blaise Haddock
Harrisonburg VA 22801

Call Sign: AK4BH
Blaise Haddock
Harrisonburg VA 22801

Call Sign: AJ4QY
George B Haddock
Harrisonburg VA 22801

Call Sign: KI4BXJ
Inc Massanutten ARA
Harrisonburg VA 22801

Call Sign: K4MRA
Inc Massanutten ARA
Harrisonburg VA 22801

Call Sign: KJ4MWT
Kathleen T Haddock

Harrisonburg VA 22801

Call Sign: KJ4RGG
Earl C Litten
Harrisonburg VA 22803

Call Sign: N4UZA
Earl C Litten
Harrisonburg VA 22803

Call Sign: KJ4CSA
Robert P Hume
Harrisonburg VA 22803

Call Sign: W4TMV
Robert P Hume
Harrisonburg VA 22803

FCC Amateur Radio Licenses in Hartfield

Call Sign: KB3EWA
Marjorie S Goettle
136B Mariners Point Ln
Hartfield VA 23071

Call Sign: KG4PMG
Jocelyn C Dunstan
63 C Mariners Point Ln
Hartfield VA 23071

Call Sign: KC0LIK
Trudith V Feigum
164 Mariners Point Ln Apt A
Hartfield VA 23071

Call Sign: KF4ZNB
Alan D Lundin
132 River Run Dr
Hartfield VA 23071

Call Sign: KB4JIR
Eleanor G Hall
Rt 1035 River Run Dr
Hartfield VA 23071

Call Sign: K3ZXV
James W Cornpropst Jr
275 River Run Dr

Hartfield VA 23071

Call Sign: KD4IYV
Richard A Hall
Rt 1035
Hartfield VA 230710405

Call Sign: AA4HQ
Verlan R Hall Sr
Rte 1035
Hartfield VA 23071

Call Sign: KJ4FBY
Richard J Marquardt Jr
302 Scoggins Creek Trl
Hartfield VA 23071

Call Sign: K7IBM
Richard J Marquardt Jr
302 Scoggins Creek Trl
Hartfield VA 23071

Call Sign: KK4AIH
Raymond P Campbell Jr
1037 Twiggs Ferry Rd
Hartfield VA 23071

Call Sign: KK4RAY
Raymond P Campbell Jr
1037 Twiggs Ferry Rd
Hartfield VA 23071

Call Sign: KJ4HTV
David G OConnor
98 C Villa Ridge Dr
Hartfield VA 23071

Call Sign: KC4QCF
Salvatore C Messina
156 Wilton Creek Rd
Hartfield VA 23071

Call Sign: KJ4IRS
Maureen E Fairbrother
517 Wilton Creek Rd
Hartfield VA 23071

Call Sign: KK4AUV
Paul F Fairbrother

517 Wilton Creek Rd
Hartfield VA 23071

Call Sign: KJ4TYU
Robert R Lovell
1938 Wilton Creek Rd
Hartfield VA 23071

Call Sign: WB2IEX
Doris E Rice
236C Wilton Creek Rd
Hartfield VA 23071

Call Sign: WB2WKU
Arthur V Rice Jr
236C Wilton Creek Rd
Hartfield VA 23071

FCC Amateur Radio Licenses in Hartwood

Call Sign: WD4RPQ
Jerry R Jernigan
107 Richards Ferry Rd
Hartwood VA 22404

Call Sign: KA4RLJ
Norman P Steak
259 Richards Ferry Rd
Hartwood VA 224064817

Call Sign: KO4OX
Thomas N Harmon
162 Shacklefords Well Rd
Hartwood VA 22406

Call Sign: AK1E
Thomas N Harmon
162 Shacklefords Well Rd
Hartwood VA 22406

Call Sign: KD4CVC
Dorothea L Horne
162 Shacklesford Well Rd
Hartwood VA 22406

Call Sign: KG4SOM
Ruth A Braun
2 Winslow Rd

Hartwood VA 22406

Call Sign: N2OTP
David D Smith
Hartwood VA 22471

Call Sign: AD5QA
Thomas A Jenkins
Hartwood VA 22471

FCC Amateur Radio Licenses in Hayes

Call Sign: WB4HZO
Garland W Shelton
Rt 4 Box 1365
Hayes VA 23072

Call Sign: KD4YJF
George H Henderson
Rt 4 Box 286
Hayes VA 23072

Call Sign: KC4OOX
Stephen M Dirle
Rt 4 Box 612
Hayes VA 23072

Call Sign: KC4VOM
Amy L Dirle
Rt 4 Box 612
Hayes VA 23072

Call Sign: KC4EVO
Susan H Pettyjohn
Rt 3 Box 806
Hayes VA 23072

Call Sign: KJ4YQT
Richard J Pearce
9870 Breezy Point Ln
Hayes VA 23072

Call Sign: N4RJP
Richard J Pearce
9870 Breezy Point Ln
Hayes VA 23072

Call Sign: KB4KNI

Louis E Serio
8620 Broad Marsh Ln
Hayes VA 23072

Call Sign: KB4DPF
Todd E Mc Coy
3100 Browns Bay Rd
Hayes VA 230724217

Call Sign: N4SUB
Terence P Szabo
9130 Butner Ln
Hayes VA 230723926

Call Sign: KJ4JSO
Walter P Coscia
8226 Circle Dr
Hayes VA 23072

Call Sign: KE4JXJ
Fred E Weymouth II
3789 Coates Ln
Hayes VA 23072

Call Sign: KF3X
Joseph P Ross
1848 Dockside Dr
Hayes VA 230723627

Call Sign: KB4WAT
Joanne C Bell
701 Dockside Village
Hayes VA 23072

Call Sign: KB4WAU
Vernon L Bell Jr
701 Dockside Village
Hayes VA 23072

Call Sign: K4FBQ
Roy A Miller Jr
1936 E Snug Harbor Dr
Hayes VA 23072

Call Sign: KE4SBB
Eric A Miller
1936 E Snug Harbor Dr
Hayes VA 23072

Call Sign: N0ZDP
Gary M Tripp
3681 George Washington Mem
Hwy
Hayes VA 23072

Call Sign: KJ4IEV
Gary M Tripp
3681 George Washington Mem
Hwy
Hayes VA 23072

Call Sign: KI4RNP
Thomas N Maclay
8399 Glass Rd
Hayes VA 23062

Call Sign: W4JWL
Thomas N Maclay
8399 Glass Rd
Hayes VA 23072

Call Sign: KC4ANN
Anna G Holloway
2281 Hayes Rd
Hayes VA 23072

Call Sign: WA4WPO
Linda L Breeden
5737 Horsley Rd
Hayes VA 23072

Call Sign: KC5LOC
John A Retikis
6931 Lakeside Dr
Hayes VA 23072

Call Sign: KE4VCX
Michael M Mahler
3765 Laurellye Ln
Hayes VA 23072

Call Sign: W4OVI
Thomas H Arnold
8175 Little England Rd
Hayes VA 23072

Call Sign: KC4ROT
Kenneth Roberts

1906 Mallard Point Ln
Hayes VA 23072

Call Sign: KJ4RBL
William L Slusher
1950 Merrick Dr
Hayes VA 23072

Call Sign: KJ4RBK
William H Slusher
1950 Merrick Dr
Hayes VA 23072

Call Sign: KD4OQI
Alfred B Little Jr
4123 Mile Gate Ln
Hayes VA 23072

Call Sign: KC4ZDC
Barbara M Little
4321 Mile Gate Ln
Hayes VA 23072

Call Sign: KG4ABI
Rebecca L Little
4321 Milegate Ln
Hayes VA 23072

Call Sign: WB7URZ
Randal S Pryor
6739 Powhatan Dr
Hayes VA 23072

Call Sign: KA7AZS
Joan R Pryor
6632 Quail Hollow Dr
Hayes VA 23072

Call Sign: KA7AZT
Loren S Pryor
6632 Quail Hollow Dr
Hayes VA 23072

Call Sign: KB4KHZ
Barbara F Stevens
2073 River Rd
Hayes VA 23072

Call Sign: WD4ONE

James R Stevens
2073 River Rd
Hayes VA 23072

Call Sign: KE4OVQ
John H Hagens III
2065 Sarahs Cove Dr
Hayes VA 230723746

Call Sign: KG4DJY
Kurt W Oest
7088 Tandems Way
Hayes VA 23072

Call Sign: K3RUM
Walter J Tillman Sr
1981 Tillage Ln
Hayes VA 23072

Call Sign: N1VW
Didier Van Went
3536 Vaughan Creek Dr
Hayes VA 23072

Call Sign: N8RK
Ralf S Klingler
3536 Vaughan Creek Dr
Hayes VA 23072

Call Sign: KC4GYO
Barbara M Stephens
Hayes VA 23072

Call Sign: KC4ROS
Mark T Matthews
Hayes VA 23072

Call Sign: KG4YAM
James R Debaun
Hayes VA 23072

Call Sign: KI4BES
William L Graham
Hayes VA 23072

Call Sign: KC4GYP
Arline S Lanciano
Hayes VA 23072

FCC Amateur Radio Licenses in Haymarket

Call Sign: N4ENW
Lowell E Puckett Sr
5519 Antioch Rd
Haymarket VA 20169

Call Sign: KJ4MTS
Michelle S Park
14850 China Ct
Haymarket VA 20169

Call Sign: WD4MPG
David O Buschow
2319 Contest Ln
Haymarket VA 220691209

Call Sign: KK4AQW
Michael W Barrett
16082 Crusade Ct
Haymarket VA 20169

Call Sign: KK4ARG
Zachary E Barrett
16082 Crusade Ct
Haymarket VA 20169

Call Sign: KE4HOT
James A Field
14980 Gaines Mill Cir
Haymarket VA 20169

Call Sign: W1MYR
Henry A Wilkins
15145 Golf View Dr
Haymarket VA 201693147

Call Sign: KC4PVA
Kevin M Loch
2307 Gore Dr
Haymarket VA 20169

Call Sign: WR5E
Jeffrey J Lambert
5047 Grand Beech Ct
Haymarket VA 20169

Call Sign: KD5OCU

Nathaniel J Lambert
5047 Grand Beech Ct
Haymarket VA 20169

Call Sign: KK4CFX
Zoeallene M Lambert
5047 Grand Beech Ct
Haymarket VA 20169

Call Sign: KJ4KGA
Kristofer Lambert
5047 Grand Beech Ct
Haymarket VA 20169

Call Sign: N3MWJ
Barbara L Sever
14793 Greenhill Crossing Dr
Haymarket VA 20169

Call Sign: AD3U
James F Ness
4001 Greenville Dr
Haymarket VA 220692412

Call Sign: KC5TJN
Jeffrey M Shapiro
4025 Greenville Dr
Haymarket VA 201692412

Call Sign: KA3MQV
William J Winkler
15505 Hagen Way
Haymarket VA 20169

Call Sign: KJ4AZX
Stephanie L Reed
6821 Hartzell Hill Ln
Haymarket VA 20169

Call Sign: KK4ARN
Timothy M Simon
6821 Hartzell Hill Ln
Haymarket VA 20169

Call Sign: KJ4OCD
Jason E Lee
14518 Holshire Way
Haymarket VA 20169

Call Sign: KJ4OCJ
John H Lee
14518 Holshire Way
Haymarket VA 20169

Call Sign: KI4GZZ
Joy E Lee
14518 Holshire Way
Haymarket VA 20169

Call Sign: KJ4ZIH
Richard M Shannon Jr
6872 Hurd Ln
Haymarket VA 20169

Call Sign: AA1EQ
Shannon M Rogers
2911 Jackson Dr
Haymarket VA 20169

Call Sign: WM2L
Michael J Coker
14930 Largo Vista Dr
Haymarket VA 20169

Call Sign: KD4ZRV
Alicia D Coker
14930 Largo Vista Dr
Haymarket VA 22069

Call Sign: N6XBC
Nathaniel J Coker
14930 Largo Vista Dr
Haymarket VA 22069

Call Sign: KF4VLR
Helena M Coker
14930 Largo Vista Dr
Haymarket VA 201691238

Call Sign: W1TQS
George A Bowley
15434 Legacy Way
Haymarket VA 20169

Call Sign: WA2CAU
Terry L Kuraner
2526 Little River Rd
Haymarket VA 20169

Call Sign: K2DK
David J Kuraner
2526 Little River Rd
Haymarket VA 22069

Call Sign: KD4TKH
Calvin D White
2625 Logmill Rd
Haymarket VA 22069

Call Sign: KJ4VPW
Thomas J Rowland Jr
5605 Mendelmore Way
Haymarket VA 20169

Call Sign: K4DSL
Fred A Johnson
5622 Mendelmore Way
Haymarket VA 201692676

Call Sign: KJ4HSW
David Vinson Jr
5501 Merchants View Sq 238
Haymarket VA 20169

Call Sign: K4TMV
David Vinson Jr
5501 Merchants View Sq 238
Haymarket VA 20169

Call Sign: KI4WGC
Philip L Simerly
4102 Mtn Rd
Haymarket VA 20169

Call Sign: KF4IRR
Teresa C Wyrick
4330 Mtn View Dr
Haymarket VA 20169

Call Sign: N4USI
Michael J Wyrick
4330 Mtn View Dr
Haymarket VA 20169

Call Sign: N3UC
Michael J Wyrick
4330 Mtn View Dr

Haymarket VA 20169

Call Sign: KI4EEC
Ao-27 Control Operator Assoc
4330 Mtnview Dr
Haymarket VA 20169

Call Sign: N4USI
Ao-27 Control Operator Assoc
4330 Mtnview Dr
Haymarket VA 20169

Call Sign: KJ4KII
James M Wyrick
4330 Mtnview Dr
Haymarket VA 20169

Call Sign: KI4WPV
Keith D Morrison
15756 Oak Ln
Haymarket VA 20169

Call Sign: KJ4UNK
Donald Brauninger
6227 Olga Ct
Haymarket VA 20169

Call Sign: WA2KLF
Donald Brauninger
6227 Olga Ct
Haymarket VA 20169

Call Sign: KA9KUJ
Vincent G Trobbiani
14402 Otis Ct
Haymarket VA 20169

Call Sign: K4MRL
Garrison C Cavell
15806 Palmer Ln
Haymarket VA 20169

Call Sign: KI4AFQ
Larry L Snead
13203 Piedmont Virst Dr
Haymarket VA 20169

Call Sign: K8WTF
Robert J Ayres

6018 Popes Creek Pl
Haymarket VA 20169

Call Sign: W4XP
Charles R Watts
1905 Ridge Rd
Haymarket VA 201691521

Call Sign: K8ISK
Terrence V Price
2702 Rodgers Ter
Haymarket VA 20169

Call Sign: W8ZN
Terrence V Price
2702 Rodgers Ter
Haymarket VA 20169

Call Sign: K4MEP
Marjorie E Price
2702 Rodgers Ter
Haymarket VA 20169

Call Sign: KG4NXY
Marjorie E Price
2702 Rodgers Ter
Haymarket VA 20169

Call Sign: AC4N
Jay I Watkins Jr
2805 Rodgers Ter
Haymarket VA 22069

Call Sign: N2NAR
Michael P Zingaro Jr
2902 Rodgers Ter
Haymarket VA 20169

Call Sign: KG4AVR
Angela G Brown-Garasic
2911 Rodgers Ter
Haymarket VA 20169

Call Sign: KG6YFP
Matthew C Meek
15724 Rothschild Ct
Haymarket VA 20169

Call Sign: K4FNV

Thomas H Nyman
5843 Seven Pines Ct
Haymarket VA 20169

Call Sign: KC4YMF
Thomas M Bohacek
16078 Simon Kenton Rd
Haymarket VA 22069

Call Sign: AI4UZ
Thomas M Bohacek
16078 Simon Kenton Rd
Haymarket VA 22069

Call Sign: KJ4VIU
Bull Run Mountain ARA
1708 Summit Dr
Haymarket VA 20169

Call Sign: W4BRM
Bull Run Mountain ARA
1708 Summit Dr
Haymarket VA 20169

Call Sign: KE2N
Kenneth Jamrogowicz
1708 Summit Dr
Haymarket VA 20169

Call Sign: KJ4VRX
Holger C Morgan
1804 Summit Dr
Haymarket VA 20169

Call Sign: N4ACH
Holger C Morgan
1804 Summit Dr
Haymarket VA 20169

Call Sign: KR4ZN
Geoffrey K Hicks
17030 Thousand Oaks Dr
Haymarket VA 20169

Call Sign: N4GKH
Geoffrey K Hicks
17030 Thousand Oaks Dr
Haymarket VA 20169

Call Sign: KI4OWG
Morgan D Jones
16810 Thunder Rd
Haymarket VA 20169

Call Sign: KJ4RDJ
Roger K Blinn
5340 Trevino Dr
Haymarket VA 20169

Call Sign: KA4WCQ
Christian M Oudar
5406 Trevino Dr
Haymarket VA 20169

Call Sign: N4QDD
Theodore L Gausmann
7023 Venus Ct
Haymarket VA 20169

Call Sign: KB8SSV
Sonji A Thee
5905 Wandering Run Ct
Haymarket VA 20169

Call Sign: KF8OI
Paul L Thee
5905 Wandering Run Ct
Haymarket VA 20169

Call Sign: WB8HPH
David A Dobis
5001 Warwick Hills Ct
Haymarket VA 20169

Call Sign: KE4GCY
William M Washington
15604 Waterfall Rd
Haymarket VA 22069

Call Sign: KJ4HSM
Alexander Graham Bell Pioneer
Repeater Association
15855 Waterfall Rd
Haymarket VA 20169

Call Sign: W3AGB
Alexander Graham Bell Pioneer
Repeater Association

15855 Waterfall Rd
Haymarket VA 20169

Call Sign: W4YP
Robert L Spindle Jr
15855 Waterfall Rd
Haymarket VA 201692128

Call Sign: KK4DOV
Quentin L Pennington II
5757 Waterloo Bridge Cir
Haymarket VA 20169

Call Sign: KJ4MFA
Russell Keaveny
6264 Woodruff Springs Way
Haymarket VA 20169

Call Sign: N3HIG
Mark D Swartz
2513 Youngs Dr
Haymarket VA 20169

Call Sign: WB4GDU
Donald J Ertel
2516 Youngs Dr
Haymarket VA 22069

Call Sign: KD4UWW
Russell B Henley
2713 Youngs Dr
Haymarket VA 201691621

FCC Amateur Radio Licenses in Haynesville

Call Sign: KE4RMF
Sara E Bronner
Haynesville VA 22472

FCC Amateur Radio Licenses in Haysi

Call Sign: N4ZEJ
Avery G Yates
Rt 2 Box 201
Haysi VA 24256

Call Sign: NM4G

Anthony M Jones
Rt 1 Box 400
Haysi VA 24256

Call Sign: KA4RYJ
Harold E Rush
Haysi VA 24256

Call Sign: N8RGQ
Terry L Oquin
Haysi VA 242560211

Call Sign: KI4LBL
Michael L Oquin
Haysi VA 242560211

FCC Amateur Radio Licenses in Haywood

Call Sign: KG4VEC
Darren S Estes
2544 W Hoover Rd
Haywood VA 22722

FCC Amateur Radio Licenses in Heathsville

Call Sign: KC4YJ
Gordon C Oehler
192 Blue Heron Dr
Heathsville VA 224732335

Call Sign: WA4SOU
Edmund T Brown
135 Bowsprit Ln
Heathsville VA 22473

Call Sign: AC4SG
Victor O Chicoine
Rt 3 Box 253E
Heathsville VA 22473

Call Sign: KE4FAV
Catherine R Morhard
Rt 1 Box 275Z
Heathsville VA 22473

Call Sign: KA4DEO
William C Morhard

Rt 1 Box 275Z
Heathsville VA 22473

Call Sign: N4PJ
Paul W Johnson
916 Canvasback Ln
Heathsville VA 22473

Call Sign: WD4JZN
Rita W Johnson
916 Canvasback Ln
Heathsville VA 22473

Call Sign: K4KBA
Charles A Vinroot
1966 Clarketown Rd
Heathsville VA 22473

Call Sign: AC4AC
Henry R Owen
114 Compass Dr
Heathsville VA 22473

Call Sign: KD8UD
Lewis B Ridgway
4198 Hacks Neck Rd
Heathsville VA 22473

Call Sign: K4PZC
Howard H Mullins III
39 Holly Dr
Heathsville VA 22473

Call Sign: AJ4XN
Ronald P Denton Sr
4 Ingram Bay Dr
Heathsville VA 22473

Call Sign: KD4GKA
Frank P Pisciotta
187 Ingram Bay Dr
Heathsville VA 224734502

Call Sign: W2NGC
Albert L Brown Jr
64 Keel Ct
Heathsville VA 22473

Call Sign: KN3E

Edwin B Hoeck Jr
63 Laser Ct
Heathsville VA 22473

Call Sign: K4AAB
Ernest L White Jr
217 Marshalls Beach Rd
Heathsville VA 224732270

Call Sign: AJ4EU
Carl G Wigginton
11 Pintail Ln
Heathsville VA 22473

Call Sign: N8HGS
Robert D Cleland
67 Pintail Ln
Heathsville VA 22473

Call Sign: W4HH
Joseph A Schlatter Jr
196 Potomac Dr
Heathsville VA 22473

Call Sign: KK4AIO
Charles R Lawson
671 Spring Rd
Heathsville VA 22473

Call Sign: KF4PQF
David C Harrell
Wittstatt Ln
Heathsville VA 22473

FCC Amateur Radio Licenses in Henrico

Call Sign: N4YNU
Guy L Edwards
2418 Alycia Ave
Henrico VA 232283813

Call Sign: N4THA
Sanford T Terry III
819A Arlington Cir
Henrico VA 23229

Call Sign: WD8CHP
Michael Billie III

9411 Brightway Ct
Henrico VA 23294

Call Sign: KJ4SEM
Chad M Martin
8203 Bronwood Rd
Henrico VA 23229

Call Sign: KC4YVE
George R Pristas
1303 Careybrook Dr
Henrico VA 232385017

Call Sign: N4DWK
David W Kiefer
1219 Condover Rd
Henrico VA 232295409

Call Sign: KJ4CMA
Scott F Avery
2600 Dancer Rd
Henrico VA 23294

Call Sign: KJ4SCZ
Christina R Donohue-Bannister
3100 Danville St
Henrico VA 23231

Call Sign: K5JAJ
John A Janssen
2616 Duffy Ct
Henrico VA 232332189

Call Sign: N5WXB
Brian W Neundorff
7007 Flagstaff Ln
Henrico VA 23228

Call Sign: W4SBI
Kevin J Fields
7608 Glendale Acres Pl
Henrico VA 23231

Call Sign: KC4TJR
William J Selph
4371 Lakefield Mews Dr Apt C
Henrico VA 232314146

Call Sign: KD4LUC

David D Whalen
1686 Liberty Bell Ct
Henrico VA 23238

Call Sign: KD4LEH
James V Tomasello
3001 Manor Dr
Henrico VA 232301931

Call Sign: KG4LJG
Hannah E Combs
110 N New Ave
Henrico VA 23075

Call Sign: W4MEV
Mark E Veney
1737 New Market Rd
Henrico VA 23231

Call Sign: KF4WNU
Stephen D Whitson
3014 Ruthland Rd
Henrico VA 23228

Call Sign: NK4H
Robert A Ladd
10500 Sancrest Rd
Henrico VA 23238

Call Sign: KK4GXG
Susan B Hackett
12251 Shoreview Dr
Henrico VA 23233

Call Sign: KI4AXW
Eddie C Klebau III
3909 Sunburst Rd
Henrico VA 23294

Call Sign: W1MTN
Paul M Gaitanis
2431 Vandover Rd
Henrico VA 23229

Call Sign: KI4WCK
Charles G John
2304 Viking Ln
Henrico VA 23228

Call Sign: KD4GAO
Carter B Dudley
807 Wales Dr
Henrico VA 23075

Call Sign: WD4PKP
Brian E Berger
1537 Westshire Ln
Henrico VA 23238

Call Sign: W4PKP
Brian E Berger
1537 Westshire Ln
Henrico VA 23238

Call Sign: KC4NYJ
Robert I Wall
1808 Windingridge Dr
Henrico VA 232384137

Call Sign: KJ4QZI
Mary D Brooks
6935 Yahley Mill Rd
Henrico VA 23231

Call Sign: KC4YVA
Robert M Brooks
6935 Yahley Mill Rd
Henrico VA 232316416

Call Sign: KJ4VSE
Ralph W Russell II
Henrico VA 23242

Call Sign: KI4TLQ
Laura A Bouharoun
Henrico VA 23255

Call Sign: N4SIR
Wade F Bouharoun
Henrico VA 23255

FCC Amateur Radio Licenses in Henry

Call Sign: KF4SHU
Doris C Wheeler
10735 Henry Rd
Henry VA 24102

Call Sign: KE4HOA
Franklin E Gaver
1569 Log Cabin Dr
Henry VA 24102

Call Sign: N4FEG
Franklin E Gaver
1569 Log Cabin Dr
Henry VA 24102

Call Sign: K4HOA
Franklin E Gaver
1569 Log Cabin Dr
Henry VA 24102

Call Sign: N3JGY
Albert J Young III
150 Scout Dr
Henry VA 24102

FCC Amateur Radio Licenses in Herndon

Call Sign: WA3WDR
Robert E Bruhns
602 Adams St
Herndon VA 201704613

Call Sign: KO4EX
Troy T Collinsworth
656 Alabama Dr
Herndon VA 22070

Call Sign: KD4HAT
Donna L Smith
13518 Apple Barrel Ct
Herndon VA 22071

Call Sign: N4PBI
Christine Wise
13152 Applegrove Ln
Herndon VA 201713943

Call Sign: WB2IOM
Michael J Gedzelman
13159 Applegrove Ln
Herndon VA 20171

Call Sign: KI4CUG
Tracy L Macfawn Hibbard
1333 April Way
Herndon VA 20170

Call Sign: N2PZH
Robert M Verdon
12534 Arnsley Ct
Herndon VA 210172538

Call Sign: KG4VNP
Robert M Verdon
12534 Arnsley Ct
Herndon VA 210172538

Call Sign: W2HVN
George T Anderson
902 Ashburn St
Herndon VA 22070

Call Sign: KK4ADR
John R Dixon
3118 Ashburton Ave
Herndon VA 20171

Call Sign: KB8ORO
Matthew J Dilber
2157 Astoria Cir 109
Herndon VA 20170

Call Sign: N3IGH
Peter J Tivol
2160 Astoria Cir Apt 114
Herndon VA 20170

Call Sign: KG4UUZ
Youth Tech ARC
2242 Astoria Cir Apt 303
Herndon VA 20170

Call Sign: K4YTC
Youth Tech ARC
2242 Astoria Cir Apt 303
Herndon VA 20170

Call Sign: W4KVI
William M Stone
602 Austin Ln
Herndon VA 22070

Call Sign: KF4RKL
Clark J Rhoades
1523 Bal Harbor Ct
Herndon VA 20170

Call Sign: KJ4PSN
Joseph R Friel
1173 Bandy Run Rd
Herndon VA 20170

Call Sign: K7CS
Don C Sambol
1419 Bayshire Ln
Herndon VA 20170

Call Sign: KJ4YNF
Herndon Dx Association
1312 Benicia Ln
Herndon VA 20170

Call Sign: KJ4YNG
Herndon Dx Association
1312 Benicia Ln
Herndon VA 20170

Call Sign: W2RPX
Herndon Dx Association
1312 Benicia Ln
Herndon VA 20170

Call Sign: W6CDH
Herndon Dx Association
1312 Benicia Ln
Herndon VA 20170

Call Sign: KA3FMX
Herndon Dx Association
1312 Benicia Ln
Herndon VA 201703667

Call Sign: AB3H
Robert F Boughton
1312 Benicia Ln
Herndon VA 201703667

Call Sign: KA3FMY
Sandra J Boughton
1312 Benicia Ln

Herndon VA 201703667

Call Sign: KB3BSA
James M Boughton
1312 Benicia Ln
Herndon VA 201703667

Call Sign: W6CDH
Herndon Dx Association
1312 Benicia Ln
Herndon VA 201703667

Call Sign: AC3H
James M Boughton
1312 Benicia Ln
Herndon VA 201703667

Call Sign: KB4TCT
Sharla L Cerra
12216 Bennett Rd
Herndon VA 22071

Call Sign: KI4TGP
Timothy J Keller
3231 Betsy Ln
Herndon VA 20171

Call Sign: WB4ZBU
Thomas D Trenkle
1202 Bicksler Ct
Herndon VA 221703106

Call Sign: KA7WNW
Michael C Hunsaker
1204 Bicksler Ct
Herndon VA 201703106

Call Sign: KC4OUF
Susanta Heendeniya
1131 Bicksler Dr
Herndon VA 22070

Call Sign: KJ4VHY
Coleman Blake
502 Bowers Ln
Herndon VA 20170

Call Sign: KJ4VTI
Sandra L Blake

502 Bowers Ln
Herndon VA 201705108

Call Sign: N3TKI
Frank B Scalzo
815 Branch Dr Unit 401
Herndon VA 20170

Call Sign: KH6UT
Karen M Wood
2502 Branding Iron Ct
Herndon VA 22071

Call Sign: N4OIY
Jay E Patterson
12816 Briery River Ter
Herndon VA 22070

Call Sign: AD6YC
Bruce O Benson
13529 Brightfield Ln
Herndon VA 201713362

Call Sign: KD4PWW
Hai H Nguyen
903 Broad Oaks Dr
Herndon VA 22070

Call Sign: KI4VDA
Adam Issahaku
2449 Brook Overlook Ct 302
Herndon VA 20171

Call Sign: KE4KGN
David J Schwartz
12546 Browns Ferry Rd
Herndon VA 20170

Call Sign: KG4RRL
Sean S Lawrence
1109 Burwick Dr
Herndon VA 20170

Call Sign: KB3CNE
Theodore P Woo
703 Campbell Way
Herndon VA 20170

Call Sign: WB4PHJ

Michael E Anderson
1438 Cellar Creek Way
Herndon VA 201702805

Call Sign: KI4FVY
Erik R Shafer
560 Center St
Herndon VA 20170

Call Sign: W4HPD
Michael E Rubin
12504 Chasbarb Ter
Herndon VA 20171

Call Sign: KK4FRB
Paresh Y Karandikar
12505 Chasbarb Ter
Herndon VA 20171

Call Sign: W4OUM
N L Cox
12018 Cheviot Dr
Herndon VA 22070

Call Sign: KG4ICG
Ronald E Collins Jr
2227 Christy Pl
Herndon VA 20170

Call Sign: WA4EZY
Jack D Martin
12920 Cinnamon Oaks Ct
Herndon VA 20171

Call Sign: KE4JET
Phillips Nguyen
2618 Claxton Dr
Herndon VA 22071

Call Sign: N8XOS
Gregory W Romaniak
12496 Cliff Edge Dr
Herndon VA 20170

Call Sign: KI4VYF
John F Pholeric
1120 Clinch Rd
Herndon VA 20170

Call Sign: KJ4UXY
Kevin J Tierney
13599 Cobra Dr
Herndon VA 20171

Call Sign: KG4PPU
Jason S Kohles
848 Colvin Ct
Herndon VA 20170

Call Sign: KF4QOI
Elbert J Mays Jr
13602 Copper Ridge Dr
Herndon VA 20171

Call Sign: KE4OHZ
Desiree M Wilkinson
13614 Copper Ridge Dr
Herndon VA 20171

Call Sign: KE4PGA
Mark S Wilkinson
13614 Copper Ridge Dr
Herndon VA 20171

Call Sign: KG4UPJ
William L Laubernds
12701 Coronation Rd
Herndon VA 20171

Call Sign: KA3LPN
Martin A Schulman
1105 Criton St
Herndon VA 20170

Call Sign: NV3H
Martin A Schulman
1105 Criton St
Herndon VA 20170

Call Sign: AL7CZ
Gary L Tarbet
1106 Criton St
Herndon VA 22070

Call Sign: AL7DA
Vivian Y Tarbet
1106 Criton St
Herndon VA 22070

Call Sign: KK4HDO
Danny F Caudill
2356 Cypress Cove Cir Apt 402
Herndon VA 20171

Call Sign: KC6BQN
Byung Uk Lee
1191 Cypress Tree Pl
Herndon VA 20170

Call Sign: KC4RKT
Adrian K Pierce
2331 Darius Ln
Herndon VA 22071

Call Sign: KK4HMX
Mary C Boatman
1125 Devon St
Herndon VA 20170

Call Sign: KB0NRK
Earl A Boatman
1125 Devon St
Herndon VA 20170

Call Sign: KA4OMU
Len Joy
1558 Dranesville Rd
Herndon VA 22070

Call Sign: KJ4FQJ
S Joseph Vajda IV
1180 Dublin Pl
Herndon VA 20170

Call Sign: WB7EJT
Harry S Kent
12141 Eddyspark Dr
Herndon VA 201702548

Call Sign: KI4YCS
Robert A Lasky
12150 Eddyspark Dr
Herndon VA 20170

Call Sign: KI4YPF
Harold L Singer
12161 Eddyspark Dr

Herndon VA 20170

Call Sign: KG4PXE
Louis T Gnecco
112 F Elden St
Herndon VA 20170

Call Sign: N2FT
Stephen P Johnson
2972 Emerald Chase Dr
Herndon VA 201712321

Call Sign: N4TS
William F Fenn
3031 Emerald Chase Dr
Herndon VA 22071

Call Sign: KC4WVD
Daniel E Lynberg
12606 Etruscan Dr
Herndon VA 22071

Call Sign: N4ACQ
Peter F Enghauser
12609 Etruscan Dr
Herndon VA 20171

Call Sign: AB2S
Howard De Felice
804 Fall Pl
Herndon VA 20170

Call Sign: KF6JCZ
James M Butler
12731 Fantasia Dr
Herndon VA 20170

Call Sign: KG4NXS
Steven C Gibson
12826 Fantasia Dr
Herndon VA 20170

Call Sign: KJ4PSF
Douglas J Halonen
12833 Fantasia Dr
Herndon VA 20170

Call Sign: KJ4CNX
Jonathan B Walker

12848 Fantasia Dr
Herndon VA 20170

Call Sign: KD4PWS
Mary F Daffron
2529 Farm Crest Dr Apt 438
Herndon VA 22071

Call Sign: KI4ISX
Joseph H Cotellessa
2505 Farmcrest Dr Apt 1201
Herndon VA 20171

Call Sign: N4XKO
Karen A Geriak
495 Fillmore St
Herndon VA 22070

Call Sign: W1IMX
Gerald I Francer
12708 Firenze Ct
Herndon VA 20171

Call Sign: KG4YLX
Scott C Allen
1116 Floyd Pl
Herndon VA 20170

Call Sign: AA3NJ
Robin A Finesmith
12110 Folkstone Dr
Herndon VA 20171

Call Sign: N3YOJ
Ariana S Finesmith
12110 Folkstone Dr
Herndon VA 20171

Call Sign: KF4BPH
Meghan R Edwards
12118 Folkstone Dr
Herndon VA 20171

Call Sign: WA3LVH
John A Edwards
12118 Folkstone Dr
Herndon VA 20171

Call Sign: N1RN

Ronald B Natalie Jr
12305 Folkstone Dr
Herndon VA 22071

Call Sign: N2JRG
Margery A Natalie
12305 Folkstone Dr
Herndon VA 201711816

Call Sign: K4JYF
Ned K Gressle
2954 Fort Lee St
Herndon VA 22071

Call Sign: WB0LLF
Robert B Weidlich
12505 Forty Oaks Ct
Herndon VA 22070

Call Sign: N3HEU
Augustine A Dolcich
2561 Fox Hound Ct
Herndon VA 20171

Call Sign: KC7GDE
Harold L Brooke
13163 Fox Hunt Ln
Herndon VA 20171

Call Sign: K4GMU
Curt A Klun
13171 Fox Hunt Ln Apt 258
Herndon VA 201715387

Call Sign: N4NLN
Michael D O Dell
2901 Fox Mill Rd
Herndon VA 20171

Call Sign: W3CGZ
Gilbert L Heller
2945 Fox Mill Rd
Herndon VA 201711527

Call Sign: KD4IJB
Larry R Blair
12711 Franklin Farm Rd
Herndon VA 22071

Call Sign: KE4LBN
Andrew R Riehl
12723 Franklin Farm Rd
Herndon VA 22071

Call Sign: KG4OTK
James J Dean
2864 Franklin Oaks Dr
Herndon VA 20171

Call Sign: KG4YIP
Krishna K Kanakasapapathi
723 Gentle Breeze Ct
Herndon VA 20170

Call Sign: KI4PRI
Phillip J Marlow
2811 Gibson Oaks Dr
Herndon VA 20171

Call Sign: KG4DUL
James M Callaghan
11657 Gilman Ln
Herndon VA 20170

Call Sign: AF4WS
James M Callaghan
11657 Gilman Ln
Herndon VA 20170

Call Sign: KD4EMS
Gregory F Bock
11682 Gilman Ln
Herndon VA 22070

Call Sign: KA1MAY
Robert C Carmen
875 Grace St Apt 308
Herndon VA 20170

Call Sign: KF5LR
Eric H Boll
792 Grant St
Herndon VA 20170

Call Sign: KJ4BRZ
Dennis T Mirr
1357 Grant St
Herndon VA 201703012

Call Sign: KC7QOP
Lee K Shissler
404 Greear Pl
Herndon VA 20170

Call Sign: KD4LTG
John R Sherbert III
3215 Greenstone Way
Herndon VA 22071

Call Sign: KE4IBX
Larry R Brown
186 Heather Glen Rd
Herndon VA 20165

Call Sign: KG4CGT
Anthony E Trojanowski
516 Herndon Woods Ct
Herndon VA 20170

Call Sign: KI4PXN
Alex E Peake
13426 Hidden Meadow Ct
Herndon VA 20171

Call Sign: K4AEP
Alex E Peake
13426 Hidden Meadow Ct
Herndon VA 20171

Call Sign: KC4QFK
Ruben E Gonzalez
1508 Hidenbrook Dr
Herndon VA 22070

Call Sign: KE4ZPY
Susan M Gibson
12636 Holkein Dr
Herndon VA 20171

Call Sign: N1CVX
Robert J Brown
510 Hollingsworth Ter
Herndon VA 20170

Call Sign: KG4SUN
Walter R King Jr
1414 Horizon Ct

Herndon VA 201703934

Call Sign: KJ4NJB
James A Rose
3023 Hughsmith Ct
Herndon VA 201714060

Call Sign: WA3FFD
James A Rose
3023 Hughsmith Ct
Herndon VA 201714060

Call Sign: KA4KKS
John P Pope Jr
13508 Huntsfield Ct
Herndon VA 22071

Call Sign: AJ4EI
Paul Caporossi
2506 Iron Forge Rd
Herndon VA 20171

Call Sign: KA4VZM
Todd D Harding
730 Jackson St
Herndon VA 22070

Call Sign: N4HUJ
Kenneth B Weinstein
3057 Jeannie Anna Ct
Herndon VA 20171

Call Sign: AA4IP
Francis E Slim
1029 Jeff Ryan Dr
Herndon VA 22070

Call Sign: WB2DCZ
Roy E Burdette
1050 Jeff Ryan Dr
Herndon VA 22070

Call Sign: N4YTZ
Wayne R Huffman
2458 Jefferson Way 103
Herndon VA 201714520

Call Sign: N4KL
Kevin S Lewis

710 Jenny Ann Ct
Herndon VA 22070

Call Sign: KK4ADT
Samuel E Spencer
1600 Jubilation Ct
Herndon VA 20170

Call Sign: WA2NGH
Michael F Weins
1504 Judd Ct
Herndon VA 201702564

Call Sign: KC4KOW
Donald W Kling
1506 Judd Ct
Herndon VA 20170

Call Sign: KC4QVN
Cynthia E Greaves
2465 Keele Dr
Herndon VA 20171

Call Sign: N4EGX
Stuart F Crump Jr
1566 Kingstream Cir
Herndon VA 20170

Call Sign: KA4YZF
Margaret P Crump
1566 Kingstream Cir F
Herndon VA 22070

Call Sign: KB0INK
Stephen M Hall
1419 Kingstream Dr
Herndon VA 20170

Call Sign: KJ4GYL
Kenneth E Sullivan
1492 Kingstream Dr
Herndon VA 20170

Call Sign: KF4KHD
Talmage C Carawan Jr
1459 Kingsvale Cir
Herndon VA 22070

Call Sign: KC4QND

Leon D Chichester
1041 Knight Ln
Herndon VA 22070

Call Sign: KK4CBP
James R Ferrier
1062 Knight Ln
Herndon VA 20170

Call Sign: KF4SJG
Dan E Burnham
13189 Ladybank Ln
Herndon VA 20171

Call Sign: KJ4CNT
Kathleen M Walsh
13055 Laurel Tree Ln 403
Herndon VA 20171

Call Sign: AJ4HH
Kathleen M Walsh
13055 Laurel Tree Ln 403
Herndon VA 20171

Call Sign: KJ4CNK
Gregory Maxwell
13055 Laurel Tree Ln Apt 403
Herndon VA 20171

Call Sign: KF4ZXF
Neil G Corbett
130 Laurel Way 3A
Herndon VA 20170

Call Sign: KJ4QKM
Johnathan C Berlin
192 Laurel Way Apt 3A
Herndon VA 20170

Call Sign: K4DSU
Johnathan C Berlin
192 Laurel Way Apt 3A
Herndon VA 20170

Call Sign: K4KJ
John J Nagle
12330 Lawyers Rd
Herndon VA 22071

Call Sign: W7RRH
Richard A Martini
2936 Leefield Dr
Herndon VA 201711525

Call Sign: N4NFZ
Lester M Overhultz
3009 Leefield Dr
Herndon VA 22071

Call Sign: KJ4ALK
Timothy M Fenton
13663 Legacy Cir Apt A
Herndon VA 20171

Call Sign: KI4YPK
Olivette Severino
563 Legacy Pride Dr
Herndon VA 20170

Call Sign: KE6GOC
Daniel K Shirey III
1049 Lexus Way
Herndon VA 20170

Call Sign: KJ4CNO
Mark W Mellinger
2440 Little Current Dr Apt 4032
Herndon VA 20171

Call Sign: KI4ZYI
Douglas M Disabello
2440 Little Current Dr Apt 4041
Herndon VA 201714622

Call Sign: KA3UIE
Robert E Mc Culley
815 Locust St
Herndon VA 22070

Call Sign: KD4OUX
Kenneth W Mulloy
12715 Longleaf Ln
Herndon VA 22070

Call Sign: N4WXZ
Jennifer A Horne
846 Longview Pl
Herndon VA 22070

Call Sign: KF4OHH
Alan P Delaune
2028 Maleady Dr
Herndon VA 201704018

Call Sign: KI4ADX
Carl S King
1074 Methuen Ct
Herndon VA 20170

Call Sign: KJ4SZI
Sadayappan Chidambaram
12727 Mill Heights Ct
Herndon VA 20171

Call Sign: WA4SOR
Francis C Crotty Jr
863 Moffett Forge Rd
Herndon VA 201703262

Call Sign: KE4IBV
Suzanne L Hurley
2106 Monaghan Dr
Herndon VA 22070

Call Sign: W1LLC
Charles E Williams
2182 Monaghan Dr
Herndon VA 20170

Call Sign: W4PMB
Jerry L Snellbaker
1190 Monroe St
Herndon VA 22070

Call Sign: N4LXI
Lee Love
485 Montalto Dr
Herndon VA 20170

Call Sign: N4LED
Lee Love
485 Montalto Dr
Herndon VA 20170

Call Sign: N2LEE
Lee Love
485 Montalto Dr

Herndon VA 20170

Call Sign: KD4WGO
Priscilla D Love
485 Montalto Dr
Herndon VA 22070

Call Sign: N2GCC
Richard D Murad
487 Montalto Dr
Herndon VA 201703324

Call Sign: KG4NXU
Matthew J Cutler
13034 Monterey Estate Dr
Herndon VA 20171

Call Sign: KG4OTJ
Christine A Cutler
13034 Monterey Estate Dr
Herndon VA 20171

Call Sign: KD4ITN
Michael J Cutler
13034 Monterey Estates Dr
Herndon VA 20171

Call Sign: AF4WR
Michael J Cutler
13034 Monterey Estates Dr
Herndon VA 201712636

Call Sign: W4BOS
George F Lake
819 Mosby Hollow Dr
Herndon VA 20170

Call Sign: N4QHY
Michael E Rubin
2902 Mother Well Ct
Herndon VA 22071

Call Sign: KD4YIJ
David W Eisenberg
3229 Nestle Wood Dr
Herndon VA 22071

Call Sign: KQ4AK
Richard B Bubeck

3131 Nestlewood Dr
Herndon VA 22071

Call Sign: KB3IPD
Mark R Webber
13016 New Austin Ct
Herndon VA 20171

Call Sign: W4MRW
Mark R Webber
13016 New Austin Ct
Herndon VA 20171

Call Sign: AC4BT
Jerry Weisskohl
2617 New Concorde Ct
Herndon VA 201712669

Call Sign: KB4XR
Andrew L Hamm
12802 New Parkland Dr
Herndon VA 201712687

Call Sign: KF4PQC
Kenneth L Rice
12815 New Parkland Dr
Herndon VA 22071

Call Sign: KJ4BYG
Kevin C Miller
13510 Nickleback Ct
Herndon VA 20171

Call Sign: N4FXP
Michael Rosati
12707 Nureyev Ln
Herndon VA 22070

Call Sign: N4QGT
Ruth A Rosati
12707 Nureyev Ln
Herndon VA 22070

Call Sign: KC5NWQ
Gary W Duff
2523 Oakhampton Pl
Herndon VA 20171

Call Sign: WA4BUR

Stephen F Hackley
12460 Oliver Cromwell Dr
Herndon VA 20171

Call Sign: AG4DM
John L Moring III
1010 Page Ct
Herndon VA 20170

Call Sign: KF4FJH
Randy F Buchanan
763 Palmer Dr
Herndon VA 20170

Call Sign: AG4NA
Randy F Buchanan
763 Palmer Dr
Herndon VA 20170

Call Sign: NT4TN
Gregory Maxwell
719 Palmer Dr
Herndon VA 20170

Call Sign: KG4TDD
Kenji Niimi
14040 Park Center Rd
Herndon VA 210713227

Call Sign: KJ4LBB
Adolph M Essigmann Jr
12230 Parkstream Ter
Herndon VA 20170

Call Sign: KD4UNT
Earl I Rigsbee
413 Patrick Ln
Herndon VA 22070

Call Sign: KA2ETG
Scott B Deutschman
1315 Pellow Cir Trl
Herndon VA 20170

Call Sign: KI4PXO
Jolie S Deutschman
1315 Pellow Cir Trl
Herndon VA 20170

Call Sign: KD4EJF
David A Gibson
2655 Petersborough St
Herndon VA 22071

Call Sign: KI4WZW
John R Ledgerwood
12539 Philmont Dr
Herndon VA 20170

Call Sign: KB4UGH
William M Obenauer
402 Pickett Ln
Herndon VA 22070

Call Sign: KB0YYI
Mark L Spinar
12614 Pinecrest Rd
Herndon VA 20171

Call Sign: N3HNL
Louis A Schmuckler
12624 Pinecrest Rd
Herndon VA 201712611

Call Sign: KI4OBV
Blake H Gillenwater
12626 Pinecrest Rd
Herndon VA 20171

Call Sign: WA6SEI
Cheryl L Plummer
13346 Point Rider Ln
Herndon VA 201713811

Call Sign: WB6SEJ
Terry L Plummer
13346 Point Rider Ln
Herndon VA 201713811

Call Sign: KG4AUY
Eric F Fox
1450 Powells Tavern Pl
Herndon VA 20170

Call Sign: KC4UBT
Gregory P Mc Cutcheon
1490 Powells Tavern Pl
Herndon VA 22070

Call Sign: KU5U
Larry K Ziegler
1500 Powells Tavern Pl
Herndon VA 20170

Call Sign: KC4HPL
Mark H Whitaker
1633 Purple Sage Dr
Herndon VA 22070

Call Sign: AC4CT
Geoff S Manns
1021 Queens Ct
Herndon VA 20170

Call Sign: KE4SVB
Winston M Gadsby
3004 Rayjohn La
Herndon VA 20171

Call Sign: K5CHH
John M Spencer
3013 Rayjohn Ln
Herndon VA 22071

Call Sign: KD4FUE
Robert S Thompson
1264 Redwood Ct
Herndon VA 20170

Call Sign: K4JI
Robert S Thompson
1264 Redwood Ct
Herndon VA 20170

Call Sign: KC6PWY
Robert A Gregor
2909 Rock Manor Ct
Herndon VA 20171

Call Sign: KD6MJU
Sallie O Gregor
2909 Rock Manor Ct
Herndon VA 20171

Call Sign: KF4AUX
Robert A Rauh
12591 Rock Ridge Rd

Herndon VA 201702876

Call Sign: KI4LGN
Samantha A Kaplan
2361 Rolling Fork Cir Apt 206
Herndon VA 20171

Call Sign: KT4YV
Mark A Goforth
3301 Rosemere Ct
Herndon VA 20171

Call Sign: WB0TFG
Paul E Travis
1004 Saber Ln
Herndon VA 22070

Call Sign: KC4ITS
Michael E Nelson
1034 Saber Ln
Herndon VA 22070

Call Sign: KD4GSX
James P Hogarty
1517 Sadlers Wells Dr
Herndon VA 22070

Call Sign: KD4GSY
Thomas P Hogarty
1517 Sadlers Wells Dr
Herndon VA 22070

Call Sign: KC4AXN
David R Gardy
12107 Sandy Ct
Herndon VA 20170

Call Sign: KD4GST
Benjamin T Preston
12610 Saylers Creek Ln
Herndon VA 22070

Call Sign: KF4GDE
Victor R Hewett
12807 Scranton Ct
Herndon VA 22070

Call Sign: KE4KKJ
Richard R Fabian

2157 Seaman Ct
Herndon VA 20170

Call Sign: KT4HH
Thomas F Heinan
1202 Shaker Dr
Herndon VA 22070

Call Sign: KA4GTR
Kenton L Waddell
1307 Shallow Ford Rd
Herndon VA 201702042

Call Sign: KG4SPZ
Kirk M Anzengruber
1130 Shannon Pl
Herndon VA 20170

Call Sign: KI4CTU
Anthony A Aiello
1605 Society Ct
Herndon VA 20170

Call Sign: KI4CTT
Augustine A Aiello Jr
1605 Society Ct
Herndon VA 20170

Call Sign: W4KSN
Augustine A Aiello Jr
1605 Society Ct
Herndon VA 20170

Call Sign: KE4GFL
Steven T Hood
12664 Still Pond Ln
Herndon VA 22071

Call Sign: KA1LM
Stephan A Greene
2605 Stone Mtn Ct
Herndon VA 201702883

Call Sign: KS1G
Stephan A Greene
2605 Stone Mtn Ct
Herndon VA 201702883

Call Sign: KG4MCO

Gordon R Miller
12315 Streamvale Cir
Herndon VA 20170

Call Sign: NQ4K
Gordon R Miller
12315 Streamvale Cir
Herndon VA 20170

Call Sign: WA3TSN
Thomas A Bruce
1706 Stuart Pointe Ln
Herndon VA 20170

Call Sign: KG4WXD
Thomas J Lyons
1718 Stuart Pointe Ln
Herndon VA 20170

Call Sign: KH2RL
Ramon G Sarmiento
1738 Stuart Pointe Ln
Herndon VA 201704470

Call Sign: W4PKU
Fred W Hurd Jr
1534 Stuart Rd
Herndon VA 22170

Call Sign: KB2SHY
Joanne Chisena
705 Tamarach Way Apt 1A
Herndon VA 20170

Call Sign: KA2ZEV
Michael F Chisena
705 Tamarack Way Apt 1A
Herndon VA 20170

Call Sign: KB8PEX
Marc S Goldberg
2601 Tarleton Corner Dr
Herndon VA 20171

Call Sign: W0PSO
Marc S Goldberg
2601 Tarleton Corner Dr
Herndon VA 20171

Call Sign: N4PCM
Ron M Staley
2501 Tatnuck Ct
Herndon VA 201712701

Call Sign: KA4JYG
Jeffery L Hagstrom
12650 Tereymill Dr
Herndon VA 22070

Call Sign: KB3CRS
Elizabeth M Witting
12649 Terrymill Dr
Herndon VA 20170

Call Sign: KJ4ERB
Elizabeth M Witting
12649 Terrymill Dr
Herndon VA 20170

Call Sign: KD4WGM
Bryan A James
12806 Tewksbury Dr
Herndon VA 22071

Call Sign: AC4EK
Francis E Rock
12831 Tewksbury Dr
Herndon VA 22070

Call Sign: K3SR
Charles F Rothrock
1505 Thurber St
Herndon VA 22070

Call Sign: N1PQI
Arlindo L Ferreira
13219 Topsfield Ct
Herndon VA 20171

Call Sign: KG4PSB
Donald B Falkenberg
2969 Treadwell Ln
Herndon VA 20171

Call Sign: AG4PT
Donald B Falkenberg
2969 Treadwell Ln
Herndon VA 20171

Call Sign: N1FA
Donald B Falkenberg
2969 Treadwell Ln
Herndon VA 20171

Call Sign: KG4QBJ
Lucy M Falkenberg
2969 Treadwell Ln
Herndon VA 201711826

Call Sign: AG4SK
Lucy M Falkenberg
2969 Treadwell Ln
Herndon VA 201711826

Call Sign: N5WDA
Charles R Tinney
1015 Trinity Gate St
Herndon VA 22070

Call Sign: KJ4JWJ
Terry A Lowe
13204 Tuckaway Dr
Herndon VA 20171

Call Sign: KA8EFA
Terry A Lowe
13204 Tuckaway Dr
Herndon VA 22071

Call Sign: KD4UNQ
David D Devine
415 VA Ave
Herndon VA 22070

Call Sign: KK4HDI
Bradford J Wilkins
1407 Valebrook Ln
Herndon VA 20170

Call Sign: KA4MXD
James A Crocker
909 Van Buren St
Herndon VA 22070

Call Sign: KI4OWJ
Brian F Gilleran
912 Van Buren St

Herndon VA 201703253

Call Sign: WB5CUQ
Carol Ann M Babcock
12459 Wendell Holmes Rd
Herndon VA 22071

Call Sign: WB5YAE
William H Arey
12606 Westlodge Ct
Herndon VA 201702854

Call Sign: KA4NAP
Anthony J Lutkus
3260 White Barn Ct
Herndon VA 22071

Call Sign: KG4WBU
Donald J Connolly
1731 Whitewood Ln
Herndon VA 20170

Call Sign: KB5LAM
David G Terrell
2631 William Short Cir Apt 201
Herndon VA 20171

Call Sign: KB9PKG
Randy Larke
3284 Willow Glen Dr
Herndon VA 20171

Call Sign: N1LBP
Gregory C York
1686 Winterwood Ct
Herndon VA 201702990

Call Sign: KE4NFJ
Gerald J Stueve
1621 Winterwood Pl
Herndon VA 201702984

Call Sign: K4INT
Gerald J Stueve
1621 Winterwood Pl
Herndon VA 201702984

Call Sign: AF4MO
James A Chappell

1623 Winterwood Pl
Herndon VA 20170

Call Sign: WB4FQH
Robert F Burnett
400 Woodgrove Ct
Herndon VA 20170

Call Sign: KK4GOY
Christopher J Harvey
12206 Woodvale Ct
Herndon VA 20170

Call Sign: KK4GOX
Duncan S Harvey
12206 Woodvale Ct
Herndon VA 20170

Call Sign: KC4YHK
Jeffrey P Sander
504 Worchester St
Herndon VA 22070

Call Sign: KK4HDJ
Janet L Boger
626 Worchester St
Herndon VA 20170

Call Sign: KD4JCA
William E Clinger
892 Young Dairy Ct
Herndon VA 22070

Call Sign: KD4WGZ
Robert M Gresham
899 Young Dairy Ct
Herndon VA 22070

Call Sign: KJ4GZY
Craig Pinto
2204 Zosimo Pl
Herndon VA 20170

Call Sign: K7HNR
A Thomas Moyer
Herndon VA 20172

Call Sign: KB3CBJ
David Comings

Herndon VA 20172

Call Sign: WV3H
Michael J Sever
Herndon VA 20172

Call Sign: KG4JBJ
Maria T Norton
Herndon VA 20172

Call Sign: KF4EWI
Dale A Mackey
Herndon VA 22070

Call Sign: KD4WGS
Robert G Ziegler
Herndon VA 201720229

FCC Amateur Radio Licenses in Highland Springs

Call Sign: KE4VLS
James C Wakefield
414 Adamson St
Highland Springs VA 28573

Call Sign: KG4GMW
Diane B Atkins
344 Argyll Cir
Highland Springs VA 23075

Call Sign: K4DBA
Diane B Atkins
344 Argyll Cir
Highland Springs VA 23075

Call Sign: N1EJ
Edward C Johnston Jr
107 Beauregard Ave
Highland Springs VA 23075

Call Sign: KG4AOJ
Thomas E Marlow III
245 Carlstone Ct
Highland Springs VA 230752501

Call Sign: KE4LRC
Loretta A Thomas

320 Colonel Dr
Highland Springs VA 23075

Call Sign: KD7CCD
John A Balint
436 E Washington St
Highland Springs VA 23075

Call Sign: WA4OIM
Ernest L Osborne
511 Heather Cir
Highland Springs VA 23075

Call Sign: KD4NIV
Richard S Brummitt
224 Hodder Ln
Highland Springs VA 23075

Call Sign: KE4HDW
Janet M Brummitt
224 Hodder Ln
Highland Springs VA 23075

Call Sign: KG4ZTD
Jonathan S Brummitt
224 Hodder Ln
Highland Springs VA 23075

Call Sign: KC4DOB
Ronald W Roop
19 N Battery Ave
Highland Springs VA 23075

Call Sign: KI4BKI
Dewey W Martin Jr
7 N Daisy
Highland Springs VA 23075

Call Sign: KJ4DAV
Dewey W Martin Jr
7 N Daisy Ave
Highland Springs VA 23075

Call Sign: WA4GSZ
Grady D Knott
407 N Daisy Ave
Highland Springs VA 23075

Call Sign: KD4ZOU

Ron J H Austin
103 N Fern Ave
Highland Springs VA 23075

Call Sign: KA4GKJ
Adrian L Cook
11 N Grove Ave
Highland Springs VA 23075

Call Sign: KD4UYB
Theresa D Brady
18 N Mapleleaf Ave
Highland Springs VA 23075

Call Sign: KW4DW
Dennis E Wyman
114 S Elm Ave
Highland Springs VA
230751319

Call Sign: KE4AUG
Chester L Edwards
227 S Elm Ave
Highland Springs VA 23075

Call Sign: KG4RPO
Larry A Edwards
227 S Elm Ave
Highland Springs VA 23075

Call Sign: W4KSM
William A Miller
528 S Kalmia Ave
Highland Springs VA 23075

Call Sign: KG4PTG
Charles R Hutchinson
523 S Oak Ave
Highland Springs VA 23075

Call Sign: K1TKR
Charles R Hutchinson
523 S Oak Ave
Highland Springs VA 23075

Call Sign: KE4HVC
Edward L Shipley Jr
900 W Nine Mile Rd
Highland Springs VA 23075

FCC Amateur Radio Licenses in Hightown

Call Sign: KJ4VVN
Charles William Rich
6058 Mtn Tpke
Hightown VA 24465

FCC Amateur Radio Licenses in Hillsboro

Call Sign: KB2YUM
Jefferson K Whitten
15255 Ashbury Church Rd
Hillsboro VA 20132

Call Sign: KJ4BXC
Seth D Walton
36903 Charles Town Pike
Hillsboro VA 20132

FCC Amateur Radio Licenses in Hillsville

Call Sign: KB4YFV
Randall S Mc Kenzie
3661 Airport Rd
Hillsville VA 24343

Call Sign: KK4EJ
Randall S Mc Kenzie
3719 Airport Rd
Hillsville VA 24343

Call Sign: KE4FQD
Bernie R Primm
3878 Airport Rd
Hillsville VA 24343

Call Sign: KG4ITI
Bobby D Parks
77 Amelia Ln
Hillsville VA 24343

Call Sign: WB2RLK
Robert W Billings
Rr 2 Box 180C
Hillsville VA 24343

Call Sign: W4YDC
Elbert L Marshall
Rt 2 Box 239
Hillsville VA 24343

Call Sign: KE4LKF
Alan L Alexander
Rt 2 Box 416
Hillsville VA 24343

Call Sign: KF4KMY
Rena K Alexander
Rt 2 Box 416
Hillsville VA 24343

Call Sign: W4PKM
Harvey G Cross
Rt 2 Box 446A
Hillsville VA 24343

Call Sign: KE4GGT
Janet M Primm
Rt 1 Box 484
Hillsville VA 24343

Call Sign: WA4WKU
Kenneth J Easter
308 Cherokee Ln
Hillsville VA 24343

Call Sign: KI4TSN
Elizabeth G Farris
1414 Coon Ridge Rd
Hillsville VA 24343

Call Sign: KI4JTH
Nancy C Sharp
21 Cottonwood Ln
Hillsville VA 243434478

Call Sign: KI4JTJ
Roy H Sharp
21 Cottonwood Ln
Hillsville VA 243434478

Call Sign: KI4GIQ
Glen O Watson
94 Cottonwood Ln

Hillsville VA 24343

Call Sign: KI4TYS
Ruth A Newman
4553 Coulson Ch Rd
Hillsville VA 24343

Call Sign: KB1ACQ
Joan A Severance
4323 Coulson Church Rd
Hillsville VA 243433863

Call Sign: N1NDZ
Donald S Severance
4323 Coulson Church Rd
Hillsville VA 243433863

Call Sign: KG4CUN
Gleaves E Newman Jr
4553 Coulson Church Rd
Hillsville VA 24343

Call Sign: KI4TSL
Adam S Newman
4553 Coulson Church Rd
Hillsville VA 24343

Call Sign: KI4TWJ
Jason R Newman
4607 Covlson Ch Rd
Hillsville VA 24343

Call Sign: KI4JTD
Clifford W Edmonds
1806 Crestview Dr
Hillsville VA 24343

Call Sign: KG4VTP
Sharleen L Sage
1928 Crooked Oak Rd
Hillsville VA 24343

Call Sign: W1SLS
Sharleen L Sage
1928 Crooked Oak Rd
Hillsville VA 24343

Call Sign: W4GHS
Glen H Sage

1928 Crooked Oak Rd
Hillsville VA 243438350

Call Sign: KF4ESW
Freddie W Horton
2078 Crooked Oak Rd
Hillsville VA 24343

Call Sign: W4FWH
Freddie W Horton
2078 Crooked Oak Rd
Hillsville VA 24343

Call Sign: WB4AZZ
Lester W Horton
335 December Ln
Hillsville VA 24343

Call Sign: KI4NFO
Emory F Bearden
525 Dogwood Rd
Hillsville VA 24343

Call Sign: K4EFB
Emory F Bearden
525 Dogwood Rd
Hillsville VA 24343

Call Sign: W1ZFP
Robert L Johnson
222 Edgewood Dr
Hillsville VA 243431225

Call Sign: N4XNE
Charles H Mackey
1003 Edgewood Dr
Hillsville VA 24343

Call Sign: KE4NJY
Larry J Bryant
5697 Fancy Gap Hwy
Hillsville VA 24343

Call Sign: KG4AVI
Lynn E Rucker
1758 Farmer Market Dr
Hillsville VA 24343

Call Sign: KG4CFR

Sara J Rucker
1758 Farmers Market Dr
Hillsville VA 24343

Call Sign: KA4GQN
Edsel D Stanley
4529 Groundhog Mtn Rd
Hillsville VA 24343

Call Sign: KA4JIQ
Linda S Newman
1001 Hanging Tree Rd
Hillsville VA 24343

Call Sign: NA4L
David C Newman
1001 Hanging Tree Rd
Hillsville VA 24343

Call Sign: KD4SPX
Kathleen M Waller
42 Hidden Pines
Hillsville VA 24343

Call Sign: AC4SS
Robert G Waller
42 Hidden Pines Ln
Hillsville VA 24343

Call Sign: KG4AVG
Anthony P Babcock
42 Hidden Pines Ln
Hillsville VA 24343

Call Sign: KQ4AZ
Richard W Beaver
167 John Edward Ln
Hillsville VA 24343

Call Sign: N4JBY
Ronald D Jones
518 Jones Rd Box 236
Hillsville VA 24343

Call Sign: KG4GZM
Billy J Ogle
1514 Mitchells Crossroads
Hillsville VA 24343

Call Sign: KD4DUW
James A Alderman Jr
296 Moorewood Ln
Hillsville VA 24343

Call Sign: KF4GUT
Bertha F Alderman
296 Morewood Ln
Hillsville VA 24343

Call Sign: KK4DEL
Jesse C Webb
707 N Main St Apt 5
Hillsville VA 24328

Call Sign: W4VL
Joseph A Kolb
1789 Peacock Dr
Hillsville VA 24343

Call Sign: KI4TSP
Thomas F Restuccia
145 R Way Dr
Hillsville VA 24343

Call Sign: KI4BMU
Tina L Puckett
268 Renfro Ridge
Hillsville VA 24343

Call Sign: KI4CPJ
Brandy N Puckett
268 Renfro Ridge Rd
Hillsville VA 24343

Call Sign: KI4AVS
David O Puckett
268 Renfro Ridge Rd
Hillsville VA 24343

Call Sign: KI4CPI
Tabitha R Puckett
268 Renfro Ridge Rd
Hillsville VA 24343

Call Sign: KB4GHT
Dennis N Puckett
284 Renfro Ridge Rd
Hillsville VA 24343

Call Sign: KD4PXJ
Melanie G Puckett
284 Renfro Ridge Rd
Hillsville VA 24343

Call Sign: KI4JTR
Sarah E Puckett
284 Renfro Ridge Rd
Hillsville VA 24343

Call Sign: KI4URK
Chemene Restuccia
145 Rway Dr
Hillsville VA 24343

Call Sign: KG4GZO
Barry G Lyon
1157 S Main St
Hillsville VA 243431241

Call Sign: K4EZ
Larry M Fariss
1441 S Main St
Hillsville VA 24343

Call Sign: WB0BMS
Robert J Kell
569 Snake Creek Rd
Hillsville VA 24343

Call Sign: NO4Z
Bernard R Alderman Sr
705 Snake Creek Rd
Hillsville VA 24343

Call Sign: KG4HRA
Rebecca C Alderman
705 Snake Creek Rd
Hillsville VA 24343

Call Sign: KB4SSW
Janet M Jackson
2615 Snake Creek Rd
Hillsville VA 24343

Call Sign: N4RQ
Terry E Jackson
2615 Snake Creek Rd

Hillsville VA 24343

Call Sign: KI4OND
Joan C Jennings
286 Sylvatus Hwy
Hillsville VA 24343

Call Sign: KI4IRZ
Jack E Kline
507 Troutland Rd
Hillsville VA 24343

Call Sign: KI4OMV
Kenny A Newman
620 W Grayson St Apt 12 B
Hillsville VA 24343

Call Sign: WA4APV
Robert D Morgan Jr
42 Wildcat Rd
Hillsville VA 24343

Call Sign: WD4CQC
Robert D Morgan
42 Wildcat Rd
Hillsville VA 24343

Call Sign: N4ZDA
Michael R Hall
715 Winding Ridge Rd
Hillsville VA 243433558

Call Sign: KI4TSO
John T Hall
Hillsville VA 24343

Call Sign: WD4DKH
James A Smith
Hillsville VA 24343

Call Sign: KK4CWH
Anthony S Harmon
Hillsville VA 24343

Call Sign: KI4TYT
Michelle L Hall
Hillsville VA 24343

Call Sign: KI4AVT

Rene M Neff
Hillsville VA 24343

Call Sign: WD8AOS
Roger E Young
Hillsville VA 24343

Call Sign: N4GZB
Carl D Davis
Hillsville VA 243430162

FCC Amateur Radio Licenses in Hiltons

Call Sign: KF4GMR
Jeff L Hartsock
2197 Ap Carter Hwy
Hiltons VA 24258

Call Sign: N4RXD
Charles W Moore
Rt 1 Box 140
Hiltons VA 24258

Call Sign: N4RZL
Jan D Moore
Rt 1 Box 140
Hiltons VA 24258

Call Sign: KF4PXG
Dwayne L Mc Nutt
Rt 1 Box 280 A
Hiltons VA 24258

Call Sign: WB4MSK
Earl W Hickam
Rt 1 Box 29
Hiltons VA 24258

Call Sign: KI4YYD
Marshall D Tipton
474 Cavalry Dr
Hiltons VA 24258

Call Sign: K4UNZ
Donald L Smallwood
409 Eaton Hill Rd
Hiltons VA 24258

Call Sign: KD4WPR
Matthew G Williams
17633 Federal Rd
Hiltons VA 24258

Call Sign: KD4ZVM
Roger W Mullins
420 Fowlers Branch Rd
Hiltons VA 24258

FCC Amateur Radio Licenses in Hinton

Call Sign: KG4DXE
Kelly P Mc Donald
232 Last Left Ln
Hinton VA 22831

Call Sign: KS4SP
Ronald E May Sr
10161 Rawley Pike
Hinton VA 22831

Call Sign: KN4U
Ronald E May Sr
10161 Rawley Pike
Hinton VA 22831

Call Sign: KJ4LDM
Aaron K Mcdonaldson
10352 Rawley Pike
Hinton VA 22831

Call Sign: KI4JRR
Timothy A Kile
10827 Rawley Pike
Hinton VA 22831

Call Sign: KE4GKQ
Donnie W Simmons
11081 Rawley Pike
Hinton VA 22831

Call Sign: KG4QMV
James C Hiles Jr
11270 Rawley Pike
Hinton VA 22831

Call Sign: KG4OMF

Gerald L Kile Jr
Rt 612
Hinton VA 22831

Call Sign: KD4OXR
Donald W Klotz
Hinton VA 22831

Call Sign: KE4SSG
Robert S Byrnes
Hinton VA 228310097

FCC Amateur Radio Licenses in Hiwassee

Call Sign: KC4ART
Lee A Ratcliff
2361 Bethel Church Rd
Hiwassee VA 24347

Call Sign: KR4LQ
Robert F Steffen
7015 Bleak Ridge Rd
Hiwassee VA 24347

Call Sign: N4AZL
John L Smith
6492 Cecils Chapel Rd
Hiwassee VA 24347

Call Sign: WR4VT
John L Smith
6492 Cecils Chapel Rd
Hiwassee VA 24347

Call Sign: KI4SIP
Anthony D Phillips
3414 Greenhouse Rd
Hiwassee VA 24347

Call Sign: WX4SNO
Anthony D Phillips
3414 Greenhouse Rd
Hiwassee VA 24347

Call Sign: KD4QDM
Michael D Keitz
3479 Gum Log Rd
Hiwassee VA 243472807

Call Sign: KD4LYT
Curtis D Smith
3520 Simpkinstown Rd
Hiwassee VA 24347

Call Sign: KI4JRS
Lyndell L Taylor
Hiwassee VA 24347

Call Sign: WW4LT
Lyndell L Taylor
Hiwassee VA 24347

FCC Amateur Radio Licenses in Honaker

Call Sign: KC4ZIQ
Sunset C Salyers
Hc 3 Box 120A
Honaker VA 24260

Call Sign: WD4OTE
John D Crockett Jr
Rt 1 Box 285
Honaker VA 24260

Call Sign: KC4HRQ
Johnny L Martin
Rt 2 Box 482C
Honaker VA 24260

Call Sign: KC4HRR
Betty A Martin
Rt 2 Box 482C
Honaker VA 24260

Call Sign: KF4YWO
Cora B Mc Glothlin
5132 Old Grissom Creek Rd
Honaker VA 24260

Call Sign: KC4WLR
Roger L Wallace
6824 Red Bud Hwy
Honaker VA 24260

Call Sign: KF4NSI
Adrin D Mc Glothlin

1161 Sugar Cane Rd
Honaker VA 24260

Call Sign: KF4QKP
Barbara S Mc Glothlin
1161 Sugarcane Rd
Honaker VA 24260

Call Sign: KJ4QPT
Kathy L Hale
60 Tennessee St
Honaker VA 24260

Call Sign: KJ4HTY
James A Boyd
26 Trackside Dr
Honaker VA 24260

Call Sign: KK4CDF
Karen L Boyd
26 Trackside Dr
Honaker VA 24260

Call Sign: KJ4UEK
William D Newton
1285 Wysor Valley Rd
Honaker VA 24260

Call Sign: KD4IOJ
James M Keen
Honaker VA 24260

Call Sign: KD4VEZ
Teresa K Keen
Honaker VA 24260

Call Sign: KE4UUG
Benjamin O Compton
Honaker VA 24260

Call Sign: KJ4VQU
Stanley D Bostic
Honaker VA 24260

FCC Amateur Radio Licenses in Hopewell

Call Sign: KE4NEH
Alan D Bean

401 Allen Ave
Hopewell VA 23860

Call Sign: KK4EMO
Kenneth L Bage
421 Atwater Rd
Hopewell VA 23860

Call Sign: KK4IEV
Aubrey J Taylor
1102 Black Stone Ave
Hopewell VA 23860

Call Sign: KK4XL
James L Young
3009 Boston St
Hopewell VA 23860

Call Sign: KD4IQY
James A Viars
252 Bullrun Dr
Hopewell VA 23860

Call Sign: KA4NXV
Irene L Mc Call
1405 Central Ave
Hopewell VA 23860

Call Sign: KF4YGZ
William J Bell
3406 Clay St
Hopewell VA 23860

Call Sign: AE4FL
Thelma A Mc Clanahan
2906 Clingman St
Hopewell VA 23860

Call Sign: NX4P
Ronnie L Mc Clanahan Sr
2906 Clingman St
Hopewell VA 23860

Call Sign: KK4BHK
Jerry D Vaughan Jr
2409 Danville St
Hopewell VA 23860

Call Sign: KJ4PBS

Edward B Curry
1818 Dinwiddie Ave
Hopewell VA 23860

Call Sign: KE4HDY
Carl E Anderson
621 Eppes St
Hopewell VA 23860

Call Sign: KC4AMD
Sterling R Neblett Jr
717 Francis St
Hopewell VA 23860

Call Sign: KI4KER
Deborah B Harvey
1002 Haskell
Hopewell VA 23860

Call Sign: WD4RNJ
Ronald L Douglas
1702 Lee St
Hopewell VA 23860

Call Sign: AB4JK
Robert O Brown Jr
2511 Liverman Dr
Hopewell VA 23860

Call Sign: W4WUY
Furman S Brigman
1204 Lynchburg St Apt 1
Hopewell VA 23860

Call Sign: K4CEC
Stephen D Eitelman
606 Mansion Dr
Hopewell VA 238601919

Call Sign: W4PWT
John R Hosea
811 Mansion Dr
Hopewell VA 23860

Call Sign: KF4UBF
Jerry L Draper
2305 Maple St
Hopewell VA 23860

Call Sign: WD4CLW
Joel C Hadley
10921 Merchants Hope Rd
Hopewell VA 23860

Call Sign: AD4TE
Evelyn L Bailey
506 Miles Ave
Hopewell VA 23860

Call Sign: KE4MAK
David Adorno
221 N 14 Ave
Hopewell VA 23860

Call Sign: K4FWX
Patricia M Lundquist
632 N 21st Ave
Hopewell VA 23860

Call Sign: N6MEI
Oscar E Dillon
508 N 4th Ave
Hopewell VA 238602604

Call Sign: KD4NHE
Paul S Hios
203 N 5th St
Hopewell VA 23860

Call Sign: KF4YRW
Kelli C Marks
414 N 7th Ave
Hopewell VA 23860

Call Sign: KD4IGQ
Luther C Gray
509 N 7th St
Hopewell VA 23860

Call Sign: KG4AVD
Charles D Lamb
624 N Bacons Chase
Hopewell VA 23860

Call Sign: W4VUY
John J Cuddihy Jr
711 Nth 8th Ave
Hopewell VA 23860

Call Sign: WA4LTO
James T Parsons
208 Oakwood Ave
Hopewell VA 23860

Call Sign: W4JTP
James T Parsons
208 Oakwood Ave
Hopewell VA 23860

Call Sign: KD4MJM
Jeremy N Marlowe
1915 Old Iron Rd
Hopewell VA 23860

Call Sign: KA2EGV
Alvin E Jenkins
1815 Owens Ct
Hopewell VA 23860

Call Sign: KD4OSX
Earl E A Corbett III
1600 Peachtree Dr
Hopewell VA 23860

Call Sign: KD4OSW
Earl E Corbett II
1600 Peachtree Dr
Hopewell VA 238607609

Call Sign: KE4GQI
James G O Brien
2090 Pickett St
Hopewell VA 23860

Call Sign: KJ4DWN
Philip E Andrews
3022 Pickett St
Hopewell VA 23860

Call Sign: WA4KXM
Homer L Barnes
3008 Portsmouth
Hopewell VA 23860

Call Sign: KG4KXV
Thomas E Hudgins
2802 Princess Anne St

Hopewell VA 23860

Call Sign: NI4G
Donald S Howlett
99 Queen Anne Dr
Hopewell VA 23860

Call Sign: KG4FZC
Patrick H Mason
367 Red Oak Dr
Hopewell VA 23860

Call Sign: W4PHM
Patrick H Mason
367 Red Oak Dr
Hopewell VA 23860

Call Sign: KF4DUC
Brian A Lawrence
11410 Ridge Rd
Hopewell VA 23860

Call Sign: KN4CF
Robert J Turner
134 S 11th Ave
Hopewell VA 23860

Call Sign: K4BPQ
Raymond L Stanley Sr
310 S 14th Ave
Hopewell VA 23860

Call Sign: KG4FGV
Lyne Y Clay
409 S 20th Ave
Hopewell VA 23860

Call Sign: KE4BRF
Thomas A Nichols Jr
110 S Marion Ave
Hopewell VA 23860

Call Sign: KE4HVG
Mark A Mc Chesney
406 Sherman Ave
Hopewell VA 23860

Call Sign: KI4FDE
Jonathan D Mcgill

503 Sherman Ave
Hopewell VA 23860

Call Sign: K9CH
Curtis R Holsopple
408 Spruance St
Hopewell VA 23860

Call Sign: K1EH
Edith B Holsopple
408 Spruance St
Hopewell VA 238601550

Call Sign: KF4ADH
Rick C Davis
103 Stonewall Ave
Hopewell VA 23860

Call Sign: KJ4EEL
Brian E Davis
103 Stonewall Ave
Hopewell VA 23860

Call Sign: KD4IQX
James H England
1403 Tabb Ave
Hopewell VA 23860

Call Sign: KM4R
James H England
1403 Tabb Ave
Hopewell VA 23860

Call Sign: KQ4CW
David K Ellison
11323 Uhrich Ln
Hopewell VA 23860

Call Sign: K4LTK
William W Lundquist
2807 W Broadway
Hopewell VA 23860

Call Sign: WB5DID
Jimmy L Hallcom
3505 W Broadway St
Hopewell VA 23860

Call Sign: NT4H

Harold V Williams Jr
900 W Poythress St
Hopewell VA 23860

Call Sign: KG4DCX
David S Clements
2913 Western St
Hopewell VA 23860

Call Sign: KG4HMQ
William R Soles
3909 Willamsburg Dr
Hopewell VA 23860

Call Sign: KG4ZTE
Thomas C Allen
3605 Wlimington Ave Apt C
Hopewell VA 23860

Call Sign: KD4RJM
Gerald S Uba
310 Woodbine St
Hopewell VA 23860

Call Sign: KA4TYZ
Donald C Bowers Sr
11601 Yorkdale Dr
Hopewell VA 23860

Call Sign: WW4DB
Donald C Bowers Sr
11601 Yorkdale Dr
Hopewell VA 23860

Call Sign: KC4ZIU
William J Leatherman III
Hopewell VA 23860

**FCC Amateur Radio Licenses
in Horsepen**

Call Sign: KB4QDS
Frank D Bowman
Rt 1 Box 5
Horsepen VA 24619

**FCC Amateur Radio Licenses
in Hot Springs**

Call Sign: K4WOB
Carl V Mullins
Rt 2 Box 225D
Hot Springs VA 24445

Call Sign: WA4OFT
Raymond E Cauley Jr
Rt 2 Box 24
Hot Springs VA 24445

Call Sign: KD4WXH
Yvette M Woodzell
Rt 2 Box 598
Hot Springs VA 24445

Call Sign: KR4KJ
Teddy J Woodzell Jr
Rt 1 Box 603
Hot Springs VA 24445

Call Sign: WA4NVD
Curtis E Pursley
Rt 2 Box 643
Hot Springs VA 24445

Call Sign: KC8EOB
Amanda M Sargent
5008 Jackson River Rd
Hot Springs VA 24445

Call Sign: KF8TQ
Harry L Sargent
5008 Jackson River Rd
Hot Springs VA 24445

Call Sign: KK4AEI
Todd C Hathaway
10401 McGraw Gap Rd
Hot Springs VA 24445

Call Sign: KF4UYI
John B Kershner Jr
3842 Switzerland Trl
Hot Springs VA 24445

Call Sign: WD0ETG
Michael L Spurgeon
284 Thomastown Rd
Hot Springs VA 24445

Call Sign: WL7AX
Patricia Z Spurgeon
284 Thomastown Rd
Hot Springs VA 24445

Call Sign: KI4BAT
Jeffrey Z Lemon
202 Treetop Rd
Hot Springs VA 24445

Call Sign: KI4FJV
Bettie F Armstrong
Hot Springs VA 24445

Call Sign: KI4FJU
James A Greer
Hot Springs VA 24445

Call Sign: KI4GCB
Richard L Armstrong
Hot Springs VA 24445

Call Sign: KG4UPO
Wiley B Kling Jr
Hot Springs VA 24445

Call Sign: AB4RI
David L Morrison
Hot Springs VA 244450057

FCC Amateur Radio Licenses in Howardsville

Call Sign: K4JBD
Joe S Dickerson
Rt 3 Box 171
Howardsville VA 24562

Call Sign: WA4OEW
Ellyn S Moore
2783 James River Rd
Howardsville VA 24562

Call Sign: KG4VWA
Jonathan E Moore
839 Rockfish Woods Cir
Howardsville VA 24562

FCC Amateur Radio Licenses in Howerton

Call Sign: KC4GDL
William F Ellis III
Howerton VA 22475

Call Sign: N4TSX
Michele A Ellis
Howerton VA 22475

FCC Amateur Radio Licenses in Huddleston

Call Sign: WB4ZCG
William F Mc Millen Sr
1081 Angel Pl
Huddleston VA 241043890

Call Sign: KC4VJL
David A Bates Jr
Rt 2 Box 191
Huddleston VA 24104

Call Sign: KC4HWW
Clyde D Bays
Rt 2 Box 433
Huddleston VA 24104

Call Sign: N4PMB
Brian C Peters
1035 Carters Mill Rd
Huddleston VA 241044058

Call Sign: WA4JSS
Douglas L Cooper
4115 Crab Orchard Rd
Huddleston VA 24104

Call Sign: KE4GTX
Sandra K Beazell
6352 Johnson Mtn Rd
Huddleston VA 24104

Call Sign: WD8CEB
Richard J Beazell
6352 Johnson Mtn Rd
Huddleston VA 24104

Call Sign: N4PVU
August Meidling Jr
1206 Lighthouse Ln
Huddleston VA 241042936

Call Sign: N4IMD
Timothy S Witt Sr
115 Mtwood Dr
Huddleston VA 24104

Call Sign: N4LIN
Linda F Witt
115 Mtwood Dr
Huddleston VA 24104

Call Sign: W9JUZ
Casimer Ryle
2110 Preston Mill Rd
Huddleston VA 24104

Call Sign: WA3DZS
John J Mc Closkey Sr
1207 Roach Rd
Huddleston VA 241044260

Call Sign: K1TT
Harlan S Miller
207 Spyglass Ln
Huddleston VA 241043547

Call Sign: W8LKS
Thomas W Plymale
101 Valley Mill Rd
Huddleston VA 24104

FCC Amateur Radio Licenses in Hudgins

Call Sign: W9QF
David A Lehew
7448 Buckley Hall Rd
Hudgins VA 23076

Call Sign: N8EZQ
Eugene C Strable
1493 Cricket Hill Rd
Hudgins VA 23076

Call Sign: W4VAH

William J Harden
84 Lanes Creek Rd
Hudgins VA 230760215

Call Sign: KF4PKH
Waldo W Scheid
Trader Point 144 Lillies Ln
Hudgins VA 23076

Call Sign: NH2K
Alan W Moe
Hudgins VA 23076

Call Sign: K4AWM
Alan W Moe
Hudgins VA 23076

FCC Amateur Radio Licenses in Hume

Call Sign: N3DT
David W Thomas
12137 McDonalds Ln
Hume VA 22639

FCC Amateur Radio Licenses in Huntly

Call Sign: K2WV
Clyde L Koral
Jordan River Farm
Huntly VA 22640

Call Sign: KB4SIL
Timothy J Pagano
213 Mill Hill Rd
Huntly VA 22640

Call Sign: KG4QVT
Christopher E Shroyer
33 VA Pines Ln
Huntly VA 22640

Call Sign: KG4FUA
Allan A Delmare
1482 Zachary Taylor Hwy
Huntly VA 22640

FCC Amateur Radio Licenses in Hurley

Call Sign: KG4WEK
Christopher S Lester
Hc 60 Box 156
Hurley VA 24620

Call Sign: KG4VKX
David W Datson
Hc 60 Box 219A
Hurley VA 24620

Call Sign: KG4EBV
Regina L Wolford
Hurley VA 24620

FCC Amateur Radio Licenses in Hurt

Call Sign: WB4VEU
Sandi B Clark
Rt 2 Box 261
Hurt VA 24563

Call Sign: WA4NPW
John L Clark
Rt 2 Box 363
Hurt VA 24563

Call Sign: KD4BVN
Roy E St John Jr
Rt 3 Box 391K
Hurt VA 24563

Call Sign: KC4HWV
Tammy A Wooldridge
Rt 3 Box 482
Hurt VA 24563

Call Sign: KD4QBE
Cheryl S Hasson
Rt 3 Box 489B
Hurt VA 24563

Call Sign: KF4EGH
Samuel T Tucker
Rt 1 Box 58B
Hurt VA 24563

Call Sign: W4IKN
Terrell H Arthur Sr
Rfd 1 Box 87
Hurt VA 24563

Call Sign: KE4TJD
Dwayne L Craft
344 Compton Dr
Hurt VA 24563

Call Sign: KE4TJH
Darrell L Craft
344 Compton Dr
Hurt VA 24563

Call Sign: KE4JRY
Lee E Vaughan
4489 Dews Rd
Hurt VA 24563

Call Sign: KD4WHE
Albert S Dewberry
209 Dogwood Ln
Hurt VA 24563

Call Sign: KE4LIL
Roy E St John
215 Dogwood Ln
Hurt VA 24563

Call Sign: KJ4QBZ
Eddie A Keene Sr
2572 Easome Rd
Hurt VA 24563

Call Sign: KD4JJH
Brian K Burnette
2541 Level Run Rd
Hurt VA 24563

Call Sign: KI4BOI
Christopher D Brooks
4214 Level Run Rd
Hurt VA 24563

Call Sign: KI4BOH
Kristie M Brooks
4214 Level Run Rd

Hurt VA 24563

Call Sign: KK4HLR
Jason B Hill
218 Longview Rd
Hurt VA 24563

Call Sign: N4NCQ
Naomi A Myers
414 Oakwood Dr
Hurt VA 24563

Call Sign: N4KSS
Mark T Myers
414 Oakwood Dr
Hurt VA 245632137

Call Sign: KJ4SND
Amy K Johnson
316 School Rd
Hurt VA 24563

Call Sign: KJ4DSJ
Eric D Johnson
316 School Rd
Hurt VA 24563

Call Sign: AJ4VN
Eric D Johnson
316 School Rd
Hurt VA 24563

Call Sign: K4ABA
Auburn B Adams
214 A School Rd
Hurt VA 245632113

Call Sign: KG4VLM
Robert L Hunt III
553 Spaniel Rd
Hurt VA 24563

Call Sign: KG4LKG
Timothy R Bowling
204 Tanyard Rd
Hurt VA 24563

Call Sign: KG4POP
Steve A Shelton Jr

233 Tanyard Rd
Hurt VA 24563

Call Sign: KI4CIK
David R Duffer
6581 Telegraph Rd
Hurt VA 24563

Call Sign: KC4OFM
Walter C Bruce
Hurt VA 24563

Call Sign: KE4HVA
David E Tuck
Hurt VA 24563

Call Sign: N5HZI
Mark T Campbell
Hurt VA 24563

Call Sign: NJ2Y
Harry Kane Sr
Hurt VA 24563

Call Sign: KK4EIW
Mary A Dziabas
Hurt VA 24563

FCC Amateur Radio Licenses in Independence

Call Sign: KC4DHJ
Montie R Sutherland
Rt 2 Box 12 I
Independence VA 24348

Call Sign: KC4IHA
Ernest E Sutherland
Rt 2 Box 12I
Independence VA 24348

Call Sign: KF4ZIG
Ronald C Tate
Rr 3 Box 664
Independence VA 24348

Call Sign: KE4RUM
James E Tarvid Sr
61 Caprine Ln

Independence VA 24348

Call Sign: KI4NEP
Daniel K Taylor
333 Cloverdale Ln
Independence VA 24348

Call Sign: KI4NEO
John M Taylor
333 Cloverdale Ln
Independence VA 24348

Call Sign: W4RCT
Ronald C Tate
1768 Gold Hill Rd
Independence VA 24348

Call Sign: KI4NER
Robert D Wingate
160 Granite Ln
Independence VA 24348

Call Sign: KK4HNP
Samuel D Parks
1951 New River Pkwy
Independence VA 24348

Call Sign: KF4ZXN
Joseph W Kennedy
2378 Old Bridle Creek Dr
Independence VA 24348

Call Sign: KF4EBV
Derek R Halsey
956 Orchid Ln
Independence VA 24348

Call Sign: KJ4WKW
Kelly D Carpenter
618 Pine Mtn Rd
Independence VA 24348

Call Sign: KC4REC
Kelly D Carpenter
618 Pine Mtn Rd
Independence VA 24348

Call Sign: N4PAA
Carl D Brown

1059 Pine Mtn Rd
Independence VA 24348

Call Sign: KG4AVH
Donald R Phipps
125 Pond View Ln
Independence VA 24348

Call Sign: KG4BQU
Alex B Phipps
125 Pond View Ln
Independence VA 24348

Call Sign: KG4BQV
Glenda H Phipps
125 Pond View Ln
Independence VA 24348

Call Sign: K4RQK
Walter E O Neal
502 Powerhouse Rd
Independence VA 24348

Call Sign: KI4NEQ
Joan M Race
68 River Ridge Ln
Independence VA 24348

Call Sign: KI4JTI
Thomas A Race
68 River Ridge Ln
Independence VA 24348

Call Sign: KF4DUV
William S Sexton
1413 Saddle Creek Rd
Independence VA 24348

Call Sign: KF4YKE
Earl D Hackler
21 Summer Set Ln
Independence VA 243489784

Call Sign: N4YXU
Roy E Absher
185 White Oak Ln
Independence VA 24348

Call Sign: KI4URL

Richard R Toler
Independence VA 24348

FCC Amateur Radio Licenses in Indian Valley

Call Sign: KK4ESK
Lorie B Taylor
1707 Indian Valley Rd
Indian Valley VA 24105

FCC Amateur Radio Licenses in Iron Gate

Call Sign: KD4BAU
James W Nuckols
415 Chalybeate Ave
Iron Gate VA 24448

Call Sign: KD4HJL
William E Simmons Jr
Iron Gate VA 24448

Call Sign: KF4IZQ
John E Norvell Jr
Iron Gate VA 24448

FCC Amateur Radio Licenses in Irvington

Call Sign: WB8QLC
Edward J Roccella
316 Cottage Ln
Irvington VA 22480

Call Sign: N5DJB
Reginald D Boudinot
656 Glebe Rd
Irvington VA 224800586

Call Sign: K4ELH
Edgar L Hannum Jr
132 Lancaster Dr 802
Irvington VA 22480

Call Sign: KC4EXA
Carlton J Schmidt Jr
Irvington VA 22480

Call Sign: KD4SGB
Susan E Wilbar Russell
Irvington VA 22480

Call Sign: KI4ZUS
Lancaster County Ares
Irvington VA 22480

Call Sign: WE4LC
Lancaster County Ares
Irvington VA 22480

Call Sign: AD4WC
Richard R Miller
Irvington VA 22480

Call Sign: KE4OFF
Walter S Johnson Jr
Irvington VA 22480

Call Sign: KE6PA
Ralph K Hallett Jr
Irvington VA 22480

Call Sign: N3YUD
Nancy L Anderson
Irvington VA 22480

Call Sign: W3UAL
Harry W Anderson
Irvington VA 22480

Call Sign: AJ4OA
Henry A Little
Irvington VA 22480

Call Sign: KJ4BOU
Henry H Little
Irvington VA 22480

Call Sign: W4RSP
Robert C Morrison
Irvington VA 22480

Call Sign: KD3EP
Robert S Butts
Irvington VA 224800740

FCC Amateur Radio Licenses in Isle of Wight

Call Sign: N4WXS
Tom D Stanfield
Isle Of Wight VA 233970002

FCC Amateur Radio Licenses in Ivanhoe

Call Sign: KD4OLY
William C Bracknell
1137 Gleaves Rd
Ivanhoe VA 24350

FCC Amateur Radio Licenses in Ivor

Call Sign: KJ4ZFE
John M Herman
12325 Appleton Rd
Ivor VA 23866

Call Sign: KD4IEP
Richard H Hobson
13494 Corinth Rd
Ivor VA 23866

Call Sign: KF4QFH
Thomas O Marstein
37321 General Mahone Blvd
Ivor VA 23866

Call Sign: WT0MM
Thomas O Marstein
37321 General Mahone Blvd
Ivor VA 23866

Call Sign: KJ4SCU
Sherri M Radtke
37345 General Mahone Blvd
Ivor VA 23866

Call Sign: KI4ROB
Timothy A Radtke
37345 General Mahone Blvd
Ivor VA 23866

Call Sign: KJ4SCV

Angela M Marstein
37321 General Mohone Blvd
Ivor VA 23866

Call Sign: WD4EKS
James H Sourbeer
9273 Tucker Swamp Rd
Ivor VA 23866

Call Sign: KJ4CER
Clayton E Gaskins
Ivor VA 23866

FCC Amateur Radio Licenses in Ivy

Call Sign: WA4UXD
Thomas F Kelsey
Ivy VA 22945

Call Sign: KF4AGU
VA A Kelsey
Ivy VA 22945

Call Sign: WR4I
Dennis F Terribile
Ivy VA 22945

Call Sign: W2CK
Allen B Graves
Ivy VA 22945

Call Sign: KB6UST
Beatrice S Stannard
Ivy VA 229450121

Call Sign: N6AAR
Robert A Stannard
Ivy VA 229450121

FCC Amateur Radio Licenses in Jamaica

Call Sign: KK4CNE
Maryanne Gibson
937 Canoe House Rd
Jamaica VA 23079

FCC Amateur Radio Licenses in Jarratt

Call Sign: K4WKG
John L Zimmerman
411 Fields Cir
Jarratt VA 23867

Call Sign: K4SVA
Timothy P Mattox
26374 Grizzard Rd
Jarratt VA 23867

Call Sign: KG4ZPL
Jordan D Mattox
26374 Grizzard Rd
Jarratt VA 23867

Call Sign: N4LLE
Timothy P Mattox
26374 Grizzard Rd
Jarratt VA 23867

Call Sign: W4MXS
John F Zimmerman
412 Lincoln Ave
Jarratt VA 23867

Call Sign: KI4WIT
Catherine H Dieter
2405 Orion Rd
Jarratt VA 23867

Call Sign: KI4OQI
David R Dieter
2405 Orion Rd
Jarratt VA 23867

FCC Amateur Radio Licenses in Java

Call Sign: KI4KAJ
Elizabeth C Geyer
3820 Coleman Mtn Rd
Java VA 24565

FCC Amateur Radio Licenses in Jeffersonton

Call Sign: KK4DWK
Christopher G Zitzman
20105 Aberdeen Ln
Jeffersonton VA 22724

Call Sign: KD4TWQ
John A Burner
Hcr 1 Box 518
Jeffersonton VA 22724

Call Sign: KD4RM
Douglas W Kay
2374 Brighton Pl
Jeffersonton VA 227241749

Call Sign: KC0KLG
Glenn W Olsen
5426 Countryside Cir
Jeffersonton VA 22724

Call Sign: KG4TZL
Richard G Bingler
5566 Countryside Cir
Jeffersonton VA 22724

Call Sign: KA4ORK
Jay L Aceto
3015 Donnington Ct
Jeffersonton VA 22724

Call Sign: AB2NA
Joseph D Wilbur
4412 Oak Springs Ln
Jeffersonton VA 22724

Call Sign: W2IRO
Donald F Webb
17290 S Cambridge Way
Jeffersonton VA 22724

Call Sign: W4KXS
Robert C Black
6216 Scottsville Rd
Jeffersonton VA 22724

FCC Amateur Radio Licenses in Jersey

Call Sign: KC4AUV
Barbara E Stello
14151 Marshall Pl
Jersey VA 22481

Call Sign: KI4BIC
Skywatchers ARC
Jersey VA 22481

Call Sign: WX4SKY
Skywatchers ARC
Jersey VA 22481

Call Sign: KK4VR
Samuel L Stello
Jersey VA 22481

Call Sign: KG4EHN
James E Price III
Jersey VA 224810073

Call Sign: N4KUP
Marla K Price
Jersey VA 224810073

Call Sign: N4ST
James E Price Jr
Jersey VA 224810073

Call Sign: K4JEP
James E Price III
Jersey VA 224810073

FCC Amateur Radio Licenses in Jetersville

Call Sign: WB3EHA
Ernest R Ovando
10530 Amelia Springs Rd
Jetersville VA 23083

Call Sign: KF4HLA
Joseph M Landschoot
6321 Amelia Springs Rd Tr 2
Jetersville VA 23083

Call Sign: KF4HLB
Angela W Landschoot
6321 Amelia Springs Rd Tr 2
Jetersville VA 23083

Call Sign: KE4RHS
David A Webb
6700 Buckskin Cr Rd
Jetersville VA 23083

Call Sign: K4UMM
Robert F Johnston
19750 Dusty Hill Ln
Jetersville VA 23083

Call Sign: KF4LZH
John C Wilkinson Jr
20611 Patrick Henry Hwy
Jetersville VA 230832135

Call Sign: KG4JIH
Michelle L Rogers
8315 Richardsons Rd
Jetersville VA 23083

FCC Amateur Radio Licenses in Jewell Ridge

Call Sign: KF4FFA
Vivian George
Hc 66 Box 507
Jewell Ridge VA 24622

Call Sign: KE4YLO
Garland George
Hcr 66 Box 507
Jewell Ridge VA 24622

Call Sign: KE4SSL
Dawneda S Cole
Hcr 66 Box 508
Jewell Ridge VA 24622

Call Sign: KD4BLR
Steve V Cole
5898 Pea Patch Rd
Jewell Ridge VA 24622

FCC Amateur Radio Licenses in Jonesville

Call Sign: KD4YGH
James B Travis

Rt 1 Box 103
Jonesville VA 24263

Call Sign: KG4GDM
Marvin G Matlock
Rt 1 Box 112
Jonesville VA 24263

Call Sign: KG4HMM
Faye B Matlock
Rt 1 Box 112 Couk St
Jonesville VA 24263

Call Sign: KE4RJD
David M Ball
Rt 2 Box 123
Jonesville VA 24263

Call Sign: KE4FFP
Robin A Travis
Rt 2 Box 212 B
Jonesville VA 24263

Call Sign: N4TUX
Boyd K Travis
Rt 2 Box 2400
Jonesville VA 24263

Call Sign: KE4TXV
James D Byington
Rt 4 Box 278
Jonesville VA 24263

Call Sign: K4VCP
Bill Collier
Rr 4 Box 302
Jonesville VA 24263

Call Sign: N4WTX
James E Rasnic
Rt 4 Box 393
Jonesville VA 24263

Call Sign: WA4RFI
Cynthia H Rasnic
Rt 4 Box 393
Jonesville VA 24263

Call Sign: KA4BWZ

Emory C Penley
Rt 4 Box 398
Jonesville VA 24263

Call Sign: KG4CYV
James Lee Laningham
Rt 1 Box 440
Jonesville VA 24263

Call Sign: WA4ZZI
Robert R Bowman
Rt 4 Box 504
Jonesville VA 24263

Call Sign: KA4BHF
Stephen E Pennington
Rt 2 Box 737
Jonesville VA 24263

Call Sign: KE4PVL
William M Graham
Rte 3 Box 742
Jonesville VA 24263

Call Sign: KK4AFJ
Paul W Clawson
2020 Clawson Rd
Jonesville VA 24263

Call Sign: K7CSX
Paul W Clawson
2020 Clawson Rd
Jonesville VA 24263

Call Sign: KE4RPJ
Sonny G Stapleton
6 Hill St Apt 22
Jonesville VA 24263

Call Sign: W4TUX
Robin A Travis
954 Red Fletcher Rd Box 2400
Jonesville VA 24263

Call Sign: WD4BNA
Claude A Pennington
3141 Rr 2
Jonesville VA 24263

Call Sign: W4BNB
John D Collier
155 Strod Dr
Jonesville VA 24263

Call Sign: WD4CBL
Howard E Bledsoe Jr
Jonesville VA 24263

Call Sign: KT4SG
Roderick Q Griffith
Jonesville VA 24263

Call Sign: N1NQZ
John P Wagner
Jonesville VA 24263

Call Sign: N4LQC
Eldon W Bonham
Jonesville VA 24263

Call Sign: N4VHS
David E Barker
Jonesville VA 24263

Call Sign: KG4OIM
Roy L Sexton
Jonesville VA 24277

FCC Amateur Radio Licenses in Keeling

Call Sign: KJ4OUK
Amanda E Deel
526 Buck Home Rd
Keeling VA 24566

Call Sign: KG4NXH
Anthony R Deel
664 Buck Horne Rd
Keeling VA 24566

Call Sign: KI4URM
Anthony R Deel
664 Buck Horne Rd
Keeling VA 24566

Call Sign: KQ4YT
Sheila D Davidson

813 Oak Grove Rd
Keeling VA 24566

Call Sign: KQ4ZI
Timothy R Davidson
813 Oak Grove Rd
Keeling VA 24566

Call Sign: KI4EJY
Kevin D Briggs
13200 Old Richmond Rd
Keeling VA 24566

FCC Amateur Radio Licenses in Keene Mountain

Call Sign: W4LSM
Rufus A Keene
Keene Mountain VA 24624

FCC Amateur Radio Licenses in Keezletown

Call Sign: KG4KKV
Louis Murray
3182 Flook Ln
Keezletown VA 228322233

Call Sign: KK4IEU
Zachary D Werner
2061 Indian Trl Rd
Keezletown VA 22832

Call Sign: KG4IUJ
Jason R Armentrout
3028 Indian Trl Rd
Keezletown VA 22832

Call Sign: KG4JBE
Dale R Armentrout
3028 Indian Trl Rd
Keezletown VA 22832

Call Sign: N4ATF
Dale R Armentrout
3028 Indian Trl Rd
Keezletown VA 22832

Call Sign: N4DSL

Jason R Armentrout
3074 Indian Trl Rd
Keezletown VA 22832

Call Sign: KG4ERB
Somer A Williams
3711 Paulington Ln
Keezletown VA 22832

Call Sign: N3DLB
Victor L Buckwalter
3272 Rainbow Trl
Keezletown VA 22832

FCC Amateur Radio Licenses in Keller

Call Sign: WA4GZA
Austin J Byrd Jr
1 2nd St Box 97
Keller VA 23401

FCC Amateur Radio Licenses in Kenbridge

Call Sign: N4KDG
William H Gary
718 Broad St
Kenbridge VA 23944

Call Sign: KO4FR
Robert W Strohmeyer
1413 Oakes Rd
Kenbridge VA 239443528

Call Sign: WB2ICM
Gail E Witty
1019 S Broad St
Kenbridge VA 23944

Call Sign: KI4KDN
John G Spease
7247 S Hill Rd
Kenbridge VA 23944

Call Sign: KI4KDL
Walter E Rich
7247 S Hill Rd
Kenbridge VA 23944

Call Sign: KI4KDK
Iris E Rich
7247 Southhill Rd
Kenbridge VA 23944

FCC Amateur Radio Licenses in Kents Store

Call Sign: WD4BAZ
Michael E Redell
3735 Broad St Rd
Kents Store VA 23084

Call Sign: N4PKP
Michael V Cottrell
595 Covered Bridge Rd
Kents Store VA 23084

Call Sign: W4CZY
Billy R Cottrell
633 Covered Bridge Rd
Kents Store VA 23084

Call Sign: KD4NFN
Jeffrey D Potter
474 Covered Bridge Rd
Kents Store VA 23084

Call Sign: K4MUD
Jeffrey D Potter
474 Covered Bridge Rd
Kents Store VA 23084

Call Sign: W4YJR
Richard W Crumley
351 Ferncliff Farms Ln
Kents Store VA 230849718

Call Sign: AA4KP
Carol A Metzger
954 Perkins Rd
Kents Store VA 23084

Call Sign: WG4T
David L Metzger
954 Perkins Rd
Kents Store VA 230842344

FCC Amateur Radio Licenses in Keokee

Call Sign: KG4VFP
Carolyn K Robbins
Rt 1 Box 196
Keokee VA 24265

Call Sign: KF4KFF
Jeremy N Penley
Rt 1 Box 268
Keokee VA 24265

Call Sign: KI4TOK
Glenda F Parsons
Rt 1 Box 275
Keokee VA 24265

Call Sign: KI4SJH
Jerry R Parsons
Rt 1 Box 275
Keokee VA 24265

Call Sign: AF4MU
Charles F Christian
Rt 1 Box 420
Keokee VA 24265

Call Sign: KF4LXR
David P Harless
Rt 1 Box 91
Keokee VA 24265

Call Sign: KG4OXG
Dan Robbins
5434 State Rt 606
Keokee VA 24265

Call Sign: KJ4TUL
Anthoney C Robbins
5434 State Rt 606
Keokee VA 24265

Call Sign: W6ACR
Anthoney C Robbins
5434 State Rt 606
Keokee VA 24265

Call Sign: KF4YJH

Dusty S Estep
Keokee VA 24265

FCC Amateur Radio Licenses in Keswick

Call Sign: KG4ZWG
Sue O Kell
641 Campbell Rd
Keswick VA 22947

Call Sign: KB4JNI
Harry L Beazell Jr
680 Campbell Rd
Keswick VA 22947

Call Sign: KB3LZE
Lois S Post
3392 Darby Rd
Keswick VA 22947

Call Sign: KI4CGK
Michael E Patterson
1095 E Keswick Dr
Keswick VA 22947

Call Sign: KA1KYO
Robert B Miller
228 Fieldstone Dr
Keswick VA 229473218

Call Sign: W4RBM
Robert B Miller
228 Fieldstone Dr
Keswick VA 229473218

Call Sign: KG4DGS
Matthew W Sommer
6478 Gordonsville Rd
Keswick VA 229471619

Call Sign: KG4ZWH
Stephen G Dobmeier
5530 Hackingwood Ln
Keswick VA 22947

Call Sign: KG4ZWI
Roger C Burket
1366 Huntersfield Close

Keswick VA 22947

Call Sign: W4BZW
Richard A Mullikin
1781 Shelbourn Ln
Keswick VA 22947

Call Sign: KC4TWE
Edward F Joachim II
3968 Stony Point Pass
Keswick VA 22947

Call Sign: KD4NNL
Michael L Johnson
4964 Stony Point Pass
Keswick VA 22947

Call Sign: KB0VFX
Kelly A Youngblood
Keswick VA 22947

Call Sign: KE4HTS
Darryl W Youngblood
Keswick VA 22947

**FCC Amateur Radio Licenses
in Keysville**

Call Sign: WF4DX
Robert M Driskill Jr
553 Abilene Rd
Keysville VA 23947

Call Sign: KB4GET
Robert M Driskill Jr
Rt 2 Box 107D
Keysville VA 23947

Call Sign: W4KD
Robert M Driskill Jr
Rt 2 Box 107D
Keysville VA 23947

Call Sign: KF4NEB
Carl J Crigger
Rr 2 Box 110 B
Keysville VA 23947

Call Sign: KB4TLZ

Gene E Lyles
16648 Farmville Rd
Keysville VA 23947

Call Sign: W4KPX
Herbert C Taylor Jr
4757 Hwy Fifty Nine
Keysville VA 23947

Call Sign: KD4NWE
Austin A Hobgood
Keysville VA 23947

Call Sign: WD4KTP
Earl N Newcomb
Keysville VA 23947

Call Sign: KI4EOE
Mark C Daniel
Keysville VA 23947

**FCC Amateur Radio Licenses
in Kilmarnock**

Call Sign: W2KNU
C Everett Coon
Rt 1 Box 1039
Kilmarnock VA 22482

Call Sign: KC4BCY
Donald W Lynch
Rt 1 Box 1752
Kilmarnock VA 22482

Call Sign: N4GHF
Harold J Sutphen
163 Castle Ln
Kilmarnock VA 224823803

Call Sign: N4GPH
Stanley R Mc Cord
191 Castle Ln
Kilmarnock VA 224829812

Call Sign: WJ4V
Carl A Broaddus Jr
558 E Fairview Dr
Kilmarnock VA 22482

Call Sign: KF4SLX
Herbert M Harlan II
235 Irvington Rd
Kilmarnock VA 22482

Call Sign: KA4ZIP
Gary E Mapes
458 Keith Ave
Kilmarnock VA 22482

Call Sign: KD4AA
Thomas D Kelley
122 Kent Cove Rd
Kilmarnock VA 22482

Call Sign: KC4QCG
Kelley K Davis
15 Lawler Ln
Kilmarnock VA 22482

Call Sign: W4CBC
Douglas A Cotter
176 Little Cove Ln
Kilmarnock VA 22482

Call Sign: KI4IUA
Morris W Dillingham
174 Prentice Point Dr
Kilmarnock VA 22482

Call Sign: AK4RM
Morris W Dillingham
174 Prentice Point Dr
Kilmarnock VA 22482

Call Sign: K2DUV
Floyd H Hollister
41 Raleigh Dr
Kilmarnock VA 22482

Call Sign: N4FRZ
Paul R Ticer
29 Roseneath Ave
Kilmarnock VA 22482

Call Sign: KA5GZR
Iris G Panzetta
244 South Dr
Kilmarnock VA 22482

Call Sign: WD5CVR
James J Panzetta
244 South Dr
Kilmarnock VA 22482

Call Sign: KD4YVT
Daniel F Hoppes II
122 Way Point
Kilmarnock VA 22482

Call Sign: KI4NAM
David C Bennett
134 Way Point Ln
Kilmarnock VA 22482

Call Sign: KA1WG
Ann G Carl
Kilmarnock VA 22482

Call Sign: KA3YYV
Francene M Carver
Kilmarnock VA 22482

Call Sign: KD4QHO
Francis J Sweeney Jr
Kilmarnock VA 22482

Call Sign: WB2NEK
Daniel J Binney
Kilmarnock VA 22482

Call Sign: KI4NGA
Michael D Nickerson Sr
Kilmarnock VA 22482

FCC Amateur Radio Licenses in King George

Call Sign: AC4MB
Adrian K Shaw
16494 10th St
King George VA 22485

Call Sign: KD4PAO
Deanne P Shaw
16494 10th St
King George VA 22485

Call Sign: KC5EMN
Daniel S Holmes
1149 Alberta Ct
King George VA 22485

Call Sign: KC5RHE
Katherine E Holmes
1149 Alberta Ct
King George VA 22485

Call Sign: N5YLA
Eugene A Holmes
1149 Alberta Ct
King George VA 22485

Call Sign: N5TTL
Gregg E Holmes
1149 Alberta Ct
King George VA 22485

Call Sign: KC4PDS
John A Berton
15 Allen Ave
King George VA 22485

Call Sign: KD4EOF
Gloria D Berton
15 Allen Ave
King George VA 22485

Call Sign: KJ4OHY
Jerry A Sanders Jr
12132 Allen Ave
King George VA 22485

Call Sign: KJ4NPA
David A Niemi
9566 Barbaras Way
King George VA 22485

Call Sign: N1FSU
Jo Rachel Jordon
15151 Belle Isle Rd
King George VA 22485

Call Sign: WA3GIN
David Jordan
15151 Belle Isle Rd
King George VA 22485

Call Sign: W4KGC
Northern Neck ARC
15151 Belle Isle Rd
King George VA 22485

Call Sign: K4FGK
Roy A Knight
15045 Big Timber Rd
King George VA 22485

Call Sign: KG4TKA
James R Nash Jr
Cedar Grove Farm
King George VA 22485

Call Sign: KI4SDP
Robert L Wernsman
7005 Chatterton Ln
King George VA 22485

Call Sign: KE5TNK
Johnny M Chandler
4327 Chesapeake Pl
King George VA 22485

Call Sign: KJ4KQB
King George Amateur Radio
Operators
7404 Cleveland Dr
King George VA 22485

Call Sign: KC4YYX
William D Collins
7404 Cleveland Dr
King George VA 224852033

Call Sign: N4WDC
William D Collins
7404 Cleveland Dr
King George VA 224852033

Call Sign: KJ4CKG
King George Dept Of
Emergency Services
Communications Group
10459 Courthouse Dr Ste 200
King George VA 22485

Call Sign: KJ4ELI
Jack W Deem Jr
8412 Dahlgren Rd
King George VA 22485

Call Sign: KF4YYA
Joseph D Mowery
8434 Dahlgren Rd
King George VA 224853205

Call Sign: AG4BW
Joseph D Mowery
8434 Dahlgren Rd
King George VA 224853205

Call Sign: KB4HUU
Raymond H Hughey Jr
11200 Dahlgren Rd
King George VA 22485

Call Sign: N4MHD
Nancy K Hughey
11200 Dahlgren Rd
King George VA 22485

Call Sign: K4SGQ
Gilbert F Comstock
14511 Dahlgren Rd
King George VA 22485

Call Sign: WA4MQJ
Craig S Johnson
4284 Danube Dr
King George VA 22485

Call Sign: KD4YHS
Daniel C Hunt
106 Delaware Dr
King George VA 22485

Call Sign: W9DMK
Robert E Lay Jr
15517 Delaware Dr
King George VA 22485

Call Sign: K9PHT
Roy K Braddy
11259 Dixie Dr
King George VA 22485

Call Sign: K8EAC
Robert N Sparbel
8216 Eden Dr
King George VA 22485

Call Sign: KE4CEG
Mary B Landino
12 Fleming St
King George VA 22485

Call Sign: KA9WNW
Joseph L Boysha
15472 Fleming St
King George VA 22485

Call Sign: N4UXN
Nels W Marvin
16400 Forrest Rd
King George VA 22485

Call Sign: KQ4XC
Steven J Shannon
8369 Independence Cir
King George VA 22485

Call Sign: KK4DEH
Christopher T Braccini
8370 Independence Cir
King George VA 22485

Call Sign: KI4OQA
Nicholas J Hirsch
15097 James Madison Pkwy
King George VA 22485

Call Sign: KQ4EE
Larry A Willis
6323 James Madison Pky
King George VA 22485

Call Sign: KF4DFA
Daniel W Dolan
7236 Jefferson Dr
King George VA 22485

Call Sign: KE4TMU
Rita G Wons
9221 Kings Dr

King George VA 22485

Call Sign: KE4TMV
Richard T Wons
9221 Kings Dr
King George VA 22485

Call Sign: KK4GXB
Clinton P Titsworth
16498 Kings Hwy
King George VA 22485

Call Sign: NV8U
Dale J Robertson
10268 Landfall Ln
King George VA 22485

Call Sign: KE4LPQ
Frank Stello Jr
8194 Lincoln Dr
King George VA 22485

Call Sign: KD4IQP
Richard L Roberts Jr
8317 Lincoln Dr
King George VA 22485

Call Sign: W4PFI
Boyd E Braden Jr
5112 Litchford Ln
King George VA 224853728

Call Sign: NO3B
David W Garvin Jr
9161 Lothian Rd
King George VA 22485

Call Sign: K4QS
Charles K Stover
13116 Mattox Dr
King George VA 22485

Call Sign: NP3ZK
Luis J Rodriguez
6113 McCarthy Dr
King George VA 22485

Call Sign: KA3DWW
Howard J Stickley

11432 Mt Rose Dr
King George VA 22485

Call Sign: KA6GWP
Rhea L Stickley
11432 Mt Rose Dr
King George VA 22485

Call Sign: WA2FHB
Gary E Carrer
9052 Mullen Rd
King George VA 22485

Call Sign: KB8IYA
Shawn E Allen
9156 Mullen Rd
King George VA 22485

Call Sign: KE4IAO
Christina M Sokolowski
8485 Newton Ln
King George VA 22485

Call Sign: K4URT
Kurt D Sokolowski
8485 Newton Ln
King George VA 22485

Call Sign: K0PT
Paul E Travis Jr
13351 Ormond Way
King George VA 22485

Call Sign: KG6FAM
Cindee A Dickens
11291 Pine Hill Rd
King George VA 22485

Call Sign: KD4TTP
Michael F Ambrose
12057 Potts Ln
King George VA 22485

Call Sign: KJ4VFI
Lucien V Casey
9050 Pumpkin Neck Rd
King George VA 22485

Call Sign: KI4PVQ

James W Otoole
10386 Rectory Ln
King George VA 22485

Call Sign: KI4PVR
Margaret E Otoole
10386 Rectory Ln
King George VA 22485

Call Sign: KB4GEZ
Alice F Whalen
10389 Rectory Ln
King George VA 22485

Call Sign: KD4IQB
Terence R Whalen
10389 Rectory Ln
King George VA 22485

Call Sign: KD4KBV
Caroline P Whalen
10389 Rectory Ln
King George VA 22485

Call Sign: KD4KBW
Patrick L Whalen
10389 Rectory Ln
King George VA 22485

Call Sign: KB4GEY
Edward R Whalen
10389 Rectory Ln
King George VA 22485

Call Sign: KD4SNO
Michael J Whalen
10389 Rectory Ln
King George VA 22485

Call Sign: W4LZY
James E John Jr
12351 Ridge Rd
King George VA 22485

Call Sign: KG4AGQ
Todd A Olivas
11405 Rocky Rd No 5
King George VA 224854032

Call Sign: KD6BAD
William H Thomas II
14354 Round Hill Rd
King George VA 224854342

Call Sign: KE4UMA
Mary K Thomas
14354 Round Hill Rd
King George VA 224854342

Call Sign: KJ4CLY
Philip M Irey IV
8335 Saddle Dr
King George VA 22485

Call Sign: K4PMI
Philip M Irey IV
8335 Saddle Dr
King George VA 22485

Call Sign: KD4BYB
Joseph J Mc Glade Jr
13131 Salem Church Rd
King George VA 22485

Call Sign: KG4SCP
Carol D Mcglade
13131 Salem Church Rd
King George VA 224852704

Call Sign: KJ4AEP
Troy A Bentz
6454 St Pauls Rd
King George VA 22485

Call Sign: AC4LS
Eric D Guinn
6444 St Pauls Rd
King George VA 22485

Call Sign: N6OJB
Robert C Getty
4226 Stafford Ln
King George VA 22485

Call Sign: KD4BHT
David R E Richardson
7 Strawberry Ln
King George VA 22485

Call Sign: K1JOZ
Robert E Richardson Jr
5412 Strawberry Ln
King George VA 22485

Call Sign: KI4DRI
Myron F Samson Jr
8087 Washington Dr
King George VA 22485

Call Sign: KI4EVQ
Myron F Samson Jr
8087 Washington Dr
King George VA 22485

Call Sign: KE4QXR
Robert W Hix Jr
7462 Washington Dr
King George VA 22485

Call Sign: KE4TQN
Jacquelyn L Hix
7462 Washington Dr
King George VA 22485

Call Sign: KJ4KX
Curtis A Parker Sr
8166 Weedonville Dr
King George VA 22485

Call Sign: KC8YSD
Jonathan W Carney
17738 Wilmont Rd
King George VA 22485

Call Sign: K8DH
David P Head
6187 Winston Pl
King George VA 22485

Call Sign: N4KZO
Michael D Smith
11440 Woodside Dr Apt 301C
King George VA 22485

Call Sign: KK4EOT
Caleb J Hull
1191 Woodstock Rd

King George VA 22485

Call Sign: KK4EOU
James W Hull
1191 Woodstock Rd
King George VA 22485

Call Sign: W4MHQ
Joshua H Cockey Jr
1225 Woodstock Rd
King George VA 22485

Call Sign: N2PLM
Frank J Redding
1394 Woodstock Rd
King George VA 224856007

Call Sign: KC4QWU
John D Jenkins
King George VA 22485

Call Sign: KD4CVG
Teresa M Jenkins
King George VA 22485

Call Sign: AF4GZ
Lynn H Gilliland
King George VA 22485

Call Sign: KB8BWG
Charles E Wilson Jr
King George VA 22485

Call Sign: KC2BHD
Greg M Hamilton
King George VA 22485

FCC Amateur Radio Licenses in King William

Call Sign: K4CNF
Guy K Carlsen
107 Ayletts Mill Dr
King William VA 23086

Call Sign: KE4CXO
Michael J Belda
Rt 1 Box 2285
King William VA 23086

Call Sign: KD4KYI
William A White Jr
Rt 1 Box 68 King William
King William VA 23086

Call Sign: KJ4SSX
Joseph M Fijol Jr
7696 E River Rd
King William VA 23086

Call Sign: KG4PET
Carol L Valdez
315 Fairfield Dr
King William VA 23086

Call Sign: KG4PEU
Stephen M Valdez Jr
315 Fairfield Dr
King William VA 23086

Call Sign: KG4CEQ
Charles E Davis
4709 Greenlevel Rd
King William VA 230862320

Call Sign: KJ4JPR
Jesse R Wise
98 Jackson Rd
King William VA 23086

Call Sign: KO4OP
Richard H Meador
230 Roane Oak Trl
King William VA 23086

FCC Amateur Radio Licenses in Kingstonwe

Call Sign: KD8FRG
Kent L Harper
7572 Cross Gate Ln
Kingstonwe VA 22315

FCC Amateur Radio Licenses in Kinsale

Call Sign: W3OVH
Robert A Kuhn

518 Plainview Rd
Kinsale VA 22488

Call Sign: KE4DKP
Herbert C Conley
Kinsale VA 22488

Call Sign: KG4RCO
Sharon E Eddy
Kinsale VA 22488

Call Sign: AG4OQ
Sharon E Eddy
Kinsale VA 22488

FCC Amateur Radio Licenses in Lackey

Call Sign: WB4KDY
Talmadge D Huckabee
Lackey VA 23694

FCC Amateur Radio Licenses in Lacrosse

Call Sign: KB2TZD
Matthew L C Denney
443 Butchers Ln
Lacrosse VA 23950

Call Sign: N3VPU
Ronald A Fells
487 Cole Ln
Lacrosse VA 23950

Call Sign: KJ4KSZ
Mark W Clemmons
2299 Country Club Rd
Lacrosse VA 23950

Call Sign: KF4MQA
Stephen D Clary
1519 Nellie Jones Rd
Lacrosse VA 23950

Call Sign: KF4KBS
Andrew B Moseley
Lacrosse VA 23950

Call Sign: KF4MFW
Marcia J Moseley
Lacrosse VA 23950

Call Sign: KI4TXE
James R Mills Jr
Lacrosse VA 23950

Call Sign: KJ4VJK
James R Telfer
Lacrosse VA 23950

FCC Amateur Radio Licenses in Ladysmith

Call Sign: KD4ZSZ
Donald R Rush
Ladysmith VA 22501

Call Sign: W8HYS
Richard E Burkhammer
Ladysmith VA 22501

FCC Amateur Radio Licenses in Laft Hampton

Call Sign: KF4CDO
Richard J O Hearn
2063 B Canberra Ct
Laft Hampton VA 23605

FCC Amateur Radio Licenses in Lake Frederick

Call Sign: W4YUR
Charles E Morris
115 Harvester Dr
Lake Frederick VA 226302094

Call Sign: NV4AA
Dr0Nk Radio Network - East
115 Turnstone Ln
Lake Frederick VA 22630

Call Sign: KB7ZZ
David P Weik
115 Turnstone Ln
Lake Frederick VA 22630

Call Sign: K3VAT
Richard D Kennedy
121 Turnstone Ln
Lake Frederick VA 22630

FCC Amateur Radio Licenses in Lake Monticello

Call Sign: KD6WVA
Jeff S Spinello
4 Lewis Ct
Lake Monticello VA 22963

Call Sign: KG4VVZ
Dale R Wagner
54 Maplevale Dr
Lake Monticello VA 229632757

FCC Amateur Radio Licenses in Lake Ridge

Call Sign: KE4DGN
Donald J Blauvelt
3444 Caledonia Cir
Lake Ridge VA 22192

Call Sign: KI4BEE
Elena B Nugent
11975 Cotton Mill Dr
Lakc Ridgc VA 22192

Call Sign: WB6ULK
Mark J Redlinger
3270 Grady Ln
Lake Ridge VA 22192

Call Sign: W6ZP
Mark J Redlinger
3270 Grady Ln
Lake Ridge VA 22192

Call Sign: W4QP
Mark J Redlinger
12074 Greatbridge Rd
Lake Ridge VA 22192

Call Sign: W3SR
Mark J Redlinger
12074 Greatbridge Rd

Lake Ridge VA 22192

Call Sign: KA3KFJ
Floyd D Mc Leroy
1916 Mariner Ln
Lake Ridge VA 22192

Call Sign: W7CLR
Craig L Rieben
12301 Mulberry Ct
Lake Ridge VA 221922004

Call Sign: KG4QXP
Jeffrey S Brown
3231 Ridgeview Ct 202
Lake Ridge VA 22192

Call Sign: N2BVS
Ronald N Livingston
12202 Stevenson Ct
Lake Ridge VA 22192

FCC Amateur Radio Licenses in Lambsburg

Call Sign: W3POW
Joseph A Gibbs
1263 Chestnut Grove
Lambsburg VA 24351

Call Sign: AF4DF
Louis B Knueppel
706 York Thicket Rd
Lambsburg VA 24351

FCC Amateur Radio Licenses in Lancaster

Call Sign: AC4SW
Richard L Kahler
156 Bayberry Ln
Lancaster VA 22503

Call Sign: N3QYW
John F Davis
362 Beach Creek Rd
Lancaster VA 225034312

Call Sign: KD4UNC

Christopher J Taylor
Rt 3 Box 1096F
Lancaster VA 22503

Call Sign: N4TCA
Charles H Braun
Rte 2 Box 1107
Lancaster VA 22503

Call Sign: N4GVQ
Arthur L Hicks
Rt 1 Box 393
Lancaster VA 22503

Call Sign: KE4QX
Richard B Libbey
Rr 1 Box 573
Lancaster VA 22503

Call Sign: KF4BED
Donald F Reilly
Rr 1 Box 726
Lancaster VA 22503

Call Sign: N3YSE
Robert J Schneider
114 Club View Dr
Lancaster VA 225033516

Call Sign: KG4VBU
Edward F Richardson Jr
530 Cove Colony Rd
Lancaster VA 22503

Call Sign: KG4VBT
Lynn K Richardson
530 Cove Colony Rd
Lancaster VA 22503

Call Sign: KK4FOP
Michele D Tucker
1212 Eagles Trace
Lancaster VA 22503

Call Sign: KJ4YSB
Richard W Tucker
1212 Eagles Trace
Lancaster VA 22503

Call Sign: AK4EE
Richard W Tucker
1212 Eagles Trace
Lancaster VA 22503

Call Sign: KF4PKU
Robert M Mac Lead
Heritage Pointe
Lancaster VA 22503

Call Sign: N4DXP
John W Riley
654 Lancaster Crk Dr
Lancaster VA 22503

Call Sign: KE4CBM
James A Charbeneau
2065 Laurel Pt Rd
Lancaster VA 22503

Call Sign: KB3CWY
Kathy C Bearden
201 Mastons Wharf Rd
Lancaster VA 22503

Call Sign: KB3CXZ
James R Bearden
201 Mastons Wharf Rd
Lancaster VA 22503

Call Sign: KD4KYQ
Linda H Mc Makin
251 Mastons Wharf Rd
Lancaster VA 22503

Call Sign: K4RET
Kenneth A Vincent
536 Mastons Wharf Rd
Lancaster VA 22503

Call Sign: K3GUF
Frederick N Lee
395 Oak Hill
Lancaster VA 225034006

Call Sign: AJ4KH
Erin H Weik
463 Ottoman Ferry Rd
Lancaster VA 22503

Call Sign: N3RIN
Erin H Weik
463 Ottoman Ferry Rd
Lancaster VA 22503

Call Sign: KJ4BXW
Benjamin B Nickerson
1220 Riverwood Dr
Lancaster VA 22503

Call Sign: KO4MB
Clark L Dorsey Jr
37 Trobrador Ln
Lancaster VA 22503

Call Sign: KG4WNU
Charles B Hearns
277 Yankee Point Rd
Lancaster VA 22503

Call Sign: KF4PKT
Melanie S Neale
Lancaster VA 22503

Call Sign: WA4DBL
Lionel O Lincoln
Lancaster VA 22503

Call Sign: WB4TJJ
Edward E Nicholas Jr
Lancaster VA 225030276

Call Sign: N3MTJ
Walter L Woody
1157 Country Ln
Laneview VA 22504

Call Sign: KE4DVJ
Douglas E Thorp
7600 Beechwood Dr
Lanexa VA 230899307

Call Sign: KJ4TYW
Philip G Stowell
314 Colony Trl
Lanexa VA 23089

Call Sign: KJ4EAU
New Kent For Amateur Radio
13732 Cypress Dr
Lanexa VA 23089

Call Sign: KJ4HIK
New Kent 4 D Star Amateur
Radio
13732 Cypress Dr
Lanexa VA 23089

Call Sign: NK4DS
New Kent 4 D Star Amateur
Radio
13732 Cypress Dr
Lanexa VA 23089

Call Sign: KJ4ADC
James E Donohue
13732 Cypress Dr
Lanexa VA 23089

Call Sign: AJ4HA
James E Donohue
13732 Cypress Dr
Lanexa VA 23089

Call Sign: KJ4TJP
Ronald B Stowell
3076 N Riverside Dr
Lanexa VA 23089

Call Sign: W1RVR
Ronald B Stowell
3076 N Riverside Dr
Lanexa VA 23089

Call Sign: N8AAG
Roger L Shakley
3420 N Waterside Dr
Lanexa VA 230895542

Call Sign: KJ4HTU
Anthony C Belcastro

15400 New Kent Hwy
Lanexa VA 23089

Call Sign: KJ4HTW
Yvonne C Smith
15400 New Kent Hwy
Lanexa VA 23089

Call Sign: AB4QF
Alvin Lipson
6005 Tabiatha Ln
Lanexa VA 23089

Call Sign: K4EBX
George T Groves
766 W Riverside Dr
Lanexa VA 230890056

Call Sign: KF4WST
Charles R Cooper
Lanexa VA 23089

Call Sign: KG4PRV
Stephen P Walker
Lanexa VA 23089

Call Sign: KF4WMI
Keith W Bickford
1552 A 4th St
Langley AFB VA 23665

Call Sign: KJ4MZH
Jason K Wampler
2074 E Keystone Dr
Langley AFB VA 23665

Call Sign: KK4EMP
Chadwick E Barber
49 Spruce St Box 33
Langley AFB VA 23665

Call Sign: KD5CUA
Brian K Rice
2005A Talon Dr
Langley AFB VA 23665

Call Sign: KE6YQI
Ermelinda Doncell
Langley AFB VA 23665

FCC Amateur Radio Licenses in Landsowne

Call Sign: W3ZME
William A Luther
19355 Cypres Ridge Ter
Lansdowne VA 20176

Call Sign: KA4KAX
Renva M Shrout
19365 Cypress Ridge Ter 503
Lansdowne VA 20176

Call Sign: KB2ULZ
Bruce E Meyers
19365 Cypress Ridge Ter 903
Lansdowne VA 20176

Call Sign: W1HRE
Wilmah M Getchell Sr
19385 Cypress Ridge Ter Apt
610
Lansdowne VA 20176

Call Sign: KN4PY
Axel R Granholm
19365 Cypres Ridge Ter Unit
401
Lansdowne VA 201768433

Call Sign: KF4VLK
Michael D Olson
19365 Cypress Ridge Ter Unit
721
Lansdowne VA 20176

Call Sign: KC4IUP
Andrew J Daffron IV
19090 Parallel Bluffs Ct
Lansdowne VA 20176

Call Sign: KI4FYK
Andrew J Daffron IV
19090 Parallel Bluffs Ct
Lansdowne VA 20176

Call Sign: K4AJD
Andrew J Daffron IV
19090 Parallel Bluffs Ct
Lansdowne VA 20176

Call Sign: KE4NIE
Howard W Deer III
43408 Riverpoint Dr
Lansdowne VA 20176

Call Sign: N4VBK
William C Wells
19287 Winmeade Dr
Lansdowne VA 20176

FCC Amateur Radio Licenses in Laurel Fork

Call Sign: KI4ONB
Blaine B Barnard
16247 Danville Pike
Laurel Fork VA 24352

Call Sign: KK4ALM
Aimee J Shanks
487 Dry Twig Rd
Laurel Fork VA 24352

Call Sign: KK4ALN
Kenneth R Shanks
487 Dry Twig Rd
Laurel Fork VA 24352

Call Sign: KG4CNI
Patricia A Dubeck
999 Excelsior School Rd
Laurel Fork VA 24352

Call Sign: W3JJV
John R Dubeck
999 Excelsior School Rd
Laurel Fork VA 243523726

Call Sign: WB5VNQ
John A Staples
Fm 640 Keno Rd
Laurel Fork VA 24352

Call Sign: KI4ONC
Phillip D Norman
2125 Laurel Fork Rd
Laurel Fork VA 24352

FCC Amateur Radio Licenses in Lawrenceville

Call Sign: KA8LNO
Mike Lupshu Jr
291 Iron Bridge Rd
Lawrenceville VA 23868

Call Sign: K4RVA
Steven S Spiroff
1147 Planters Rd Bwcc 368599
Lawrenceville VA 23868

Call Sign: KI4VAT
Shirley J Walker
13312 Western Mill Rd
Lawrenceville VA 23868

Call Sign: KG4ZPJ
William G Turner
13312 Western Mill Rd
Lawrenceville VA 23868

Call Sign: W4WGT
William G Turner
13312 Western Mill Rd
Lawrenceville VA 23868

Call Sign: KJ4BMV
Judy E Turner
13312 Western Mill Rd
Lawrenceville VA 23868

Call Sign: WW4JET
Judy E Turner
13312 Western Mill Rd
Lawrenceville VA 23868

Call Sign: KJ4LZY
Joseph S Turner
13312 Western Mill Rd
Lawrenceville VA 23868

Call Sign: KE4MPA

Martin L Lewis
Lawrenceville VA 23868

**FCC Amateur Radio Licenses
in Lebanon**

Call Sign: KB4VGH
William A Bottiglierie
Rt 2 Box 104
Lebanon VA 24266

Call Sign: KB4UOH
Donald L Cook
Rt 4 Box 195
Lebanon VA 24266

Call Sign: N4SCF
Robert D Riggs
Rt 2 Box 27 B
Lebanon VA 24266

Call Sign: W4GXD
Berton L Monk
Rt 4 Box 4
Lebanon VA 24266

Call Sign: KB4LUP
Conard M Powers
Rte 3 Box 65
Lebanon VA 24266

Call Sign: KB4RXB
Vernon L Salyers
Rt 1 Box 97
Lebanon VA 24266

Call Sign: WD4EYU
Curtis W Cox
682 Brumley Cir
Lebanon VA 24266

Call Sign: KB4WTO
Patricia D Bratton
5924 Clinch Mtn Rd
Lebanon VA 24266

Call Sign: KB4WTP
Garland T Bratton
5924 Clinch Mtn Rd

Lebanon VA 24266

Call Sign: KK4AFN
Roger S Dishman
986 E Cross Rds Dr
Lebanon VA 24266

Call Sign: WD4MLU
Freddie E Shreve
Hillcrest Trailer Pk Lot 25
Lebanon VA 24266

Call Sign: KE4LLW
James A Combs II
118 Horton Dr
Lebanon VA 24266

Call Sign: K4CWP
Charles W Peake
284 Jessee St
Lebanon VA 24266

Call Sign: KJ4VQV
Teena J Peake
284 Jessee St
Lebanon VA 24266

Call Sign: N4RCC
Charles H Lowdermilk
Box 33 Lively Ave
Lebanon VA 24266

Call Sign: KI4PNJ
Michael Compton
349 Moccasin Ct
Lebanon VA 24266

Call Sign: KC4SIL
David V Cook
2326 Pioneer Dr
Lebanon VA 24266

Call Sign: KD4PBF
Christopher S Newton
272 Rose Dr
Lebanon VA 24266

Call Sign: KF4PFD
Michael A Stone

114 Salyer St
Lebanon VA 24266

Call Sign: KB4FZI
Roy D Worley
Lebanon VA 24266

Call Sign: N4ZHZ
Robert J Cox
Lebanon VA 24266

Call Sign: W4GMN
Billy L Jessee
Lebanon VA 24266

Call Sign: WA4GML
Billy J Campbell
Lebanon VA 24266

Call Sign: KC4MSR
Billy R Salyers Sr
Lebanon VA 24266

Call Sign: KG4VTJ
Russell County ARC
Lebanon VA 24266

Call Sign: WR4RC
Russell County ARC
Lebanon VA 24266

Call Sign: KB4DCD
Rita J Vandyke
Lebanon VA 24266

Call Sign: KE4RIX
Marcy D Shaw
Lebanon VA 24266

Call Sign: KF4GCM
Theodore C Slack
Lebanon VA 24266

Call Sign: KF4NFO
David L Jenks
Lebanon VA 24266

Call Sign: KF4OFI
David C Justice

Lebanon VA 24266

Call Sign: KF4SGE
Daniel J Mc Glothlin
Lebanon VA 24266

Call Sign: K4COX
Robert J Cox
Lebanon VA 24266

Call Sign: KG4SGN
Sarah J Lee
Lebanon VA 24266

Call Sign: KG4YKL
Cody A Stinson
Lebanon VA 24266

Call Sign: KJ4JDD
Marquis J Bolton
Lebanon VA 24266

Call Sign: KG4YKM
Randall K Stinson
Lebanon VA 24266

Call Sign: N4ZHZ
Robert J Cox
Lebanon VA 24266

Call Sign: KJ4QYI
Robert L Dorton
Lebanon VA 24266

FCC Amateur Radio Licenses in Lebanon Church

Call Sign: KG4FLM
Don R Himelright
5677 John Marshall Hwy
Lebanon Church VA 22641

Call Sign: N4TRX
Ray L Williams
541 Laurel Hill Way
Lebanon Church VA 22641

FCC Amateur Radio Licenses in Leemont

Call Sign: KE4AKS
Connie M Cunningham
19249 Bayside Rd
Leemont VA 23403

FCC Amateur Radio Licenses in Leesburg

Call Sign: N4HWB
Michael L Hatzimanolis
18843 Accokeek Ter
Leesburg VA 201768453

Call Sign: KH6WY
Jack A Hearn Sr
811 Anne St
Leesburg VA 22075

Call Sign: WA0LIJ
James J Heinen
507 Appletree Dr NE
Leesburg VA 22075

Call Sign: KK4ELI
David J Houman
294 Ariel Dr
Leesburg VA 20176

Call Sign: KE4IHG
Winfield S Heagy
270 Ariel Dr NE
Leesburg VA 20176

Call Sign: KC2JDX
Joseph C Picolla
220 Ashton Dr SW
Leesburg VA 20175

Call Sign: KD4AIF
Mercel D Skaggs
320 Ayrlee Ave NW
Leesburg VA 20176

Call Sign: N4TGA
Mercel D Skaggs
320 Ayrlee Ave NW
Leesburg VA 20176

Call Sign: W4TZO
William C Whitmore Jr
21 Ayrst NW
Leesburg VA 20176

Call Sign: N3AHA
Stacey L Jansen
105 Balch Springs Cir
Leesburg VA 20175

Call Sign: KI4TXP
John H Ives
42052 Bald Hill Rd
Leesburg VA 20176

Call Sign: K4FW
James E Stowers
40056 Basque Ct
Leesburg VA 20175

Call Sign: KE4NFG
John J Bideganeta
600 Beauregard Dr SE
Leesburg VA 20175

Call Sign: K4NFG
John J Bideganeta
600 Beauregard Dr SE
Leesburg VA 20175

Call Sign: KG4LVT
Yvette Castro-Green
107 Belmont Dr SW
Leesburg VA 20175

Call Sign: KE4ZGG
Nelson C Davis
315 Belmont Pl SW
Leesburg VA 22075

Call Sign: KW4US
Udo Schilcher
43672 Bermuda Dunes Ter
Leesburg VA 20176

Call Sign: KC3UF
Michael R Densmore
761 Bonnie Ridge Dr
Leesburg VA 20176

Call Sign: KE4IMB
David H Mac Anlis
Rte 2 Box 101D
Leesburg VA 22075

Call Sign: W4JEC
Orville L Martin
Rt 3 Box 126
Leesburg VA 22075

Call Sign: KD4JQT
Andrew H Lamothe Jr
Rt 3 Box 267
Leesburg VA 22075

Call Sign: W4GYP
John M Ciganek
Rte 1 Box 380
Leesburg VA 22075

Call Sign: KB4DAD
La Verte W Dowd
Rt 2 Box 59
Leesburg VA 22075

Call Sign: WB4GZU
Larry L Tucker
1218 Bradfield Dr SW
Leesburg VA 22075

Call Sign: KE4JEH
Gloria M Borgrink
41180 Bridges Farm Ln
Leesburg VA 20175

Call Sign: W4LFO
Charles W Borgrink
41180 Bridges Farm Ln
Leesburg VA 20175

Call Sign: KI4DTK
William Shoemaker
41107 Bryn Bach Ln
Leesburg VA 20175

Call Sign: KK4GJX
Leonard Buckwalter
649 Burnside Ter St

Leesburg VA 20175

Call Sign: KB2SBI
Bradley M Eckert
102 Cagney Ter SE
Leesburg VA 20175

Call Sign: KI4NX
Kenneth R Harrigan
103 Cagney Ter SE
Leesburg VA 20175

Call Sign: AG4TW
Kenneth R Harrigan
103 Cagney Ter SE
Leesburg VA 20175

Call Sign: KZ4Y
Kenneth R Harrigan
103 Cagney Ter SE
Leesburg VA 20175

Call Sign: KD4NFA
Kelly M Harrigan
103 Cagney Ter SE
Leesburg VA 22175

Call Sign: N3CKI
David Sippel
43044 Caledonia Ct
Leesburg VA 20176

Call Sign: K5NOB
Luther P Guise
1403 Campbell Ct NE
Leesburg VA 20176

Call Sign: KJ4LWO
Sally M Guise
1403 Campbell Ct NE
Leesburg VA 20176

Call Sign: K4NOB
Sally M Guise
1403 Campbell Ct NE
Leesburg VA 20176

Call Sign: AI2C
Norman W Styer Jr

18062 Canby Rd
Leesburg VA 201756914

Call Sign: KA2IJU
Kay A Styer
18062 Canby Rd
Leesburg VA 201756914

Call Sign: KE4IGI
Gregory A Kope
18685 Canby Rd
Leesburg VA 20175

Call Sign: KJ4PUM
Kenneth W Linder Jr
726 Catoctin Cir NE
Leesburg VA 20176

Call Sign: KA4RRS
Douglas G Rambo
18314 Cattail Branch Ct
Leesburg VA 20176

Call Sign: KF4VBZ
Shirley A Bee
14368 Chapel Ln
Leesburg VA 20176

Call Sign: W4POF
Robert W Bee
14368 Chapel Ln
Leesburg VA 22075

Call Sign: AI4XE
Timothy C Boan
14703 Chapel Ln
Leesburg VA 20176

Call Sign: AE4TB
Timothy C Boan
14703 Chapel Ln
Leesburg VA 20176

Call Sign: KJ4SMF
Stirling E West II
206 Chatfield Ct NE
Leesburg VA 20176

Call Sign: KC3BM

John I Brown III
604 Cherry Ln NE
Leesburg VA 20176

Call Sign: KD4TNN
John I Brown IV
604 Cherry Ln NE
Leesburg VA 22075

Call Sign: W0MPM
John I Brown III
604 Cherry Ln NE
Leesburg VA 201764534

Call Sign: KE6SA
David N Rosenblum
1616 Chickasaw Pl
Leesburg VA 20176

Call Sign: WB4DWE
David C Frye
109 Church St NE
Leesburg VA 20176

Call Sign: W0MAZ
James R Banks
402 Clagett St SW
Leesburg VA 201754356

Call Sign: KA4CYJ
David S Nordby
414 Clagett St SW
Leesburg VA 201754357

Call Sign: N4QIV
Abigail Horner
125G Clubhouse Dr 2
Leesburg VA 22075

Call Sign: KJ4BRS
Andrew S Borgquist
13331 Cool Hollow Ln
Leesburg VA 20176

Call Sign: KF4VVY
Kenneth H Ward
19238 Coton Hall St
Leesburg VA 20176

Call Sign: KD4WOZ
Kevin A Noll
502 Country Club Dr SW
Leesburg VA 20175

Call Sign: KJ4VHT
Nathaniel I Cummings
20409 Crimson Pl
Leesburg VA 20175

Call Sign: KI4ZYL
Bruce H Burnette
39381 Crooked Bridge Ln
Leesburg VA 20175

Call Sign: KJ4VHW
Samantha Z Sheedy
39392 Crooked Bridge Ln
Leesburg VA 20175

Call Sign: AI4ID
Sean K Sheedy
39392 Crooked Bridge Ln
Leesburg VA 20175

Call Sign: KB3IU
Brian J Withnell
506 Currant Ter NE
Leesburg VA 201762452

Call Sign: KK4ELH
Thomas F Lindsey
19385 Cypress Ridge Ter 110
Leesburg VA 20176

Call Sign: W3NN
Norman A Heck
19385 Cypress Ridge Ter 1115
Leesburg VA 20176

Call Sign: W4OWA
Robert W Ruedisueli
19385 Cypress Ridge Ter 416
Leesburg VA 20176

Call Sign: W3VAR
Charles B Weaver
19355 Cypress Ridge Ter 701
Leesburg VA 20176

Call Sign: W4DM
Dale S Harris
19355 Cypress Ridge Ter Unit 315
Leesburg VA 20176

Call Sign: WA6TQA
James A Webb
1107 Dailey Pl SW
Leesburg VA 201754317

Call Sign: KI4PRK
Brennen P Ernst
41456 Daleview Ln
Leesburg VA 20176

Call Sign: WB4JCY
Paul F Supan
105 F Davis Ave
Leesburg VA 20175

Call Sign: KG4RMV
American Wire And Wireless Association
105F Davis Ave
Leesburg VA 20175

Call Sign: N4WLE
Elaine T Eliezer
105 F Davis Ave SW
Leesburg VA 20175

Call Sign: K4ETE
Elaine T Eliezer
105 F Davis Ave SW
Leesburg VA 20175

Call Sign: K6PS
Paul F Supan
105 Davis Ave SW Apt F
Leesburg VA 201753441

Call Sign: K6PI
American Wire And Wireless Association
105 Davis Ave SW Apt F
Leesburg VA 201753441

Call Sign: N5OIW
Douglas T Bond
336 Deer Path Ave SW
Leesburg VA 20175

Call Sign: KK4HBY
Ernest A Gomez
19442 Diamond Lake Dr
Leesburg VA 20176

Call Sign: KI4LGM
Malcolm H Teas
709 Donaldson Ln SW
Leesburg VA 20175

Call Sign: N2MZN
Harold B Hindley Jr
215 Dry Mill Rd SW
Leesburg VA 20175

Call Sign: KC8DTT
Georga L Hackworth
324 Dry Mill Rd SW
Leesburg VA 20175

Call Sign: N8PHU
Christopher J Hackworth
324 Dry Mill Rd SW
Leesburg VA 20175

Call Sign: KC4IVB
Frederick B Adams
315 Dry Mill Rd SW Apt 136
Leesburg VA 20175

Call Sign: WB2UNA
John Covici
220 Dry Mill Rd SW H
Leesburg VA 22075

Call Sign: N3TZK
Irene M Haldeman
716 Duncan Pl SE
Leesburg VA 20175

Call Sign: N3TZL
Mark M Haldeman
716 Duncan Pl SE
Leesburg VA 20175

Call Sign: KJ4JMO
Michael D Mcburnett
102 Duvall Ct
Leesburg VA 20175

Call Sign: KJ4KGB
Michael D Mcburnett
102 Duvall Ct
Leesburg VA 20175

Call Sign: KJ4ZTP
Brian W Bacon
586 Edmonton Ter
Leesburg VA 20176

Call Sign: KJ4BSF
Robert W Kemner
587 Edmonton Ter
Leesburg VA 20176

Call Sign: KF4YCE
Craig W Metz
932 Edwards Ferry Rd 105
Leesburg VA 20176

Call Sign: W2YE
Richard W Maylott
19277 Evergreen Mill Rd
Leesburg VA 20175

Call Sign: WB4SFF
Elsie M Maylott
19277 Evergreen Mill Rd
Leesburg VA 20175

Call Sign: WA4ZRG
John A Olsen
23168 Evergreen Mills Rd
Leesburg VA 22075

Call Sign: AJ4WF
John Kotrosa Jr
1306 Featherstone Ln
Leesburg VA 20176

Call Sign: N3EEP
Donald R Mattmueller
1206 Featherstone Ln NE

Leesburg VA 22075

Call Sign: KE4JOZ
Craig R Everett
1219 Featherstone Ln NE
Leesburg VA 20176

Call Sign: KA3AOK
Michael E Malarkey
1237 Featherstone Ln NE
Leesburg VA 20176

Call Sign: KB9SVY
Amy C Chaput
1237 Featherstone Ln NE
Leesburg VA 20176

Call Sign: KI4BCT
Joseph T Pisula
43547 Firestone Pl
Leesburg VA 20176

Call Sign: W3CZJ
Joseph T Pisula
43547 Firestone Pl
Leesburg VA 20176

Call Sign: KG8JA
Steven M Johnson
662A Fort Evans Rd N E 108
Leesburg VA 20176

Call Sign: W4SSN
Stanley E Steele
117D Fort Evans Rd S E
Leesburg VA 20175

Call Sign: NU3F
James M Freire
106B Fort Evans Rd SE
Leesburg VA 20175

Call Sign: WB4JCH
Stanley E Steele
117D Fort Evans Rd SE
Leesburg VA 20175

Call Sign: WA4WDI
Joseph Evon

21095 Fox Hollow Ln
Leesburg VA 20175

Call Sign: KI4NHV
Eric F Paul
404 Fox Ridge Dr SW
Leesburg VA 201752500

Call Sign: KA6LOW
Scott Adams
211 Fox Trot Way
Leesburg VA 201762048

Call Sign: KB6MUQ
Gail L Adams
211 Fox Trot Way
Leesburg VA 201762048

Call Sign: KK4DLO
Kevin J Teska
209 Fox Trot Way NW
Leesburg VA 20176

Call Sign: N2ALA
Dwight A Dopilka
210 Foxborough Dr SW
Leesburg VA 201752541

Call Sign: KF4EKA
Sandra R Bowen
808 Ft Macleod Ter
Leesburg VA 20176

Call Sign: K4OIP
Gary K Pritchard
1409 Garrison Ct NE
Leesburg VA 201764905

Call Sign: KD4SBQ
Sharon Y Elliott
674 Gateway Dr 706
Leesburg VA 22075

Call Sign: KJ4BSE
B Radcliff
668 401 Gateway Dr SE
Leesburg VA 20175

Call Sign: KA3GWW

Dolores M Kearns
775 Gateway Dr SE 510
Leesburg VA 22075

Call Sign: N8GKI
Chris M Kearns
775 Gateway Dr SE 510
Leesburg VA 22075

Call Sign: N2KTA
Carolyn M Corbett
775 Gateway Dr SE 925
Leesburg VA 20175

Call Sign: N7MTC
Michael T Corbett
775 Gateway Dr SE 925
Leesburg VA 20175

Call Sign: KF4PTH
Sean T Bowers
544 Glade Fern Ter SE
Leesburg VA 20175

Call Sign: KI4ZZO
Christopher K Clance
41715 Glaydin Woods Ln
Leesburg VA 20176

Call Sign: KJ4DER
Matthew A Gloe
20540 Gleedsville Rd
Leesburg VA 20175

Call Sign: KN6WQ
Timothy A Doncaster
18275 Glen Oak Way
Leesburg VA 20176

Call Sign: WR3D
Iain Philipps
18275 Glen Oak Way
Leesburg VA 20176

Call Sign: KI4CEG
David T Lang
13354 Goodhart Ln
Leesburg VA 20176

Call Sign: K4NSX
David T Lang
13354 Goodhart Ln
Leesburg VA 20176

Call Sign: KG4HRI
James D Waldron
13359 Goodhart Ln
Leesburg VA 20176

Call Sign: N9GDH
James D Waldron
13359 Goodhart Ln
Leesburg VA 20176

Call Sign: N4MT
Philip W Flack
38359 Goose Creek Ln
Leesburg VA 20175

Call Sign: KA4UFI
William F Bowman
205 Greenmont Way NE
Leesburg VA 20176

Call Sign: KI4WZX
David P Kajut
19064 Grouse Ter
Leesburg VA 20176

Call Sign: KK4PR
Frank D Kirschner
43617 Habitat Cir
Leesburg VA 20176

Call Sign: AF4FJ
James A Bates Jr
750 Hetzel Ter SE
Leesburg VA 20175

Call Sign: KE4PRH
Eric J G Du Pont
405 Huntfield Ct NE
Leesburg VA 20176

Call Sign: N2FID
Paul C Krein
728 Hunton Pl NE
Leesburg VA 20176

Call Sign: N3BS
Nils V Jespersen
38134 Hunts End Pl
Leesburg VA 20175

Call Sign: WA4UDQ
Ralph L Lamm
12841 James Monroe Hwy
Leesburg VA 22075

Call Sign: WA9ZPB
Michael J Sare
13723 James Monroe Hwy
Leesburg VA 201765437

Call Sign: KJ4BRH
Bonnie J Greeley
1209 James Rifle Ct
Leesburg VA 20176

Call Sign: KI4UTB
Jay R Greeley Sr
1209 James Rifle Ct
Leesburg VA 20176

Call Sign: KC3QT
Darwin B Bingham
803 Kenneth Pl S E
Leesburg VA 20175

Call Sign: KK4GJV
David K Thornton
19061 Kipheart Dr
Leesburg VA 20176

Call Sign: KD4LSV
Paul Horenberger
43118 Lake Ridge Pl
Leesburg VA 201766816

Call Sign: KE5APC
Jeffery A Slusher
211 Lake View Way NW
Leesburg VA 20176

Call Sign: KI4HS
Thomas J Matason
18474 Lanier Island Sq

Leesburg VA 201763936

Call Sign: KA4LDP
Roseanne M Gilligan
18490 Lanier Island Sq
Leesburg VA 20176

Call Sign: KF4UUU
Craig H Smith
207 Lawnhill Ct SW
Leesburg VA 201755814

Call Sign: KJ4BRM
Deborah G Blasdell
120 Lawson Rd SE
Leesburg VA 20175

Call Sign: KJ4BRL
Joshua D Blasdell
120 Lawson Rd SE
Leesburg VA 20175

Call Sign: KI4UL
Margaret G Craun
131 Lawson Rd SE
Leesburg VA 22075

Call Sign: KB4PFY
Roy B Liggett Jr
16320 Limestone Ct
Leesburg VA 20176

Call Sign: KC6GEA
Walter L Raheb
15679 Limestone School Rd
Leesburg VA 20176

Call Sign: KD4CSO
Arthur H Laurent
4 Linden Hill Way SW
Leesburg VA 20175

Call Sign: KF4EOM
Ken E Kizzee
19558 Loudoun Orchard Rd
Leesburg VA 20175

Call Sign: KB3RUR
Christopher J Painter

244 Loudoun St SW
Leesburg VA 20175

Call Sign: KJ4VHU
Paul Davies
241 Loudoun St SW I
Leesburg VA 20175

Call Sign: KI4KEY
Jack E Brown Jr
316 Lucust Knoll Dr NW
Leesburg VA 20176

Call Sign: N7RPA
Paul H Greenfield
844 Macalister Dr SE
Leesburg VA 201758905

Call Sign: KJ4BXG
Jeffrey A Van Etten
201 Magruder Pl SE
Leesburg VA 201754408

Call Sign: KI4RSJ
Christopher G Turner
608 Marshall Dr NE
Leesburg VA 20176

Call Sign: KB3NKY
Karl B Harrison
123 Maryanne Ave SW
Leesburg VA 20175

Call Sign: KF4TJI
Paul D Boehler
101 Masons Ln SE
Leesburg VA 20175

Call Sign: KF4TJJ
Carol L Boehler
101 Masons Ln SE
Leesburg VA 20175

Call Sign: N9YQF
Sujatha Perepa
520 McArthur Ter NE
Leesburg VA 20176

Call Sign: N9YQE

Bhargav V R Perepa
520 McArthur Ter NE
Leesburg VA 201761832

Call Sign: KC4EWT
Dan Johnson
603 McLeary Sq
Leesburg VA 20175

Call Sign: NN4EA
Dan Johnson
603 McLeary Sq
Leesburg VA 20175

Call Sign: KD6DRT
Brandon B Buhler
669 McLeary Sq SE
Leesburg VA 201755651

Call Sign: KK4ELD
Allen K Warner Jr
625 Meade Dr
Leesburg VA 20175

Call Sign: KK4ELC
Corwin A Warner
625 Meade Dr
Leesburg VA 20175

Call Sign: KA4DPO
John W Long
123 Meade Dr SW
Leesburg VA 20175

Call Sign: KB2UHW
Kurt E Hassler
627 Meade Dr SW
Leesburg VA 201755011

Call Sign: KI4TZE
Richard S Will
110 Meherrin Ter SW
Leesburg VA 20175

Call Sign: KI4YHA
Douglas A Knott
18202 Mill House Sq
Leesburg VA 20176

Call Sign: KJ4BSB
Karl J Brown
247 Mindy Ct SE
Leesburg VA 20175

Call Sign: AG4EC
Mark A Goforth
1412 Moore Pl SW
Leesburg VA 20175

Call Sign: KI4NAP
Janice L Fristad
1206 Musket Ct NE
Leesburg VA 20176

Call Sign: KI4BRG
Arvid C Fristad
1206 Musket Ct NE
Leesburg VA 201764805

Call Sign: KT9N
Arvid C Fristad
1206 Musket Ct NE
Leesburg VA 201764805

Call Sign: KC4JZ
Clarence J Zarobila
1208 Musket Ct NE
Leesburg VA 201764805

Call Sign: KG4CGR
Larry D Hughes
321 Nansemond St SE
Leesburg VA 20175

Call Sign: K3HE
Larry D Hughes
321 Nansemond St SE
Leesburg VA 20175

Call Sign: KK4ELG
Brian J Zabela
619 Nathan Pl
Leesburg VA 20176

Call Sign: KD8IJX
Michael R Roddewig
104 Newhall Pl SW
Leesburg VA 20175

Call Sign: KI4OWI
Gregory M Ayers
506 North St NE
Leesburg VA 20176

Call Sign: WW4GR
George F Reitz
905 North St NE
Leesburg VA 20176

Call Sign: AI4UT
George F Reitz
905 North St NE
Leesburg VA 20176

Call Sign: KI4HVH
Jay A Gibble
43105 Northlake Overlook Ter
Leesburg VA 20176

Call Sign: KJ1G
Jay A Gibble
43105 Northlake Overlook Ter
Leesburg VA 20176

Call Sign: N4SAS
Anthony L Davis
18264 Oak Lake Ct
Leesburg VA 20176

Call Sign: KB0ENH
Richard E Unis
320 Oakcrest Manor Dr NE
Leesburg VA 201762233

Call Sign: AF1U
John L Moring III
43241 Overview Pl
Leesburg VA 20176

Call Sign: KF4UUW
Mark R Turgeon
107 Paddington Way NE
Leesburg VA 20176

Call Sign: KJ4GZV
Matthew D Stevens
310 Pathway Pl SW

Leesburg VA 20175

Call Sign: WA4MWO
David E Pearce
40949 Pearce Cir
Leesburg VA 20176

Call Sign: K7TCP
Robert J Ballard II
18474 Perdido Bay Ter
Leesburg VA 20176

Call Sign: KB4ZVO
Barbara G Talbott
13192 Pinnacle Ln
Leesburg VA 20176

Call Sign: K3ICH
Charles F Talbott
13192 Pinnacle Ln
Leesburg VA 201766146

Call Sign: WX4FOX
Kevin J Smith
673 Potomac Station Dr 634
Leesburg VA 20176

Call Sign: KG4OTI
Dale K Harrison
103 Prospect Dr SW
Leesburg VA 20175

Call Sign: K3CN
Dale K Harrison
103 Prospect Dr SW
Leesburg VA 201753525

Call Sign: KK4HVX
David R Smith
119 Prosperity Ave Apt F
Leesburg VA 20175

Call Sign: K4BEO
Kenneth A Owen
621 Radford Ter NE
Leesburg VA 201762463

Call Sign: KG4OAP
James R Sheafer

41911 Raspberry Dr
Leesburg VA 20176

Call Sign: WA9LAZ
Chester A Kmak
41260 Red Hill Rd
Leesburg VA 20175

Call Sign: KM6PT
James K Boyce
41263 Red Hill Rd
Leesburg VA 20175

Call Sign: WA4PT
James K Boyce
41263 Red Hill Rd
Leesburg VA 20175

Call Sign: KM4GC
Douglas W Mc Nulty
43920 Riverpoint Dr
Leesburg VA 20176

Call Sign: N4TOJ
Mary Ann Mc Nulty
43920 Riverpoint Dr
Leesburg VA 20176

Call Sign: KF4HCW
Peter G Mc Neil
550 Rockbridge Dr
Leesburg VA 22075

Call Sign: KD4AMU
Randall P Tremblay
552 Rockbridge Dr
Leesburg VA 22075

Call Sign: KF4UUX
Earl M Haussling
567 Rockbridge Dr
Leesburg VA 20175

Call Sign: AJ4EY
Dodson B Brown
1022 Rolling Dr SW
Leesburg VA 20175

Call Sign: KJ4GYH

Marcia L Brown
1022 Rollins Dr SW
Leesburg VA 20175

Call Sign: KJ4GYI
Patrick T Brown
1022 Rollins Dr SW
Leesburg VA 20175

Call Sign: N1NCY
Nancy D Dluehosh
1106 Rollins Pl
Leesburg VA 20175

Call Sign: KE4RTP
Nancy D Dluehosh
1106 Rollins Pl
Leesburg VA 22075

Call Sign: N4PD
Paul H Dluehosh
1106 Rollins Pl
Leesburg VA 201754336

Call Sign: KI4GFI
Karen C Minichino
14388 Rosefinch Cir
Leesburg VA 20176

Call Sign: WA3CZT
Glenn R Markus
Rt 1
Leesburg VA 22075

Call Sign: K4RWK
Robert W Kemner
812 Rust Dr NE
Leesburg VA 20176

Call Sign: KG4OIR
Loudon County Chapter
American Red Cross
604 S King St Ste 006
Leesburg VA 20175

Call Sign: N1AZU
Marion L Wiehl
104 Salem Ct SE
Leesburg VA 20175

Call Sign: WA1AMA
James F Wiehl
104 Salem Ct SE
Leesburg VA 20175

Call Sign: N3YYO
Gerald M Dudley
1501 Shields Ter NE
Leesburg VA 211081552

Call Sign: KJ4RNN
Stephen Rhee
18431 Sierra Springs Sq
Leesburg VA 20176

Call Sign: KB2RMK
Brian C Rogers
605 Smartts Ln
Leesburg VA 20176

Call Sign: KE4UNL
Thomas P Walker
1001 Smartts Ln
Leesburg VA 22075

Call Sign: KI4IEO
Charles R Graham
908 Smartts Ln NE
Leesburg VA 20176

Call Sign: WD4BNO
John L Judge Jr
1095 Smartts Ln NE
Leesburg VA 20176

Call Sign: K4LEK
Judith A Wodynski
17189 Southern Planter Ln
Leesburg VA 20178

Call Sign: KH6IMX
Robert H Meurer
43247 Spinks Ferry Rd
Leesburg VA 201765629

Call Sign: KJ4LAY
Robert L Isaacs
43455 Spinks Ferry Rd

Leesburg VA 20176

Call Sign: KG4EBO
Robin Claud L Henderson
42690 St Clair Ln
Leesburg VA 20176

Call Sign: WY3E
Carmine A Petrillo
306 Stable View Ter
Leesburg VA 20176

Call Sign: KA2EOM
Adi P Da Luz
306 Stallion Sq NE
Leesburg VA 20176

Call Sign: K2ADI
Adi P Da Luz
306 Stallion Sq NE
Leesburg VA 20176

Call Sign: WB9RXJ
Thomas L Carney
41780 Stumptown Rd
Leesburg VA 201766067

Call Sign: KG4JNA
Michael A Virgilio
504 Sunset View Ter SE 203
Leesburg VA 20175

Call Sign: KE4JRZ
Kevin S Cunningham
902 Sweet William Ct SE
Leesburg VA 20175

Call Sign: KI4COM
Alexander G Miller
610 Tammy Ter
Leesburg VA 20175

Call Sign: KG4ZIX
Arthur R Taylor
43143 Teaberry Dr
Leesburg VA 20176

Call Sign: KF6RBP
Jeffrey B Williams

1201 Tennessee Dr NE
Leesburg VA 20176

Call Sign: KG4KZZ
David C Putman
20878 The Woods Rd
Leesburg VA 20175

Call Sign: KE4S
David C Putman
20878 The Woods Rd
Leesburg VA 20175

Call Sign: KE2HT
Alan G Skutt
39835 Thomas Mill Rd
Leesburg VA 20175

Call Sign: N4KWO
Kirk E Maskalenko
17760 Tobermory Pl
Leesburg VA 20175

Call Sign: KD4ATG
David V Di Girolamo
569 Tuliptree Sq
Leesburg VA 20176

Call Sign: AI2P
Jacobus P Engelbrecht
590 Tuliptree Sq NE
Leesburg VA 20176

Call Sign: AJ4EZ
Robert W Jensen
43422 Turnberry Isle Ct
Leesburg VA 201763910

Call Sign: KI4CTZ
Reeves B Smith
1003 Tuscarora Dr
Leesburg VA 20175

Call Sign: WA4VVJ
James B Anderson II
308 Valley View Ave SW
Leesburg VA 201753527

Call Sign: K4USO

Donald R Dailey
309 Valley View Ave SW
Leesburg VA 22075

Call Sign: KC4BMY
Twilla J Rowe
108 Washington St NE
Leesburg VA 22075

Call Sign: W4JCV
John R Gill
1010 White Pl SW
Leesburg VA 22075

Call Sign: KW5Y
John D Thomas
43430 Wild Dunes Sq
Leesburg VA 201763940

Call Sign: KE4FYL
Allon J Stern
202 Wild Turkey Way SW
Leesburg VA 20175

Call Sign: KB4WKK
Stephen F Hood
211 Wildman St NE
Leesburg VA 201762319

Call Sign: KF4ARX
Scott A Macdonald
212 Wilson Ave NW
Leesburg VA 22075

Call Sign: KG4RDI
Hilary H U Seymour
233 Wirt St NW
Leesburg VA 20176

Call Sign: N4QE
Gene L Harrison
Leesburg VA 20177

Call Sign: KA3JWL
Kenneth F Eliezer
Leesburg VA 20177

Call Sign: KF4UUY
Mary T Oliphant

Leesburg VA 20177

Call Sign: N4XT
Glen M Moon
Leesburg VA 20177

Call Sign: WD4MZG
Peter B Arnold
Leesburg VA 20177

Call Sign: W4CGT
Christopher G Turner
Leesburg VA 20177

Call Sign: KJ4EZG
Christopher M Patton
Leesburg VA 20177

Call Sign: KG4YXN
Warren A Pelton
Leesburg VA 20177

Call Sign: N3EV
Gene Harrison
Leesburg VA 20177

Call Sign: KI4RSL
Misty K Turner
Leesburg VA 20177

Call Sign: N4LND
Misty K Turner
Leesburg VA 20177

Call Sign: KK4GJW
Judith A Wodynski
Leesburg VA 20178

Call Sign: W1RHW
Robert H Wilson
Leesburg VA 20178

Call Sign: KD4TWR
David E Bachschmid
Leesburg VA 201771260

Call Sign: WB4NGC
Gene L Harrison
Leesburg VA 201771584

Call Sign: KG4IIR
Joel A Glass
Leesburg VA 201777595

Call Sign: KJ4JAG
Joel A Glass
Leesburg VA 201777595

FCC Amateur Radio Licenses in Lexington

Call Sign: KG4YIL
Roland G Stetler Jr
73 Avalon Ln
Lexington VA 24450

Call Sign: KD4JJK
William B Still
400 Battery Ln
Lexington VA 24450

Call Sign: KE4AAS
Kenneth L Harris
2338 Big Hill Rd
Lexington VA 244506516

Call Sign: KE4NRI
Julie L Whitesell
Rt 6 Box 107A
Lexington VA 24450

Call Sign: KC4SYK
James W Holland III
Rte 4 Box 160
Lexington VA 24450

Call Sign: KE6ORE
Kara B Seymour
Rt 1 Box 232
Lexington VA 24450

Call Sign: N4KBR
Albert S J Tucker Jr
Rt 2 Box 363B
Lexington VA 24450

Call Sign: KC4IKY
Aaron M Grunewald

Rt 2 Box 80
Lexington VA 24450

Call Sign: N4YBW
Mark H Grunewald
Rt 2 Box 80
Lexington VA 24450

Call Sign: AI4MV
William A Solomon
85 Broad Wing Trl
Lexington VA 244507039

Call Sign: KC4VJW
Gabriel G Balazs
503 Brooke Ln
Lexington VA 24450

Call Sign: KI4RAO
Thomas L Owens
122 Chavis Ave
Lexington VA 244501797

Call Sign: KI4ZR
Daniel M Welsh
159 Cliff View Ln
Lexington VA 24450

Call Sign: KC4CSX
George D Larsen
2 Courtland Center
Lexington VA 24450

Call Sign: KJ4KVW
George D Larsen
2 Courtland Center
Lexington VA 24450

Call Sign: K4AOV
Ronald H Mac Donald
5 Courtland Ctr
Lexington VA 24450

Call Sign: KU4WE
Don B Heckman
115 Deer Dr
Lexington VA 24450

Call Sign: KI4AVZ

Barbara J Heckman
115 Deer Dr
Lexington VA 24450

Call Sign: N4OQO
George B Bush
148 Discovery Ln
Lexington VA 24450

Call Sign: KI4QMG
John D Canellas
26 Ford Hill Rd
Lexington VA 24450

Call Sign: N4XKA
Daniel P Brinson
251 Forge Hill Ln
Lexington VA 24450

Call Sign: WA4MFH
Jerry R Roscoe
3 Gaines Ct
Lexington VA 24450

Call Sign: KF4GHX
Joaquin Ponce
11 Grey Dove Rd
Lexington VA 24450

Call Sign: KE4NRE
Michael R Sexton
14 Grey Dove Rd
Lexington VA 24450

Call Sign: N4VMI
Michael R Sexton
14 Grey Dove Rd
Lexington VA 24450

Call Sign: K4WHE
Dave H Wheeler
3 Hamric St
Lexington VA 24450

Call Sign: KJ4UEC
David H Wheeler
3 Hamric St
Lexington VA 24450

Call Sign: KJ4KVU
Stephen J Feldman
25 High Meadow Dr
Lexington VA 24450

Call Sign: KJ4KVV
Nathan S Feldman
25 High Meadow Dr
Lexington VA 24450

Call Sign: N4QPB
Bonnie M Vogel
176 Honey Hollow Rd
Lexington VA 24450

Call Sign: KB4MDG
Ted A Whiteside Sr
122 Houston St
Lexington VA 24450

Call Sign: WA4DOO
Weldon D Tolley
303 Houston St
Lexington VA 24450

Call Sign: K4IPC
Joseph Goldsten
401 Jackson Ave
Lexington VA 24450

Call Sign: KC4UUI
Richard H Bidlack
511 Jackson Ave
Lexington VA 24450

Call Sign: KG4EHJ
David C Keifer
2010 Jacktown Rd
Lexington VA 24450

Call Sign: K4JFK
Robert M Harper Sr
160 Kendal Dr Apt 322
Lexington VA 24450

Call Sign: W4PIH
Ronald L Jackson
140 Lacy Ln
Lexington VA 24450

Call Sign: KC4NWS
Trevor S Cox
107 Lee Ave
Lexington VA 24450

Call Sign: K4VPL
Jorge R Piercy
527 Limekiln Rd
Lexington VA 24450

Call Sign: KK4KZ
George E Mohler
1472 Maury River Rd
Lexington VA 24450

Call Sign: KJ4KV
Walter A Hutchens
2121 Maury River Rd
Lexington VA 24450

Call Sign: N7BGP
Elburn W Eubank
75 Mohlers Loop
Lexington VA 24450

Call Sign: WA4LJI
Manly L Curry
105 Monticello Dr
Lexington VA 24450

Call Sign: KA4VJT
Frederick A Arndt
111 Monticello Rd
Lexington VA 24450

Call Sign: KG4ZBX
Gregory P Dresden
116 N Main St Robinson Hall
Lexington VA 24450

Call Sign: AI4AC
Gregory P Dresden
116 N Main St Robinson Hall
Lexington VA 24450

Call Sign: KJ4WQ
Thomas W Tinsley
305 Overhill Dr

Lexington VA 24450

Call Sign: K2ANV
Donald J Kunar
304 Patrick Dr
Lexington VA 24450

Call Sign: KF4JT
Leonard J Reiss Jr
447 Patterson Hollow Rd
Lexington VA 24450

Call Sign: KC4NWT
Danek H Duvall
106 Paxton St
Lexington VA 24450

Call Sign: AB4JB
Kenneth C Falk
1282 Poplar Hill Rd
Lexington VA 244507332

Call Sign: N1YEM
Robert E Gough
201 Ross Rd
Lexington VA 24450

Call Sign: K3YEO
Ronald E Telsch
260 Round Hill Rd
Lexington VA 24450

Call Sign: KG4YBD
Gregory P Dresden
908 Ruffner Pl
Lexington VA 24450

Call Sign: KJ4KVR
Amber M Clark
825 Shenandoah Rd
Lexington VA 24450

Call Sign: KJ4KVS
Dallas B Clark
825 Shenandoah Rd
Lexington VA 24450

Call Sign: WA4ZMP
Charles L Taylor

19 Skyline Rd
Lexington VA 24450

Call Sign: KJ4KWD
Michael D Smith
1273 Smokey Row Rd
Lexington VA 24450

Call Sign: WB2DTH
William C Hunter
73 Southwest View Dr
Lexington VA 24450

Call Sign: KA1FR
William E Hunter
1248 Sycamore Valley Dr
Lexington VA 244503616

Call Sign: KJ4EXY
Wanda Z Dunnigan
1125 Toad Run
Lexington VA 24450

Call Sign: W4SED
Wanda Z Dunnigan
1125 Toad Run
Lexington VA 24450

Call Sign: KI4QME
Donald C Reid
3058 Tpke Rd
Lexington VA 24450

Call Sign: KI4QMF
Joyce M Reid
3058 Tpke Rd
Lexington VA 24450

Call Sign: N4DAV
David C Whitesell
15 Traveler Cir
Lexington VA 24450

Call Sign: KC4UVG
David C Whitesell
34 Traveler Cir
Lexington VA 24450

Call Sign: KE4ZXX

V M I ARC
VA Military Institute Ece Dept
Rm 508
Lexington VA 24450

Call Sign: KF4CQX
Joshua C Hahnlen
Vmi Box 814
Lexington VA 24450

Call Sign: KA3EMW
Mary S Mc Ginn
402 Vmi Parade
Lexington VA 24450

Call Sign: WA2QAP
Vincent P Mc Ginn
402 Vmi Parade
Lexington VA 24450

Call Sign: KJ4KVX
Ward R Lockett Jr
163 White Rock Rd
Lexington VA 24450

Call Sign: W4VAT
Ward R Lockett Jr
163 White Rock Rd
Lexington VA 24450

Call Sign: KF4GHY
Harry E Hughes
105 White St
Lexington VA 24450

Call Sign: KD4NIZ
C Elizabeth Jackson
Lexington VA 24450

Call Sign: N4YDM
Allan B Massie
Lexington VA 24450

Call Sign: AC4BN
David L Du Puy
Lexington VA 24450

Call Sign: KE4AAR
Henry E Ravenhorst

Lexington VA 244500904

FCC Amateur Radio Licenses in Lightfoot

Call Sign: KC4CMR
Chris B Courson
Rt 60 Box 22
Lightfoot VA 230900022

Call Sign: NK4AR
New Kent For Amateur Radio
Lightfoot VA 23090

Call Sign: WB3HUZ
Stephen M Ickes
Lightfoot VA 23090

Call Sign: KB3UPA
Carl J Wyche
Lightfoot VA 23090

Call Sign: KJ4VSF
Geraldine M Wyche
Lightfoot VA 23090

Call Sign: K4HX
Stephen M Ickes
Lightfoot VA 23090

Call Sign: NJ2WB
Colonial ARS
Lightfoot VA 230900053

Call Sign: K2QIJ
George C Ford Jr
Lightfoot VA 230900053

Call Sign: KF4ADM
Colonial ARS
Lightfoot VA 230900053

FCC Amateur Radio Licenses in Lignum

Call Sign: K4OSS
Charles W Ross
Lignum VA 22726

FCC Amateur Radio Licenses in Lincoln

Call Sign: KK4GC
Christopher G Dean
Lincoln VA 22078

FCC Amateur Radio Licenses in Linden

Call Sign: KJ4TJY
Paul S Savidge III
293 Bifrost Way
Linden VA 22642

Call Sign: N4PSS
Paul S Savidge III
293 Bifrost Way
Linden VA 22642

Call Sign: KJ4ZPS
Moriah R Bacon
4673 Blue Mtn Rd
Linden VA 22642

Call Sign: KG4TBW
Emmett B Snyder
72 Blue Valley Rd
Linden VA 22642

Call Sign: KK4CJI
Jami A Bladen
23 Broadway Ln
Linden VA 22642

Call Sign: KD4IIV
Joseph B Nichols
321 Cashmere Ct
Linden VA 22642

Call Sign: KR4DO
Thomas J Blicharz
3688 Cherry Hill Rd
Linden VA 22642

Call Sign: WB3BIC
Harry C Richmond
3906 Fiery Run Rd
Linden VA 226421812

Call Sign: N4HBY
Richard Bill
2889 Freezeland Rd
Linden VA 226425301

Call Sign: KG4KMB
Dorotea E Flores-Kestner
2987 Freezeland Rd
Linden VA 22642

Call Sign: KF4VED
Christine E Kestner
2987 Freezeland Rd
Linden VA 226425302

Call Sign: KB3MBM
Richard I Carpenter
3833 Freezeland Rd
Linden VA 226425310

Call Sign: KF4JNA
Marlon O Mills
8 Granny Smith Rd
Linden VA 22642

Call Sign: KF4LWW
Paul D Burton
746 High Top Rd
Linden VA 22642

Call Sign: N4LWW
Paul D Burton
746 High Top Rd
Linden VA 22642

Call Sign: KF4JZ
Val J Burt
71 Jericho Rd
Linden VA 22642

Call Sign: WA3F
Milburn E Altvater
282 Jericho Rd
Linden VA 22642

Call Sign: KF4KVJ
Jason W Norton
110 Longview Rd

Linden VA 226425418

Call Sign: W4CWX
Jason W Norton
110 Longview Rd
Linden VA 226425418

Call Sign: KF4LGV
James S Dodd
3133 Snow Hill Ln
Linden VA 22642

Call Sign: KG4ICJ
Joseph W Starr
75 Stayman Turn Ct
Linden VA 22642

Call Sign: KG4ICK
Valerie W Starr
75 Stayman Turn Ct
Linden VA 22642

Call Sign: KD4GVQ
Stanley K F Stocker
1 Wealthy Rd
Linden VA 22642

Call Sign: KG4VXK
Lorne W Cooper
49 Wild Cherry Way
Linden VA 22642

Call Sign: KF4CQD
Jeff M Rash
Linden VA 22642

Call Sign: N9PSE
Mark A Clausen
Linden VA 22642

Call Sign: K4LDN
Jeff M Rash
Linden VA 22642

FCC Amateur Radio Licenses
in Linville

Call Sign: K4SAD
Timothy N Taylor

7015 Joes Creek Rd
Linville VA 22834

Call Sign: KE4EXE
Jay A Carper
Linville VA 228340141

FCC Amateur Radio Licenses
in Lively

Call Sign: KA9OKG
Art C Jenson
263 Catch Penny Ln
Lively VA 22507

Call Sign: KG4DUP
Lauri L Jenson
263 Catch Penny Ln
Lively VA 22507

Call Sign: KK4PU
Douglas B Trittipoe
Lively VA 22507

FCC Amateur Radio Licenses
in Locust Dale

Call Sign: WA9JFW
Christopher C Allen
8048 Oak Park Rd
Locust Dale VA 229484898

Call Sign: W9CCA
Christopher C Allen
8048 Oak Park Rd
Locust Dale VA 229484898

FCC Amateur Radio Licenses
in Locust Grove

Call Sign: KJ4SDD
Robert N Cole
11810 Ashwood Ct
Locust Grove VA 22508

Call Sign: KK4QY
David G Agsten
100 Birch Ct
Locust Grove VA 22508

Call Sign: W4TXS
David G Agsten
100 Birch Ct
Locust Grove VA 22508

Call Sign: N8AG
David G Agsten
100 Birch Ct
Locust Grove VA 22508

Call Sign: KA2TUX
Edward F Martell
Hc 73 Box 1077
Locust Grove VA 22508

Call Sign: KD4OCJ
Donald W Houston
Hc 75 Box 1212
Locust Grove VA 22508

Call Sign: KB4UZK
Mark D Smith
Hcr 73 Box 804A
Locust Grove VA 22508

Call Sign: KE4UNK
Patricia A Robinson
Hc 73 Box 841B
Locust Grove VA 22508

Call Sign: WB2DQN
Richard R Viladesau
Hc 73 Box 905
Locust Grove VA 22508

Call Sign: WM3C
William M Minnick
108 Cedar Ct
Locust Grove VA 225085673

Call Sign: KG4OJX
Howard J Skinner
1302 Confederate Dr
Locust Grove VA 22508

Call Sign: K4HZN
Donald B Nowakoski
128 Cumberland Cir Box 408

Locust Grove VA 22508

Call Sign: KJ4YNI
Robert H Johnson Jr
830 Eastover Pkwy
Locust Grove VA 22508

Call Sign: K4ZBJ
Robert H Johnson Jr
830 Eastover Pkwy
Locust Grove VA 22508

Call Sign: KE4OMG
James D Harkness
200 Edgehill Dr
Locust Grove VA 22508

Call Sign: KC7SAH
Stephen A Birgells
303 Freedom Rd
Locust Grove VA 225085142

Call Sign: W4KK
Kenneth L Keyseear
7621 Gold Dale Rd
Locust Grove VA 22508

Call Sign: NR4M
Steve C Bookout
6480 Governor Almond Rd
Locust Grove VA 22508

Call Sign: KJ4ZRZ
William T Fecke Sr
125 Green St
Locust Grove VA 22508

Call Sign: KI4AEY
Robert J Welsh
138 Green St
Locust Grove VA 22508

Call Sign: KG4WJI
Faith M Olen
118 Independence St
Locust Grove VA 22508

Call Sign: KG4SGZ
Stephen A Mccarthy

510 Lake View Pkwy
Locust Grove VA 22508

Call Sign: KJ4YCR
Harry S Lovell
507 Lakeview Pkwy
Locust Grove VA 22508

Call Sign: WB4GOR
George Codoley
1903 Lakeview Pkwy
Locust Grove VA 225085320

Call Sign: WA4SFC
Robert E Eamigh
3604 Lakeview Pkwy
Locust Grove VA 225085605

Call Sign: KC4DPW
Martha J Goodman Dunne
Box 144 Low
Locust Grove VA 22508

Call Sign: W2OUV
Kenneth F Hackbarth
Box 507A Low Hc72
Locust Grove VA 22508

Call Sign: KA0IWV
Frank P Turvey
217 Meadow View Ln
Locust Grove VA 22508

Call Sign: AG4PG
Frank P Turvey
217 Meadow View Ln
Locust Grove VA 22508

Call Sign: KJ4YCT
Kim N Sawyer
30521 Mine Run Rd
Locust Grove VA 22508

Call Sign: KJ4YCV
Philip R Sawyer
30521 Mine Run Rd
Locust Grove VA 22508

Call Sign: KJ4YCU

Robert F Sawyer
30521 Mine Run Rd
Locust Grove VA 22508

Call Sign: KI4IGP
Posey L Brim Jr
535 Monticello Cir
Locust Grove VA 22508

Call Sign: AJ4QD
Donald W Keehan
704 Mt Pleasant Dr
Locust Grove VA 22508

Call Sign: KF4ICU
Howard W Hollis Jr
35264 Pheasant Ridge Rd
Locust Grove VA 22508

Call Sign: K9SP
James J Buongiovanni
7 Rapidan Rd
Locust Grove VA 22508

Call Sign: KB4KLU
Frank J Snow
303 Spotswood Rd
Locust Grove VA 22508

Call Sign: W4MCH
Marc C Hawkins
4180 Trail Of Faith Ct
Locust Grove VA 22508

Call Sign: K4FFD
Howard J Skinner
4231 Trail Of Faith Ct
Locust Grove VA 22508

Call Sign: KJ4DTN
Robert A Halstead
101 Woodland Trl
Locust Grove VA 22508

Call Sign: AJ4HU
Robert A Halstead
101 Woodland Trl
Locust Grove VA 22508

Call Sign: N8AN
Robert A Halstead
101 Woodland Trl
Locust Grove VA 22508

Call Sign: KE4YOB
Jon Z Ali
401 Yorktown Blvd
Locust Grove VA 22508

Call Sign: KD4IGO
George E Wright Jr
32040 Yucca Ln
Locust Grove VA 22805

Call Sign: KG4WAV
Rappackers Contest Group
Locust Grove VA 22508

Call Sign: NR4AA
Rappackers Contest Group
Locust Grove VA 22508

Call Sign: KB4EDU
Carolyn W Bookout
Locust Grove VA 22508

FCC Amateur Radio Licenses in Locust Hill

Call Sign: WD4IDK
Kenneth L Green
3 Egret Point Dr
Locust Hill VA 230929710

Call Sign: KC4PFQ
Edwin L Green
Rt 620
Locust Hill VA 23092

Call Sign: AC4OG
Patricia A Muller
Locust Hill VA 23092

Call Sign: KC4WED
James A Bakunas
Locust Hill VA 23092

FCC Amateur Radio Licenses in Long Island

Call Sign: KG4POS
Jason L Carter
152 Wyatts Rd
Long Island VA 24569

FCC Amateur Radio Licenses in Lorton

Call Sign: N4RYL
Randy R Harvey
9229 Ashland Woods Ln Apt B2
Lorton VA 22079

Call Sign: KE4JPB
James R Krear
8104 Bard St
Lorton VA 22079

Call Sign: KK4EYC
Jason Iaci
8528 Barrow Furnace La
Lorton VA 22079

Call Sign: KG4WNE
Ronald L Holtz
7500 Billsam Ct
Lorton VA 22079

Call Sign: AI4CB
Ronald L Holtz
7500 Billsam Ct
Lorton VA 22079

Call Sign: NN4RH
Ronald L Holtz
7500 Billsam Ct
Lorton VA 22079

Call Sign: WN9HJW
Ronald L Holtz
7500 Billsam Ct
Lorton VA 22079

Call Sign: KG4EXX
Douglas L Needham

8559 Blackfoot Ct
Lorton VA 22079

Call Sign: KD4BBE
James L Le Croy
8550 Blue Rock Ln
Lorton VA 22079

Call Sign: KE4BUP
Teresa A Kellogg
8554 Blue Rock Ln
Lorton VA 22079

Call Sign: KQ4VK
Kevin G Kellogg
8554 Blue Rock Ln
Lorton VA 22079

Call Sign: WH7YY
Aaron G Amacher III
8120 Bluebonnet Dr
Lorton VA 22079

Call Sign: KD4OKM
Hugo J Miller
6724 Bulkley Rd
Lorton VA 22079

Call Sign: K3PCC
Mahlon C Hawker
8009 Cardiff St
Lorton VA 22079

Call Sign: KG4SHD
Stephen J Hennessy
6024 Chapman Rd
Lorton VA 22079

Call Sign: N3QQP
Roy C Perry
8176 301 Cockburn Ct
Lorton VA 22079

Call Sign: KJ6RL
Joseph H Schafer
9305 Elkhorn Run Ct
Lorton VA 22079

Call Sign: KF9CJ

Donald J Brooks
8505 Enochs Dr
Lorton VA 22079

Call Sign: KJ4VAB
Gregory T Longacre
8538 Enochs Dr
Lorton VA 22079

Call Sign: KB8TNU
Carol M Cutchall Jr
5929 Fox Glove Trl
Lorton VA 220794215

Call Sign: KE4LYF
Glendon M Frick
10541 Greene Dr
Lorton VA 22079

Call Sign: W1WR
David L Durand
10724 Greene Dr
Lorton VA 220793533

Call Sign: WA1VAK
Charles W Rhodes
9525 Hagel Cir
Lorton VA 22079

Call Sign: KK4COR
Adil Usman
7666 Henry Knox Dr
Lorton VA 22079

Call Sign: KK4DOW
James M Phalin
8015 Horseshoe Cottage Cir
Lorton VA 22079

Call Sign: KI4MIO
James E Ruf
8036 Horseshoe Cottage Cir
Lorton VA 220792326

Call Sign: KB4WST
Edward L Gorham Jr
9018 Igoe St
Lorton VA 22079

Call Sign: WD4DQF
Martin A Torre
8466 Indian Paintbrush Way
Lorton VA 22079

Call Sign: NQ4A
Kevin A Falls
8822 Jandell Rd
Lorton VA 22079

Call Sign: W4ABQ
Kevin A Falls
8822 Jandell Rd
Lorton VA 22079

Call Sign: WA4ZPE
Floyd W Harrison Jr
8821 La Grange St
Lorton VA 22079

Call Sign: KG4HTJ
Leila H Cutchall
8908 Lagrange St
Lorton VA 22079

Call Sign: KG4HTK
Carol M Cutchall Sr
8908 Lagrange St
Lorton VA 22079

Call Sign: WN4OXC
Leila H Cutchall
8908 Lagrange St
Lorton VA 22079

Call Sign: WA4GFW
Carol M Cutchall Sr
8908 Lagrange St
Lorton VA 22079

Call Sign: WN4PP
Leila H Cutchall
8908 Lagrange St
Lorton VA 22079

Call Sign: KI4IAL
Amy J Cutchall
8908 Lagrange St
Lorton VA 22079

Call Sign: KI4BDY
Nicholas R Fratus
8908 Lagrange St
Lorton VA 22079

Call Sign: KG4CKF
Thomas J Lally
8803 Lake Hill Dr
Lorton VA 22079

Call Sign: W1NSS
Thomas J Lally
8803 Lake Hill Dr
Lorton VA 22079

Call Sign: KD5HVM
Cheryl L Casson
9231 Lee Masey Dr
Lorton VA 22079

Call Sign: KG4FIF
Kevin K Durand
8711 Legrange St
Lorton VA 22079

Call Sign: KB4EGF
Robert A Lang
7459 Lone Star Rd
Lorton VA 22079

Call Sign: KJ4SET
Michelle E West
9036 Lorton Station Blvd 229
Lorton VA 22079

Call Sign: KJ4CNR
David L Reed
7226 Lyndam Hill Cir
Lorton VA 22079

Call Sign: AA4UJ
Brian D Robertson
7228 Lyndam Hill Cir
Lorton VA 22079

Call Sign: KF6VBJ
James B Dooley
9352 Occoquan Overlook Dr

Lorton VA 22079

Call Sign: AF4JH
George R Corron
9205 Ox Rd
Lorton VA 22079

Call Sign: KG4KUN
Sean P Corron
9205 Ox Rd
Lorton VA 22079

Call Sign: KI4THD
Douglas C Spalding
9409 Ox Rd
Lorton VA 22079

Call Sign: KF4KTW
Roger D Birtcil
9411 Ox Rd
Lorton VA 22079

Call Sign: WA1ASU
Henry J Maciog Jr
8216 Paper Birch Dr
Lorton VA 22079

Call Sign: KO4IV
Drake Wilson
8922 Pink Carnation Ct
Lorton VA 22079

Call Sign: KI4YBK
Bradford M Grane
8908 Purple Lilac Cir
Lorton VA 22079

Call Sign: AG4KX
Christopher E Lee
8906 Rhododendron Cir
Lorton VA 220795685

Call Sign: KJ4FUR
Donald G Goff
8943 Rhododendron Cir
Lorton VA 22079

Call Sign: KF7LHY
Tim J Strobell

7866 Seafarer Way
Lorton VA 22079

Call Sign: KM4AD
Steven R Suarez
8300 Southern Oaks Ct
Lorton VA 22079

Call Sign: KI4IPU
Lee R Burton
6806 Springfield Dr
Lorton VA 22079

Call Sign: WA4YCK
Christopher S Compton
8229 Springwood Meadow Ln
Apt 201
Lorton VA 22079

Call Sign: KG6CQY
Don J Payette
8204 Springwood Meadow Ln
Apt B02
Lorton VA 22079

Call Sign: KG4TDK
Everett E Gayle
8229 Springwood Meadows Ln
301
Lorton VA 22079

Call Sign: KJ4WCS
Michael D Pagdanganan
9124 Stonegarden Dr
Lorton VA 22079

Call Sign: N4VSS
Alan E Norman
8762 Susquehanna St
Lorton VA 220793050

Call Sign: N4GGR
Linda A Botbyl
7913 Timarand Ct
Lorton VA 22079

Call Sign: KC5MLP
Michael Reyna
9231 Treasure Oak Ct

Lorton VA 22079

Call Sign: AC6KU
D J Mc Cann
9005 VA Ter
Lorton VA 220793252

Call Sign: KE3YK
Joel K Harding
8949 Waldren Way
Lorton VA 208172207

Call Sign: KI4RFP
Young-Tae Shin
8862 Western Hemlock Way
Lorton VA 22079

Call Sign: N2MBH
Dorothy A Lake
7602 Whitly Way
Lorton VA 22079

Call Sign: KI4BXW
David N Collyer
7620 Wiley Dr
Lorton VA 220792516

Call Sign: KJ4EAB
Todd C Lurker
7662 Wolford Way
Lorton VA 22079

Call Sign: WQ0TXG
Todd C Lurker
7662 Wolford Way
Lorton VA 22079

Call Sign: KG4IBZ
Chris C Conway Jr
7500 Woodside Ln 23
Lorton VA 22079

Call Sign: KG4LGI
Paul R Otto Jr
7511 Woodside Ln Apt 33
Lorton VA 22079

Call Sign: KE4VIL
Wade C Brown

7466 Wounded Knee Rd
Lorton VA 22079

Call Sign: KE4ULJ
Charles A Brown
7966 Wounded Knee Rd
Lorton VA 22079

Call Sign: KB4YKQ
Jeffrey A Baker
Lorton VA 221991535

FCC Amateur Radio Licenses in Lottsburg

Call Sign: KB4KOT
Warren A Stansbury
Bon Harbors Box 461
Lottsburg VA 22511

Call Sign: KJ4GVB
Northumberland County Ares
2705 Northumberland Hwy
Lottsburg VA 22511

Call Sign: WE4NC
Northumberland County Ares
2705 Northumberland Hwy
Lottsburg VA 22511

Call Sign: KD4QIT
Jefferson T Newsome Jr
2705 Northumberland Hwy
Lottsburg VA 22511

Call Sign: WB4GBS
James W Curlin
168 Snows Cove Ln
Lottsburg VA 22511

Call Sign: KE4OFI
R Deane Conrad
Sr 623
Lottsburg VA 22511

Call Sign: N4QJB
Robert R Petersen
Lottsburg VA 22511

Call Sign: N4XFK
Thomas K Boots
Lottsburg VA 22511

FCC Amateur Radio Licenses in Louisa

Call Sign: WR4VA
Michael E Sharp
5050 3 Chopt Rd
Louisa VA 23093

Call Sign: N5ZBA
Wade C Welch
5097 3 Notch Rd
Louisa VA 23093

Call Sign: KC4ZIH
Herbert L Evans
Rt 5 Box 156A
Louisa VA 23093

Call Sign: KS4ZQ
Jensen R Montambault
Rt 5 Box 156A
Louisa VA 23093

Call Sign: KD4IGU
Ruth W Randall
Rte 2 Box 220
Louisa VA 23093

Call Sign: N4KGN
Charles H Pettey
Rt 4 Box 51
Louisa VA 23093

Call Sign: K4NZ
David L Jones
1874 Brickhouse Rd
Louisa VA 23093

Call Sign: KG4JAO
Millard C Scott
1403 Courthouse Rd
Louisa VA 23093

Call Sign: N4CF
Michael M Dodd

114 Creek Rd
Louisa VA 23093

Call Sign: N2EME
Mark S Bouillon
737 Doctors Rd
Louisa VA 23093

Call Sign: AA4VI
Larry E Carpenter
921 Doctors Rd
Louisa VA 23093

Call Sign: KF4WMB
James G Corle
410 Ellisville Dr
Louisa VA 23093

Call Sign: KI4FVX
Linda J Tiblis
176 Ferndale Dr
Louisa VA 23093

Call Sign: KD4OUZ
John W Walter
176 Ferndale Dr
Louisa VA 230935724

Call Sign: KK4AIU
Christopher L Smith
444 Firehouse Dr
Louisa VA 23093

Call Sign: KK4AIW
Gwen T Taylor
444 Firehouse Dr
Louisa VA 23093

Call Sign: WB2JRR
Maurice M Burns
1007 Hickory Creek Rd
Louisa VA 230935905

Call Sign: KF4SE
Jimmy L Mc Whorter
635 Hidden Creek Rd
Louisa VA 23093

Call Sign: AF4DU

Francis I Luck
134 Holland Creek Rd
Louisa VA 23093

Call Sign: AF4DV
Jeffrey A Luck
439 Holland Creek Rd
Louisa VA 23093

Call Sign: KS4ZR
Kenneth K Reitz
1403 Holland Creek Rd
Louisa VA 23093

Call Sign: WW4JM
Jensen R Montambault
1403 Holland Creek Rd
Louisa VA 23093

Call Sign: KF4NOS
Jesse I Rosenthal
877 Holland Creek Rd
Louisa VA 23093

Call Sign: KF4OZE
Lisa D Luck
439 Holland Crk Rd
Louisa VA 23093

Call Sign: KF4LMP
Margaret H Reitz
1403 Hollandcreek Rd
Louisa VA 23093

Call Sign: KF4NOR
Alan C Gage
868 Lasley Ln
Louisa VA 230938829

Call Sign: KB4GX
Marvin G Duke
4265 Old Fredericksburg Rd
Louisa VA 23093

Call Sign: KC6YYO
Garland E Eavey Jr
261 Ordinary Way
Louisa VA 23093

Call Sign: KF4PIZ
Philip N Hepler
104 Pinehurst Dr
Louisa VA 23093

Call Sign: KB4FNF
Freddie C Drymond
Box 231 Rt 5
Louisa VA 23093

Call Sign: WB0AJQ
Thomas M Porter
26 S Lakeshore Dr
Louisa VA 23093

Call Sign: KI4MIM
John E Ross Jr
13761 Shannon Hill Rd
Louisa VA 23093

Call Sign: KK4DCL
Michael C Taylor
201 Taylor Rd
Louisa VA 23093

Call Sign: KD4OCG
Elizabeth Ann Stokes Bateman
962 Walnut Shade Rd
Louisa VA 23093

Call Sign: KG4QIR
Daniel L Bateman
962 Walnut Shade Rd
Louisa VA 23093

Call Sign: KK4FOS
Daniel L Bateman
962 Walnut Shade Rd
Louisa VA 23093

Call Sign: KD4LEF
John A Haksch
1087 Waltons Store Rd
Louisa VA 23093

Call Sign: KA4NNN
Presley L Travis III
324 Yanceyville Rd
Louisa VA 23093

Call Sign: KA4NPT
Diane L Travis
324 Yanceyville Rd
Louisa VA 23093

Call Sign: KB4UVO
Kathleen M Pierce
Louisa VA 23093

Call Sign: KG6SXY
Anthony C May
Louisa VA 230933678

FCC Amateur Radio Licenses in Lovettsville

Call Sign: N4XBU
Charles M Schwab Jr
12859 Axline Rd
Lovettsville VA 20180

Call Sign: KI4FWB
Kurt J Reber
11207 Berlin Tpke
Lovettsville VA 20180

Call Sign: KF4BCU
Howard A Dotson
12006 Berlin Tpke
Lovettsville VA 20180

Call Sign: W4HAD
Howard A Dotson
12006 Berlin Tpke
Lovettsville VA 20180

Call Sign: KG4TAF
Douglas A Henderson
13535 Berlin Tpke
Lovettsville VA 20180

Call Sign: KJ4GZX
Gregory P Jablonski
13886 Berlin Tpke
Lovettsville VA 20180

Call Sign: KF4YBW
Gabriel F Marcus

39334 Bolington Rd
Lovettsville VA 201803404

Call Sign: AB4XV
Arthur E Brendel
39465 Bolington Rd
Lovettsville VA 20180

Call Sign: KB4MTZ
Wilmer W Lloyd Jr
Rt 1 Box 182
Lovettsville VA 22080

Call Sign: N3KGE
James D Morris
Rte 2 Box 293C
Lovettsville VA 22080

Call Sign: KI4NAO
James J Johnston
39854 Canterfield Ct
Lovettsville VA 20180

Call Sign: W4MMP
Ronald L Patton
39066 Dobbins Farm Ln
Lovettsville VA 20180

Call Sign: KK4HWA
Christopher C Howlett
11465 Dutchmans Creek Rd
Lovettsville VA 20180

Call Sign: K8EI
Loyd E Davis
12659 Elvan Rd
Lovettsville VA 201802761

Call Sign: KB3BWU
Steven Cavallo
12872 Furance Mtn Rd
Lovettsville VA 20180

Call Sign: W4TLQ
Clark A Baker Jr
13106 Furnace Mtn Rd
Lovettsville VA 201802418

Call Sign: KI4BCR

Dominic M Mason
41470 Lovettsville Rd
Lovettsville VA 20180

Call Sign: KI4BCQ
Jacob X Mason
41470 Lovettsville Rd
Lovettsville VA 20180

Call Sign: K4STL
Jacob X Mason
41470 Lovettsville Rd
Lovettsville VA 20180

Call Sign: KC8MNS
Brian K Biggs
40891 Meadow Vista Pl
Lovettsville VA 20180

Call Sign: W7DTD
Michael L Schaff
40899 Meadow Vista Pl
Lovettsville VA 20180

Call Sign: KA2MNC
Irene M Kosman
17 Mills Ct
Lovettsville VA 20180

Call Sign: WD5JDQ
Lloyd W Mansfield
13167 Milltown Rd
Lovettsville VA 220803507

Call Sign: N3GMW
Mark D Gillam
11 N Light St
Lovettsville VA 201808613

Call Sign: N4MFK
Barry S Parks
4 Newmarket Ct
Lovettsville VA 22080

Call Sign: KB5CXS
Kimberly S Lewis
13290 Norsire Ln
Lovettsville VA 20180

Call Sign: KF5XN
John D Lewis
13290 Norsire Ln
Lovettsville VA 20180

Call Sign: KJ4EYP
Zachary T Pruckowski
13504 Picnic Woods Rd
Lovettsville VA 20180

Call Sign: KB7UDG
Charles V Fair
32 Potterfield Dr
Lovettsville VA 201808628

Call Sign: KB9SZW
Scott E Brock
14215 Rehobeth Church Rd
Lovettsville VA 20180

Call Sign: K4LRG
Loudoun Amateur Radio Group
14282 Rehobeth Church Rd
Lovettsville VA 20180

Call Sign: NC4S
Gary N Quinn
14282 Rehobeth Church Rd
Lovettsville VA 20180

Call Sign: KI4TQT
Richard W Denney Jr
39604 Rickard Rd
Lovettsville VA 20180

Call Sign: AI4TT
Richard W Denney Jr
39604 Rickard Rd
Lovettsville VA 20180

Call Sign: KR9D
Richard W Denney Jr
39604 Rickard Rd
Lovettsville VA 20180

Call Sign: KD4CQH
James G Shipe
39430 Rodeffer Rd
Lovettsville VA 20180

Call Sign: K4MDG
Mark D Gillam
39518 Rodeffer Rd
Lovettsville VA 201803500

Call Sign: W4RAH
Rodney A Hignite
11910 Rolling Hills Ln
Lovettsville VA 201802518

Call Sign: KK4IJV
Robert P Geisler
11767 Ropp Ln
Lovettsville VA 20180

Call Sign: KJ4VHR
Sherrill Blauer
12087 Ropp Ln
Lovettsville VA 20180

Call Sign: WB4OHD
Bruce N C Patterson
23 S Berlin Pike
Lovettsville VA 201808502

Call Sign: W3OW
Bruce N C Patterson
23 S Berlin Pike
Lovettsville VA 201808502

Call Sign: WB5ODJ
John W Westerman
38668 Sierra Ln
Lovettsville VA 20180

Call Sign: KD4ZZJ
Clarence W Thomas III
38173 Stevens Rd
Lovettsville VA 20180

Call Sign: KC4YMJ
Thomas E Ayers
38413 Stevens Rd
Lovettsville VA 20180

Call Sign: WX3Q
Alexander Benitez
39560 Sweetfern Ln

Lovettsville VA 20180

Call Sign: W4UMA
Floyd A Demory
12978 Taylorstown Rd
Lovettsville VA 201809209

Call Sign: KJ4KIE
Robert C Hyatt
Lovettsville VA 20180

Call Sign: WB4FUJ
Franklin C Lamm
Lovettsville VA 201800285

FCC Amateur Radio Licenses in Lovingston

Call Sign: KG4NBD
Helene R Dodge
2401 Davis Creek Ln
Lovingston VA 22949

Call Sign: KB4JNK
Ronald W Mauer
49 Stargate Ln
Lovingston VA 22949

FCC Amateur Radio Licenses in Lowery

Call Sign: W4IVN
Ivan A Lowery
6658 E Lynchburg Salem Tpk
Lowery VA 24570

FCC Amateur Radio Licenses in Lowesville

Call Sign: KG4RUK
William F Cash Jr
710 Dillard Hill Rd
Lowesville VA 22967

Call Sign: KG4SKO
Sheila C Cash
710 Dillard Hill Rd
Lowesville VA 22967

Call Sign: KI4YCP
Sherrie Carel
2820 Lowesville Rd
Lowesville VA 22967

FCC Amateur Radio Licenses in Lozton

Call Sign: KI4BCS
Guy V Holsten
7650 Graysons Mill Ln
Lozton VA 22079

FCC Amateur Radio Licenses in Luray

Call Sign: K4RTS
Richard T Seal
603 8th Ave Ext
Luray VA 228351572

Call Sign: KJ4HFU
Robert M Forrest III
323 Almond Dr
Luray VA 22835

Call Sign: AK4BS
Robert M Forrest III
323 Almond Dr
Luray VA 22835

Call Sign: WO4MI
Robert M Forrest III
323 Almond Dr
Luray VA 228353520

Call Sign: KA4LAF
Carol A Terry
30 Blue Ridge Ave
Luray VA 228350649

Call Sign: KD4KL
Michael P Terry
30 Blue Ridge Ave
Luray VA 228350649

Call Sign: KC4QFI
Andy B Roberts
Rt 1 Box 204A

Luray VA 22835

Call Sign: N4QIC
Clarence W Truax Jr
238 Bugle Hill Ln
Luray VA 22835

Call Sign: WA3WIP
George J Mc Culloch
15 Canaan St
Luray VA 22835

Call Sign: KG4ALT
Charles E Roach
13 Charles St
Luray VA 22835

Call Sign: KG4EYX
Chester D Fields
13 Charles St
Luray VA 22835

Call Sign: W4GGX
Charles S Newman Jr
331 Cottage Dr
Luray VA 22835

Call Sign: N4SFG
Benjamin E Endicott Jr
260 Creekside Dr
Luray VA 22835

Call Sign: KT4CB
John V Spillman
295 Cross Mtn Rd
Luray VA 22835

Call Sign: N4UXA
Bryan A Tennyson
162 Deer Track Rd
Luray VA 228355930

Call Sign: KF4JSN
Timothy L Ramey
10 E Ridge Ln
Luray VA 22835

Call Sign: AK4CJ
Timothy L Ramey

10 E Ridge Ln
Luray VA 22835

Call Sign: W4GSB
Gary S Beaver
1417 Ganders Dr
Luray VA 22835

Call Sign: KI8DM
Stephen R Statts
108 High St
Luray VA 22835

Call Sign: KE4JSV
Christopher A Miller
1 Hillside Dr
Luray VA 22835

Call Sign: KG4CGO
Rebecca L Strickler
1 Hillside Dr
Luray VA 22835

Call Sign: N4LDR
Loren D Ristola
1971 Hollow Run Rd
Luray VA 22835

Call Sign: KA4KUE
Daniel W Davidson
2030 Jewell Hollow Rd
Luray VA 22835

Call Sign: KA4LAW
Pamela S Davidson
2030 Jewell Hollow Rd
Luray VA 22835

Call Sign: WA4ROJ
William N Amonette
772 Kauffmans Mill Rd
Luray VA 22835

Call Sign: WD4LYO
Geoffrey K Phillips
466 Lake Arrowhead Rd
Luray VA 22835

Call Sign: KI4VFP

Harold F Mckay
273 Long Fort Rd
Luray VA 22835

Call Sign: W9NCJ
Jack A Russell
301 Martin St
Luray VA 22835

Call Sign: K4LDM
Larry D Moyer
331 Mtn Run Rd
Luray VA 22835

Call Sign: KN4CB
Mark C Pickett
577 Old Farm Rd
Luray VA 22835

Call Sign: KE4RMC
Chad C Painter
2767 Old Forge Rd
Luray VA 22835

Call Sign: KE4FEF
Wayne M Stanley
1202 Parkview Est Rd
Luray VA 22835

Call Sign: N4RWW
Walter L Wilson
642 Parkview Est Rd
Luray VA 22835

Call Sign: KU4TY
Robert Minetta
235 Parkview Estates Rd
Luray VA 22835

Call Sign: KA4LER
Maurice D Baliles
255 Riverside Dr
Luray VA 22835

Call Sign: KI4LLB
Bryan M Fleming
1250 S Antioch Rd
Luray VA 22835

Call Sign: KI4HAB
Jason L Temple
123 S Deford Ave
Luray VA 228351331

Call Sign: KG4IJE
Robert R Beahm Sr
1913 US Hwy 340 N
Luray VA 22835

Call Sign: K4RRB
Robert R Beahm Sr
1913 US Hwy 340 N
Luray VA 22835

Call Sign: WD4HLG
Ernest F Brown
722 W Main St
Luray VA 22835

Call Sign: W4KXE
Howard A Miller
198 Woodland Dr
Luray VA 228352919

Call Sign: KE4CKM
Maxwell Y Butler
Luray VA 22835

Call Sign: KJ4LNI
Page Valley ARC
Luray VA 22835

Call Sign: K4PMH
Page Valley ARC
Luray VA 22835

Call Sign: KD4JEA
Thomas A Coffey Jr
Luray VA 22835

**FCC Amateur Radio Licenses
in Lynch Station**

Call Sign: KG4DDQ
Mel R West
1010 Bedford Hwy
Lynch Station VA 24571

Call Sign: KN4RW
Rick A Protz
Rt 1 Box 132
Lynch Station VA 24571

Call Sign: KF4EGM
John L Green Jr
Rt 1 Box 251
Lynch Station VA 24571

Call Sign: KF4FYG
Nathan L Dowdy
Rt 1 Box 298 A
Lynch Station VA 24571

Call Sign: KD4OOL
Hastin L Brooks
Rt 1 Box 78
Lynch Station VA 24571

Call Sign: KE4RWV
Francis T Phillips III
Rt 1 Box 99C22
Lynch Station VA 24571

Call Sign: KU4TM
Robert L Morris
1095 Castle Rock Ln
Lynch Station VA 24571

Call Sign: KG4UQS
Ruth A Morris
1095 Castle Rock Ln
Lynch Station VA 24571

Call Sign: KG4KCI
Timothy D Rhodes
555 Leesville Rd
Lynch Station VA 24571

Call Sign: KG4DDM
Charles A Dowdy
5928 Leesville Rd
Lynch Station VA 24571

Call Sign: KF4JOS
Kathy M Rheault
1059 Powell Rd
Lynch Station VA 24571

Call Sign: KG4JTZ
Phillip A Oakes
2725 Wileman Rd
Lynch Station VA 24571

Call Sign: WB4UJR
Larry C Hunley
266 Windsong Dr
Lynch Station VA 24571

FCC Amateur Radio Licenses in Lynchburg

Call Sign: N4SKU
Everett M Harvey II
1982 Abert Rd
Lynchburg VA 245039737

Call Sign: W4VPO
Everet M Harvey II
1982 Abert Rd
Lynchburg VA 245039737

Call Sign: KU4TN
James L Thompson
1264 Abert Rd
Lynchburg VA 245036511

Call Sign: K4KLS
Kerri L Sowers
4620 Alabama Ave
Lynchburg VA 24502

Call Sign: KG4KQZ
Paul B Stinnett
410 Alta Ln 40
Lynchburg VA 24502

Call Sign: K5GHP
Ray L Sullivan
2700 Anthony Pl
Lynchburg VA 24501

Call Sign: W4BGQ
William M Hodnett
1020 Ardmore Dr
Lynchburg VA 24501

Call Sign: KF4UKJ
Warnie H Crews
32 Arrowhead Dr
Lynchburg VA 24502

Call Sign: W4OKM
Stephen W Tolley
237 Arrowhead Dr
Lynchburg VA 245024584

Call Sign: W6SFG
Bruce E Braun
322 Arrowhead Dr
Lynchburg VA 24502

Call Sign: KF4ZBL
Barbara J Braun
322 Arrowhead Dr
Lynchburg VA 24502

Call Sign: KR4FS
William H Anderson Jr
344 Arrowhead Dr
Lynchburg VA 24502

Call Sign: WB4GMR
Phillip C Reid
1106 Ashbourne Dr
Lynchburg VA 245015302

Call Sign: KI4BUP
Blue Ridge Farms Wireless
1106 Ashbourne Dr
Lynchburg VA 245015302

Call Sign: KN4YPO
Blue Ridge Farms Wireless
1106 Ashbourne Dr
Lynchburg VA 245015302

Call Sign: KG4KCH
Charles D Bible Jr
200 Avondale Dr
Lynchburg VA 24502

Call Sign: WA4PDJ
Stephen F Ronk
307 Bedford Spring Rd
Lynchburg VA 24502

Call Sign: W4NEX
Gerald E Nemetz
367 Beechwood Dr
Lynchburg VA 245023193

Call Sign: KK4GDI
David L Mays
110 Bellwood Dr
Lynchburg VA 24501

Call Sign: KK4GDH
Lyndon W Huggins
122 Bellwood Dr
Lynchburg VA 24501

Call Sign: K4CQ
Everett H Vatcher
101 Berkshire Pl
Lynchburg VA 24502

Call Sign: W4RJH
Robert L Dole
103 Berkshire Pl
Lynchburg VA 24502

Call Sign: KF4NUN
Joseph G Kislo
205 Beverly Hills Cir
Lynchburg VA 24502

Call Sign: KG4UAH
Joseph G Kislo
205 Beverly Hills Cir
Lynchburg VA 24502

Call Sign: WD4KFZ
Benjamin W Clark
112 Beverly Hills Ct
Lynchburg VA 24502

Call Sign: K3SJ
Steven D Joseph
902 Biltmore Ave
Lynchburg VA 24502

Call Sign: KG4PKB
Barbara J Amos
902 Biltmore Ave

Lynchburg VA 24502

Call Sign: WA2OMT
Randy N Davis
184 Bishops Ln
Lynchburg VA 24503

Call Sign: KC4HXB
Michael T Mayo
310 Blue Ridge St
Lynchburg VA 24501

Call Sign: KI4MFX
Thomas A Savage
110 Blumont Dr
Lynchburg VA 24503

Call Sign: WA4DGA
George H Floyd Jr
775 Bon Air Cir
Lynchburg VA 24503

Call Sign: KD7MBO
Johnny Waters
112 Boonsboro Dr
Lynchburg VA 24503

Call Sign: KD4HVV
John B Scales
122 Boonsboro Dr
Lynchburg VA 245032102

Call Sign: KG4RUI
Steven M Kepler
5151 Boonsboro Rd
Lynchburg VA 24503

Call Sign: KE4RBS
Mahesh A Makhijani
5105 B Boonsboro Rd
Lynchburg VA 24503

Call Sign: KF4NKJ
Scott W Adams
5139 Boonsboro Rd 4
Lynchburg VA 24503

Call Sign: KI4RIT
Richard F Watson

5001 Boonsboro Rd 402
Lynchburg VA 24503

Call Sign: KD4RBY
Anthony M Brown
4715 Boonsboro Rd Apt 123
Lynchburg VA 24503

Call Sign: KC4HXC
Melaney C Davis
4715 Boonsboro Rd Apt 91
Lynchburg VA 24503

Call Sign: N4SLE
James R Giles Jr
Rt 2 Box 239 37
Lynchburg VA 24502

Call Sign: KG4DDO
Richard D Hulser Jr
Rt 3 Box 270 A5
Lynchburg VA 24504

Call Sign: WD4FTG
Walter J Kent
Rt 2 Box 271
Lynchburg VA 24501

Call Sign: KD4AZV
Calvin S Perdieu Sr
Rt 2 Box 29 Evergreen Trl Pk
Lynchburg VA 24501

Call Sign: KE4TYX
Betty V Cartrett
Rt 5 Box 856
Lynchburg VA 24501

Call Sign: KI4TTA
Carlton R Albritton
1 Box Ln
Lynchburg VA 24501

Call Sign: WB4MBO
Donald R Seay
1209 Brandon Rd
Lynchburg VA 24502

Call Sign: KC4PAV

James D Bourne
126 Breezewood Dr
Lynchburg VA 24502

Call Sign: KD4GXG
Jason K Moorefield
594 Briar Cliff Cir
Lynchburg VA 24502

Call Sign: KA8INL
David E Thomas
605 Briarcliff Cir
Lynchburg VA 245023601

Call Sign: N2JUP
David E Thomas
605 Briarcliff Cir
Lynchburg VA 245023601

Call Sign: KD4WCM
William C Myers
205 Bryant Rd
Lynchburg VA 24502

Call Sign: K4WCM
William C Myers
205 Bryant Rd
Lynchburg VA 24502

Call Sign: KC0LBE
Marcos A Gallego
285 Buckhead Rd Apt 303
Lynchburg VA 24502

Call Sign: N4DRY
John A Mc Cormick
203 Buckingham Dr
Lynchburg VA 24502

Call Sign: KK4BIW
Kimberly R Mac Pherson
2004 Burnt Bridge Rd
Lynchburg VA 24503

Call Sign: K4ITH
Donald B Brah
1920 Burnt Bridge Rd Apt 211
Lynchburg VA 245032248

Call Sign: N4WK
Wallace F Kabler
262 Burr Oak Rd
Lynchburg VA 245025612

Call Sign: KG4IAX
James S Garber Jr
50 Callaway Ct
Lynchburg VA 24502

Call Sign: N4JSG
James S Garber Jr
50 Callaway Ct
Lynchburg VA 245023902

Call Sign: WB9VQQ
Thomas K Gregory
417 Cambridge Dr
Lynchburg VA 24502

Call Sign: WB4NYE
Carl G Summy
1842 Camp Hwy Rd
Lynchburg VA 24501

Call Sign: W4RLA
Earl W Talley Sr
3410 Campbell Ave
Lynchburg VA 24501

Call Sign: KE4OQK
Patrick D Hkartzell
507 Cape Charles Sq
Lynchburg VA 24502

Call Sign: KF4WBF
VA D Vallastro
24 Cape Lookout Ct
Lynchburg VA 24502

Call Sign: KE4SVS
Walter N Jones
2237 Carroll Ave
Lynchburg VA 24501

Call Sign: W4SLS
Robert F Maschal
94 Cavalier Ct
Lynchburg VA 24502

Call Sign: N4TZE
Marc A Rowley
107 Cedar Branch Rd
Lynchburg VA 24502

Call Sign: W4TZI
Edwin S Bolen Jr
1208 Cedar Hill Dr
Lynchburg VA 24502

Call Sign: KE4JGU
John W Orban
207 Chadwick Dr
Lynchburg VA 24502

Call Sign: KI4FQM
Maria S Groshner
407 Chadwick Dr
Lynchburg VA 24502

Call Sign: KG4GCB
Michael R Marsh
378 Charldon Rd
Lynchburg VA 24501

Call Sign: KC4OFL
Carlos E Gutierrez
127 Cheese Creek Rd
Lynchburg VA 24503

Call Sign: KG4KDM
David M Regney
212 Chesterfield Rd
Lynchburg VA 24502

Call Sign: N4JAX
David M Regney
212 Chesterfield Rd
Lynchburg VA 24502

Call Sign: KK4CSJ
Daniel B Van Atta
222 Chesterfield Rd
Lynchburg VA 24502

Call Sign: N4RSU
Everett C Twining
631 Chestnut Mt Dr

Lynchburg VA 24504

Call Sign: KJ4WTG
Jared Wight
735 Chinook Pl
Lynchburg VA 24502

Call Sign: KJ4VZT
David R Bourque
414 Clay St
Lynchburg VA 24504

Call Sign: KC4OFH
Jeff W Nash
235 Cleveland Ave
Lynchburg VA 24503

Call Sign: W9VSW
Richard J Skulina
1408 Club Dr
Lynchburg VA 245032504

Call Sign: KD4WWM
David R Glenn
1436 Club Dr
Lynchburg VA 24503

Call Sign: KB4RDH
Terry F Bebo
117 Clubhouse Dr Ste 102
Lynchburg VA 245027279

Call Sign: KF4EVH
Robert H Mason
2330 Cobbs St
Lynchburg VA 24501

Call Sign: N4LGJ
Willie L Langford Jr
2373 Cobbs St
Lynchburg VA 24501

Call Sign: KC4CWX
Barbara F Hamilton
2410 Cobbs St
Lynchburg VA 24501

Call Sign: NJ4Q
William K Smiley

2935 Coffee Rd
Lynchburg VA 24503

Call Sign: KF4WBG
Sahr J Ngayenga
221 Coffee Rd Apt 39
Lynchburg VA 24503

Call Sign: KM4WM
Vernon R Frank
225 Coffee Rd Apt 57
Lynchburg VA 24501

Call Sign: KA4MOQ
Charles F Flaugher
107 College Park Dr
Lynchburg VA 24502

Call Sign: KD4MZG
James S Vames
308 College Park Dr
Lynchburg VA 24502

Call Sign: KI4RVV
Johnny M Lawson
297 Collington Dr
Lynchburg VA 24502

Call Sign: KQ4NS
Wayne A Brindle
315 Collington Dr
Lynchburg VA 24502

Call Sign: K4DMG
Robert A Johnston
308 Cornerstone St
Lynchburg VA 24502

Call Sign: W4FKY
Charles V Krantz
1027 Coronado Ln
Lynchburg VA 24502

Call Sign: KE4VVA
Jason M Wright
1935 Cottontown Rd
Lynchburg VA 24503

Call Sign: W4PBS

Jason M Wright
1935 Cottontown Rd
Lynchburg VA 24503

Call Sign: NG4K
Nelson K Drinkard
1552 Country Rd
Lynchburg VA 24504

Call Sign: WA4WFR
James W Martin
2076 Country Rd
Lynchburg VA 245044162

Call Sign: KD4YFI
Douglas J Mc Daniel Jr
4109 Crescent Rd
Lynchburg VA 24502

Call Sign: N4WHQ
Rufus H Parker Jr
585 Cresthill Rd
Lynchburg VA 245044466

Call Sign: WA8RCB
Mike B Gorbutt
885 Cresthill Rd
Lynchburg VA 24504

Call Sign: K4QXS
Frederick E White
715 Custer Dr
Lynchburg VA 23502

Call Sign: KJ4WND
Christina L Matson
105 Dale Ave
Lynchburg VA 24502

Call Sign: KJ4WNE
Kaleb Matson
105 Dale Ave
Lynchburg VA 24502

Call Sign: N4BVP
Rachel S Bush
1109 Dandridge Dr
Lynchburg VA 24501

Call Sign: W4FOD
John V A Bush
1109 Dandridge Dr
Lynchburg VA 245012219

Call Sign: KI4SAK
William L Burton Jr
1227 Dandridge Dr
Lynchburg VA 24501

Call Sign: AC4RN
Thomas C Rehrer
193 Deerfield Ln
Lynchburg VA 24502

Call Sign: WA4UKZ
Paul R Smith Jr
300 Dianne Dr
Lynchburg VA 24504

Call Sign: N4IW
David E Simms
3218 Downing Dr
Lynchburg VA 245033106

Call Sign: W4VRG
Robert T Gordon
3233 Downing Dr
Lynchburg VA 24503

Call Sign: KA4MVO
Michael Montgomery
3242 Downing Dr
Lynchburg VA 24503

Call Sign: KG4LKI
William T Strayhorn
7 Duiguid Dr
Lynchburg VA 24502

Call Sign: AG4HM
William T Strayhorn
7 Duiguid Dr
Lynchburg VA 24502

Call Sign: KC4OFQ
Michael T Howard
1518 E Overbrook Rd
Lynchburg VA 24502

Call Sign: KG4PKA
Ronald M Buchanan
3579 Eastbrook Rd
Lynchburg VA 24501

Call Sign: KG4EUN
Richard J Pannell
131 Easton Ave
Lynchburg VA 24503

Call Sign: KD6BUV
Gregory A Hoag
52 Easton Ave
Lynchburg VA 24501

Call Sign: KJ4WNG
Scott R Gresham
44 Easton Ave Apt B
Lynchburg VA 24503

Call Sign: K4HOP
Robert W Colby
1915 Eastwood Ln
Lynchburg VA 245034314

Call Sign: WA4BDF
Calvin L Crance
6020 Edgewood Ave
Lynchburg VA 24502

Call Sign: AB4FU
Jerry D Hartley
16 Edgewood Ct E
Lynchburg VA 245023224

Call Sign: KD4WHB
Lynnette K Hartley
16 Edgewood Ct E
Lynchburg VA 245023224

Call Sign: KI4OJC
Bevin R Alexander Jr
1400 Edley Pl
Lynchburg VA 24502

Call Sign: K4ALE
Bevin R Alexander Jr
1400 Edley Pl

Lynchburg VA 24502

Call Sign: WB6HMS
John M Keegan
428 Elmwood Ave
Lynchburg VA 24503

Call Sign: KJ4HJZ
Michael S James
500 Elmwood Ave
Lynchburg VA 24503

Call Sign: K4MSJ
Michael S James
500 Elmwood Ave
Lynchburg VA 24503

Call Sign: WA4AAX
Robert T Forrest
1556 English Tavern Rd
Lynchburg VA 245017105

Call Sign: W4VKT
James W Yates
1400 Enterprise Dr N128
Lynchburg VA 245022045

Call Sign: KG4FBV
Lucy M Spinner
504 Euclid Ave
Lynchburg VA 24501

Call Sign: KD4WWK
Stephen C Stanton
708 Farfields Dr
Lynchburg VA 24502

Call Sign: KG4JUD
Tony L Shrader
948 Farfields Dr
Lynchburg VA 24502

Call Sign: KJ4GHC
James L Quattlebaum
2724 Farmington Pl
Lynchburg VA 24503

Call Sign: W4QQI
James L Quattlebaum

2724 Farmington Pl
Lynchburg VA 24503

Call Sign: KG4KDJ
Daryl W Rexrode
68 Farmington Rd
Lynchburg VA 24502

Call Sign: KF4YGC
Stephen W Stilwell Jr
61 Federal St
Lynchburg VA 24504

Call Sign: KC4NZI
Thomas G Klein
1331 Fenwick Dr
Lynchburg VA 24502

Call Sign: WB2DWC
Marc D Kaufman
1721 Fillmore St
Lynchburg VA 245012019

Call Sign: KD4LJR
David J Widgeon III
303 Fleetwood Dr
Lynchburg VA 24501

Call Sign: KF4ZBM
Ricky L Burns
600 Fleetwood Dr
Lynchburg VA 24501

Call Sign: KC2IWG
Marc P Vanleer
711 Fleetwood Dr
Lynchburg VA 24501

Call Sign: KG4DEC
Ronald W Anderson
915 Floyd St 2
Lynchburg VA 24501

Call Sign: N4YLD
James D Austin
3310 Fort Ave
Lynchburg VA 24501

Call Sign: WB4IFD

Edward L Keaton
3917 Fort Ave
Lynchburg VA 24502

Call Sign: KG4POO
Joseph M Monopoli Jr
4359 Fort Ave
Lynchburg VA 245021231

Call Sign: KG4PUC
Joshua S Matheny
4396 Fort Ave
Lynchburg VA 24502

Call Sign: KE4NPH
Jesse L Dunaway
4916 Fort Ave
Lynchburg VA 245020314

Call Sign: N4SOY
John W Northcutt
206 Fox Crest Dr
Lynchburg VA 24502

Call Sign: KF4MQW
William S Harding
105 Fox Hollow Rd
Lynchburg VA 245033858

Call Sign: KE4DHS
David F Schlemmer
117 Frederick Dr
Lynchburg VA 24502

Call Sign: KG4PJZ
Michael L Drumheller
102 Gala Dr
Lynchburg VA 24503

Call Sign: KC4HXD
Scott D Driskill
172 George St
Lynchburg VA 245023518

Call Sign: WB4ZHF
Edwin R Page
2316 Glencove Pl
Lynchburg VA 24503

Call Sign: W4PEF
Marvin C Tweedy
4330 Gorman Dr
Lynchburg VA 24503

Call Sign: WB4ESX
William E Wright
1602 A Graves Mill Rd
Lynchburg VA 24502

Call Sign: W8KZX
Frank R Terrant
1604 Graves Mill Rd 210
Lynchburg VA 24502

Call Sign: AA4SA
Norman S Cromwell
2748 Greenhill Ln
Lynchburg VA 24503

Call Sign: KK4BIR
Betty J Clifton
115 Greenwell Ct
Lynchburg VA 24502

Call Sign: W4ODA
Herman E Parker
128 Greenwell Ct
Lynchburg VA 24502

Call Sign: KC4KZK
Arthur L Nickerson Jr
2111 Hanover St
Lynchburg VA 24501

Call Sign: KG4OLR
Diane P Nickerson
2111 Hanover St
Lynchburg VA 24501

Call Sign: KG4NBT
Nathan L Nickerson
2113 Hanover St
Lynchburg VA 245014617

Call Sign: KG4MPR
Garland R Harper
3920 Harbor St
Lynchburg VA 245031002

Call Sign: KC4VWE
Jeremy W Rusher
3259 Hawkins Mill Rd
Lynchburg VA 24503

Call Sign: KG4TCM
Gary V Clark
2420 Hawthorne Rd
Lynchburg VA 24503

Call Sign: AI4BY
Gary V Clark
2420 Hawthorne Rd
Lynchburg VA 24503

Call Sign: KG4PTX
Jack R Crandall
712 Hayes Dr
Lynchburg VA 24502

Call Sign: N4MQW
Fredrick A Alvis
4709 Heritage Dr
Lynchburg VA 245031105

Call Sign: N8ONQ
Nathan D Mc Clure III
2308 Heron Hill Pl
Lynchburg VA 24503

Call Sign: N8TE
Nathan D Mc Clure III
2308 Heron Hill Pl
Lynchburg VA 24503

Call Sign: WB4BVA
Charles W Mayo
5348 Hickory Hill Rd
Lynchburg VA 24503

Call Sign: KG4COX
Artemus S Dixon
2355 High St
Lynchburg VA 24501

Call Sign: WA4SNY
David L Suchodolski
1816 Hillsdale Rd

Lynchburg VA 245011002

Call Sign: AG4DJ
David L Suchodolski
1816 Hillsdale Rd
Lynchburg VA 245011002

Call Sign: KG4JTV
Christopher B Fritz
5925 Hines Cir B
Lynchburg VA 24502

Call Sign: KD4AZT
Hans K Schubert III
218 Holcomb Path Rd
Lynchburg VA 24501

Call Sign: KD4AZU
Hans K Schubert
218 Holcomb Path Rd
Lynchburg VA 24501

Call Sign: KD4WWJ
Joseph A Whitehead
104B Holcombe Rd
Lynchburg VA 24502

Call Sign: KD4PYV
Marianne C Branch
212 Honey Tree Ln
Lynchburg VA 24502

Call Sign: N4MUV
Robert H Branch Jr
212 Honey Tree Ln
Lynchburg VA 24502

Call Sign: K4JQG
Cantrell Smith
300 Hopkins Rd
Lynchburg VA 24502

Call Sign: KD4ZSF
Matt O Hannam
142 Howard Dr
Lynchburg VA 24503

Call Sign: KC4GBD
David C Fraley

213 Huntingwood Blvd
Lynchburg VA 24503

Call Sign: W4DF
Frederic D Fraley
213 Huntingwood Blvd
Lynchburg VA 24503

Call Sign: KJ4IFZ
Charles E Burgess
194 Huron Ave
Lynchburg VA 24503

Call Sign: N4ZYW
Robin G Carter
5923 Igloe Dr
Lynchburg VA 24502

Call Sign: KI4PYI
George R Devenport
2044 Indian Hill Rd
Lynchburg VA 24503

Call Sign: WA4JXY
Arvil K Guthrie Jr
2044 Indian Hill Rd
Lynchburg VA 245034327

Call Sign: KD4JJG
Glenn A Huddleston
948 Indian Ridge Dr
Lynchburg VA 24502

Call Sign: KJ4ATF
Robert L Mcghee
5019 Inglewood Rd
Lynchburg VA 24503

Call Sign: K6JGS
James G Switzer
144 Irvington Springs Rd
Lynchburg VA 24503

Call Sign: WA4RTS
Gordon P Howell Jr
201 Irvington St
Lynchburg VA 24503

Call Sign: KB4HFG

Peter J Perrone
3400 Ivylink Pl
Lynchburg VA 24503

Call Sign: N4IZG
Roger W Graybill
1349 Jennings Dr
Lynchburg VA 24503

Call Sign: KG4JUB
Reuben C Johnson Jr
913 Johnson Rd
Lynchburg VA 245025025

Call Sign: WB2DLK
Charles L Seals
32 Juniper Dr
Lynchburg VA 245026638

Call Sign: KJ4SNE
James Neel
108 Keenland Ct
Lynchburg VA 24503

Call Sign: KG4JTX
Carey S West Jr
104 Keswick Dr
Lynchburg VA 24503

Call Sign: KC4WNA
Dudley K Stafford
4201 Keystone Rd
Lynchburg VA 24503

Call Sign: KB4HPQ
Steven L Hough
301 F Killarney Ct
Lynchburg VA 24502

Call Sign: KI4FHZ
Jeffrey B Lambert
303 A Killarney Ct
Lynchburg VA 24502

Call Sign: WE4ENG
Jeffrey B Lambert
303 A Killarney Ct
Lynchburg VA 24502

Call Sign: KD4WWG
Steven G Keefer
314G Killarney Ct
Lynchburg VA 24502

Call Sign: KI4EAR
Seshagiri Krishnamoorthy
305 Killarney St Apt B
Lynchburg VA 24502

Call Sign: KD4WWH
Bonnie P Smith
402 Kings Way
Lynchburg VA 24502

Call Sign: KG4AHI
Mark E Poole
134 Kingswood Ln
Lynchburg VA 24504

Call Sign: KG4CDT
Victoria S Reed
337 Kitty Hawk Sq
Lynchburg VA 24502

Call Sign: KJ4ILG
Ronald W Brown
1245 Krise Cir
Lynchburg VA 24503

Call Sign: KF4ICM
Damon R Smith
1309 Krise Cir
Lynchburg VA 245032613

Call Sign: KA4UTG
Edgar J Stone
316 Lake Forest Dr
Lynchburg VA 24502

Call Sign: KK4EXN
Marvin W Lane Jr
2134 Lakeside Dr Lot 119
Lynchburg VA 24501

Call Sign: KE4VVB
Cledus O Neighbors
1020 Lakeview Dr
Lynchburg VA 24502

Call Sign: KC4ZWZ
Barry G Turner
1209 Lakeview Dr
Lynchburg VA 245022809

Call Sign: AJ4LZ
Barry G Turner
1209 Lakeview Dr
Lynchburg VA 245022809

Call Sign: KC4CWT
Tracy L Proehl
1211 Lakeview Dr
Lynchburg VA 24502

Call Sign: WT4B
Tyler B Burdick
1409 Landon Ct
Lynchburg VA 24503

Call Sign: KD4MIU
Ronald L Hooper
3423 Landon St
Lynchburg VA 24503

Call Sign: KD4HAE
Douglas C Renalds
310 Langhorne Ln
Lynchburg VA 245013628

Call Sign: WB2QHE
Jeremiah J Tell
1818 Langhorne Sq Apt 318
Lynchburg VA 24501

Call Sign: WD4NEI
Wilson W Noel
1701 Laxton Rd
Lynchburg VA 24502

Call Sign: KG4PTW
Matthew R Hughes
709 Laxton Rd Apt 4
Lynchburg VA 24502

Call Sign: KB4MQW
William J Cary Jr
648 Leesville Rd

Lynchburg VA 24502

Call Sign: KE4WPH
Wayne D Lipscomb
739 Leesville Rd
Lynchburg VA 24502

Call Sign: KE4GKR
Raymond E Kimpton
826 Leesville Rd
Lynchburg VA 24502

Call Sign: KG4BAD
Catherine D Royster
18584 Leesville Rd
Lynchburg VA 245015169

Call Sign: KG4BAE
Charles E Royster
18584 Leesville Rd
Lynchburg VA 245015169

Call Sign: KA8MOZ
Timothy G Current
521B Leesville Rd
Lynchburg VA 24502

Call Sign: KF4UER
Kenneth R Crews
791 A Leesville Rd
Lynchburg VA 24502

Call Sign: N9PKQ
Russell L Bolstad
762 Leesville Rd Apt 2002
Lynchburg VA 24502

Call Sign: KA4KQI
Philip E Weeks
208 Leewood Dr
Lynchburg VA 24503

Call Sign: KJ4NED
Timothy L Soyars
400 Legacy Oaks Cir
Lynchburg VA 24501

Call Sign: K3KER
Diana M Lester

410 Legacy Oaks Dr
Lynchburg VA 24501

Call Sign: KG4AIQ
Charles K Hurt
1663 Link Rd
Lynchburg VA 24503

Call Sign: KG4BAB
Scott T Judy
3101 Link Rd 40
Lynchburg VA 245033238

Call Sign: N4JDY
Scott T Judy
3101 Link Rd 40
Lynchburg VA 245033238

Call Sign: N4ZEG
Richard L Von Gemmingen
3101 Link Rd 69
Lynchburg VA 24503

Call Sign: KI4WQO
Jason M Thompson
89 Logan Ln
Lynchburg VA 245027321

Call Sign: KC4VJF
Lewis E Padgett
1110 Lone Jack Rd
Lynchburg VA 24501

Call Sign: KI4CMU
Bryant J Lampmon
1276 Lone Jake Rd Apt 2
Lynchburg VA 24501

Call Sign: KI4CQW
James Fisher
1021 Long Meadows Dr
Lynchburg VA 24502

Call Sign: WA6QBJ
Kenneth L Brown
1213 Long Meadows Dr Apt
109
Lynchburg VA 24502

Call Sign: W4SBX
Leroy E Glass
1213 Long Meadows Dr Apt
426
Lynchburg VA 24502

Call Sign: W4FUR
James L Cox
1213 Long Measows Dr Apt
325
Lynchburg VA 24502

Call Sign: KD4NYM
Duane D Davis III
112 Lookout Dr
Lynchburg VA 24502

Call Sign: KG4OFT
Gary L Howard
1605 Lynndale Pl
Lynchburg VA 24502

Call Sign: K4IUS
Melvin T Anderson
200 Lynview Dr
Lynchburg VA 24502

Call Sign: AG4GL
Jerzy G Kowalczyk
111 Macarthur Dr
Lynchburg VA 24502

Call Sign: N4QWF
John B Price Jr
1190 Macon Loop
Lynchburg VA 24503

Call Sign: KC4RAX
Nancy D Price
1190 Macon Loop Rd
Lynchburg VA 24503

Call Sign: KF4ZBY
Mathhew G Sullivan
320 Madison St
Lynchburg VA 24504

Call Sign: K1BEE
Louis E Kibby

1420 Madison St
Lynchburg VA 24504

Call Sign: KC4RBC
Lois E Dameron
617 Madison St
Lynchburg VA 24503

Call Sign: KG4KQY
Anthony L Iovinetti
104 Majestic Cricle
Lynchburg VA 24502

Call Sign: W4NRW
Robert L Nunley
305 Mallard Dr
Lynchburg VA 24503

Call Sign: N4BTM
David F Conner
Nr 36 Mallows Mhp
Lynchburg VA 24502

Call Sign: KG4WCW
Daniel P Morgan
3614 Manton Dr
Lynchburg VA 24503

Call Sign: KB3AZL
Louisa A Morgan
3614 Manton Dr
Lynchburg VA 245033014

Call Sign: W4QE
James V Morgan Jr
3614 Manton Dr
Lynchburg VA 245033014

Call Sign: WD9DEM
Diane W Morgan
3614 Manton Dr
Lynchburg VA 245033014

Call Sign: K4TM
Hunsdon Cary III
3701 Manton Dr
Lynchburg VA 245033015

Call Sign: K4IAK

William T Powell
3809 Manton Ln
Lynchburg VA 24503

Call Sign: KG4MPP
Mark A Tinsley
229 Maple Hills Dr
Lynchburg VA 24502

Call Sign: N4TEF
James H Catlett Jr
3232 Maryland Ave
Lynchburg VA 24501

Call Sign: N4TQF
Pamela L Lygon
3703 Mathews St
Lynchburg VA 24503

Call Sign: KE4MAC
Jeffrey J Pullen
200 McIntosh Dr
Lynchburg VA 24503

Call Sign: KJ4HZG
David Whiteley Jr
1500 McKinney Ave
Lynchburg VA 24502

Call Sign: WA4HYE
Etta T Bennett
1504 McVeigh Rd
Lynchburg VA 24502

Call Sign: KN4GB
Joe W Ernsberger
7123 Meadowbrook Rd
Lynchburg VA 24502

Call Sign: KJ4JBD
Jeffrey N Pantoja
113 Meadowridge Dr
Lynchburg VA 24503

Call Sign: N4NIB
Daniel L Bathurst
147 Melinda Dr
Lynchburg VA 24502

Call Sign: W4GCE
George D Rose Jr
105 Middleboro Pl
Lynchburg VA 245022121

Call Sign: KB4MPX
Tyrone B Jones
114 Middleboro Pl
Lynchburg VA 24502

Call Sign: N4LBF
Frank J Pursley
517 Midvale St
Lynchburg VA 24502

Call Sign: K4HK
Robert J Martin III
600 Midvale St
Lynchburg VA 24502

Call Sign: KE4SVR
Michael A Spires
604 Mill Stream Ln
Lynchburg VA 24502

Call Sign: KG4VLI
Tarah V Jordan
308 Mill View Ln
Lynchburg VA 24502

Call Sign: N5SUN
Steven A Gross
1215 Millstream Ln
Lynchburg VA 245024356

Call Sign: W4FTV
Junior I Rhodes
2121 Mimosa Dr
Lynchburg VA 245034305

Call Sign: KC4RAT
Sidney G Hall
2207 Mimosa Dr
Lynchburg VA 24503

Call Sign: W3SYS
Stanier E Brayshaw
2416 Mimosa Dr
Lynchburg VA 24503

Call Sign: WD4AYK
Bryan J Cox
2424 Mimosa Dr
Lynchburg VA 24503

Call Sign: KC8ZHN
Robert G Cropp
1009 Misty Mtn Rd Apt 1702
Lynchburg VA 24502

Call Sign: KC4DYW
Kendall E Giles
721 Mohawk Dr
Lynchburg VA 24502

Call Sign: KF4WBD
Jason Be Jarrett
733 Mohawks Dr
Lynchburg VA 245021407

Call Sign: KG4NGU
Mark C Early
1405 Monroe St
Lynchburg VA 24504

Call Sign: KG4PKZ
Zandra M Pavicic
3701 Montridge Pl
Lynchburg VA 24501

Call Sign: KC4RAW
Mihail Dinu Jr
1020 Moreview Dr
Lynchburg VA 24502

Call Sign: N4HUZ
Kenneth B Bryan
1113 Moreview Dr
Lynchburg VA 24502

Call Sign: N4RB
Richard I Bain
1140 Moreview Dr
Lynchburg VA 24502

Call Sign: KI4GJZ
David S Murphy
4109 Morningside Dr

Lynchburg VA 24503

Call Sign: N7LKB
David S Murphy
4109 Morningside Dr
Lynchburg VA 24503

Call Sign: AJ4AL
David S Murphy
4109 Morningside Dr
Lynchburg VA 24503

Call Sign: KI4FGV
Joshua Bates
297 Morton Creek Rd
Lynchburg VA 24504

Call Sign: KD4JJL
Gregory A Whorley II
2387 Mosby Ave
Lynchburg VA 24501

Call Sign: W4KCS
Carlyle A Shields
391 Mt Olivet Ch Rd
Lynchburg VA 24504

Call Sign: WA4JNL
Oxford Furnace Vhf Club
391 Mt Olivet Ch Rd
Lynchburg VA 24504

Call Sign: KE4OQJ
Roy A Shields
519 Mt Olivet Church Rd
Lynchburg VA 24504

Call Sign: WA4DMU
John F Simmons Jr
130 Mtn Peak Dr
Lynchburg VA 245025560

Call Sign: W4RCY
W Conrad Richardson
326 Mtn Peak Dr
Lynchburg VA 24502

Call Sign: KC4AHS
Donald L Turner

326 Munford St
Lynchburg VA 24501

Call Sign: KE4YLT
Ralph L Puckett
448 Neighbors Pl
Lynchburg VA 24501

Call Sign: WA6CAL
Joseph S Herman
1432 Nelson Dr
Lynchburg VA 24502

Call Sign: WA6QFG
Linda L Herman
1432 Nelson Dr
Lynchburg VA 24502

Call Sign: N4IYV
Allan F Johnson
1441 Nelson Dr
Lynchburg VA 24502

Call Sign: N5BTP
Laurence A La Fratta
123 New London Dr
Lynchburg VA 24502

Call Sign: AG4JQ
Patrick A La Fratta
123 New London Dr
Lynchburg VA 24502

Call Sign: KI4YWH
Jordan W Goulder
413 Newberne St
Lynchburg VA 24501

Call Sign: KA4JKV
Penelope H Cline
1512 Northwood Cir
Lynchburg VA 24503

Call Sign: WD4EXG
William C Cline
1512 Northwood Cir
Lynchburg VA 24503

Call Sign: KJ4WTF

Christopher A Malone
111 Northwynd Cir 4
Lynchburg VA 24502

Call Sign: KI4SAL
Jeremy R Dillinger
220 Norwood St
Lynchburg VA 24504

Call Sign: KA4YOX
Ingeborg K Mann
211 Nottingham Cir
Lynchburg VA 24502

Call Sign: WA4RJP
Friedrich H Mann
211 Nottingham Cir
Lynchburg VA 24502

Call Sign: KC4OFN
Gregory W Furr
215 Nottingham Cir
Lynchburg VA 24502

Call Sign: KG4WSR
Kenneth F Wallace
95 Oak Hill Dr Apt E
Lynchburg VA 24502

Call Sign: KD4PUG
Octavio De Marchena
2001 Oak Park Pl
Lynchburg VA 24503

Call Sign: AG4HN
Octavio De Marchena
2001 Oak Park Pl
Lynchburg VA 24503

Call Sign: K4WCK
Walter C Kelly
330 Oak Ridge Blvd
Lynchburg VA 24502

Call Sign: KI4CQX
Peter J Beland
52 Oak Trl
Lynchburg VA 24502

Call Sign: KG4FOW
Stephen R Wynn
169 Oak Trl
Lynchburg VA 24502

Call Sign: KE4JGT
Fran B Dallison
124 Oakdale Cir
Lynchburg VA 24502

Call Sign: WA4FHQ
J Russell Dallison
124 Oakdale Cir
Lynchburg VA 24502

Call Sign: W4MLQ
Harry W Dallison
124 Oakdale Cir
Lynchburg VA 24502

Call Sign: N4YVI
John D Reed
166 Oakdale Cir
Lynchburg VA 245023422

Call Sign: W4JGI
Howard B Cannaday
9107 Oakland Cir
Lynchburg VA 24502

Call Sign: KC4FPP
Vincent E Mc Candless
198 Oakley Ave
Lynchburg VA 24501

Call Sign: KD4CAU
Stephen P Leonard
309 Oakridge Blvd
Lynchburg VA 24502

Call Sign: W4KNC
Joe T Guthrie
327 Oakridge Blvd
Lynchburg VA 24502

Call Sign: KI4AOA
Marlin E Schrock
808 Old Forest Rd
Lynchburg VA 24501

Call Sign: KD4HVU
Donald E Olmstead
3205 Old Forest Rd
Lynchburg VA 24501

Call Sign: KC7LMS
Daniel A Torres
3315 Old Forest Rd Of 53
Lynchburg VA 24506

Call Sign: KF4ZBS
Ryan E Petrey
3600 Old Forest Rd Unit 117
Lynchburg VA 24501

Call Sign: KF4ZBR
Justin T Petrey
3600 Old Forest Rd Unit 117
Lynchburg VA 24503

Call Sign: KG4DEZ
D M Harrington
417 Old Graves Mill Rd
Lynchburg VA 24502

Call Sign: KF4HCJ
Vincent L Goodman
1023 Old Graves Mill Rd
Lynchburg VA 24502

Call Sign: KF4ABK
James E Hyler
326 Old Plum Branch Rd
Lynchburg VA 24504

Call Sign: KA4BAS
James I Phillips Jr
925 Old Trents Ferry Rd
Lynchburg VA 24503

Call Sign: W3CQ
Boonsboro Brasspounders
117 Overstreet Ln
Lynchburg VA 24503

Call Sign: KC4D
William W Perkins
117 Overstreet Ln

Lynchburg VA 245033741

Call Sign: W4MNW
Daniel J Lynch
3088 Oxford Furnace Rd
Lynchburg VA 24504

Call Sign: WB4MNL
Lynn W Seipp
114 Pacos St
Lynchburg VA 24502

Call Sign: KG4EWE
Michael S Mann
99 Page St
Lynchburg VA 24501

Call Sign: K4IEE
Melvin L Clark Sr
107 Page St
Lynchburg VA 24501

Call Sign: KF4UKI
Freddy T Ling
2005 Park Ave
Lynchburg VA 24501

Call Sign: KF4BGG
Lawrence J Brennan
2105 Park Ave
Lynchburg VA 245012728

Call Sign: KC4FPI
Frederick J Kee II
2216 Park Pl
Lynchburg VA 24501

Call Sign: KA2SPH
Michael J Edelson
8 Parkwood Ave Apt B
Lynchburg VA 24501

Call Sign: KG4KQX
Joseph D Dowdy
198 Patricia Dr
Lynchburg VA 24501

Call Sign: K3VFD
Joseph D Dowdy

198 Patricia Dr
Lynchburg VA 245015136

Call Sign: KD4YFF
Robert W Windle
6240 Pawnee Dr
Lynchburg VA 24502

Call Sign: KC4NGV
Daniel S Smith
6312 Pawnee Dr
Lynchburg VA 24302

Call Sign: KA3LOY
Ronald S Smith
6312 Pawnee Dr
Lynchburg VA 24502

Call Sign: KG4DEY
Keith G Staples
226 Payne St
Lynchburg VA 24501

Call Sign: KK4GDJ
Daniel F Savage III
3840 Peakland Pl
Lynchburg VA 24503

Call Sign: AK4SQ
Daniel F Savage III
3840 Peakland Pl
Lynchburg VA 24503

Call Sign: KF4ZBZ
Benjamin R Whitehouse
3853 Peakland Pl
Lynchburg VA 24503

Call Sign: KB8CVG
John F Boye
90 Peg Ln
Lynchburg VA 245023417

Call Sign: WD0HBA
Mark L Cooksey
207 Pennsylvania Ave
Lynchburg VA 24502

Call Sign: KI4EDM

Jerome A Minnis
217 Pennsylvania Ave
Lynchburg VA 24502

Call Sign: W4LTF
Layard T Fortune Jr
416 Perrymont Ave
Lynchburg VA 245021104

Call Sign: KC4PBK
Tim L Johnson
120 Phillips Cir
Lynchburg VA 24502

Call Sign: KF4TGA
Blake A Edmondson
102 Pilgrim Rd
Lynchburg VA 24502

Call Sign: KI4IC
Allen G Edmondson
102 Pilgrim Rd
Lynchburg VA 24502

Call Sign: N4TOI
Carolyn B Edmondson
102 Pilgrim Rd
Lynchburg VA 24502

Call Sign: KG4OFV
Gregory S Simms
1406 Pine Bluff
Lynchburg VA 24503

Call Sign: N4LFD
Gregory S Simms
1406 Pine Bluff
Lynchburg VA 245034947

Call Sign: W4FLU
William A Dooley
537 Pine Dr
Lynchburg VA 24503

Call Sign: KI4IXH
Daniel B Dugger
238 Pine Haven Dr
Lynchburg VA 24502

Call Sign: KD4TZM
Timothy B Cartrett
Lot 26 Pine Ln Mhp
Lynchburg VA 24501

Call Sign: KI4EDN
Thomas D Brendle
41 Point Dr Apt 4
Lynchburg VA 24502

Call Sign: N4LTB
Thomas A Johnson
101 Quail Rd
Lynchburg VA 245044227

Call Sign: W4WGE
James L Whiting Jr
471 Rainbow Forest Dr
Lynchburg VA 24502

Call Sign: W4VTT
Donald C Gordon
527 Rainbow Forest Dr
Lynchburg VA 24502

Call Sign: KD4OMB
Garry M Ford
531 Rainbow Forest Dr
Lynchburg VA 24502

Call Sign: KD4WOA
Walter S Eanes Jr
1264 Rainbow Forest Dr
Lynchburg VA 24502

Call Sign: WA4IUB
Rupert R Armentrout
1766 Rainbow Forest Dr
Lynchburg VA 24502

Call Sign: KG4POM
Jennifer K Carey
208 Reno Dr
Lynchburg VA 24502

Call Sign: N4JFR
Jennifer K Carey
208 Reno Dr
Lynchburg VA 245024365

Call Sign: KC4CDX
Steven C Groves
600 Reusens Rd Apt F67
Lynchburg VA 24503

Call Sign: KK4VZ
Ralph Etherington
5824 Rhonda Rd
Lynchburg VA 24502

Call Sign: N4RXK
Barbara C Etherington
5824 Rhonda Rd
Lynchburg VA 245024918

Call Sign: KB4EFQ
John A Rayhill Jr
7006 Richland Dr
Lynchburg VA 24502

Call Sign: KG4PPB
Galen A Wright
7218 Richland Dr
Lynchburg VA 24502

Call Sign: W4KSV
Lawrence W Falwell
4132 Richmond Hwy
Lynchburg VA 24501

Call Sign: KF4YPL
Kathlene M Hand
2005 Ridge Ave
Lynchburg VA 24501

Call Sign: W4WTR
William D Marlin Jr
107 Riverbirch Trace
Lynchburg VA 24502

Call Sign: KF4PHS
Harold E Smith
115 Riverbirch Trace
Lynchburg VA 245025597

Call Sign: KE4TJG
Thomas L Womack
1534 Rivermont Ave

Lynchburg VA 24503

Call Sign: KJ4HJY
Jacob A Grimes
1800 Rivermont Ave
Lynchburg VA 24503

Call Sign: KF4FYK
Josh Q Famorca
2401 Rivermont Ave
Lynchburg VA 24503

Call Sign: KB4DTD
E G Wood
3305 Rivermont Ave
Lynchburg VA 245032029

Call Sign: KB4CWX
Dave Rubinberg
3101 Rivermont Ave
Lynchburg VA 24503

Call Sign: KA4HIU
Hester Hastings
2939 Rivermont Ave 21
Lynchburg VA 24503

Call Sign: KJ4BFI
Charlotte K Baldwin
2934 Rivermont Ave 30
Lynchburg VA 24503

Call Sign: AJ4CX
Wesley L Baldwin
2934 Rivermont Ave 30
Lynchburg VA 24503

Call Sign: KA2NJQ
Everett G Mc Laren
2910 Rivermont Ave Apt 52
Lynchburg VA 24503

Call Sign: KF4UKM
Mark J Adams
2925 Rivermont Ave Apt 6
Lynchburg VA 24503

Call Sign: WB4WDL
John R Mc Clenon

712 Riverside Dr
Lynchburg VA 24503

Call Sign: WB5QNA
David T Schwartz
3 Riverview Pl
Lynchburg VA 24503

Call Sign: KB4DPE
George S Bieri
800 Rockbridge Ave
Lynchburg VA 245015820

Call Sign: KA2M
Ellis Glazebrook
3540 Round Hill Rd
Lynchburg VA 24503

Call Sign: W4IEF
Homer C Shirlen
716 Russell Woods Dr
Lynchburg VA 24502

Call Sign: KG4OYS
Kevin S Dodgion
2240 Sackett St
Lynchburg VA 24501

Call Sign: W4LJR
Ralph R Sherman Jr
168 Salisbury Cir
Lynchburg VA 24502

Call Sign: KZ4D
Frederick W Morris
207 Sandown Cir
Lynchburg VA 245033736

Call Sign: NI4R
Mary U Morris
207 Sandown Cir
Lynchburg VA 245033736

Call Sign: K4MKR
Boonsboro Radio Experimental
Wireless
212 Sandown Cir
Lynchburg VA 24503

Call Sign: WD4GPS
John D White III
601 Sandusky Dr
Lynchburg VA 24502

Call Sign: K4LBG
John D White III
601 Sandusky Dr
Lynchburg VA 24502

Call Sign: N4LSY
Alfred E White
621 Sandusky Dr
Lynchburg VA 24502

Call Sign: WD4FSS
Cecilia E Cox
744 Sandusky Dr
Lynchburg VA 24502

Call Sign: N4TEM
Dwayne S Bradley
556 Savannah Ave
Lynchburg VA 24502

Call Sign: WB6NFT
James M Mc Kellips
160 Scotts Farm Rd
Lynchburg VA 245044040

Call Sign: W4NFT
James M Mc Kellips
160 Scotts Farm Rd
Lynchburg VA 245044040

Call Sign: KD4HVY
Cecil W Waddle
1151 Sheffield Dr
Lynchburg VA 24502

Call Sign: KE4ISE
Michael S Mc Navish
1532 Sherbrooke Dr
Lynchburg VA 24502

Call Sign: KC4NZH
Tony A Little
122 Silver Spring Dr
Lynchburg VA 24502

Call Sign: KJ4GVK
William T Dorr
98 Silver Springs Dr
Lynchburg VA 24502

Call Sign: KC4VOK
Chris S Roder
38 Sky Pl Apt 40
Lynchburg VA 24502

Call Sign: KI4SAN
Frank Carter
3317 Sky View Pl
Lynchburg VA 24503

Call Sign: KC4WGP
Brigetta G Eshleman
14 Skylark Pl
Lynchburg VA 245031708

Call Sign: KK4HJ
Curtis R Eshleman
14 Skylark Pl
Lynchburg VA 245031708

Call Sign: N4ZTI
Lester M Bell
220 Sleepy Hollow Rd
Lynchburg VA 245023040

Call Sign: KJ4JNV
Braden T Kinzie
576 Spicer Rd
Lynchburg VA 24504

Call Sign: KC4RBB
Shirley L Crouch
205 Springvale Dr
Lynchburg VA 24502

Call Sign: N4TEQ
Eddie D Crouch
205 Springvale Dr
Lynchburg VA 24502

Call Sign: WD4RMK
Michael R Clark
110 Spruce Ln

Lynchburg VA 24501

Call Sign: KC4RAY
Robert E Coalson
1337 St Cloud Ave
Lynchburg VA 24502

Call Sign: WD4SCF
Bernard D Reams
128 St Johns Dr
Lynchburg VA 24503

Call Sign: KG4FBU
Martha A Lind
205 St Paul Dr
Lynchburg VA 24503

Call Sign: K4GBG
William J Blackburn
1153 Stevens Rd
Lynchburg VA 24501

Call Sign: WD4BQM
Thomas S Kirby
1130 Stratford Rd
Lynchburg VA 24502

Call Sign: KI4FOP
Thomas S Kirby
516 Stuart St
Lynchburg VA 24501

Call Sign: KK4FPN
Aaron D Mills
401 Suburban Rd
Lynchburg VA 24501

Call Sign: WB8ZEF
Betty J Fisher
434 Sunburst Rd
Lynchburg VA 24501

Call Sign: KJ4KNJ
Johnny M Lawson
434 Sunburst Rd
Lynchburg VA 24501

Call Sign: W4JML
Johnny M Lawson

434 Sunburst Rd
Lynchburg VA 24501

Call Sign: KI4FGU
Reid C Bristow
612 Susannah Pl
Lynchburg VA 24502

Call Sign: KJ4RIW
Dean E Mosteller
197 Sweetwater Rd
Lynchburg VA 24501

Call Sign: KF4RJP
Marc S Long
4906 Sycamore Pl
Lynchburg VA 24502

Call Sign: WA4CJT
Elton W Staton
204 Tanglewood Dr
Lynchburg VA 24502

Call Sign: KD4JJI
April M Slayton
1108 Taylor St
Lynchburg VA 24504

Call Sign: KU4WL
Tara A Eskey
83 Timber Ct
Lynchburg VA 24501

Call Sign: KG4VEJ
Jason E Gallagher
40 Timber E Dr Apt 202
Lynchburg VA 24502

Call Sign: KC4VJK
David M Smith
1200 Timberlake Dr
Lynchburg VA 24502

Call Sign: AB4M
William L Dail
1994 Timberlake Dr
Lynchburg VA 245026942

Call Sign: KE4JUF

Mark A Jacobsen
9511 Timberlake Rd
Lynchburg VA 24502

Call Sign: KC4OFO
James A Hahn
8108 Timberlake Rd 144
Lynchburg VA 24502

Call Sign: KG4KCL
Emmanuel Castellon
8022 Timberlake Rd 32
Lynchburg VA 24502

Call Sign: KG4KCK
Jonathan R Harris
5020 Tineeanna Rd
Lynchburg VA 24504

Call Sign: KF4YGD
Kevin R Thayer
1512 Toledo Ave
Lynchburg VA 24502

Call Sign: KC4FPU
Richard G Johnson
43 Tunnel St
Lynchburg VA 24501

Call Sign: KD4ILE
Brian D Loomis
117 Turtle Creek Rd
Lynchburg VA 24501

Call Sign: KD4HVX
Lawrence G Mehaffey Jr
220 Twin Oak Dr
Lynchburg VA 24502

Call Sign: KF4ZBN
Jay W Cesafsky
225 Twin Oak Dr
Lynchburg VA 24502

Call Sign: KC4VJI
Robert M Smith
238 Twin Oak Dr
Lynchburg VA 24502

Call Sign: KE4MMV
Randy S Grubbs
1 Valorie Ct
Lynchburg VA 24502

Call Sign: W4VES
Lawrence R Graham
249 Ves Rd
Lynchburg VA 24503

Call Sign: KI4WQR
Lawrence R Graham
400 Ves Rd
Lynchburg VA 24505

Call Sign: W4JJD
Robert A Farmer
501 VES Rd
Lynchburg VA 24503

Call Sign: WA4GMW
Joseph P Johann
501 Ves Rd Apt Bt15
Lynchburg VA 24503

Call Sign: W8CXD
H Warren Middleton Jr
501 VES Rd Apt C510
Lynchburg VA 24503

Call Sign: N4LVF
Elizabeth S Hannell
501 VES Rd Apt W426
Lynchburg VA 24503

Call Sign: W4EZE
Francis D Hannell
501 Ves Rd Apt W426
Lynchburg VA 24503

Call Sign: K4EPM
Milton S Ridgeway
5225 Village Hwy
Lynchburg VA 24504

Call Sign: WA4BWY
Arthur L Ridgeway
5225 Village Hwy
Lynchburg VA 24504

Call Sign: K4BWY
Arthur L Ridgeway
5225 Village Hwy
Lynchburg VA 24504

Call Sign: WA4BWB
Russell F Streeper
5283 Village Hwy
Lynchburg VA 24504

Call Sign: WA4LQA
Floyd E Kanode
104 Vista Ln
Lynchburg VA 245022934

Call Sign: K4SQW
Joseph E A Duprey
111 Vista Ln
Lynchburg VA 24502

Call Sign: KG4PJY
Jorge O Saavedra
18 W Princeton Cr 149
Lynchburg VA 24503

Call Sign: KE4NGY
Thomas R Griffin
221 Wadsworth St
Lynchburg VA 24501

Call Sign: KI4EUP
Jonathan D Clough
1414 Wakefield Rd
Lynchburg VA 24503

Call Sign: NS4L
Jonathan D Clough
1414 Wakefield Rd
Lynchburg VA 24503

Call Sign: KI4OIQ
Roxanna C Clough
1414 Wakefield Rd
Lynchburg VA 24503

Call Sign: KG4JTS
Subrina W Clark
1818 B Wards Ferry Rd

Lynchburg VA 24502

Call Sign: KC4NDK
Steven E Bruffy
4418 Wards Rd
Lynchburg VA 24502

Call Sign: N4QNX
De Witt L R Clay
617 Washington St
Lynchburg VA 245042621

Call Sign: KK4EWS
John D Towles
112A Water Gate Dr
Lynchburg VA 24502

Call Sign: KD4WHF
Gregory Coudoures
3413 Waterlick Dr
Lynchburg VA 24502

Call Sign: N4ZNY
Emil L Hansen
103 Watkins Pl
Lynchburg VA 24502

Call Sign: KE4YEU
Dennis L Kemppainen
5016 Wedgewood Rd
Lynchburg VA 24503

Call Sign: WB8LDN
Dave L Grissom
3300F Weeping Willow
Lynchburg VA 24501

Call Sign: KF4GCR
Leonard T Lee
2900 D Weeping Willow Dr
Lynchburg VA 24501

Call Sign: KF4RMU
Crystal J Compton
600 A Weeping Willow Dr
Lynchburg VA 24501

Call Sign: K4ZGN
James P Hanway Jr

2127 Westerly Dr
Lynchburg VA 24501

Call Sign: KI4AAI
Matthew R Ripley
2608 Westhaven Pl
Lynchburg VA 24501

Call Sign: KG6JAW
Bridger J Smith
2619 Westhaven Pl
Lynchburg VA 24501

Call Sign: KE4FKG
Warren C Light
127 Westminster Way
Lynchburg VA 24503

Call Sign: K4YPF
Clarence N Mc Bride
418 Westover Blvd
Lynchburg VA 24501

Call Sign: KK4GDK
Randy S Williamson
380 Westview Cir
Lynchburg VA 24504

Call Sign: WB4ZPF
Gary D Gill
501 Westview Cir
Lynchburg VA 245044063

Call Sign: W4GDG
Gary D Gill
501 Westview Cir
Lynchburg VA 245044063

Call Sign: KG4KCJ
William D Wilkins
909 Westview Dr
Lynchburg VA 24502

Call Sign: K4WDW
William D Wilkins
909 Westview Dr
Lynchburg VA 24502

Call Sign: N4RAM

Robert A Merkle
202 Whistlewood Ct
Lynchburg VA 245024680

Call Sign: KG4JTW
Joseph L Porter Jr
207 Whistlewood Ct
Lynchburg VA 24502

Call Sign: WD4IKL
William S Rowse
5613 White Oak Dr
Lynchburg VA 24502

Call Sign: WA2UNJ
Charles H Zane
30 Whitestone Dr
Lynchburg VA 24502

Call Sign: N4UTB
Edwin C Lafferty
76 Whitestone Dr
Lynchburg VA 24502

Call Sign: KS4HT
Michael P Rausch
38 Wildcrest Dr
Lynchburg VA 24502

Call Sign: KG4WCX
Douglas C Mekanik
3513 Willow Lawn Dr
Lynchburg VA 24503

Call Sign: KD4LRX
Gregory C Mick Sr
53 Winding Way Rd
Lynchburg VA 24502

Call Sign: K4BA
Phillip L Brown
227 Windsor Rd
Lynchburg VA 24502

Call Sign: KJ4IGA
Derek W Cate
203 Windy Ridge Pl
Lynchburg VA 24503

Call Sign: KG4IAY
Chris S Towler
265 Winebarger Cir
Lynchburg VA 245017146

Call Sign: K4VFD
Chris S Towler
265 Winebarger Cir
Lynchburg VA 245017146

Call Sign: KJ4VIA
Brian C Markey
101 Winesap Dr
Lynchburg VA 24503

Call Sign: KE4GKE
Patrick A Lafratta
201 Woodbourne Dr
Lynchburg VA 24502

Call Sign: KC4HZC
Vivian M Royal
2039 Woodcrest Dr
Lynchburg VA 24503

Call Sign: N4IHB
Rodney L Perdue
2050 Woodcrest Dr
Lynchburg VA 24503

Call Sign: KJ4IGH
Thomas H Willman
2223 Woodcrest Dr
Lynchburg VA 24503

Call Sign: KD4BSG
Jerzy G Kowalczyk
196 Woodhaven Dr
Lynchburg VA 24502

Call Sign: K4RHH
Randolph W Cunningham
411 Woodhaven Dr
Lynchburg VA 24502

Call Sign: K4NRF
O L Durham Jr
496 Woodhaven Dr
Lynchburg VA 24502

Call Sign: W3HBP
Lyman G Hailey
209 Woodland Ave
Lynchburg VA 24503

Call Sign: KD4YFG
Ian J Smith
115 Woodridge Cir
Lynchburg VA 24502

Call Sign: N4JMK
Thomas D Jamerson
1209 Woods Rd
Lynchburg VA 24502

Call Sign: N4WHP
Nancy B Jamerson
1209 Woods Rd
Lynchburg VA 24502

Call Sign: KK4EXP
Robert J Anglin
106 Wooldridge Cir
Lynchburg VA 24502

Call Sign: WB4ASE
William V Suchodolski
305 Wyndale Dr No 8
Lynchburg VA 24501

Call Sign: KG4IIU
Thomas Cabrera
106 Wyndhurst Dr
Lynchburg VA 245023145

Call Sign: KJ4K
Jack B Freeman
201 Wyndhurst Dr
Lynchburg VA 24502

Call Sign: K4WTS
William T Strayhorn
309 Wyndhurst Dr
Lynchburg VA 24502

Call Sign: KF4PHP
Sheldon E Smith
313 Wyndhurst Dr

Lynchburg VA 24502

Call Sign: K4VWT
Quinton D Overman Jr
107 Yorkshire Cir
Lynchburg VA 24502

Call Sign: KD4FGG
Robert A Hahn
126 Yorkshire Cr
Lynchburg VA 24502

Call Sign: KG4POU
Brandon R Coleman
2217 Yorktown Ave Apt D 7
Lynchburg VA 24501

Call Sign: KD4RBX
Charles W Brooks Jr
Lynchburg VA 24501

Call Sign: KC4VJJ
Christopher T Harris
Lynchburg VA 24502

Call Sign: KD4PYU
Arthur G Schlumpf
Lynchburg VA 24506

Call Sign: KB4RGE
William M Screen
Lynchburg VA 24502

Call Sign: KG4JMN
Samuel Adams
Lynchburg VA 24502

Call Sign: AD6YX
David F Barber
Lynchburg VA 24502

Call Sign: KK4BIX
Paul J Merriam
Lynchburg VA 24502

Call Sign: KE4YLS
Danny F Terry Sr
Lynchburg VA 24505

Call Sign: KE4LZF
Valerie A Merchent
Lynchburg VA 24506

Call Sign: N8JKX
Thomas T Butterfield
Lynchburg VA 24506

Call Sign: WB2CYJ
Paul D Jasiewicz
Lynchburg VA 24506

Call Sign: KJ4JNW
Arthur G Schlumpf
Lynchburg VA 24506

Call Sign: KJ4WXB
Gregory R Alkire
Lynchburg VA 24506

Call Sign: KG4VEK
John M Hazlehurst
Lynchburg VA 24506

Call Sign: N4BDL
Brian D Loomis
Lynchburg VA 24506

Call Sign: KJ4MHJ
Carlos C Whaley Jr
Lynchburg VA 245060576

Call Sign: N8KZS
Carlos C Whaley Jr
Lynchburg VA 245060576

Call Sign: KG4HFQ
Eugenia E Petke
Lynchburg VA 245062026

Call Sign: KG4HFY
Matthew Petke
Lynchburg VA 245062026

FCC Amateur Radio Licenses in Lyndhurst

Call Sign: KB4SSD
Dennis R Simmons Sr

110 Back Creek Ln
Lyndhurst VA 22952

Call Sign: KB4JGD
Sharon E Hupp
Rt 1 Box 161
Lyndhurst VA 22952

Call Sign: KF4HEX
Lynwood R Hutchens Sr
Rt 1 Box 241
Lyndhurst VA 22952

Call Sign: N4EAU
Lois M Risley
Rd 1 Box 7 Mt Torrey Rd
Lyndhurst VA 22952

Call Sign: KE4HCR
Herman E Kern
Rt 1 Box 8
Lyndhurst VA 22952

Call Sign: KF4KNM
David O Grimmett
16 Inch Run Ln
Lyndhurst VA 22952

Call Sign: KF4KNN
Marvin S Henderson
642 Love Rd
Lyndhurst VA 22952

Call Sign: K4GSP
Arthur C Hupp
596 Mt Torrey Rd
Lyndhurst VA 22952

Call Sign: KI4FDG
John W Schlabach
671 Mt Torrey Rd
Lyndhurst VA 22952

Call Sign: KD4KAU
John L Huffman
1165 Mt Torrey Rd
Lyndhurst VA 22952

Call Sign: KA4RWR

Robert W Ryder Jr
1225 Mt Torrey Rd
Lyndhurst VA 22952

Call Sign: KE4GMI
Gertrude D Hale
1765 Mt Torrey Rd
Lyndhurst VA 22952

Call Sign: KE4NRG
Brian K Mays
73 Rising Sun Ln
Lyndhurst VA 22952